10-3-83

Instant Facts

The World Book
Desk Reference Set

Instant Facts

Published by

World Book Encyclopedia, Inc.
a Scott Fetzer company

Chicago

Staff

Editorial director
William H. Nault

Editorial

Executive editor
Robert O. Zeleny

Senior editor
Seva Johnson

Editors
Kathleen L. Florio
Mike Urban

Administrative assistant
Janet T. Peterson

Editorial assistant
Valerie Steward

Cartographic services
H. George Stoll

Statistics
Katherine Norgel

Index editor
Dawn Tanis

Art

Executive art director
William Hammond

Art director
Roberta Dimmer

Assistant art director
Joe Gound

Cover design
David Doty

Product production

Executive director
Peter Mollman

Manufacturing
Joseph C. LaCount

Research and development
Henry Koval

Pre-press services
J. J. Stack
George Luehring
Barbara Podczerwinski

Film separations
Alfred Mozdzen
Barbara McDonald

Editorial services

Director
Susan C. Kilburg

Research services
Mary Norton, head
Edna Capehart
Rebecca Chekouras
Karen Fleischer
Frances Lee Fu
Robert Hamm
Yogamani Leo Hamm
Cheryl Prihoda

Rights and permissions
Paul Rafferty

Contents

7 Introduction
8 Abbreviations
13 Alphabets and codes
17 Animals
28 Area codes
29 Astrology
30 Awards
62 Calendars
65 Canada
73 Chemical elements
76 Decorations and medals
78 Disasters
80 Earth
90 Explorations
94 Flags
96 Holidays
97 Human being
101 Human body
109 Library classification system
110 Money

112 Mythology
114 Parliamentary procedure
116 People
138 Plants
145 Presidents
149 Religion
156 Scientific inventions and inventors
158 Signs and symbols
193 Space
203 Sports winners
232 Time zones
234 Transportation
241 United Nations
245 United States
276 Universe
284 Weather
287 Weights and measures
290 Wonders of the world
291 World
310 Index

Acknowledgments

All photographs unless otherwise noted were created exclusively for *The World Book Encyclopedia*.

165   *Beagle*—Hans Reinhard, Bruce Coleman Inc.

167   *Belgian sheepdog*—Walter Chandoha; *Bouvier des Flandres*—Walter Chandoha

168   *Miniature schnauzer*—William P. Gilbert

169   *Bichon frise*—Mar-Jon's

170   *American saddle horse*—Fritz Prenzel, Bruce Coleman Inc.; *Tennessee walking horse*—Tom Clark, Shostal; *Morgan*—American Morgan Horse Assoc., Inc.; *Quarter horse*—Becky Hance

171   *Thoroughbred*—Alix Coleman; *Standardbred*—Ira Haas, Photo Researchers; *Appaloosa*—Appaloosa Horse Club; *Palomino*—Robert Shiflet, Palomino Horse Breeders of America; *Lipizzaner*—Jerry Cooke, Photo Researchers

172   *Percheron*—Walter Chandoha

173   *Przewalski's horse*—Chicago Zoological Society; *Clydesdale*—Anheuser-Busch, Inc.

Introduction

On what day of the week will your birthday be in the year 1992? What are the seven wonders of the ancient world? How do plants make food from sunlight? Who was the first person to set foot on the moon? Which baseball team has won the most World Series championships? How does a bill become law in the United States? The answers to these questions and many more may be found in *Instant Facts*.

This book contains information on a wide variety of subjects. Refer to the "People" and "Presidents" sections for brief descriptions of some of the most important people in history. Concise descriptions of life on earth are given in the "Animals," "Human being," "Human body," and "Plants" sections. The "Canada," "Religion," "United Nations," "United States," and "World" sections explain the political, economic, cultural, and geographic makeup of two important countries and the world in general. The physical makeup of the earth, its relation to the rest of the universe, and attempts to explore the unknown are outlined in the "Earth," "Explorations," "Space," and "Universe" sections.

In addition to these narrative sections, *Instant Facts* also contains almanac-type listings of information that are useful in school and in everyday life. Winners of some of the most important awards and events are listed in the "Awards" and "Sports winners" sections. Aids to reading, writing, research, calculating, and converting may be found in the "Abbreviations," "Alphabets and codes," "Library classification system," "Money," "Signs and symbols," and "Weights and measures" sections.

Numerous maps, photographs, and illustrations also help bring greater understanding to the topics covered in this book. The time zones of the world, telephone area codes in the United States and Canada, and world climate regions are all depicted on easy-to-read maps. Full-color photos and illustrations of cats, dogs, horses, decorations and medals, and flags appear on pages 161–192. Charts outlining the history of the earth and the development of the human race supplement the "Earth" and "Human being" sections.

Whether you are writing a report for school, looking for answers to trivia questions, or simply satisfying your curiosity about the world around you, *Instant Facts* serves as your one-stop reference source for a wide variety of information.

Abbreviations

The table below lists many abbreviations commonly used in writing and speaking, in medical prescriptions and records, and to indicate college degrees. Abbreviations for the states, provinces, and territories appear in a separate table. For the abbreviations, called *symbols,* of chemical elements, see "Chemical elements" section. Other common abbreviations appear in the "Signs and symbols," "United Nations," and "Weights and measures" sections.

A.A.—Alcoholics Anonymous; Associate in Arts

AAA—American Automobile Association

AAAS—American Association for the Advancement of Science

AAU—Amateur Athletic Union

ABC—American Broadcasting Companies, Inc.

a.c.—*ante cibum* (before meals)

AC—alternating current

ACLU—American Civil Liberties Union

ACTH—adrenocorticotropic hormone

A.D.—*anno Domini* (in the year of our Lord)

ad lib—*ad libitum* (as one pleases)

ad us. exter.—*ad usum externum* (for external use)

Adj., Adjt.—Adjutant

Adm.—Admiral; Admiralty

AFL-CIO—American Federation of Labor and Congress of Industrial Organizations

agit. a. us.—*agita ante usum* (shake before using)

agit. bene—*agita bene* (shake well)

AID—Agency for International Development

a.k.a.—also known as

ALA—American Library Association

AM—amplitude modulation

A.M., a.m.—*ante meridiem* (before noon)

AMA—American Medical Association

amp.—ampere

AMVETS—American Veterans of World War II, Korea, and Vietnam

anon.—anonymous

AP—Associated Press

aq.—*aqua* (water)

A.S.—Associate in Science

ASCAP—American Society of Composers, Authors and Publishers

assn.—association

assoc.—associate; association

asst.—assistant

astrol.—astrology

astron.—astronomy

AT&T—American Telephone and Telegraph Company

atty.—attorney

Aug.—August

ave.—avenue

AWOL—absent without leave

b.—born

B.A., A.B.—Bachelor of Arts

B.A. in Ed.—Bachelor of Arts in Education

B.Arch.—Bachelor of Architecture

B.B.A.—Bachelor of Business Administration

BBC—British Broadcasting Corporation

B.C.—before Christ

B.C.P.—Book of Common Prayer

B.D.—Bachelor of Divinity

B.Ed.—Bachelor of Education

B.E.E.—Bachelor of Electrical Engineering

B.F.A.—Bachelor of Fine Arts

bib.—*bibe* (drink)

bibliog.—bibliography

b.i.d.—*bis in die* (twice a day)

biog.—biography

BLM—Bureau of Land Management

B.L.S.—Bachelor of Library Science

BLS—Bureau of Labor Statistics

blvd.—boulevard

B.M., B.Mus.—Bachelor of Music

B.M.E., B.Mus.Ed.—Bachelor of Music Education

bol.—*bolus* (large pill)

bot.—botany; botanical

Br.—Britain; British; Brother

Brig.—Brigade; Brigadier

B.S.—Bachelor of Science

B.S. in B.A., B.S.B.A.—Bachelor of Science in Business Administration

B.S. in C.E., B.S.C.E.—Bachelor of Science in Civil Engineering

B.S. in Ch.E., B.S.Ch.E.—Bachelor of Science in Chemical Engineering

B.S. in Chemistry, B.S.Chem. —Bachelor of Science in Chemistry

B.S. in Ed., B.S.Ed.—Bachelor of Science in Education

B.S. in E.E., B.S.E.E.—Bachelor of Science in Electrical Engineering

B.S. in Elem.Ed.—Bachelor of Science in Elementary Education

B.S. in L.S.—Bachelor of Science in Library Science

B.S. in M.E., B.S.M.E.—Bachelor of Science in Mechanical Engineering

B.S. in Med. Tech.—Bachelor of Science in Medical Technology

B.S.J., J.B.S.—Bachelor of Science in Journalism

B.S.N.—Bachelor of Science in Nursing

B.S.Pharm.—Bachelor of Science in Pharmacy

B.T.U.—British thermal unit

c.—*circa* (about); *centum* (century); copy; copyright

ca.—*circa* (about)

CAB—Civil Aeronautics Board

cal, cal.—calorie (heat)

Cal, Cal.—calorie (nutrition)

cap.—capital; capital letter

CAP—Civil Air Patrol

Capt.—Captain

CB—citizens band

CBC—Canadian Broadcasting Corporation

CBO—Congressional Budget Office

CBS—Columbia Broadcasting System

CD—civil defense; certificate of deposit

CEA—Council of Economic Advisors

CED—Committee for Economic Development

cent.—century

CEQ—Council on Environmental Quality

ch., chap.—chapter

chm., chmn.—chairman

Chron.—Chronicles

CIA—Central Intelligence Agency

CO—commanding officer

c/o—in care of

co.—company; county

ibid.—*ibidem* (in the same place)

ICBM—**i**ntercontinental **b**allistic **m**issile

ICC—Interstate Commerce Commission

id.—*idem* (the same)

i.e.—*id est* (that is)

ill.—illustrated

IMF—International Monetary Fund

inc.—incorporated; including

incog.—incognito

ind.—independent; industrial; index

INS—Immigration and Naturalization Service

int.—interest; international

int. cib.—*inter cibos* (between meals)

int. noct.—*inter noctem* (during the night)

INTERPOL—International Criminal Police Organization

I.O.U.—I owe you

IQ—intelligence quotient

IRA—Irish Republican Army; Individual Retirement Account

IRS—Internal Revenue Service

Is.—Isaiah; islands

I T T—International Telephone and Telegraph Corporation

J.—joule

Jan.—January

Jas.—James

J.D.—Juris Doctor

Jer.—Jeremiah

Josh.—Joshua

Jr.—Junior

Judg.—Judges

k.—carat; knot

K.C., K. of C.—Knights of Columbus

kHz—kilohertz

KP—kitchen police

kwh—kilowatt-hour

lab.—laboratory

Lam.—Lamentations

lang.—language

lat.—latitude

L.C.—Library of Congress

l.c.—lower case

LDL—low-density lipoproteins

Lev.—Leviticus

LH—luteinizing hormone

*L.H.D.—Doctor of Humane Letters

lib.—librarian; library; liberal

liq.—liquid

lit.—literature

*Lit.D., D.Lit.—Doctor of Literature

*Litt.D.—Doctor of Letters

LL.B.—Bachelor of Laws

---

*Honorary degree only

*LL.D.—Doctor of Laws

LL.M.—Master of Laws

loc. cit.—*loco citato* (in the place cited)

log.—logarithm

lon., long.—longitude

l.t.—long ton

Lt.—Lieutenant

Ltd.—Limited

m.—minute

M.—*misce* (mix)

M.A., A.M.—Master of Arts

M.A. in Ed.—Master of Arts in Education

Maj.—Major

Mal.—Malachi

M.A.T.—Master of Arts in Teaching

Matt.—Matthew

max.—maximum

M.B.A.—Master of Business Administration

MBS—Mutual Broadcasting System

M.D.—Doctor of Medicine

M.Div.—Master of Divinity

mdse.—merchandise

meas.—measure

med.—medicine; medium

M.Ed.—Master of Education

met.—metropolitan

M.F.A.—Master of Fine Arts

mfd.—manufactured

mfg.—manufacturing

mfr.—manufacturer

MHz—megahertz

M.I.A.—missing in action

Mic.—Micah

min.—minimum; minute

misc.—miscellaneous

M.L.S.—Master of Library Science

M.M., M.Mus.—Master of Music

M.M.Ed., M.Mus.Ed.—Master of Music Education

mo.—month

M.O.—money order; mail order; *modus operandi* (method of working)

Mon.—Monday

mor. dict.—*moro dicto* (as directed)

mor. sol.—*moro solito* (in the usual way)

m.p.—melting point

M.P.—Member of Parliament

MP—Military Police

mph—miles per hour

M.R.E.—Master of Religious Education

Ms.—Miss or Mrs.

M.S.—Master of Science

M.S. in C.E., M.S.C.E.—Master of Science in Civil Engineering

M.S. in Ch.E.—Master of Science in Chemical Engineering

M.S. in Ed.—Master of Science in Education

M.S. in E.E., M.S.E.E.—Master of Science in Electrical Engineering

M.S. in L.S.—Master of Science in Library Science

M.S. in M.E.—Master of Science in Mechanical Engineering

M.S.J.—Master of Science in Journalism

mss.—manuscripts

MST—Mountain Standard Time

M.S.W.—Master of Social Work

Mt.—Mount

n.—noun; note (footnote)

n—neutron

N.—north

NAACP—National Association for the Advancement of Colored People

Nah.—Nahum

N.A.I.A.—National Association of Intercollegiate Athletics

NASA—National Aeronautics and Space Administration

natl.—national

NATO—North Atlantic Treaty Organization

naut.—nautical

N.B., n.b.—*nota bene* (note well)

NBC—National Broadcasting Company

NBS—National Bureau of Standards

NCAA—National Collegiate Athletic Association

NCO—noncommissioned officer

n.d.—no date

NEA—National Educational Association

Neh.—Nehemiah

neut.—neuter

n.g.—no good; not good

NIE—National Institute of Education

NIH—National Institutes of Health

NLRB—National Labor Relations Board

no.—*numero;* number

non. rep., n.r.—*non repetatur* (do not repeat; do not refill)

non seq.—*non sequitur* (it does not follow)

Nov.—November

NOW—National Organization for Women

N.P.—notary public

n.p.—no publisher, no place of publication

NRC—Nuclear Regulatory Commission

N/S, N.S.F.—not sufficient funds

10

coch.—*cochleare* (spoonful)
COD—cash on delivery; collect on delivery
Col.—Colonel; Colossians
colloq.—colloquial
comp.—compiled; composer
con.—*contra* (against)
Cong.—Congress
cont.—continued
cont. rem.—*continuentur remedia* (continue the medicines)
coop.—cooperative
Cor.—Corinthians
corp.—corporation
cp.—compare
CPA—certified public accountant
CPB—Corporation for Public Broadcasting
Cpl.—Corporal
CPO—Chief Petty Officer
CST—Central Standard Time
D—Democrat
d.—died
D.A.—district attorney; Doctor of Arts
Dan.—Daniel
DAR—Daughters of the American Revolution
D.A.V.—Disabled American Veterans
db, dB—decibel
D.B.A.—Doctor of Business Administration
D.C.—District of Columbia; Doctor of Chiropractic
DC—direct current
*D.D.—Doctor of Divinity
D.D.S.—Doctor of Dental Surgery
DDT—dichloro-diphenyl-trichloroethane
DEA—Drug Enforcement Administration
dec.—deceased
Dec.—December
Dem.—Democrat
dept.—department
Deut.—Deuteronomy
D.M.D.—Doctor of Dental Medicine
*D.Mus., Mus.D.—Doctor of Music
DNA—deoxyribonucleic acid
D.O.—Doctor of Osteopathy
D.O.A.—dead on arrival
DOD—Department of Defense
DOE—Department of Energy
DOT—Department of Transportation
DP—displaced person
DPT—diphtheria, pertussis, and tetanus (vaccine)
Dr.—doctor
DST—daylight-saving time

*Honorary degree only
†Commonly known as "Fannie Mae"

dup.—duplicate
dur. dol.—*durante dolore* (while pain lasts)
D.V.M.—Doctor of Veterinary Medicine
E.—east
ea.—each
EC—European Community
Eccles.—Ecclesiastes
ECT—electroconvulsive therapy
ed.—edition; editor; edited
Ed.D., D.Ed.—Doctor of Education
educ.—education
EEC—European Economic Community
EEG—electroencephalgram
EEOC—Equal Employment Opportunity Commission
EFT—electronic funds transfer
e.g.—*exempli gratia* (for example)
EKG—electrocardiogram
elem.—elementary
emf—electromotive force
EMG—electromyogram
e.m.p.—*ex modo praescripto* (in the manner prescribed)
eng., engr.—engraving; engineering
ENT—ear, nose, and throat
e.o.—*ex officio* (by virtue of office)
EPA—Environmental Protection Agency
Eph.—Ephesians
eq.—equal; equation
ERA—Equal Rights Amendment; earned run average
ESP—extrasensory perception
esp.—especially
EST—Eastern Standard Time; electroshock therapy
Esth.—Esther
E.T.A.—estimated time of arrival
et al.—*et alibi* (and elsewhere); *et alii* (and others)
et seq.—*et sequens, et sequentis, et sequentia* (and what follows)
etc.—*et cetera* (and so forth)
ethnog.—ethnography
ethnol.—ethnology
etym., etymol.—etymology
Exod.—Exodus
Ezek.—Ezekiel
FAA—Federal Aviation Administration
FBI—Federal Bureau of Investigation
FCC—Federal Communications Commission
FDA—Food and Drug Administration
FDIC—Federal Deposit Insurance Corporation

Feb.—February
ff.—folios (page numbers); follo (pages)
FFA—Future Farmers of Americ
FHA—Federal Housing Admini tion; Future Homemakers of Ar ica
FICA—Federal Insurance Contr tions Act
fig.—figure
fl.—*floruit* (flourished)
FM—frequency modulation
FMCS—Federal Mediation and Co ciliation Service
†FNMA—Federal National Mortga Association
f.o.b.—free on board
Fr.—Father; French; Friar
Fri.—Friday
FSH—follicle-stimulating hormone
FSLIC—Federal Savings and Loa Insurance Corporation
FTC—Federal Trade Commission
Gal.—Galatians
GAO—General Accounting Office
G.A.R.—Grand Army of the Republic
GED—General Educational Develop ment
Gen.—General; Genesis
geog.—geography
geol.—geology
GI—general issue; government issue; gastrointestinal
GNP—gross national product
Gov.—Governor
Govt.—government
GPO—Government Printing Office
GSA—General Services Administra tion; Girl Scouts of America
h.—hour
Hab.—Habakkuk
Hag.—Haggai
HDL—high-density lipoproteins
hdqrs.—headquarters
Heb.—Hebrews
HHS—Department of Health an Human Services
hi-fi—high fidelity
HMO—health maintenance organiza tion
H.M.S.—His (or Her) Majesty's Sh
Hon.—Honorable
Hos.—Hosea
H.P., h.p.—horsepower
hr.—hour
h.s.—*hora somni* (at bedtime)
HUD—Department of Housing a Urban Development
Hz—hertz
I.—island

NSC—National Security Council
NSF—National Science Foundation
N.T.—New Testament
Num.—Numbers
OAS—Organization of American States
ob.—*obiit* (died)
Obad.—Obadiah
obs.—obsolete
Oct.—October
o.d.—*omni die* (every day)
OECD—Organization for Economic Cooperation and Development
o.h., omn. hor.—*omni hora* (every hour)
OK, O.K.—correct; all right
OMB—Office of Management and Budget
o.n., omn. noct.—*omni nocte* (every night)
o.p.—out of print
op. cit.—*opere citato* (in the work cited)
OPEC—Organization of Petroleum Exporting Countries
orch.—orchestra
OSHA—Occupational Safety and Health Administration
O.T.—Old Testament
p.—page; part
p—pence; penny
par.—paragraph; parenthesis
Parl.—Parliament
pass.—*passim* (throughout, here and there)
pat.—patent; patented
PBS—Public Broadcasting System
P.C.—*post cibum* (after meals)
PCB—polychlorinated biphenyl
pd.—paid
pen.—peninsula
Pet.—Peter
Pfc.—Private first class
phar.—pharmacy
Ph.B.—Bachelor of Philosophy
Phil.—Philippians
Philem.—Philemon
PHS—Public Health Service
phys.—physics; physical
pk.—park; peak; peck
PKU—phenylketonuria
pl.—plural; place; plate
PLO—Palestine Liberation Organization
p.m.—postmaster; post mortem
P.M., p.m.—*post meridiem* (after noon)
p.o.—*per os* (by mouth)

‡Usually honorary

P.O.—post office
pop.—population
POW—prisoner of war
p.p.—parcel post
pp.—pages
ppd.—prepaid
pref.—preface
Pres.—President
p.r.n.—*pro re nata* (as occasion arises; given when necessary)
pro tem.—*pro tempore* (for the time being)
pro us. ext.—*pro usu externo* (for external use)
Prof.—Professor
Prov.—Proverbs
prov.—province
Ps.—Psalms
P.S.—*post scriptum* (postscript)
pseud.—pseudonym
PST—Pacific Standard Time
PTA—Parent-Teacher Association
Pvt.—Private
Q.E.D.—*quod erat demonstrandum* (which was to be shown or proved)
q.h.—*quaque hora* (every hour)
q.i.d.—*quater in die* (four times a day)
Q.M.—quartermaster
q.p.—*quantum placet* (as much as you please)
quot.—quotation; *quoties* (as often as needed)
quotid.—*quotidie* (daily)
q.v.—*quod vide* (which see)
R.—*rex* (king); *regina* (queen); Republican; River
RAF—Royal Air Force
RBC—red blood cell
R.C.—Red Cross; Roman Catholic
R.D.—rural delivery
rd.—road
RDA—recommended dietary allowance
ref.—refer; reference
reg.—region; regulation
Rep.—Republic; Republican; Representative
rev.—revised
Rev.—Revelation; Reverend
R.I.P.—*requiescat in pace* (rest in peace)
riv.—river
R.N.—Royal Navy; registered nurse
RNA—ribonucleic acid
Rom.—Romans
ROTC—Reserve Officers Training Corps
rpm—revolutions per minute
rpt.—reprinted; report
R.R.—railroad; rural route

R.S.V.—Revised Standard Version (Bible)
R.S.V.P.—*Répondez, s'il vous plaît* (Answer, if you please)
Rt. Rev.—Right Reverend
RV—recreational vehicle
R.V.—Revised Version (Bible)
S.—south
s.—second
SAC—Strategic Air Command
Sam.—Samuel
Sat.—Saturday
SBA—Small Business Administration
‡Sc.D., D.Sc., D.S.—Doctor of Science
sci.—science; scientific
sec.—second
SEC—Securities and Exchange Commission
secy.—secretary
Sen.—Senator
Sept.—September
Sgt.—Sergeant
SIDS—sudden infant death syndrome
Sig.—*signa* (write, label)
sig.—signature
S.J.—Society of Jesus
soc.—society
Song of Sol.—Song of Solomon
s.o.s.—*si opus sit* (if necessary)
SP—Shore Patrol
sp.—spelling; species
SPCA—Society for the Prevention of Cruelty to Animals
sq.—square
Sr.—Senior
SS.—Saints
S.S.—steamship
SSA—Social Security Administration
SSS—Selective Service System
SST—supersonic transport
s.t.—short ton
St.—Saint; strait; street
Ste.—Sainte
S.T.M.—Master of Sacred Theology
subj.—subject
Sun.—Sunday
Supt.—Superintendent
syn.—synonym
TB—tuberculosis
tech.—technical; technology
temp.—temperature
ter., terr.—territory
Test.—Testament (Bible)
theol.—theological; theology
Thess.—Thessalonians
Th.M.—Master of Theology
Thurs.—Thursday
Tim.—Timothy

Tit.—Titus
TNT—trinitrotoluene
tp., twp.—township
tr.—translation; transpose
treas.—treasurer
trig.—trigonometry
TSH—thyroid-stimulating hormone
Tues.—Tuesday
TVA—Tennessee Valley Authority
typ., typo., typog.—typography
UAW—United Automobile Workers
UFO—unidentified flying object
UHF—ultrahigh frequency
UMTA—Urban Mass Transportation Administration
ung.—*unguentum* (ointment)
univ.—university
UPI—United Press International
U.S.—United States
USA—United States Army
U.S.A.—United States of America
USAF—United States Air Force

USCG—United States Coast Guard
USDA—United States Department of Agriculture
USMC—United States Marine Corps
USN—United States Navy
USO—United Service Organizations
USPS—United States Postal Service
U.S.S.—United States Ship
ut dict.—*ut dictum* (as directed)
ut sup.—*ut supra* (as above)
v.—verb
V—volt
v., vid.—*vide* (see)
v., vs.—*versus* (against)
VA—Veterans Administration
VAT—value-added tax
VD—venereal disease
vet.—veteran; veterinarian
VFW—Veterans of Foreign Wars of the United States
VHF—very high frequency
VIP—very important person

viz.—*videlicet* (namely)
VOA—Voice of America
vol.—volume
V.P.—Vice President
Vulg.—Vulgate (Bible)
W—watt
W.—west
W.C.T.U.—Woman's Christian Temperance Union
Wed.—Wednesday
wt.—weight
Xmas—Christmas
YMCA—Young Men's Christian Association
YWCA—Young Women's Christian Association
YM-YWHA—Young Men's and Young Women's Hebrew Association
Zech.—Zechariah
Zeph.—Zephaniah
ZIP—Zoning Improvement Plan
zool.—zoology

Postal and traditional abbreviations for the United States and Canada

The table below lists the states and certain outlying areas of the United States, and the provinces and territories of Canada. After the full name of each political unit, its postal abbreviation appears, followed by its traditional abbreviation.

Alabama AL, Ala.
Alaska AK,*
Arizona AZ, Ariz.
Arkansas AR, Ark.
California CA, Calif.
Colorado CO, Colo.
Connecticut CT, Conn.
Delaware DE, Del.
Florida FL, Fla.
Georgia GA, Ga.
Hawaii HI,*
Idaho ID, Ida.
Illinois IL, Ill.
Indiana IN, Ind.
Iowa IA, Ia.
Kansas KS, Kans. or Kan.
Kentucky KY, Ky. or Ken.
Louisiana LA, La.
Maine ME, Me.
Maryland MD, Md.
Massachusetts MA, Mass.
Michigan MI, Mich.
Minnesota MN, Minn.

Mississippi MS, Miss.
Missouri MO, Mo.
Montana MT, Mont.
Nebraska NE, Nebr. or Neb.
Nevada NV, Nev.
New Hampshire NH, N.H.
New Jersey NJ, N.J.
New Mexico NM, N. Mex. or N.M.
New York NY, N.Y.
North Carolina NC, N.C.
North Dakota ND, N. Dak. or N.D.
Ohio OH, O.
Oklahoma OK, Okla.
Oregon OR, Ore. or Oreg.
Pennsylvania PA, Pa. or Penn.
Rhode Island RI, R.I.
South Carolina SC, S.C.
South Dakota SD, S. Dak. or S.D.
Tennessee TN, Tenn.
Texas TX, Tex.
Utah UT, Ut.
Vermont VT, Vt.
Virginia VA, Va.

Washington WA, Wash.
West Virginia WV, W. Va.
Wisconsin WI, Wis.
Wyoming WY, Wyo.
District of Columbia DC, D.C.
Guam GU,*
Puerto Rico PR, P.R.
Virgin Islands VI, V.I.

Alberta AB, Alta.
British Columbia BC, B.C.
Manitoba MB, Man.
New Brunswick NB, N.B.
Newfoundland NF, Nfld.
Northwest Territories NT, N.W. Terr. or N.W.T.
Nova Scotia NS, N.S.
Ontario ON, Ont.
Prince Edward Island PE, P.E.I.
Quebec PQ, Que.
Saskatchewan SK, Sask.
Yukon Territory YT, Y.T.
Labrador LB, Lab.

*No traditional abbreviation

Alphabets and codes

The Roman alphabet is used to write English and many other languages spoken in different parts of the world. This section presents examples of certain non-Roman alphabets. It also includes codes that communicate the Roman alphabet and other information in various ways. For lists of special symbols used in such fields as map-making, and mathematics, see the "Signs and symbols" section.

Greek alphabet

Greek alphabet			Approximate English Sound	Greek alphabet			Approximate English Sound
A	α	alpha	*a*rm	N	ν	nu	*no*w
B	β	beta	*b*ut	Ξ	ξ	xi	a*x*
Γ	γ	gamma	*g*et	O	o	omicron	*fo*r
Δ	δ	delta	*d*o	Π	π	pi	*pi*e
E	ε	epsilon	*he*ld	Π	ρ	rho	*ra*n
Z	ζ	zeta	a*dz*e	Σ	σ ,ς	sigma	*s*at
H	η	eta	*the*y	T	τ	tau	*ta*r
Θ	θ	theta	*th*in	Y	υ	upsilon	r*u*de
I	ι	iota	mach*i*ne	Φ	φ	phi	*f*ill
K	κ	kappa	*k*ite	X	χ	chi	el*kh*orn
Λ	λ	lambda	*l*amb	Ψ	ψ	psi	u*ps*et
M	μ	mu	*m*an	Ω	ω	omega	*ho*ld

Russian (Cyrillic) alphabet

Russian		Roman Equivalent	Approximate Sound in English	Russian		Roman Equivalent	Approximate Sound in English
А	а	a	*fa*r	У	у	u	*foo*l
Б	б	b	*bo*g	Ф	ф	f	*f*or
В	в	v	*v*ault	Х	х	kh	lo*ch*
Г	г	g	*go*	Ц	ц	ts	i*ts*
Д	д	d	*do*g	Ч	ч	ch	*ch*urch
Е	е	ye	*ye*t	Ш	ш	sh	*sch*nauzer
Ё	ё	yo	*ya*wl	Щ	щ	shch	fre*sh ch*eese
Ж	ж	zh	a*z*ure	Ъ	ъ	—	indicates a break
З	з	z	*z*one				for syllable and
И	и	i	*fee*t				y-sound before
Й	й	y	bo*y*				vowel following
К	к	k	*k*id	Ы	ы	y	rh*y*thm
Л	л	l	*l*aw	Ь	ь	—	usually softens
М	м	m	*m*oose				preceding
Н	н	n	*n*ot				consonant, with
О	о	o	*aw*e				attached y-sound,
П	п	p	*p*ot				as *n* in canyon
Р	р	r	th*r*ice (rolled)	Э	э	e	*me*t
С	с	s	*s*oot	Ю	ю	yu	*u*se
Т	т	t	*t*oe	Я	я	ya	*ya*rd

13

Hebrew alphabet

The Hebrew Alphabet has 26 consonants. Five of them—Kaph, Mem, Nun, Peh, and Tsadi—are formed differently when they come at the ends of words. The illustration below shows the consonants in alphabetical order from right to left, which is the way the Hebrew language is read and written.

| Khaph | Kaph | Yod | Teth | Heth | Zayin | Vav | He | Daleth | Gimel | Veth | Beth | Aleph |

| Tav | Sin | Shin | Resh | Koph | Tsadi | Feh | Peh | Ayin | Samekh | Nun | Mem | Lamed |

Hebrew Vowels are indicated by vowel points placed with a consonant. Some of the vowel points are shown below with Daleth.

| Dih | Dee | Deh | Day | Dah | Daw | Duh | Doh | Doh | Doo | Doo |

Finger alphabet

The Finger alphabet is one of the special systems that help deaf people communicate. Each letter of this alphabet is represented by a different position of the fingers of one hand.

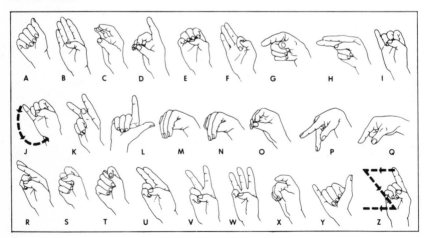

14

Braille

Braille is a code of small raised dots pressed on paper. Blind persons read Braille by running their fingertips over the raised dots. The complete code has 63 characters, including letters, numerals, punctuation marks, word symbols, and speech sounds. Louis Braille invented the code (see "People").

A	B	C	D	E	F	G	H	I	J	K	L	M	N	O

P	Q	R	S	T	U	V	X	Y	Z	and	for	of	the	with

Morse code and international Morse code

Morse code uses a system of long and short signals to send messages. In its written form, a dot represents a short signal, and a dash represents a long signal. Morse code can also be used with flashes of light or with long and short sounds, such as those made by a telegraph machine. The original Morse code includes spaces between the dots used to form some letters. The International Morse Code is a later version. The code was invented by Samuel F. B. Morse (see "People" section).

Morse code

A	B	C	D	E	F	G
●▬	▬●●●	●●●	▬●●	●	●▬●	▬▬●

H	I	J	K	L	M	N
●●●●	●●	▬●▬●	▬●▬	▬	▬▬	▬●

O	P	Q	R	S	T	U
●●	●●●●●	●●▬●	●●●	●●●	▬	●●▬

V	W	X	Y	Z
●●●▬	●▬▬	●▬●●	●● ●●	●●●● ●

Numerals

1	2	3	4
●▬▬●	●●▬●●	●●●▬●	●●●●▬

5	6	7	8
▬▬▬	●●●●●●	▬▬●●	▬●●●●

9	0
▬●●▬	▬

Punctuation

Comma	Period	Semicolon	Interrogation
●▬●▬	●●▬▬●●	●●● ●●	▬●●▬

International Morse code

A	B	C	D	E	F
●▬	▬●●●	▬●▬●	▬●●	●	●●▬●

G	H	I	J	K
▬▬●	●●●●	●●	●▬▬▬	▬●▬

L	M	N	O	P
●▬●●	▬▬	▬●	▬▬▬	●▬▬●

Q	R	S	T	U
▬▬●▬	●▬●	●●●	▬	●●▬

V	W	X	Y	Z
●●●▬	●▬▬	▬●●▬	▬●▬▬	▬▬●●

Numerals

1	2	3	4
●▬▬▬▬	●●▬▬▬	●●●▬▬	●●●●▬

5	6	7	8
●●●●●	▬●●●●	▬▬●●●	▬▬▬●●

9	0
▬▬▬▬●	▬▬▬▬▬

Punctuation and other signs

Period	Comma	Interrogation	Colon
●▬●▬●▬	▬▬●●▬▬	●●▬▬●●	▬▬▬●●●

Semicolon	Quotation marks
▬●▬●▬●	●▬●●▬●

S O S	Start	Wait	Error
●●●▬▬▬●●●	▬●▬	●▬●●●	●●●●●●●●

End of Message	Understand
●▬●▬●	●▬●

International flag code

The International flag code is used on ships.

blue | yellow
white | red | black

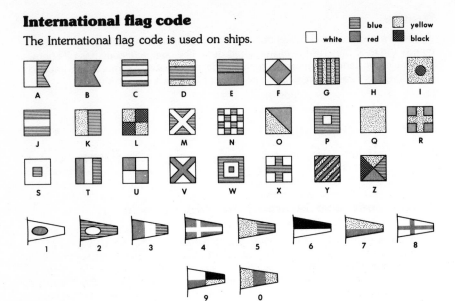

Semaphore

Semaphore is a code system that uses two flags held in various positions. The numerals 1 through 0 are signaled by showing the numeral signal before the first 10 letters of the alphabet.

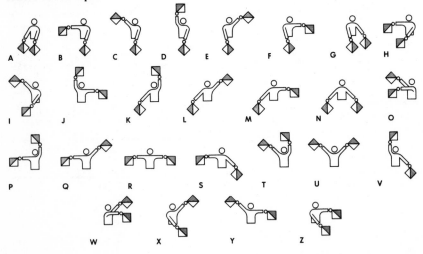

Animals

This section consists mainly of general information about the animal kingdom. For information about the early development of animal life on earth, see the table in the "Earth" section. The Biomes map and table, also in the "Earth" section, show the regions where certain kinds of animals live.

Interesting facts about animals

Kinds of animals. Scientists have classified nearly a million kinds of animals. There are more than 800,000 kinds of insects alone. They make up by far the largest animal group. Scientists believe there may be from 1 million to 10 million kinds of insects not yet discovered. The animal kingdom also includes more than 20,000 kinds of fishes, over 8,600 kinds of birds, about 6,000 kinds of reptiles, about 4,000 kinds of mammals, and about 3,000 kinds of amphibians.

The largest animal that has ever lived is the blue whale. This mammal measures up to 100 feet (30 meters) long when fully grown. The largest land animal is the elephant. The giraffe is the tallest animal of all.

The smallest animals of all are one-celled protozoans, which can be seen only with a microscope.

The smallest mammals are certain kinds of shrews that are less than 3 inches (8 centimeters) long and weigh about as much as a penny.

The largest fish is the whale shark. It weighs more than twice as much as an African elephant, and it is harmless to people. It eats small water plants and animals.

The smallest bird is the bee hummingbird. Fully grown, it measures about 2 inches (5 centimeters) long and weighs about 1/10 ounce (3 grams). Its nest is the size of half a walnut shell.

Animal intelligence. Apes and monkeys have more learning ability than any other animals except humans. The bottle-nosed dolphin is the smartest water animal. Among hoofed animals, the pig is the best problem solver. The squirrel is the brightest rodent.

Insect population. There are at least four times as many insects in the world as all other animals combined. Scientists estimate that in every square mile (2.6 square kilometers) of land, there are as many insects as there are people in the entire world.

Animal senses are very well developed among certain species. Dogs, for example, can detect odors that are millions of times too faint to be recognized by people. Dragonflies can see a gnat flying 18 feet (5.5 meters) away. The amount of sugar in water that a monarch butterfly can taste would have to be increased 2,000 times before a person would be able to taste it.

The life spans of animals range from a few hours or days for adult mayflies to more than 100 years for the giant tortoise.

The first animal to be tamed was probably the dog. Prehistoric people used dogs to help them hunt other animals for food. Cattle were raised for food as early as 12,000 years ago.

Birds that can't fly include ostriches and penguins. Ostriches—the largest of all birds—walk or run on their long legs. Penguins waddle on land and use their wings to swim underwater.

The greatest animal travelers are birds called Arctic terns. They travel about 11,000 miles (17,700 kilometers) each way between their breeding grounds in the Arctic and their winter home in the Antarctic.

A champion weight lifter is the ant. It can lift 50 times its own weight. To be as strong as an ant, a 175-pound (79-kilogram) person would have to be able to lift more than 4 short tons (3.6 metric tons)—with his or her teeth.

The largest ears of all animals are those of the African elephant. They grow as large as 4 feet (1.2 meters) across. The largest eyes of all land animals are those of the horse and the ostrich. They are about one and a half times as large as human eyes.

Caterpillars have from 2,000 to 4,000 muscles. In comparison, human beings have fewer than 700.

Scientific classification of the animal kingdom

The animal kingdom can be divided into two large groups: *vertebrates* (animals with backbones) and *invertebrates* (animals without backbones). The backbone of a vertebrate helps protect its main nerve cord, or spinal cord. Vertebrates, commonly called *higher animals,* include amphibians, birds, fishes, reptiles, and mammals. Invertebrates, commonly called *lower animals,* have an unprotected main nerve cord. There are many kinds of invertebrates, including amebas, centipedes, insects, mollusks, sponges, starfish, and worms. A small sea animal called the *amphioxus* is considered a link between the higher and lower animals. It has a rod of cartilage called a *notochord* that serves as a backbone and gives some protection to the main nerve.

Scientists classify animals by separating them according to their differences and grouping them according to their likenesses. The scientific classification below lists animals according to their *phylum* (major grouping) and gives a few of the characteristics that the members of each phylum have in common.

Phylum	Characteristics

Subkingdom Protozoa (One-celled animals)

Protozoa	The bodies consist of one cell. The animals live alone or in colonies. They grow in fresh water or salt water, in the soil, or in the bodies of other animals. Classes include Mastigophora, Sarcodina, Sporozoa, Ciliata, and Suctoria.

Subkingdom Parazoa (Many-celled animals without a true digestive cavity)

Porifera (Sponges)	Body walls consist of two layers of cells. Internal cavities or canals connect with pores in the body wall. Most of these animals grow in colonies and are found in fresh water or in salt water.

Subkingdom Metazoa (Many-celled animals with true digestive cavities)

Mesozoa	These are the smallest of the multicelled animals. Their bodies are small, slender, and wormlike. They have a layer of digestive cells on the outside wall of the body. They live as parasites in the bodies of animals without backbones.

Phylum	Characteristics
Coelenterata (Coelenterates)	The bodies of these animals contain a jellylike material between two layers of cells. The baglike digestive cavity has a single opening. Classes include Scyphozoa (jellyfishes) and Anthozoa (sea anemones and corals).
Ctenophora (Comb jellies)	The bodies are round or almost flat, and contain a jellylike material. The animals live in salt water and swim by means of eight *combs* (rows of platelike tissues). The ribbonlike *Venus's-girdle* is a member of this phylum.
Platyhelminthes (Flatworms)	These animals have soft, thin, flattened bodies that consist of three layers of cells. Most flatworms live as parasites in other animals. Classes include Turbellaria (free-living flatworms), Trematoda (flukes), and Cestoda (tapeworms).
Nemertinea or Nemertea (Ribbon worms)	The bodies of these animals are soft, slender, and elastic. They are not divided into segments. Most ribbon worms live in salt water, but a few kinds live in fresh water or on land. None of these animals is a parasite.
Aschelminthes	Most animals of this group have small, slender bodies. They move about and get food by means of cilia. Classes include Rotifera (wheel animalcules or wheel worms), Nematoda (roundworms), and Nematomorpha (hair snakes).
Acanthocephala (Spiny-headed worms)	These animals have flat, rough bodies, and rows of curved spines on the "head." The young are parasites in arthropods. The adults are parasites in vertebrates. They use their head spines to attach themselves to other animals.
Entoprocta	These animals resemble flowers. They have stalklike parts of the body attached to objects or other animals in the water. A *calyx* (cuplike structure) at the top of the stalk has a single circle of tentacles on top, like flower petals.
Phoronidea	The bodies of these marine animals are wormlike, but are not divided into segments. They have a pair of "arms" that bear tentacles. The animals live in mud, encased in a membranous tube formed from a body secretion.
Ectoprocta or Bryozoa (Moss animals)	These are plantlike water animals that usually grow in colonies. They cannot move about. The colonies form crusts on rocks, shells, and water plants. Each animal has tentacles around the mouth that sweep food into the mouth.
Brachiopoda (Lamp shells)	These marine animals have two-piece shells. They attach themselves to rocks by means of fleshy stalks. One member of this phylum, the genus *Lingula*, is believed by some scientists to be the oldest living genus of animals.
Mollusca (Mollusks)	The soft bodies of these animals are covered by a *mantle* (layer of tissue) that usually secretes a limy shell. Classes include Gastropoda (univalve mollusks such as limpets) and Pelecypoda (bivalve mollusks such as clams).
Sipunculoidea (Peanut worms)	These animals have slender, gourd-shaped bodies without segments. They live along the seashore, where they burrow into the sand and mud. When disturbed, they pull their bodies together so they look like a peanut.
Echiuroidea	The bodies of these marine animals are soft and fleshy. The mouth is at the base of a long, trough-shaped *proboscis* (snout). They dig and live in U-shaped burrows in mud or sand, or find shelter between rocks in shallow water.
Priapuloidea	These marine animals have sausage-shaped bodies, with a slightly enlarged "head." The head can be pushed forward or pulled backward. Animals of this group live in mud or sand, and often use empty shells for protection.
Annelida (Segmented worms)	These animals have long bodies divided into many segments. Most of them are covered with bristles, which they use to move about. Classes include Polychaeta (sandworms), Oligochaeta (earthworms), and Hirudinea (leeches).
Arthropoda (Arthropods or joint-footed animals)	These animals have a head, thorax, abdomen, and three or more pairs of jointed legs. Classes include Arachnida (spiders), Crustacea (lobsters), Insecta (insects), Chilopoda (centipedes), and Diplopoda (millipedes).
Chaetognatha (Arrowworms)	These animals have slender, transparent bodies divided into three distinct sections: (1) head, (2) trunk, and (3) tail. They have fins on the trunk and a tail fin for moving about. They are an important part of ocean plankton.

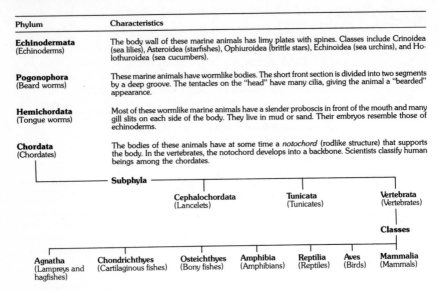

Phylum	Characteristics
Echinodermata (Echinoderms)	The body wall of these marine animals has limy plates with spines. Classes include Crinoidea (sea lilies), Asteroidea (starfishes), Ophiuroidea (brittle stars), Echinoidea (sea urchins), and Holothuroidea (sea cucumbers).
Pogonophora (Beard worms)	These marine animals have wormlike bodies. The short front section is divided into two segments by a deep groove. The tentacles on the "head" have many cilia, giving the animal a "bearded" appearance.
Hemichordata (Tongue worms)	Most of these wormlike marine animals have a slender proboscis in front of the mouth and many gill slits on each side of the body. They live in mud or sand. Their embryos resemble those of echinoderms.
Chordata (Chordates)	The bodies of these animals have at some time a *notochord* (rodlike structure) that supports the body. In the vertebrates, the notochord develops into a backbone. Scientists classify human beings among the chordates.

Subphyla

Cephalochordata (Lancelets)	Tunicata (Tunicates)	Vertebrata (Vertebrates)

Classes

Agnatha (Lampreys and hagfishes)	Chondrichthyes (Cartilaginous fishes)	Osteichthyes (Bony fishes)	Amphibia (Amphibians)	Reptilia (Reptiles)	Aves (Birds)	Mammalia (Mammals)

Animal terms

Amphibians are cold-blooded vertebrates that live both on land and in water. Frogs are an example of amphibians.

Carnivorous animals eat animal flesh. Examples include lions, wolves, dolphins, and hyenas.

Cold-blooded animals have an internal body temperature that changes according to their surroundings. They are hot on hot days and cold on cold days. All animals except birds and mammals are cold-blooded. This group includes many animals that have no blood at all, such as jellyfish and sponges.

Domesticated animals are those that have been tamed to serve as pets, as working animals, or as sources of food and other products. Examples include dogs, horses, and cattle.

Endangered species are animals that are in danger of becoming extinct. Some have become endangered as a result of too much hunting or fishing. Other animals are threatened by expanding human settlement and other changes in their environment.

Estivate means to sleep through the summer. In places where summers are very hot, some animals estivate to escape the heat. Estivating animals include lungfish and some kinds of snails.

Herbivorous animals are plant eaters. Examples include cattle, elephants, and horses.

Hibernate means to sleep through the cold winter months. Many hibernating animals use stored body fat as food while they are inactive. Animals that hibernate include bats, frogs, skunks, and woodchucks.

Insectivorous animals are those that eat insects. Examples include bats, shrews, and anteaters.

Mammals are vertebrates that feed their young on their mother's milk. Mammals include such familiar animals as cats, dogs, monkeys, cows, mice, whales, and humans.

Marsupials are mammals that give birth to tiny, poorly developed young. The newborns attach themselves to the mother's nipples immediately after birth and remain there until they develop more fully. In most marsupials, the nipples are located on the stomach. Marsupials include kangaroos, opossums, and koala bears.

Migration is a journey by a large group of animals at a certain time of year. Migrating animals include deer, whales, monarch butterflies, salmon, and robins.

Molting is the regular process of shedding of hair, skin, or feathers that some animals go through.

Omnivorous animals eat both plants and animals. Examples include bears, hogs, and humans.

Parasite is a small animal that feeds on or lives inside plants or other animals. They carry a variety of diseases, some of which can cause death.

Predators are animals that hunt other animals as food. Examples include coyotes, lions, and wolves.

Protective coloration is a form of defense in which an animal's color makes it blend in with its surroundings so that its enemies are unlikely to notice it.

Protective resemblance is a defense mechanism in which an animal's shape enables it to hide from its enemies. Some insects, for example, look like the leaves of plants.

Reptile is a cold-blooded vertebrate that has lungs for breathing and dry, scaly skin. Examples include alligators, snakes, and turtles.

Warm-blooded animals maintain about the same internal body temperature all the time, regardless of the temperature of their surroundings. Birds and mammals are the only warm-blooded animals.

Life processes

Animal reproduction occurs in two ways: (1) *asexual reproduction,* and (2) *sexual reproduction.* In asexual reproduction, one parent produces the offspring. In sexual reproduction, two parents produce the offspring. Many simple animals, such as sponges, flatworms, and protozoans, reproduce asexually most of the time and sexually some of the time. Most other animals reproduce only sexually.

Asexual reproduction can occur in several ways. In *binary fission,* the simplest method, a one-celled animal, such as a paramecium, develops into a two-celled structure, which then splits apart into two new organisms. Planarians and some other multicelled animals reproduce by a process called *fragmentation.* The animal breaks into two or more parts, and each part develops into a new animal. The missing parts on the parent animal grow back through a process called *regeneration.* *Budding* is a process in which the parent animal forms small extensions, called *buds,* which eventually may detach themselves. In *sporulation,* an animal produces and releases one-celled structures called *spores* that develop into new organisms.

Almost all animals that reproduce sexually have special organs or tissues that produce either *eggs* (female sex cells) or *sperm* (male sex cells). The reproduction process begins with fertilization, the union of an egg and a sperm. Among most higher animals, including almost all birds, mammals, and reptiles, *internal fertilization* takes place within the female's body, after the male releases sperm into the female. *External fertilization* occurs among most fish and amphibians. In this process, male and female animals release their sex cells into the water, and some of the cells unite.

Among most mammals, the growth and development of the new organisms occur within the female, and the young are eventually born alive. This internal development is called *viviparity.* Among most reptiles and birds, the young develop within fertilized eggs that have shells and are laid outside the female's body. This is called *oviparity.* Some amphibians, fish, and reptiles produce eggs that remain within the female until the young hatch. This process is called *ovoviviparity.*

A *hermaphrodite* is an animal that produces both eggs and sperm. Examples include earthworms and some sponges. Among some hermaphrodites, an egg and a sperm from the same organism can fertilize each other in a process called *self-fertilization.* In most cases, however, a hermaphrodite must unite with another individual of its species for fertilization to occur.

Parthenogenesis is a process in which an unfertilized egg can develop into an adult animal. This process occurs among wasps and honeybees. Many animals that reproduce this way also reproduce by other sexual methods.

Respiration is the process by which animals take in oxygen and give off carbon dioxide. Almost all animals breathe air in order to get the oxygen they need to survive. Most vertebrates breathe through lungs if they live on land and through gills if they live in water. Lungs of land animals work in various ways. But in all cases, air is drawn into the lungs, where oxygen is absorbed by the bloodstream and then transported to all parts of the body. A fish gulps water and then expels it through its gills, which absorb the oxygen the water contains. Insects, the most common invertebrates, take in air through tiny openings called *spiracles* in the sides of their bodies. Each spiracle leads to a tube called a *trachea.* The tubes branch out into a complex system that leads to all parts of the insect's body. Some worms and other invertebrates simply absorb all the oxygen they need through the surface of their bodies. A few kinds of animals live in places where oxygen is not readily available. For example, certain kinds of parasites live in intestinal organs of other animals. They depend on a special digestive process to get oxygen from their food.

Metabolism is the conversion of food into energy and living tissue. It takes place in *all* living things—animals and plants. It actually consists of two chemical processes: (1) *catabolism,* the breaking down of food to release energy and digest food, and (2) *anabolism,* the building and repair of cells and tissues.

During digestion, food is broken down chemically into "food fuels" that enter the bloodstream. The blood carries these food fuels to all parts of the body where they can be used as building blocks for new tissue or as energy sources for tissue building. The oxygen that an animal takes in during breathing is used to burn the food fuels in a process called *tissue respiration.* Tissue respiration thus supplies the energy needed for tissue building. It also supplies the heat that warm-blooded animals need to maintain their body temperatures.

Growth is the process of increasing in size. All animals begin life as a single cell. The cell may then grow, multiply, and divide to form other cells. Some cells may grow into specific structures, such as skin, muscles, or body organs. This development into specific structures is called *differentiation.* The form that an organism develops depends on its *heredity*—the passing on of characteristics from parents to offspring. For more information about heredity, see the "Plants" section.

In many animals, including most vertebrates, the developing offspring closely resemble the animal in adult form. As these animals grow, the proportions of their body parts may change; but basically, the young animals are simply small versions of the adults. Along with food, the steady growth of these animals depends on heredity and substances called *hormones* that are produced by various glands in the body.

Other animals go through a process called *metamorphosis,* in which the form of an animal changes drastically at different stages of life. A frog is an example of a vertebrate that undergoes metamorphosis. The frog develops first into an egg. The egg hatches into a water-dwelling tadpole. The tadpole eventually grows legs and lungs and becomes an adult frog, able to live both in and out of water.

Complete metamorphosis occurs in most insects, including butterflies, flies, bees, and ants. This four-staged process begins with an egg. A wormlike larva—a caterpillar, for example—hatches from the egg. After the larva completes its growth it stops eating and becomes a pupa. Some larvae spin a cocoon or some other kind of covering around themselves at this point. During this stage, the larva undergoes a complete change in form, until it finally emerges as a fully developed adult. Some kinds of insects, including grasshoppers and roaches, go through a three-staged process called *incomplete metamorphosis.* In this process, an egg hatches into a nymph. The nymph *molts* (sheds) its outer covering several times as it grows before emerging as an adult.

Animal life spans

Figures in this list are from animals in captivity, because of the difficulty of determining the ages of wild animals.

Mammals
(Average life span in years)

Buffalo	10
Cat	13-17
Chimpanzee	40-50
Deer (fallow)	10
Dog	13
Elephant	60
Goat	10
Grizzly bear	20
Hippopotamus	40
Horse	20-30
Jaguar	14
Lion	20-25
Monkey (rhesus)	15
Mouse	1-2
Sheep	10-15
Squirrel	9
Tiger	11
Wolf	12
Zebra	22

Birds
(Maximum life span in years)

Blue jay	4
Canada goose	32
Canary	24
Cardinal	22
Chickadee	7
Condor	52
Heron	24
Macaw (red and blue)	64
Ostrich (African)	50
Owl (snowy)	24½
Penguin (king)	26
Pigeon	35
Raven	69
Robin	12
Skylark	24
Sparrow	20
Starling	15

Fish
(Maximum life span in years)

Dogfish	2
Electric eel	11½
Flounder	10
Goldfish	25
Halibut	40
Lamprey	5
Lungfish (African)	17
Mackerel (Pacific)	11
Perch	11
Pike	24
Sea horse	6
Sole (Dover)	15
Sturgeon	50
Trout (rainbow)	4

Reptiles and amphibians
(Maximum life span in years)

Alligator	56
Boa constrictor	23
Bullfrog	15½
Chameleon	3½
Cottonmouth	21
Crocodile	13½
Frog (leopard)	6
Garter snake	6
Gila monster	20
King snake	14½
Puff adder	14
Rattlesnake	18½
Salamander (spotted)	25
Turtle (box)	123
Water snake	7

Breeds of cats

This table lists the breeds commonly recognized by most cat associations in the United States. Pictures of many of these breeds appear in color on pages 161–162.

Breed	Characteristics
Short-haired group	
Abyssinian	Medium-sized; *agouti* coat pattern (each hair has alternating bands of light and dark)
American shorthair	Medium-sized to large; color varies
Burmese	Medium-sized; dark brown
Havana brown	Medium-sized; reddish-brown
Japanese bobtail	Medium-sized; color varies
Korat	Medium-sized; silvery gray
Manx	Small; some varieties have no tail; color varies
Rex	Small to medium-sized; color varies
Russian blue	Large; bluish-gray
Siamese	Medium-sized; *colorpoint* (light body with darker face, ears, feet and tail)

Breed	Characterstics
Long-haired group	
Balinese	Medium-sized; colorpoint
Birman	Large; colorpoint except paws are white
Himalayan	Medium-sized to large; brown, light gray, or colorpoint
Maine coon	Large; color varies
Persian	Medium-sized to large; color varies
Somali	Medium-sized; agouti coat
Turkish angora	Medium-sized; color varies

Breeds of purebred dogs

Pictures of some of the most popular dog breeds appear in color on pages 163–169.

Breed	Average Weight in lbs.	in kg	Breed	Average Weight in lbs.	in kg
Sporting group			**Toy group**		
American water spaniel	25-45	11-20	Affenpinscher	7-8	3-4
Brittany	30-40	14-18	Brussels griffon	8-10	4-5
Chesapeake Bay retriever	55-75	25-34	Chihuahua	1-6	0.5-3
Clumber spaniel	35-65	15-29	English toy spaniel	9-12	4-5
Cocker spaniel	22-28	10-13	Italian greyhound	6-10	3-5
Curly-coated retriever	60-70	27-32	Japanese chin	7	3
English cocker spaniel	26-34	12-15	Maltese	4-6	2-3
English setter	50-70	23-32	Miniature pinscher	6-10	3-5
English springer spaniel	49-55	22-25	Papillon	5-11	2-5
Field spaniel	35-50	16-23	Pekingese	6-10	3-5
Flat-coated retriever	60-70	27-32	Pomeranian	3-7	1-3
German short-haired pointer	45-70	20-32	Pug	14-18	6-8
German wire-haired pointer	55-65	25-29	Shih tzu	12-15	5-9
			Silky terrier	8-10	4-5
Golden retriever	60-75	27-34	Yorkshire terrier	4-8	2-4
Gordon setter	45-80	20-36			
Irish setter	60-70	27-32	**Working group**		
Irish water spaniel	45-65	20-29	Akita	80-120	36-54
Labrador retriever	55-75	25-34	Alaskan malamute	75-85	34-39
Pointer	45-60	20-27	Bernese mountain dog	50-75	23-34
Sussex spaniel	35-45	16-20	Boxer	60-75	27-34
Vizsla	50	23	Bullmastiff	100-130	45-59
Weimaraner	55-85	25-39	Doberman pinscher	60-75	27-34
Welsh springer spaniel	40	18	Giant schnauzer	75	34
Wire-haired pointing griffon	50-60	23-27	Great Dane	120-150	54-68
			Great Pyrenees	90-125	41-57
Hound group			Komondor	90	41
Afghan hound	50-60	23-27	Kuvasz	70	32
American foxhound	60-70	27-32	Mastiff	165-185	75-84
Basenji	22-24	10-11	Newfoundland	110-150	50-68
Basset hound	25-45	11-20	Rottweiler	80-90	36-41
Beagle	18-30	8-14	St. Bernard	165-200	75-90
Black and tan coonhound	50-60	23-27	Samoyed	35-60	16-27
Bloodhound	80-110	36-50	Siberian husky	35-60	16-27
Borzoi	60-105	27-48	Standard schnauzer	35-40	16-18
Dachshund	5-20	2-9			
English foxhound	60-75	27-34	**Herding group**		
Greyhound	60-70	27-32	Australian cattle dog	35-55	16-25
Harrier	40-50	18-23	Bearded collie	50	23
Ibizan hound	42-50	19-23	Belgian malinois	50-55	23-25
Irish wolfhound	105-140	48-64	Belgian sheepdog	55-60	25-27
Norwegian elkhound	50	23	Belgian tervuren	55	25
Otter hound	65	29	Bouvier des Flandres	70	32
Rhodesian ridgeback	65-75	29-34	Briard	70-80	32-36
Saluki	60	27	Cardigan Welsh corgi	20-26	9-12
Scottish deerhound	75-110	34-50	Collie	50-75	23-34
Whippet	18-23	8-10	German shepherd dog	60-85	27-39
			Old English sheepdog	50-65	23-29
			Pembroke Welsh corgi	18-30	8-14
			Puli	30-35	14-16
			Shetland sheepdog	16-24	7-11

Breed	Average Weight in lbs.	in kg
Terrier group		
Airedale terrier	40-50	18-23
American Staffordshire terrier	35-50	16-23
Australian terrier	12-14	5-6
Bedlington terrier	17-23	8-10
Border terrier	11½-15½	5-7
Bull terrier	30-60	14-27
Cairn terrier	13-14	6
Dandie Dinmont terrier	18-24	8-11
Fox terrier	15-19	7-9
Irish terrier	25-27	11-12
Kerry blue terrier	30-40	14-18
Lakeland terrier	15-17	7-8
Manchester terrier*	5-22	2-10
Miniature schnauzer	15	7
Norfolk terrier	10-15	5-7
Norwich terrier	10-15	5-7
Scottish terrier	18-22	8-10
Sealyham terrier	20-21	9-10
Skye terrier	25	11

Breed	Average Weight in lbs.	in kg
Soft-coated wheaten terrier	35-45	16-20
Staffordshire bull terrier	35	16
Welsh terrier	20	9
West highland white terrier	13-19	6-9
Nonsporting group		
Bichon frise	12-15	5-7
Boston terrier	12-25	5-11
Bulldog	40-50	18-23
Chow chow	50-60	23-27
Dalmatian	40-50	18-23
French bulldog	18-28	8-13
Keeshond	35-40	16-18
Lhasa apso	15	7
Poodle†	7-55	3-25
Schipperke	15	7
Tibetan terrier	22-23	10

*Manchester terriers weighing 12 pounds (5 kilograms) or less are entered in dog shows in Toy group.
†Poodles measuring 10 inches (21 centimeters) or less are entered in dog shows in the Toy group.

Some types and breeds of horses

Pictures of some of the most popular types and breeds of horses appear in color on pages 170–173.

Type	Weight in lbs.	in kg	Height in hands*
Saddle horses			
American saddle horse	900 to 1,200	410 to 540	14.3 to 16.1
American quarter horse	900 to 1,200	410 to 540	14.2 to 15.3
Appaloosa	950 to 1,175	430 to 530	14.2 to 15.2
Arabian	850 to 1,000	390 to 450	14.2 to 15.3
Morgan	800 to 1,100	360 to 500	14.2 to 15.2
Palomino	900 to 1,300	410 to 590	14.1 to 16
Tennessee walking horse	900 to 1,200	410 to 540	15 to 16
Thorough-bred	1,000 to 1,300	450 to 590	15 to 17
Light harness or roadster horses			
Hackney	900 to 1,200	410 to 540	14.3 to 16.2
Standard-bred or American trotter	800 to 1,200	360 to 540	15 to 16

Type	Weight in lbs.	in kg	Height in hands*
Draft horses			
Belgian	1,700 to 2,200	770 to 1,000	16 to 19
Clydesdale	1,500 to 2,000	680 to 910	16 to 17.1
Percheron	1,600 to 2,100	730 to 950	15 to 17
Shire	1,800 to 2,300	820 to 1,040	16 to 17
Suffolk	1,500 to 1,900	680 to 860	15.2 to 16.2
Heavy harness or coach horses			
Cleveland bay	1,250 to 1,550	570 to 700	15.3 to 16.3
French coach	1,100 to 1,400	500 to 640	15.1 to 16.3
German coach	1,200 to 1,500	540 to 680	15.2 to 16.3
Ponies			
Hackney pony	600 to 850	270 to 390	12 to 14.2
Shetland pony	300 to 500	140 to 230	9 to 11.2
Welsh pony	400 to 650	180 to 290	10 to 12

*One hand equals 4 inches (10 centimeters)

Comparative speeds of animals

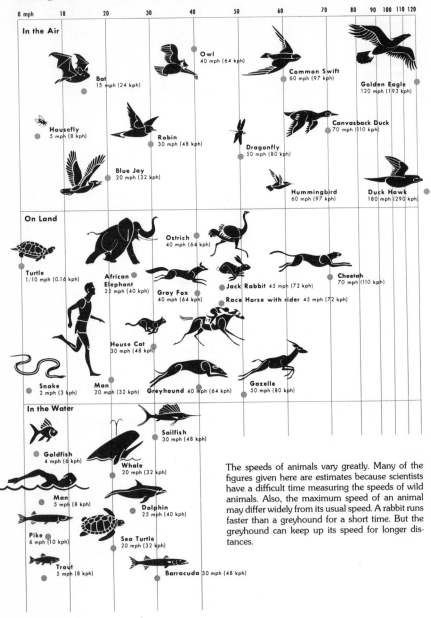

0 mph 10 20 30 40 50 60 70 80 90 100 110 120

In the Air

Bat
15 mph (24 kph)

Owl
40 mph (64 kph)

Common Swift
60 mph (97 kph)

Golden Eagle
120 mph (193 kph)

Housefly
5 mph (8 kph)

Robin
30 mph (48 kph)

Dragonfly
50 mph (80 kph)

Canvasback Duck
70 mph (110 kph)

Blue Jay
20 mph (32 kph)

Hummingbird
60 mph (97 kph)

Duck Hawk
180 mph (290 kph)

On Land

Turtle
1/10 mph (0.16 kph)

Ostrich
40 mph (64 kph)

African Elephant
25 mph (40 kph)

Gray Fox
40 mph (64 kph)

Jack Rabbit 45 mph (72 kph)

Race Horse with rider 45 mph (72 kph)

Cheetah
70 mph (110 kph)

House Cat
30 mph (48 kph)

Snake
2 mph (3 kph)

Man
20 mph (32 kph)

Greyhound 40 mph (64 kph)

Gazelle
50 mph (80 kph)

In the Water

Sailfish
30 mph (48 kph)

Goldfish
4 mph (6 kph)

Whale
20 mph (32 kph)

Man
5 mph (8 kph)

Dolphin
25 mph (40 kph)

Pike
6 mph (10 kph)

Sea Turtle
20 mph (32 kph)

Trout
5 mph (8 kph)

Barracuda 30 mph (48 kph)

The speeds of animals vary greatly. Many of the figures given here are estimates because scientists have a difficult time measuring the speeds of wild animals. Also, the maximum speed of an animal may differ widely from its usual speed. A rabbit runs faster than a greyhound for a short time. But the greyhound can keep up its speed for longer distances.

26

Names of animals and their young

Animal	Male	Female	Young	Group	Approximate gestation period
Albatross (royal)			fledgling	flock	81 days*
Antelope	buck	doe	kid	herd	9 months
Bear	boar	sow	cub	sloth	6-8 months
Beaver			kit pup	colony family	3 months
Bobcat	tom	lioness	kit		50 days
Camel			calf	herd	11 months
Cat	tom	puss, queen	kitten	clowder	63 days
Cattle	bull	cow	calf	herd drove	9 months
Chicken	cock rooster	hen	chick	flock	21 days*
Deer	buck hart stag	doe hind roe	fawn	herd	7 months
Dog	dog	bitch	pup	kennel	58-63 days
Dolphin	bull	cow	calf	school	10-12 months
Donkey	jackass	jennet jenny	foal colt	pace	12 months
Duck	drake	duck	duckling	flock	23-30 days*
Elephant	bull	cow	calf	herd	20-22 months
Fish			fry, larva	school	1 day-5 months
Fox	dog	vixen	cub pup	skulk	49-55 days
Giraffe	bull	cow	calf	herd	14-15 months
Goat	billy buck	nanny doe	kid	herd	51 days
Goose	gander	goose	gosling	flock gaggle	30 days*
Hog	boar	sow	shoat farrow piglet	herd drove	114 days
Horse	stallion stud	dam mare	foal colt (male) filly (female)	herd	11 months
Kangaroo	buck boomer	doe flier	joey	herd troop mob	30-40 days
Lion	lion	lioness	cub	pride	108 days
Ostrich	cock	hen	chick	flock	42 days*
Rabbit	buck	doe	kit kitten	warren	30-32 days
Rat	buck	doe			22 days
Seal	bull	cow	pup whelp	herd trip	8-12 months
Sheep	buck ram	dam ewe	lamb lambkin teg	flock herd	5 months
Swan	cob	pen	cygnet	flock	35 days*
Tiger	tiger	tigress	cub		98–109 days
Turkey	cock gobbler tom	hen	poult	flock	28 days*
Whale	bull	cow	calf	herd	10-17 months
Wolf			pup	pack	65 days
Zebra	stallion	mare	colt	herd	11-12 months

*Approximate incubation period.

27

Area codes

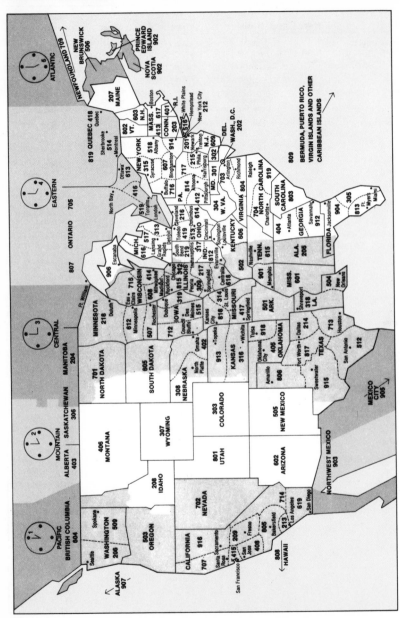

Astrology

Astrology is the study of how the sun, moon, planets, and stars are supposedly related to life and events on earth. It is based on the belief that the heavenly bodies form patterns that can reveal a person's character or future. Astrology originated sometime before 2000 B.C. in Babylonia (now southeastern Iraq). Although many people throughout the world believe in astrology, others consider it merely a form of entertainment with no scientific basis.

One element of astrology is the *zodiac,* a band of stars that appears to encircle the earth. It is divided into 12 equal parts called *signs.* Each sign has certain characteristics, determined by a particular planet and other factors. Astrologers believe that every person is influenced by a particular sign, depending on the person's date of birth. The chart below shows the dates and some of the characteristics associated with each sign.

The signs of the zodiac

Nov. 22- Dec. 21 **Sagittarius** Cheerful, generous, restless	Dec. 22- Jan. 19 **Capricornus** Ambitious, cautious, practical	Jan. 20- Feb. 18 **Aquarius** Curious, outgoing, independent	Feb. 19- Mar. 20 **Pisces** Artistic, emotional, sensitive
Mar. 21- Apr. 19 **Aries** Bold, courageous, energetic	Apr. 20- May 20 **Taurus** Conservative, possessive, loyal	May 21- June 20 **Gemini** Lively, talkative, intelligent	June 21- July 22 **Cancer** Emotional, patriotic, home loving
July 23- Aug. 22 **Leo** Cheerful, proud, powerful	Aug. 23- Sept. 22 **Virgo** Modest, practical, tidy	Sept. 23- Oct. 22 **Libra** Companionable, diplomatic, pleasant	Oct. 23- Nov. 21 **Scorpius** Secretive, intense, passionate

Awards

The following tables list some of the most famous and prestigious awards given in various fields, including entertainment, literature, journalism, and science. For military and other special service awards, see the section "Decorations and medals."

Academy Awards (Oscars)

The Academy Awards, or "Oscars," are presented each spring by the Academy of Motion Picture Arts and Sciences. The awards recognize outstanding achievements in filmmaking during the preceding year.

Best Picture

1927-28	Wings	1947	Gentleman's Agreement	1964	My Fair Lady
1928-29	The Broadway Melody	1948	Hamlet	1965	The Sound of Music
1929-30	All Quiet on the Western Front	1949	All the King's Men	1966	A Man for All Seasons
		1950	All About Eve	1967	In the Heat of the Night
1930-31	Cimarron	1951	An American in Paris	1968	Oliver!
1931-32	Grand Hotel	1952	The Greatest Show on Earth	1969	Midnight Cowboy
1932-33	Cavalcade			1970	Patton
1934	It Happened One Night	1953	From Here to Eternity	1971	The French Connection
1935	Mutiny on the Bounty	1954	On the Waterfront	1972	The Godfather
1936	The Great Ziegfeld	1955	Marty	1973	The Sting
1937	The Life of Emile Zola	1956	Around the World in 80 Days	1974	The Godfather, Part II
1938	You Can't Take It with You			1975	One Flew Over the Cuckoo's Nest
1939	Gone with the Wind	1957	The Bridge on the River Kwai		
1940	Rebecca			1976	Rocky
1941	How Green Was My Valley	1958	Gigi	1977	Annie Hall
1942	Mrs. Miniver	1959	Ben-Hur	1978	The Deer Hunter
1943	Casablanca	1960	The Apartment	1979	Kramer vs. Kramer
1944	Going My Way	1961	West Side Story	1980	Ordinary People
1945	The Lost Weekend	1962	Lawrence of Arabia	1981	Chariots of Fire
1946	The Best Years of Our Lives	1963	Tom Jones	1982	Ghandi

Best Director

1927-28	Frank Borzage (Seventh Heaven), Lewis Milestone (Two Arabian Knights)	1942	William Wyler (Mrs. Miniver)
1928-29	Frank Lloyd (The Divine Lady)	1943	Michael Curtiz (Casablanca)
1929-30	Lewis Milestone (All Quiet on the Western Front)	1944	Leo McCarey (Going My Way)
1930-31	Norman Taurog (Skippy)	1945	Billy Wilder (The Lost Weekend)
1931-32	Frank Borzage (Bad Girl)	1946	William Wyler (The Best Years of Our Lives)
1932-33	Frank Lloyd (Cavalcade)	1947	Elia Kazan (Gentleman's Agreement)
1934	Frank Capra (It Happened One Night)	1948	John Huston (The Treasure of Sierra Madre)
1935	John Ford (The Informer)	1949	Joseph L. Mankiewicz (A Letter to Three Wives)
1936	Frank Capra (Mr. Deeds Goes to Town)	1950	Joseph L. Mankiewicz (All About Eve)
1937	Leo McCarey (The Awful Truth)	1951	George Stevens (A Place in the Sun)
1938	Frank Capra (You Can't Take It with You)	1952	John Ford (The Quiet Man)
1939	Victor Fleming (Gone with the Wind)	1953	Fred Zinnemann (From Here to Eternity)
1940	John Ford (The Grapes of Wrath)	1954	Elia Kazan (On the Waterfront)
1941	John Ford (How Green Was My Valley)	1955	Delbert Mann (Marty)
		1956	George Stevens (Giant)
		1957	David Lean (The Bridge on the River Kwai)

1958	Vincente Minnelli (*Gigi*)	1970	Franklin J. Schaffner (*Patton*)
1959	William Wyler (*Ben-Hur*)	1971	William Friedkin (*The French Connection*)
1960	Billy Wilder (*The Apartment*)	1972	Bob Fosse (*Cabaret*)
1961	Robert Wise and Jerome Robbins (*West Side Story*)	1973	George Roy Hill (*The Sting*)
1962	David Lean (*Lawrence of Arabia*)	1974	Francis Ford Coppola (*The Godfather, Part II*)
1963	Tony Richardson (*Tom Jones*)	1975	Milos Forman (*One Flew Over the Cuckoo's Nest*)
1964	George Cukor (*My Fair Lady*)	1976	John Avildsen (*Rocky*)
1965	Robert Wise (*The Sound of Music*)	1977	Woody Allen (*Annie Hall*)
1966	Fred Zinnemann (*A Man for All Seasons*)	1978	Michael Cimino (*The Deer Hunter*)
1967	Mike Nichols (*The Graduate*)	1979	Robert Benton (*Kramer vs. Kramer*)
1968	Sir Carol Reed (*Oliver!*)	1980	Robert Redford (*Ordinary People*)
1969	John Schlesinger (*Midnight Cowboy*)	1981	Warren Beatty (*Reds*)
		1982	Richard Attenborough (*Ghandi*)

Best Actor

1927-28	Emil Jannings (*The Way of All Flesh, The Last Command*)	1955	Ernest Borgnine (*Marty*)
1928-29	Warner Baxter (*In Old Arizona*)	1956	Yul Brynner (*The King and I*)
1929-30	George Arliss (*Disraeli*)	1957	Alec Guinness (*The Bridge on the River Kwai*)
1930-31	Lionel Barrymore (*A Free Soul*)	1958	David Niven (*Separate Tables*)
1931-32	Fredric March (*Dr. Jekyll and Mr. Hyde*), Wallace Beery (*The Champ*)	1959	Charlton Heston (*Ben-Hur*)
		1960	Burt Lancaster (*Elmer Gantry*)
1932-33	Charles Laughton (*The Private Life of Henry VIII*)	1961	Maximilian Schell (*Judgment at Nuremberg*)
		1962	Gregory Peck (*To Kill a Mockingbird*)
1934	Clark Gable (*It Happened One Night*)	1963	Sidney Poitier (*Lilies of the Field*)
1935	Victor McLaglen (*The Informer*)	1964	Rex Harrison (*My Fair Lady*)
1936	Paul Muni (*The Story of Louis Pasteur*)	1965	Lee Marvin (*Cat Ballou*)
1937	Spencer Tracy (*Captains Courageous*)	1966	Paul Scofield (*A Man for All Seasons*)
1938	Spencer Tracy (*Boys Town*)	1967	Rod Steiger (*In the Heat of the Night*)
1939	Robert Donat (*Goodbye, Mr. Chips*)	1968	Cliff Robertson (*Charly*)
1940	James Stewart (*The Philadelphia Story*)	1969	John Wayne (*True Grit*)
1941	Gary Cooper (*Sergeant York*)	1970	George C. Scott (*Patton*)
1942	James Cagney (*Yankee Doodle Dandy*)	1971	Gene Hackman (*The French Connection*)
1943	Paul Lukas (*Watch on the Rhine*)	1972	Marlon Brando (*The Godfather*)
1944	Bing Crosby (*Going My Way*)	1973	Jack Lemmon (*Save the Tiger*)
1945	Ray Milland (*The Lost Weekend*)	1974	Art Carney (*Harry and Tonto*)
1946	Fredric March (*The Best Years of Our Lives*)	1975	Jack Nicholson (*One Flew Over the Cuckoo's Nest*)
1947	Ronald Colman (*A Double Life*)	1976	Peter Finch (*Network*)
1948	Laurence Olivier (*Hamlet*)	1977	Richard Dreyfuss (*The Goodbye Girl*)
1949	Broderick Crawford (*All the King's Men*)	1978	Jon Voight (*Coming Home*)
1950	José Ferrer (*Cyrano de Bergerac*)	1979	Dustin Hoffman (*Kramer vs. Kramer*)
1951	Humphrey Bogart (*The African Queen*)	1980	Robert De Niro (*Raging Bull*)
1952	Gary Cooper (*High Noon*)	1981	Henry Fonda (*On Golden Pond*)
1953	William Holden (*Stalag 17*)	1982	Ben Kingsley (*Ghandi*)
1954	Marlon Brando (*On the Waterfront*)		

Best Actress

1927-28	Janet Gaynor (*Seventh Heaven, Street Angel, Sunrise*)	1932-33	Katharine Hepburn (*Morning Glory*)	1939	Vivien Leigh (*Gone with the Wind*)
		1934	Claudette Colbert (*It Happened One Night*)	1940	Ginger Rogers (*Kitty Foyle*)
1928-29	Mary Pickford (*Coquette*)			1941	Joan Fontaine (*Suspicion*)
1929-30	Norma Shearer (*The Divorcee*)	1935	Bette Davis (*Dangerous*)	1942	Greer Garson (*Mrs. Miniver*)
		1936	Luise Rainer (*The Great Ziegfeld*)		
1930-31	Marie Dressler (*Min and Bill*)	1937	Luise Rainer (*The Good Earth*)	1943	Jennifer Jones (*The Song of Bernadette*)
1931-32	Helen Hayes (*The Sin of Madelon Claudet*)	1938	Bette Davis (*Jezebel*)	1944	Ingrid Bergman (*Gaslight*)

31

Academy Awards *(cont.)*

1945	Joan Crawford (*Mildred Pierce*)	1958	Susan Hayward (*I Want to Live!*)	1969	Maggie Smith (*The Prime of Miss Jean Brodie*)
1946	Olivia de Havilland (*To Each His Own*)	1959	Simone Signoret (*Room at the Top*)	1970	Glenda Jackson (*Women in Love*)
1947	Loretta Young (*The Farmer's Daughter*)	1960	Elizabeth Taylor (*Butterfield 8*)	1971	Jane Fonda (*Klute*)
1948	Jane Wyman (*Johnny Belinda*)	1961	Sophia Loren (*Two Women*)	1972	Liza Minnelli (*Cabaret*)
1949	Olivia de Havilland (*The Heiress*)	1962	Anne Bancroft (*The Miracle Worker*)	1973	Glenda Jackson (*A Touch of Class*)
1950	Judy Holliday (*Born Yesterday*)	1963	Patricia Neal (*Hud*)	1974	Ellen Burstyn (*Alice Doesn't Live Here Anymore*)
1951	Vivien Leigh (*A Streetcar Named Desire*)	1964	Julie Andrews (*Mary Poppins*)	1975	Louise Fletcher (*One Flew Over the Cuckoo's Nest*)
1952	Shirley Booth (*Come Back, Little Sheba*)	1965	Julie Christie (*Darling*)	1976	Faye Dunaway (*Network*)
		1966	Elizabeth Taylor (*Who's Afraid of Virginia Woolf?*)	1977	Diane Keaton (*Annie Hall*)
1953	Audrey Hepburn (*Roman Holiday*)			1978	Jane Fonda (*Coming Home*)
1954	Grace Kelly (*The Country Girl*)	1967	Katharine Hepburn (*Guess Who's Coming to Dinner*)	1979	Sally Field (*Norma Rae*)
1955	Anna Magnani (*The Rose Tattoo*)	1968	Katharine Hepburn (*The Lion in Winter*),	1980	Sissy Spacek (*Coal Miner's Daughter*)
1956	Ingrid Bergman (*Anastasia*)		Barbra Streisand (*Funny Girl*)	1981	Katharine Hepburn (*On Golden Pond*)
1957	Joanne Woodward (*The Three Faces of Eve*)			1982	Meryl Streep (*Sophie's Choice*)

Best Supporting Actor

1927-28	No Award	1956	Anthony Quinn (*Lust for Life*)
1928-29	No Award	1957	Red Buttons (*Sayonara*)
1929-30	No Award	1958	Burl Ives (*The Big Country*)
1930-31	No Award	1959	Hugh Griffith (*Ben-Hur*)
1931-32	No Award	1960	Peter Ustinov (*Spartacus*)
1932-33	No Award	1961	George Chakiris (*West Side Story*)
1934	No Award	1962	Ed Begley (*Sweet Bird of Youth*)
1935	No Award	1963	Melvyn Douglas (*Hud*)
1936	Walter Brennan (*Come and Get It*)	1964	Peter Ustinov (*Topkapi*)
1937	Joseph Schildkraut (*The Life of Émile Zola*)	1965	Martin Balsam (*A Thousand Clowns*)
1938	Walter Brennan (*Kentucky*)	1966	Walter Matthau (*The Fortune Cookie*)
1939	Thomas Mitchell (*Stagecoach*)	1967	George Kennedy (*Cool Hand Luke*)
1940	Walter Brennan (*The Westerner*)	1968	Jack Albertson (*The Subject Was Roses*)
1941	Donald Crisp (*How Green Was My Valley*)	1969	Gig Young (*They Shoot Horses, Don't They?*)
1942	Van Heflin (*Johnny Eager*)	1970	John Mills (*Ryan's Daughter*)
1943	Charles Coburn (*The More the Merrier*)	1971	Ben Johnson (*The Last Picture Show*)
1944	Barry Fitzgerald (*Going My Way*)	1972	Joel Grey (*Cabaret*)
1945	James Dunn (*A Tree Grows in Brooklyn*)	1973	John Houseman (*The Paper Chase*)
1946	Harold Russell (*The Best Years of Our Lives*)	1974	Robert De Niro (*The Godfather, Part II*)
1947	Edmund Gwenn (*Miracle on 34th Street*)	1975	George Burns (*The Sunshine Boys*)
1948	Walter Huston (*The Treasure of Sierra Madre*)	1976	Jason Robards (*All the President's Men*)
1949	Dean Jagger (*Twelve O'Clock High*)	1977	Jason Robards (*Julia*)
1950	George Sanders (*All About Eve*)	1978	Christopher Walken (*The Deer Hunter*)
1951	Karl Malden (*A Streetcar Named Desire*)	1979	Melvyn Douglas (*Being There*)
1952	Anthony Quinn (*Viva Zapata!*)	1980	Timothy Hutton (*Ordinary People*)
1953	Frank Sinatra (*From Here to Eternity*)	1981	Sir John Gielgud (*Arthur*)
1954	Edmond O'Brien (*The Barefoot Contessa*)	1982	Louis Gossett, Jr. (*An Officer and a Gentleman*)
1955	Jack Lemmon (*Mister Roberts*)		

Best Supporting Actress

1927-28	No Award	1929-30	No Award
1928-29	No Award	1930-31	No Award

32

Year			Year	
1931-32	No Award		1957	Miyoshi Umeki (*Sayonara*)
1932-33	No Award		1958	Wendy Hiller (*Separate Tables*)
1934	No Award		1959	Shelley Winters (*The Diary of Anne Frank*)
1935	No Award		1960	Shirley Jones (*Elmer Gantry*)
1936	Gale Sondergaard (*Anthony Adverse*)		1961	Rita Moreno (*West Side Story*)
1937	Alice Brady (*In Old Chicago*)		1962	Patty Duke (*The Miracle Worker*)
1938	Fay Bainter (*Jezebel*)		1963	Margaret Rutherford (*The V.I.P.'s*)
1939	Hattie McDaniel (*Gone with the Wind*)		1964	Lila Kedrova (*Zorba the Greek*)
1940	Jane Darwell (*The Grapes of Wrath*)		1965	Shelley Winters (*A Patch of Blue*)
1941	Mary Astor (*The Great Lie*)		1966	Sandy Dennis (*Who's Afraid of Virginia Woolf?*)
1942	Teresa Wright (*Mrs. Miniver*)		1967	Estelle Parsons (*Bonnie and Clyde*)
1943	Katina Paxinou (*For Whom the Bell Tolls*)		1968	Ruth Gordon (*Rosemary's Baby*)
1944	Ethel Barrymore (*None But the Lonely Heart*)		1969	Goldie Hawn (*Cactus Flower*)
1945	Anne Revere (*National Velvet*)		1970	Helen Hayes (*Airport*)
1946	Anne Baxter (*The Razor's Edge*)		1971	Cloris Leachman (*The Last Picture Show*)
1947	Celeste Holm (*Gentleman's Agreement*)		1972	Eileen Heckart (*Butterflies Are Free*)
1948	Claire Trevor (*Key Largo*)		1973	Tatum O'Neal (*Paper Moon*)
1949	Mercedes McCambridge (*All the King's Men*)		1974	Ingrid Bergman (*Murder on the Orient Express*)
1950	Josephine Hull (*Harvey*)		1975	Lee Grant (*Shampoo*)
1951	Kim Hunter (*A Streetcar Named Desire*)		1976	Beatrice Straight (*Network*)
1952	Gloria Grahame (*The Bad and the Beautiful*)		1977	Vanessa Redgrave (*Julia*)
1953	Donna Reed (*From Here to Eternity*)		1978	Maggie Smith (*California Suite*)
1954	Eva Marie Saint (*On the Waterfront*)		1979	Meryl Streep (*Kramer vs. Kramer*)
1955	Jo Van Fleet (*East of Eden*)		1980	Mary Steenburgen (*Melvin and Howard*)
1956	Dorothy Malone (*Written on the Wind*)		1981	Maureen Stapleton (*Reds*)
			1982	Jessica Lange (*Tootsie*)

Caldecott Medal

The Caldecott Medal is presented annually by the American Library Association. It honors the most distinguished children's picture book of the year. Winners must be U.S. citizens or residents. The medal is named for Randolph Caldecott, an English illustrator.

Caldecott Medal winners

Year	Illustrator	Winning Book
1938	Dorothy P. Lathrop	*Animals of the Bible*
1939	Thomas Handforth	*Mei Li*
1940	Ingri and Edgar Parin d'Aulaire	*Abraham Lincoln*
1941	Robert Lawson	*They Were Strong and Good*
1942	Robert McCloskey	*Make Way for Ducklings*
1943	Virginia Lee Burton	*The Little House*
1944	Louis Slobodkin	*Many Moons*
1945	Elizabeth Orton Jones	*Prayer for a Child*
1946	Maud and Miska Petersham	*The Rooster Crows*
1947	Leonard Weisgard	*The Little Island*
1948	Roger Duvoisin	*White Snow, Bright Snow*
1949	Berta and Elmer Hader	*The Big Snow*
1950	Leo Politi	*Song of the Swallows*
1951	Katherine Milhous	*The Egg Tree*

Caldecott Medal winners

Year	Illustrator	Winning Book
1952	Nicolas Mordvinoff	*Finders Keepers*
1953	Lynd K. Ward	*The Biggest Bear*
1954	Ludwig Bemelmans	*Madeline's Rescue*
1955	Marcia Brown	*Cinderella; or The Little Glass Slipper*
1956	Feodor Rojankovsky	*Frog Went A-Courtin'*
1957	Marc Simont	*A Tree Is Nice*
1958	Robert McCloskey	*Time of Wonder*
1959	Barbara Cooney	*Chanticleer and the Fox*
1960	Marie Hall Ets	*Nine Days to Christmas*
1961	Nicolas Sidjakov	*Baboushka and the Three Kings*
1962	Marcia Brown	*Once a Mouse*
1963	Ezra Jack Keats	*The Snowy Day*
1964	Maurice Sendak	*Where the Wild Things Are*
1965	Beni Montresor	*May I Bring a Friend?*
1966	Nonny Hogrogian	*Always Room for One More*
1967	Evaline Ness	*Sam, Bangs, & Moonshine*

Year	Illustrator	Winning Book	Year	Illustrator	Winning Book
1968	Ed Emberley	Drummer Hoff	1976	Leo and Diane Dillon	Why Mosquitoes Buzz in People's Ears: A West African Tale
1969	Uri Shulevitz	The Fool of the World and the Flying Ship			
1970	William Steig	Sylvester and the Magic Pebble	1977	Leo and Diane Dillon	Ashanti to Zulu: African Traditions
1971	Gail E. Haley	A Story—A Story	1978	Peter Spier	Noah's Ark
1972	Nonny Hogrogian	One Fine Day	1979	Paul Goble	The Girl Who Loved Wild Horses
1973	Blair Lent	The Funny Little Woman	1980	Barbara Cooney	Ox-Cart Man
1974	Margot Zemach	Duffy and the Devil	1981	Arnold Lobel	Fables
1975	Gerald McDermott	Arrow to the Sun: A Pueblo Indian Tale	1982	Chris Van Allsburg	Jumanji

Newbery Medal

The Newbery Medal is awarded annually for the outstanding children's book written by an American. Frederic G. Melcher, an American publisher, established the award. He named it for John Newbery, an English publisher and bookseller who was the first person to print and sell books for children. The award is presented by the American Library Association.

Newbery Medal winners

Year	Author	Winning Book	Year	Author	Winning Book
1922	Hendrik Van Loon	The Story of Mankind	1946	Lois Lenski	Strawberry Girl
1923	Hugh Lofting	The Voyages of Dr. Dolittle	1947	Carolyn S. Bailey	Miss Hickory
			1948	William Pène du Bois	The Twenty-One Balloons
1924	Charles Hawes	The Dark Frigate			
1925	Charles Finger	Tales from Silver Lands			
			1949	Marguerite Henry	King of the Wind
1926	Arthur Chrisman	Shen of the Sea	1950	Marguerite de Angeli	The Door in the Wall
1927	Will James	Smoky	1951	Elizabeth Yates	Amos Fortune, Free Man
1928	Dhan Mukerji	Gay-Neck			
1929	Eric P. Kelly	The Trumpeter of Krakow	1952	Eleanor Estes	Ginger Pye
			1953	Ann Nolan Clark	Secret of the Andes
1930	Rachel Field	Hitty, Her First Hundred Years	1954	Joseph Krumgold	. . . And Now Miguel
1931	Elizabeth Coatsworth	The Cat Who Went to Heaven	1955	Meindert DeJong	The Wheel on the School
1932	Laura Armer	Waterless Mountain	1956	Jean Lee Latham	Carry on, Mr. Bowditch
1933	Elizabeth Lewis	Young Fu of the Upper Yangtze	1957	Virginia Sorensen	Miracles on Maple Hill
			1958	Harold V. Keith	Rifles for Watie
1934	Cornelia Meigs	Invincible Louisa	1959	Elizabeth G. Speare	The Witch of Blackbird Pond
1935	Monica Shannon	Dobry			
1936	Carol Ryrie Brink	Caddie Woodlawn	1960	Joseph Krumgold	Onion John
1937	Ruth Sawyer	Roller Skates	1961	Scott O'Dell	Island of the Blue Dolphins
1938	Kate Seredy	The White Stag			
1939	Elizabeth Enright	Thimble Summer	1962	Elizabeth G. Speare	The Bronze Bow
1940	James Daugherty	Daniel Boone	1963	Madeleine L'Engle	A Wrinkle in Time
1941	Armstrong Sperry	Call It Courage	1964	Emily C. Neville	It's Like This, Cat
1942	Walter D. Edmonds	The Matchlock Gun	1965	Maia Wojciechowska	Shadow of a Bull
1943	Elizabeth Janet Gray	Adam of the Road	1966	Elizabeth Borton de Treviño	I, Juan de Pareja
1944	Esther Forbes	Johnny Tremain			
1945	Robert Lawson	Rabbit Hill	1967	Irene Hunt	Up a Road Slowly

Year	Author	Winning Book	Year	Author	Winning Book
1968	Elaine Konigsburg	From the Mixed-Up Files of Mrs. Basil E. Frankweiler	1976	Susan Cooper	The Grey King
			1977	Mildred Taylor	Roll of Thunder, Hear My Cry
1969	Lloyd Alexander	The High King	1978	Katherine Paterson	Bridge to Terabithia
1970	William H. Armstrong	Sounder	1979	Ellen Raskin	The Westing Game
1971	Betsy Byars	The Summer of the Swans	1980	Joan Blos	A Gathering of Days: A New England Girl's Journal
1972	Robert C. O'Brien	Mrs. Frisby and the Rats of NIMH	1981	Katherine Paterson	Jacob Have I Loved
1973	Jean C. George	Julie of the Wolves	1982	Nancy Willard	A Visit to William Blake's Inn
1974	Paula Fox	The Slave Dancer			
1975	Virginia Hamilton	M. C. Higgins, the Great			

Hall of Fame for Great Americans

The Hall of Fame for Great Americans is a museum in New York City that honors distinguished Americans in various fields. The museum was founded by New York University in 1900. Members of the Hall of Fame are listed below according to the year of their selection.

Members of the Hall of Fame for Great Americans

1900
George Washington†
Abraham Lincoln†
Daniel Webster*
Benjamin Franklin†
Ulysses S. Grant†
John Marshall*
Thomas Jefferson†
Ralph Waldo Emerson*
Robert Fulton*
Henry Wadsworth Longfellow*
Washington Irving*
Jonathan Edwards
Samuel F. B. Morse*
David G. Farragut*
Henry Clay*
Nathaniel Hawthorne*
George Peabody
Peter Cooper
Robert E. Lee*
Eli Whitney*
John James Audubon*
Horace Mann*
Henry Ward Beecher
James Kent
Joseph Story
John Adams†
William Ellery Channing
Gilbert Stuart*
Asa Gray

1905
John Quincy Adams†
James Russell Lowell
William T. Sherman*
Emma Willard*
Mary Lyon
James Madison†
John Greenleaf Whittier
Maria Mitchell

1910
Harriet Beecher Stowe*
Oliver Wendell Holmes*
Edgar Allan Poe*
James Fenimore Cooper*
Phillips Brooks
William Cullen Bryant
Frances E. Willard
Andrew Jackson†
George Bancroft
John Lothrop Motley

1915
Mark Hopkins
Francis Parkman
Elias Howe*
Joseph Henry
Louis Agassiz
Charlotte Cushman
Rufus Choate
Daniel Boone*
Alexander Hamilton*

1920
Mark Twain*
James B. Eads
William T. G. Morton
Augustus Saint-Gaudens
Patrick Henry*
Roger Williams*
Alice Freeman Palmer

1925
Edwin Booth
John Paul Jones*

1930
Walt Whitman*
Matthew F. Maury
James A. McNeill Whistler*
James Monroe†

1935
William Penn*
Simon Newcomb
Grover Cleveland†

1940
Stephen Foster

1945
Booker T. Washington*
Sidney Lanier
Thomas Paine*
Walter Reed

1950
Woodrow Wilson†
Alexander Graham Bell*
Susan B. Anthony*
William C. Gorgas*
Theodore Roosevelt†
Josiah W. Gibbs

1955
Wilbur Wright*
Stonewall Jackson*
George Westinghouse

1960
Thomas Alva Edison*
Henry David Thoreau*
Edward MacDowell

1965
Jane Addams*
Oliver Wendell Holmes, Jr.*
Sylvanus Thayer
Orville Wright*

1970
Albert Abraham Michelson
Lillian D. Wald

1973
George Washington Carver*
Louis D. Brandeis
Franklin D. Roosevelt†
John Philip Sousa

1976
Clara Barton*
Luther Burbank
Andrew Carnegie*

*See "People" section for biographical information.
†See "Presidents" section for biographical information.

National Book Awards

The National Book Awards were given annually from 1950 to 1979 for outstanding books written or translated by U.S. citizens. The awards were discontinued in 1979 and replaced by the American Book Awards. A table of American Book Award winners appears on page 39.

Fiction

1950	Nelson Algren, *The Man with the Golden Arm.*
1951	William Faulkner,* *Collected Stories of William Faulkner.*
1952	James Jones, *From Here to Eternity.*
1953	Ralph Ellison, *Invisible Man.*
1954	Saul Bellow,* *The Adventures of Augie March.*
1955	William Faulkner,* *A Fable.*
1956	John O'Hara, *Ten North Frederick.*
1957	Wright Morris, *The Field of Vision.*
1958	John Cheever,* *The Wapshot Chronicle.*
1959	Bernard Malamud, *The Magic Barrel.*
1960	Philip Roth, *Goodbye, Columbus.*
1961	Conrad Richter, *The Waters of Kronos.*
1962	Walker Percy, *The Moviegoer.*
1963	J. F. Powers, *Morte D'Urban.*
1964	John Updike,* *The Centaur.*
1965	Saul Bellow,* *Herzog.*
1966	Katherine Anne Porter, *The Collected Stories of Katherine Anne Porter.*
1967	Bernard Malamud, *The Fixer.*
1968	Thornton Wilder, *The Eighth Day.*
1969	Jerzy Kosinski, *Steps.*
1970	Joyce Carol Oates, *Them.*
1971	Saul Bellow,* *Mr. Sammler's Planet.*
1972	Flannery O'Connor, *The Complete Stories.*
1973	John Barth, *Chimera;* John Williams, *Augustus.*
1974	Isaac Bashevis Singer, *A Crown of Feathers;* Thomas Pynchon, *Gravity's Rainbow.*
1975	Robert Stone, *Dog Soldiers;* Thomas Williams, *The Hair of Harold Roux.*
1976	William Gaddis, *JR.*
1977	Wallace Stegner, *The Spectator Bird.*
1978	Mary Lee Settle, *Blood Tie.*
1979	Tim O'Brien, *Going After Cacciato.*

Poetry

1950	William Carlos Williams, *Paterson III and Selected Poems.*
1951	Wallace Stevens, *The Auroras of Autumn.*
1952	Marianne Moore, *Collected Poems.*
1953	Archibald MacLeish, *Collected Poems: 1917-1952.*
1954	Conrad Aiken, *Collected Poems.*
1955	Wallace Stevens, *The Collected Poems of Wallace Stevens.*
1956	W. H. Auden, *The Shield of Achilles.*
1957	Richard Wilbur, *Things of This World.*
1958	Robert Penn Warren, *Promises: Poems 1954-1956.*
1959	Theodore Roethke, *Words for the Wind.*
1960	Robert Lowell, *Life Studies.*
1961	Randall Jarrell, *The Woman at the Washington Zoo.*
1962	Alan Dugan, *Poems.*
1963	William Stafford, *Traveling Through the Dark.*
1964	John Crowe Ransom, *Selected Poems.*
1965	Theodore Roethke, *The Far Field.*
1966	James Dickey, *Buckdancer's Choice.*
1967	James Merrill, *Nights and Days.*
1968	Robert Bly, *The Light Around the Body.*
1969	John Berryman, *His Toy, His Dream, His Rest.*
1970	Elizabeth Bishop, *The Complete Poems.*
1971	Mona Van Duyn, *To See, To Take.*
1972	Howard Moss, *Selected Poems;* Frank O'Hara, *The Collected Poems.*
1973	A. R. Ammons, *Collected Poems: 1951-1971.*
1974	Allen Ginsberg, *The Fall of America: Poems of These States, 1965-1971;* Adrienne Rich, *Diving into the Wreck: Poems, 1971-1972.*
1975	Marilyn Hacker, *Presentation Piece.*
1976	John Ashbery, *Self-Portrait in a Convex Mirror.*
1977	Richard Eberhart, *Collected Poems, 1930-1976.*
1978	Howard Nemerov, *Collected Poems.*
1979	James Merrill, *Mirabell: Books of Number.*

Nonfiction

1950	Ralph L. Rusk, *Ralph Waldo Emerson.*
1951	Newton Arvin, *Herman Melville.*
1952	Rachel Carson, *The Sea Around Us.*
1953	Bernard De Voto, *The Course of Empire.*
1954	Bruce Catton, *A Stillness at Appomattox.*
1955	Joseph Wood Krutch, *The Measure of Man.*
1956	Herbert Kubly, *American in Italy.*
1957	George F. Kennan, *Russia Leaves the War.*
1958	Catherine Drinker Bowen, *The Lion and the Throne.*

*See "People" section for biographical information.

Awards

1959	J. Christopher Herold, *Mistress to an Age*.
1960	Richard Ellmann, *James Joyce*.
1961	William L. Shirer, *The Rise and Fall of the Third Reich*.
1962	Lewis Mumford, *The City in History*.
1963	Leon Edel, *Henry James: The Conquest of London: 1870-1881* and *Henry James: The Middle Years: 1882-1895*.
1964	Award divided into three groups: Arts and Letters; History and Biography; and Science, Philosophy, and Religion.

Arts and letters

1964	Aileen Ward, *John Keats: The Making of a Poet*.
1965	Eleanor Clark, *The Oysters of Locmariaquer*.
1966	Janet Flanner, *Paris Journal (1944-1965)*.
1967	Justin Kaplan, *Mr. Clemens and Mark Twain*.
1968	William Troy, *Selected Essays*.
1969	Norman Mailer, *The Armies of the Night*.
1970	Lillian Hellman, *An Unfinished Woman*.
1971	Francis Steegmuller, *Cocteau*.
1972	Charles Rosen, *The Classical Style*.
1973	Arthur M. Wilson, *Diderot*.
1974	Pauline Kael, *Deeper into Movies*.
1975	Roger Shattuck, *Marcel Proust*; Lewis Thomas, *The Lives of a Cell: Notes of a Biology Watcher*.
1976	Paul Fussell, *The Great War and Modern Memory*.
1977	Award discontinued.

History and biography

1964	William H. McNeill, *The Rise of the West*.
1965	Louis Fischer, *The Life of Lenin*.
1966	Arthur M. Schlesinger, Jr., *A Thousand Days*.
1967	Peter Gay, *The Enlightenment: An Interpretation*.
1968	George F. Kennan, *Memoirs: 1925-1950*.
1969	Winthrop Jordan, *White Over Black*.
1970	T. Harry Williams, *Huey Long*.
1971	James MacGregor Burns, *Roosevelt: The Soldier of Freedom*.
1972-75	Award divided into two groups: History and Biography.
1976	David Brion Davis, *The Problem of Slavery in the Age of Revolution: 1770-1823*.
1977	Award divided into two groups: History, and Biography and Autobiography.

History

1972	Allan Nevins, *The War for the Union: The Organized War, 1863-1864* and *The War for the Union: The Organized War to Victory, 1864-1865*.
1973	Robert M. Myers, *The Children of Pride: A True Story of Georgia and the Civil War*; Isaiah Trunk, *Judenrat: The Jewish Councils in Eastern Europe Under Nazi Occupation*.
1974	John Clive, *Macaulay: The Shaping of the Historian*.
1975	Bernard Bailyn, *The Ordeal of Thomas Hutchinson*.
1976	Award became History and Biography.
1977	Irving Howe, *World of Our Fathers*.
1978	David McCullough, *The Path Between the Seas*.
1979	Richard Beale Davis, *Intellectual Life in the Colonial South, 1585-1763*.

Biography

1972	Joseph P. Lash, *Eleanor and Franklin*.
1973	James Thomas Flexner, *George Washington: Anguish and Farewell (1793-1799)*.
1974	Douglas Day, *Malcolm Lowry: A Biography*.
1975	Richard B. Sewall, *The Life of Emily Dickinson*.
1976	Award became History and Biography.

Biography and autobiography

1977	W. A. Swanberg, *Norman Thomas: The Last Idealist*.
1978	W. Jackson Bate, *Samuel Johnson*.
1979	Arthur M. Schlesinger, Jr., *Robert Kennedy and His Times*.

Science, philosophy, and religion

1964	Christopher Tunnard and Boris Pushkarev, *Man-Made America: Chaos or Control?*
1965	Norbert Wiener, *God and Golem, Inc.*
1966	No Award.
1967	Oscar Lewis, *La Vida*.
1968	Jonathan Kozol, *Death at an Early Age*.
1969	Award divided into two groups: The Sciences, and Philosophy and Religion.

37

The sciences

1969	Robert J. Lifton, *Death in Life: Survivors of Hiroshima.*	**1973**	George B. Schaller, *The Serengeti Lion: A Study of Predator-Prey Relations.*
1970	No Award.	**1974**	S. E. Luria, *Life: The Unfinished Experiment.*
1971	Raymond Phineas Stearns, *Science in the British Colonies of America.*	**1975**	Silvano Arieti, *Interpretation of Schizophrenia.*
1972	George L. Small, *The Blue Whale.*	**1976**	Award discontinued.

Philosophy and religion

1969	No Award.	**1973**	Sydney E. Ahlstrom, *A Religious History of the American People.*
1970	Erik H. Erikson, *Gandhi's Truth: On the Origins of Militant Nonviolence.*	**1974**	Maurice Nathanson, *Edmund Husserl: Philosopher of Infinite Tasks.*
1971	No Award.	**1975**	Robert Nozick, *Anarchy, State and Utopia.*
1972	Martin E. Marty, *Righteous Empire: The Protestant Experience in America.*	**1976**	Award discontinued.

Contemporary affairs

1972	Stewart Brand, *The Last Whole Earth Catalog.*	**1975**	Theodore Rosengarten, *All God's Dangers: The Life of Nate Shaw.*
1973	Frances FitzGerald, *Fire in the Lake: The Vietnamese and the Americans in Vietnam.*	**1976**	Michael J. Arlen, *Passage to Ararat.*
1974	Murray Kempton, *The Briar Patch: The People of New York v. Lumumba Shakur Et Al.*	**1977**	Award discontinued.

Contemporary thought

1977	Bruno Bettelheim, *The Uses of Enchantment: The Meaning and Importance of Fairy Tales.*	**1978**	Gloria Emerson, *Winners and Losers.*
		1979	Peter Matthiessen, *The Snow Leopard.*

Children's literature

1969	Meindert DeJong, *Journey from Peppermint Street.*	**1974**	Eleanor Cameron, *The Court of the Stone Children.*
1970	Isaac Bashevis Singer, *A Day of Pleasure: Stories of a Boy Growing Up in Warsaw.*	**1975**	Virginia Hamilton, *M. C. Higgins, the Great.*
		1976	Walter D. Edmonds, *Bert Breen's Barn.*
1971	Lloyd Alexander, *The Marvelous Misadventures of Sebastian.*	**1977**	Katherine Paterson, *The Master Puppeteer.*
1972	Donald Barthelme, *The Slightly Irregular Fire Engine or the Hithering Thithering Djinn.*	**1978**	Herbert and Judith Kohl, *The View from the Oak: The Private Worlds of Other Creatures.*
1973	Ursula Le Guin, *The Farthest Shore.*	**1979**	Katherine Paterson, *The Great Gilly Hopkins.*

Translation

1967	Gregory Rabassa, for his translation of *Hopscotch* by Julio Cortazar; Willard Trask, for his translation of *History of My Life* by Giacomo Casanova.	**1973**	Allen Mandelbaum, *The Aeneid of Virgil.*
		1974	Karen Brazell for her translation of *The Confessions of Lady Nijo;* Helen R. Lane for her translation of *Alternating Current* by Octavio Paz; Jackson Mathews for his translation of *Monsieur Teste* by Paul Valéry.
1968	Howard and Edna Hong for their translation of *Søren Kierkegaard's Journals and Papers.*
1969	William Weaver for his translation of *Cosmicomics* by Italo Calvino.
1970	Ralph Manheim for his translation of *Castle to Castle* by Louis-Ferdinand Celine.	**1975**	Anthony Kerrigan for his translation of *The Agony of Christianity and Essays on Faith* by Miguel de Unamuno.
		1976	No award.
1971	Frank Jones for his translation of *Saint Joan of the Stockyards* by Bertolt Brecht; Edward G. Seidensticker for his translation of *The Sound of the Mountain* by Yasunari Kawabata.	**1977**	Li-li Ch'en for her translation of *Master Tung's Western Chamber Romance.*
		1978	Richard and Clara Winston for their translation of *In the Deserts of this Earth* by Uwe George.
1972	Austryn Wainhouse for his translation of *Chance and Necessity: An Essay on the Natural Philosophy of Modern Biology* by Jacques Monod.	**1979**	Clayton Eshleman and José Rubia Barcia for their translation of *The Complete Posthumous Poetry* by César Vallejo.

American Book Awards

The American Book Awards were first presented in 1980. They honor American achievements in various categories of literature. The awards are presented by the Association of American Publishers.

National Medal for Literature*

1980	Eudora Welty	**1982**	John Cheever†
1981	Kenneth Burke		

General fiction

1980	William Styron, *Sophie's Choice*	**1982**	John Updike,† *Rabbit Is Rich*
1981	Wright Morris, *Plains Song*		

General nonfiction

1980	Tom Wolfe, *The Right Stuff*	**1982**	Tracy Kidder, *The Soul of a New Machine*
1981	Maxine Hong Kingston, *China Men*		

First novel

1980	William Wharton, *Birdy*	**1982**	Robb Forman Dew, *Dale Loves Sophie to Death*
1981	Ann Arensberg, *Sister Wolf*		

Autobiography

1980	Lauren Bacall, *By Myself*	**1981**	Award became Autobiography and Biography.

Biography

1980	Edmund Morris, *The Rise of Theodore Roosevelt*	**1981**	Award became Autobiography and Biography.

Autobiography and biography

1981	Justin Kaplan, *Walt Whitman*	**1982**	David McCullough, *Mornings on Horseback*

Children's books

1980	Joan W. Blos, *A Gathering of Days: A New England Girl's Journal, 1830–32*	**1981**	Award divided into two categories: Children's Fiction and Children's Nonfiction.

Children's fiction

1981	Betsy Byars, *The Night Swimmers*	**1982**	Lloyd Alexander, *Westmark*

Children's nonfiction

1981	Alison Cragin Herzig and Jane Lawrence Mali, *Oh, Boy! Babies*	**1982**	Susan Bonners, *A Penguin Year*

Children's picture books

1982	Maurice Sendak, *Outside Over There*

---

*Recipients of this award are cited for lifetime contributions to literature.
†See "People" section for biographical information.

History

1980	Henry Kissinger, *White House Years*	**1982**	Rev. Peter John Powell, *People of the Sacred Mountain*
1981	John Boswell, *Christianity, Social Tolerance and Homosexuality*		

Poetry

1980	Philip Levine, *Ashes*	**1981**	Lisel Mueller, *The Need to Hold Still*
1982	William Bronk, *Life Supports*		

Science

1980	Douglas Hofstadter, *Godel, Escher, Bach: An Eternal Golden Braid; A Metaphorical Fugue on Minds and Machines in the Spirit of Lewis Carroll*	**1981**	Stephen Jay Gould, *The Panda's Thumb*
		1982	Donald Johanson and Maitland Edey, *Lucy*

Translation

1980	Jane Gary Harris and Constance Link, for their translation of *The Complete Critical Prose and Letters* by Osip E. Mandelstam	**1982**	Robert Lyons Danly, for *In the Shade of Spring Leaves*, a biography of Higushi Ichiyo; Ian Hideo Levy, for *The Ten Thousand Leaves*, the first volume of the Man'yoshu collection of Japanese poetry
1981	Francis Steegmuller, for her translation of *The Letters of Gustave Flaubert 1830–1857;* John E. Woods, for his translation of *Evening Edged in Gold* by Arno Schmidt		

Nobel prizes

Nobel prizes are awarded annually for outstanding contributions to the "good of humanity" in six fields: physics; chemistry; physiology or medicine; literature; world peace; and economics. Persons of any nationality may receive the prizes. Alfred Nobel, a Swedish chemist, established the prizes (see "People"). The peace prize is awarded in Oslo, Norway, and the others are awarded in Stockholm, Sweden.

Nobel prizes for physics

1901	Wilhelm K. Roentgen* (German) for discovering X rays.	**1909**	Guglielmo Marconi* (Italian) and Karl Ferdinand Braun (German) for developing the wireless telegraph.
1902	Hendrik Antoon Lorentz and Pieter Zeeman (Dutch) for discovering the Zeeman effect of magnetism on light.	**1910**	Johannes D. van der Waals (Dutch) for studying the relationships of liquids and gases.
1903	Antoine Henri Becquerel and Pierre and Marie Curie (French) for discovering radioactivity and studying uranium.	**1911**	Wilhelm Wien (German) for his discoveries on the heat radiated by black objects.
1904	Baron Rayleigh (British) for studying the density of gases and discovering argon.	**1912**	Nils Dalén (Swedish) for inventing automatic gas regulators for lighthouses.
1905	Philipp Lenard (German) for studying the properties of cathode rays.	**1913**	Heike Kamerlingh Onnes (Dutch) for experimenting with low temperatures and liquefying helium.
1906	Sir Joseph John Thomson* (British) for studying electrical discharge through gases.	**1914**	Max T. F. von Laue (German) for using crystals to measure X rays.
1907	Albert A. Michelson (American) for inventing optical instruments and measuring the speed of light.	**1915**	Sir William Henry Bragg and Sir William L. Bragg (British) for using X rays to study crystal structure.
1908	Gabriel Lippmann (French) for his method of color photography.	**1916**	No Award
		1917	Charles Barkla (British) for studying the diffusion of light and the radiation of X rays from elements.

*See "People" section for biographical information.

1918 Max Planck (German) for stating the quantum theory of light.

1919 Johannes Stark (German) for discovering the Stark effect of spectra in electric fields.

1920 Charles E. Guillaume (French) for discovering nickel-steel alloys with slight expansion, and the alloy invar.

1921 Albert Einstein* (German) for contributing to mathematical physics and stating the law of the photoelectric effect.

1922 Niels Bohr* (Danish) for studying the structure of atoms and their radiations.

1923 Robert A. Millikan (American) for measuring the charge on electrons and working on the photoelectric effect.

1924 Karl M. G. Siegbahn (Swedish) for working with the X-ray spectroscope.

1925 James Franck and Gustav Hertz (German) for stating laws on the collision of an electron with an atom.

1926 Jean Baptiste Perrin (French) for studying the discontinuous structure of matter and measuring the sizes of atoms.

1927 Arthur H. Compton (American) for discovering the Compton effect on X rays reflected from atoms, and Charles T. R. Wilson (British) for discovering a method for tracing the paths of ions.

1928 Owen W. Richardson (British) for studying thermionic effect and electrons sent off by hot metals.

1929 Louis Victor de Broglie (French) for discovering the wave character of electrons.

1930 Sir Chandrasekhara Venkata Raman (Indian) for discovering a new effect in radiation from elements.

1931 No Award

1932 Werner Heisenberg (German) for founding quantum mechanics, which led to discoveries in hydrogen.

1933 Paul Dirac (British) and Erwin Schrödinger (Austrian) for discovering new forms of atomic theory.

1934 No Award

1935 Sir James Chadwick (British) for discovering the neutron.

1936 Carl David Anderson (American) for discovering the positron, and Victor F. Hess (Austrian) for discovering cosmic rays.

1937 Clinton Davisson (American) and George Thomson (British) for discovering the diffraction of electrons by crystals.

1938 Enrico Fermi* (Italian) for discovering new radioactive elements beyond uranium.

1939 Ernest O. Lawrence (American) for inventing the cyclotron and working on artificial radioactivity.

1940-42 No Award

1943 Otto Stern (American) for discovering the molecular beam method of studying the atom.

1944 Isidor Isaac Rabi (American) for recording the magnetic properties of atomic nuclei.

1945 Wolfgang Pauli (Austrian) for discovering the exclusion principle (Pauli principle) of electrons.

1946 Percy Williams Bridgman (American) for his work in the field of very high pressures.

1947 Sir Edward V. Appleton (British) for exploring the ionosphere.

1948 Patrick M. S. Blackett (British) for his discoveries in cosmic radiation.

1949 Hideki Yukawa (Japanese) for discovering the meson.

1950 Cecil Frank Powell (British) for his photographic method of studying atomic nuclei and his discoveries concerning mesons.

1951 Sir John D. Cockcroft (British) and Ernest T. S. Walton (Irish) for working on the transmutation of atomic nuclei by artificially accelerated atomic particles.

1952 Felix Bloch and Edward Mills Purcell (American) for developing magnetic measurement methods for atomic nuclei.

1953 Frits Zernike (Dutch) for inventing the phase contrast microscope for cancer research.

1954 Max Born (German) for research in quantum mechanics, and Walther Bothe (German) for discoveries he made with his coincidence method.

1955 Willis E. Lamb, Jr. (American), for discoveries on the structure of the hydrogen spectrum, and Polykarp Kusch (American) for determining the magnetic moment of the electron.

1956 John Bardeen, Walter H. Brattain, and William Shockley (American) for inventing the transistor.

1957 Tsung Dao Lee and Chen Ning Yang (American) for disproving the law of conservation of parity.

1958 Pavel A. Cherenkov, Ilya M. Frank, and Igor Y. Tamm (Russian) for discovering and interpreting the Cherenkov effect in studying high-energy particles.

1959 Emilio Segrè and Owen Chamberlain (American) for their work in demonstrating the existence of the antiproton.

1960 Donald A. Glaser (American) for inventing the bubble chamber to study subatomic particles.

1961 Robert Hofstadter (American) for his studies of nucleons, and Rudolf L. Mössbauer (German) for his research on gamma rays.

1962 Lev Davidovich Landau (Russian) for his research on liquid helium.

1963 Eugene Paul Wigner (American) for his contributions to the understanding of atomic nuclei and the elementary particles, and Maria Goeppert Mayer (American) and J. Hans Jensen (German) for their work on the structure of atomic nuclei.

1964 Charles H. Townes (American) and Nikolai G. Basov and Alexander M. Prokhorov (Russian) for developing masers and lasers.

1965 Sin-itiro Tomonaga (Japanese) and Julian S. Schwinger and Richard P. Feynman (American) for basic work in quantum electrodynamics.

1966 Alfred Kastler (French) for his work on the energy level of atoms.

1967 Hans Albrecht Bethe (American) for his contributions to the theory of nuclear reactions, especially his discoveries on the energy production in stars.

1968 Luis W. Alvarez (American) for his contributions to the knowledge of subatomic particles.

1969 Murray Gell-Mann (American) for his discoveries concerning the classification of nuclear particles and their interactions.

1970 Hannes Olof Gosta Alfven (Swedish) for his work in magnetohydrodynamics, the study of electrical and magnetic effects in fluids that conduct electricity, and Louis Eugène Félix Néel (French) for his discoveries of magnetic properties that applied to computer memories.

---

*See "People" section for biographical information.

1971	Dennis Gabor (British) for his work in *holography*, a method of making a three-dimensional photograph with coherent light produced by a laser.	1977	Philip W. Anderson and John H. Van Vleck (American) and Sir Nevill F. Mott (British) for helping develop semiconductor devices.
1972	John Bardeen, Leon N. Cooper, and John Robert Schrieffer (American) for their work on *superconductivity*, the disappearance of electrical resistance.	1978	Pyotr Kapitsa (Russian) for his research in low-temperature physics, and Arno Penzias and Robert Wilson (American) for their discovery and study of cosmic microwave background radiation.
1973	Ivar Giaever (American), Leo Esaki (Japanese), and Brian Josephson (British) for their work on the phenomena of electron "tunneling" through semiconductor and superconductor materials.	1979	Sheldon L. Glashow and Steven Weinberg (American) and Abdus Salam (Pakistani) for developing a principle that unifies the weak nuclear force and the force of electromagnetism.
1974	Antony Hewish (British) for the discovery of *pulsars*, celestial objects that give off bursts of radio waves, and Sir Martin Ryle (British) for his use of small radio telescopes to "see" into space with great accuracy.	1980	James W. Cronin and Val L. Fitch (American) for their research on subatomic particles that revealed that the fundamental laws of symmetry in nature could be violated.
1975	L. James Rainwater (American) and Aage N. Bohr and Ben R. Mottelson (Danish) for their work on the structure of the atomic nucleus.	1981	Nicolaas Bloembergen and Arthur L. Schawlow (American) for their contribution to the development of laser spectroscopy, and Kai Siegbahn (Swedish) for his contribution to the development of high-resolution electron spectroscopy.
1976	Burton Richter and Samuel Chao Chung Ting (American) for their discovery of an elementary nuclear particle called the *psi*, or *J, particle.*	1982	Kenneth G. Wilson (American) for his method of analyzing the behavior of matter when it changes form—for example, from water to steam.

Nobel prizes for chemistry

1901	Jacobus Henricus Van't Hoff (Dutch) for discovering laws of chemical dynamics and osmotic pressure.	1918	Fritz Haber (German) for the Haber-Bosch process of synthesizing ammonia from nitrogen and hydrogen.
1902	Emil Fischer (German) for synthesizing sugars, purine derivatives, and peptides.	1919	No Award
1903	Svante August Arrhenius (Swedish) for his dissociation theory of ionization in electrolytes.	1920	Walther Nernst (German) for his discoveries concerning heat changes in chemical reactions.
1904	Sir William Ramsay (British) for discovering helium, neon, xenon, and krypton, and determining their place in the periodic system.	1921	Frederick Soddy (British) for studying radioactive substances and isotopes.
1905	Adolph von Baeyer (German) for his work on dyes and organic compounds, and for synthesizing indigo and arsenicals.	1922	Francis W. Aston (British) for discovering many isotopes by means of the mass spectrograph and discovering the whole number rule on the structure and weight of atoms.
1906	Henri Moissan (French) for preparing pure fluorine and developing the electric furnace.	1923	Fritz Pregl (Austrian) for inventing a method of microanalyzing organic substances.
1907	Eduard Buchner (German) for his biochemical researches and for discovering cell-less fermentation.	1924	No Award
		1925	Richard Zsigmondy (German) for his method of studying colloids.
1908	Ernest Rutherford* (British) for discovering that alpha rays break down atoms and studying radioactive substances.	1926	Theodor Svedberg (Swedish) for his work on dispersions and on colloid chemistry.
1909	Wilhelm Ostwald (German) for his work on catalysis, chemical equilibrium, and the rate of chemical reactions.	1927	Heinrich O. Wieland (German) for studying gall acids and related substances.
1910	Otto Wallach (German) for his work in the field of alicyclic substances.	1928	Adolf Windaus (German) for studying sterols and their connection with vitamins.
1911	Marie Curie* (French) for discovering radium and polonium, and for isolating radium and studying its compounds.	1929	Sir Arthur Harden (British) and Hans August Simon von Euler-Chelpin (German) for their research on sugar fermentation and enzymes.
1912	François Auguste Victor Grignard (French) for discovering the Grignard reagent to synthesize organic compounds, and Paul Sabatier (French) for his method of adding hydrogen to organic compounds, using metals as catalysts.	1930	Hans Fischer (German) for studying the coloring matter of blood and leaves and synthesizing hemin.
		1931	Carl Bosch and Friedrich Bergius (German) for inventing high-pressure methods of manufacturing ammonia and liquefying coal.
1913	Alfred Werner (Swiss) for his coordination theory on the arrangement of atoms.	1932	Irving Langmuir (American) for his discoveries about molecular films absorbed on surfaces.
1914	Theodore W. Richards (American) for determining the atomic weights of many elements.	1933	No Award
1915	Richard Willstätter (German) for his research concerning chlorophyll and other coloring matter in plants.	1934	Harold Clayton Urey (American) for discovering deuterium (heavy hydrogen).
1916-17	No Award	1935	Frédéric and Irène Joliot-Curie (French) for synthesizing new radioactive elements.
		1936	Peter J. W. Debye (Dutch) for his studies on molecules, dipole moments, the diffraction of electrons, and X rays in gases.

*See "People" section for biographical information.

1937 Sir Walter N. Haworth (British) for his research on carbohydrates and vitamin C, and Paul Karrer (Swiss) for studying carotenoids, flavins, and vitamins A and B_2.

1938 Richard Kuhn (German) for his work on carotenoids and vitamins (declined).

1939 Adolph Butenandt (German) for studying sex hormones (declined), and Leopold Ružicka (Swiss) for his work on polymethylenes.

1940-42 No Award

1943 Georg von Hevesy (Hungarian) for using isotopes as indicators in chemistry.

1944 Otto Hahn (German) for his discoveries in fission.

1945 Artturi Virtanen (Finnish) for inventing new methods in agricultural biochemistry.

1946 James B. Sumner (American) for discovering that enzymes can be crystallized, and Wendell M. Stanley and John H. Northrop (American) for preparing pure enzymes and virus proteins.

1947 Sir Robert Robinson (British) for his research on biologically significant plant substances.

1948 Arne Tiselius (Swedish) for his discoveries on the nature of the serum proteins.

1949 William Francis Giauque (American) for studying reactions to extreme cold.

1950 Otto Diels and Kurt Alder (German) for developing a method of synthesizing organic compounds of the diene group.

1951 Edwin M. McMillan and Glenn T. Seaborg (American) for discovering plutonium and other elements.

1952 Archer J. P. Martin and Richard Synge (British) for developing the partition chromatography process, a method of separating compounds.

1953 Hermann Staudinger (German) for discovering a way to synthesize fiber.

1954 Linus Pauling (American) for his work on the forces that hold matter together.

1955 Vincent Du Vigneaud (American) for discovering a process for making synthetic hormones.

1956 Sir Cyril Hinshelwood (British) and Nikolai N. Semenov (Russian) for their work on chemical chain reactions.

1957 Lord Todd (British) for his work on the protein composition of cells.

1958 Frederick Sanger (British) for discovering the structure of the insulin molecule.

1959 Jaroslav Heyrovský (Czech) for developing the polarographic method of analysis.

1960 Willard F. Libby (American) for developing a method of radiocarbon dating.

1961 Melvin Calvin (American) for his research on photosynthesis.

1962 Sir John Cowdery Kendrew and Max Ferdinand Perutz (British) for their studies on globular proteins.

1963 Giulio Natta (Italian) for his contributions to the understanding of *polymers*, and Karl Ziegler (German) for his production of *organometallic compounds*. Their work resulted in improved plastics.

1964 Dorothy C. Hodgkin (British) for X-ray studies of compounds such as vitamin B_{12} and penicillin.

1965 Robert Burns Woodward (American) for his contributions to organic synthesis.

1966 Robert S. Mulliken (American) for developing the *molecular-orbital* theory of chemical structure.

1967 Manfred Eigen (German) and Ronald G. W. Norrish and George Porter (British) for developing techniques to measure rapid chemical reactions.

1968 Lars Onsager (American) for developing the theory of reciprocal relations of various kinds of thermodynamic activity.

1969 Derek H. R. Barton (British) and Odd Hassel (Norwegian) for their studies relating chemical reactions with the three-dimensional shape of molecules.

1970 Luis Federico Leloir (Argentine) for his discovery of chemical compounds that affect the storage of chemical energy in living things.

1971 Gerhard Herzberg (Canadian) for his research in the structure of molecules, particularly for his work on molecular fragments that are called *free radicals*.

1972 Christian B. Anfinsen, Stanford Moore, and William H. Stein (American) for their fundamental contributions to the chemistry of *enzymes*, basic substances of living things.

1973 Geoffrey Wilkinson (British) and Ernst Fischer (German) for their work on *organometallic compounds*, substances which consist of organic compounds and metal atoms.

1974 Paul John Flory (American) for his work in polymer chemistry.

1975 John Warcup Cornforth (Australian-born) and Vladimir Prelog (Swiss) for their work on the chemical synthesis of important organic compounds.

1976 William N. Lipscomb, Jr. (American), for his studies on the structure and bonding mechanisms of *boranes*, complex compounds that consist of boron and hydrogen.

1977 Ilya Prigogine (Belgian) for his contributions to nonequilibrium thermodynamics.

1978 Peter Mitchell (British) for his studies of cellular energy transfer.

1979 Herbert C. Brown (American) and Georg Wittig (German) for developing compounds capable of producing chemical bonds useful in the manufacture of drugs and in other industrial processes.

1980 Paul Berg and Walter Gilbert (American) and Frederick Sanger (British) for their studies of the chemical structure of nucleic acids.

1981 Kenichi Fukui (Japanese) and Roald Hoffmann (American) for applying the theories of quantum mechanics to predict the course of chemical reactions.

1982 Aaron Klug (South African-born) for his study of the structure of viruses and other important molecular complexes.

Nobel prizes for physiology or medicine

1901 Emil von Behring (German) for discovering the diphtheria antitoxin.

1902 Sir Ronald Ross (British) for working on malaria and discovering how malaria is transmitted.

1903 Niels Ryberg Finsen (Danish) for treating diseases, especially *lupus vulgaris,* with concentrated light rays.

1904 Ivan Petrovich Pavlov (Russian) for his work on the physiology of digestion.

1905 Robert Koch* (German) for working on tuberculosis and discovering the tubercule bacillus and tuberculin.

1906 Camillo Golgi (Italian) and Santiago Ramon y Cajal (Spanish) for their studies of nerve tissue.

1907 Charles Louis Alphonse Laveran (French) for studying diseases caused by protozoans.

1908 Paul Ehrlich (German) and Élie Metchnikoff (Russian) for their work on immunity.

1909 Emil Theodor Kocher (Swiss) for his work on the physiology, pathology, and surgery of the thyroid gland.

1910 Albrecht Kossel (German) for studying cell chemistry, proteins, and nucleic substances.

1911 Allvar Gullstrand (Swedish) for his work on dioptrics, the refraction of light through the eye.

1912 Alexis Carrel (French) for suturing blood vessels and grafting vessels and organs.

1913 Charles Robert Richet (French) for studying allergies caused by foreign substances, as in hay fever.

1914 Robert Bárány (Austrian) for work on function and diseases of equilibrium organs in the inner ear.

1915-18 No Award

1919 Jules Bordet (Belgian) for his discoveries on immunity.

1920 August Krogh (Danish) for discovering the system of action of blood capillaries.

1921 No Award

1922 Archibald V. Hill (British) for his discovery on heat production in the muscles, and Otto Meyerhof (German) for his theory on the production of lactic acid in the muscles.

1923 Sir Frederick Grant Banting (Canadian) and John J. R. Macleod (Scottish) for discovering insulin.

1924 Willem Einthoven (Dutch) for inventing the electrocardiograph.

1925 No Award

1926 Johannes Fibiger (Danish) for discovering a parasite that causes cancer.

1927 Julius Wagner von Jauregg (Austrian) for discovering the fever treatment for paralysis.

1928 Charles Nicolle (French) for his work on typhus.

1929 Christiaan Eijkman (Dutch) for discovering vitamins that prevent beriberi, and Sir Frederick G. Hopkins (British) for discovering vitamins that help growth.

1930 Karl Landsteiner (American) for discovering the four main human blood types.

1931 Otto H. Warburg (German) for discovering that enzymes aid in respiration by tissues.

1932 Edgar D. Adrian and Sir Charles S. Sherrington (British) for discoveries on the function of neurons.

1933 Thomas H. Morgan (American) for studying the function of chromosomes in heredity.

1934 George Minot, William P. Murphy, and George H. Whipple (American) for their discoveries on liver treatment for anemia.

1935 Hans Spemann (German) for discovering the organizer-effect in the growth of an embryo.

1936 Sir Henry H. Dale (British) and Otto Loewi (Austrian) for their discoveries on the chemical transmission of nerve impulses.

1937 Albert Szent-Györgyi (Hungarian) for his discoveries in connection with oxidation in tissues, vitamin C, and fumaric acid.

1938 Corneille Heymans (Belgian) for his discoveries concerning the regulation of respiration.

1939 Gerhard Domagk (German) for discovering prontosil, the first sulfa drug (declined).

1940-42 No Award

1943 Henrik Dam (Danish) for discovering vitamin K, and Edward Doisy (American) for synthesizing it.

1944 Joseph Erlanger and Herbert Gasser (American) for their work on single nerve fibers.

1945 Sir Alexander Fleming,* Howard W. Florey, and Ernst B. Chain (British) for discovering penicillin.

1946 Hermann Joseph Muller (American) for discovering that X rays can produce mutations.

1947 Carl F. and Gerty Cori (American) for their work on insulin, and Bernardo Houssay (Argentine) for studying the pancreas and the pituitary gland.

1948 Paul Mueller (Swiss) for discovering the insect-killing properties of DDT.

1949 Walter R. Hess (Swiss) for discovering how certain parts of the brain control organs of the body, and Antônio E. Moniz (Portuguese) for originating prefrontal lobotomy.

1950 Philip S. Hench, Edward C. Kendall (American), and Tadeus Reichstein (Swiss) for their discoveries on cortisone and ACTH.

1951 Max Theiler (South African who worked in the United States) for developing the yellow fever vaccine known as 17-D.

1952 Selman A. Waksman (American) for his work in the discovery of streptomycin.

1953 Fritz Albert Lipmann (American) and Hans Adolf Krebs (British) for their discoveries in biosynthesis and metabolism.

1954 John F. Enders, Thomas H. Weller, and Frederick C. Robbins (American) for discovering a simple method of growing polio virus in test tubes.

1955 Hugo Theorell (Swedish) for his discoveries on the nature and action of oxidation enzymes.

1956 André F. Cournand, Dickinson W. Richards, Jr. (American), and Werner Forssmann (German) for using a catheter to chart the interior of the heart.

1957 Daniel Bovet (Italian) for discovering antihistamines.

1958 George Wells Beadle and Edward Lawrie Tatum (American) for their work in biochemical genetics, and Joshua Lederberg (American) for his studies of genetics in bacteria.

1959 Severo Ochoa and Arthur Kornberg (American) for producing nucleic acid by artificial means.

1960 Sir Macfarlane Burnet* (Australian) and Peter B. Medawar (British) for research in transplanting human organs.

1961 Georg von Békésy (American) for demonstrating how the ear distinguishes between various sounds.

1962 James D. Watson (American) and Francis H. C. Crick and Maurice H. F. Wilkins (British) for their work on nucleic acid.

---

*See "People" section for biographical information.

1963	Sir John Carew Eccles (Australian) for his research on the transmission of nerve impulses, and Alan Lloyd Hodgkin (British) and Andrew Fielding Huxley (British) for their description of the behavior of nerve impulses.
1964	Konrad E. Bloch (American) and Feor Lynen (German) for their work on cholesterol and fatty acid metabolism.
1965	Francois Jacob, André Lwoff, and Jacques Monod (French) for their discoveries concerning genetic control of enzyme and virus synthesis.
1966	Francis Peyton Rous (American) for discovering a cancer-producing virus, and Charles B. Huggins (American) for discovering uses of hormones in treating cancer.
1967	Ragnar Granit (Swedish) and H. Keffer Hartline and George Wald (American) for their work on the chemical and physiological processes that take place in the eye.
1968	Robert W. Holley, H. Gobind Khorana, and Marshall W. Nirenberg (American) for explaining how genes determine the function of cells.
1969	Max Delbrück, Alfred Hershey, and Salvador Luria (American) for their work with *bacteriophages (viruses that attack bacteria).*
1970	Julius Axelrod (American), Bernard Katz (British), and Ulf Svante von Euler (Swedish) for their discoveries of the role played by certain chemicals in the transmission of nerve impulses.
1971	Earl W. Sutherland, Jr. (American), for his discovery of the ways hormones act, including the discovery of cyclic AMP, a chemical that influences the actions of hormones on body processes.
1972	Gerald M. Edelman (American) and Rodney R. Porter (British) for their discovery of the chemical structure of antibodies.

1973	Nikolaas Tinbergen (Dutch-born) and Konrad Z. Lorenz and Karl von Frisch (Austrian) for their studies on animal behavior.
1974	Christian de Duve (Belgian) and Albert Claude and George E. Palade (American) for their pioneer work in cell biology.
1975	David Baltimore, Renato Dulbecco, and Howard M. Temin (American) for their research on how certain viruses affect the genes of cancer cells.
1976	Baruch S. Blumberg and D. Carleton Gajdusek (American) for their discoveries concerning the origin and spread of infectious diseases.
1977	Roger Guillemin, Andrew Schally, and Rosalyn Yalow (American) for their research concerning the role of hormones in the chemistry of the body.
1978	Werner Arber (Swiss) and Daniel Nathans and Hamilton O. Smith (American) for their discoveries in molecular genetics.
1979	Allan MacLeod Cormack (American) and Godfrey Newbold Hounsfield (British) for their contributions to the development of the computerized axial tomographic (CAT) scanner, an X-ray machine that makes a cross-sectional view of the body.
1980	Baruj Benacerraf and George D. Snell (American) and Jean Dausset (French) for their discoveries concerning the genetic regulation of the body's immune system.
1981	Roger W. Sperry and David H. Hubel (American) and Torsten N. Wiesel (Swedish) for their research on the organization and functioning of the brain.
1982	Sune Karl Bergstrom and Bengt Ingemar Samuelsson (Swedish) and John R. Vane (British) for their study of prostaglandins.

Nobel prizes for literature

1901	René Sully-Prudhomme (French) for his poems.
1902	Theodor Mommsen (German) for his historical narratives, particularly his history of Rome.
1903	Bjørnstjerne Bjørnson (Norwegian) for his novels, poems, and dramas.
1904	Frédéric Mistral (French) for his poems, and José Echegaray y Eizaguirre (Spanish) for his dramas.
1905	Henryk Sienkiewicz (Polish) for his novels.
1906	Giosuè Carducci (Italian) for his poems.
1907	Rudyard Kipling* (British) for his stories, novels, and poems.
1908	Rudolf Eucken (German) for his philosophic writings.
1909	Selma Lagerlöf (Swedish) for her novels and poems.
1910	Paul von Heyse (German) for his poems, novels, and dramas.
1911	Maurice Maeterlinck (Belgian) for his dramas.
1912	Gerhart Hauptmann (German) for his dramas.
1913	Sir Rabindranath Tagore (Indian) for his poems.
1914	No Award
1915	Romain Rolland (French) for his novels.
1916	Verner von Heidenstam (Swedish) for his poems.
1917	Karl Gjellerup (Danish) for his poems and novels, and Henrik Pontoppidan (Danish) for his novels and short stories.
1918	No Award

1919	Carl Spitteler (Swiss) for his epics, short stories, and essays.
1920	Knut Hamsun (Norwegian) for his novels.
1921	Anatole France (French) for his novels, short stories, and essays.
1922	Jacinto Benavente (Spanish) for his dramas.
1923	William Butler Yeats (Irish) for his poems.
1924	Władysław S. Reymont (Polish) for his novels.
1925	George Bernard Shaw* (Irish-born) for his plays.
1926	Grazia Deledda (Italian) for her novels.
1927	Henri Bergson (French) for his philosophic writings.
1928	Sigrid Undset (Norwegian) for her novels.
1929	Thomas Mann* (German) principally for his novel, *Buddenbrooks.*
1930	Sinclair Lewis (American) for his novels.
1931	Erik Axel Karlfeldt (Swedish) for his lyric poetry.
1932	John Galsworthy (British) for his novels, plays, and short stories.
1933	Ivan Alexeyevich Bunin (Russian) for his novels, short stories, and poems.
1934	Luigi Pirandello (Italian) for his dramas.
1935	No Award
1936	Eugene O'Neill* (American) for his dramas.
1937	Roger Martin du Gard (French) for his novels.
1938	Pearl S. Buck (American) for her novels.

*See "People" section for biographical information.

45

1939	Frans Eemil Sillanpää (Finnish) for his novels.	**1964**	Jean-Paul Sartre (French) for his philosophical works (declined).

1939 Frans Eemil Sillanpää (Finnish) for his novels.

1940-43 No Award

1944 Johannes V. Jensen (Danish) for his poems and novels.

1945 Gabriela Mistral (Chilean) for her poems.

1946 Hermann Hesse (German) for his novels, poems, and essays.

1947 André Gide (French) for his novels.

1948 T. S. Eliot* (British) for his poems, essays, and plays.

1949 William Faulkner* (American) for his novels. (Award delayed until 1950.)

1950 Bertrand Russell* (British) for his philosophic writings.

1951 Pär Fabian Lagerkvist (Swedish) for his novels, particularly *Barabbas.*

1952 François Mauriac (French) for his novels, essays, and poems.

1953 Sir Winston Churchill* (British) for his essays, speeches, and historical writings.

1954 Ernest Hemingway* (American) for his novels and short stories.

1955 Halldór K. Laxness (Icelandic) for his novels.

1956 Juan Ramón Jiménez (Spanish) for his poems.

1957 Albert Camus (French) for his novels.

1958 Boris Pasternak (Russian) for his novels, especially *Dr. Zhivago* (declined).

1959 Salvatore Quasimodo (Italian) for his lyric poems.

1960 Saint-John Perse (French) for his poems.

1961 Ivo Andrić (Yugoslav) for his novels, especially *The Bridge on the Drina.*

1962 John Steinbeck* (American) for his novels, especially *The Winter of Our Discontent.*

1963 George Seferis (Greek) for his lyric poetry.

1964 Jean-Paul Sartre (French) for his philosophical works (declined).

1965 Mikhail Sholokhov (Russian) for his novels.

1966 Shmuel Yosef Agnon (Israeli) for his stories of Eastern European Jewish life, and Nelly Sachs (German-born) for her poetry and plays about the Jewish people.

1967 Miguel Angel Asturias (Guatemalan) for his writings rooted in national individuality and Indian traditions.

1968 Kawabata Yasunari (Japanese) for his novels about the Japanese people.

1969 Samuel B. Beckett (Irish-born) for his novels and plays.

1970 Alexander Solzhenitsyn (Russian) for his novels.

1971 Pablo Neruda (Chilean) for his poems.

1972 Heinrich Böll (German) for his novels, short stories, and plays.

1973 Patrick White (Australian) for his novels.

1974 Eyvind Johnson (Swedish) for his novels and short stories, and Harry Edmund Martinson (Swedish) for his essays, plays, novels, and poems.

1975 Eugenio Montale (Italian) for his poems.

1976 Saul Bellow* (American) for his novels.

1977 Vicente Aleixandre (Spanish) for his poems.

1978 Isaac Bashevis Singer (Polish-born) for his novels and short stories.

1979 Odysseus Elytis (Greek) for his poems.

1980 Czeslaw Milosz (Polish) for his poems.

1981 Elias Canetti (Bulgarian-born) for his fiction and nonfiction.

1982 Gabriel García Márquez (Colombian) for his novels and short stories.

Nobel prizes for peace

1901 Jean Henri Dunant (Swiss) for founding the Red Cross and originating the Geneva Convention, and Frédéric Passy (French) for founding a French peace society.

1902 Élie Ducommun (Swiss) for his work as honorary secretary of the International Peace Bureau, and Charles Albert Gobat (Swiss) for his work as administrator of the Inter-Parliamentary Union.

1903 Sir William R. Cremer (British) for his activities as founder and secretary of the International Arbitration League.

1904 The Institute of International Law for its studies on the laws of neutrality and other phases of international law.

1905 Baroness Bertha von Suttner (Austrian) for promoting pacifism and founding an Austrian peace society.

1906 Theodore Roosevelt† (American) for negotiating peace in the Russo-Japanese War.

1907 Ernesto T. Moneta (Italian) for his work as president of the Lombard League for Peace, and Louis Renault (French) for organizing international conferences and representing France at two peace conferences.

1908 Klas Pontus Arnoldson (Swedish) for founding the Swedish Society for Arbitration and Peace, and Fredrik Bajer (Danish) for his work on the International Peace Bureau.

1909 Auguste M. F. Beernaert (Belgian) for his work on the Permanent Court of Arbitration, and Paul d'Estournelles (French) for founding and directing the French Parliamentary Arbitration Committee and League of International Conciliation.

1910 The International Peace Bureau for promoting international arbitration and organizing many peace conferences.

1911 Tobias M. C. Asser (Dutch) for organizing conferences on international law, and Alfred H. Fried (Austrian) for his writings on peace as editor of *Die Friedenswarte.*

1912 Elihu Root (American) for settling the problem of Japanese immigration to California and organizing the Central American Peace Conference.

1913 Henri Lafontaine (Belgian) for his work as president of the International Peace Bureau.

1914-16 No Award

1917 The International Red Cross for doing relief work during World War I.

1918 No Award

1919 Woodrow Wilson† (American) for attempting a just settlement of World War I and advocating the League of Nations. (Award delayed until 1920.)

1920 Léon Bourgeois (French) for his contribution as the president of the Council of the League of Nations.

---

*See "People" section for biographical information.
†See "Presidents" section for biographical information.

1921 Karl Hjalmar Branting (Swedish) for promoting social reforms in Sweden and serving as the Swedish delegate to the League of Nations, and Christian Louis Lange (Norwegian) for his contribution as secretary-general of the Inter-Parliamentary Union.

1922 Fridtjof Nansen (Norwegian) for doing relief work among Russian prisoners of war and in famine areas in Russia.

1923-24 No Award

1925 Sir Austen Chamberlain (British) for helping to work out the Locarno Peace Pact, and Charles G. Dawes (American) for originating a plan for payment of German reparations.

1926 Aristide Briand (French) for his part in forming the Locarno Peace Pact, and Gustav Stresemann (German) for persuading Germany to accept plans for reparations.

1927 Ferdinand Buisson (French) for his contribution as president of the League of Human Rights, and Ludwig Quidde (German) for his writings on peace and his work in international peace congresses.

1928 No Award

1929 Frank Billings Kellogg (American) for negotiating the Kellogg-Briand Peace Pact.

1930 Nathan Söderblom (Swedish) for writing on and working for peace.

1931 Jane Addams* (American) for her work with the Women's International League for Peace and Freedom, and Nicholas M. Butler (American) for his work with the Carnegie Endowment for International Peace.

1932 No Award

1933 Sir Norman Angell (British) for his work with the Royal Institute of International Affairs, the League of Nations, and the National Peace Council.

1934 Arthur Henderson (British) for his contribution as president of the World Disarmament Conference.

1935 Carl von Ossietzky (German) for promoting world disarmament. (Award delayed until 1936.)

1936 Carlos Saavedra Lamas (Argentine) for negotiating a peace settlement between Bolivia and Paraguay in the Chaco War.

1937 Edgar Algernon Robert Gascoyne Cecil (British) for promoting the League of Nations and working with peace movements.

1938 The International Office for Refugees for directing relief work among refugees.

1939-43 No Award

1944 The International Red Cross for doing relief work during World War II.

1945 Cordell Hull (American) for his peace efforts as Secretary of State.

1946 John R. Mott (American) for his YMCA work and for aiding displaced persons, and Emily Greene Balch (American) for her work with the Women's International League for Peace and Freedom.

1947 The Friends Service Council and the American Friends Service Committee for humanitarian work.

1948 No Award

1949 John Boyd Orr (British) for directing the United Nations Food and Agriculture Organization.

---

*See "People" section for biographical information.

1950 Ralph J. Bunche (American) for his work as UN mediator in Palestine in 1948 and 1949.

1951 Léon Jouhaux (French) for his work helping to organize national and international labor unions.

1952 Albert Schweitzer* (German) for his humanitarian work in Africa. (Award delayed until 1953.)

1953 George C. Marshall (American) for his work in promoting peace through the European Recovery Program.

1954 Office of the United Nations High Commissioner for Refugees for providing protection for millions of refugees and seeking permanent solutions to their problems. (Award delayed until 1955.)

1955-56 No Award

1957 Lester B. Pearson (Canadian) for organizing a United Nations force in Egypt.

1958 Dominique Georges Pire (Belgian) for his work in resettling displaced persons.

1959 Philip Noel-Baker (British) for his work in promoting peace and disarmament.

1960 Albert John Luthuli (African) for his peaceful campaign against racial restrictions in South Africa.

1961 Dag Hammarskjöld (Swedish) for his efforts to bring peace to the Congo (awarded posthumously).

1962 Linus Pauling (American) for trying to effect a ban on nuclear weapons.

1963 The International Committee of the Red Cross and The League of Red Cross Societies for humanitarian work.

1964 Martin Luther King, Jr.* (American), for leading the black struggle for equality in the United States through nonviolent means.

1965 United Nations Children's Fund (UNICEF) for its aid to children.

1966-67 No Award

1968 René Cassin (French) for promoting human rights.

1969 International Labor Organization (ILO) for its efforts to improve working conditions.

1970 Norman E. Borlaug (American) for his role in developing high-yield grains that increased food production in developing countries.

1971 Willy Brandt (German) for his efforts to improve relations between Communist and non-Communist nations.

1972 No Award

1973 Henry A. Kissinger (American) and Le Duc Tho (North Vietnamese) for their work in negotiating the Vietnam War cease-fire agreement (Le Duc Tho declined).

1974 Sean MacBride (Irish) for working to guarantee human rights through international law, and Eisaku Sato (Japanese) for his efforts to improve international relations and stop the spread of nuclear weapons.

1975 Andrei D. Sakharov (Russian) for his work in promoting peace and opposing violence and brutality.

1976 Mairead Corrigan and Betty Williams (Irish) for organizing a movement to end Protestant-Catholic fighting in Northern Ireland. (Award delayed until 1977.)

1977 Amnesty International for its work to help political prisoners.

1978 Menachem Begin (Israeli) and Anwar el-Sadat (Egyptian) for their efforts to bring about a settlement of the Arab-Israeli conflict.

1979 Mother Teresa (Indian) for aiding India's poor.

1980 Adolfo Pérez Esquivel (Argentine) for his role in Service for Peace and Justice in Latin America, a group promoting the cause of human rights.

1981 Office of the United Nations High Commissioner for Refugees for protection of millions of Vietnamese and other refugees.

1982 Alfonso Garcia Robles (Mexican) and Alva Myrdal (Swedish) for their efforts on behalf of international nuclear disarmament.

Nobel prizes for economics

The prize in economics was established in 1969.

1969 Ragnar Frisch (Norwegian) and Jan Tinbergen (Dutch) for their work in *econometrics*, a method of analyzing economic activity.

1970 Paul A. Samuelson (American) for raising the level of scientific analysis in economic theory.

1971 Simon Kuznets (American) for his interpretation of economic growth.

1972 Kenneth J. Arrow (American) and Sir John Hicks (British) for their pioneering contribution to general equilibrium theory and to welfare theory.

1973 Wassily Leontief (American) for his development of the input-output method of economic analysis.

1974 Friedrich von Hayek (Austrian) and Gunnar Myrdal (Swedish) for their work in the theory of money and economic change and in the relationship between economic and social factors.

1975 Leonid V. Kantorovich (Russian) and Tjalling C. Koopmans (American) for their work on how economic resources should be distributed and used.

1976 Milton Friedman (American) for his work in the fields of economic consumption, monetary history and theory, and price stabilization policy.

1977 James Meade (British) and Bertil Ohlin (Swedish) for their studies of international trade and international finance.

1978 Herbert A. Simon (American) for his research on the decision-making process in business.

1979 Sir Arthur Lewis (St. Lucian-born) and Theodore W. Schultz (American) for their research into the economic problems of developing countries.

1980 Lawrence R. Klein (American) for using econometric models to analyze economic policies and the rise and fall in business activity.

1981 James Tobin (American) for his analyses of financial markets and their effect on how businesses and families spend and save money.

1982 George J. Stigler (American) for his study of government regulation and its effect on industry and the economy.

Pulitzer prizes

Pulitzer prizes are awarded annually for distinguished achievements in journalism, literature, and music in the United States. Joseph Pulitzer, an American newspaper publisher, established the prizes (see the "People" section).

Pulitzer prizes in journalism

Meritorious public service

1917	No Award.
1918	*The New York Times.*
1919	*The Milwaukee Journal.*
1920	No Award.
1921	*Boston Post.*
1922	*The World* (New York).
1923	*Memphis Commercial Appeal.*
1924	*The World* (New York).
1925	No Award.
1926	*The Enquirer Sun* (Columbus, Ga.).
1927	*Canton* (Ohio) *Daily News.*
1928	*Indianapolis Times.*
1929	*The Evening World* (New York).
1930	No Award.
1931	*Atlanta Constitution.*
1932	*Indianapolis News.*

1933	*New York World-Telegram.*
1934	*Medford* (Ore.) *Mail Tribune.*
1935	*The Sacramento* (Calif.) *Bee.*
1936	*The Cedar Rapids* (Iowa) *Gazette.*
1937	*St. Louis Post-Dispatch.*
1938	*The Bismarck* (N.Dak.) *Tribune.*
1939	*The Miami* (Fla.) *Daily News.*
1940	*Waterbury* (Conn.) *Republican and American.*
1941	*St. Louis Post-Dispatch.*
1942	*Los Angeles Times.*
1943	*The World-Herald* (Omaha).
1944	*The New York Times.*
1945	*The Detroit Free Press.*
1946	*The Scranton* (Pa.) *Times.*
1947	*The Sun* (Baltimore).
1948	*St. Louis Post-Dispatch.*

1949	*Nebraska State Journal* (Lincoln).	1965	*Hutchinson* (Kans.) *News.*
1950	*Chicago Daily News; St. Louis Post-Dispatch.*	1966	*The Boston Globe.*
1951	*Miami* (Fla.) *Herald; Brooklyn Daily Eagle.*	1967	*Courier-Journal* (Louisville); *Milwaukee Journal.*
1952	*St. Louis Post-Dispatch.*	1968	*The Riverside* (Calif.) *Press-Enterprise.*
1953	*The News Reporter* (Whiteville, N.C.); *Tabor City* (N.C.) *Tribune.*	1969	*Los Angeles Times.*
		1970	*Newsday* (Garden City, N.Y.).
1954	*Newsday* (Garden City, N.Y.).	1971	*Winston-Salem* (N.C.) *Journal and Sentinel.*
1955	*Columbus* (Ga.) *Ledger* and *Sunday Ledger-Enquirer.*	1972	*The New York Times.*
		1973	*The Washington* (D.C.) *Post.*
1956	*Watsonville* (Calif.) *Register-Pajaronian.*	1974	*Newsday* (Garden City, N.Y.).
1957	*Chicago Daily News.*	1975	*The Boston Globe.*
1958	*Arkansas Gazette* (Little Rock).	1976	*Anchorage* (Alaska) *Daily News.*
1959	*Utica* (N.Y.) *Observer-Dispatch; Utica Daily Press.*	1977	*Lufkin* (Tex.) *News.*
		1978	*The Philadelphia Inquirer.*
1960	*Los Angeles Times.*	1979	*Point Reyes* (Calif.) *Light.*
1961	*Amarillo* (Tex.) *Globe-Times.*	1980	*Gannett News Service.*
1962	*The Panama City* (Fla.) *News-Herald.*	1981	*Charlotte* (N.C.) *Observer.*
1963	*Chicago Daily News.*	1982	*The Detroit News*
1964	*The St. Petersburg* (Fla.) *Times.*		

Reporting

1917	Herbert B. Swope, *The World* (New York).	1937	John J. O'Neill, *New York Herald Tribune;* William L. Laurence, *The New York Times;* Howard W. Blakeslee, The Associated Press; Gobind Behari Lal, Universal Service; David Dietz, The Scripps-Howard Newspapers.
1918	Harold A. Littledale, *New York Evening Post.*		
1919	No Award.		
1920	John J. Leary, Jr., *The World* (New York).		
1921	Louis Seibold, *The World* (New York).	1938	Raymond Sprigle, *Pittsburgh Post-Gazette.*
1922	Kirke L. Simpson, The Associated Press.	1939	Thomas L. Stokes, Scripps-Howard Newspaper Alliance.
1923	Alva Johnston, *The New York Times.*		
1924	Magner White, *San Diego* (Calif.) *Sun.*	1940	S. Burton Heath, *New York World-Telegram.*
1925	James W. Mulroy, Alvin H. Goldstein, *Chicago Daily News.*	1941	Westbrook Pegler, *New York World-Telegram.*
		1942	Stanton Delaplane, *San Francisco Chronicle.*
1926	William B. Miller, *The Courier-Journal* (Louisville).	1943	George Weller, *Chicago Daily News.*
		1944	Paul Schoenstein and associates, *New York Journal-American.*
1927	John T. Rogers, *St. Louis Post-Dispatch.*		
1928	No Award.	1945	Jack S. McDowell, *The Call-Bulletin* (San Francisco).
1929	Paul Y. Anderson, *St. Louis Post-Dispatch.*		
1930	Russell D. Owen, *The New York Times.*	1946	William L. Laurence, *The New York Times.*
1931	A. B. MacDonald, *The Kansas City* (Mo.) *Star.*	1947	Frederick Woltman, *New York World-Telegram.*
1932	W. C. Richards, D. D. Martin, J. S. Pooler, F. D. Webb, J. N. W. Sloan, *The Detroit Free Press.*	1948	George E. Goodwin, *The Atlanta Journal.*
		1949	Malcolm Johnson, *The Sun* (New York).
1933	Francis A. Jamieson, The Associated Press.	1950	Meyer Berger, *The New York Times.*
1934	Royce Brier, *San Francisco Chronicle.*	1951	Edward S. Montgomery, *San Francisco Examiner.*
1935	William H. Taylor, *New York Herald Tribune.*	1952	George de Carvalho, *San Francisco Chronicle.*
1936	Lauren D. Lyman, *The New York Times.*	1953	Award divided into the two categories listed below.

Local reporting (Under Pressure of Edition Time)

1953	*The Providence* (R.I.) *Journal and Evening Bulletin.*	1960	Jack Nelson, *The Constitution* (Atlanta, Ga.).
		1961	Sanche de Gramont, *New York Herald Tribune.*
1954	*Vicksburg* (Miss.) *Sunday Post-Herald.*	1962	Robert D. Mullins, *Salt Lake City Deseret News.*
1955	Caro Brown, *Alice* (Tex.) *Daily Echo.*	1963	Sylvan Fox, William Longgood, and Anthony Shannon, *The New York World-Telegram & Sun.*
1956	Lee Hills, *Detroit Free Press.*		
1957	*Salt Lake* (Utah) *Tribune.*		
1958	*Fargo* (N.Dak.) *Forum.*	1964	Award became local general or spot news reporting.
1959	Mary Lou Werner, *The Evening Star* (Washington).		

Local reporting (Not Under Pressure of Edition Time)

1953	Edward J. Mowery, *The New York World-Telegram & Sun.*	1959	John H. Brislin, *Scranton* (Pa.) *Tribune* and *Sunday Scrantonian.*
1954	Alvin S. McCoy, *The Kansas City* (Mo.) *Star.*	1960	Miriam Ottenberg, *The Evening Star* (Washington).
1955	Roland K. Towery, *Cuero* (Tex.) *Record.*		
1956	Arthur Daley, *The New York Times.*	1961	Edgar May, *Buffalo* (N.Y.) *Evening News.*
1957	Wallace Turner, William Lambert, *Portland* (Ore.) *Oregonian.*	1962	George Bliss, *Chicago Tribune.*
		1963	Oscar Griffin, Jr., *Pecos* (Tex.) *Independent Enterprise.*
1958	George Beveridge, *The Evening Star* (Washington).		
		1964	Award became local specialized reporting.

Local general or spot news reporting

1964	Norman C. Miller, Jr., *The Wall Street Journal.*	1973	The staff of the *Chicago Tribune.*
1965	Melvin H. Ruder, *Hungry Horse News* (Columbia Falls, Mont.)	1974	Art Petacque and Hugh Hough, *Chicago Sun-Times.*
1966	The staff of the *Los Angeles Times.*	1975	The staff of the *Xenia* (Ohio) *Daily Gazette.*
1967	Robert V. Cox, *The Chambersburg* (Pa.) *Public Opinion.*	1976	Gene Miller, *The Miami Herald.*
		1977	Margo Huston, *The Milwaukee Journal.*
1968	The staff of *The Detroit Free Press.*	1978	Richard Whitt, *The Courier-Journal* (Louisville).
1969	John Fetterman, *The Courier-Journal* (Louisville).	1979	The staff of the *San Diego Evening Tribune.*
1970	Thomas Fitzpatrick, *Chicago Sun-Times.*	1980	The staff of *The Philadelphia Inquirer.*
1971	The staff of the *Akron Beacon Journal.*	1981	The staff of the *Longview* (Wash.) *Daily News.*
1972	Richard I. Cooper and John W. Machacek, *The Rochester* (N.Y.) *Times-Union.*	1982	The staffs of *The Kansas City* (Mo.) *Star* and *The Kansas City* (Mo.) *Times.*

Local specialized reporting

1964	Albert V. Gaudiosi, James V. Magee, and Frederick A. Meyer, *The Philadelphia Bulletin.*	1974	William Sherman, *Daily News* (New York).
		1975	The staff of the *Indianapolis Star.*
1965	Gene Goltz, *The Houston Post.*	1976	The staff of the *Chicago Tribune.*
1966	John A. Frasca, *The Tampa Tribune.*	1977	Acel Moore and Wendell Rawls, Jr., *The Philadelphia Inquirer.*
1967	Gene Miller, *The Miami Herald.*		
1968	J. Anthony Lukas, *The New York Times.*	1978	Anthony R. Dolan, *Stamford* (Conn.) *Advocate.*
1969	Albert L. Delugach, Denny Walsh, *St. Louis Globe-Democrat.*	1979	Gilbert M. Gaul and Elliot G. Jaspin, *Pottsville* (Pa.) *Republican.*
1970	Harold Eugene Martin, *The Montgomery* (Ala.) *Journal.*	1980	Nils Bruzelius, Alexander B. Hawes, Jr., Stephen A. Kurkjian, Robert Porterfield, and Joan Vennochi, *The Boston Globe.*
1971	William Hugh Jones, *Chicago Tribune.*		
1972	Ann DeSantis, Stephen A. Kurkjian, Timothy Leland, and Gerard M. O'Neill, *The Boston Globe.*	1981	Clark Hallas and Robert B. Lowe, *The Arizona Daily Star* (Tucson).
1973	The staff of the Sun Newspapers, Omaha, Nebr.	1982	Paul Henderson, *The Seattle Times.*

Correspondence

1929	Paul S. Mowrer, *Chicago Daily News.*	1939	Louis P. Lochner, The Associated Press.
1930	Leland Stowe, *New York Herald Tribune.*	1940	Otto D. Tolischus, *The New York Times.*
1931	H. R. Knickerbocker, *Philadelphia Public Ledger* and *New York Evening Post.*	1941	Bronze plaque honoring American reporters serving in the war zones of Asia, Africa, and Europe.
1932	Walter Duranty, *The New York Times;* Charles G. Ross, *St. Louis Post-Dispatch.*	1942	Carlos P. Romulo, *The Philippines Herald.*
1933	Edgar A. Mowrer, *Chicago Daily News.*	1943	Hanson W. Baldwin, *The New York Times.*
1934	Frederick T. Birchall, *The New York Times.*	1944	Ernie Pyle, Scripps-Howard Newspaper Alliance.
1935	Arthur Krock, *The New York Times.*	1945	Harold V. Boyle, The Associated Press.
1936	Wilfred C. Barber, *Chicago Tribune.*	1946	Arnaldo Cortesi, *The New York Times.*
1937	Anne O'Hare McCormick, *The New York Times.*	1947	Brooks Atkinson, *The New York Times.*
1938	Arthur Krock, *The New York Times.*	1948	Award discontinued.

National reporting

1942	Louis Stark, *The New York Times.*
1943	No Award.
1944	Dewey L. Fleming, *The Sun* (Baltimore).
1945	James B. Reston, *The New York Times.*
1946	Edward A. Harris, *St. Louis Post-Dispatch.*
1947	Edward T. Folliard, *The Washington* (D.C.) *Post.*
1948	Bert Andrews, *New York Herald Tribune;* Nat S. Finney, *The Minneapolis Tribune.*
1949	Charles P. Trussell, *The New York Times.*
1950	Edwin O. Guthman, *The Seattle Times.*
1951	No Award.
1952	Anthony Leviero, *The New York Times.*
1953	Don Whitehead, The Associated Press.
1954	Richard L. Wilson, The Cowles Newspapers.
1955	Anthony Lewis, *Washington* (D.C.) *Daily News.*
1956	Charles L. Bartlett, *Chattanooga* (Tenn.) *Times.*
1957	James B. Reston, *The New York Times.*
1958	Relman Morin, Associated Press; Clark Mollenhoff, *The Register & Tribune* (Des Moines, Iowa).
1959	Howard Van Smith, *Miami* (Fla.) *News.*
1960	Vance Trimble, Scripps-Howard Newspaper Alliance.
1961	Edward R. Cony, *The Wall Street Journal.*
1962	Nathan G. Caldwell and Gene S. Graham, *Nashville Tennessean.*
1963	Anthony Lewis, *The New York Times.*
1964	Merriman Smith, United Press International.
1965	Louis M. Kohlmeier, *The Wall Street Journal.*
1966	Haynes Johnson, *The Evening Star* (Washington).
1967	Monroe W. Karmin and Stanley Penn, *The Wall Street Journal.*
1968	Howard James, *The Christian Science Monitor;* Nathan K. Kotz, *The Des Moines* (Iowa) *Register.*
1969	Robert Kahn, *The Christian Science Monitor.*
1970	William J. Eaton, *Chicago Daily News.*
1971	Lucinda Franks and Thomas Powers, United Press International.
1972	Jack Anderson, syndicated columnist.
1973	Robert Boyd and Clark Hoyt, Knight Newspapers.
1974	James R. Polk, *Star-News* (Washington, D.C.); Jack White, *Providence* (R.I.) *Journal* and *Evening Bulletin.*
1975	Donald L. Barlett and James B. Steele, *The Philadelphia Inquirer.*
1976	James Risser, *The Des Moines* (Iowa) *Register.*
1977	Walter Mears, The Associated Press.
1978	Gaylord D. Shaw, *Los Angeles Times.*
1979	James Risser, *The Des Moines* (Iowa) *Register.*
1980	Bette Swenson Orsini and Charles Stafford, *St. Petersburg* (Fla.) *Times.*
1981	John M. Crewdson, *The New York Times.*
1982	Rick Atkinson, *The Kansas City* (Mo.) *Times.*

International reporting

1942	Laurence E. Allen, The Associated Press.
1943	Ira Wolfert, North American Newspaper Alliance.
1944	Daniel DeLuce, The Associated Press.
1945	Mark S. Watson, *The Sun* (Baltimore).
1946	Homer W. Bigart, *New York Herald Tribune.*
1947	Eddy Gilmore, The Associated Press.
1948	Paul W. Ward, *The Sun* (Baltimore).
1949	Price Day, *The Sun* (Baltimore).
1950	Edmund Stevens, *The Christian Science Monitor.*
1951	Keyes Beech, Fred Sparks, *Chicago Daily News;* Homer Bigart, Marguerite Higgins, *New York Herald Tribune;* Relman Morin, Don Whitehead, The Associated Press.
1952	John M. Hightower, The Associated Press.
1953	Austin C. Wehrwein, *The Milwaukee Journal.*
1954	Jim G. Lucas, The Scripps-Howard Newspapers.
1955	Harrison E. Salisbury, *The New York Times.*
1956	William R. Hearst, Jr., Frank Conniff, Kingsbury Smith, International News Service.
1957	Russell Jones, The United Press.
1958	*The New York Times.*
1959	Joseph Martin and Philip Santora, *Daily News* (N.Y.).
1960	A. M. Rosenthal, *The New York Times.*
1961	Lynn Heinzerling, The Associated Press.
1962	Walter Lippmann, *New York Herald Tribune.*
1963	Hal Hendrix, *Miami* (Fla.) *News.*
1964	Malcolm W. Browne, The Associated Press, and David Halberstam, *The New York Times.*
1965	J. A. Livingston, *The Philadelphia Bulletin.*
1966	Peter Arnett, The Associated Press.
1967	R. John Hughes, *The Christian Science Monitor.*
1968	Alfred Friendly, *The Washington* (D.C.) *Post.*
1969	William Tuohy, *Los Angeles Times.*
1970	Seymour M. Hersh, Dispatch News Service.
1971	Jimmie Lee Hoagland, *The Washington* (D.C.) *Post.*
1972	Peter R. Kann, *The Wall Street Journal.*
1973	Max Frankel, *The New York Times.*
1974	Hedrick Smith, *The New York Times.*
1975	William Mullen and Ovie Carter, *Chicago Tribune.*
1976	Sidney H. Schanberg, *The New York Times.*
1977	No Award.
1978	Henry Kamm, *The New York Times.*
1979	Richard Ben Cramer, *The Philadelphia Inquirer.*
1980	Joel Brinkley and Jay Mather, *The Courier-Journal* (Louisville).
1981	Shirley Christian, *Miami* (Fla.) *Herald.*
1982	John Darnton, *The New York Times.*

Editorial writing

1917	New York Tribune.	1950	Carl M. Saunders, Jackson (Mich.) Citizen Patriot.
1918	The Courier-Journal (Louisville).		
1919	No Award.	1951	William H. Fitzpatrick, New Orleans States.
1920	Harvey E. Newbranch, Evening World-Herald (Omaha).	1952	Louis LaCoss, St. Louis Globe-Democrat.
		1953	Vermont C. Royster, The Wall Street Journal.
1921	No Award.	1954	Donald M. Murray, The Boston Herald.
1922	Frank M. O'Brien, The New York Herald.	1955	Royce Howes, The Detroit Free Press.
1923	William Allen White, The Emporia (Kans.) Gazette.	1956	Lauren K. Soth, The Register & Tribune (Des Moines, Iowa).
1924	The Boston Herald. Special prize to Frank I. Cobb, The World (New York).	1957	Buford Boone, Tuscaloosa (Ala.) News.
		1958	Harry S. Ashmore, Arkansas Gazette (Little Rock).
1925	Charleston (S.C.) News and Courier.		
1926	Edward M. Kingsbury, The New York Times.	1959	Ralph McGill, The Constitution (Atlanta).
1927	F. Lauriston Bullard, The Boston Herald.	1960	Lenoir Chambers, The Virginian-Pilot (Norfolk, Va.).
1928	Grover C. Hall, Montgomery (Ala.) Advertiser.		
1929	Louis I. Jaffe, Norfolk (Va.) Virginian-Pilot.	1961	William J. Dorvillier, San Juan (P.R.) Star.
1930	No Award.	1962	Thomas M. Storke, Santa Barbara (Calif.) News-Press.
1931	Charles S. Ryckman, Fremont (Nebr.) Tribune.		
1932	No Award.	1963	Ira B. Harkey, Jr., Pascagoula (Miss.) Chronicle.
1933	The Kansas City (Mo.) Star.	1964	Hazel Brannon Smith, The Lexington (Miss.) Advertiser.
1934	E. P. Chase, Atlantic (Iowa) News Telegraph.		
1935	No Award.	1965	John R. Harrison, The Gainesville (Fla.) Sun.
1936	Felix Morley, The Washington (D.C.) Post; George B. Parker, The Scripps-Howard Newspapers.	1966	Robert Lasch, St. Louis Post-Dispatch.
		1967	Eugene Patterson, The Atlanta Constitution.
		1968	John S. Knight, Knight Newspapers.
1937	John W. Owens, The Sun (Baltimore).	1969	Paul Greenberg, Pine Bluff (Ark.) Commercial.
1938	W. W. Waymack, The Register and Tribune (Des Moines, Iowa).	1970	Philip L. Geyelin, The Washington (D.C.) Post.
		1971	Horance G. Davis, Jr., The Gainesville (Fla.) Sun.
1939	Ronald G. Callvert, The Oregonian (Portland).	1972	John Strohmeyer, The Bethlehem (Pa.) Globe-Times.
1940	Bart Howard, St. Louis Post-Dispatch.		
1941	Reuben Maury, Daily News (New York).	1973	Roger B. Linscott, The Berkshire Eagle (Pittsfield, Mass.).
1942	Geoffrey Parsons, New York Herald Tribune.		
1943	Forrest W. Seymour, The Register & Tribune (Des Moines, Iowa).	1974	F. Gilman Spencer, The Trentonian (Trenton, N.J.).
1944	Henry J. Haskell, The Kansas City (Mo.) Star.	1975	John Daniell Maurice, Charleston (W.Va.) Daily Mail.
1945	George W. Potter, The Providence (R.I.) Journal-Bulletin.		
		1976	Philip P. Kerby, Los Angeles Times.
1946	Hodding Carter, The Delta Democrat-Times (Greenville, Miss.).	1977	Warren L. Lerude, Foster Church, and Norman F. Cardoza, Reno (Nev.) Evening Gazette and Nevada State Journal.
1947	William H. Grimes, The Wall Street Journal.		
1948	Virginius Dabney, Richmond (Va.) Times-Dispatch.	1978	Meg Greenfield, The Washington (D.C.) Post.
		1979	Edwin M. Yoder, Jr., The Washington (D.C.) Star.
1949	John H. Crider, The Boston Herald; Herbert Elliston, The Washington (D.C.) Post.	1980	Robert L. Bartley, The Wall Street Journal.
		1981	No Award.
		1982	Jack Rosenthal, The New York Times.

Feature writing

1979	Jon D. Franklin, Baltimore Evening Sun.	1981	Teresa Carpenter, Village Voice (New York).
1980	Madeleine Blais, Miami Herald.	1982	Saul Pett, The Associated Press.

Criticism

1970	Ada Louise Huxtable, The New York Times.	1977	William McPherson, The Washington (D.C.) Post.
1971	Harold C. Schonberg, The New York Times.	1978	Walter Kerr, The New York Times.
1972	Frank L. Peters, Jr., St. Louis Post-Dispatch.	1979	Paul Gapp, Chicago Tribune.
1973	Ronald Powers, Chicago Sun-Times.	1980	William A. Henry III, The Boston Globe.
1974	Emily Genauer, Newsday Syndicate.	1981	Jonathan Yardley, The Washington (D.C.) Star.
1975	Roger Ebert, Chicago Sun-Times.	1982	Martin Bernheimer, Los Angeles Times.
1976	Alan M. Kriegsman, The Washington (D.C.) Post.		

Commentary

1970	Marquis Childs, *St. Louis Post-Dispatch.*
1971	William A. Caldwell, *The Record* (Hackensack, N.J.).
1972	Mike Royko, *Chicago Daily News.*
1973	David S. Broder, *The Washington* (D.C.) *Post.*
1974	Edwin A. Roberts, Jr., *The National Observer.*
1975	Mary McGrory, *Star-News* (Washington, D.C.).
1976	Red Smith, *The New York Times.*
1977	George F. Will, Washington Post Writers Group.
1978	William Safire, *The New York Times.*
1979	Russell Baker, *The New York Times.*
1980	Ellen H. Goodman, *The Boston Globe.*
1981	Dave Anderson, *The New York Times.*
1982	Art Buchwald, *Los Angeles Times Syndicate.*

Cartoon

1922	Rollin Kirby, *The World* (New York).
1923	No Award.
1924	Ding Darling, *New York Tribune.*
1925	Rollin Kirby, *The World* (New York).
1926	D. R. Fitzpatrick, *St. Louis Post-Dispatch.*
1927	Nelson Harding, *Brooklyn Daily Eagle.*
1928	Nelson Harding, *Brooklyn Daily Eagle.*
1929	Rollin Kirby, *The World* (New York).
1930	Charles R. Macauley, *Brooklyn Daily Eagle.*
1931	Edmund Duffy, *The Sun* (Baltimore).
1932	John T. McCutcheon, *Chicago Tribune.*
1933	Harold M. Talburt, *Washington* (D.C.) *Daily News.*
1934	Edmund Duffy, *The Sun* (Baltimore).
1935	Ross A. Lewis, *The Milwaukee Journal.*
1936	No Award.
1937	Clarence D. Batchelor, *Daily News* (New York).
1938	Vaughn Shoemaker, *Chicago Daily News.*
1939	Charles G. Werner, *The Daily Oklahoman* (Oklahoma City).
1940	Edmund Duffy, *The Sun* (Baltimore).
1941	Jacob Burck, *The Times* (Chicago).
1942	Herbert L. Block, Newspaper Enterprise Assn.
1943	Ding Darling, *New York Herald Tribune.*
1944	Clifford K. Berryman, *The Washington* (D.C.) *Evening Star.*
1945	Bill Mauldin, United Feature Syndicate, Inc.
1946	Bruce A. Russell, *Los Angeles Times.*
1947	Vaughn Shoemaker, *Chicago Daily News.*
1948	Rube Goldberg, *The Sun* (New York).
1949	Lute Pease, *Newark* (N.J.) *Evening News.*
1950	James T. Berryman, *The Washington* (D.C.) *Evening Star.*
1951	Reginald W. Manning, *Arizona Republic* (Phoenix).
1952	Fred L. Packer, *New York Mirror.*
1953	Edward D. Kuekes, *Plain Dealer* (Cleveland).
1954	Herbert L. Block, *The Washington* (D.C.) *Post.*
1955	Daniel R. Fitzpatrick, *St. Louis Post-Dispatch.*
1956	Robert York, *Louisville* (Ky.) *Times.*
1957	Tom Little, *Nashville Tennessean.*
1958	Bruce M. Shanks, *Buffalo* (N.Y.) *Evening News.*
1959	Bill Mauldin, *St. Louis Post-Dispatch.*
1960	No Award.
1961	Carey Orr, *Chicago Tribune.*
1962	Edmund S. Valtman, *The Hartford* (Conn.) *Times.*
1963	Frank Miller, *The Des Moines* (Iowa) *Register.*
1964	Paul Conrad, *The Denver Post.*
1965	No Award.
1966	Don Wright, *Miami News.*
1967	Patrick B. Oliphant, *The Denver Post.*
1968	Eugene G. Payne, *The Charlotte* (N.C.) *Observer.*
1969	John Fischetti, *Chicago Daily News.*
1970	Thomas F. Darcy, *Newsday* (Garden City, N.Y.).
1971	Paul Conrad, *Los Angeles Times.*
1972	Jeffrey K. MacNelly, *The Richmond* (Va.) *News Leader.*
1973	No Award.
1974	Paul Szep, *The Boston Globe.*
1975	Garry Trudeau, Universal Press Syndicate.
1976	Tony Auth, *The Philadelphia Inquirer.*
1977	Paul Szep, *The Boston Globe.*
1978	Jeffrey K. MacNelly, *The Richmond* (Va.) *News Leader.*
1979	Herbert L. Block, *The Washington* (D.C.) *Post.*
1980	Don Wright, *Miami News.*
1981	Mike Peters, *Dayton* (Ohio) *Daily News.*
1982	Ben Sargent, *Austin* (Tex.) *American-Statesman.*

News photography

1942	Milton Brooks, *The Detroit News.*
1943	Frank Noel, The Associated Press.
1944	Frank Filan, The Associated Press; Earle L. Bunker, *The World-Herald* (Omaha).
1945	Joe Rosenthal, The Associated Press.
1946	No Award.
1947	Arnold Hardy.
1948	Frank Cushing, *Boston Traveler.*
1949	Nathaniel Fein, *New York Herald Tribune.*
1950	Bill Crouch, *Oakland Tribune* (Calif.).
1951	Max Desfor, The Associated Press.
1952	John Robinson, Don Ultang, *The Register & Tribune* (Des Moines, Iowa).
1953	William M. Gallagher, *The Flint* (Mich.) *Journal.*
1954	Mrs. Walter M. Schau.
1955	John L. Gaunt, Jr., *Los Angeles Times.*
1956	*Daily News* (New York).
1957	Harry A. Trask, *Boston Traveler.*
1958	William C. Beall, *Washington* (D.C.) *Daily News.*
1959	William Seaman, *The Minneapolis Star.*

1960	Andrew Lopez, United Press International.
1961	Yasushi Nagao *Mainichi* (Tokyo).
1962	Paul Vathis, The Associated Press.
1963	Hector Rondon, *La República* (Caracas, Venezuela).
1964	Robert H. Jackson, *The Dallas Times Herald.*
1965	Horst Faas, The Associated Press.
1966	Kyoichi Sawada, United Press International.
1967	Jack R. Thornell, The Associated Press.
1968	Award divided into the two categories listed below.

Spot news photography

1968	Rocco Morabito, *The Jacksonville* (Fla.) *Journal.*
1969	Edward T. Adams, The Associated Press.
1970	Steve Starr, The Associated Press.
1971	John Paul Filo, *Valley Daily News* (Tarentum, Pa.) and *The Daily Dispatch* (New Kensington, Pa.).
1972	Horst Faas and Michel Laurent, The Associated Press.
1973	Huynh Cong Ut, The Associated Press.
1974	Anthony K. Roberts, free-lance photographer.
1975	Gerald H. Gay, *Seattle Times.*
1976	Stanley Forman, *The Boston Herald-American.*
1977	Neal Ulevich, The Associated Press; Stanley Forman, *The Boston Herald-American.*
1978	John Blair, free-lance photographer.
1979	Thomas J. Kelly III, *Pottstown* (Pa.) *Mercury.*
1980	Name withheld, United Press International.
1981	Larry Price, *Fort Worth* (Tex.) *Star-Telegram.*
1982	Ron Edmonds, The Associated Press.

Feature news photography

1968	Toshio Sakai, United Press International.
1969	Moneta Sleet, Jr., *Ebony.*
1970	Dallas Kinney, *The Palm Beach* (Fla.) *Post.*
1971	Jack Dykinga, *Chicago Sun-Times.*
1972	Dave Kennerly, United Press International.
1973	Brian Lanker, *Topeka* (Kans.) *Capital-Journal.*
1974	Slava Veder, The Associated Press.
1975	Matthew Lewis, *The Washington* (D.C.) *Post.*
1976	The staff of the *Courier-Journal and Times* (Louisville).
1977	Robin Hood, *Chattanooga* (Tenn.) *News-Free Press.*
1978	J. Ross Baughman, The Associated Press.
1979	The staff of *The Boston Herald-American.*
1980	Erwin H. Hagler, *Dallas Times Herald.*
1981	Taro M. Yamasaki, *The Detroit Free Press.*
1982	John H. White, *Chicago Sun-Times.*

Pulitzer prizes in literature and music

Fiction

1917	No Award.
1918	Ernest Poole, *His Family.*
1919	Booth Tarkington, *The Magnificent Ambersons.*
1920	No Award.
1921	Edith Wharton, *The Age of Innocence.*
1922	Booth Tarkington, *Alice Adams.*
1923	Willa Cather, *One of Ours.*
1924	Margaret Wilson, *The Able McLaughlins.*
1925	Edna Ferber, *So Big.*
1926	Sinclair Lewis, *Arrowsmith* (declined).
1927	Louis Bromfield, *Early Autumn.*
1928	Thornton Wilder, *The Bridge of San Luis Rey.*
1929	Julia M. Peterkin, *Scarlet Sister Mary.*
1930	Oliver H. P. La Farge, *Laughing Boy.*
1931	Margaret A. Barnes, *Years of Grace.*
1932	Pearl S. Buck, *The Good Earth.*
1933	T. S. Stribling, *The Store.*
1934	Caroline Miller, *Lamb in His Bosom.*
1935	Josephine W. Johnson, *Now in November.*
1936	Harold L. Davis, *Honey in the Horn.*
1937	Margaret Mitchell, *Gone with the Wind.*
1938	John P. Marquand, *The Late George Apley.*
1939	Marjorie Kinnan Rawlings, *The Yearling.*
1940	John Steinbeck,* *The Grapes of Wrath.*
1941	No Award.
1942	Ellen Glasgow, *In This Our Life.*
1943	Upton Sinclair, *Dragon's Teeth.*
1944	Martin Flavin, *Journey in the Dark.*
1945	John Hersey, *A Bell for Adano.*
1946	No Award.
1947	Robert Penn Warren, *All the King's Men.*
1948	James A. Michener, *Tales of the South Pacific.*
1949	James G. Cozzens, *Guard of Honor.*
1950	A. B. Guthrie, Jr., *The Way West.*
1951	Conrad Richter, *The Town.*
1952	Herman Wouk, *The Caine Mutiny.*
1953	Ernest Hemingway,* *The Old Man and the Sea.*
1954	No Award.
1955	William Faulkner,* *A Fable.*
1956	MacKinlay Kantor, *Andersonville.*
1957	No Award.
1958	James Agee, *A Death in the Family.*
1959	Robert L. Taylor, *The Travels of Jaimie McPheeters.*
1960	Allen Drury, *Advise and Consent.*
1961	Harper Lee, *To Kill a Mockingbird.*
1962	Edwin O'Connor, *The Edge of Sadness.*
1963	William Faulkner,* *The Reivers.*

*See "People" section for biographical information.

54

1964	No Award.	1973	Eudora Welty, *The Optimist's Daughter.*
1965	Shirley Ann Grau, *The Keepers of the House.*	1974	No Award.
1966	Katherine Anne Porter, *The Collected Stories of Katherine Anne Porter.*	1975	Michael Shaara, *The Killer Angels.*
1967	Bernard Malamud, *The Fixer.*	1976	Saul Bellow,* *Humboldt's Gift.*
1968	William Styron, *The Confessions of Nat Turner.*	1977	No Award.
1969	N. Scott Momaday, *House Made of Dawn.*	1978	James Alan McPherson, *Elbow Room.*
1970	Jean Stafford, *Collected Stories.*	1979	John Cheever,* *The Stories of John Cheever.*
1971	No Award.	1980	Norman Mailer, *The Executioner's Song.*
1972	Wallace Earle Stegner, *Angle of Repose.*	1981	John Kennedy Toole, *A Confederacy of Dunces.*
		1982	John Updike,* *Rabbit Is Rich.*

Poetry

The Pulitzer prize for poetry was established in 1922, but earlier awards were made through gifts provided by the Poetry Society. The awards made in 1918 and 1919 are carried in the Pulitzer prize records.

1918	Sara Teasdale, *Love Songs.*	1951	Carl Sandburg,* *Complete Poems.*
1919	Margaret Widdemer, *Old Road to Paradise;* Carl Sandburg,* *Corn Huskers.*	1952	Marianne Moore, *Collected Poems.*
1920	No Award.	1953	Archibald MacLeish, *Collected Poems 1917-1952.*
1921	No Award.	1954	Theodore Roethke, *The Waking: Poems 1933-1953.*
1922	Edwin Arlington Robinson, *Collected Poems.*		
1923	Edna St. Vincent Millay, *The Ballad of the Harp-Weaver; A Few Figs from Thistles;* eight sonnets in *American Poetry, 1922: A Miscellany.*	1955	Wallace Stevens, *Collected Poems.*
		1956	Elizabeth Bishop, *Poems: North and South.*
		1957	Richard Wilbur, *Things of This World.*
1924	Robert Frost,* *New Hampshire: A Poem with Notes and Grace Notes.*	1958	Robert Penn Warren, *Promises: Poems 1954-1956.*
1925	Edwin Arlington Robinson, *The Man Who Died Twice.*	1959	Stanley Kunitz, *Selected Poems, 1928-1958.*
		1960	William DeWitt Snodgrass, *Heart's Needle.*
1926	Amy Lowell, *What's O'Clock.*	1961	Phyllis McGinley, *Times Three: Selected Verse from Three Decades.*
1927	Leonora Speyer, *Fiddler's Farewell.*		
1928	Edwin Arlington Robinson, *Tristram.*	1962	Alan Dugan, *Poems.*
1929	Stephen Vincent Benét, *John Brown's Body.*	1963	William Carlos Williams, *Pictures from Breughel.*
1930	Conrad Aiken, *Selected Poems.*	1964	Louis Simpson, *At the End of the Open Road.*
1931	Robert Frost,* *Collected Poems.*	1965	John Berryman, *Seventy-Seven Dream Songs.*
1932	George Dillon, *The Flowering Stone.*	1966	Richard Eberhart, *Selected Poems (1930-1965).*
1933	Archibald MacLeish, *Conquistador.*	1967	Anne Sexton, *Live or Die.*
1934	Robert Hillyer, *Collected Verse.*	1968	Anthony Hecht, *The Hard Hours.*
1935	Audrey Wurdemann, *Bright Ambush.*	1969	George Oppen, *Of Being Numerous.*
1936	Robert P. Tristram Coffin, *Strange Holiness.*	1970	Richard Howard, *Untitled Subjects.*
1937	Robert Frost,* *A Further Range.*	1971	W. S. Merwin, *The Carrier of Ladders.*
1938	Marya Zaturenska, *Cold Morning Sky.*	1972	James Wright, *Collected Poems.*
1939	John Gould Fletcher, *Selected Poems.*	1973	Maxine Winokur Kumin, *Up Country.*
1940	Mark Van Doren, *Collected Poems.*	1974	Robert Lowell, *The Dolphin.*
1941	Leonard Bacon, *Sunderland Capture.*	1975	Gary Snyder, *Turtle Island.*
1942	William Rose Benét, *The Dust Which Is God.*	1976	John Ashbery, *Self-Portrait in a Convex Mirror.*
1943	Robert Frost,* *A Witness Tree.*	1977	James Merrill, *Divine Comedies.*
1944	Stephen Vincent Benét, *Western Star.*	1978	Howard Nemerov, *Collected Poems.*
1945	Karl Shapiro, *V-Letter and Other Poems.*	1979	Robert Penn Warren, *Now and Then: Poems 1976-1978.*
1946	No Award.		
1947	Robert Lowell, *Lord Weary's Castle.*	1980	Donald Justice, *Selected Poems.*
1948	W. H. Auden, *The Age of Anxiety.*	1981	James Schuyler, *The Morning of the Poem.*
1949	Peter Viereck, *Terror and Decorum.*	1982	Sylvia Plath, *The Collected Poems.*
1950	Gwendolyn Brooks,* *Annie Allen.*		

*See "People" section for biographical information.

Pulitzer prizes *(cont.)*

Drama

1917	No Award.
1918	Jesse L. Williams, *Why Marry?*
1919	No Award.
1920	Eugene O'Neill,* *Beyond the Horizon.*
1921	Zona Gale, *Miss Lulu Bett.*
1922	Eugene O'Neill,* *Anna Christie.*
1923	Owen Davis, *Icebound.*
1924	Hatcher Hughes, *Hell-Bent fer Heaven.*
1925	Sidney Howard, *They Knew What They Wanted.*
1926	George E. Kelly, *Craig's Wife.*
1927	Paul Green, *In Abraham's Bosom.*
1928	Eugene O'Neill* *Strange Interlude.*
1929	Elmer Rice, *Street Scene.*
1930	Marc Connelly, *The Green Pastures.*
1931	Susan Glaspell, *Alison's House.*
1932	George S. Kaufman, Morrie Ryskind, Ira Gershwin, *Of Thee I Sing.*
1933	Maxwell Anderson, *Both Your Houses.*
1934	Sidney Kingsley, *Men in White.*
1935	Zoe Akins, *The Old Maid.*
1936	Robert E. Sherwood, *Idiot's Delight.*
1937	George S. Kaufman, Moss Hart, *You Can't Take It With You.*
1938	Thornton Wilder, *Our Town.*
1939	Robert E. Sherwood, *Abe Lincoln in Illinois.*
1940	William Saroyan, *The Time of Your Life* (declined).
1941	Robert E. Sherwood, *There Shall Be No Night.*
1942	No Award.
1943	Thornton Wilder, *The Skin of Our Teeth.*
1944	No Award.
1945	Mary Chase, *Harvey.*
1946	Howard Lindsay, Russel Crouse, *State of the Union.*
1947	No Award.
1948	Tennessee Williams, *A Streetcar Named Desire.*
1949	Arthur Miller, *Death of a Salesman.*
1950	Richard Rodgers, Oscar Hammerstein II, and Joshua Logan, *South Pacific.*
1951	No Award.
1952	Joseph Kramm, *The Shrike.*
1953	William Inge, *Picnic.*
1954	John Patrick, *The Teahouse of the August Moon.*
1955	Tennessee Williams, *Cat on a Hot Tin Roof.*
1956	Frances Goodrich, Albert Hackett, *The Diary of Anne Frank.*
1957	Eugene O'Neill,* *Long Day's Journey into Night.*
1958	Ketti Frings, *Look Homeward, Angel.*
1959	Archibald MacLeish, *J.B.*
1960	George Abbott, Jerry Bock, Sheldon Harnick, and Jerome Weidman, *Fiorello!*
1961	Tad Mosel, *All the Way Home.*
1962	Abe Burrows and Frank Loesser, *How to Succeed in Business Without Really Trying.*
1963	No Award.
1964	No Award.
1965	Frank D. Gilroy, *The Subject Was Roses.*
1966	No Award.
1967	Edward Albee, *A Delicate Balance.*
1968	No Award.
1969	Howard Sackler, *The Great White Hope.*
1970	Charles Gordone, *No Place to Be Somebody.*
1971	Paul Zindel, *The Effect of Gamma Rays on Man-in-the-Moon Marigolds.*
1972	No Award.
1973	Jason Miller, *That Championship Season.*
1974	No Award.
1975	Edward Albee, *Seascape.*
1976	Michael Bennett, James Kirkwood, Nicholas Dante, Marvin Hamlisch, and Edward Kleban, *A Chorus Line.*
1977	Michael Cristofer, *The Shadow Box.*
1978	D. L. Coburn, *The Gin Game.*
1979	Sam Shepard, *Buried Child.*
1980	Lanford Wilson, *Talley's Folly.*
1981	Beth Henley, *Crimes of the Heart.*
1982	Charles Fuller, *A Soldier's Play.*

Biography or autobiography

1917	Laura E. H. Richards, Maude H. Elliott, Florence H. Hall, *Julia Ward Howe.*
1918	William C. Bruce, *Benjamin Franklin, Self-Revealed.*
1919	Henry Adams, *The Education of Henry Adams.*
1920	Albert J. Beveridge, *The Life of John Marshall.*
1921	Edward W. Bok, *The Americanization of Edward Bok.*
1922	Hamlin Garland, *A Daughter of the Middle Border.*
1923	Burton J. Hendrick, *The Life and Letters of Walter H. Page.*
1924	Michael I. Pupin, *From Immigrant to Inventor.*
1925	M. A. DeWolfe Howe, *Barrett Wendell and His Letters.*
1926	Harvey Cushing, *The Life of Sir William Osler.*
1927	Emory Holloway, *Whitman.*
1928	Charles E. Russell, *The American Orchestra and Theodore Thomas.*
1929	Burton J. Hendrick, *The Training of An American: The Earlier Life and Letters of Walter H. Page.*
1930	Marquis James, *The Raven.*
1931	Henry James, *Charles W. Eliot.*
1932	Henry F. Pringle, *Theodore Roosevelt.*
1933	Allan Nevins, *Grover Cleveland.*
1934	Tyler Dennett, *John Hay.*
1935	Douglas Southall Freeman, *R. E. Lee.*
1936	Ralph B. Perry, *The Thought and Character of William James.*
1937	Allan Nevins, *Hamilton Fish.*
1938	Odell Shepard, *Pedlar's Progress;* Marquis James, *Andrew Jackson.*

*See "People" section for biographical information.

1939	Carl Van Doren, *Benjamin Franklin.*	**1963**	Leon Edel, *The Conquest of London* and *The Middle Years,* volumes II and III of *Henry James.*
1940	Ray S. Baker, *Woodrow Wilson, Life and Letters.*		
1941	Ola E. Winslow, *Jonathan Edwards.*	**1964**	W. Jackson Bate, *John Keats.*
1942	Forrest Wilson, *Crusader in Crinoline.*	**1965**	Ernest Samuels, *Henry Adams.*
1943	Samuel E. Morison, *Admiral of the Ocean Sea.*	**1966**	Arthur M. Schlesinger, Jr., *A Thousand Days.*
1944	Carlton Mabee, *The American Leonardo: The Life of Samuel F. B. Morse.*	**1967**	Justin Kaplan, *Mr. Clemens and Mark Twain.*
1945	Russell B. Nye, *George Bancroft: Brahmin Rebel.*	**1968**	George F. Kennan, *Memoirs (1925-1950).*
1946	Linnie M. Wolfe, *Son of the Wilderness.*	**1969**	Benjamin Lawrence Reid, *The Man from New York: John Quinn and His Friends.*
1947	William Allen White, *The Autobiography of William Allen White.*	**1970**	T. Harry Williams, *Huey Long.*
1948	Margaret Clapp, *Forgotten First Citizen: John Bigelow.*	**1971**	Lawrance R. Thompson, *Robert Frost: The Years of Triumph, 1915-1938.*
1949	Robert E. Sherwood, *Roosevelt and Hopkins.*	**1972**	Joseph P. Lash, *Eleanor and Franklin: The Story of Their Relationship Based on Eleanor Roosevelt's Private Papers.*
1950	Samuel F. Bemis, *John Quincy Adams and the Foundations of American Foreign Policy.*		
1951	Margaret L. Coit, *John C. Calhoun: American Portrait.*	**1973**	W. A. Swanberg, *Luce and His Empire.*
		1974	Louis Sheaffer, *O'Neill, Son and Artist.*
1952	Merlo J. Pusey, *Charles Evans Hughes.*	**1975**	Robert A. Caro, *The Power Broker: Robert Moses and the Fall of New York.*
1953	David J. Mays, *Edmund Pendleton, 1721-1803.*		
1954	Charles A. Lindbergh,* *The Spirit of St. Louis.*	**1976**	R. W. B. Lewis, *Edith Wharton: A Biography.*
1955	William S. White, *The Taft Story.*	**1977**	John E. Mack, *A Prince of Our Disorder: The Life of T. E. Lawrence.*
1956	Talbot F. Hamlin, *Benjamin Henry Latrobe.*		
1957	John F. Kennedy,† *Profiles in Courage.*	**1978**	W. Jackson Bate, *Samuel Johnson.*
1958	Douglas Southall Freeman, Mary W. Ashworth, John A. Carroll, *George Washington.*	**1979**	Leonard Baker, *Days of Sorrow and Pain: Leo Baeck and the Berlin Jews.*
1959	Arthur Walworth, *Woodrow Wilson, American Prophet.*	**1980**	Edmund Morris, *The Rise of Theodore Roosevelt.*
1960	Samuel E. Morison, *John Paul Jones.*	**1981**	Robert K. Massie, *Peter the Great: His Life and World.*
1961	David Donald, *Charles Sumner and the Coming of the Civil War.*	**1982**	William S. McFeely, *Grant: A Biography.*
1962	No Award.		

History

1917	J. J. Jusserand, *With Americans of Past and Present Days.*	**1933**	Frederick J. Turner, *The Significance of Sections in American History.*
1918	James Rhodes, *A History of the Civil War, 1861-1865.*	**1934**	Herbert Agar, *The People's Choice.*
1919	No Award.	**1935**	Charles M. Andrews, *The Colonial Period of American History.*
1920	Justin H. Smith, *The War with Mexico.*	**1936**	Andrew C. McLaughlin, *The Constitutional History of the United States.*
1921	William S. Sims, *The Victory at Sea.*		
1922	James T. Adams, *The Founding of New England.*	**1937**	Van Wyck Brooks, *The Flowering of New England.*
1923	Charles Warren, *The Supreme Court in United States History.*		
1924	Charles H. McIlwain, *The American Revolution—A Constitutional Interpretation.*	**1938**	Paul H. Buck, *The Road to Reunion, 1865-1900.*
		1939	Frank L. Mott, *A History of American Magazines.*
1925	Frederic Paxson, *A History of the American Frontier.*	**1940**	Carl Sandburg,* *Abraham Lincoln: The War Years.*
1926	Edward Channing, *The War for Southern Independence,* volume 6 of *The History of the United States.*	**1941**	Marcus Hansen, *The Atlantic Migration, 1607-1860.*
		1942	Margaret Leech, *Reveille in Washington.*
1927	Samuel F. Bemis, *Pinckney's Treaty.*	**1943**	Esther Forbes, *Paul Revere and the World He Lived In.*
1928	Vernon L. Parrington, *Main Currents in American Thought.*		
1929	Fred A. Shannon, *The Organization and Administration of the Union Army, 1861-1865.*	**1944**	Merle Curti, *The Growth of American Thought.*
		1945	Stephen Bonsal, *Unfinished Business.*
1930	Claude H. Van Tyne, *The War of Independence.*	**1946**	Arthur M. Schlesinger, Jr., *The Age of Jackson.*
1931	Bernadotte E. Schmitt, *The Coming of the War: 1914.*	**1947**	James P. Baxter III, *Scientists Against Time.*
		1948	Bernard DeVoto, *Across the Wide Missouri.*
1932	John J. Pershing,* *My Experiences in the World War.*	**1949**	Roy F. Nichols, *The Disruption of American Democracy.*
		1950	Oliver W. Larkin, *Art and Life in America.*
		1951	R. Carlyle Buley, *The Old Northwest, Pioneer Period 1815-1840.*

*See "People" section for biographical information.
†See "Presidents" section for biographical information.

1952	Oscar Handlin, *The Uprooted.*
1953	George Dangerfield, *The Era of Good Feelings.*
1954	Bruce Catton, *A Stillness at Appomattox.*
1955	Paul Horgan, *Great River: The Rio Grande in North American History.*
1956	Richard Hofstadter, *The Age of Reform.*
1957	George F. Kennan, *Russia Leaves the War: Soviet-American Relations, 1917-1920.*
1958	Bray Hammond, *Banks and Politics in America: From the Revolution to the Civil War.*
1959	Leonard D. White and Jean Schneider, *The Republican Era: 1869-1901.*
1960	Margaret Leech, *In the Days of McKinley.*
1961	Herbert Feis, *Between War and Peace: The Potsdam Conference.*
1962	Lawrence Henry Gipson, *The Triumphant Empire: Thunder-Clouds Gather in the West, 1763-1766.*
1963	Constance McLaughlin Green, *Washington, Village and Capital, 1800-1878.*
1964	Sumner Chilton Powell, *Puritan Village: The Formation of a New England Town.*
1965	Irwin Unger, *The Greenback Era.*
1966	Perry Miller, *The Life of the Mind in America: From the Revolution to the Civil War.*
1967	William H. Goetzmann, *Exploration and Empire.*
1968	Bernard Bailyn, *The Ideological Origins of The American Revolution.*

1969	Leonard W. Levy, *Origins of the Fifth Amendment.*
1970	Dean Gooderham Acheson, *Present at the Creation: My Years in the State Department.*
1971	James MacGregor Burns, *Roosevelt: The Soldier of Freedom.*
1972	Carl N. Degler, *Neither Black Nor White: Slavery and Race Relations in Brazil and the United States.*
1973	Michael Kammen, *People of Paradox: An Inquiry Concerning the Origins of American Civilization.*
1974	Daniel J. Boorstin, *The Americans: The Democratic Experience.*
1975	Dumas Malone, volumes 1 through 5 of *Jefferson and His Time.*
1976	Paul Horgan, *Lamy of Santa Fe.*
1977	David M. Potter, *The Impending Crisis.*
1978	Alfred D. Chandler, Jr., *The Invisible Hand: The Managerial Revolution in American Business.*
1979	Don E. Fehrenbacher, *The Dred Scott Case: Its Significance in American Law and Politics.*
1980	Leon F. Litwack, *Been in the Storm So Long: The Aftermath of Slavery.*
1981	Lawrence A. Cremin, *American Education: The National Experience, 1783-1876.*
1982	C. Van Woodward, ed. *Mary Chesnut's Civil War.*

General nonfiction

1962	Theodore H. White, *The Making of the President, 1960.*
1963	Barbara W. Tuchman, *The Guns of August.*
1964	Richard Hofstadter, *Anti-Intellectualism in American Life.*
1965	Howard Mumford Jones, *O Strange New World.*
1966	Edwin Way Teale, *Wandering Through Winter.*
1967	David Brion Davis, *The Problem of Slavery in Western Culture.*
1968	Will and Ariel Durant, *Rousseau and Revolution.*
1969	Norman Mailer, *The Armies of the Night.* René Jules Dubos, *So Human An Animal: How We Are Shaped by Surroundings and Events.*
1970	Erik H. Erikson, *Gandhi's Truth: On the Origins of Militant Nonviolence.*
1971	John Toland, *The Rising Sun.*
1972	Barbara W. Tuchman, *Stilwell and the American Experience in China, 1911-1945.*

1973	Frances FitzGerald, *Fire in the Lake: The Vietnamese and the Americans in Vietnam.* Robert M. Coles, volumes two and three of *Children of Crisis.*
1974	Ernest Becker, *The Denial of Death.*
1975	Annie Dillard, *Pilgrim at Tinker Creek.*
1976	Robert N. Butler, *Why Survive? Being Old in America.*
1977	William W. Warner, *Beautiful Swimmers: Watermen, Crabs and the Chesapeake Bay.*
1978	Carl Sagan, *The Dragons of Eden: Speculations on the Evolution of Human Intelligence.*
1979	Edward O. Wilson, *On Human Nature.*
1980	Douglas R. Hofstadter, *Gödel, Escher, Bach: An Eternal Golden Braid.*
1981	Carl E. Schorske, *Fin-de-Siècle Vienna: Politics and Culture.*
1982	Tracy Kidder, *The Soul of a New Machine.*

Music

1943	William Schuman, *Secular Cantata No. 2.*
1944	Howard Hanson, *Symphony No. 4, opus 34.*
1945	Aaron Copland, *Appalachian Spring.*
1946	Leo Sowerby, *The Canticle of the Sun.*
1947	Charles Ives, *Symphony No. 3.*
1948	Walter Piston, *Symphony No. 3.*
1949	Virgil Thomson, *Louisiana Story.*
1950	Gian Carlo Menotti, *The Consul.*
1951	Douglas Moore, *Giants in the Earth.*
1952	Gail Kubik, *Symphony Concertante.*
1953	No Award.

1954	Quincy Porter, *Concerto for Two Pianos and Orchestra.*
1955	Gian Carlo Menotti, *The Saint of Bleecker Street.*
1956	Ernst Toch, *Symphony No. 3.*
1957	Norman Dello Joio, *Meditations on Ecclesiastes.*
1958	Samuel Barber, *Vanessa.*
1959	John La Montaine, *Concerto for Piano and Orchestra.*
1960	Elliott Carter, *Second String Quartet.*
1961	Walter Piston, *Symphony No. 7.*
1962	Robert Ward, *The Crucible.*
1963	Samuel Barber, *Piano Concerto No. 1.*

1964	No Award.	1975	Dominick Argento, *From the Diary of Virginia Woolf.*
1965	No Award.	1976	Ned Rorem, *Air Music.*
1966	Leslie Bassett, *Variations for Orchestra.*	1977	Richard Wernick, *Visions of Terror and Wonder.*
1967	Leon Kirchner, *String Quartet No. 3.*	1978	Michael Colgrass, *Déjà Vu for Percussion Quartet and Orchestra.*
1968	George Crumb, *Echoes of Time and the River.*	1979	Joseph Schwantner, *Aftertones of Infinity.*
1969	Karel Husa, *String Quartet No. 3.*	1980	David Del Tredici, *In Memory of a Summer Day.*
1970	Charles W. Wuorinen, *Time's Encomium.*	1981	No Award.
1971	Mario Davidovsky, *Synchronisms No. 6.*	1982	Roger Sessions, *Concerto for Orchestra.*
1972	Jacob Druckman, *Windows.*		
1973	Elliott Carter, *String Quartet No. 3.*		
1974	Donald Martino, *Notturno.*		

Special Citations

1938	*Edmonton* (Alberta) *Journal,* for its defense of the freedom of the press in Alberta.	1952	*The Kansas City* (Mo.) *Star,* for its news coverage of the 1951 flood in Kansas and Missouri.
1941	*The New York Times,* for the public educational value of its foreign news reports.	1953	*The New York Times,* for the "Review of the Week" section in its Sunday edition.
1944	Byron Price, Director of the United States Office of Censorship, for creating and administering newspaper and radio codes during World War II.	1957	Kenneth Roberts, for his historical novels that have helped create greater interest in early American history.
1944	Mrs. William Allen White, for her husband's services on the Advisory Board on Pulitzer Prizes.	1958	Walter Lippmann, syndicated columnist, for the wisdom and sense of responsibility in his comments on national and international affairs.
1944	Richard Rodgers and Oscar Hammerstein II, for their musical play *Oklahoma!*	1960	Garrett Mattingly, for his book *The Armada.*
1945	The cartographers of the American press, for their war maps that helped increase public information on the progress of the armed forces in World War II.	1961	*American Heritage Picture History of the Civil War.*
		1964	The Gannett newspaper group, for its special series *The Road to Integration.*
1947	Columbia University and its Graduate School of Journalism, for efforts to maintain and advance the high standards governing the Pulitzer prizes.	1973	James Thomas Flexner, for his four-volume biography *George Washington.*
		1974	Roger Sessions, for his life's work as a distinguished composer.
1947	*St. Louis Post-Dispatch,* for unswerving adherence to the ideals of its founder and its constructive leadership in American journalism.	1976	Scott Joplin, for his contribution to American music; John Hohenberg, for services for 22 years as administrator of the Pulitzer prizes and for achievements as teacher and journalist.
1948	Frank D. Fackenthal, Provost of Columbia University, for his interest in and service to the advisory board.	1977	Alex Haley, for his book *Roots.*
1951	Cyrus L. Sulzberger, *The New York Times,* for his exclusive interview with Archbishop Aloysius Stepinac.	1978	E. B. White, for the full body of his works; Richard L. Strout, for many years of journalistic dedication.
1952	Max Kase, *New York Journal-American,* for his exclusive exposure of bribery in basketball.	1982	Milton Babbitt, for his life's work as a distinguished and seminal American composer.

Tony awards

The Tony awards honor outstanding achievements in various categories in New York theater productions. The awards are named for Antoinette Perry, an American producer and director. They are presented by the American Theatre Wing.

Best play (dramatic)

1947	No award	1954	*The Teahouse of the August Moon*	1960	*The Miracle Worker*
1948	*Mister Roberts*			1961	*Becket*
1949	*Death of a Salesman*	1955	*The Desperate Hours*	1962	*A Man for All Seasons*
1950	*The Cocktail Party*	1956	*The Diary of Anne Frank*	1963	*Who's Afraid of Virginia Woolf?*
1951	*The Rose Tattoo*	1957	*Long Day's Journey Into Night*		
1952	*The Fourposter*			1964	*Luther*
1953	*The Crucible*	1958	*Sunrise at Campobello*	1965	*The Subject Was Roses*
		1959	*J.B.*		

1966	Marat/Sade (The Persecution and Assassination of Marat as Performed by the Inmates of the Asylum of Charenton Under the Direction of the Marquis de Sade)	1969	The Great White Hope	1977	The Shadow Box
1967	The Homecoming	1970	Borstal Boy	1978	Da
1968	Rosencrantz and Guildenstern Are Dead	1971	Sleuth	1979	The Elephant Man
		1972	Sticks and Bones	1980	Children of a Lesser God
		1973	The Championship Season	1981	Amadeus
		1974	The River Niger	1982	The Life and Adventures of Nicholas Nickleby
		1975	Equus		
		1976	Travesties		

Best play (musical)

1947	No award	1960	Fiorello! and The Sound of Music	1970	Applause
1948	No award			1971	Company
1949	Kiss Me Kate	1961	Bye, Bye Birdie	1972	Two Gentlemen of Verona
1950	South Pacific	1962	How to Succeed in Business Without Really Trying	1973	A Little Night Music
1951	Guys and Dolls			1974	Raisin
1952	The King and I	1963	A Funny Thing Happened on the Way to the Forum	1975	The Wiz
1953	Wonderful Town			1976	A Chorus Line
1954	Kismet	1964	Hello, Dolly!	1977	Annie
1955	The Pajama Game	1965	Fiddler on the Roof	1978	Ain't Misbehavin'
1956	Damn Yankees	1966	Man of La Mancha	1979	Sweeney Todd
1957	My Fair Lady	1967	Cabaret	1980	Evita
1958	The Music Man	1968	Hallelujah, Baby!	1981	42nd Street
1959	Redhead	1969	1776	1982	Nine

Best actor (dramatic)

1947	José Ferrer (Cyrano de Bergerac) Fredric March (Years Ago)	1958	Ralph Bellamy (Sunrise at Campobello)	1970	Fritz Weaver (Child's Play)
1948	Henry Fonda (Mister Roberts) Paul Kelly (Command Decision) Basil Rathbone (The Heiress)	1959	Jason Robards, Jr. (The Disenchanted)	1971	Brian Bedford (The School for Wives)
		1960	Melvyn Douglas (The Best Man)	1972	Cliff Gorman (Lenny)
		1961	Zero Mostel (Rhinoceros)	1973	Alan Bates (Butley)
1949	Rex Harrison (Anne of the Thousand Days)	1962	Paul Scofield (A Man for All Seasons)	1974	Michael Moriarty (Find Your Way Home)
1950	Sidney Blackmer (Come Back, Little Sheba)	1963	Arthur Hill (Who's Afraid of Virginia Woolf?)	1975	John Kani and Winston Ntshona (The Island and Sizwe Banzi Is Dead)
1951	Claude Rains (Darkness at Noon)	1964	Alec Guinness (Dylan)	1976	John Wood (Travesties)
1952	José Ferrer (The Shrike)	1965	Walter Matthau (The Odd Couple)	1977	Al Pacino (The Basic Training of Pavlo Hummel)
1953	Tom Ewell (The Seven Year Itch)	1966	Hal Holbrook (Mark Twain Tonight!)	1978	Barnard Hughes (Da)
1954	David Wayne (The Teahouse of the August Moon)	1967	Paul Rogers (The Homecoming)	1979	Tom Conti (Whose Life Is It, Anyway?)
1955	Alfred Lunt (Quadrille)	1968	Martin Balsam (You Know I Can't Hear You When the Water's Running)	1980	John Rubinstein (Children of a Lesser God)
1956	Paul Muni (Inherit the Wind)	1969	James Earl Jones (The Great White Hope)	1981	Ian McKellen (Amadeus)
1957	Fredric March (Long Day's Journey Into Night)			1982	Roger Rees (The Life and Adventures of Nicholas Nickleby)

Best actress (dramatic)

1947	Ingrid Bergman (Joan of Lorraine) Helen Hayes (Happy Birthday)	1948	Judith Anderson (Medea) Katharine Cornell (Antony and Cleopatra) Jessica Tandy (A Streetcar Named Desire)	1950	Shirley Booth (Come Back, Little Sheba)
		1949	Martita Hunt (The Madwoman of Chaillot)	1951	Uta Hagen (The Country Girl)
				1952	Julie Harris (I Am a Camera)
				1953	Shirley Booth (Time of the Cuckoo)

1954	Audrey Hepburn (Ondine)	1964	Sandy Dennis (Any Wednesday)	1974	Colleen Dewhurst (A Moon for the Misbegotten)
1955	Nancy Kelly (The Bad Seed)	1965	Irene Worth (Tiny Alice)	1975	Ellen Burstyn (Same Time, Next Year)
1956	Julie Harris (The Lark)	1966	Rosemary Harris (The Lion in Winter)		
1957	Margaret Leighton (Separate Tables)	1967	Beryl Reid (The Killing of Sister George)	1976	Irene Worth (Sweet Bird of Youth)
1958	Helen Hayes (Time Remembered)	1968	Zoe Caldwell (The Prime of Miss Jean Brodie)	1977	Julie Harris (The Belle of Amherst)
1959	Gertrude Berg (A Majority of One)	1969	Julie Harris (Forty Carats)	1978	Jessica Tandy (The Gin Game)
1960	Anne Bancroft (The Miracle Worker)	1970	Tammy Grimes (Private Lives)	1979	Constance Cummings (Wings)
1961	Joan Plowright (A Taste of Honey)	1971	Maureen Stapleton (Gingerbread Lady)		Carole Shelley (The Elephant Man)
1962	Margaret Leighton (Night of the Iguana)	1972	Sada Thompson (Twigs)	1980	Phyllis Frelich (Children of a Lesser God)
1963	Uta Hagen (Who's Afraid of Virginia Woolf?)	1973	Julie Harris (The Last of Mrs. Lincoln)	1981	Jane Lapotaire (Piaf)
				1982	Zoe Caldwell (Medea)

Best actor (musical)

1947	No award	1960	Jackie Gleason (Take Me Along)	1971	Hal Linden (The Rothschilds)
1948	Paul Hartman (Angel in the Wings)	1961	Richard Burton (Camelot)	1972	Phil Silvers (A Funny Thing Happened on the Way to the Forum)
1949	Ray Bolger (Where's Charley?)	1962	Robert Morse (How to Succeed in Business Without Really Trying)		
1950	Ezio Pinza (South Pacific)			1973	Ben Vereen (Pippin)
1951	Robert Alda (Guys and Dolls)	1963	Zero Mostel (A Funny Thing Happened on the Way to the Forum)	1974	Christopher Plummer (Cyrano)
1952	Phil Silvers (Top Banana)	1964	Bert Lahr (Foxy)	1975	John Cullum (Shenandoah)
1953	Thomas Mitchell (Hazel Flagg)	1965	Zero Mostel (Fiddler on the Roof)	1976	George Rose (My Fair Lady)
1954	Alfred Drake (Kismet)	1966	Richard Kiley (Man of La Mancha)	1977	Barry Bostwick (The Robber Bridegroom)
1955	Walter Slezak (Fanny)				
1956	Ray Walston (Damn Yankees)	1967	Robert Preston (I Do! I Do!)	1978	John Cullum (On the Twentieth Century)
1957	Rex Harrison (My Fair Lady)	1968	Robert Goulet (The Happy Time)	1979	Len Cariou (Sweeney Todd)
1958	Robert Preston (The Music Man)	1969	Jerry Orbach (Promises, Promises)	1980	Jim Dale (Barnum)
				1981	Kevin Kline (The Pirates of Penzance)
1959	Richard Kiley (Redhead)	1970	Cleavon Little (Purlie)	1982	Ben Harney (Dreamgirls)

Best actress (musical)

1947	No award	1959	Gwen Verdon (Redhead)	1969	Angela Lansbury (Dear World)
1948	Grace Hartman (Angel in the Wings)	1960	Mary Martin (The Sound of Music)		
1949	Nanette Fabray (Love Life)	1961	Elizabeth Seal (Irma la Douce)	1970	Lauren Bacall (Applause)
1950	Mary Martin (South Pacific)			1971	Helen Gallagher (No, No, Nanette)
1951	Ethel Merman (Call Me Madam)	1962	Anna Maria Alberghetti (Carnival)	1972	Alexis Smith (Follies)
1952	Gertrude Lawrence (The King and I)		Diahann Carroll (No Strings)	1973	Glynis Johns (A Little Night Music)
1953	Rosalind Russell (Wonderful Town)	1963	Vivien Leigh (Tovarich)	1974	Virginia Capers (Raisin)
		1964	Carol Channing (Hello, Dolly!)	1975	Angela Lansbury (Gypsy)
1954	Dolores Gray (Carnival in Flanders)	1965	Liza Minnelli (Flora, the Red Menace)	1976	Donna McKechnie (A Chorus Line)
1955	Mary Martin (Peter Pan)			1977	Dorothy Loudon (Annie)
1956	Gwen Verdon (Damn Yankees)	1966	Angela Lansbury (Mame)	1978	Liza Minelli (The Act)
1957	Judy Holliday (Bells Are Ringing)	1967	Barbara Harris (The Apple Tree)	1979	Angela Lansbury (Sweeney Todd)
1958	Thelma Ritter (New Girl in Town)	1968	Patricia Routledge (Darling of the Day)	1980	Patti LuPone (Evita)
	Gwen Verdon (New Girl in Town)		Leslie Uggams (Hallelujah, Baby!)	1981	Lauren Bacall (Woman of the Year)
				1982	Jennifer Holliday (Dreamgirls)

Calendars

The Gregorian calendar is used by most people in the Western World. It was devised in the 1580's by Pope Gregory XIII to correct errors in the earlier Julian calendar. The Gregorian calendar has 12 months, 11 of which have 30 or 31 days. The other month, February, normally has 28 days. Every fourth year, called a *leap year*, it has 29 days. In century years that cannot be divided by 400, such as 1700, 1800, and 1900, the extra day is dropped.

In A.D. 532, a monk named Dionysius Exiguus worked out a Christian system for dating events starting with the year he believed Christ was born. He called the years after this event *anno Domini* (in the year of our Lord), as in A.D. 532. The years before the birth of Christ are *before Christ*, or B.C. Non-Christians sometimes substitute B.C.E. for *before Christian era*, and C.E., for *Christian era.*

The Julian calendar was developed in 46 B.C., after Julius Caesar asked an astronomer to suggest ways to improve an earlier Roman calendar. Acting on those suggestions, Caesar divided the year into 12 months of 30 or 31 days, except for February, which had 29 days. Every fourth year, February had 30 days. Caesar also moved the start of the year from March 1 to January 1. The Roman months were *January, February, Martius, Aprilis, Maius, Junius, July, August, September, October, November,* and *December.* The Julian calendar was widely used for more than 1,500 years. It provided for a year that lasted 365¼ days, but was actually about 11 minutes and 14 seconds longer than the solar year. This difference led to a gradual change in the dates on which the seasons began and the eventual reforms accomplished by the Gregorian calendar.

The church calendar is regulated by both the sun and the moon. *Immovable feasts,* which are based on the solar calendar, include Christmas and the Nativity of the Blessed Virgin. *Movable feasts*—including Easter, Ash Wednesday, Palm Sunday, Good Friday, Ascension, and Pentecost—are based on the phases of the moon, and their dates vary from year to year.

The Hebrew calendar, according to tradition, supposedly started with the Creation, at a moment 3,760 years and 3 months before the beginning of the Christian era. To find the year in the Hebrew calendar, a person must add 3,760 to the date in the Gregorian calendar. This method is not precise, however, because the Hebrew year begins in autumn, rather than in midwinter. The Hebrew year is based

(continued on page 64)

A perpetual calendar

The perpetual calendar that follows tells you quickly on what day of the week any date falls between 1753 and 2000. Notice that January and February occur twice in the headings—once in Roman type, once in *italic.* Use the Roman headings for all months, including January and February, when looking for a date in nonleap years. Use the *italic* headings for a January or a February date in leap years, which appear in **Bold.**

Step 1. Read down from the month, and across from the date you are working with. You will note a letter (from a to g) at the point of intersection. Remember this letter.

Step 2. Look in the year columns for the year you are seeking. Go *up* the same column until you find the letter you obtained in Step 1. Then read to the right end of the horizontal line to find the day your date falls on.

Example: What day of the week was Nov. 11, 1917?

Step 1. Read down from November and across from 11. At the intersection, you will find the letter b.

Step 2. Find the year 1917 (first column). Read directly above that column of years until you find the letter b. By reading horizontally to your right you will find that Nov. 11, 1917 fell on a Sunday.

Day of the month	Jan. Oct.	Apr. July *Jan.*	Sept. Dec.	June	Feb. Mar. Nov.	Aug. *Feb.*	May	Day of the week
1 8 15 22 29	a	b	c	d	e	f	g	Monday
2 9 16 23 30	g	a	b	c	d	e	f	Tuesday
3 10 17 24 31	f	g	a	b	c	d	e	Wednesday
4 11 18 25	e	f	g	a	b	c	d	Thursday
5 12 19 26	d	e	f	g	a	b	c	Friday
6 13 20 27	c	d	e	f	g	a	b	Saturday
7 14 21 28	b	c	d	e	f	g	a	Sunday

Jan./Oct.	Apr./July/Jan.	Sept./Dec.	June	Feb./Mar./Nov.	Aug./Feb.	May
1753 1759 **1764** 1770 1781 1787 **1792** 1798	1754 1765 1771 **1776** 1782 1793 1799	1755 **1760** 1766 1777 1783 **1788** 1794	1761 1767 **1772** 1778 1789 1795	**1756** 1762 1773 1779 **1784** 1790	1757 1763 **1768** 1774 1785 1791 **1796**	1758 1769 1775 **1780** 1786 1797
1804 1810 1821 1827 **1832** 1838 1849	1805 1811 1806 1822 1833 1839 **1844**	1800 1806 1817 1823 **1828** 1834 1845	1801 1807 **1812** 1818 1829 1835 **1840** 1846	1802 1813 1819 **1824** 1830 1841 1847	1803 **1808** 1814 1825 1831 **1836** 1842	1809 1815 **1820** 1826 1837 1843 **1848**
1855 **1860** 1866 1877 **1888** 1894	1850 1861 1867 **1872** 1878 1889 1895	1851 **1856** 1862 1873 1879 **1884** 1890	1857 1863 **1868** 1874 1885 1891 **1896**	**1852** 1858 1869 1875 **1880** 1886 1897	1853 1859 **1864** 1870 1881 1887 **1892** 1898	1854 1865 1871 **1876** 1882 1893 1899
1900 1906 1917 1923 **1928** 1934 1945	1901 1907 **1912** 1918 1929 1935 **1940** 1946	1902 1913 1919 **1924** 1930 1941 1947	1903 **1908** 1914 1925 1931 **1936** 1942	1909 1915 **1920** 1926 1937 1943 **1948**	1803 1910 1921 1927 **1932** 1938 1949	1905 1911 **1916** 1922 1933 1939 **1944**
1951 **1956** 1962 1973 1979 **1984** 1990	1957 1963 **1968** 1974 1985 1991 **1996**	**1952** 1958 1969 1975 **1980** 1986 1997	1953 1959 **1964** 1970 1981 1987 **1992** 1998	1954 1965 1971 **1976** 1982 1993 1999	1955 **1960** 1966 1977 1983 **1988** 1994	1950 1961 1967 **1972** 1978 1989 1995 **2000**

Year	Ash Wednesday
1983	February 16
1984	March 7
1985	February 20
1986	February 12
1987	March 4
1988	February 17
1989	February 8
1990	February 28
1991	February 13
1992	March 4
1993	February 24
1994	February 16
1995	March 1
1996	February 21
1997	February 12
1998	February 25
1999	February 17
2000	March 8

Year	Easter Sunday
1983	April 3
1984	April 22
1985	April 7
1986	March 30
1987	April 19
1988	April 3
1989	March 26
1990	April 15
1991	March 31
1992	April 19
1993	April 11
1994	April 3
1995	April 16
1996	April 7
1997	March 30
1998	April 12
1999	April 4
2000	April 23

on the moon and normally consists of 12 months: *Tishri, Heshvan, Kislev, Tebet, She-bat, Adar, Nisan, Iyar, Sivan, Tammuz, Ab,* and *Elul.* The months are alternately 30 and 29 days long. Seven times during every 19-year period, an *embolismic,* or extra 29-day month—called *Veadar—*is inserted between Adar and Nisan. At the same time, Adar is given 30 days instead of 29.

The Islamic calendar begins with Muhammad's flight from Mecca to Medina. This event, called the *Hegira,* took place in A.D. 622 according to the Gregorian calendar. The Islamic year is much shorter than the solar year, with only 354 days. As a result, the Islamic New Year moves backward through the seasons, completing a full backward course every 32½ years. The Islamic calendar divides time into 30-year cycles. During each cycle, 19 years have the regular 354 days and 11 years have an extra day each. The Islamic year is based on the moon and has 12 months, alternately 30 and 29 days long. The months are *Muharram, Safar, Rabi I, Rabi II, Jumada I, Jumada II, Rajab, Shaban, Ramadan, Shawwal, Zulkadah,* and *Zulhij-jah.* The extra day in leap years occurs in Zulhijjah.

The Chinese calendar begins with the Gregorian year 2637 B.C., which is when the legendary Emperor Huang-Ti supposedly invented it. The calendar designates years in cycles of 60. For example, the Gregorian year 1985 is the second year in the 78th cycle of the Chinese calendar. The years in each cycle are identified by a word combination formed from two series of terms, one of which involves the name of any of 12 animals. The year 1985, for example, is the *year of the ox.* The Chinese year is based on the moon and generally consists of 12 months. Each month begins at the new moon and has 29 or 30 days. A month is repeated seven times during each 19-year period, so that the calendar stays approximately in line with the seasons. The year starts at the second new moon after the beginning of winter. Thus, the Chinese New Year occurs no earlier than January 20 and no later than February 20.

Canada

Facts in brief

Capital: Ottawa.
Official languages: English and French.
Form of government: Constitutional monarchy.
Divisions: 10 provinces, 2 territories.
Head of state: Elizabeth II of Great Britain, who is also queen of Canada, appoints a governor general as her representative.
Head of government: Prime minister, leader of the majority party in the House of Commons.
Parliament: *Senate*—104 members appointed by the governor general. *House of Commons*—282 members elected by the people.
Area: 3,831,033 sq. mi. (9,922,330 km²), including 291,571 sq. mi. (755,165 km²) of inland water. *Greatest distances*—east-west, 3,223 mi. (5,187 km), from Cape Spear, Nfld., to Mount St. Elias, Y.T.; north-south, 2,875 mi. (4,627 km), from Cape Columbia on Ellesmere Island to Middle Island in Lake Erie. *Coastline*—151,488 mi. (243,797 km), including mainland and islands; Atlantic Ocean, 28,019 mi. (45,092 km); Arctic Ocean, 82,698 mi. (133,089 km); Hudson Bay, Hudson Strait, and James Bay, 24,786 mi. (39,890 km); Pacific Ocean, 15,985 mi. (25,726 km). *Shoreline*—Great Lakes, 4,726 mi. (7,606 km).
Elevation: *Highest*—Mount Logan, 19,520 ft. (5,950 m) above sea level. *Lowest*—sea level.
Climate: January temperatures average below 0° F. (−18° C) in two-thirds of the country. Pacific coastal areas are the only region with average January temperatures above freezing. Average July temperatures range from below 40° F. (4° C) in the northern Arctic Islands to more than 70° F. (21° C) in southern Ontario. Precipitation is heaviest along the Pacific coast, where more than 80 inches (200 centimeters) falls annually, mainly in autumn and winter. Central prairies receive from 8 to 20 inches (20 to 50 centimeters) of precipitation, mainly during the summer. In the southeast, average annual precipitation ranges from about 30 inches (76 centimeters) in southern Ontario to about 60 inches (150 centimeters) along the Atlantic coast. Snowfall totals more than 100 inches (250 centimeters) annually in parts of the east. (See also "Weather.")
Population: *Estimated 1983 population*—24,541,000; distribution, 76 per cent urban, 24 per cent rural; density, 5 persons per sq. mi. (2 persons per km²). *1981 Census*—24,104,873. *Estimated 1988 population*—25,665,000.
Chief products: *Agriculture*—beef cattle, wheat, milk, hay, hogs, rapeseed, poultry, barley, eggs, vegetables, tobacco, fruits. *Fishing industry*—salmon, herring, cod, lobster, scallops. *Forest industry*—logs and bolts, pulpwood. *Fur industry*—mink, beaver, fox, lynx. *Manufacturing*—food products; transportation equipment; paper products; fabricated metal products; primary metals; chemicals; lumber and wood products; electric machinery and equipment; nonelectric machinery; printed materials; stone, clay, and glass products; textiles; clothing. *Mining*—petroleum, natural gas, iron ore, copper, natural gas liquids, zinc, coal, nickel, uranium, asbestos, potash, sand and gravel.
Flag: Adopted Feb. 15, 1965. (For illustration, see page 192. See also "Flags" section.)
National symbols: Beaver and maple leaf.
National holiday: Dominion Day (Canada Day), July 1.
Coat of arms: The shield bears the royal arms of England (upper left); Scotland (upper right); Ireland (lower left); and France (lower right); and three red maple leaves. A British lion holds the Union Jack and a unicorn holds the fleur-de-lis of France.
Anthems: "O Canada" (national); "God Save the Queen" (royal).
National motto: *A Mari Usque ad Mare* (From Sea to Sea).
Money: *Basic unit*—dollar.

The provinces and territories of Canada

Provincial and territorial flags appear on page 192. See "Abbreviations" for a list of postal and traditional abbreviations for the provinces and territories.

Provinces

Province	Capital	Area In sq. mi.	In km²	Rank in Area	Population (1976 Census)	Floral Emblem	Date Became Province
Alberta	Edmonton	255,285	661,185	4	1,838,037	Wild Rose	1905
British Columbia	Victoria	366,255	948,596	3	2,466,608	Flowering Dogwood	1871
Manitoba	Winnipeg	251,000	650,087	6	1,021,506	Pasqueflower	1870
New Brunswick	Fredericton	28,354	73,436	8	677,250	Violet	1867
Newfoundland	St. John's	156,185	404,517	7	557,725	Pitcher Plant	1949
Nova Scotia	Halifax	21,425	55,491	9	828,571	Trailing Arbutus	1867
Ontario	Toronto	412,582	1,068,582	2	8,264,465	White Trillium	1867

Provinces	Capital	Area In sq. mi.	in km²	Rank in Area	Population (1976 Census)	Floral Emblem	Date Became Province
Prince Edward Island	Charlottetown	2,184	5,657	10	118,229	Lady's-Slipper	1873
Quebec	Quebec	594,860	1,540,680	1	6,234,445	White Garden Lily	1867
Saskatchewan	Regina	251,700	651,900	5	921,323	Prairie Lily	1905

Territories

Territory	Capital	Area In sq. mi.	In km²	Population (1976 Census)	Floral Emblem
Northwest Territories	Yellowknife	1,304,903	3,379,684	42,609	Mountain Avens
Yukon Territory	Whitehorse	186,300	482,515	21,836	Fireweed

The population of Canada

Canada's population has grown steadily since the first census was taken in 1851. Rapid growth occurred between 1851 and 1861, between 1901 and 1911, and between 1951 and 1961.

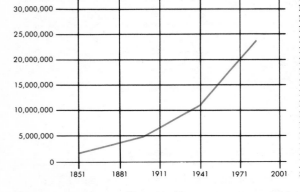

Census year	Population
1851	2,436,297
1861	3,229,633
1871	3,689,257
1881	4,324,810
1891	4,833,239
1901	5,371,315
1911	7,206,643
1921	8,787,949
1931	10,376,786
1941	11,506,655
1951	14,009,429
1956	16,080,791
1961	18,238,247
1966	20,014,880
1971	21,568,311
1976	22,992,604
1981	24,104,873

Source: Statistics Canada.

50 Largest cities and towns in Canada

1. **Montreal** 1,080,546
2. **Toronto** 633,318
3. **Winnipeg** 560,874
4. **Calgary** 469,917
5. **Edmonton** 461,361
6. **Vancouver** 410,188
7. **Hamilton** 312,003
8. **Ottawa** 304,462
9. **Mississauga** 250,017
10. **Laval** 246,243
11. **London** 240,392
12. **Windsor** 196,526

13. **Quebec** 177,082
14. **Regina** 149,593
15. **Saskatoon** 133,750
16. **Kitchener** 131,870
17. **St. Catharines** 123,351
18. **Longueuil** 122,429
19. **Halifax** 117,882
20. **Thunder Bay** 111,476
21. **Oshawa** 107,023
22. **Burlington** 104,314
23. **Brampton** 103,459
24. **Sudbury** 97,604

25. **Montréal-Nord** 97,250
26. **St. John's** 86,576
27. **Saint John** 85,956
28. **Sault Ste. Marie** 81,048
29. **St.-Léonard** 78,452
30. **Sherbrooke** 76,804
31. **LaSalle** 76,713
32. **Gatineau** 73,479
33. **Cambridge** 72,383
34. **Ste.-Foy** 71,237
35. **Niagara Falls** 69,423
36. **Oakville** 68,950

37. **Verdun** 68,013
38. **Guelph** 67,538
39. **Brantford** 66,950
40. **Dartmouth** 65,341
41. **St.-Laurent** 64,404

42. **Charlesbourg** 63,147
43. **Victoria** 62,551
44. **Hull** 61,039
45. **Jonquière** 60,691
46. **Prince George** 59,929

47. **Peterborough** 59,683
48. **Kamloops** 58,311
49. **Chicoutimi** 57,737
50. **Markham** 56,206

Cultural and economic regions of Canada

The Atlantic Provinces (Newfoundland, New Brunswick, Prince Edward Island, and Nova Scotia)—Most of the inhabitants are of English, Irish, Scottish, or French descent. The region provides most of Canada's fish catch, but manufacturing is the leading economic activity. Agriculture, mining, shipping, and tourism are also important.

Quebec—About 80 per cent of the people are of French descent, and French is the official language. Most of the people are Roman Catholics. Montreal, Quebec's largest city, is the cultural and economic hub of the province and ranks as Canada's leading transportation center. Manufacturing and service industries are the chief economic activities.

Ontario—About 60 per cent of the people are of British or Irish descent, and about 10 per cent are of French ancestry. Ontario has more American Indians than any other province. It produces about half of Canada's manufactured goods and is also a major agricultural area. The city of Toronto is the leading manufacturing, financial, and communications center of English-speaking Canada.

The Prairie Provinces (Alberta, Saskatchewan, and Manitoba)—Many inhabitants are descendants of settlers who arrived during the late 1800's and early 1900's from eastern Canada, the United States, and various European countries. The region produces most of Canada's grain and cattle and also has considerable mineral wealth, including oil and natural gas.

British Columbia—Most inhabitants are of British ancestry. Others include persons of Chinese, German, Italian, or Scandinavian descent. Known for its scenic coastline and mountains, the province attracts many tourists. Huge evergreen forests provide jobs in the logging and wood-processing industries. Other major economic activities include agriculture, fishing, and mining.

The Territories—The Yukon Territory and the Northwest Territories cover more than a third of Canada's land area, but have less than 1 per cent of its population. Indians and Eskimos make up much of the population. Forested mountains occupy most of the Yukon and the southwestern parts of the Northwest Territories. Most of the rest of the region is frozen and barren much of the year. The territories have rich mineral deposits, and mining is the chief economic activity.

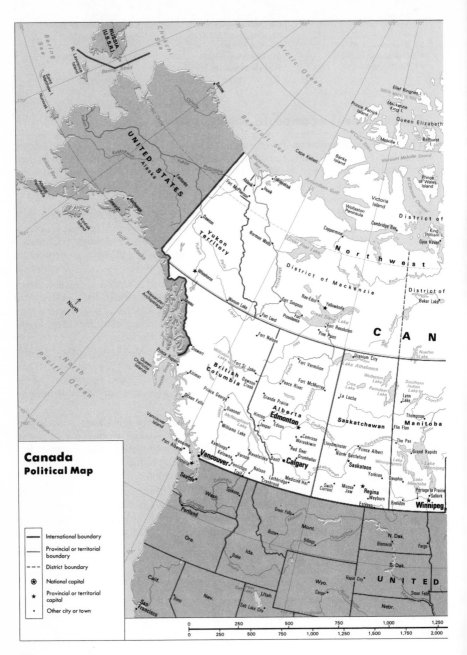

Canada
Political Map

International boundary
Provincial or territorial boundary
District boundary
⊛ National capital
★ Provincial or territorial capital
· Other city or town

| 0 | 250 | 500 | 750 | 1,000 | 1,250 |
| 0 | 250 | 500 | 750 | 1,000 | 1,250 | 1,500 | 1,750 | 2,000 |

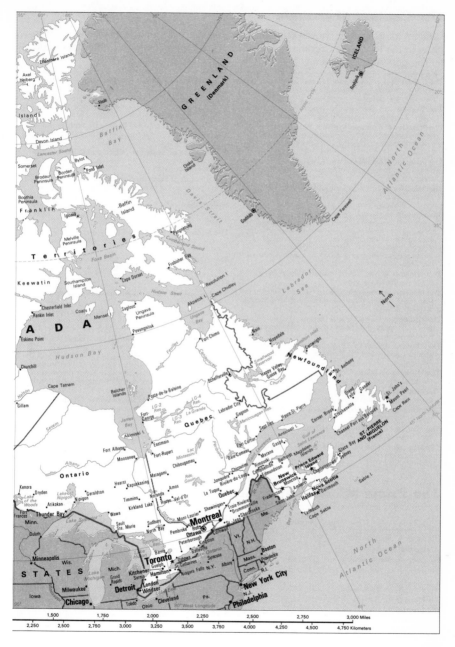

The Cabinet of Canada

Cabinet ministers are chosen by the prime minister from members of the majority party in the House of Commons—or occasionally the Senate—and are appointed by the governor general.

The Leader of the Government in the Senate is a Senator who sponsors legislation in the Senate that has been passed by the House of Commons.

The Minister of Agriculture supervises federal programs of land reclamation and price stabilization.

The Minister of Communications coordinates research on communications technology, operates the national galleries and museums, and regulates the broadcasting industry.

The Minister of Consumer and Corporate Affairs administers regulations concerning pure food standards and deceptive advertising.

The Minister of Employment and Immigration handles all matters concerning immigration and the development of Canada's labor resources.

The Minister of Energy, Mines, and Resources supervises the development of Canada's energy supply and the surveying of natural resources. The minister is assisted by the Minister of State for Mines. The Minister of State for Mines heads two special agencies—the Advisory Council on the Status of Women and the Office of the Coordinator, Status of Women.

The Minister of the Environment oversees programs to protect the environment.

The Minister of Finance presents the annual budget to Parliament. The minister is assisted by the Minister of State for Finance.

The Minister of Fisheries and Oceans administers programs to control water pollution and to manage the nation's fisheries.

The Minister of Indian Affairs and Northern Development administers the Northwest Territories, Yukon Territory, and Eskimo and Indian affairs.

The Minister of Justice interprets laws passed by Parliament and acts as legal adviser to the national government.

The Minister of Labour helps prevent or settle labor disputes, and watches over the interests of labor.

The Minister of National Defence controls and manages the Canadian Armed Forces.

The Minister of National Health and Welfare manages national public-health and social-welfare activities.

The Minister of National Revenue assesses and collects federal taxes and customs and excise duties.

The Minister of Public Works controls the construction and repair of public roads, buildings, and bridges.

The Minister of Regional Industrial Expansion supervises manufacturing, tourism, and trade in Canada. The minister is assisted by the Minister of State for Trade.

The Minister of State for Economic and Regional Development develops policies for promoting the Canadian economy.

The Minister of State for Science and Technology coordinates research on science and technology within the federal government.

The Minister of State for Social Development directs programs in aid of individual, family, and community development.

The Ministers of State. The Cabinet includes two Ministers of State, who handle special government assignments.

The Minister of Supply and Services handles government purchases and provides management services to other departments.

The Minister of Transport regulates nearly all commercial transportation and communications. The minister is assisted by the Minister of State for the Canadian Wheat Board.

The Minister of Veterans Affairs has charge of all matters concerning war veterans.

The President of the Queen's Privy Council for Canada supervises preparation of the government's legislative program and manages it in the House of Commons.

The President of the Treasury Board reviews proposed spending programs of all government agencies.

The Secretary of State of Canada controls state records and documents. The secretary is assisted by the Minister of State for Multiculturalism, who directs programs to promote the preservation and sharing of cultural heritages.

The Secretary of State for External Affairs handles relations with the Commonwealth nations, with other countries, and with the United Nations.

The Solicitor General of Canada supervises federal prisons and the Royal Canadian Mounted Police.

The Prime Ministers of Canada

	Served	Political Party	Born	Birthplace
Sir John A. Macdonald	1867-1873	Conservative	Jan. 11, 1815	Glasgow, Scotland
Alexander Mackenzie	1873-1878	Liberal	Jan. 28, 1822	Logierait, Scotland
Sir John A. Macdonald	1878-1891	Conservative	Jan. 11, 1815	Glasgow, Scotland
Sir John J. C. Abbott	1891-1892	Conservative	Mar. 12, 1821	St. Andrews, Lower Canada (now Quebec)
Sir John S. D. Thompson	1892-1894	Conservative	Nov. 10, 1844	Halifax, N.S.
Sir Mackenzie Bowell	1894-1896	Conservative	Dec. 27, 1823	Rickinghall, England
Sir Charles Tupper	1896	Conservative	July 2, 1821	Amherst, N.S.

	Served	Political Party	Born	Birthplace
Sir Wilfrid Laurier	1896-1911	Liberal	Nov. 20, 1841	St. Lin (now Laurentide), Que.
Sir Robert L. Borden	1911-1917	Conservative	June 26, 1854	Grand Pre, N.S.
Sir Robert L. Borden	1917-1920	Unionist	June 26, 1854	Grand Pre, N.S.
Arthur Meighen	1920-1921	Unionist	June 16, 1874	near St. Mary's, Ont.
W. L. Mackenzie King	1921-1926	Liberal	Dec. 17, 1874	Berlin (now Kitchener), Ont.
Arthur Meighen	1926	Conservative	June 16, 1874	near St. Mary's, Ont.
W. L. Mackenzie King	1926-1930	Liberal	Dec. 17, 1874	Berlin (now Kitchener), Ont.
Richard B. Bennett	1930-1935	Conservative	July 3, 1870	near Hopewell Cape, N.B.
W. L. Mackenzie King	1935-1948	Liberal	Dec. 17, 1874	Berlin (now Kitchener), Ont.
Louis S. St. Laurent	1948-1957	Liberal	Feb. 1, 1882	Compton, Que.
John Diefenbaker	1957-1963	Progressive Conservative	Sept. 18, 1895	Neustadt, Ont.
Lester B. Pearson	1963-1968	Liberal	April 23, 1897	Toronto, Ont.
Pierre E. Trudeau	1968-1979	Liberal	Oct. 18, 1919	Montreal, Que.
Charles Joseph Clark	1979-1980	Progressive Conservative	June 5, 1939	High River, Alta.
Pierre E. Trudeau	1980	Liberal	Oct. 18, 1919	Montreal, Que.

Important dates in Canadian history

A.D. 1000's Vikings sail along the east coast, possibly establishing a temporary settlement at the northern tip of Newfoundland.

1497 John Cabot lands on Canada's east coast. As a result, Britain lays claim to all of Canada.

1534 French explorer Jacques Cartier reaches the Gulf of St. Lawrence and claims the surrounding territory for France.

1583 Sir Humphrey Gilbert lands on Newfoundland and claims it for England.

1603 French explorer Samuel de Champlain lands at what is now Prince Edward Island and claims it for France.

1608 Champlain founds the city of Quebec.

1610 English explorer Henry Hudson arrives at the great bay that later bears his name.

1642 Roman Catholic missionaries found the settlement of Ville-Marie, later renamed Montreal.

1663 King Louis XIV of France officially proclaims Canada a province of France, called New France.

1689–1763 British and French forces clash over territorial claims in a series of four wars known collectively as the French and Indian Wars.

1713 The Treaty of Utrecht gives Britain control of the mainland of Nova Scotia, Newfoundland, and the Hudson Bay region.

1759 French forces led by the Marquis de Montcalm are defeated by the British under General James Wolfe at the Battle of Quebec. The French defeat marks a turning point in the battle for control of Canada.

1763 The Treaty of Paris brings a formal end to the French and Indian Wars. Under the terms of the treaty, Britain wins control of Canada. France retains control of two tiny islands south of Newfoundland—Saint Pierre and Miquelon.

1774 The Quebec Act guarantees freedom of religion to Roman Catholic French Canadians. It also makes French civil law valid in British courts in Quebec.

1791 The Constitutional Act of 1791 divides the province of Quebec into Upper Canada (now Ontario) and Lower Canada (now Quebec).

1793 British troops establish a permanent settlement at York (now Toronto).

1812 U.S. forces based in Detroit, on the Niagara River, and at the foot of Lake Champlain launch an invasion of Canada at the start of the War of 1812. The invasion attempts fail completely.

1813 U.S. troops capture York (now Toronto) and hold the city briefly, burning several public buildings.

1814 The Treaty of Ghent ends the War of 1812. All territorial holdings of the two sides are returned to their pre-war status.

1836 Canada's first railroad begins operations between La prairie and St. Jean, Quebec.

1837–1838 Louis Joseph Papineau leads a brief, unsuccessful rebellion against British rule in Lower Canada. In Upper Canada, William Lyon Mackenzie leads an unsuccessful revolt demanding more self-government.

1839 Lord Durham submits a report to Queen Victoria urging Britain to grant self-government to the North American colonies.

1840 The British Parliament adopts the Act of Union, which combines Upper and Lower Canada into the new province of Canada.

1843 The Hudson's Bay Company establishes the first permanent settlement on Vancouver Island at what is now Victoria.

1857 Queen Victoria designates Ottawa as the capital of the province of Canada.

1864 Leaders of British North American colonies meet and draw up a plan to form a confederation called the Dominion of Canada.

1867 The British Parliament adopts the British North America Act, formally establishing the Dominion of Canada.

1869–1870 Louis Riel, a leader of the métis (persons of mixed Indian and European descent), leads a rebellion against the Canadian government in what is now Manitoba.

1885 The Canadian Pacific Railway is completed, linking Canada's Atlantic and Pacific coasts.

1885 Louis Riel leads an unsuccessful revolt of the métis in Saskatchewan. Riel is later hanged in spite of widespread protests among French Canadians.

1896 Sir Wilfrid Laurier becomes the first French Canadian to serve as prime minister.

1896 Gold is discovered on a tributary of the Klondike River, leading to a major gold rush.

1914–1918 Canada joins the British war effort in World War I and sends its troops overseas.

1918 The Canadian Parliament grants women the right to vote in federal elections.

1920 Canada becomes a charter member of the League of Nations.

1926 After a constitutional crisis over the question of the power of the governor general, the Imperial Conference in London decides that all British dominions have equal status and are completely self-governing.

1939–1945 All branches of the Canadian armed forces contribute to the Allied effort in World War II.

1945 Canada joins 49 other nations to become a charter member of the United Nations.

1949 The Supreme Court of Canada becomes the country's final court of appeals. Before this time, the Privy Council in England had heard appeals of Canadian cases.

1949 Canada wins the right to amend its constitution in federal matters.

1949 Canada becomes a charter member of the North Atlantic Treaty Organization (NATO).

1959 Queen Elizabeth II and U.S. President Dwight D. Eisenhower preside at the opening of the St. Lawrence Seaway.

1960 The government approves a Bill of Rights, which includes a provision that no individual may be denied rights because of sex, race, national origin, color, or religion.

1962 The Trans-Canada Highway is opened.

1967 Canada observes its centennial with a world's fair in Montreal, called *Expo 67*.

1970 A national crisis erupts when members of the militant French-Canadian separatist group, the Front de Libération du Québec (FLQ) kidnap two government officials and murder one.

1974 Quebec's provincial legislature enacts laws making French the sole official language for education, commerce, and government.

1976 The Parti Québécois, a separatist party, wins control of the provincial government of Quebec.

1980 Voters in a referendum in Quebec vote overwhelmingly against withdrawing from Canada and becoming an independent nation.

1982 Britain approves a new constitution for Canada, ending British control over constitutional amendments.

Major documents in Canadian history

Date	Document	Significance
1774	Quebec Act	Guaranteed freedom of religion to French Canadians; validated French civil law in Quebec's British courts.
1791	Constitutional Act	Divided Quebec into two self-governing parts: Upper Canada (now Ontario) and Lower Canada (now Quebec).
1839	Report on the Affairs of British North America (Durham Report)	Submitted by Lord Durham to Queen Victoria. Urged Britain to grant self-government to its North American colonies.
1840	Act of Union	Combined Upper and Lower Canada into a single province of Canada.
1867	British North America Act	Established the Dominion of Canada and served as Canada's written constitution until 1982.
1931	Statute of Westminster	Passed by the British Parliament; made Canada one of several independent dominions joined in a voluntary union called the Commonwealth of Nations.
1960	Bill of Rights	Guaranteed freedom of speech, religion, and other basic rights in areas under federal jurisdiction.
1982	Constitution Act	Replaced the British North America Act as the basic governing document of Canada and ended British control over constitutional amendments. Includes a new bill of rights called the *Canadian Charter of Rights and Freedoms*.

Chemical elements

Name	Symbol	Atomic Weight*	Atomic Number	Density (g/cm³) at 20° C	Discoverer	Country of Discovery	Date of Discovery
Actinium	Ac	[227]	89	10.07†	André Debierne	France	1899
Aluminum	Al	26.9815	13	2.70	Hans Christian Oersted	Denmark	1825
Americium	Am	[243]	95	13.67	G. T. Seaborg; R. A. James; L. O. Morgan; A. Ghiorso	United States	1945
Antimony	Sb	121.75	51	6.691		Known to Ancients	
Argon	Ar	39.948	18	0.00166	Sir William Ramsay; Baron Rayleigh	Scotland	1894
Arsenic	As	74.9216	33	5.73		Known to Ancients	
Astatine	At	[210]	85	0.0175†	D. R. Corson; K. R. MacKenzie; E. Segrè	United States	1940
Barium	Ba	137.33	56	3.5	§Sir Humphry Davy	England	1808
Berkelium	Bk	[247]	97	14.0‡	G. T. Seaborg; S. G. Thompson; A. Ghiorso	United States	1949
Beryllium	Be	9.0122	4	1.848	Friedrich Wöhler; A. A. Bussy	Germany; Fr.	1828
Bismuth	Bi	208.980	83	9.747		Known to Ancients	
Boron	B	10.811	5	2.34	§H. Davy; J. L. Gay-Lussac; L. J. Thenard	England; Fr.	1808
Bromine	Br	79.909	35	3.12	Antoine J. Balard	France	1826
Cadmium	Cd	112.41	48	8.65	Friedrich Stromeyer	Germany	1817
Calcium	Ca	40.08	20	1.55	§Sir Humphry Davy	England	1808
Californium	Cf	[251]	98	————	G. T. Seaborg; S. G. Thompson; A. Ghiorso; K. Street, Jr.	United States	1950
Carbon	C	12.01115	6	2.25		Known to Ancients	
Cerium	Ce	140.12	58	6.768	W. von Hisinger; J. Berzelius; M. Klaproth	Sweden; Germany	1803
Cesium	Cs	132.905	55	1.873	Gustav Kirchhoff, Robert Bunsen	Germany	1860
Chlorine	Cl	35.453	17	0.00295	Carl Wilhelm Scheele	Sweden	1774
Chromium	Cr	51.996	24	7.19	Louis Vauquelin	France	1797
Cobalt	Co	58.9332	27	8.9	Georg Brandt	Sweden	1737
Copper	Cu	63.54	29	8.96		Known to Ancients	
Curium	Cm	[247]	96	13.51†	G. T. Seaborg; R. A. James; A. Ghiorso	United States	1944
Dysprosium	Dy	162.50	66	8.550	Paul Émile Lecoq de Boisbaudran	France	1886
Einsteinium	Es	[254]	99	————	Argonne; Los Alamos; U. of Calif.	United States	1952
Element 104	—	————	104	————	Claimed by G. Flerov and others	Russia	1964
					Claimed by A. Ghiorso and others	United States	1969
Element 105	—	————	105	————	Claimed by G. Flerov and others	Russia	1968
					Claimed by A. Ghiorso and others	United States	1970
Element 106	—	————	106	————	Claimed by G. Flerov and others	Russia	1974
					Claimed by A. Ghiorso and others	United States	1974

*A number in brackets indicates the mass number of the most stable isotope.
†The density is calculated and not based on an actual measurement.
‡Estimated.
§See the "People" section for biographical information.

Name	Symbol	Atomic Weight*	Atomic Number	Density (g/cm³) at 20° C	Discoverer	Country of Discovery	Date of Discovery
Element 107	—	————	107		Claimed by G. Flerov; Y. Oganessian; and others	Russia	1976
					Claimed by P. Armbruster and others	Germany	1981
Erbium	Er	167.26	68	9.15	Carl Mosander	Sweden	1843
Europium	Eu	151.96	63	5.245	Eugène Demarçay	France	1901
Fermium	Fm	[257]	100	————	Argonne; Los Alamos; U. of Calif.	United States	1953
Fluorine	F	18.998403	9	0.00158	Henri Moissan	France	1886
Francium	Fr	[223]	87		Marguerite Perey	France	1939
Gadolinium	Gd	157.25	64	7.86	Jean de Marignac	Switzerland	1880
Gallium	Ga	69.72	31	5.907	Paul Émile Lecoq de Boisbaudran	France	1875
Germanium	Ge	72.59	32	5.323	Clemens Winkler	Germany	1886
Gold	Au	196.967	79	19.32		Known to Ancients	
Hafnium	Hf	178.49	72	13.31	Dirk Coster; Georg von Hevesy	Denmark	1923
Helium	He	4.0026	2	0.0001664	Sir William Ramsay; Nils Langlet; P. T. Cleve	Scotland; Sweden	1895
Holmium	Ho	164.930	67	8.79	J. L. Soret	Switzerland	1878
Hydrogen	H	1.00797	1	0.00008375	Henry Cavendish	England	1766
Indium	In	114.82	49	7.31	Ferdinand Reich; H. Richter	Germany	1863
Iodine	I	126.9044	53	4.93	Bernard Courtois	France	1811
Iridium	Ir	192.2	77	22.65	Smithson Tennant	England	1804
Iron	Fe	55.847	26	7.874		Known to Ancients	
Krypton	Kr	83.80	36	0.003488	Sir William Ramsay; M. W. Travers	Great Britain	1898
Lanthanum	La	138.91	57	6.189	Carl Mosander	Sweden	1839
Lawrencium	Lr	[256]	103	————	A. Ghiorso; T. Sikkeland; A. E. Larsh; R. M. Latimer	United States	1961
Lead	Pb	207.19	82	11.35		Known to Ancients	
Lithium	Li	6.939	3	0.534	Johann Arfvedson	Sweden	1817
Lutetium	Lu	174.97	71	9.849	Georges Urbain	France	1907
Magnesium	Mg	24.312	12	1.738	§Sir Humphry Davy	England	1808
Manganese	Mn	54.9380	25	7.3	Johan Gahn	Sweden	1774
Mendelevium	Md	[258]	101	————	G. T. Seaborg; A. Ghiorso; B. Harvey; G. R. Choppin; S. G. Thompson	United States	1955
Mercury	Hg	200.59	80	13.546		Known to Ancients	
Molybdenum	Mo	95.94	42	10.22	Carl Wilhelm Scheele	Sweden	1778
Neodymium	Nd	144.24	60	7.0	C. F. Auer von Welsbach	Austria	1885
Neon	Ne	20.183	10	0.0008387	Sir William Ramsay; M. W. Travers	England	1898
Neptunium	Np	[237]	93	20.25	E. M. McMillan; P. H. Abelson	United States	1940
Nickel	Ni	58.71	28	8.902	Axel Cronstedt	Sweden	1751
Niobium	Nb	92.906	41	8.57	Charles Hatchett	England	1801
Nitrogen	N	14.0067	7	0.001165	Daniel Rutherford	Scotland	1772
Nobelium	No	[255]	102	————	Nobel Institute for Physics	Sweden	1957
Osmium	Os	190.2	76	22.57	Smithson Tennant	England	1804
Oxygen	O	15.9994	8	0.001332	Joseph Priestley; Carl Wilhelm Scheele	England; Sweden	1774

Name	Symbol	Atomic Weight*	Atomic Number	Density (g/cm³) at 20° C	Discoverer	Country of Discovery	Date of Discovery
Palladium	Pd	106.4	46	12.02	William Wollaston	England	1803
Phosphorus	P	30.9738	15	1.83	Hennig Brand	Germany	1669
Platinum	Pt	195.09	78	21.45	Julius Scaliger	Italy	1557
Plutonium	Pu	[244]	94	19.84	G. T. Seaborg; J. W. Kennedy; E. M. McMillan; A. C. Wahl	United States	1940
Polonium	Po	[210]	84	9.24	§Pierre and Marie Curie	France	1898
Potassium	K	39.0983	19	0.862	§Sir Humphry Davy	England	1807
Praseodymium	Pr	140.907	59	6.769	C. F. Auer von Welsbach	Austria	1885
Promethium	Pm	[145]	61	7.22	J. A. Marinsky; Lawrence E. Glendenin; Charles D. Coryell	United States	1945
Protactinium	Pa	[231]	91	15.37†	Otto Hahn; Lise Meitner; Frederick Soddy; John Cranston	Germany; England	1917
Radium	Ra	[226]	88	5.0	§Pierre and Marie Curie	France	1898
Radon	Rn	[222]	86	0.00923	Friedrich Ernst Dorn	Germany	1900
Rhenium	Re	186.2	75	21.02	Walter Noddack; Ida Tacke; Otto Berg	Germany	1925
Rhodium	Rh	102.905	45	12.41	William Wollaston	England	1803
Rubidium	Rb	85.47	37	1.532	R. Bunsen; G. Kirchhoff	Germany	1861
Ruthenium	Ru	101.07	44	12.41	Karl Klaus	Russia	1844
Samarium	Sm	150.35	62	7.49	Paul Émile Lecoq de Boisbaudran	France	1879
Scandium	Sc	44.956	21	2.989	Lars Nilson	Sweden	1879
Selenium	Se	78.96	34	4.79	Jöns Berzelius	Sweden	1817
Silicon	Si	28.0855	14	2.33	Jöns Berzelius	Sweden	1823
Silver	Ag	107.870	47	10.50		Known to Ancients	
Sodium	Na	22.9898	11	0.971	§Sir Humphry Davy	England	1807
Strontium	Sr	87.62	38	2.60	A. Crawford	Scotland	1790
Sulfur	S	32.064	16	2.07		Known to Ancients	
Tantalum	Ta	180.948	73	16.6	Anders Ekeberg	Sweden	1802
Technetium	Tc	[97]	43	11.50†	Carlo Perrier; Émilio Segrè	Italy	1937
Tellurium	Te	127.60	52	6.24	Franz Müller von Reichenstein	Romania	1782
Terbium	Tb	158.924	65	8.25	Carl Mosander	Sweden	1843
Thallium	Tl	204.37	81	11.85	Sir William Crookes	England	1861
Thorium	Th	232.038	90	11.66	Jöns Berzelius	Sweden	1828
Thulium	Tm	168.934	69	9.31	Per Theodor Cleve	Sweden	1879
Tin	Sn	118.69	50	7.2984		Known to Ancients	
Titanium	Ti	47.90	22	4.507	William Gregor	England	1791
Tungsten	W	183.85	74	19.3	Fausto and Juan José de Elhuyar	Spain	1783
Uranium	U	238.03	92	19.07	Martin Klaproth	Germany	1789
Vanadium	V	50.942	23	6.1	Nils Sefström	Sweden	1830
Xenon	Xe	131.30	54	0.005495	Sir William Ramsay; M. W. Travers	England	1898
Ytterbium	Yb	173.04	70	6.959	Jean de Marignac	Switzerland	1878
Yttrium	Y	88.905	39	4.472	Johann Gadolin	Finland	1794
Zinc	Zn	65.37	30	7.133	Andreas Marggraf	Germany	1746
Zirconium	Zr	91.22	40	6.506	Martin Klaproth	Germany	1789

*A number in brackets indicates the mass number of the most stable isotope.
†The density is calculated and not based on an actual measurement.
§See the "People" section for biographical information.

Decorations and medals

The following tables list the most important military and civilian decorations and medals awarded in the United States and other nations. Many of the entries are illustrated on pages 176–177.

United States military decorations and medals

(Listed in order of importance)

Name of Medal	Year Established	Persons Eligible	Awarded For
Medal of Honor	1861 (Navy) 1862 (Army, Air Force*)	All ranks of the U.S. armed forces only	Gallantry in action
Distinguished Service Cross (Army)	1918	All ranks of the armed forces	Exceptional heroism in combat
Navy Cross	1919		
Air Force Cross	1960		
Distinguished Service Medal	1918 (Army, Air Force*) 1919 (Navy) 1951 (Coast Guard)	Usually, only high-ranking officers	Exceptional meritorious service in a duty of great responsibility
Silver Star	1932	All ranks of the armed forces	Gallantry in action
Legion of Merit	1942	Normally to officers	Exceptionally meritorious service in peace or war
Distinguished Flying Cross	1926	All ranks of the armed forces	Heroism or extraordinary achievement in flight
Soldier's Medal	1926	All ranks of the armed forces	Heroism not involving conflict with the enemy
Navy and Marine Corps Medal	1942		
Airman's Medal	1960		
Coast Guard Medal	1951		
Bronze Star	1944	All ranks of the armed forces	Heroic or meritorious achievement during military operations
Air Medal	1942	All ranks of the armed forces	Meritorious achievement in flight
Commendation Medal	1944 (Navy) 1945 (Army) 1947 (Coast Guard) 1958 (Air Force)	All members of the armed forces	Meritorious service in war or peace
Purple Heart†	1932 (Army) 1942 (Navy)	All ranks of the armed forces	Wounds or death in combat

United States civilian decorations and medals

Presidential Medal of Freedom	1963	Any person	Service connected with U.S. or national interest, or cultural or public service
Gold and Silver Lifesaving Medals	1874	Any person	Lifesaving in maritime waters at personal risk of life
National Security Medal	1953	Any person	Distinguished achievement in the field of national security
President's Award for Distinguished Federal Civilian Service	1957	Federal employees	Outstanding service
Young American Medals for Bravery and for Service	1950	U.S. residents under 19	Courage or public service
National Aeronautics and Space Administration Distinguished Service Medal	1959	Astronauts and NASA personnel	Heroism or distinguished service

76

Decorations and medals of other countries

(Listed in order of importance)

Country	Name of Medal	Year Estab- lished	Persons Eligible	Awarded For
British Commonwealth	**Victoria Cross**	1856	All ranks of the armed forces	Conspicuous bravery in action
	George Cross	1940	Civilians and military	Conspicuous bravery
	Order of Merit	1902	Civilians and military	Distinguished service
	Distinguished Service Order	1886	All officers	Distinguished service in combat
	Military Cross	1914	Army officers	Distinguished service in action
	Distinguished Flying Cross	1918	All officers	Bravery in combat flying
Canada	**Canada Medal**	1943	All Canadians and citizens of other countries	Meritorious service beyond the call of duty
	Canadian Forces Decoration	1951	All armed forces	12 years' service
Russia	**Order of Lenin**	1930	Russian individuals and organizations	General merit
	Gold Star Medal	1939	Russians	General merit
France	**Legion of Honor**	1802	Frenchmen and citizens of other countries	General merit
	Croix de Guerre	1915	All ranks of the armed forces	Bravery in combat
West Germany	**Iron Cross**	1813	All ranks of the armed forces	Bravery or general merit in combat
Japan	**Order of the Chrysanthemum**	1877	Japanese men and men of other countries	Great service to Japan
Sweden	**Order of the Seraphim**	1748	Royalty and heads of state	Service to humanity
Denmark	**Order of the Dannebrog**	1671	Danes and citizens of other countries	General merit
Belgium	**Order of Leopold**	1832	Belgians and citizens of other countries	General civilian and military merit
The Vatican	**Order of Pius**	1847	Any person	Personal merit
Israel	**Hero of Israel**	1949	Military personnel	Gallantry in combat
Greece	**Order of the Redeemer**	1829	Greeks and citizens of other countries	General merit
United Nations	**Korean Service Medal**	1951	Personnel of UN forces	Service in Korean War
	United Nations Medal	1959	Personnel of UN forces	Service in UN police actions

*A separate Air Force medal was designed in 1965.
†In 1782, General George Washington created a heart-shaped badge made of purple cloth to honor his soldiers for extraordinary bravery during the Revolutionary War. It was called the *Badge of Military Merit* and was the first U.S. military decoration. In 1932, the badge was revived and renamed the *Purple Heart*. Soldiers could claim the award if they had been wounded in any earlier war or had received a special commendation certificate in World War I. In 1941, the War Department restricted the award to persons wounded in combat.

Disasters

Year	Location	Dead	Disaster
64	Rome	Unknown	City fire
79	Pompeii and Herculaneum	2,000	Vesuvius eruption
856	Corinth, Greece	45,000	Earthquake
1268	Silicia, Asia Minor	60,000	Earthquake
1290	Hopeh Province, China	100,000	Earthquake
1293	Kamakura, Japan	30,000	Earthquake
1531	Lisbon, Portugal	30,000	Earthquake
1556	Shensi Province, China	830,000	Earthquake
1666	London	Unknown	City fire
1667	Shemaka, Russia	80,000	Earthquake
1669	Sicily	20,000	Mount Etna eruption
1693	Catania, Italy	60,000	Earthquake
1737	Calcutta, India	300,000	Earthquake; tornado
1755	Lisbon, Portugal	60,000	Earthquake
1755	Northern Persia (now Iran)	40,000	Earthquake
1759	Baalbek, Lebanon	30,000	Earthquake
1783	Calabria, Italy	50,000	Earthquake
1797	Quito, Ecuador	41,000	Earthquake
1815	Indonesia	12,000	Mount Tambora eruption
1865	Mississippi River	1,653	Steamboat explosion
1867	West Indies	1,000	Hurricane; ship-wrecks
1871	Chicago	300	City fire
1871	Peshtigo, Wis.	1,200	Forest fire
1877	Ecuador	1,000	Cotopaxi eruption
1878	Thames R.	640	Ship collision
1883	Indonesia	36,000	Krakatoa eruption; tidal wave
1887	Honan Province, China	900,000	Huang Ho flood
1889	Johnstown, Pa.	2,200	Burst dam; flood
1900	Galveston, Tex.	6,000	Hurricane; storm tide
1902	Martinique	38,000	Mont Pélee eruption
1903	Chicago	575	Iroquois Theater fire
1904	New York City	1,030	Excursion boat fire
1904	Scotland	651	Shipwreck
1906	San Francisco	700	Earthquake; fire
1907	Monongah, W. Va.	361	Coal mine explosion
1908	Messina, Italy	75,000	Earthquake
1912	North Atlantic	1,500	Liner *Titanic* collision with iceberg
1913	Indiana; Ohio	467	Ohio River Basin flood
1914	Saint Lawrence R.	1,029	Ship collision
1915	Chicago R.	812	Excursion boat capsized
1915	Avezzano, Italy	29,970	Earthquake
1917	Modane, France	550	Train derailment
1917	Halifax, N. S.	1,635	Ship explosion
1918	Nashville, Tenn.	101	Train collision
1920	Kansu Province, China	200,000	Earthquake; landslide
1923	Tokyo-Yokohama	142,802	Earthquake; fire
1925	Alabama; Illinois; Indiana; Kentucky; Missouri; Tennessee	792	Tornadoes
1928	Florida	2,136	Hurricane
1932	Alabama, Georgia, Mississippi, Tennessee	268	Tornadoes
1932	Kansu Province, China	70,000	Earthquake
1935	Quetta, India (now Pakistan)	60,000	Earthquake
1935	Tampa, Fla.	400	Hurricane
1936	Alabama, Arkansas, Georgia, S. Carolina, Tennessee	498	Tornadoes
1937	Ohio and Mississippi valleys	135	Floods
1937	New London, Tex.	296	Gas explosion in school
1939	Chillan, Chile	30,000	Earthquake
1942	Manchuria, China	1,549	Coal mine explosion
1942	Boston	492	Nightclub fire
1947	Texas City, Tex.	512	Ship explosion
1948	China Sea	1,100	Ship explosion
1948	China coast	600	Ship collision
1952	Alabama, Kentucky, Mississippi, Missouri, Tennessee	208	Tornadoes
1953	North Sea	2,000	Floods
1953	Michigan, Ohio	116	Tornadoes
1953	Waco, Tex.	114	Tornado
1954	Tsugaru St., Japan	794	Shipwreck
1955	Eastern U.S.	184	Hurricane (Diane)
1957	Louisiana, Mississippi, Texas	550	Hurricane (Audrey)
1960	Agadir, Morocco	12,000	Earthquake

Year	Location	Dead	Disaster
1962	Iran	10,000	Earthquake
1962	Peru	3,500	Huascaran avalanche
1963	Bali	1,022	Mount Agung eruption
1963	Cuba; Haiti	6,000	Hurricane (Flora)
1963	Belluno, Italy	1,800	Burst dam; flood
1964	Alaska	131	Earthquake; tidal waves
1965	Illinois, Indiana, Iowa, Michigan, Ohio, Wisconsin	256	Tornadoes
1966	Aberfan, Wales	144	Coal mine avalanche
1968	Iran	11,588	Earthquake
1969	Southeastern U.S.	250	Hurricane (Camille)
1970	East Pakistan (now Bangladesh)	266,087	Cyclone; tidal wave
1970	Peru	66,794	Earthquake
1971	Los Angeles	64	Earthquake
1971	Mississippi, Louisiana	115	Tornadoes
1972	Managua, Nicaragua	10,000	Earthquake
1972	Rapid City, S. Dak.	238	Burst dam; flood
1972	Iran	5,374	Earthquake
1972	Buffalo Creek, W. Va.	125	Burst dam; flood

*Includes dead and missing.

Year	Location	Dead	Disaster
1972	Eastern U.S.	122	Hurricane (Agnes); floods
1974	Pakistan	5,200	Earthquake
1974	Southern and central U.S.	315	Tornadoes
1974	Near Paris	346	Airliner crash
1974	Honduras	8,000	Hurricane (Fifi)
1976	Guatemala	23,000	Earthquake
1976	Hopeh Province, China	240,000	Earthquake
1976	Baja California Sur, Mexico	400	Hurricane (Liza)
1977	Canary Islands	583	Airliner collision
1977	India	15,000	Cyclone; tidal wave
1978	Iran	15,000	Earthquake
1979	Chicago	273	Airliner crash
1979	Dominica, Dominican Republic	2,068	Hurricane (David)
1980	El Asnam, Algeria	5,000	Earthquake
1980	Italy	3,000	Earthquake
1980	Las Vegas, Nev.	85	Hotel fire
1980	Washington	61*	Mount St. Helens eruption
1980	Riyadh, Saudi Arabia	301	Airliner fire
1982	Mexico	187	El Chichón eruption
1982	New Orleans, La.	154	Airliner crash

Earth

This section discusses the planet earth and its physical characteristics. Information about the solar system as a whole appears in the "Universe" section. For information about the earth's population and human events, see the "World" section.

The earth at a glance

Age: 4,500,000,000 (4½ billion) years.

Weight: 6,600,000,000,000,000,000,000 (6.6 sextillion) short tons (6.0 sextillion metric tons).

Area: *Total Surface Area*—196,951,000 square miles (510,100,000 square kilometers). *Land Area*—approximately 57,259,000 square miles (148,300,000 square kilometers), about 30 per cent of total surface area. *Water Area*—approximately 139,692,000 square miles (361,800,000 square kilometers), about 70 per cent of total surface area.

Surface features: *Highest Land*—Mount Everest, 29,028 feet (8,848 meters) above sea level. *Lowest Land*—shore of Dead Sea, 1,299 feet (396 meters) below sea level.

Ocean depths: *Deepest Part of Ocean*—area of the Mariana Trench in Pacific Ocean southwest of Guam, 36,198 feet (11,033 meters) below surface. *Average Ocean Depth*—12,450 feet (3,795 meters).

Temperature: *Highest,* 136° F. (58° C) at Al Aziziyah, Libya. *Lowest,* −126.9° F. (−88.29° C) at Vostok in Antarctica. *Average Surface Temperature,* 57° F. (14° C).

Atmosphere: *Height*—99 per cent of the atmosphere is less than 100 miles (160 kilometers) above the earth's surface, but particles of the atmosphere are 1,000 miles (1,600 kilometers) above the surface. *Chemical makeup of atmosphere*—78 per cent nitrogen, 21 per cent oxygen, 1 per cent argon with small amounts of other gases.

Chemical makeup of the earth's crust (in per cent of the crust's weight): oxygen 46.6, silicon 27.7, aluminum 8.1, iron 5.0, calcium 3.6, sodium 2.8, potassium 2.6, magnesium 2.0, and other elements totaling 1.6.

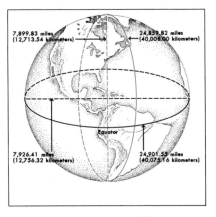

7,899.83 miles (12,713.54 kilometers)

24,859.82 miles (40,008.00 kilometers)

Equator

7,926.41 miles (12,756.32 kilometers)

24,901.55 miles (40,075.16 kilometers)

The earth is not perfectly round. Distances measured through the poles are shorter than those at the equator.

Three motions of the earth

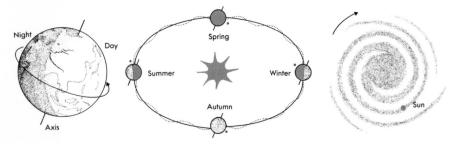

The illustrations show how the earth moves in three ways. (1) The earth spins around its axis once every 23 hours, 56 minutes, and 4.09 seconds. This motion creates day and night. The earth's axis is an imaginary line that connects the North and South poles and tilts at an angle of about 23½°. (2) The earth travels around the sun once every 365 days, 6 hours, 9 minutes, and 9.54 seconds. This motion creates years. The moon's gravitation makes the earth follow a wobbly path *(dotted line)*. The trip around the sun, combined with the earth's tilt, creates the four seasons. (3) The earth moves with the sun as the sun circles the center of the Milky Way once every 225 million years.

Inside the earth

The earth can be thought of as a huge ball covered with water, rock, and soil that is surrounded by air. All the bodies of water make up the *hydrosphere*. The largest landforms are the *continents*. The *biosphere* is the region where life is found—on land, underground, underwater, or in the atmosphere.

A rocky *crust* covers the earth. Three kinds of rocks make up the crust. *Igneous rocks* were formed when melted rock deep inside the crust cooled and hardened. *Sedimentary rocks* were formed by material that collected in layers and hardened. *Metamorphic rocks* were formed by heat and pressure acting upon igneous and sedimentary rocks.

The continents form a layer of the crust called *sial*. It consists chiefly of silicon, oxygen, aluminum, calcium, sodium, and potassium. The sial rests atop another layer of rock, called *sima*, made up mainly of silicon, oxygen, iron, and magnesium. The sima extends under the oceans and forms the ocean floors. The bottom of the crust, the *Mohorovičic discontinuity*, or *Moho*, marks the boundary between the crust and the inner earth.

The inside of the earth has three parts: the *mantle*, the *outer core*, and the *inner core*. The mantle is a thick layer of solid rock made up of silicon, oxygen, aluminum, iron, and magnesium. Scientists believe the outer core is made of melted iron and nickel and the inner core consists of solid iron and nickel.

Plate Tectonics

Plate tectonics is a theory that many earth scientists use to explain certain changes in the earth's crust, such as the creation of mountains and the occurrence of earthquakes and volcanoes. According to this theory, the earth's crust and upper mantle consist of about 20 plates that move slowly—½ to 4 inches (1.3 to 10 centimeters) a year. The plates carry the continents and ocean floor with them. Most earthquakes, mountains, and volcanoes occur along the boundaries between the plates, where the plates slide past one another or collide. (See "Disasters" section for a list that includes major earthquakes and volcanic eruptions.)

The moon at a glance

Age: More than 4,500,000,000 (4½ billion) years.

Distance from the earth: *Shortest*—221,456 miles (356,399 kilometers); *Greatest*—252,711 miles (406,699 kilometers); *Mean*—238,857 miles (384,403 kilometers).

Diameter: About 2,160 miles (3,476 kilometers).

Circumference: About 6,790 miles (10,927 kilometers).

Surface area: About 14,650,000 square miles (37,943,000 square kilometers).

Rotation period: 27 days, 7 hours, 43 minutes.

Revolution period around the earth: 29 days, 12 hours, 44 minutes.

Average speed around the earth: 2,300 miles (3,700 kilometers) per hour.

Length of day and night: About 14 earth-days each.

Temperature at equator: *Sun at zenith over maria,* 260 ° F. (127° C); *Lunar night on maria,* −280° F. (−173° C).

Surface gravity: About $\frac{1}{6}$ that of the earth.

Escape velocity: 1½ miles (2.4 kilometers) per second.

Mass: $\frac{1}{81}$ that of the earth.

Volume: $\frac{1}{50}$ that of the earth.

Atmosphere: Little or none.

81

Major geographic features

Continents

Name	Area Square miles	Area Square kilometers
Africa	11,714,000	30,339,000
Antarctica	5,100,000	13,209,000
Asia	17,011,000	44,059,000
Australia	2,966,000	7,682,000
Europe*	4,063,000	10,524,000
North America	9,400,000	24,345,000
South America	6,883,000	17,828,000

*Many persons consider Europe and Asia to form a single continent, called Eurasia, with a total area of 21,074,000 square miles (54,583,000 square kilometers).

Largest islands

Name	Area Square miles	Area Square kilometers
Greenland	840,004	2,175,600
New Guinea	311,737	807,396
Borneo	291,420	754,744
Madagascar	226,658	587,042
Sumatra	208,948	541,174
Baffin	195,927	507,449
Great Britain	88,797	229,984
Honshu	87,805	227,414
Victoria	83,896	217,290
Ellesmere	75,767	196,236

Largest natural lakes

Name	Location	Area Square miles	Area Square kilometers	Maximum depth Feet	Maximum depth Meters
Caspian Sea*	Asia, Europe	143,630	372,000	3,264	995
Lake Superior	North America	31,700	82,103	1,333	406
Lake Victoria	Africa	26,828	69,484	270	82
Aral Sea*	Asia	25,660	66,459	223	68
Lake Huron	North America	23,050	59,699	750	229
Lake Michigan	North America	22,300	57,757	923	281
Lake Tanganyika	Africa	12,700	32,893	4,708	1,435
Great Bear Lake	North America	12,275	31,792	1,350	411
Lake Baikal	Asia	12,162	31,499	5,315	1,620
Lake Nyasa	Africa	11,100	28,749	2,300	701

*Saltwater.

Famous waterfalls

Name	Location	Height Feet	Height Meters
Angel*	Venezuela	2,648	807
Cuquenán	Venezuela	2,000	610
Gavarnie	France	1,385	422
Giessbach	Switzerland	1,982	604
King George VI	Guyana	1,600	488
Niagara	New York	182	55
	Ontario	173	53
Ribbon	California	1,612	491
Silver Strand	California	1,170	357
Sutherland†	New Zealand	815	248
Takakkaw	British Columbia	1,200	366
Victoria	Zambia-Zimbabwe border	355	108
Yosemite Upper Falls	California	1,430	436

*Highest in a series of falls with a total height of 3,212 feet (979 meters).
†Highest in a series of falls with a total height of 1,904 feet (580 meters).

Longest rivers

Name	Location	Length Miles	Length Kilometers
Nile	Africa	4,145	6,671
Amazon	South America	4,000	6,437
Yangtze	Asia	3,915	6,300
Huang Ho	Asia	2,903	4,672
Congo	Africa	2,900	4,667
Amur	Asia	2,744	4,416
Lena	Asia	2,734	4,400
Irtysh	Asia	2,640	4,248
Mackenzie	North America	2,635	4,241
Mekong	Asia	2,600	4,184
Niger	Africa	2,590	4,168
Yenisey	Asia	2,543	4,093
Paraná	South America	2,485	3,999
Mississippi	North America	2,348	3,779
Missouri	North America	2,315	3,726
Murray-Darling	Australia	2,310	3,718

Major mountain ranges

Name	Location
Alaska Range	North America
Alps	Europe
Andes Mountains	South America
Appalachian Mountains	North America
Atlas Mountains	Africa
Himalaya	Asia
Rocky Mountains	North America
Ural Mountains	Asia, Europe

Famous volcanoes

Name	Location	Height Feet	Meters
Cotopaxi	Ecuador	19,347	5,897
El Chichón	Mexico	3,478	1,060
Erebus	Antarctica	12,448	3,794
Krakatoa	Indonesia	2,667	813
Lassen Peak	California	10,457	3,187
Maipu, or Maipo	Chile-Argentina border	17,464	5,323
Mauna Loa	Hawaii	13,677	4,169
Mont Pelée	Martinique	4,583	1,397
Mount Etna	Sicily	11,122	3,390
Mount St. Helen's	Washington	8,364	2,549
Mount Tambora	Indonesia	9,350	2,850
Paricutín	Mexico	9,213	2,808
Stromboli	Mediterranean Sea	3,031	924
Tolima	Colombia	17,110	5,215
Vesuvius	Italy	4,190	1,277

Editor's note: See "Disasters" section for a table that includes famous volcanic eruptions.

Famous mountains

Asia has more than 60 mountain peaks over 23,000 feet (7,015 meters) high. Many are in the Himalaya Range. This table lists notable peaks in various parts of the world. Famous active volcanoes appear in a separate table.

Name	Range and location	Height Feet	Meters
Aconcagua	Andes in Argentina	22,831	6,959
Ararat	Armenian Plateau in Turkey	17,011	5,185
Chimborazo	Andes in Ecuador	20,561	6,267
Communism Peak	Pamir-Alai in Russia	24,590	7,495
Elbert	Rocky Mountains in Colorado	14,433	4,399
Elbrus, or Elbruz	Caucasus in Russia	18,481	5,633
Everest	Himalaya on Nepal-Tibet border	29,028	8,848
Fuji	On volcanic island in Japan	12,388	3,776
Godwin Austen, or K2, or Dapsang	Karakoram in Kashmir	28,250	8,611
Hood	Cascade in Oregon	11,235	3,427
Kanchenjunga, or Kinchinjunga	Himalaya on Nepal-India border	28,208	8,598
Kenya	Isolated peak in Kenya	17,058	5,199
Kilimanjaro	Isolated peak in Tanzania	19,340	5,895
Logan	St. Elias in Canada	19,520	5,950
Longs Peak	Rocky Mountains in Colorado	14,255	4,345
Makalu	Himalaya on Nepal-Tibet border	27,824	8,481
Matterhorn	Pennine Alps on Switzerland-Italy border	14,692	4,478
McKinley	Alaska Range in Alaska	20,320	6,194
Mitchell	Appalachians in North Carolina	6,684	2,037
Mont Blanc	Pennine Alps in France	15,771	4,807
Orizaba	Mexican Plateau in Mexico	18,701	5,700
Pikes Peak	Rocky Mountains in Colorado	14,110	4,301
Rainier	Cascade in Washington	14,410	4,392
Shasta	Cascade in California	14,162	4,317
Whitney	Sierra Nevada in California	14,494	4,418

Oceans, seas, bays, and gulfs

This table lists the earth's oceans and, in parentheses, some of the smaller bodies of water—seas, bays, and gulfs—that are parts of the oceans or are linked to them.

Name	Approximate area		Maximum depth	
	Square miles	Square kilometers	Feet	Meters
Atlantic Ocean				
(Baffin Bay, Baltic Sea, Caribbean Sea, Gulf of Mexico, Gulf of Saint Lawrence, Hudson Bay, Labrador Sea, Mediterranean Sea, North Sea)	31,530,000	81,662,000	28,374	8,648
Arctic Ocean				
(Barents Sea, Beaufort Sea, Chuckchi Sea, East Siberian Sea, Greenland Sea, Kara Sea, Laptev Sea)	3,662,000	9,485,100	17,880	5,450
Indian Ocean				
(Arabian Sea, Bay of Bengal, Great Australian Bight, Mozambique Channel, Persian Gulf, Red Sea)	28,356,000	73,441,700	25,344	7,725
Pacific Ocean				
(Bering Sea, Coral Sea, East China Sea, Gulf of Alaska, Philippine Sea, Sea of Japan, Sea of Okhotsk, South China Sea, Tasman Sea, Yellow Sea)	63,800,000	165,200,000	36,198	11,033

Editor's note: Some geographers identify a fifth ocean—the Antarctic Ocean. But many others say the waters surrounding Antarctica are the southern parts of the Atlantic, Pacific, and Indian oceans. Similarly, some geographers say the Arctic Ocean is really a sea of the Atlantic, rather than a separate ocean.

Natural resources

The earth's natural resources include water and land, plant and animal life, coal, oil, and various minerals. Air, sunshine, and climate are also natural resources. All natural resources are not evenly distributed over the earth, and they vary in quality from place to place. For example, only about a third of the earth's land can be used for farming and raising livestock. Much of the rest is either too dry, too cold, or too mountainous. See the *Biomes* map and table on page 89 to locate regions in terms of their climate and plant and animal life.

Deposits of coal and oil, two of the earth's most important energy resources, occur on every continent. But the United States alone has about a third of the world's coal deposits, and more than half the world's oil lies in the Middle East. The earth has more than 2,000 different kinds of minerals. However, only about 100 are common. Graphite, gypsum, salt, and talc are some of the earth's most common minerals. Scarce minerals include diamonds, gold, and platinum. Other important minerals include aluminum, copper, iron, lead, magnesium, nickel, silver, tin, uranium, and zinc.

Air

The *atmosphere* (air) that surrounds the earth consists of nitrogen, oxygen, and other gases. Water vapor and tiny particles of solid materials such as dust float in the air. Scientists divide the atmosphere into four layers. The chart below describes the layers, their depths, and temperatures, beginning with the outermost layer from the earth's surface.

Thermosphere

300 miles (480 kilometers)

+2700° F. (+1500°C)

More than 99 per cent of all air is below the thermosphere. The sun heats the very thin air in this layer to high temperatures. Atomic particles from the sun cause the *aurora borealis* (northern lights) to occur in the thermosphere.

The upper part of the thermosphere is the *exosphere*. Satellites or spacecraft orbiting the earth find little resistance here. The *ionosphere,* centered in the lower thermosphere, has air particles that are electrically charged by radiation from the sun and outer space. Radio waves of certain frequencies bounce off the ionosphere and can be received thousands of miles or kilometers from their source.

Mesosphere

50 miles (80 kilometers)

−135° F. (−93°C)

The top of the mesosphere has the lowest temperatures in the atmosphere. Trails left by meteors appear in the upper mesosphere.

Stratosphere

30 miles (48 kilometers)

+28° F. (−3°C)

The stratosphere has a lower layer of nearly constant temperature and an upper layer in which the temperature increases with increasing altitude. The upper layer is warmed by the sun's rays striking a chemical compound called *ozone*. Jet planes fly in the stratosphere.

Troposphere

10 miles (16 kilometers)

−67° F. (−56°C)

The troposphere is the layer of atmosphere closest to earth. Here the temperature drops rapidly as the altitude increases. This layer has most of the air, moisture, and dust of the atmosphere. The most rapid changes in temperature take place in the troposphere, and it is where most clouds and weather occur.

Earth's surface

Outline of earth history

This geological time chart outlines the development of the earth and of life on the earth. The earth's earliest history appears at the bottom of the chart, and its most recent history is at the top. For more information about the origins and development of human life on earth, see the section "Human Being."

Period or Epoch and Its Length			Beginning (Years Ago)	Development of Life on Earth	
CENOZOIC ERA	Quaternary Period	HOLOCENE EPOCH 10-25 Thousand Years	10 Thousand	Human beings hunted and tamed animals; developed agriculture; learned to use metals, coal, oil, gas, and other resources; and put the power of wind and rivers to work.	Cultivated Plants
CENOZOIC ERA	Quaternary Period	PLEISTOCENE EPOCH 1¾ Million Years	1¾ Million	Modern human beings developed from a primitive form of human being. Mammoths, woolly rhinos, and other animals flourished but died out near the end of the epoch.	Human Beings
CENOZOIC ERA	Tertiary Period	PLIOCENE EPOCH 12¼ Million Years	14 Million	Sea life became much like today's. Birds and many mammals became like modern kinds and spread around the world. Human beings appeared near the end of the epoch.	Horses
CENOZOIC ERA	Tertiary Period	MIOCENE EPOCH 12 Million Years	26 Million	Apes appeared in Asia and Africa. Other animals included bats, monkeys, and whales, and primitive bears and raccoons. Flowering plants and trees resembled modern kinds.	Apes
CENOZOIC ERA	Tertiary Period	OLIGOCENE EPOCH 14 Million Years	40 Million	Primitive apes appeared. Camels, cats, dogs, elephants, horses, rhinos, and rodents developed. Huge rhinoceroslike animals disappeared near the end of the epoch.	Early Horses
CENOZOIC ERA	Tertiary Period	EOCENE EPOCH 15 Million Years	55 Million	Fruits, grains, and grasses developed. Birds, amphibians, small reptiles, and fish were plentiful. Primitive bats, camels, cats, horses, monkeys, rhinoceroses, and whales appeared.	Grasses
CENOZOIC ERA	Tertiary Period	PALEOCENE EPOCH 10 Million Years	65 Million	Flowering plants became plentiful. Invertebrates, fish, amphibians, reptiles, and small mammals were common.	Small Mammals
MESOZOIC ERA		CRETACEOUS PERIOD 65 Million Years	130 Million	Flowering plants appeared. Invertebrates, fish, and amphibians were plentiful. Dinosaurs with horns and armor became common. Dinosaurs died out at the end of the period.	Flowering Plants
MESOZOIC ERA		JURASSIC PERIOD 50 Million Years	180 Million	Cone-bearing trees were plentiful. Sea life included primitive squids. Dinosaurs reached their largest size. The first birds appeared. A few small, primitive mammals lived on land.	Birds
MESOZOIC ERA		TRIASSIC PERIOD 45 Million Years	225 Million	Cone-bearing trees were plentiful. Many fish resembled modern kinds. Insects were plentiful. The first turtles, crocodiles, and dinosaurs appeared, as did the first mammals.	Dinosaurs
PALEOZOIC ERA		PERMIAN PERIOD 50 Million Years	275 Million	Algae were plentiful. The first seed plants—cone-bearing trees—appeared. Fish, amphibians, and reptiles were plentiful. Trilobites and eurypterids died out near the end of the period.	Seed Plants
PALEOZOIC ERA	Carboniferous Period	PENNSYLVANIAN PERIOD 35 Million Years	310 Million	Algae were plentiful. Fern trees grew from seedlike bodies. Fish and amphibians were plentiful. The first reptiles appeared. Giant insects lived in forests where coal later formed.	Reptiles
PALEOZOIC ERA	Carboniferous Period	MISSISSIPPIAN PERIOD 35 Million Years	345 Million	Algae were plentiful and the first mosses appeared. Trilobites were dying out. Shelled animals, fish, and amphibians were plentiful. Many coral reefs were formed.	Amphibians
PALEOZOIC ERA		DEVONIAN PERIOD 60 Million Years	405 Million	The first forests grew in swamps. Many kinds of fish, including sharks, armored fish, and lungfish, swam in the sea and in fresh waters. The first amphibians and insects appeared.	Fish
PALEOZOIC ERA		SILURIAN PERIOD 30 Million Years	435 Million	Algae were plentiful and spore-bearing land plants appeared. Trilobites, fish, and mollusks were common. Coral reefs formed, and air-breathing animals called eurypterids appeared.	Eurypterids
PALEOZOIC ERA		ORDOVICIAN PERIOD 45 Million Years	480 Million	Algae became plentiful. Trilobites, corals, and shelled animals were common. Tiny animals called graptolites grouped together and formed branching colonies. Jawless fish appeared.	Mollusks
PALEOZOIC ERA		CAMBRIAN PERIOD 120 Million Years (?)	600 Million (?)	Plentiful fossils appeared for the first time. Insectlike animals called trilobites, and some shelled animals were common in the sea. Fossil teeth give evidence of the first fish.	Trilobites
PRECAMBRIAN TIME Almost 4 Billion Years (?)			4½ Billion (?)	Corals, jellyfish, sponges, and worms lived in the sea about 1,100 million years ago. Bacteria lived as long ago as 3½ billion years. Before that, no living things are known.	Bacteria

Development of the Earth	Mountain Building North America Europe and Asia	Development of North America
Streams, glaciers, and oceans eroded the land. Present river deltas and coastlines were formed. Ice Age glaciers melted and water collected, forming the Great Lakes in North America.		These maps compare North America's present shape with its shape (white) during four periods. Brown represents oceans.
Several times during the Ice Age, glaciers covered large areas of North America and Europe. The climate was cool. Mountains rose in western North America, and volcanoes erupted.	Cascade Mountains	
The Oligocene, Miocene, and Pliocene epochs were much alike. Rocks that formed during these epochs included clays, limestones, and sands. The climate was uniform and mild through the Oligocene and Miocene, but began to get cooler during the Pliocene, leading up to the following Ice Age. Mountain making was common, and many volcanoes erupted. Oil and natural gas formed in rocks made during these epochs.	Alps and Himalaya	 Miocene Epoch
Seas flooded the shores of the continents. Large areas were covered by swamps where lignite, a kind of coal, later formed. Oil and gas also formed in clays, limestones, and sands.		
Thick soil formed in hot, rainy lands. Mountains, not yet worn by erosion, were high. The climate was varied. Coal, gas, and oil formed in clays, limestones, and sands.	Rocky Mountains	
Oceans flooded large areas. Coal swamps developed. Rocks included chalk, limestones, sandstones, and shales. Coal, gas, oil, and ores of gold, silver, and other metals were formed.		
Shallow seaways cut across the continents. Some volcanic action occurred. Rocks included limestones, sandstones, and shales. Gas, oil, salt, and ores of gold and uranium formed.	Sierra Nevada, California Coast Ranges	
Layers called red beds developed along with shales, sandstones, and limestones. Gas, oil, and ores of copper and uranium formed. Faults (cracks) occurred in eastern North America.	Palisades Caucasus Mountains	Late Triassic Period
Glaciers in the southern hemisphere melted and left sedimentary layers. Rocks in the northern hemisphere included limestones, sandstones, and shales. Gas, oil, gypsum, and salt formed.	Ural Mountains	
Swamps covered the lowlands. Oil, gas, and large amounts of coal formed among limestones, sandstones, and shales. River deltas partially filled the Appalachian seaway.	Appalachian Mountains	
Large amounts of limestone formed among layers of shale and sandstone in deltas in the Appalachian and Cordilleran seaways. Coal, gas, oil, and deposits of lead and zinc formed.	Variscan Mountains	
Red sandstones, shales, and limestones formed in Europe, and black shales, reef limestones, and sandstones formed in North America. Gas, oil, and quartz sand formed.	Acadian Mountains Caledonian Mountains	Early Devonian Period
Limestones, coral reefs, sandstones, and shales formed, with the deepest deposits in the Appalachian and Cordilleran seaways. Gas, oil, gypsum, iron ore, and salt formed.		
Greatest floods of the era covered two-thirds of North America. A delta formed in the Appalachian seaway. Gas, oil, lead, and zinc formed in limestones, sandstones, and shales.	Taconian Mountains	
Seas spread across North America from the Appalachian seaway in the east and the Cordilleran seaway in the west. Lead and zinc formed in sandstones, shales, and limestones.	Vermont Mountains	
Copper, gold, iron, nickel, and silver formed in shales, siltstones, lava, volcanic ash, and metamorphic rocks. The earth's crust melted and cooled repeatedly during this time.	Killarneyan Mountains Algoman Mountains Laurentian Mountains	 Early Cambrian Period

Data for maps from *Historical Geology*, Second Edition by Carl O. Dunbar, Copyright ©1960 by John Wiley & Sons, Inc. Reprinted by permission of John Wiley & Sons, Inc.

Wind

Wind results from the uneven heating of the atmosphere by the sun. Warm air expands and rises and is replaced by cooler air in a process called *circulation.* Two kinds of circulation produce wind. *General circulation* extends around the earth and produces *prevailing winds. Secondary circulation* occurs around smaller areas. General circulation is caused by warm air rising up and then returning and flowing across the earth's surface. This moving surface air produces the six belts of prevailing winds around the earth. The turning of the earth causes the prevailing winds to blow toward the east in belts where the air moves away from the equator. In belts where the air moves toward the equator, the prevailing winds blow toward the west. The *doldrums* is a belt of calm air that extends about 700 miles (1,100 kilometers) on either side of the equator. Here, air is rising, instead of moving across the earth. Similarly, the *horse latitudes* are calm areas where air is moving downward, producing no wind.

Seasons

The earth's motion around the sun determines the astronomical seasons. (See the drawing, "Three Motions of the Earth," on page 80.) In the Northern Hemisphere, summer begins when the *summer solstice* occurs, on June 20 or 21. The summer solstice marks the time when the sun is at its northernmost position in the sky. The *winter solstice,* when the sun is at its southernmost position, occurs on December 21 or 22. The *equinoxes* are the two days of the year when the sun is directly above the earth's equator. The *vernal equinox,* on March 20 or 21, marks the start of spring in the Northern Hemisphere. The *autumnal equinox,* on September 22 or 23, is the beginning of autumn. The seasons are reversed in the Southern Hemisphere.

First day of the astronomical seasons in the northern hemisphere*

Year	Spring	Summer	Autumn	Winter	Year	Spring	Summer	Autumn	Winter
1981	March 20	June 21	Sept. 22	Dec. 21	1986	March 20	June 21	Sept. 23	Dec. 21
1982	March 20	June 21	Sept. 23	Dec. 21	1987	March 20	June 21	Sept. 23	Dec. 21
1983	March 20	June 21	Sept. 23	Dec. 22	1988	March 20	June 20	Sept. 22	Dec. 21
1984	March 20	June 20	Sept. 22	Dec. 21	1989	March 20	June 21	Sept. 22	Dec. 21
1985	March 20	June 21	Sept. 22	Dec. 21	1990	March 20	June 21	Sept. 23	Dec. 21

*Central Standard Time

Major land biomes

A biome is a community of animals and plants that live in a large geographical area with a similar climate.

Biome	Climate	Dominant plants*	Examples of common animals*
Tundra	Extremely cold, dry; permanently frozen subsoil	Lichens, low shrubs, sedges	Arctic foxes, lemmings, polar bears, caribou, wolves, many migratory birds

88

Biome	Climate	Dominant plants*	Examples of common animals*
Boreal forest (taiga)	Cold winters, short growing season	Coniferous evergreen trees, chiefly balsam fir, black spruce, jack pine, and white spruce	Bears, moose, wolves, ducks, loons
Temperate coniferous forest	Cool, moist middle and upper mountain slopes; coastal areas with mild winters and heavy rainfall	Coniferous evergreen trees, including cedar, hemlock, pine, and redwood	Bears, elk, mountain lions, wolves
Temperate deciduous forest	Cold winters, warm summers, moist	Broadleaf deciduous trees, such as elm, maple, and oak	Deer, raccoons, squirrels, many kinds of small birds
Chaparral	Rainy, mild winter, hot, dry summer; fires common	Low shrubs with small, hard leaves, such as scrub oak and manzanita	Coyotes, mule deer, many species of lizards
Desert	Extremely dry	Cacti and other fleshy plants, sparse grasses, small-leaved shrubs	Lizards, snakes, many small rodents, such as kangaroo rats and wood rats
Treeless grassland	Temperate, subhumid	Grasses and many herbaceous plants	Antelope, buffaloes, wolves, coyotes
Savanna and woodland	Long dry season	Grasses and scattered clumps of trees, such as acacia and baobab trees†	Giraffes, zebras, jackals, lions†
Tropical rain forest	Warm and wet all year	Broadleaf evergreen trees, some palms and tree ferns, climbing vines	Bats, colorful birds, lizards, monkeys, snakes

*Species representative of North American biomes, except for savanna and tropical rain forest.
†Species representative of African tropical savanna.

Biomes of the world

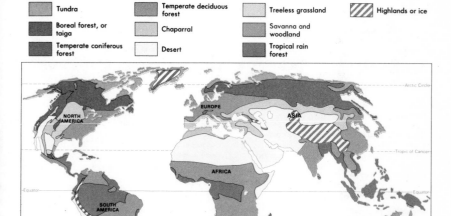

WORLD BOOK map; adapted from *Physical Elements of Geography* by Trewartha, Robinson, and Hammond.
Copyright © 1967 by McGraw-Hill, Inc. Used with permission of McGraw-Hill Book Company.

Explorations

The tables in this section list famous explorers of earth and space from ancient times to the present. For more detailed information about space explorations, see the various tables and other information in the "Space" section of this book.

Explorers

Explorer	Nationality	Main Achievements	Date

Famous ancient and medieval explorers

Explorer	Nationality	Main Achievements	Date
Alexander the Great*	Macedonian	Reached Afghanistan, western India.	c.331 B.C.–326 B.C.
Chang Ch'ien	Chinese	Traveled from China to central Asia.	128–126 B.C.
Eric the Red	Norwegian	Sailed to Greenland from Iceland.	c.982
Ericson, Leif*	Norwegian	Probably the first European to reach mainland North America.	c.1000
Ibn Batuta	Arabian	Traveled through the Middle East and India; visited China and the East Indies.	1325–1354
Polo, Marco*	Italian	Visited Sri Lanka, China, India, Iran, and Sumatra.	1271–1295
Pytheas	Greek	Sailed from the Mediterranean Sea to the North Atlantic Ocean.	c.300 B.C.
Odoric of Pordenone	Italian	Traveled in Turkey, Iran, across central Asia, and in the Indian and South Pacific oceans.	c.1314–c.1330
Rubruck, William of	Flemish	Traveled through central Asia to Mongolia.	1253–1255

Explorers of the great age of European discovery

Explorer	Nationality	Main Achievements	Date
Balboa, Vasco Núñez de*	Spanish	Led expedition across Isthmus of Panama; sighted Pacific Ocean	1513
Cabeza de Vaca, Álvar Núñez	Spanish	Explored Gulf Plains from Texas to Mexico.	1528–1536
Cabot, John*	Italian	Sailed across the North Atlantic to what is now Canada.	1497–1498
Cabot, Sebastian	Italian	Explored South American coast to the Río de la Plata.	1526–1530
Cabral, Pedro Álvares	Portuguese	Reached Brazilian coast; sailed around Africa to India.	1500–1501
Cartier, Jacques*	French	Sailed up the St. Lawrence River.	1535
Columbus, Christopher*	Italian	Made four voyages to the West Indies and Caribbean lands.	1492–1504
Coronado, Francisco de*	Spanish	Explored the American Southwest.	1540–1542
Cortés, Hernando*	Spanish	Conquered Mexico.	1519–1521
Da Gama, Vasco*	Portuguese	First European to reach India by sea.	1498
De Soto, Hernando*	Spanish	Explored American Southeast; reached Mississippi River.	1539–1542
Dias, Bartolomeu*	Portuguese	First European to round the Cape of Good Hope.	1487–1488
Drake, Sir Francis*	English	First English explorer to sail around the world.	1577–1580
Frobisher, Sir Martin*	English	Searched North American coast for a Northwest Passage.	1576–1578
Magellan, Ferdinand*	Portuguese	Commanded first globe-circling voyage, completed in 1522 after his death.	1519–1521
Oñate, Juan de	Spanish	Explored American Southwest.	1598–1605

*See "People" section for biographical information.

Explorer	Nationality	Main Achievements	Date
Orellana, Francisco de	Spanish	Explored Amazon River.	1541
Pizarro, Francisco*	Spanish	Conquered Peru; founded Lima.	1531–1535
Ponce de León, Juan*	Spanish	Explored Florida.	1513
Verrazano, Giovanni da	Italian	Searched for a Northwest Passage.	1524
Vespucci, Amerigo*	Italian	Sailed to the West Indies and South America.	1499–1504

Famous explorers of North America

Bridger, James	American	Probably the first white person to reach Great Salt Lake.	1824–1825
Champlain, Samuel de*	French	Explored eastern coast of North America, and St. Lawrence River west to Lake Huron; reached Lake Champlain.	1603–1616
Clark, William	American	Led an expedition across the Rocky Mountains to the Pacific Ocean with Meriwether Lewis.	1804–1806
Duluth, Sieur	French	Explored Lake Superior region.	1678–1687
Frémont, John Charles*	American	Explored the American West.	1842–1846
Hennepin, Louis	Belgian	Explored upper Mississippi River region.	1679–1680
Hudson, Henry*	English	Explored Hudson Bay, Hudson River, and Hudson Strait.	1609–1611
Jolliet, Louis	French-Canadian	Explored northern Mississippi River region with Jacques Marquette.	1673
La Salle, Sieur de*	French	Traveled down the Mississippi River with Henri de Tonti.	1679–1682
La Vérendrye, Sieur de	French-Canadian	Explored western Canada.	1731–1743
Lewis, Meriwether*	American	Led an expedition across the Rocky Mountains to the Pacific Ocean with William Clark.	1804–1806
Mackenzie, Sir Alexander	Canadian	Explored western Canada; followed the Mackenzie River to the Arctic Ocean.	1789–1793
Marquette, Jacques*	French	Explored northern Mississippi River region with Louis Jolliet.	1673
Pike, Zebulon	American	Explored Middle West and Rocky Mountain region.	1805–1807
Radisson, Pierre Esprit	French	Explored Lake Superior and northern Mississippi River regions.	1659–1661
Smith, Jedediah Strong	American	Explored Great Basin region; blazed trails across the Rocky Mountains to California and the Pacific Northwest.	1824–1829
Thompson, David	Canadian	Explored western Canada.	1789–1812
Tonti, Henri de	French	Traveled down the Mississippi River with Sieur de la Salle.	1679–1682

Famous explorers of Africa

Bruce, James	Scottish	Rediscovered source of the Blue Nile.	1770
Burton, Sir Richard	English	Explored Arabia and East Africa; reached Lake Tanganyika.	1853–1858
Caillié, René	French	Explored western Africa; crossed the Sahara.	1826–1828
Clapperton, Hugh	Scottish	Explored northern Nigeria and Lake Chad region.	1822–1827
Emin Pasha	German	Explored east-central Africa.	1878–1892
Laing, Alexander Gordon	Scottish	Explored Niger River Basin; reached Timbuktu.	1822; 1826

*See "People" section for biographical information.

Explorer	Nationality	Main Achievements	Date
Livingstone, David*	Scottish	Traced upper course of the Zambezi River; reached Victoria Falls and Lake Ngami.	1849–1873
Park, Mungo	Scottish	Explored course of the Niger River.	1795–1797; 1805–1806
Speke, John Hanning	English	Reached Lake Tanganyika and Lake Victoria.	1858
Stanley, Sir Henry	Welsh	Explored the Congo River.	1874–1889

Explorers of Australia and the Pacific Ocean

Bougainville, Louis Antoine de	French	Led first French expedition around the world.	1766–1769
Burke, Robert O'Hara	Irish	One of the first explorers to cross Australia from south to north, with William John Wills.	1860–1861
Cook, James*	English	Explored South Pacific.	1768–1779
Dampier, William	English	Explored coasts of Australia, New Guinea, and New Britain.	1691–1701
Eyre, Edward John	English	Explored southern coast of Australia.	1840–1841
Jansz, Willem	Dutch	First known European to sight and land in Australia.	1606
Stuart, John McDouall	Scottish	Made six trips into the interior of Australia.	1858–1862
Sturt, Charles	English	Explored southeastern Australia; reached Darling River.	1829–1830
Tasman, Abel Janszoon	Dutch	Sailed to Tasmania and New Zealand.	1642
Warburton, Peter Egerton	English	Crossed Australia from Alice Springs to Roebourne.	1873
Wills, William John	English	One of the first explorers to cross Australia from south to north, with Robert O'Hara Burke.	1860–1861

Famous polar explorers

Amundsen, Roald*	Norwegian	First explorer to reach South Pole overland; flew over North Pole.	1911–1926
Baffin, William	English	Reached Baffin Bay.	1616
Bartlett, Robert A.	Canadian-American	Explored Alaska, Greenland, Labrador, and Siberia.	1897–1941
Bellingshausen, Fabian von	Russian	Sailed around Antarctica.	1819–1821
Bering, Vitus	Danish	Proved that Asia and North America are separated by water.	1727–1729
Bransfield, Edward	English	Explored northern coast of Antarctic Peninsula.	1820
Byrd, Richard Evelyn*	American	Flew over North Pole; flew over South Pole.	1926; 1929
Franklin, Sir John	English	Led three expeditions to the Arctic.	1819; 1825; 1845
Fuchs, Sir Vivian	English	Led first expedition across Antarctica.	1957–1958
Henson, Matthew A.	American	Member of first expedition to reach the North Pole.	1909
Hillary, Sir Edmund*	New Zealander	Scouted route from McMurdo Sound to South Pole for Sir Vivian Fuchs' transatlantic expedition.	1957–1958
McClure, Sir Robert	English	Sailed through most of the Northwest Passage.	1850–1854
Nansen, Fridtjof	Norwegian	First to cross the icefields of Greenland; attempted to reach the North Pole.	1888; 1893–1895

*See "People" section for biographical information.

Explorer	Nationality	Main Achievements	Date
Nobile, Umberto	Italian	Flew over North Pole in an airship.	1926
Nordenskjöld, Nils A. E.	Swedish	First to sail Northeast Passage to Asia.	1878–1879
Parry, Sir William E.	English	Attempted to reach North Pole.	1827
Peary, Robert Edwin*	American	Led first expedition to reach North Pole.	1909
Ross, Sir James Clark	British	Located the north magnetic pole; explored Antarctica.	1831; 1839–1843
Scott, Robert Falcon	British	Reached South Pole.	1912
Shackleton, Sir Ernest H.	Irish	Explored Antarctica.	1907–1916
Stefansson, Vilhjalmur	American	Explored many parts of the Arctic.	1906–1918
Wilkes, Charles	American	Explored the coast of Antarctica.	1840

Famous undersea explorers

Anderson, William R.	American	Commanded U.S. Navy submarine *Nautilus* during voyage under Arctic waters to the North Pole.	1958
Beebe, William*	American	Descended one-half mile (0.8 kilometer) into the ocean in a bathysphere.	1934
Cousteau, Jacques-Yves	French	Explored the world's oceans with his research ship *Calypso*.	1951–1970's
Piccard, Jacques*	Swiss	Descended into the Mariana Trench, the lowest known place in the world, with Don Walsh of the U.S. Navy.	1960
Walsh, Don	American	Descended into the Mariana Trench with Jacques Piccard.	1960

Famous space explorers

Aldrin, Edwin E., Jr.	American	Landed on the moon with Neil A. Armstrong.	1969
Anders, William A.	American	Orbited the moon with James A. Lovell, Jr., and Frank Borman.	1968
Armstrong, Neil A.*	American	First person to set foot on the moon.	1969
Borman, Frank	American	Commanded the first space flight to orbit the moon.	1968
Crippen, Robert L.	American	Piloted the first space shuttle flight with John W. Young.	1981
Gagarin, Yuri A.*	Russian	First person to travel in space.	1961
Leonov, Alexei A.	Russian	First person to leave a spacecraft and float freely in space.	1965
Lovell, James A., Jr.	American	Orbited the moon.	1968
Tereshkova, Valentina V.*	Russian	First woman to travel in space.	1963
Young, John W.	American	Commanded the first space shuttle flight.	1981

*See "People" section for biographical information.

Flags

This section presents information about flags in general, and the flags of the United States and Canada in particular. See pages 178–192 for color illustrations of the flags of the nations of the world, of the states and territories of the United States, of the Canadian provinces and territories, and of historical American flags.

Flag terms

Badge is an emblem or design, usually on the fly.

Battle flag is carried by armed forces on land.

Battle streamer, attached to the flag of a military unit, names battles or campaigns where the unit served with distinction.

Bend on means to attach signal flags to a halyard.

Breadth, a measurement for flags, is 9 inches (23 centimeters) wide. A four-breadth flag is 36 inches (91 centimeters) wide. The term originated when flag cloth was made in 9-inch (23-centimeter) strips.

Bunting is cloth decorated with stripes of the national colors. The term is also used for the woolen cloth used in making flags.

Burgee is a flag or pennant that ends in a swallow-tail of two points.

Canton is the upper corner of a flag next to the staff where a special design, such as a union, appears.

Color is a special flag carried by a military unit or officer. In the armed forces of many countries, regiments and larger units often carry two colors—the national flag and a unit flag.

Courtesy flag is the national flag of the country a merchant ship visits, hoisted as the ship enters port.

Device is an emblem or design, usually on the fly.

Ensign is a national flag flown by a naval ship. Some countries also have ensigns for other armed services.

Ensign staff is the staff at the stern of a ship.

Field is the background color of a flag.

Fimbriation is a narrow line separating two other colors in a flag.

Flag hoist is a group of signal flags attached to the same halyard and hoisted as a unit.

Fly is the free end of a flag, farthest from the staff. The term is also used for the horizontal length of the flag.

Garrison flag, in the U.S. Army, flies over military posts on holidays and special days. It is 20 feet (6 meters) wide by 38 feet (12 meters) long, twice as wide and long as a post flag.

Ground is the background color of a flag.

Guidon is a small flag carried at the front or right of a military unit to guide the marchers.

Halyard is a rope used to hoist and lower a flag.

Hoist is the part of the flag closest to the staff. The term is also used for the vertical width of a flag.

House flag is flown by a merchant ship to identify the company that owns it.

Jack is a small flag flown at the bow of a ship.

Jackstaff is the staff at the bow of a ship.

Merchant flag is a flag flown by a merchant ship.

National flag is the flag of a country.

Pennant is a triangular or tapering flag.

Pilot flag is flown from a ship that wants the aid of a pilot when entering port.

Post flag, in the U.S. Army, flies regularly over every army base. It is 10 feet (3 meters) wide by 19 feet (5.8 meters) long.

Reeve means to pull the halyard through the truck, raising or lowering a flag.

Staff is the pole a flag hangs on.

Standard is a flag around which people rally. Today, the term usually refers to the personal flag of a ruler, such as Great Britain's *Royal Standard.*

State flag is the flag flown by the government of a country. Many state flags are the same as national flags but with the country's coat of arms added.

Storm flag, in the U.S. Army, flies over an army base in stormy weather. It is 5 feet (1.5 meters) wide by 9 feet 6 inches (2.9 meters) long, half as wide and half as long as a post flag.

Truck is the wooden or metal block at the top of a flagpole below the *finial* (staff ornament). It includes a pulley or holes for the halyards.

Union is a design that symbolizes unity. It may appear in the canton, as the stars do in the U.S. flag. Or it may be the entire flag, as in the *Union Flag* of Great Britain.

Vexillology is the study of flag history and symbolism. The name comes from the Latin word *vexillum,* which means flag.

Rules for displaying and honoring the flag

The following rules apply to the U.S. flag in particular but may be observed for any national flag.

Salute the flag at the moment it passes in a parade or when it is raised or lowered as part of a ceremony. A person in military uniform should give a hand salute. Persons not in uniform should place their right hand over their heart. A man removes his hat before saluting; a woman does not.

In a parade, carry the national flag on the marching right. If there are many other flags, the colorbearer with the national flag marches alone in front of the center of the line.

As a colorbearer, hold the staff at a slight angle away from your body; or carry it with one hand, resting the staff on your right shoulder.

On a float, hang a national flag from a staff with its folds falling free, or hang it flat.

On a car, tie the flag to the antenna or to a staff that is fixed firmly to the right fender.

From a building, hang the flag on a staff or on a rope over the sidewalk, with its canton away from the building.

In a window, hang the flag vertically with its canton to the left of a person who is seeing it from outside the building.

Over the street, hang the flag with its canton to the east on a north-south street or to the north on an east-west street.

Behind a speaker, hang the flag flat against the wall. The U.S. flag may not be used to decorate the speaker's platform. Use bunting instead. The Canadian flag may be gathered up like bunting in a display.

Beside a speaker, put the flag on the person's right. Any other flag on display should be put at the speaker's left.

In a corridor or lobby, hang the flag vertically opposite the main entrance with its canton to the left of a person coming in the door.

With other flags on the same halyard, hang the national flag above the others. Never hang one national flag above another national flag in time of peace.

National flags flying together should be hung on staffs of equal length. Hang the national flag of the host country on its own right, hoisting it first and lowering it last.

In a group of flags with clustered staffs, place the national flag at the center and highest point.

In a pair of flags with crossed staffs, put the national flag on its own right, with its staff on top.

On a casket, drape the flag with its canton at the head and over the left shoulder of the body. Do not lower the flag into the grave.

At half-mast, the flag is a symbol of mourning. Hoist the flag to the peak before you lower it to half-mast. Raise it to the peak again before lowering it at the end of the day.

Hung upside down, the flag is a recognized distress signal. Never hang the flag upside down unless you mean it as a signal of a serious emergency.

The United States flag

On June 14, 1777, the Continental Congress resolved that "the Flag of the united states be 13 stripes alternate red and white, and the Union be 13 stars white in a blue field representing a new constellation." The stripes stand for the 13 original colonies. Congress did not indicate how the stars should be arranged, and various designs were used. By 1794, two new states had joined the Union, and Congress decided to add two stars and two stripes to the flag. Five more states had joined the Union by 1817, but Congress did not want a flag with 20 stars and 20 stripes, because it would be too cluttered. On April 4, 1818, Congress set the number of stripes at 13, with a star for each state. It ordered that a new star be added to the flag on the July 4th after a state had joined the Union. The arrangement of the stars varied until presidential orders fixed their position in 1912 (for 48 stars), in 1959 (for 49), and in 1960 (for 50).

The U.S. flag flies over the White House and the Capitol every day. It customarily flies from sunrise to sunset, but it is not illegal to fly the flag 24 hours a day. It should be spotlighted when flown at night. The United States observes June 14 as Flag Day, and the flag is flown on many other public holidays.

The Canadian flag

Until 1965, Canada's national flag was the Red Ensign, which included the British Union Jack. In 1964, Prime Minister Lester Pearson proposed a new flag, with no symbols of Canada's ties to Great Britain. In December, 1964, after debating the flag issue for 33 days, the Canadian Parliament adopted a new flag design recommended by a parliamentary committee. The flag features an 11-point red maple leaf (Canada's national symbol) on a broad white center stripe, with a broad red vertical stripe at each end. This flag became Canada's official flag on Feb. 15, 1965.

The Canadian flag flies over the Parliament Buildings in Ottawa when Parliament is in session, and on holidays and special days. It flies at half-mast only on occasions of national mourning, such as the death of the sovereign.

Holidays

Holidays observed around the world

Ascension Day —40 days after Easter; Christian holiday celebrating the rising of Jesus Christ into heaven.

Christmas —December 25; Christian celebration of the birth of Jesus Christ.

Easter —March or April; Christian celebration of the Resurrection of Jesus Christ.

Epiphany —January; Christian festival which, in Roman Catholic and Protestant churches, commemorates the adoration of the infant Jesus by the wise men; in Eastern churches it celebrates the baptism of Jesus.

Good Friday —Friday before Easter; Christian holiday commemorating the anniversary of Christ's death on the cross.

Great Festival —(Festival of Sacrifice) Muslim festival in the last month of the Muslim year, at the end of pilgrimages to the holy city of Mecca.

Hanukkah —(Feast of Lights) Usually in December; Jewish celebration of a Jewish victory over the Syrians in 165 B.C.

Lesser Festival —(Little Bairam, or Festival of the Break-ing of the Fast) Muslim celebration at the end of Ramadan, the ninth month in the Muslim year and the holy month of fasting.

Muhammad's Birthday —Date varies; Muslim celebration of the birth of the Prophet Muhammad, the founder of Islam.

Passover —March or April; Jewish holiday celebrating the exodus of the Jews from Egypt.

Purim —February or March; Jewish celebration of the rescue of the Jews of Persia (now Iran) from a plot to kill them.

Rosh Hashanah —Usually observed in September or October; Jewish New Year and High Holiday.

Shabuot —(Pentecost) Jewish holiday celebrated 50 days after the beginning of Passover to commemorate the giving of the Torah to Moses on Mount Sinai.

Sukkot —Jewish harvest festival that begins five days after Yom Kippur.

Yom Kippur —(Day of Atonement) Jewish High Holiday and fast day 10 days after Rosh Hashanah.

U.S. holidays

The holidays listed below have been declared legal federal holidays by Congress.

New Year's Day —January 1

Washington's Birthday —February 22, but observed on the third Monday in February

Memorial Day —last Monday in May

Independence Day —July 4

Labor Day —first Monday in September

Columbus Day —second Monday in October

Veterans Day —November 11

Thanksgiving Day —fourth Thursday in November

Christmas Day —December 25

Canadian public holidays

New Year's Day —January 1

Good Friday —March or April; date varies

Easter Monday —March or April; date varies

Queen's Birthday (Victoria Day) —Monday before May 25

Dominion Day —July 1

Labour Day —first Monday in September

Thanksgiving Day —second Monday in October

Remembrance Day —November 11

Christmas Day —December 25

Human being

This section discusses the physical and cultural characteristics that distinguish human beings from other animals and traces the development of those characteristics. For details about the human body and how it works, see "Human Body."

Human beings are the most highly developed of all animals. In the scientific classification of the animal kingdom, human beings belong to the class of animals called *mammals* and the order called *primates.* Human beings and apes form the superfamily *Hominoidea.* The family *Hominidae* consists of humans and their closest prehuman ancestors. Human beings alone make up the genus *Homo,* which consists of one species with living members—*Homo sapiens*—and several extinct species known only through fossil remains. Modern human beings make up a subspecies called *Homo sapiens sapiens.*

Human beings and other primates share certain physical characteristics, such as fingers and thumbs that can grasp things. Human beings and apes both have excellent vision and a highly developed nervous system. The human brain, however, is twice as large as an ape's brain and is more highly developed than that of any other animal. Other important physical differences are related to posture and walking. Humans stand upright and walk on two legs. An ape's body is designed for walking on four legs and for climbing and swinging in trees.

The highly developed human brain enables human beings to use language, a special ability that distinguishes humans from all other animals. Over the years, human beings have developed about 3,000 different spoken languages. (See "World" for a table of major languages.) Through language, humans use symbols to communicate complex ideas, to talk about objects and events that are distant in time and space, and to reason and solve problems. Language has enabled human beings to develop culture, which consists of ways of thinking and behaving that are passed on from one generation to the next. Culture also includes technology—the tools and techniques that people invent to help them satisfy their needs and desires.

Human culture has developed in three major phases. These are: (1) the hunting and gathering phase, (2) the agricultural phase, and (3) the industrial phase.

For almost the entire period of prehistoric human existence, people lived by hunting game and gathering fruit, nuts, and other plant foods. They probably lived in isolated groups of 25 to 50 persons, wandering over large areas in search of food. They invented weapons and cutting tools for hunting, and devised containers for gathering plant foods.

Agricultural societies developed around 9000 B.C., as people began to domesticate wild animals and plants. Farming provided a larger and more reliable food supply that could support growing populations. Permanent villages were formed; later, towns and cities grew up. Because not everyone was needed to provide food, some people became involved in such activities as trade and manufacturing. Governments and systems of writing were devised.

The development of prehistoric human beings

Human Cultural Development

For about 2½ million years, prehistoric people lived by hunting and by gathering plants. About 9000 B.C., people learned to farm. They then began to develop a way of life that led to the invention of writing about 3000 B.C. Writing ended prehistoric times. The chart below shows some steps in human cultural development. Note that the scale of dates changes after 1,000,000 B.C. and after 10,000 B.C.

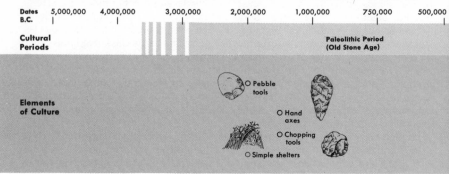

| Dates B.C. | 5,000,000 | 4,000,000 | 3,000,000 | 2,000,000 | 1,000,000 | 750,000 | 500,000 |

Cultural Periods

Paleolithic Period (Old Stone Age)

Elements of Culture

O Pebble tools

O Hand axes

O Chopping tools

O Simple shelters

Human Physical Development

Scientists do not know exactly when or how the various species of human beings and their ancestors developed. For example, scientists have found evidence that the first human beings lived about 2,600,000 B.C. The chart at the right shows approximately when the various species of human beings and their ancestors lived. The drawings below show examples of these species and how their skulls, heads, and bodies probably looked. The maps indicate where fossils of these species have been found.

Omo · Rudolf and Olduvai · Java

Early Primitive Human Beings

Humanlike Ancestors

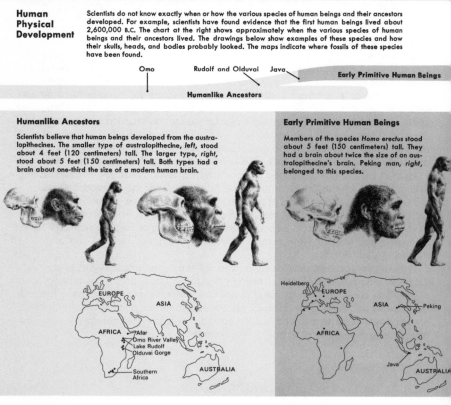

Humanlike Ancestors

Scientists believe that human beings developed from the australopithecines. The smaller type of australopithecine, *left*, stood about 4 feet (120 centimeters) tall. The larger type, *right*, stood about 5 feet (150 centimeters) tall. Both types had a brain about one-third the size of a modern human brain.

EUROPE
ASIA
AFRICA — Afar
Omo River Valley
Lake Rudolf
Olduvai Gorge
Southern Africa
AUSTRALIA

Early Primitive Human Beings

Members of the species *Homo erectus* stood about 5 feet (150 centimeters) tall. They had a brain about twice the size of an australopithecine's brain. Peking man, *right*, belonged to this species.

Heidelberg
EUROPE
ASIA — Peking
AFRICA
Java
AUSTRALIA

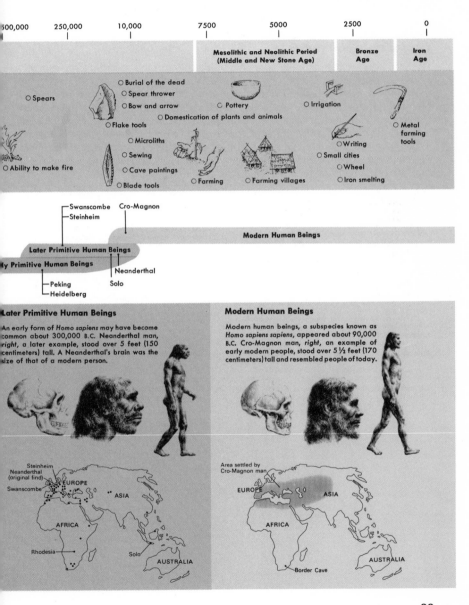

500,000	250,000	10,000	7500	5000	2500	0

			Mesolithic and Neolithic Period (Middle and New Stone Age)		Bronze Age	Iron Age

○ Spears

○ Burial of the dead
○ Spear thrower
○ Bow and arrow
○ Flake tools

○ Pottery

○ Irrigation

○ Domestication of plants and animals

○ Ability to make fire

○ Microliths
○ Sewing
○ Cave paintings
○ Blade tools

○ Farming

○ Farming villages

○ Writing
○ Small cities
○ Wheel
○ Iron smelting

○ Metal farming tools

─Swanscombe
─Steinheim

Cro-Magnon

Modern Human Beings

Later Primitive Human Beings

My Primitive Human Beings

Neanderthal

─Peking
─Heidelberg

Solo

Later Primitive Human Beings

An early form of *Homo sapiens* may have become common about 300,000 B.C. Neanderthal man, *right*, a later example, stood over 5 feet (150 centimeters) tall. A Neanderthal's brain was the size of that of a modern person.

Steinheim
Neanderthal (original find)
Swanscombe
EUROPE
ASIA
AFRICA
Rhodesia
Solo
AUSTRALIA

Modern Human Beings

Modern human beings, a subspecies known as *Homo sapiens sapiens*, appeared about 90,000 B.C. Cro-Magnon man, *right*, an example of early modern people, stood over 5½ feet (170 centimeters) tall and resembled people of today.

Area settled by Cro-Magnon man
EUROPE
ASIA
AFRICA
AUSTRALIA
Border Cave

Modern industrial societies came about during the A.D. 1700's, after people learned to operate machines using energy from coal and other fuels. Great technological advances in this period have resulted in a tremendous expansion of human knowledge and a higher standard of living for many people.

Geographical races

Human races are the naturally occurring subdivisions of the species *Homo sapiens*. Races developed because groups of people lived in the same general location for thousands of years, isolated from other people by mountains, oceans, or deserts. Members of the same race developed similar physical characteristics that tended to distinguish them from members of other races. Some of these characteristics are obvious outward traits. Others are related to blood groups or other factors of body chemistry. There are various methods of classifying human races. This table describes nine geographical races, which are actually collections of similar races that extend over large geographical areas.

African, frequently called *Negroid,* is a collection of related races in Africa south of the Sahara. Members have curly or tightly coiled hair, thick lips, and large amounts of melanin in the skin, hair, and gums. They have changed genetically to meet such diseases as malaria. American blacks are mostly of African origin.

American Indian, sometimes called *Amerindian* or *American Mongoloid,* is related to the Asian geographical race but differs in various blood-group frequencies. For thousands of years, American Indians were the only people in the Western Hemisphere. Their skin ranges from light to dark brown, and they have straight, dark hair.

Asian, sometimes called *Mongoloid,* includes populations in continental Asia, except for South Asia and the Middle East. It also extends to Japan, Taiwan, the Philippines, and the major islands of Indonesia. Members have straight hair, inner eyefolds, and pads of fat over their cheekbones. Most of them are shorter than Europeans and have light brown skin.

Australian, also called *Australian Aborigine* or *Australoid,* is a group of local races in Australia. Members have large teeth, moderate to heavy skin coloring, narrow skulls, and a moderate amount of body hair.

European, sometimes called *Caucasoid,* includes populations throughout Europe, in the Middle East, and north of the Sahara. Members have lighter skins than the people of any other geographical race, though many people in the southern part of this region have dark skins. The "whites" of Australia, New Zealand, North and South America, and South Africa are members of the European geographical race.

Indian includes populations in South Asia and extends from the Himalaya to the Indian Ocean. Skin color ranges from light in the north to dark in the south. The Indian and European geographical races both have high frequencies of blood group B, but they differ in several other blood groups.

Melanesian, or *Melanesian-Papuan,* includes the dark-skinned peoples of New Britain, New Guinea, and the Solomon Islands. They resemble Africans in skin color but are unlike Africans in blood-group frequencies.

Micronesian occupies a series of islands in the Pacific, including the Carolines, Gilberts, Marianas, and Marshalls. Members are dark-skinned and most are small. Micronesians have wavy to woolly hair. Their blood-group frequencies resemble those of the Polynesians, but they have higher frequencies of blood group B.

Polynesian consists of Pacific Island peoples living far apart, ranging from Hawaii in the north to New Zealand in the south and from Easter Island in the east to the Tuvalu island group in the west. Members are tall and many are stout. Polynesians have light to moderate skin color. Like other Pacific populations, they have low frequencies of blood group B.

Human body

The human body is an incredibly complex structure. At its simplest level, it consists of various chemical elements—mainly carbon, hydrogen, nitrogen, and oxygen—put together into molecules, which, in turn, form cells. About 65 per cent of the body is water, which consists of hydrogen and oxygen. Carbon occurs in all the major molecules of the body except water. The most important carbon-containing molecules are called *macromolecules*. Four kinds of macromolecules are carbohydrates, lipids, proteins, and nucleic acids. Carbohydrates provide the body with energy. Lipids have various functions. Fats are a kind of lipid that store extra fuel for the body. Other lipids serve as one of the building materials for cells. Proteins also have various functions. Some serve as building materials. Certain others, called *enzymes,* speed up the various chemical reactions in the body. Nucleic acids carry instructions that tell each cell how to perform.

The human skeleton gives support

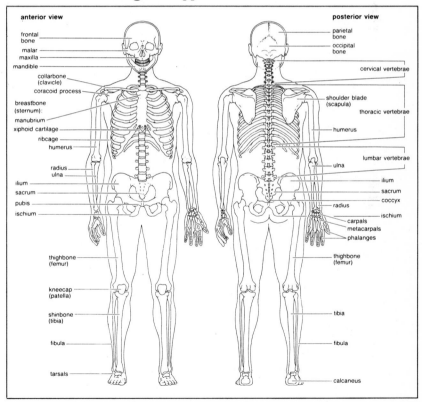

anterior view

frontal bone
malar
maxilla
mandible
collarbone (clavicle)
coracoid process
breastbone (sternum):
manubrium
xiphoid cartilage
ribcage
humerus
radius
ulna
ilium
sacrum
pubis
ischium
thighbone (femur)
kneecap (patella)
shinbone (tibia)
fibula
tarsals

posterior view

parietal bone
occipital bone
cervical vertebrae
shoulder blade (scapula)
thoracic vertebrae
humerus
lumbar vertebrae
ulna
ilium
sacrum
coccyx
radius
ischium
carpals
metacarpals
phalanges
thighbone (femur)
tibia
fibula
calcaneus

Cells are the basic building blocks of the human body. They consist mainly of water, proteins, and nucleic acids. Every cell can take in food, get rid of wastes, and grow. There are various kinds of cells, such as blood cells, muscle cells, and nerve cells, each with special features and jobs. Cells that perform the same function make up *tissues*. There are four kinds of tissues. *Connective tissue* helps support and connect various parts of the body. *Epithelial tissue* covers the body to form the skin and lines the mouth and other body openings. *Muscle tissue* makes movement possible. *Nervous tissue* carries signals from one part of the body to another. An organ consists of two or more kinds of tissue joined together to form a structure that has a particular task. Groups of organs form organ systems, which carry out a major function, such as digestion or respiration.

The skin is the body's largest organ. It has three layers. The *epidermis,* the outermost layer, acts as a barrier that prevents bacteria and other harmful substances from entering the body. It also prevents water loss from the body's inner tissues

Muscles make the body move

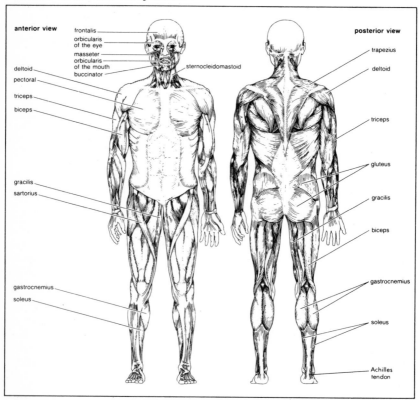

anterior view

frontalis
orbicularis of the eye
masseter
orbicularis of the mouth
buccinator
sternocleidomastoid

deltoid
pectoral
triceps
biceps

gracilis
sartorius

gastrocnemius
soleus

posterior view

trapezius
deltoid

triceps

gluteus

gracilis

biceps

gastrocnemius

soleus

Achilles tendon

and protects those tissues from harmful rays of the sun. Sweat glands in the epidermis help control body temperature. The *dermis,* the middle layer, also helps keep the body's temperature within normal range through the contraction and expansion of blood vessels. Nerve endings in the dermis respond to cold, heat, pain, pressure, and touch. *Subcutaneous tissues,* the innermost layer, help retain body heat and cushion the inner tissues against blows. Fat cells in this layer provide extra fuel for the body.

The skeletal system consists of about 200 bones, which account for approximately 25 per cent of the total body weight. The skeleton provides a strong, yet lightweight, framework to support the body and protect the internal organs. The skeleton works with the muscles to move the body. The place where two bones meet is called a joint. *Movable joints* include the elbow and knee. Bundles of strong, flexible connective tissue called *ligaments* hold the bones of a movable joint together. *Fixed joints* do not move. Most of the bones of the skull, for example, meet in fixed joints.

Bone tissue plays an important role in the production and maintenance of blood. The cells of bone marrow manufacture new blood cells. Other bone cells regulate the blood's mineral content.

The muscular system consists of more than 600 muscles, which account for about 40 per cent of the body's weight. Muscles are made of special fibers that contract, resulting in movement. *Skeletal muscles* move the bones of the arms, legs, and other parts of the skeleton. Viewed through a microscope, these muscles have alternating light and dark bands called *striations.* The skeletal muscles are attached to the bones either directly or by means of bundles of tough, elastic connective tissue called *tendons.* Because we can consciously control the movement of skeletal muscles, they are also called *voluntary muscles.*

Smooth muscles occur in most of the body's internal organs. They have no striations. They contract and relax automatically, and so are often called *involuntary muscles.* Smooth muscles cannot contract as rapidly as skeletal muscles, but they can contract more completely and over a longer period of time.

Cardiac muscle, found only in the heart, has striations like skeletal muscle. But like smooth muscle, it contracts rhythmically and automatically without tiring. The cardiac muscle enables the heart to contract, or beat, continuously, more than 100,000 times a day.

The digestive system breaks down food chemically into simple substances that the body can use, passes these substances into the bloodstream, and then eliminates leftover waste products. The digestive system consists of many parts. In the mouth, teeth tear and grind food into small pieces. *Saliva,* the first of several digestive enzymes, begins the process of chemical breakdown. After swallowing, the food moves down the esophagus to the stomach. The stomach produces an acid and an enzyme that further break down much of the food. Muscle contractions mix the partly digested food into a thick liquid called *chyme.* Chyme moves steadily from the stomach to the small intestine. More digestive enzymes complete the food breakdown in the first part of the small intestine. Some of these enzymes are made by the small intestine. The rest are made by the pancreas, which is linked to the small intestine by a duct. *Bile,* a liquid that is made by the liver and stored in the gall bladder, also enters the small intestine. Bile is not a digestive enzyme, but it breaks up large molecules of fatty foods.

Food has been completely digested by the time it leaves the first part of the small intestine. In the rest of the small intestine, special cells absorb useful substances from the digested food, and these substances then pass into the bloodstream. Some are carried directly to cells throughout the body. Others are carried to the liver, where some are stored for future use and others are chemically changed into forms needed by the body. The substances that are not absorbed into the bloodstream pass from the small intestine to the large intestine. These substances consist of water, minerals, and wastes. Most of the water and minerals are absorbed by the large intestine and then passed to the bloodstream. The wastes move down to the *rectum,* the lower end of the large intestine, and leave the body as bowel movements.

The digestive system

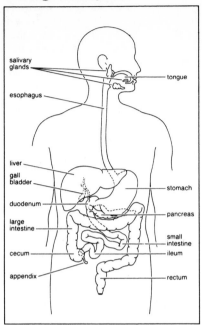

The respiratory system provides the body with oxygen and rids it of carbon dioxide. Oxygen enables the cells to break down food and release its energy. During this process, carbon dioxide forms as a waste product.

The act of breathing results chiefly from the contraction and relaxation of the *diaphragm,* a large muscle that forms the floor of the chest cavity. When we inhale, air flows through the nose. Cold air is warmed and moistened as it moves through the nasal passages, and tiny, hairlike structures and mucus filter dust and dirt from the air. From the nose, the air passes through the *pharynx* (the cavity behind the nose and mouth) and the *larynx* (the voice box). The air then enters the *trachea* (windpipe), which splits into two tubes, each entering one lung. Within the lungs, the tubes split into smaller and smaller branches, ending in hundreds of millions of thin-walled structures called *alveoli.* The exchange of oxygen and carbon dioxide occurs in the alveoli. A network of tiny, thin-walled blood vessels surrounds each alveolus. The blood entering these vessels has a large amount of carbon dioxide picked up from the body tissues, and little oxygen. The carbon dioxide passes through the walls of the blood vessels and alveoli into the lungs. Oxygen from the air in the lungs then passes through the walls of the alveoli and blood vessels and enters the blood. The oxygen-rich blood travels from the lungs to the heart, which pumps it throughout the body. The carbon dioxide leaves the lungs when we exhale.

The circulatory system moves blood throughout the body by means of the heart and a system of about 100,000 miles (160,000 kilometers) of blood vessels. These vessels consist of arteries, veins, and capillaries. The heart actually consists of two pumps side by side. The pump on the left side sends blood rich in food

Blood circulates throughout the body

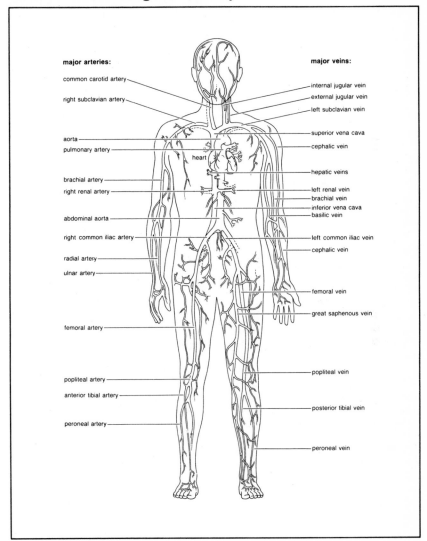

major arteries:

common carotid artery

right subclavian artery

aorta

pulmonary artery

heart

brachial artery

right renal artery

abdominal aorta

right common iliac artery

radial artery

ulnar artery

femoral artery

popliteal artery

anterior tibial artery

peroneal artery

major veins:

internal jugular vein

external jugular vein

left subclavian vein

superior vena cava

cephalic vein

hepatic veins

left renal vein

brachial vein

inferior vena cava

basilic vein

left common iliac vein

cephalic vein

femoral vein

great saphenous vein

popliteal vein

posterior tibial vein

peroneal vein

and oxygen through the arteries and the arterioles to the capillaries. The tiny, thin-walled capillaries form an exchange system for the blood. Food and oxygen pass through the capillary walls to the cells. Carbon dioxide and other wastes from the cells seep into the capillaries and so enter the bloodstream. The waste-filled blood returns to the right side of the heart through a system of venules and veins. The pump on the right side of the heart sends this blood to the lungs, where the carbon dioxide is removed and oxygen is picked up. This oxygen-rich blood returns to the left side of the heart and is pumped to all parts of the body. The liver and kidneys remove other waste materials from the blood.

More than half the total volume of blood consists of a liquid called *plasma,* which carries digested food substances and many of the waste products formed by the cells. Blood also consists of three kinds of solid particles. *Red blood cells* carry oxygen from the lungs to the body tissues and also carry some of the carbon dioxide away from the tissues. *White blood cells* attack bacteria, viruses, poisons, and other harmful substances that can cause illness. *Platelets* help prevent bleeding from broken blood vessels by working with various proteins in the plasma to form blood clots.

The lymphatic system is a network of vessels that work alongside the blood vessels and form another part of the circulatory system. Water, proteins, and dissolved food that pass through the capillary walls make up what is called *interstitial fluid.* This fluid bathes and nourishes the cells. The excess fluid, called *lymph,* drains into a series of lymphatic vessels that eventually empty into veins near the neck. *Lymph nodes,* located at various points along the lymphatic vessels, produce white blood cells that filter out and destroy harmful substances in the lymph.

The urinary system removes certain wastes from the blood and flushes them from the body. The principal organs of this system are the two kidneys. Each kidney has about a million microscopic filtering units called *nephrons.* As blood passes through the nephrons, a network of capillaries and tubes filters out a small amount of water, as well as urea, sodium chloride, and other wastes. The water and wastes form urine. Tubes called *ureters* carry the urine from the kidneys to the urinary bladder, where it is stored temporarily. Muscle contractions squeeze the urine out of the bladder and it leaves the body through a tube called the *urethra.*

The reproductive system enables people to have children. Human reproduction is a sexual process that begins when a *sperm* (male sex cell) unites with an *egg* (female sex cell). This union is called *fertilization.*

Males and females have different reproductive organs. In males, sperm are produced in two *testicles,* which are inside a pouch called the *scrotum* that hangs between the legs. Tubes carry the sperm to the *penis,* an organ in front of the scrotum. In females, eggs are produced in two glands called *ovaries,* which are near the base of the abdomen. Two *Fallopian tubes*—one for each ovary—carry the eggs to the top of the uterus, a hollow, muscular organ. The lower end of the uterus leads to the *vagina,* a canal that extends to the outside of the body. About once a month during a female's childbearing years, one egg cell is released from an ovary and travels down one of the Fallopian tubes. Infrequently, more than one egg is released.

During sexual intercourse, sperm are released from the penis into the vagina. The sperm swim to the uterus and the Fallopian tubes. If an egg is present, a sperm may fertilize it. The fertilized egg moves on through the tube and eventually becomes attached to the wall of the uterus. The single fertilized egg cell divides over and over again to form all the parts of a new human being. After about nine months, the baby is ready to be born. Strong contractions of the uterus push the baby through the vagina, which widens to let the baby pass out of the mother's body.

The nervous system regulates and coordinates the activities of every other system through an intricate communications network made up of countless *neurons* (nerve cells). The nervous system has three main divisions: (1) the central nervous system, (2) the peripheral nervous system, and (3) the autonomic nervous system.

The central nervous system consists of the brain and the spinal cord. It receives information from the senses, analyzes the information, and determines an appropriate response. It then sends instructions to carry out the necessary actions. Some simple decisions, called *spinal reflexes,* occur totally within the spinal cord. Most

The nervous system — a communications network

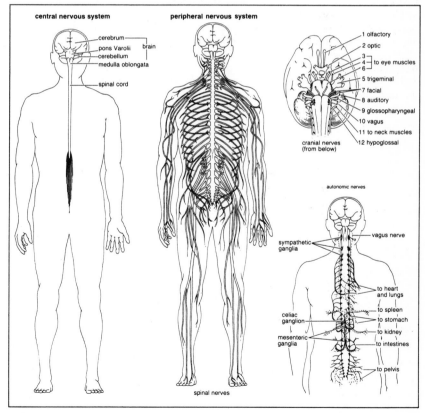

central nervous system

cerebrum
pons Varolii — brain
cerebellum
medulla oblongata

spinal cord

peripheral nervous system

1 olfactory
2 optic
3
4 — to eye muscles
6
5 trigeminal
7 facial
8 auditory
9 glossopharyngeal
10 vagus
11 to neck muscles
12 hypoglossal

cranial nerves
(from below)

autonomic nerves

vagus nerve

sympathetic
ganglia

to heart
and lungs
to spleen
to stomach
to kidney
to intestines

celiac
ganglion

mesenteric
ganglia

to pelvis

spinal nerves

decisions, however, involve the brain, a complicated collection of billions of neurons. Brain activity occurs on two levels. Voluntary decisions that we make and control take place at the brain's conscious level. The brain makes many other decisions at the subconscious level—decisions beyond voluntary control.

The peripheral nervous system is made up of nerves that link the central nervous system with every part of the body. These nerves include sensory neurons, which carry information from sense receptors to the central nervous system, and motor neurons, which carry instructions back from the central nervous system to the affected tissues.

The autonomic nervous system is part of the peripheral nervous system. It carries messages between the subconscious level of the brain and the internal organs, regulating such body functions as the heartbeat and the movement of food through the digestive tract.

The endocrine system consists of glands that produce chemical substances called hormones, which travel through the bloodstream to the cells, regulating growth and other body functions. Some hormones also help the body deal with stress and emergencies. The main endocrine glands include the adrenal glands, the pituitary gland, the parathyroid glands, the sex glands, and the thyroid gland. The brain, kidneys, stomach, and pancreas also produce hormones. The pituitary gland, which lies near the base of the brain, is known as the *master gland.* It releases many hormones that, in turn, regulate other endocrine glands. The pituitary itself is controlled by hormones produced by a part of the brain called the *hypothalamus.*

The body also has various *exocrine glands,* which do not produce hormones. Instead, they make chemicals that perform specific jobs in limited areas. Digestive juices, mucus, sweat, and tears are all examples of exocrine products.

Library classification systems

Most libraries in the United States use the Dewey Decimal Classification System to categorize nonfiction books in their collections. Many large research and university libraries use the Library of Congress Classification System.

Dewey decimal classification

000	**General works**	**300**	**Social sciences**	650	Management
010	Bibliography	310	Statistics	660	Chemical technology
020	Library and information sci-	320	Political science	670	Manufactures
	ences	330	Economics	680	Assembled products
030	General encyclopedias	340	Law	690	Buildings
040		350	Public administration		
050	General periodicals	360	Social problems and serv-	**700**	**The arts**
060	General organizations		ices	710	Civic and landscape art
070	Newspapers and journalism	370	Education	720	Architecture
080	Collected works	380	Commerce	730	Sculpture, plastic arts
090	Manuscripts and rare books	390	Customs, etiquette, folklore	740	Drawing, decorative and
					minor arts
100	**Philosophy and related**	**400**	**Language**	750	Painting
	disciplines	410	Linguistics	760	Graphic arts
110	Metaphysics	420	English and Anglo-Saxon	770	Photography
120	Epistemology, causation,	430	Germanic languages	780	Music
	humankind	440	French, Provençal, Catalan	790	Recreational and perform-
130	Paranormal phenomena	450	Italian, Romanian		ing
140	Philosophical systems	460	Spanish, Portuguese		
150	Psychology	470	Latin and other Italic	**800**	**Literature**
160	Logic	480	Classical and modern	810	American literature
170	Ethics		Greek	820	English and Anglo-Saxon
180	Ancient, medieval, Oriental	490	Other languages	830	Germanic literatures
190	Modern Western philoso-			840	French, Provençal, Catalan
	phy	**500**	**Pure sciences**	850	Italian, Romanian
		510	Mathematics	860	Spanish, Portuguese
200	**Religion**	520	Astronomy	870	Latin and other Italic
210	Natural religion	530	Physics	880	Classical and modern
220	Bible	540	Chemistry		Greek
230	Christian theology	550	Sciences of earth and other	890	Other literatures
240	Christian moral and devo-		worlds		
	tional	560	Paleontology	**900**	**History and geography**
250	Local church and religious	570	Life sciences	910	Geography and travel
	orders	580	Botanical sciences	920	Biography and genealogy
260	Social and ecclesiastical	590	Zoological sciences	930	Ancient history
	theology			940	Europe
270	History and geography of	**600**	**Technology**	950	Asia
	church	610	Medical sciences	960	Africa
280	Christian churches and	620	Engineering	970	North America
	sects	630	Agriculture	980	South America
290	Other religions	640	Home economics	990	Rest of world

Library of Congress classification

The system of classification devised by the Library of Congress uses 21 letters of the alphabet to represent the principal branches of knowledge. Subdivision is achieved by adding second letters and Arabic numerals through 9999.

A	General works: Polygraphy	H	Social sciences	Q	Science		
B	Philosophy and religion	J	Political science	R	Medicine		
C	History: Auxiliary sciences	K	Law	S	Agriculture		
D	History: General and Old World	L	Education	T	Technology		
E–F	History: America	M	Music	U	Military science		
G	Geography and anthropology	N	Fine arts	V	Naval science		
		P	Language and literature	Z	Bibliography and library science		

Money

The table below lists many world monetary units with their equivalent subdivisions. Symbols commonly used to represent the dollar, pound, yen, and other major world currencies appear in the "Signs and symbols" section.

Exchange rates, the price of a nation's currency in terms of another nation's currency, vary from day to day. Many newspapers publish daily reports on the exchange rates of major foreign currencies. Banks can also provide information about exchange rates.

Country	Monetary unit	Equivalent subdivision	Country	Monetary unit	Equivalent subdivision
Afghanistan	**Afghani**	100 puls	Chile	**Peso**	100 centavos
Albania	**Lek**	100 qin darka	China	**Yuan**	10 jiao; 100 fen
Algeria	**Dinar**	100 centimes	Colombia	**Peso**	100 centavos
Angola	**Kwanza**	100 lwei	Congo	**Franc**	100 centimes
Argentina	**Peso**	100 centavos	Costa Rica	**Colón**	100 centimos
Australia	**Dollar**	100 cents	Cuba	**Peso**	100 centavos
Austria	**Schilling**	100 groschen	Czechoslovakia	**Koruna**	100 halers
Bahamas	**Dollar**	100 cents	Denmark	**Krone**	100 öre
Bahrain	**Dinar**	1,000 fils	Dominican Republic	**Peso**	100 centavos
Bangladesh	**Taka**	100 paisa	Ecuador	**Sucre**	100 centavos
Belgium	**Franc**	100 centimes	Egypt	**Pound**	100 piasters
Benin	**Franc**	100 centimes	El Salvador	**Colón**	100 centavos
Bermuda	**Dollar**	100 cents	Ethiopia	**Birr**	100 cents
Bolivia	**Peso**	100 centavos	Finland	**Markka**	100 penni
Brazil	**Cruzeiro**	100 centavos	France	**Franc**	100 centimes
Bulgaria	**Lev**	100 stotinki	Germany, East	**Mark**	100 pfennige
Burma	**Kyat**	100 pyas	Germany, West	**Mark**	100 pfennige
Burundi	**Franc**	100 centimes	Ghana	**Cedi**	100 pesewas
Cameroon	**Franc**	100 centimes	Great Britain	**Pound**	100 pence
Canada	**Dollar**	100 cents	Greece	**Drachma**	100 lepta
Central African Republic	**Franc**	100 centimes	Guatemala	**Quetzal**	100 centavos
Chad	**Franc**	100 centimes			

Country	Monetary unit	Equivalent subdivision	Country	Monetary unit	Equivalent subdivision
Guinea	Syli	100 cauris	Norway	Krone	100 öre
Guyana	Dollar	100 cents	Oman	Rial	1,000 baiza
Haiti	Gourde	100 centimes	Pakistan	Rupee	100 paisa
Honduras	Lempira	100 centavos	Panama	Balboa	100 centésimos
Hong Kong	Dollar	100 cents	Papua New Guinea	Kina	100 toea
Hungary	Forint	100 fillér	Paraguay	Guaraní	100 céntimos
India	Rupee	100 paisa	Peru	Sol	100 centavos
Indonesia	Rupiah	100 sen	Philippines	Peso	100 centavos
Iran	Rial	100 dinars	Poland	Zloty	100 groszy
Iraq	Dinar	20 dirhams; 1,000 fils	Portugal	Escudo	100 centavos
Ireland	Pound	100 pence	Romania	Leu	100 bani
Israel	Shekel	100 new agorot	Russia	Ruble	100 kopecks
Italy	Lira	100 centesimi	Rwanda	Franc	100 centimes
Ivory Coast	Franc	100 centimes	Saudi Arabia	Riyal	100 halalas
Jamaica	Dollar	100 cents	Senegal	Franc	100 centimes
Japan	Yen	100 sen; 1,000 rin	Sierra Leone	Leone	100 cents
			Singapore	Dollar	100 cents
Jordan	Dinar	1,000 fils	Somalia	Shilling	100 cents
Kenya	Shilling	100 cents	South Africa	Rand	100 cents
Korea, South	Won	10 hwan; 100 chun	Spain	Peseta	100 céntimos
			Sri Lanka	Rupee	100 cents
Kuwait	Dinar	10 dirhams; 1,000 fils	Sudan	Pound	100 piasters; 1,000 millièmes
Laos	Kip	100 at	Sweden	Krona	100 öre
Lebanon	Pound	100 piasters	Switzerland	Franc	100 centimes
Lesotho	Loti*	100 lisente	Syria	Pound	100 piasters
Liberia	Dollar	100 cents	Taiwan	Dollar	100 cents
Libya	Dinar	1,000 dirhams	Tanzania	Shilling	100 cents
Luxembourg	Franc	100 centimes	Thailand	Baht	100 satangs
Madagascar	Franc	100 centimes	Togo	Franc	100 centimes
Malawi	Kwacha	100 tambala	Trinidad and Tobago	Dollar	100 cents
Malaysia	Ringgit	100 cents	Tunisia	Dinar	1,000 millimes
Mali	Franc	100 centimes	Turkey	Lira	100 kurus
Mauritania	Ouguiya	5 khoums	Uganda	Shilling	100 cents
Mexico	Peso	100 centavos	United Arab Emirates	Dirham	100 fils
Monaco	Franc	100 centimes	United States	Dollar	100 cents
Mongolia	Tughrik	100 möngö	Upper Volta	Franc	100 centimes
Morocco	Dirham	100 centimes	Uruguay	Peso	100 centésimos
Mozambique	Metical	100 centavos	Venezuela	Bolívar	100 céntimos
Nepal	Rupee	100 pice	Yemen (Sana)	Rial	100 fils
Netherlands	Guilder	100 cents	Yugoslavia	Dinar	100 para
New Zealand	Dollar	100 cents	Zaire	Zaire	100 makuta; 10,000 sengi
Nicaragua	Córdoba	100 centavos	Zambia	Kwacha	100 ngwee
Niger	Franc	100 centimes	Zimbabwe	Dollar	100 cents
Nigeria	Naira	100 kobo			

*Plural *Maloti*

Mythology

Greek and Roman divinities

Many gods and goddesses of Greek mythology held similar positions in Roman mythology. For example, each mythology had a goddess of love. The Greeks called her Aphrodite. The Romans called her Venus. The table below lists the most important Greek and Roman divinities.

Greek	Roman	Position	Greek	Roman	Position
Aphrodite	Venus	Goddess of love	Hera	Juno	Protector of marriage and women. In Greek mythology, sister and wife of Zeus; in Roman mythology, wife of Jupiter
Apollo	Apollo	God of light, medicine, and poetry			
Ares	Mars	God of war			
Artemis	Diana	Goddess of hunting and childbirth	Hermes	Mercury	Messenger for the gods; god of commerce and science; and protector of travelers, thieves, and vagabonds
Asclepius	Aesculapius	God of healing			
Athena	Minerva	Goddess of crafts, war, and wisdom			
Cronus	Saturn	In Greek mythology, ruler of the Titans and father of Zeus; in Roman mythology, also the god of agriculture	Hestia	Vesta	Goddess of the hearth
			Hypnos	Somnus	God of sleep
Demeter	Ceres	Goddess of growing things	Pluto, or Hades	Pluto	God of the underworld
Dionysus	Bacchus	God of wine, fertility, and wild behavior	Poseidon	Neptune	God of the sea. In Greek mythology, also god of earthquakes and horses
Eros	Cupid	God of love			
Gaea	Terra	Symbol of the earth and mother and wife of Uranus	Rhea	Ops	Wife and sister of Cronus
			Uranus	Uranus	Son and husband of Gaea and father of the Titans
Hephaestus	Vulcan	Blacksmith for the gods and god of fire and metalworking	Zeus	Jupiter	Ruler of the gods

Other Greek divinities

Aeolus	God of the winds	Muses	Nine goddess of various arts and sciences; daughters of Zeus and Mnemosyne
Fates	Three goddesses who controlled the destinies of all persons		
Clotho	Spinner of the thread that represents a person's life	Calliope	Muse of epic poetry
		Clio	Muse of history
Lachesis	Decides the length of the thread of life	Erato	Muse of love poetry
Atropos	Cuts the thread of (ends) life	Euterpe	Muse of lyric poetry
Hebe	Goddess of youth	Melpomene	Muse of tragedy
Iris	Goddess of the rainbow and a messenger of the gods	Polyhymnia	Muse of sacred song
		Terpsichore	Muse of dance
Mnemosyne	Goddess of memory	Thalia	Muse of comedy
		Urania	Muse of astronomy
		Pan	God of the forests and pastures

Other Roman divinities

Faunus	A god of nature	Terminus	God of boundaries
Pomona	Goddess of fruits and trees		
Quirinus	One of the original major gods; believed to be the divine incarnation of Romulus, one of the cofounders of Rome		

Important divinities in Teutonic (Norse) mythology

Balder A son of Odin; god of goodness, beauty, and light

Bragi God of poetry

Frey God of agriculture and fertility

Frigg Wife of Odin

Hel Goddess of the underworld

Loki God of evil; son of a giant; known as a troublemaker and trickster

Odin Ruler of Asgard, kingdom of the gods

Thor A son of Odin; god of thunder and lightning

Tyr God of war

Ve A brother of Odin

Vili A brother of Odin

Important divinities in Egyptian mythology

Amon Originally a local god worshipped in Thebes; later identified with Re, the sun god; became known as Amon-Re, the chief Egyptian god

Anubis Escort of the dead to the entrance to the afterworld; inventor of funeral rites and burial procedures

Atum Source of all gods and living things

Geb God of the earth and pharaoh of Egypt

Hathor Wife of Horus; goddess of heaven, joy, music, and love; protector of women and children

Horus Son of Osiris and Isis; god of heaven and light

Isis Sister and wife of Osiris; mother of all things; goddess of female fertility

Nephthys Sister of Isis

Nut Goddess of the heavens

Osiris God of vegetation and the afterlife

Ptah Inventor of the arts

Re, or Ra Sun god; ruler of the world and first divine pharaoh

Set God of the desert; god of evil

Shu God of the air

Tefnut Goddess of the dew

Thoth God of learning, letters, and wisdom; protector of the arts

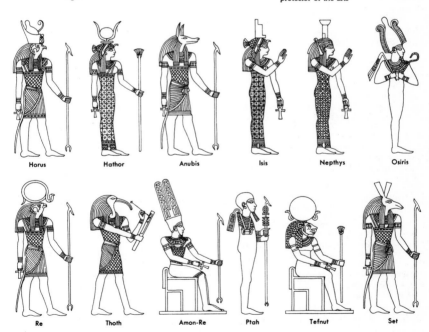

Horus   Hathor   Anubis   Isis   Nepthys   Osiris

Re   Thoth   Amon-Re   Ptah   Tefnut   Set

The ancient Egyptians portrayed many of their gods and goddesses with human bodies and the heads of birds or other animals. The divinities held or wore objects symbolizing their power. For example, the god Osiris held a scepter and a whip, which represented the authority of gods and divine pharaohs.

Parliamentary Procedure

Parliamentary procedure is a way to conduct a meeting in an orderly manner. Whenever people hold a meeting, they need rules to help them accomplish their purpose. The rules of parliamentary procedure help the chairperson keep order during a meeting. The procedure is called *parliamentary* because it comes from the rules and customs of the British Parliament. Parliamentary procedure is also known as *parliamentary law, parliamentary practice,* and *rules of order.*

Kinds of motions used in parliamentary procedure

The following motions are listed in order of their rank. When a group is considering any one of them, you may not introduce another that is listed below it. But you may introduce another that is listed above it.

To do this	You say this

Privileged motions (deal with the welfare of the group, rather than with any specific proposal. They must be disposed of before the group can consider any other type of motion).

Adjourn the meeting	"I move that we adjourn."
Recess the meeting	"I move we recess until __"
Complain about noise, room temperature, etc.	"Point of privilege"

Subsidiary motions (provide various ways of modifying or disposing of main motions. They must be acted upon before all other motions except privileged motions).

Suspend debate on a matter without calling for a vote	"I move we table the matter."
End debate	"I move the previous question."
Limit length of debate	"I move debate on this matter be limited to __"
Ask for a vote by actual count, to verify a voice vote	"I call for a division of the house."
Postpone consideration of a matter to a specific time	"I move we postpone this matter until __"
Have a matter studied further	"I move we refer this matter to a committee."
Consider a matter informally	"I move that the question be considered informally."
Amend a motion	"I move that this motion be amended by __"
Reject a main motion without voting on the motion itself	"I move the question be postponed indefinitely."

Incidental motions (grow out of other business that the group is considering. They must be decided before the group can return to the question that brought them up).

Correct an error in parliamentary procedure	"Point of order"
Object to a ruling by the chairman	"I appeal the chair's decision."
Consider a matter that violates normal procedure, but does not violate the constitution or bylaws	"I move we suspend the rules that interfere with __"
Object to considering some matter	"I object to the consideration of this matter."
Obtain advice on proper procedure	"I raise a parliamentary inquiry."
Request information	"Point of information"
Withdraw a motion	"I request leave to withdraw the motion."

Main motions (are the tools used to introduce new business).

Introduce business	"I move that __"
Take up a matter previously tabled	"I move we take from the table __"
Reconsider a matter already disposed of	"I move we reconsider our action relative to __"
Strike out a motion previously passed	"I move we rescind the motion calling for __"
Consider a matter out of its scheduled order.	"I move we suspend the rules and consider __"

Terms used in parliamentary procedure

Adjourn means to end a meeting.

Agenda is a list of items to be considered at a meeting.

Amendment is a change proposed or made in a motion, a constitution, or a set of bylaws.

Appeal is a request for a majority vote to overrule a decision of the presiding officer.

Chairman pro tempore is the temporary chairman.

Close debate refers to ending discussion on a motion by passing another motion to vote immediately.

Decorum in debate refers to the observance of normal rules of courtesy and proper procedure.

Dilatory motion is a meaningless motion. The presiding officer must rule it out of order.

Division is a count of votes by a show of hands.

Majority is one more than half of those voting.

Order of business is the series of steps covered in a meeting, from the call to order through adjournment.

Pending question is any motion open to debate.

Plurality is the largest number of votes received by any candidate in an election involving three or more candidates.

Point of order is an objection raised by a member because of improper procedure or annoying remarks. It must be ruled upon immediately by the presiding officer.

Previous question is a motion to end debate on a pending motion and vote immediately.

Privileged question is a request made by a member who asks the presiding officer to deal with an emergency, disorder in the assembly, or other matters of general welfare.

Quorum is the number of members necessary to transact business. Usually it is a majority of the total membership.

Ratify refers to a motion to approve an action already taken, such as a ruling by the president.

Recess is a temporary interruption of a meeting.

May you interrupt speaker?	Second needed?	Motion debatable?	Motion amendable?	Vote needed
no	yes	no	no	majority
no	yes	no	yes	majority
yes	no	no	no	none, chairman rules
no	yes	no	no	majority
no	yes	no	no	⅔ majority
no	yes	no	yes	⅔ majority
no	no	no	no	none*
no	yes	yes	yes	majority
no	yes	yes	yes	majority
no	yes	yes	no	majority
no	yes	yes	yes	majority
no	yes	yes	no	majority
yes	no	no	no	none, chairman rules
yes	yes	yes	no	majority
no	yes	no	no	⅔ majority
yes	no	no	no	⅔ majority
yes	no	no	no	none, chairman rules
yes	no	no	no	none
no	no	no	no	majority
no	yes	yes	yes	majority
no	yes	no	no	majority
yes	yes	yes†	no	majority
no	yes	yes	yes	majority
no	yes	no	no	⅔ majority

*But majority vote if someone objects. †If original action was debatable.

People

This section presents biographical information about famous people in various fields, from ancient times to the present. See also "Awards," "Canada," "Chemical elements," "Explorations," "Presidents," "Sports winners," "Space," "Scientific inventions and inventors," "United States," and "World" sections.

Abraham (about 1800 B.C.), whose name means "father of nations," was the founder of the ancient kingdom of Israel. A native of Ur, Abraham obeyed God's command to lead the Hebrew people to Palestine, where he established his people as a nation. He is considered a patriarch of the Jewish people.

Adams, Samuel (1722–1803), an American patriot and politician during the Revolutionary War period, was a leader of the independence movement. He opposed British tax laws such as the Stamp Act and the Tea Act and helped organize demonstrations against them. After the war, Adams served as governor of Massachusetts.

Addams, Jane (1860–1935), was a social worker and humanitarian. She established Hull House, a neighborhood center in Chicago for immigrants and the poor. Addams worked for numerous reforms, was active in women's movements and peace movements, and wrote several books.

Aeschylus (525?–456 B.C.), a tragic dramatist, ranked with Sophocles and Euripides as one of the most important playwrights of ancient Greece. His plays emphasized divine justice and power. Aeschylus wrote about 80 plays in all, of which only 7 survive, including *Seven Against Thebes*, *Prometheus Bound*, and *Agamemnon*.

Aesop (620?–560? B.C.), a legendary character and probably a Greek slave, was credited as the author of fables—short stories with moral lessons. His tales about animals such as the slow tortoise and the swift hare, and the frugal ant and the wastrel grasshopper have been enjoyed for centuries and remain popular today.

Albertus Magnus, Saint (1206?–1280), born Count Albert von Bollstadt, was a German theologian, philosopher, and scientist, generally considered to be the most learned person in the medieval world. He taught for many years in various universities, and his pupils included Thomas Aquinas. Albertus Magnus was canonized by the Roman Catholic Church in 1932.

Alcott, Louisa May (1832–1888), an American writer, is best known for her novel *Little Women*, the largely autobiographical story of the girlhood experiences of four sisters. She was a member of the New England literary group that included Henry David Thoreau, Ralph Waldo Emerson, and her father, Bronson Alcott.

Alexander the Great (356–323 B.C.), a pupil of the Greek philosopher Aristotle, at the age of 20 succeeded his father, Philip II of Macedon, to the throne. He united the Greek city-states and conquered the Persian Empire, Egypt, and northern India. Alexander ruled over the greatest empire of the time and founded the city of Alexandria in Egypt.

Alfred the Great (849–899), a Saxon king in England, defeated the Danes who tried to conquer his kingdom in Wessex. With his kingdom as the center, he paved the way for the unification of England and issued a code of laws for governing the people. A learned man, Alfred promoted education and Christianity and translated books from Latin to Anglo-Saxon.

Ampère, André Marie (1775–1836), was a French physicist and mathematician who formulated the laws of electromagnetism. He discovered that electric currents moving in the same direction attract but that those moving in opposite directions repel. Ampère also discovered that a coil of electrically charged wire acts as a magnet.

Amundsen, Roald (1872–1928), was a Norwegian explorer who determined the exact position of the North Pole and in 1911 became the first person to reach the South Pole. He also navigated the Northwest Passage through North America and crossed the North Pole in a dirigible. Amundsen disappeared on a North Pole rescue attempt.

Andersen, Hans Christian (1805–1875), Denmark's most famous author, is known for his many popular fairy tales. Although enjoyed by children, many of his works have moral meanings intended for adult audiences as well. Andersen's best known stories include "The Ugly Duckling," "The Emperor's New Clothes," and "The Tinder Box."

Anthony, Susan B. (1820–1906), was a leader of reform movements in the United States who worked for women's suffrage, temperance, and the abolition of slavery. She edited the magazine *The Revolution*, was arrested for voting in 1872, and was president of a national women's suffrage group.

Antony, Mark (82?–30 B.C.), a friend and fellow commander of Julius Caesar, became a consul in the Roman government. After Caesar's assassination, he was a member of the triumvirate that ruled Rome and later commanded the eastern empire. Pursuing Cleopatra of Egypt while trying to widen his control over the empire, he was defeated by Octavian and committed suicide.

Aquinas, Saint Thomas (1225?–1274), an Italian theologian who was influenced by the teachings of the Greek philosopher Aristotle, constructed a system of theology that became the basis for many doctrines of the Roman Catholic Church. Among his writings are *Summa contra Gentiles* and *Summa Theologica*, considered the most complete account of his theology.

Archimedes (287?–212 B.C.), although he considered himself to be a mathematician, is best remembered for his inventions. His inventions included a screw to raise irrigation water and a catapult for military use. Living in Syracuse on the island of Sicily, he also developed the laws of displacement and buoyancy in water and a more precise figure for pi.

Aristophanes (445?–385? B.C.), who wrote during the Golden Age of Athens in ancient Greece, is considered one of the greatest writers of comedy of all time. In his plays, he satirized many contemporary figures and events. His known works include *Clouds*, *Wasps*, *Birds*, *Frogs*, and *Lysistrata*.

Aristotle (384–322 B.C.), a student of Plato, was the greatest Greek philosopher after Plato's death. Considered one of the greatest of logicians, he also lectured on government and ethics and laid the foundations for psychology. Aristotle established a school in Athens.

Armstrong, Neil A. (1930–   ), an American astronaut, was the first person to set foot on the moon. A naval pilot between 1949 and 1952, he made his first space flight in 1966. A part of the crew of *Apollo XI*, Armstrong and another astronaut stepped onto the moon on July 20, 1969, and briefly explored the lunar surface. Armstrong later became a professor of engineering.

Arnold, Benedict (1741–1801), although remembered as a traitor, was one of the best Revolutionary War generals. He fought in several important battles. Passed over for promotions and court-martialed by enemies, Arnold arranged for the British to take over West Point. When the plot was discovered, he joined the British.

Astor, John Jacob (1763–1848), a German by birth, was the founder of a wealthy American family. He became successful in the fur trade and shipped furs to Europe and to China. He extended his control over the fur trade throughout much of North America and established a post at Astoria, Ore. Astor accumulated real estate in New York City and left a fortune of about $20 million.

Atahualpa (1500?–1533), became the emperor of the Inca empire after defeating his brother Huáscar in a civil war. He was the last Inca to rule Peru before Spaniards under the command of Francisco Pizarro invaded the empire and conquered it. Alleging that he might arouse his people against the Spaniards, Pizarro had Atahualpa put to death.

Atatürk, Kemal (1881–1938), was the first president of the Turkish Republic, serving from 1923 until his death. He led armies against the British in World War I, and after the war he worked for the independence and unification of Turkey. Atatürk modernized Turkey, abolishing ancient dress, old penal codes, and the practice of polygamy. He achieved many other social, economic, and religious reforms.

Attila (406?– 453), called the "Scourge of God," was a fierce leader of the Huns. He led his soldiers to conquer much of eastern and central Europe. Turned back in France, he invaded Italy but withdrew when the Pope interceded. The Huns returned to the Danube area, where Attila died while celebrating his wedding.

Attucks, Crispus (1723?–1770), often assumed to have been a black man, was a leader of the mob in the Boston Massacre. He was one of three men killed by British soldiers. His background, however, is uncertain. He may have been a mulatto, or he may have been of mixed Negro and Indian blood. Attucks' place of birth and his occupation, like his ancestry, are also unknown.

Audubon, John James (1785–1851), a failure in business, found success as a painter of American birds. His first group of 435 paintings, *Birds of America,* was first published in England between 1826 and 1838. Audubon later published numerous editions of his paintings of birds and other animals.

Augustine, Saint (354–430), as an intelligent and well-educated youth, led a carefree, worldly life before converting to Christianity at about the age of 30. He became one of the important philosophers of early Christianity and served as the bishop of Hippo in North Africa for more than 30 years. Augustine's writings include *City of God* and his autobiographical *Confessions.*

Augustus Caesar (63 B.C.–A.D. 14), known originally as Octavian, became the first Roman emperor in 27 B.C. He expanded the empire to the north and east. During his reign, the Roman Empire reached the peak of its glory in a period of peace and great artistic production.

Aurangzeb (1618–1707), the last effective Mogul emperor of India, took the throne by imprisoning his father and killing two of his brothers. He was a harsh ruler, and his religious persecutions of both Muslims and Hindus led to widespread revolts. These and other outbreaks brought about the end of the Mogul empire in India.

Austen, Jane (1775–1817), an English author, wrote six novels, including *Pride and Prejudice, Sense and Sensibility,* and *Northanger Abbey.* As she herself had experienced them, she portrayed the attitudes, hopes, fears, and superficialities of the English middle class with sympathy and understanding.

Bach, Johann Sebastian (1685–1750), a giant among composers, was also a great organist who was attached to many important churches and courts in his native Germany. Among his religious works are the *Mass in B Minor* and *The Passion According to St. Matthew.* His instrumental music includes the *Brandenburg Concertos, The Well-Tempered Clavier,* and *The Art of the Fugue.*

Bacon, Francis (1561–1626), an English philosopher, politician, and writer, is best remembered for his essays. Particularly interested in learning, he planned but never completed an encyclopedia of all knowledge. In *Novum Organum,* Bacon stressed the inductive scientific method of collecting data and arriving at tentative conclusions.

Bacon, Roger (1214?–1292?), a medieval philosopher probably born in England, emphasized experience as a means of knowing. Interested in science, he stressed the superiority of conclusions based on observation over those based on reason. A Franciscan, he was imprisoned for some of his views. His greatest work was *Opus Maius,* a discourse on scientific subjects.

Balboa, Vasco Núñez de (1475–1519), was one of the early Spanish explorers of America. He became the governor of Darién in Panama and led expeditions seeking gold. In 1513, he led 200 men on an expedition to discover the Pacific Ocean. Under charges of treason, probably false, Balboa was condemned and executed by beheading.

Balzac, Honoré de (1799–1850), a prolific French writer, studied law but turned to literature as a profession. He wrote many novels, including *The Human Comedy,* a group of novels that deal with the lives of more than 2,000 different characters representing all walks of life. Among his best-known books are *Old Goriot* and *Droll Stories.*

Banneker, Benjamin (1731–1806), was a black mathematician who published an almanac containing weather predictions and astronomical calculations. Also a surveyor, Banneker came to the attention of Thomas Jefferson, who helped him win appointment to the group that laid out the boundaries of the District of Columbia.

Barnum, Phineas T. (1810–1891), perhaps the greatest American showman, created the modern circus. Barnum presented the Swedish singer Jenny Lind, as well as the midget General Tom Thumb and the elephant Jumbo, to American audiences. Because of Barnum, expressions like *white elephant* (fake) and *ballyhoo* (strident publicity) became a part of the English language.

Barton, Clara (1821–1912), won acclaim as a battlefield nurse during the Civil War. Serving as a nurse in Europe during the Franco-Prussian War, she became interested in the Red Cross movement. Barton later organized the American National Red Cross and served as its president.

Becket, Saint Thomas à (1118?–1170), an English cleric and archbishop of Canterbury, opposed the plans of King Henry II to weaken the authority of the Roman Catholic Church in England. When Henry II indicated that he wanted to be rid of Becket, four knights took this to mean his death and killed Becket at Canterbury. Two years later, the church made him a saint.

Bede (673?–735), an English Roman Catholic priest, wrote more than 30 works on history, science, hymns, the lives of saints, grammar, and the Bible. His most famous work is the *Ecclesiastical History of the English Nation.* For his many achievements, he was given the title "the Venerable Bede" and was canonized.

Beebe, William (1877–1962), became famous for designing the bathysphere, in which he made many undersea explorations to observe marine life. Beebe served as curator of ornithology at the New York Zoological Society. His popular books include *Beneath Tropic Seas.*

Beethoven, Ludwig van (1770–1827), a German-born composer generally credited with beginning the romantic movement in music, expanded musical form and used daring harmonies. His compositions include nine symphonies, an opera, five piano concertos, a violin concerto, more than 30 sonatas, and numerous string quartets and religious works.

Bell, Alexander Graham (1847–1922), a painter and a teacher of the deaf, invented the telephone. With the aid of his assistant, Thomas A. Watson, Bell carried out many experiments that in 1876 produced one of the first instruments that successfully transmitted voices over a distance.

117

Bellow, Saul (1915–   ), an American author, has won numerous awards for his novels, including Nobel and Pulitzer prizes in 1976 and National Book Awards in 1954, 1965, and 1971. Bellow's heroes confront serious concerns in comic fashion in such works as *The Adventures of Augie March* and *Henderson the Rain King*. Other major works by Bellow include *Herzog, Mr. Sammler's Planet, Humboldt's Gift,* and *The Dean's December.*

Ben-Gurion, David (1886–1973), promoted the creation of the state of Israel and became the nation's first prime minister, serving from 1948 to 1953 and again from 1955 to 1963. Born in Poland, he emigrated to Israel and became a Zionist (independence) leader. In 1930 he formed the United Labor, now the Mapai, political party.

Bentham, Jeremy (1748–1832), an English jurist and philosopher, taught that the morality of ideas, actions, and institutions should be judged on the basis of how well they promote the greatest good for the greatest number of people. His philosophy, called utilitarianism, brought about some court and other reforms.

Bessemer, Sir Henry (1813–1898), an English inventor and engineer, developed a means of removing impurities from iron ore. Called the Bessemer process, it greatly increased the quantity and quality of steel production in the 1800's. He established steelworks at Sheffield, England, to produce parts for guns and steel rails.

Bethune, Mary McLeod (1875–1955), a black educator, founded a school for black women in 1904 in Daytona Beach, Fla., that later merged with a men's school to become Bethune-Cookman College. She was the school's president for many years and later held several positions in the federal government. Bethune also established mission schools for blacks.

Bismarck, Otto von (1815–1898), became the first chancellor of the German Empire in 1871 after he had unified his country after wars with Austria and France. To solidify and secure Germany's position, he created the Triple Alliance through a series of treaties with Austria-Hungary and Italy that lasted until the outbreak of World War I.

Blackstone, Sir William (1723–1780), an English jurist, wrote the influential *Commentaries on the Laws of England.* This extensive treatise was frequently quoted in the 1700's and became the basis for legal education in England. It was also influential in the American Colonies, where it served as a source book on English law.

Blackwell, Elizabeth (1821–1910), was the first woman physician in the United States. Born in England, she moved to the United States as a child. She graduated from medical school in 1849 and opened a hospital for women and children in 1853. Elizabeth and her sister, Emily, founded the Women's Medical College of the New York Infirmary for Women and Children in 1857.

Blake, William (1757–1827), was an English mystic, poet, engraver, and painter. He illustrated his own books as well as the writings of others. Blake's works include two volumes, both entitled *Songs of Innocence,* which treat similar subjects from contrasting points of view. His engravings include *Illustrations of the Book of Job.*

Boccaccio, Giovanni (1313?–1375), an Italian author, wrote *The Decameron,* a collection of tales supposedly related by a group of men and women isolated in Florence, Italy, during a plague. The stories are humorous and earthy and were retold by many later writers. Boccaccio also served in several diplomatic posts for the Florentine government.

Bohr, Niels (1885–1962), a Danish physicist, elaborated on Ernest Rutherford's theory that the atom consists of a positively charged nucleus with negatively charged electrons revolving around it. Bohr's research was a major step toward the practical use of nuclear energy. Bohr won the Nobel prize in physics in 1922.

Boleyn, Anne (1507–1536), was the second wife of Henry VIII of England. When Henry divorced his first wife to marry Anne, the act brought about the separation of England from the Roman Catholic Church and the establishment of the Church of England. Anne's daughter became Elizabeth I.

Bolívar, Simón (1783–1830), born into the middle class, joined the Latin-American independence movement and fought many successful battles against the Spanish. Colombia, Ecuador, Venezuela, and other countries gained their freedom from Spain because of Bolívar's military leadership. For several years, Bolívar was president of Colombia, and unsuccessfully worked for Latin-American unity.

Boone, Daniel (1734–1820), an almost legendary frontiersman, participated in the French and Indian Wars and later led an early group of first pioneers into Kentucky. He helped lay out the Wilderness Road and found settlements. In 1799, Boone moved West to become a pioneer in Missouri.

Booth, John Wilkes (1838–1865), an actor and member of a prominent theatrical family, assassinated President Abraham Lincoln in Ford's Theatre in Washington, D.C., on April 14, 1865. A Southerner, he considered Lincoln to be a tyrant and an enemy of the South. Fleeing the theater after the shooting, Booth was hunted down in Virginia, where he was shot to death.

Bradford, William (1590–1657), was the second governor of Plymouth Colony, the settlement established by the Pilgrims in 1620. In 1621, he organized the celebration of the first Thanksgiving Day held in New England. His book *History of Plimmoth Plantation* is the chief record of Pilgrim life.

Brahe, Tycho (1546–1601), a Danish astronomer, made important discoveries through systematic observation of the planets, an innovation at the time. He observed a new star and suggested that comets originate in outer space, not in the earth's atmosphere, as had been thought. Brahe's theories and astronomical tables were of great value to succeeding astronomers.

Brahms, Johannes (1833–1897), a German romantic composer, wrote in all major forms except opera and ballet. His compositions include *Variations on a Theme by Haydn, Academic Festival Overture,* four symphonies, two piano concertos and a violin concerto, Hungarian dances, and many songs.

Braille, Louis (1809–1852), a Frenchman blinded by an accident at the age of 3, studied music and became an organist. As a teacher at the National Institute for the Blind in Paris, he developed a system of writing using raised points that could be read with the fingertips. His system, called braille, opened a new means of communication for the blind.

Brontë Sisters—Charlotte (1816–1855), **Emily** (1818–1848), and **Anne** (1820–1849), were novelists whose works are associated with the lonely moors of Yorkshire, England, where they were born. Charlotte Brontë's most famous work, *Jane Eyre,* is largely autobiographical. Emily Brontë wrote only one novel, *Wuthering Heights,* a romantic masterpiece. Anne Brontë wrote two novels, *Agnes Grey* and *The Tenant of Wildfell Hall.*

Brooks, Gwendolyn (1917–   ), a black American poet and writer, published several collections of poetry, including *A Street in Bronzeville.* A Guggenheim scholar, she won the Pulitzer prize in 1950 for her volume of poetry *Annie Allen.* The first black woman to win the prize, Brooks was named poet laureate of Illinois in 1968.

Brown, John (1800–1859), an American abolitionist, embodied the hostility between the North and the South in the decade before the Civil War. He helped blacks escape from slavery and fought proslavery groups in Kansas. In 1859, Brown and his followers briefly seized the federal arsenal at Harper's Ferry, Va. The arsenal retaken, Brown was convicted of treason and hanged.

Bryan, William Jennings (1860–1925), a politician, served from 1891 to 1895 in the House of Representatives. A spokesman for the free-silver movement, he ran unsuccessfully for the presidency as a Democrat in 1896, 1900, and 1908. Bryan served as secretary of state during the administration of President Woodrow Wilson and later attacked the teaching of evolution in schools.

Buddha (563?–483? B.C.), developed a philosophy of peace based on enlightenment, on which he founded a religion. Born Prince Siddhartha Gautama in Nepal, he taught his followers to forsake desire, seek goodness, escape from sorrow, and follow an eightfold path to righteousness and enlightenment. (See "Religion.")

Burr, Aaron (1756–1836), an American politician, was Vice-President under Thomas Jefferson from 1801 to 1805. Under the system of that time, Jefferson won the Presidency over Burr on the 36th ballot in the House of Representatives. In a duel in 1804, Burr killed Alexander Hamilton, who was largely responsible for Burr's having lost the Presidency and another office. Later, he was involved in a mysterious plot to establish an independent nation in the Southwest.

Byrd, Richard (1888–1957), an American admiral and explorer, led numerous expeditions to Antarctica. During the last expedition in 1955 and 1956, he flew over the South Pole for the third time. Byrd became the foremost authority on Antarctica of his time.

Byron, Lord (1788–1824), George Gordon Byron, was an English romantic poet whose work reflects his belief that people should be free to choose their own courses in life. Byron used settings in Europe and the Near East for much of his poetry. His major works include epic *Childe Harold's Pilgrimage* and the long, unfinished epic *Don Juan*.

Cabot, John (1450?–1498?), a navigator and explorer born in Italy, made two voyages for King Henry VII of England. Although he was sailing for Asia, both times he reached islands in the North Atlantic. On the first voyage, he landed on Cape Breton Island or Newfoundland. Setting out again, Cabot and his party were lost; however, his voyages helped England establish claims on the islands.

Caesar, Julius (100?–44 B.C.), a Roman general and politician, conquered what is now France and twice invaded England. He later took over the Roman government and fought several wars, one in Egypt. Fearing a dictatorship, Caesar's enemies assassinated him.

Calhoun, John C. (1782–1850), a powerful politician, was the foremost spokesman for states' rights before the Civil War. He was a representative and a senator from South Carolina and was Vice-President from 1825 to 1832. Calhoun's last speech in the Senate opposed the Compromise of 1850, a measure that was meant to settle the slavery issue.

Calvin, John (1509–1564), a Swiss theologian born in France, developed a stern and forbidding Protestant theology based on faith rather than good works. He believed in predestination and free will. Calvinism was a highly individualistic religion, and vestiges of it can be found today in Presbyterian, Congregational, and other faiths.

Carnegie, Andrew (1835–1919), born in Scotland, became an American industrialist and philanthropist. He emigrated to the United States at age 13 and worked his way up to an important position in a railroad company. Carnegie later became a steel manufacturer and eventually accumulated a fortune of some half billion dollars. He gave away much money to philanthropic causes.

Carroll, Lewis (1832–1898), was the pen name of Charles L. Dodgson, an English mathematician and writer. For a girl named Alice, he developed imaginative stories that were later published as *Alice's Adventures in Wonderland*. When the book quickly became a children's favorite, he wrote a sequel, *Through the Looking Glass*. A professor, he also published works on mathematics.

Cartier, Jacques (1491?–1557), a French sailor, became an explorer of Canada for King Francis I. In 1534, he discovered the Gulf of St. Lawrence and the St. Lawrence River. On other voyages, he journeyed far up the St. Lawrence River and located the future sites of Quebec and Montreal. Cartier's voyages gave France huge land claims in North America.

Caruso, Enrico (1873–1921), was perhaps the greatest operatic tenor of his time. Born in Italy, he sang in opera houses in Russia, Italy, England, and in South American countries but had his greatest success with the Metropolitan Opera Company of New York City. Caruso had a large repertoire of more than 40 operas.

Carver, George Washington (1859?–1943), a black American born of slave parents, won international fame for agricultural research. He developed more than 300 products from the peanut, 118 products from the sweet potato, and 75 products from the pecan, convincing southern farmers to produce these crops instead of cotton, to provide new sources of income. He joined the staff of Tuskegee Institute in Alabama in 1896 and spent the rest of his life there.

Cassatt, Mary (1845–1926), ranks among the most famous American women painters. She became associated with the French impressionist movement in painting, and is best known for her sensitive portraits of mothers and children. Her works include *The Bath, At the Opera*, and *La Loge*.

Castro, Fidel (1926–   ), a Cuban revolutionary leader, became prime minister after he overthrew dictator Fulgencio Batista in 1959. He established a Communist state, nationalized businesses, and began land reforms.

Catherine of Aragon (1485–1536) was the first of the six wives of King Henry VIII of England. The daughter of Ferdinand and Isabella of Spain, she was the mother of Mary I. Henry's insistence on divorcing her led to England's break with the Roman Catholic Church and the establishment of the Church of England. After her divorce, Catherine lived a life of religious devotion in prison.

Catherine II (1729–1796) was an empress of Russia who became known as "the Great." When her husband Peter was deposed and murdered, Catherine took the throne. Although interested in European liberalism, she ruled autocratically, and the misery of the serfs increased during her reign. Catherine extended Russian borders to include a part of Poland and the Crimea. She also conquered Siberian tribes.

Cato, Marcus Porcius, the Elder (234–149 B.C.), a Roman consul and senator, helped bring about the destruction of Carthage in northern Africa in the Third Punic War. He viewed Carthage as Rome's mortal enemy and closed all of his speeches in the senate with a plea for its destruction.

Cavour, Camillo Benso (1810–1861), an Italian statesman, served as prime minister of Sardinia from 1852 to 1861. Under his leadership, Sardinia joined France to drive Austria from Lombardy. Sardinia then took control of Lombardy and other areas of Italy. Working with Giuseppe Garibaldi and others, Cavour succeeded in making Italy a unified nation.

Cervantes, Miguel de (1547–1616), a Spanish author, wrote *Don Quixote*, sometimes called the world's greatest novel. Begun while Cervantes was in prison, the work tells the adventures of the idealistic Don Quixote and his servant Sancho Panza and is a satire on chivalry. Cervantes held several minor military and diplomatic posts and wrote plays, poems, and other works.

Cézanne, Paul (1839–1906), a French painter, used forms such as the cone, the cube, and the sphere in his works. Trained in the impressionistic school of art, he established his own style in painting that emphasized solid masses of color. Cézanne influenced the cubist school of painters.

Champlain, Samuel de (1567?–1635), was a French explorer of the New World and for several years served as governor of the French colony at Quebec in Canada. He discovered Lake Champlain and explored extensively along the St. Lawrence River, Georgian Bay, and Lake Ontario.

Charlemagne (742–814) was king of the Franks (Germans) and emperor of the Romans. Defeating the Saxons, the Bavarians, the Avars, the Lombards, and others, he created an empire sprawling over much of central and western Europe. A patron of culture, he did much to promote scholarship and education within his realm.

Chaucer, Geoffrey (1340?–1400), an English public official, diplomat, and poet, wrote *The Canterbury Tales*. In the poem, a group of pilgrims journeying to Canterbury tell stories for their amusement as they proceed. Chaucer also wrote several other poems, including *The Book of the Duchess*.

Chavez, Cesar (1927–   ), was the first labor leader who effectively organized migrant workers. A migrant worker himself, he worked to unionize field laborers in the 1960's in spite of much opposition. Chavez established the National Farm Workers Association and in 1966 signed the first contract with California growers.

Cheever, John (1912–1982), was an American novelist and short-story writer known for his accounts of persons lost in a society of rising wealth. His major novels include *The Wapshot Chronicle, The Wapshot Scandal, Bullet Park,* and *Falconer.* He won the 1979 Pulitzer prize for fiction for *The Stories of John Cheever.*

Chekhov, Anton (1860–1904), a Russian author, wrote many plays and short stories in which he stressed human loneliness and people's failure to understand one another. Among his stories are "Kashtanka," "The Party," "The Darling," and "Ward No. 6." Chekhov's plays include *The Cherry Orchard, Uncle Vanya,* and *The Three Sisters.*

Chiang Kai-shek (1887–1975), was a military leader who headed the Nationalist government of China from 1928 to 1949, when he was defeated by the Communists. Chiang then fled to Taiwan, where he served as political and military leader of the government until his death.

Chopin, Frédéric (1810?–1849), a pianist and composer born in Poland, was a child prodigy and wrote lyrical works for the piano, many based on popular dance forms. Settling in Paris with George Sand, a woman writer, Chopin composed two piano concertos and many shorter works—mazurkas, polonaises, preludes, études, nocturnes, ballades, and songs.

Churchill, Winston (1874–1965), a British statesman and author, began his career as a soldier and reporter. He later entered Parliament and headed various ministries. In 1940, he became prime minister, leading Great Britain during World War II. He served as prime minister again from 1951 to 1955. Churchill wrote on English history and also wrote a history of World War II that won him the Nobel prize in literature in 1953.

Cicero (106–43 B.C.), a Roman lawyer, statesman, and writer, served as a consul. Exiled for refusing to support the First Triumvirate, he devoted himself to writing. He later became a leader of the senate and opposed Mark Antony's ambition to rule Rome. Feared because of his ability as an orator, Cicero was condemned to death and was killed while trying to escape.

Cincinnatus, Lucius Quinctius (519?–439? B.C.), a Roman patriot, was appointed dictator and led an army that defeated the Aequians in central Italy. After his victory, he resigned. Given absolute power a second time, he once more resigned after slaying a traitor threatening Rome. To later Romans, Cincinnatus became a symbol of old-fashioned virtue.

Clark, George Rogers (1752–1818), led troops against the British in the Northwest Territory during the Revolutionary War. He financed his own campaigns and was never reimbursed for his expenses. Clark's successes helped secure the Northwest for the United States.

Clay, Henry (1777–1852), represented Kentucky for many years in the House of Representatives, where he served several terms as speaker, and in the Senate. He tried unsuccessfully for the presidency three times. Clay's greatest renown came from the Missouri Compromise and the Compromise of 1850—agreements that he worked out to ease the conflict between the North and South over the slavery issue.

Cleopatra (69–30 B.C.), an Egyptian queen who at various times ruled with her two brothers (who were also her husbands), became the mistress of Julius Caesar and bore him a son. She later became the lover of Mark Antony and bore him twins. When Antony was defeated in Egypt by Octavian, Cleopatra committed suicide to avoid the humiliation of being taken to Rome for exhibition as a captive.

Clinton, De Witt (1769–1828), promoted the Erie Canal, completed in 1825 when he was governor of New York. The canal helped New York City develop as the country's most important port. Clinton also served as mayor of New York City, as a state senator, and as lieutenant governor.

Cochise (?–1874), a chief of the Chiricahua Apache, was captured by white soldiers under a flag of truce and accused of a crime he had not committed. Escaping, the embittered Cochise led his warriors in 10 years of intermittent warfare against whites. A brilliant leader, he finally was forced to accept life on a reservation.

Columbus, Christopher (1451–1506), an Italian navigator, made four voyages of exploration of the Americas for Spain in the 1490's and early 1500's. He was searching for a route to Asia and reached what he thought were the Indies. Because of his efforts, Spain made vast land claims in the Americas, but Columbus died in poverty.

Confucius (551?–479? B.C.), a Chinese philosopher, centered his teachings on human relationships, not gods. He taught moral responsibility, kindness and generosity, filial piety, respect for elders and superiors, and the duty of rulers to govern wisely and well. (See "Religion.")

Conrad, Joseph (1857–1924), a Polish-born British author, wrote mostly about sailors and the sea, which he knew from firsthand experience. Among his writings are *Lord Jim* and *Heart of Darkness.* Although he did not learn English until he was 20 years old, Conrad became an elegant stylist in the language.

Constantine (275?–337), called "the Great," was an emperor of the Roman Empire. He favored Christianity during his rule and moved his capital from Rome to Byzantium, renaming the city Constantinople. In 325, Constantine called Christian leaders together at the Council of Nicaea to settle disputes over doctrine.

Cook, James (1728–1779), a British mariner, made voyages of exploration throughout the world. He mapped portions of the eastern coasts of North America and of New Zealand, Australia, and New Guinea; sailed across the Antarctic Circle; reached New Caledonia; charted much of the western coast of North America; and explored the Bering Strait. Cook was killed in Hawaii.

Cooper, James Fenimore (1789–1851), an American novelist and social critic, is best known for *The Leatherstocking Tales,* five novels about a frontiersman named Natty Bumppo. With these novels, Cooper became the first author to seriously portray American scenes and characters. Cooper's conservative ideas about society are reflected in many of his writings, including several nonfiction works criticizing American life.

Copernicus, Nicolaus (1473–1543), a Polish astronomer, is considered the founder of modern astronomy. He developed the theory that the earth is a moving planet, and he attacked Ptolemy's theory—then generally accepted—that the earth was fixed in the universe and never moved. Copernicus' major work was *Concerning the Revolutions of the Celestial Spheres* (1543).

Coronado, Francisco Vásquez de (1510–1554), a Spanish explorer, led an expedition into the American Southwest in search of the legendary Seven Cities of Cibola, which were reportedly filled with gold. Coronado traveled through what is now Arizona, New Mexico, Texas, Oklahoma, and Kansas. He found Indian villages, but no golden cities.

Cortés, Hernando (1485–1547), a Spanish explorer, conquered the Aztec Indians after bitter fighting and won Mexico for Spain. As the first governor of Mexico (then called New Spain), he spread Spanish control and influence and began the first settlement in Lower California.

Cousteau, Jacques-Yves (1910–), is a French oceanographer, author, and motion-picture producer who explores the world's oceans from his research ship *Calypso*. He helped invent the aqualung and also developed the first underwater diving station and an underwater observation vehicle called the *diving saucer*. His books include *The Silent World, The Living Sea,* and *World Without Sun.*

Crane, Stephen (1871–1900), an American author, earned an international reputation as a novelist, poet, and short-story writer before dying of tuberculosis at age 28. His best known work, *The Red Badge of Courage,* is a novel that takes place during the Civil War. His most famous short stories, "The Open Boat" and "The Blue Hotel," were published while he was a correspondent in the Greek-Turkish War and the Spanish-American War.

Crockett, David (1786–1836), was a frontier hunter, scout, and soldier whose love for tall tales made him a folk hero in his own time. He eventually became a colonel in the Tennessee militia and a U.S. congressman. Crockett died defending the Alamo in San Antonio, Texas.

Cromwell, Oliver (1599–1658), an English Puritan, led parliamentary forces to defeat, depose, and behead King Charles I in 1649. Beginning in 1653, he ruled England as Lord Protector Cromwell, mostly without the aid of Parliament, until his death. After a short rule by Cromwell's son Richard, Charles II, the son of Charles I, came to the throne.

Curie, Marie (1867–1934), a Polish-born chemist, made important discoveries in radioactivity with her husband Pierre. Together, the Curies discovered radium and polonium and shared the Nobel prize in physics in 1903 with another scientist. A professor at the Sorbonne in Paris, she won the Nobel prize in chemistry in 1911.

Curie, Pierre (1859–1906), a French physicist and chemist, did his first important work on the magnetic properties of metals, and with his wife Marie made important discoveries in radioactivity. The Curies discovered radium and polonium, for which they shared the Nobel prize in physics. Curie was a professor of physics and chemistry.

Custer, George Armstrong (1839–1876), was a United States Army officer who won fame as a Civil War general and an Indian fighter in the West. In the Battle of Little Bighorn on June 25, 1876, in Montana, Sioux and Cheyenne Indians killed Custer and all of the more than 200 men under his command. Historians have never determined the reason for Custer's disastrous defeat.

Cyrus the Great (reigned 559–529 B.C.) established the ancient Persian Empire. He extended his empire by defeating several rulers—including Astyages, the king of Media; King Croesus of Lydia; and Nabonidus, the king of Babylon. Cyrus freed the Jews from captivity, allowing them to return to Palestine.

Da Gama, Vasco (1469?–1524), a Portuguese navigator, rounded the Cape of Good Hope with an expedition in 1497 and sailed to India. He was the first to establish an all-water route from Europe to the East and was instrumental in opening the spice trade of the Indies to the Portuguese.

Dalton, John (1766–1844), an English chemist, developed the first clear statements of the atomic theory of matter. He also established the law of multiple proportions, developed formulas of molecular atomic composition, and although it proved to be inaccurate, produced a table of atomic weights. He also made the first detailed description of color blindness (Daltonism).

Dante Alighieri (1265–1321), an Italian poet, wrote the *Divine Comedy.* Inspired by his love for a woman named Beatrice, the allegorical work describes the narrator's struggle through hell, purgatory, and heaven. Dante also wrote love poems, as well as prose works.

Darius I (558?–486 B.C.), called the "Great," ruled the Persian Empire as its king. In an invasion of Greece, his armies were defeated at the Battle of Marathon. Darius ran his empire efficiently, reorganizing the administration, building roads, and reforming the tax system.

Darwin, Charles (1809–1882), a British naturalist, in 1859 published *The Origin of Species,* a theory of evolution. He first began to develop the theory as the result of observations he made on a five-year voyage around the world. Darwin also wrote *The Descent of Man,* which deals with human evolution from lower animals.

David (?–973? B.C.), the successor to Saul, was the second king of Israel. He won fame as a boy for killing Goliath, the Philistine giant. A harpist, poet, and composer of psalms, David tried to make his kingdom secure with the defeat of several surrounding tribes, but his reign was troubled by rebellions.

Da Vinci, Leonardo (1452–1519), an Italian genius of the Renaissance, was a scientist, inventor, engineer, sculptor, and painter. Among his many accomplishments, he drew up plans for a flying machine, designed fortifications for Italian rulers, and wrote on astronomy and botany. His paintings include *The Last Supper* and *Mona Lisa.*

Davis, Jefferson (1808–1889), became president of the Confederate States of America in 1861. He had earlier served the United States government as a soldier, as a representative and senator, and as secretary of war. After the Civil War, he spent two years in prison and then retired to Mississippi.

Davy, Sir Humphry (1778–1829), an English chemist, was the first scientist to isolate a number of elements, including potassium, sodium, strontium, calcium, and magnesium. He invented the Davy lamp, used in coal mining, and also experimented with "laughing gas" (nitrous oxide) as an anesthetic.

Debs, Eugene V. (1855–1926), an American labor leader, formed the American Railway Union in the 1890's and as the result of a strike went to prison for contempt of court. Debs became a Socialist and ran for the presidency five times between 1900 and 1920. He conducted his last campaign while in prison for opposing United States participation in World War I.

Degas, Edgar (1834–1917), a French impressionist painter, developed a style using pastel colors for spectacular effects. Although he painted some still lifes, his favorite subjects were people in informal poses. He also enjoyed painting pictures of race-track and theatrical life.

De Gaulle, Charles (1890–1970), a French military leader and statesman, was the leader and symbol of the French resistance movement during World War II. As prime minister and later president of the Fifth Republic in the 1960's, he improved France's economy and ended the war with Algeria by granting independence to that colony. Although he was criticized for his dictatorial rule, De Gaulle brought stability to postwar France.

Demosthenes (384?–322 B.C.), an Athenian statesman who was regarded as the greatest of the Greek orators, was a lifelong defender of Greek independence. He spoke out frequently against Philip of Macedon's designs on Greece and formed an army to resist Macedonian invasion. When the Greeks met defeat, Demosthenes committed suicide rather than allow himself to be captured.

Descartes, René (1596–1650), a French mathematician and philosopher, devoted himself to settling questions about existence and reality. As a starting point, he argued that thought is proof of one's existence. From the existence of the self, he developed proofs of the existence of other realities and of the existence of God.

De Soto, Hernando (1500?–1542), a Spanish adventurer, accompanied Francisco Pizarro in the conquest of the Incas of Peru. Although he gained much wealth from the conquest, he later searched for more gold by leading a party to explore the lower Mississippi River Valley, the Ozark Mountains, and portions of the American Southeast, including Florida. De Soto died on the banks of the Mississippi and was buried in the river.

Dewey, John (1859–1952), an American philosopher, had

a great influence on American educational practices. He taught that experience is fundamental and that the value of an idea lies in its results. In education, he emphasized learning through activity rather than lectures or memorization. Dewey became one of the leaders of the "progressive" movement in education.

Dias, Bartolomeu (1457?–1500), a Portuguese navigator, discovered the Cape of Good Hope in 1488, opening the path by sea from Europe to the East. Ten years later, Vasco da Gama duplicated Dias's feat but continued eastward to India, beginning Portuguese domination of the spice trade with the Indies.

Dickens, Charles (1812–1870), an English novelist, portrayed the lives of the lower classes in the 1800's. He often included social comments on the wretched conditions under which the poor lived and was credited with some social improvements that were made. His novels include *Pickwick Papers, David Copperfield, A Tale of Two Cities, Great Expectations, Bleak House,* and *A Christmas Carol.*

Dickinson, Emily (1830–1886), a poet who was unknown to the public in her lifetime, came to be considered among the greatest writers in American literature. Apparently because of her unfulfilled love for a married man, she withdrew from society to write on death, immortality, and love. By her own wish, her poems were not published during her lifetime. The first volume of Dickinson's poems was published in 1890.

Didérot, Denis (1713–1784), a French writer, edited an encyclopedia, a task that took him 20 years. A monumental work, the encyclopedia stressed scientific objectivity. Several other important French writers aided Didérot in his project, and it contained contributions from such influential French thinkers as Rousseau and Voltaire.

Diocletian (245?–313) was proclaimed Roman emperor at a time of great disunity. Dividing the empire into four separate and self-ruled districts, he tried to bring order after 50 years of civil war. Trying to restore the traditional Roman gods, Diocletian carried on severe persecutions of the Christians during much of his reign.

Disraeli, Benjamin (1804–1881), a British politician and statesman, was the only Jewish person to serve as prime minister of England. A novelist early in his life, he was elected to Parliament in 1837, becoming prime minister in 1868 and serving again from 1874 to 1880. During his terms, Disraeli strengthened British imperialism abroad.

Dostoevsky, Fyodor (1821–1881), a Russian novelist, often wrote about people who sought salvation through suffering as they struggled with good and evil. Accused of political conspiracy, he spent several years in prison in Siberia and was plagued by poverty and misfortune throughout his life. Among his novels are *The Brothers Karamazov, The Idiot,* and *The Possessed.*

Douglas, Stephen A. (1813–1861), a powerful representative and senator from Illinois, helped pass the Compromise of 1850. He promoted the idea of popular sovereignty—that the people of a territory should decide on slavery. His Kansas-Nebraska Bill in 1854, which was based on popular sovereignty, led to civil war in Kansas. His debates with Abraham Lincoln over slavery gained national attention for Lincoln, and Douglas was defeated in his bid for the presidency in 1860.

Douglas, William Orville (1898–1980), served as an associate justice of the U.S. Supreme Court from 1939 to 1975—longer than any other justice. He became known for his strong support for government protection of civil liberties and civil rights, as well as for his wide travels and his books about important problems in American national and international life. His works include *Of Men and Mountains, Strange Lands and Friendly People, The Anatomy of Liberty,* and *Points of Rebellion.*

Douglass, Frederick (1817–1895), escaped slavery to become a writer and a leader in the antislavery movement. He founded a newspaper, during the Civil War raised black Union regiments, and later held several government posts. In the *Narrative of the Life of Frederick Douglass,*

he wrote about his upbringing as a slave in Maryland and his life after escaping.

Drake, Sir Francis (1540?–1596), an English navigator and plunderer of Spanish treasure ships, sailed the *Golden Hind* around the world between 1577 and 1580. Returning to England with much Spanish wealth, he was knighted by Queen Elizabeth I. Drake later participated in the successful battles against the Spanish Armada that was sent to invade England.

Du Bois, W. E. B. (1868–1963), a black educator, writer, and leader, argued for black-white equality rather than gradual economic improvement for blacks. Du Bois wrote several books, including *The Souls of Black Folk,* about the lives of blacks in the United States. He helped form the National Association for the Advancement of Colored People in 1909.

Dunbar, Paul Laurence (1872–1906), a black American poet, became famous for poems written in dialect that expressed blacks' feelings. His poems were often humorous and were published in volumes that include *Majors and Minors, Joggin' Erlong, Lyrics of the Hearthside,* and *Lyrics of Lowly Life.* Dunbar became a model of achievement for blacks, and many schools were named after him.

Duns Scotus (1265?–1308), an English theologian, disagreed with his contemporary Thomas Aquinas on several theological and philosophical doctrines and founded a system called Scotism. He studied at Oxford and became a professor of theology there and at Paris and Cologne. Duns Scotus wrote commentaries on the Bible and on the Greek philosopher Aristotle.

Dürer, Albrecht (1471–1528), a German painter, engraver, and designer, was a leading Renaissance artist. He influenced many later artists in northern Europe. Dürer's works include the painting *Adoration of the Magi* and the engraving *Knight, Death, and the Devil.*

Earhart, Amelia (1897–1937?), an American aviator, was the first woman passenger to cross the Atlantic Ocean by air and the first woman pilot to fly solo across the Atlantic. She was the first woman pilot to fly from Hawaii to the mainland of the United States and the first to cross the continent solo in both directions. Earhart disappeared in the Pacific Ocean under mysterious circumstances while on a round-the-world flight.

Edison, Thomas Alva (1847–1931), perhaps the foremost technological genius of his time, invented the electric light bulb and the phonograph. Edison also made improvements on the typewriter, storage battery, ticker tape machine, electric-powered train, and electric generator. Altogether, he produced more than 1,000 inventions.

Edward the Confessor (1002?–1066) codified Anglo-Saxon laws and built a church on the site of Westminster Abbey, where he is buried. Placed on the throne by the powerful Earl Godwin, Edward spent much of his reign quarreling with Godwin over policies involving both the state and religion. The king was canonized by the Roman Catholic Church in 1161.

Einstein, Albert (1879–1955), a German-born mathematician and physicist, developed the theory of relativity and contributed to the quantum theory and numerous other discoveries in modern physics. A resident of the United States after 1933, he influenced the government to begin work on an atomic bomb. Einstein was awarded the Nobel prize for physics in 1921.

Eleanor of Aquitaine (1122?–1204) was the wife of Louis VII of France and later of Henry II of England. She was the mother of two English kings—Richard I, the Lion-Hearted, and John, the signer of the Magna Carta. England fought several wars to hold her lands in France, the beginning of centuries of hostility between the two countries.

Eliot, T. S. (1888–1965), an American who became a British subject in 1927, was one of the most influential poets and critics of his time. Among his best-known poems are "The Love Song of J. Alfred Prufrock," *The Waste Land,* "Ash Wednesday," "The Hollow Men," and "Gerontion."

Many of his poems involve religious themes. Eliot won the Nobel prize for literature in 1948.

Elizabeth I (1533–1603) ruled during a time of great expansion of English power and a time of great literary production. William Shakespeare lived during her reign, and English exploration and discovery overseas increased the country's position among European nations. In 1588, Elizabeth's navy defeated the Spanish Armada to make England the greatest sea power of the age.

Elizabeth II (1926–   ) is queen of the United Kingdom of Great Britain and Northern Ireland. She is also head of the Commonwealth of Nations. Elizabeth was 25 years old when she succeeded to the throne of her father, George VI, in 1952. Her reign has been marked by frequent state visits to all parts of the Commonwealth. Elizabeth married Philip Mountbatten in 1947.

Emerson, Ralph Waldo (1803–1882), an American poet, philosopher, and essayist, was among the leading writers of his time and an associate of such literary figures as Henry David Thoreau and Walt Whitman. Emerson based his philosophy on individualism and self-reliance. *Concord Hymn* is among his most popular poems.

Engels, Friedrich (1820–1895), a German Socialist, collaborated with Karl Marx on *The Communist Manifesto.* Involved in revolutionary activity in Germany, Engels fled to England where he was a manufacturer and a leader of the Socialist movement. He edited and published many of Marx's writings. Engels' own writings include *The Condition of the Working Class in England.*

Erasmus, Desiderius (1466?–1536), a Dutch scholar, was a Christian humanist of the Renaissance. He favored internal reform of the Roman Catholic Church, rather than a break with the church. He stressed faith and grace over works. Erasmus lived and studied in several important university centers.

Ericson, Leif (about 1000), a Norse sailor and adventurer, has been credited with discovering North America long before Columbus. Sailing west, he came upon a land that he named Vinland because of the grapevines he found there. The land Ericson reached has been identified by different historians as the Labrador Peninsula, Newfoundland Island, or New England.

Euclid (about 300 B.C.), a Greek mathematician, was the founder of geometry. His work *The Elements* remained the foundation of geometry until the early 1900's. The text is a model of mathematical and logical thinking. Euclid lived in Alexandria, Egypt, during the reign of Ptolemy I, and founded a school for mathematicians there.

Euripides (c. 480–406 B.C.), one of the great writers of Greek tragedies, produced about 90 plays, of which 19 survive. Euripides dealt with mythological heroes, but showed them as ordinary Athenians, and he used his plays to criticize political, social, and religious ideas of his times. His works include *Medea, The Trojan Women,* and *Electra.*

Faraday, Michael (1791–1867), an English physicist and chemist, made important discoveries in electromagnetism. He discovered that passing a magnet through a coil of copper wire produces a flow of electric current, a principle on which the electric motor and generator are based. As a chemist, Faraday developed the law of valences.

Farragut, David G. (1801–1870), was a Union naval commander in the Civil War. Known as "Old Salamander," he commanded Union forces blockading the South along the lower Mississippi River, and won fame for his victory at Mobile Bay, Ala., in 1864. Farragut also participated in many military actions, including the Mexican War.

Faulkner, William (1897–1962), a Mississippi writer, portrayed Southern life in a place called Yoknapatawpha County that he created. He regretted the loss of traditional Southern values. Among his novels are *Sartoris, The Sound and the Fury, Absalom, Absalom!, Intruder in the Dust,* and *As I Lay Dying.* Faulkner won the Nobel prize for literature in 1949.

Fermi, Enrico (1901–1954), was a physicist whose work led to the development of the atomic bomb. He became professor of theoretical physics at the University of Rome in 1926, but he left Italy for the United States in 1938 after winning the Nobel prize for physics. At the University of Chicago in 1942, Fermi led a team that produced the first atomic chain reaction.

Fleming, Sir Alexander (1881–1955), a British bacteriologist, discovered penicillin, probably the most useful of all antibiotics. It proved to be an extremely useful drug during World War II and was credited with saving many lives. For his work in bacteriology, Fleming shared the Nobel prize in medicine in 1945.

Ford, Henry (1863–1947), a pioneer American automaker, made the automobile available to the middle class when he introduced the Model T—a plain but sturdy, reliable, and relatively inexpensive automobile. He developed the use of moving assembly lines and interchangeable parts in the manufacture of automobiles.

Francis of Assisi, Saint (1181?–1226), an Italian cleric, abandoned a life of wealth and ease to embrace poverty. He founded the Franciscan order in 1209. Known as a gentle man, Francis was a missionary in Italy, Spain, and Egypt, and he visited Palestine. He was canonized by the Roman Catholic Church two years after his death.

Franklin, Benjamin (1706–1790), was perhaps the best-known person in the American Colonies. A signer of the Declaration of Independence and the Constitution, he was a philosopher, inventor, scientist, diplomat, writer, printer, statesman, and civic leader of Philadelphia. Among his many literary works was *Poor Richard's Almanac.*

Frederick I (1121?–1190), known as Barbarossa or Red Beard, was a king of Germany and the Holy Roman emperor. Often involved in conflicts with the pope, he set out on the Third Crusade, during which he drowned while crossing a river. His reign was marked by the advancement of learning and the development of towns and cities as well as by internal peace in his kingdom.

Frémont, John C. (1813–1890), was an explorer of the Western United States who won the nickname "the Pathfinder." He explored the area that is now Oregon, Nevada, and California and organized the seizure of California during the Mexican War. In 1856, Frémont became the first Republican candidate for the presidency. He led Union troops during the Civil War. Later, he served as territorial governor of Arizona.

Freud, Sigmund (1856–1939), an Austrian physician, founded psychoanalysis, a method of treating emotional problems through recall of repressed thoughts and feelings. Freud believed that the unconscious is a collection of memories that can govern human behavior. Freud also investigated the importance of infantile experiences, sexuality, and dreams. Among his writings are *The Interpretation of Dreams, Three Essays on the Theory of Sexuality,* and *General Introduction to Psychoanalysis.*

Frobisher, Sir Martin (1535?–1594), an English navigator during the reign of Elizabeth I, searched unsuccessfully for the Northwest Passage through North America. He reached Frobisher Bay, explored Labrador, and entered the Hudson Strait. He later participated in the sea battles against the Spanish Armada.

Frost, Robert Lee (1874–1963), an American poet, found inspiration for many of his finest works in the landscapes, folkways, and speech mannerisms of New England. His poems are known for their plain language, conventional forms, and graceful style. Frost won the Pulitzer prize for poetry four times. In 1960, Congress voted him a gold medal "in recognition of his poetry, which has enriched the culture of the United States and the philosophy of the world." Some of his best known works include "Mending Wall," "Birches," and "Stopping by Woods on a Snowy Evening."

Fulton, Robert (1765–1815), an American artist, engineer, and inventor, developed the first practical steamboat, the *Clermont,* which in 1807 steamed up the Hudson River from New York City to Albany. He also invented a machine for spinning thread, a machine for weaving rope, a dredge for cutting channels for canals, and a successful submarine.

Gagarin, Yuri Alekseyevich (1934–1968), a Russian air force pilot, became the first human to travel in space. During a 1961 space flight, he circled the earth at a speed of more than 17,000 miles (27,400 kilometers) per hour, reaching a maximum height of about 203 miles (327 kilometers) above the earth. Gagarin died in a plane crash in 1968.

Galen (130?–200?), the foremost physician of the Roman world, made discoveries about human anatomy that became the basis of medicine for centuries. He studied anatomy at Alexandria, Egypt, and in Rome gave lectures, conducted anatomical demonstrations, and served as physician to gladiators. He wrote several books, and even though his works contained many errors, his authority went unquestioned throughout much of the Middle Ages.

Galileo (1564–1642), an Italian astronomer and physicist, made important astronomical observations that confirmed the Copernican theory that the planets revolve around the sun. The Roman Catholic Church rejected his evidence and forced Galileo to recant his view. He built telescopes, discovered the law of the pendulum, and experimented with gravity.

Gandhi, Mohandas K. (1869–1948), the father of modern India, led the movement that forced Great Britain to grant India its independence in 1947. Trained as a lawyer, he fought discrimination in South Africa but returned to India to work for independence. Gandhi practiced passive resistance and civil disobedience and was frequently jailed for his actions.

Garibaldi, Giuseppe (1807–1882), was a leader of the movement that united Italy and was later a member of the Italian parliament. He led troops that freed Lombardy from Austria and conquered the Kingdom of the Two Sicilies. These areas became part of the Kingdom of Italy and were joined by Rome in 1870 to form the modern nation of Italy.

Gauguin, Paul (1848–1903), a French painter, produced brilliant canvases in bright colors with sweeping brushwork. Beginning his career as an impressionist, he was not well accepted. He left France for Tahiti, where he lived for most of the remainder of his life. In Tahiti, Gauguin produced some of his greatest paintings, which won acclaim in Europe.

Gauss, Karl Friedrich (1777–1855), a German mathematician and astronomer, established the mathematical theory of electromagnetism. A child prodigy, he produced his first important original work at the age of 19. Gauss made numerous contributions to astronomy, geometry, algebra, and number theory. He also invented a form of the telescope.

Genghis Khan (1167–1227), a Mongol conqueror, successfully invaded northern China and turned his forces toward the west. He also conquered parts of the Middle East. Though a military genius, he left few permanent influences on the lands he conquered.

Geronimo (1829–1909) was a chief of the southern Apache Indians, who resisted control by whites. Rather than go to a reservation, Geronimo moved his people from Arizona to Mexico. From there he led raids on American settlements. After surrendering in 1886, he and his tribe were sent to Oklahoma, where Geronimo spent the rest of his life.

Giacometti, Alberto (1901–1966), a Swiss sculptor, portrayed exaggeratedly long and slender human figures. At first, his work brought him little attention or praise, but he began to receive recognition after World War II. His use of bronze and terra cotta and his unusual sense of space and proportion earned him a secure place among modern sculptors.

Giotto (1267?–1337), an Italian painter, architect, and

sculptor, was among the first to portray human figures realistically in three instead of two dimensions. *The Descent from the Cross* and *The Madonna Enthroned with Saints* are two of his most famous paintings.

Gladstone, William Ewart (1809–1898), a British politician, began his long tenure of more than 60 years in Parliament as a Conservative but switched to the Liberal Party. He worked to expand suffrage, to increase elementary education, and to provide relief for Irish tenant farmers. Between 1868 and 1894, Gladstone served four terms as British prime minister.

Glenn, John (1921–   ), in 1962 became the first American astronaut to orbit the earth. In the spacecraft *Friendship 7,* he made three orbits during a flight of nearly five hours. As a naval pilot in 1957, Glenn made the first transcontinental nonstop flight in a supersonic aircraft. Glenn later became active in Democratic politics and was elected a senator from Ohio.

Goddard, Robert Hutchings (1882–1945), an American physicist, was a pioneer in the development of rockets. His experiments with solid and liquid rocket fuels, his work in the mathematical foundations of rocketry, and his many other discoveries led to the development of satellites, space exploration, and nuclear missiles.

Goethe, Johann Wolfgang von (1749–1832), a German poet and writer, inaugurated the romantic and modern movements in German literature. Among his works are the novel *The Sorrows of Young Werther,* a romantic love story, and the verse play *Egmont.* His play *Faust* is considered one of the most important works in modern Western literature.

Gompers, Samuel (1850–1924), an American labor leader born in England, was, except for one year, president of the American Federation of Labor from 1886 to 1924. He worked to improve the position of trade unionists and to abolish the court injunction as means of stopping strikes. Gompers supported free collective bargaining between employees and employers.

Gorgas, William Crawford (1854–1920), a United States Army physician, led a successful battle against yellow fever in Havana, Cuba. He became the chief sanitary officer of the Panama Canal Commission and eliminated yellow fever as a threat to workers building the canal. In 1914, Gorgas was made surgeon general of the Army.

Goya, Francisco (1746–1828), a Spanish artist, became the court painter, a position that brought him prosperity. His position, however, did not prevent him from painting subjects, including the royal family, as he saw them. Among his works are *The Family of Charles IV* and *The 3rd of May,* which depicts the French invasion of Spain. Goya also painted scenes of torture and of bullfighting.

Greco, El (1541?–1614), a painter, was born Domenikos Theotokopoulos in Crete but became famous in Spain, where he produced most of his work, as "the Greek." He painted many mystical religious scenes and landscapes, including *Christ Carrying the Cross* and *View of Toledo.*

Greeley, Horace (1811–1872), a newspaper editor and publisher, founded the *New York Tribune* in 1841. Greeley was influential in the antislavery movement and in efforts to ban alcoholic beverages. A Republican, he worked for the election of Abraham Lincoln. In 1872, the Liberal Republicans and Democrats formed a coalition to nominate Greeley for the presidency, but he lost the election to Ulysses S. Grant.

Grimm, Jakob Ludwig (1785–1863) and **Wilhelm Karl** (1786–1859), are known for their *German Dictionary* and for their collection of German fairy tales, including such well known stories as "Hansel and Gretel," "Little Red Riding Hood," "Snow White," "Sleeping Beauty," and "Cinderella." The Grimms collected the stories from people who lived and worked around Kassel, Germany. Jakob also formulated *Grimm's Law,* which was basic to the later development of comparative linguistics.

Gropius, Walter (1883–1969), a German-born architect, founded the Bauhaus school to coordinate the work of architects, artists, and building craftsmen. He created spare, functional designs that used materials in innovative ways. Beginning in 1937, Gropius taught at Harvard University and designed many buildings in the United States.

Gutenberg, Johannes (1395?–1486?), a German printer, invented type molds for casting individual letters. His invention made movable type practical. Gutenberg could produce any quantity of individual letters, arrange them into words, and place the type in a frame. His most famous production was the *Mazarin* (or *Gutenberg*) *Bible*.

Hadrian (76–138), a Roman emperor, improved the empire's fortifications, patronized the arts, curbed graft, and built many edifices in Rome. He had Salvius Julianus draw up a legal code that later became the basis for the Justinian Code. Hadrian established the Euphrates River as the empire's eastern boundary and visited Britain, where he supervised the building of Hadrian's Wall.

Hale, Nathan (1755–1776), an American patriot of the Revolutionary War, was hanged by the British as a spy when he was only 21 years old. Hale was on a mission to obtain information for George Washington about the British position in the New York City area when he was captured. According to tradition, his last words before death were, "I only regret that I have but one life to lose for my country."

Hamilton, Alexander (1755?–1804), who helped draft the U.S. Constitution, was the first secretary of the treasury. As an advocate of a strong federal government, he established a tax system, a mint, and a central bank. An able but controversial politician and diplomat, Hamilton was killed in a duel with Vice-President Aaron Burr.

Hammurabi (ruled about 1850–1750 B.C.) ruled the Babylonian empire during its greatest period of growth and prosperity. He enlarged the empire, established price and wage controls, and set up an efficient system of taxation. He established the Code of Hammurabi, a set of laws containing almost 300 definitions of crime and punishment.

Hancock, John (1737–1793), an American revolutionary leader, was the first person to sign the Declaration of Independence in 1776. Hancock served as president of the Continental Congress from 1775 to 1777 and hoped to command the Continental Army that fought for independence from the British. He was disappointed when Congress chose George Washington instead. Hancock later served nine terms as governor of Massachusetts.

Handel, George Frideric (1685–1759), a composer born in Germany who became a British subject, wrote both religious and secular music. He wrote several oratorios, including the *Messiah;* more than 40 operas; and many instrumental works. A favorite of the British royalty and people, he wrote *Water Music* and *Fireworks Music* for royal occasions.

Hannibal (247–183 B.C.) became Carthage's greatest general. He fought the Romans in Spain, and led an army through the Alps to Rome in the Second Punic War. Finally defeated in North Africa by Scipio, Hannibal became the civilian leader of Carthage. Faced with Roman captivity, he committed suicide.

Hardy, Thomas (1840–1928), a British novelist and poet, studied architecture but devoted most of his life to literature, becoming one of the most popular writers of his time. Among his novels are *Tess of the D'Urbervilles, The Return of the Native, Far from the Madding Crowd, Jude the Obscure,* and *The Mayor of Casterbridge.*

Harvey, William (1578–1657), an English physician, demonstrated the route of the circulation of blood in the human body. Many who clung to the theories of the Greek physician Galen attacked Harvey vigorously. However, his conclusions, which were based on sound observations, were eventually accepted.

Hawthorne, Nathaniel (1804–1864), an American writer, used symbolism to explore moral issues and human psychology. His novels include *The Scarlet Letter* and *The House of the Seven Gables.* Hawthorne's best-known

short stories include "Young Goodman Brown" and "Ethan Brand."

Haydn, Joseph (1732–1809), an Austrian composer, mastered the forms of the symphony and string quartet and established standards that influenced later composers. He wrote masses, several operas, oratorios, including *The Creation,* trios, more than 80 string quartets, and more than 100 symphonies.

Hearst, William Randolph (1863–1951), a powerful newspaper publisher, became famous for sensational news stories called "yellow journalism." He was partly responsible for arousing public opinion against Spain, which led to the Spanish-American War in 1898. Hearst's chain of newspapers made him wealthy, and he established a 240,000-acre estate, San Simeon, in California.

Hegel, Georg Wilhelm Friedrich (1770–1831), a German philosopher, was one of the most influential thinkers of the 1800's. He integrated earlier philosophies into a new system that stressed the historical sequence of philosophical ideas. His works include *Logic, Encyclopedia of the Philosophical Sciences,* and *Philosophy of Right.*

Hemingway, Ernest (1899–1961), one of the most popular American writers, was a master of a simple, terse prose style used to describe adventures that were concerned with moral values. He won the Pulitzer prize for fiction in 1953 and the Nobel prize in literature in 1954. Among his novels are *A Farewell to Arms, To Have and Have Not, The Sun Also Rises,* and *For Whom the Bell Tolls.*

Henry, Patrick (1736–1799), an American patriot known for his oratory, supported the Revolutionary cause in Virginia. A member of the Virginia House of Burgesses, he also served in the First Continental Congress and was on the committee that wrote Virginia's first state constitution. Henry was governor of Virginia during the Revolutionary War.

Henry II (1133–1189), through his marriage to Eleanor of Aquitaine, ruled over western France as well as England. When he quarreled with Thomas à Becket, the archbishop of Canterbury, over the power of the Roman Catholic Church, four of his knights murdered Becket. Henry II established the English common law and circuit courts. Late in his reign, his two sons led rebellions against him.

Henry VIII (1491–1547), who had six wives, brought about a church-state crisis with the divorce from his first wife. The divorce led to England's break with the Roman Catholic Church and the establishment of the Church of England. Two of his wives, Anne Boleyn and Catherine Howard, were executed. Henry VIII unified power in England and improved the English navy.

Henson, Matthew (1867–1955), a black man, gained fame as the only American to accompany American explorer Robert E. Peary to the North Pole in 1909. For more than 20 years, he went on expeditions with Peary and was often honored for his part in the explorations. Henson wrote *A Negro Explorer at the North Pole.*

Heraclitus (500's or 400's B.C.), a Greek philosopher, made change the basis of his teachings. He believed that everything constantly changes but that change is guided by logos, or intelligent laws. Heraclitus became known as "the weeping philosopher" because of his gloomy view that there are no lasting things in life.

Herodotus (484?–424? B.C.), called the "Father of History," traveled throughout most of the known world of the time and reported and commented on the customs, religion, and behavior of the people he came in contact with. Born in Asia Minor, he wrote a comprehensive history of the Persian empire, describing its beginnings, rise, and unsuccessful invasions of Greece.

Hertz, Heinrich (1857–1894), a German physicist, discovered electromagnetic waves and described their important characteristics. He demonstrated that the transmission of ultrahigh-frequency waves would produce oscillations in a distant wire loop. The development of radio, radar, and television was made possible by Hertz's discoveries.

125

Heyerdahl, Thor (1914–   ), a Norwegian ethnologist, in 1947 sailed a balsa-wood raft from Peru to islands in Polynesia to demonstrate that Polynesia could have been settled by ancient Peruvians. He told of his adventures on the trip in *Kon-Tiki*. Later, Heyerdahl and others built a reed boat, called *Ra-2*, in which they sailed from Africa to the West Indies.

Hidalgo, Miguel (1753–1811), a revolutionary Mexican priest, was one of the early leaders in the Mexican independence movement. Rallying followers in the village of Dolores, he marched south toward Mexico City. Although Hidalgo won some victories, the Spanish defeated his forces and captured him. Hidalgo was put to death, but his campaign began the war for Mexican independence.

Hillary, Sir Edmund (1919–   ), a New Zealand mountain climber and author, in 1953 with a companion became the first person to reach the top of Mount Everest in the Himalayas. He later led an expedition to climb Mount Makalu I. His books describing his experiences include *High Adventure* and *High in the Thin Cold Air*.

Hippocrates (460?–377? B.C.), a Greek physician called the "Father of Medicine," was the first to show that diseases have natural causes. He prescribed medicines and diets, practiced surgery, and set broken bones. Hippocrates formulated rules of conduct for doctors that became the basis for the Hippocratic oath.

Hitler, Adolf (1889–1945), the leader of the Nazi Party, ruled Germany from 1933 to 1945. He rearmed Germany and began World War II with an invasion of Poland in 1939. Hitler planned to conquer Europe and to exterminate all Jews. At first successful, German armies later met defeat by the Allies. Hitler committed suicide in an underground bomb shelter.

Hobbes, Thomas (1588–1679), an English philosopher, developed the theory that government arises as a social contract to protect the rights of individuals. He argued that, because humans are selfish, they need the rule of an all-powerful sovereign. Also a writer on physics and psychology, he believed that only matter exists. His most famous work is *Leviathan*, in which he describes his political theory.

Ho Chi Minh (1890–1969) led Vietnam to independence from France after World War II and became the founder and president of the Democratic Republic of Vietnam (then North Vietnam). A Socialist and later a Communist, he conducted a long war to unify North and South Vietnam, a campaign that eventually succeeded in 1975, after his death.

Holmes, Oliver Wendell (1809–1894), an American physician and medical educator, was better known as an essayist, poet, and novelist. His *The Autocrat of the Break-fast-Table* is a collection of essays, many humorous. Holmes's most popular poems include "Old Ironsides," "The Last Leaf," and "The Wonderful One-Hoss Shay."

Holmes, Oliver Wendell, Jr. (1841–1935), an American jurist, served for nearly 30 years on the Supreme Court of the United States, after having been a law professor at Harvard University and a justice on the Massachusetts Supreme Judicial Court. He believed in judicial restraint and in social experimentation. Holmes won attention for his dissenting opinions on many Supreme Court cases.

Homer (about 800? B.C.) was the reputed author of the Greek epic poems *The Iliad* and *The Odyssey*, which tell the story of the Trojan War and of Odysseus' long journey from Troy back to Greece. There has been a long controversy among scholars over whether the epics were the work of several authors or of only one. Other poems once attributed to Homer are now thought to be the work of other poets.

Homer, Winslow (1836–1910), was a painter who portrayed objects realistically but with drama and vitality. A war correspondent with Union troops during the Civil War, he painted such popular war pictures as *Prisoners from the Front*. Homer painted many seascapes of the Atlantic Coast.

Hooke, Robert (1635–1703), an English scientist, described the law of elasticity and the kinetic theory of gases. He made important astronomical observations and discoveries about the earth's and the moon's gravity. He also developed a reflecting telescope, a marine barometer, and a spring to regulate watches. Hooke is also credited with having discovered plant cells.

Houston, Samuel (1793–1863), born a Virginian, represented Tennessee in Congress and was governor of the state. He moved to Texas and worked for independence from Mexico and for admission of Texas to the Union. Houston became president of the Republic of Texas and, later, governor of the state and a senator from Texas.

Howe, Elias (1819–1867), an American inventor, in 1846 became the first person to patent a workable sewing machine. He found little interest for his invention in the United States and scarcely more in England, where he sold manufacturing rights. When other people in the United States began to manufacture sewing machines, Howe began a long and successful lawsuit to protect his patent.

Hudson, Henry (?–1611), an English navigator and explorer, made discoveries in the New World for Holland and England, giving each country some claims to land. He explored the Hudson River, Hudson Strait, and Hudson Bay. On his fourth voyage, his crew mutinied and cast him and eight others adrift in a small boat that apparently was lost.

Hughes, Langston (1902–1967), was a black American poet and writer. Many of his poems were set to music, and they were translated into several languages. His works include *Not Without Laughter, Shakespeare in Harlem, I Wonder As I Wander, The Weary Blues,* and *The Ways of White Folks*.

Hugo, Victor Marie (1802–1885), a French author, led the romantic movement in French literature. His work reveals his love of liberty, his strong sense of justice, and his sympathy with the suffering of ordinary people. His most popular works include the novels *The Hunchback of Notre Dame* and *Les Misérables*. Hugo also wrote poetry and plays.

Huygens, Christian (1629–1695), was a Danish astronomer, mathematician, and physicist. The first to use a pendulum to regulate a clock, he also developed the wave theory of light, improved methods of grinding lenses, constructed telescopes, and discovered a satellite and a ring of Saturn. Huygens also invented the measuring device known as the micrometer.

Ibn Khaldun (1332–1406), considered the greatest Arab historian, wrote a history of the known world. Born in Tunis in North Africa, he saw history as a series of civilizations, each growing and expanding through cooperation and then declining because of corruption and selfishness.

Ibsen, Henrik (1828–1906), a Norwegian playwright, is often called the father of modern drama. His works deal with real-life social problems in a direct manner. Some of Ibsen's best-known plays are *A Doll's House, An Enemy of the People,* and *Hedda Gabler*.

Ikhnaton (1300's B.C.), an Egyptian pharaoh also known as Akhenaton, was married to Nefertiti and was the first Egyptian ruler to promote the worship of one deity. He tried to abolish belief in many gods among the Egyptians and to make Aton, the sun god, the only deity. The movement did not survive his death.

Innocent III (1160?–1216) exercised perhaps the greatest power of any Roman Catholic Pope. Using his power to excommunicate and to mete out spiritual punishment, he dealt harshly with European monarchs such as Otto IV of Swabia and John of England. He promoted the Fourth Crusade, which resulted in the capture of Constantinople. Innocent III convened Lateran IV, a council that dealt extensively with Church doctrine.

Irving, Washington (1783–1859), an American author, is best known for two short stories, "Rip Van Winkle" and "The Legend of Sleepy Hollow." Irving's humorous stories and satirical essays, which poked fun at New York City's fashionable society, earned him recognition in Europe as well as the United States, and influenced other American writers who followed him. At various times, Irving was also a lawyer, businessman, and U.S. diplomat to England and Spain.

Isabella I (1451–1504), queen of Castile and Aragon, supported Christopher Columbus in his plan to find a faster route to the Indies by sailing west. Her support led to the discovery of the New World and the growth of the Spanish Empire. Together with her husband, Ferdinand, she strengthened the power of the Spanish monarchy.

Ivan IV (1530–1584) was the first czar of Russia. He conquered the area along the Volga River, expanded Russia into Siberia, made Moscow the capital, and reduced the power of the nobility. He acquired the name "the Terrible" because of his cunning and cruelty and because he killed his own son.

Jackson, Thomas J. (1824–1863), a Confederate general of the Civil War, earned the nickname "Stonewall" for his stand against Union forces at the first battle at Bull Run, Va., in 1861. A religious man much loved by his troops, Jackson was considered one of the Confederacy's finest generals. He was accidentally killed by his own men during a battle at Chancellorsville, Va.

James, Henry (1843–1916), an American novelist and short-story writer, often wrote from the point of view of one of his characters and emphasized human relationships and the individual in relation to society. Among his novels are *The American, The Portrait of a Lady, Daisy Miller, Washington Square* and *The Bostonians.* James spent much of his life in Europe.

Jay, John (1745–1829), was the first chief justice of the United States. He served in the Continental Congress, conducted foreign affairs, worked for the ratification of the Constitution, and negotiated a treaty with England. Jay served on the Supreme Court from 1790 to 1795, when he was elected governor of New York.

Jenner, Edward (1749–1823), a British physician, discovered vaccination. He developed a smallpox vaccine that used cowpox virus to immunize against the disease. By 1800, Jenner's vaccine was widely accepted. He received many honors, including a grant from Parliament and an honorary degree in medicine from Oxford University.

Jesus Christ (dates uncertain, but about 8 B.C. to A.D. 29) proclaimed the moral and theological teachings that became the foundation of the Christian religion. Accompanied by twelve disciples, He was a critic and a teacher, credited with healing and other miracles. Although many accepted Jesus as the Messiah, Jewish religious leaders condemned Him. He was executed by crucifixion but, according to the Gospels, arose in three days and ascended into heaven. (See "Religion.")

Joan of Arc, Saint (1412–1431), a French peasant girl, believed that she heard voices directing her to aid her country. She led a French army to victory over the English at Orleans in 1429 and defeated the English in other battles. Later imprisoned, she was tried as a witch and heretic by the French and burned at the stake. The Roman Catholic Church canonized Joan of Arc in 1920.

Jones, John Paul (1747–1792), was an American naval commander during the Revolutionary War. He won several engagements against the British, the greatest as commander of the *Bonhomme Richard,* which defeated the British ship *Serapis.* After the war Jones wrote on naval tactics and, at the invitation of the Empress Catherine, served for a time in the Russian navy.

Jonson, Ben (1572–1637), was an English playwright and poet whose reputation and influence on English drama rivaled that of William Shakespeare for a time. In 1616, he became the first playwright to prepare an edition of his own works for publication, claiming that drama be considered a serious form of literature. His best known works include the satiric comedies *Every Man in his Humour, Volpone, The Silent Woman,* and *The Alchemist.*

Joyce, James (1882–1941), an Irish writer, created some of the most complex and difficult masterpieces of modern literature in the English language. His major works include the novels *A Portrait of the Artist as a Young Man* and *Finnegans Wake* and the short-story collection *Dubliners.* Though Joyce lived away from Ireland after 1904, he set all of his work in Ireland and continued to explore the character of the Irish people.

Juárez, Benito (1806–1872), worked to establish constitutional government in Mexico to end foreign interference in the government. An Indian, he was elected president of Mexico in 1861. When the French invaded Mexico, Juárez led a successful war against them and captured Maximilian, who had been offered the throne by Mexican nobles under French influence. Juárez was elected to two additional terms as president; he is regarded as a great hero of Mexican independence.

Jung, Carl (1875–1961), a Swiss psychologist and psychiatrist, was influenced by Sigmund Freud but also developed his own theories, called analytical psychology. Like Freud, Jung stressed the importance of the unconscious, but he also emphasized the importance of "racial memory" and the will to live. He also focused on present problems rather than childhood trauma. Jung originated the distinction between introverts and extroverts.

Justinian I (482–565), called "the Great," was an emperor of the eastern Roman Empire. In wars against Vandals, Huns, and Franks, he won back much of the original empire that had been lost. He was responsible for the Corpus Juris Civilis, known as the Justinian Code, a body of civil law he had drawn up to govern his realm. The code became the basis for most European law.

Kant, Immanuel (1724–1804), a German philosopher, examined the nature and limits of human knowledge in the *Critique of Pure Reason.* For Kant, knowledge comes from the mind's involvement with the objects it experiences, and so the nature of human knowledge depends partly on the nature of the mind. He also wrote *Critique of Practical Reason,* a work on ethics that argued for absolute moral standards.

Keats, John (1795–1821), was an English romantic poet who expressed experiences of the senses, as well as ideas, in his works. Among Keat's best known poems are "Endymion," "Hyperion," "The Eve of St. Agnes," "On a Grecian Urn," and "La Belle Dame sans Merci." Plagued by poor health, he contracted tuberculosis and died in Italy.

Keller, Helen (1880–1968), became a famous American lecturer and writer even though she had lost her sight and hearing before she was 2 years old. Taught to speak and to read and write in braille, she graduated from high school and college. She devoted her life to working on behalf of the blind and published several books about her experiences.

Kelvin, William Thomson, Lord (1824–1907), a British mathematician and physicist, invented the mirror galvanometer and the siphon recorder and was an electrical engineer in charge of laying the Atlantic cable. He established a thermodynamic scale with −273.15° C as absolute zero. Lord Kelvin also contributed inventions and discoveries in numerous other fields.

Kenyatta, Jomo (1890?–1978), a leader for African independence, fought for the freedom of Kenya from British rule after World War II. He spent some time in jail for anti-British activities. When Kenya became free in 1963 after years of strife, Kenyatta became president of the new nation and became an important spokesmen for Africa.

Kepler, Johannes (1571–1630), a German astronomer and mathematician, discovered that planets have elliptical, or oval, orbits—rather than circular orbits. Kepler was the first astronomer to support Copernicus' findings openly. He was appointed imperial mathematician by Rudolph II, the Holy Roman Emperor.

Key, Francis Scott (1779–1843), an American lawyer, wrote the poem that was used as the lyrics of "The Star-Spangled Banner." From an American warship, he

127

witnessed the bombardment of Fort McHenry in the harbor of Baltimore during the War of 1812. The successful American defense of the fort inspired Key to write the poem which Congress made the national anthem in 1931.

Keynes, John Maynard (1883–1946), an English economist who was an adviser to the British government, achieved worldwide attention with his book *The Economic Consequences of the Peace.* He argued that governments should stimulate the economy with spending during times of slowdown to prevent unemployment and depression. His writings on government and economics became very influential.

King, Martin Luther, Jr. (1929–1968), was the foremost black leader of the civil rights movement in the 1950's and 1960's. A Baptist minister who believed in passive resistance and nonviolent civil disobedience, Dr. King led many demonstrations against racial discrimination in the United States and spent time in jail. He received the Nobel peace prize in 1964. He was assassinated in Memphis, Tenn.

Kipling, Rudyard (1865–1936), an English writer, was born in India and lived there for several years. India was the setting for many of his stories, novels, and poems. Among Kipling's popular works are *The Jungle Book, The Light That Failed, Just So Stories,* and *Barrack-Room Ballads,* which includes the poems "Gunga Din" and "On the Road to Mandalay." He was awarded the Nobel prize in literature in 1907.

Klee, Paul (1879–1940), a Swiss artist, developed an original style used to express the subconscious mind and fantasy. Living much of his life in Germany, he founded a movement called Blue Four in collaboration with German abstract artists. Klee taught for a time at the Bauhaus, a German school of design founded by the architect Walter Gropius.

Knox, John (1515?–1572), a Scottish Protestant theologian, statesman, and writer, successfully worked to establish Presbyterianism as the official religion of Scotland. Knox preached a stern and righteous doctrine and was a bitter enemy of Mary, Queen of Scots, a Roman Catholic who was queen of Scotland.

Koch, Robert (1843–1910), a German physician and bacteriologist, developed a method of growing and observing bacteria and found a vaccine for preventing anthrax in cattle. He also isolated the germ that causes tuberculosis and conducted research on bubonic plague in India and on other diseases. Koch won the 1905 Nobel prize in physiology or medicine.

Kosciusko, Thaddeus (1746–1817), a Polish patriot, arrived in America in 1776 to take part in the Revolutionary War. He participated in the Battle of Saratoga and built fortifications on the Hudson River. Returning to Poland, Kosciusko fought unsuccessfully to prevent the partition of his country among Prussia, Russia, and Austria.

Kublai Khan (1216–1294), established the Yüan, or Mongol, dynasty of China after expanding the conquests of his grandfather, Genghis Khan. He completed the conquest of China and made Peking his capital. Kublai Khan attempted unsuccessfully to conquer Java and Japan. He treated the people he conquered humanely and was a patron of arts and letters.

Lafayette, Marquis de (1757–1834), a French soldier and statesman, fought in the American Revolutionary War and became a prominent leader in the French Revolution. In 1830, he became the leader of a revolution that dethroned the Bourbon kings of France. Lafayette resisted popular pressure to become president of the French republic and instead worked to make Louis Philippe the constitutional monarch of France.

La Salle, Robert Cavelier, Sieur de (1643–1687), a French explorer in the New World, explored the Mississippi River Valley and claimed to have first reached the Ohio River. He named Louisiana and claimed the Mississippi Valley for France. Named viceroy of North America by Louis XIV, La Salle attempted unsuccessfully to establish a colony at the mouth of the Mississippi.

Lavoisier, Antoine Laurent (1743–1794), a French chemist, wrote the first chemical equation. He also gave the first scientific analysis of fire. Lavoisier was the author of *Elements of Chemistry,* the first modern chemistry textbook. Because he was a member of a financial company associated with the government, Lavoisier was put to death as an aristocrat during the French Revolution.

Le Corbusier (1887–1965), was the professional name of Charles Edouard Jeanneret-Gris, a Swiss-born French architect and city planner who became a leading influence on design in the 1900's. He used reinforced concrete, geometric shapes, flat roofs, and *pilotis* (columns that raise a building above the ground) in many of his buildings. Some of his most famous works include the Villa Savoye in Poissy, France; the Unité d'Habitation apartment building in Marseille, France; and the principal buildings of Chandigarh, India.

Lee, Robert E. (1807–1870), a Confederate general, commanded troops in the East in the Civil War. For a time, he successfully fought off Northern invasion of the South. When he tried to carry the war to the North, he met disastrous defeat at Gettysburg. His army was worn down by General Ulysses S. Grant, and in 1865 Lee surrendered at Appomattox Court House in Virginia.

Lewis, Meriwether (1774–1809), an American explorer, led an expedition with William Clark to explore the Louisiana Purchase. The party moved up the Missouri River from a point near St. Louis, crossed the Great Divide, and traveled down the Columbia River to the Pacific Ocean. The expedition returned with much valuable information on the new territory.

Liliuokalani (1838–1917), the last queen of Hawaii, had only a two-year reign. Wealthy American settlers on the islands led a revolt against her and established a republic in 1893. She tried in vain to reclaim her throne. After some hesitation because of the circumstances under which the queen had been deposed, the United States Congress in 1898 voted to annex Hawaii as a territory.

Lindbergh, Charles A. (1902–1974), became in 1927 the first person to fly solo nonstop across the Atlantic Ocean. Taking off from Long Island, N.Y., he landed in Paris 33½ hours later. A rich and famous man, he promoted commercial and military aviation. The kidnapping and murder of his son was the most sensational crime of the 1930's. Lindbergh's biography, *The Spirit of St. Louis,* won a Pulitzer prize in 1954.

Linnaeus, Carolus (1707–1778), a Swedish botanist and naturalist, developed a system for classifying plants and animals according to genus and species. Also a physician, a teacher, and a writer of several books on plants, Linnaeus is considered the founder of the modern system of botanical names.

Lister, Sir Joseph (1827–1912), an English surgeon, founded antiseptic (germ-free) surgery. Realizing the role played by bacteria in infections, Lister used carbolic acid to kill bacteria in operating rooms and on instruments. Because of his work, mortality rates after surgery, formerly very high, were reduced to a small percentage of those operated on.

Livingstone, David (1813–1873), a Scottish missionary and explorer in Africa, reached Lake Ngami, explored the Zambezi River, and reached Victoria Falls. Disappearing for a time, he was found and rescued by Henry M. Stanley, a newspaperman. Livingstone continued exploration and missionary work in Africa until his death there.

Livy (59 B.C.–A.D. 17), a Roman historian during the reign of Augustus, wrote *History from the Founding of the City,* a history in 142 volumes. Written over a period of 40 years, only 35 of the books have survived. Although Livy included legends and myths in his work, it is considered a principal source on the history of Rome.

Locke, John (1632–1704), an English philosopher, also wrote on education, psychology, and political theory. Locke believed that a government exists to promote the welfare of the people, and that if it does not do so, the

People

people have a right to change it. His ideas were used to justify the American Revolution.

London, Jack (1876–1916), an American writer, became famous for novels and short stories about dogs, such as *The Call of the Wild* and *White Fang*, and his tales of the sea. An adventurer in Alaska and at sea, in his writings London reflected his interest in primitive violence as well as his socialistic political opinions.

Longfellow, Henry Wadsworth (1807–1882), was a poet and a teacher of languages and literature. He was the most popular American literary figure of his time. Longfellow spent 18 years as a professor at Harvard University. Among his best known poems are *The Courtship of Miles Standish*, an account of life among the Pilgrims, and *The Song of Hiawatha*, which he based on an Indian legend.

Louis XIV (1638–1715), the Sun King, became the ruler of France at the age of 4. Presiding over a glittering court, he encouraged the arts, and the writers of his time contributed much to French literature. Louis XIV also led France into four major wars. Although a great monarch in many respects, his wars left France in debt with declining influence in Europe.

Louis XVI (1745–1793), suffered the consequences of misrule by the French monarchy when the French Revolution began. He was forced to call a meeting of the national assembly, which had not met for 175 years. Captured while trying to flee France, Louis XVI and his queen, Marie Antoinette, were executed by guillotine.

Luther, Martin (1483–1546), originally a German priest in the Roman Catholic Church, criticized corruption and broke with the church in 1517 to establish the Protestant Reformation. He believed that faith, rather than works, is the basis of salvation. Luther's teachings became the foundation for the Lutheran and other Protestant denominations that were formed in Europe.

MacArthur, Douglas (1880–1964), commanded United States forces in the Pacific area during World War II. His "island-hopping" strategy pushed Japan toward defeat. He later headed the occupation government in Japan. MacArthur commanded United Nations forces in the Korean War until 1951 when, following disputes with President Harry S. Truman, he was relieved of his command.

Machiavelli, Niccoló (1469–1527), an Italian Renaissance literary figure and statesman, wrote *The Prince*, a book on practical politics. He was a member of the Florentine government from 1498 to 1512. Machiavelli's political writings emphasized that the first consideration of a ruler must be success, not morality.

Magellan, Ferdinand (1480?–1521), a Portuguese navigator, led the first expedition to sail around the world. Leaving Spain in 1519, the fleet rounded Cape Horn on South America and proceeded across the Pacific Ocean. Although Magellan was killed in the Philippine Islands, one ship survived the remainder of the journey and reached Spain in 1522.

Malthus, Thomas Robert (1766–1834), an English clergyman and economist, wrote *Essay on the Principle of Population*, in which he argued that population growth tends to outrun food supplies and that excessive population growth encourages war and disease epidemics. He was pessimistic about the possibility of human survival unless population growth were checked. Malthus was also a history professor.

Manet, Édouard (1832–1883), a French painter, was a forerunner of the impressionists. Influenced by painters such as Goya, Velázquez, and Rembrandt, Manet produced flatly silhouetted forms that became popular. Among his works are *Le Bon Bock, Luncheon on the Grass, The Absinthe Drinkers, Argenteuil*, and *Boating*.

Mann, Horace (1796–1859), was a politician and educational reformer who did much to promote free public schools in the United States. He founded the first state normal school in the nation, in Lexington, Mass., and improved public control and financial support for schools

in the state. He later served as president of Antioch College in Ohio.

Mann, Thomas (1875–1955), had a long literary career in which he became perhaps the foremost German novelist of the 1900's. He left Germany in 1933 when the Nazis came to power. Among his many complex and difficult works are *Buddenbrooks, Joseph and His Brothers, Doctor Faustus, Mario and the Magician, Death in Venice, Tonio Kröger*, and *The Magic Mountain*.

Mao Tse-tung (1893–1976), the leader of the Chinese Communist revolution, based his movement on the peasants. In the 1930's, he led his followers to northern China, established a government, and fought Japanese invaders. After the Communist victory over Nationalist Chinese forces in 1949, Mao became both chairman of the party and head of state.

Marconi, Guglielmo (1874–1937), an Italian engineer and inventor, developed wireless telegraphy. He produced the first practical wireless telegraph in 1895 and sent the first transatlantic signal in 1901. His other inventions included a magnetic detector and a directional aerial. In 1909, Marconi shared the Nobel prize in physics.

Marcus Aurelius (121–180), a Roman emperor, was also a learned Stoic philosopher. Although he is considered one of the few "good emperors" of Rome, his reign was marked by barbarian invasions, wars, epidemics, severe economic difficulties, and persecution of Christians.

Maria Theresa (1717–1780), was the Holy Roman empress, the archduchess of Austria, and the queen of Hungary and Bohemia. The War of the Austrian Succession and the Seven Years' War shrank her empire, but she remained an influential monarch during her reign of nearly 40 years.

Marie Antoinette (1755–1793), the daughter of Maria Theresa, was the wife of King Louis XVI of France. She was blamed for being extravagant, frivolous, and insensitive, particularly to the poor. During the French Revolution, she and the king attempted to flee the country. They were captured, tried, and executed by guillotine.

Marlowe, Christopher (1564–1593), an English playwright, was the first great Elizabethan writer of tragedy. His most famous work is *The Tragical History of Doctor Faustus*. Other works include *Tamburlaine*, the *Jew of Malta*, and *Edward II*.

Marquette, Jacques (1637–1675), a French Jesuit missionary and explorer, made an expedition with the fur trader Louis Joliet that followed the Mississippi River as far south as the Arkansas River. For a number of years, he did missionary work among American Indians. One of the most important French explorers of America, Marquette kept a journal of his Mississippi voyage, which was published posthumously.

Marshall, John (1755–1835), was one of the most influential justices of the United States. During his 34-year term, he made the Supreme Court of the United States an important branch of the government. By affirming the power to declare laws unconstitutional, many of his decisions strengthened the power of the Court. He also increased the power of the federal government over the states.

Marshall, Thurgood (1908–   ), became the first black associate justice of the Supreme Court of the United States following his nomination by President Lyndon B. Johnson in 1967. From 1938 to 1961, Marshall was chief counsel for the National Association for the Advancement of Colored People (NAACP). He presented the legal argument that resulted in the 1954 Supreme Court decision that racial segregation in public schools is unconstitutional. Marshall also served on the U.S. Court of Appeals and as solicitor general of the United States.

Marx, Karl (1818–1883), a German philosopher, collaborated with Friedrich Engels on *The Communist Manifesto*. A Socialist who was forced to leave Germany for England, he wrote *Das Kapital*, an analysis of capitalism that became the basis for the Communist movement. Marx believed that economic conditions govern human behavior.

129

Mary, Queen of Scots (1542–1587), the daughter of King James V of Scotland and the mother of James I of England, was one of the last Roman Catholic rulers of Scotland. When revolt forced her to flee Scotland in 1568, she found refuge in England with her cousin, Queen Elizabeth I. Found guilty of aiding a plot to overthrow Elizabeth, Mary was beheaded.

Mather, Cotton (1663–1728), was an influential Puritan clergyman. The son of a minister, Increase Mather, Cotton Mather was considered a prime mover behind the witchcraft trials in Massachusetts in the 1690's. He wrote on many subjects, including the history of New England. Deeply interested in science and education, Mather became one of the founders of Yale College.

Mazzini, Giuseppe (1805–1872), an Italian patriot, spent many years in exile for his efforts to unify Italy. An advocate of a republic, he was displeased when Italy, except for Rome, was unified in 1861 under a king. He tried to organize a republican revolt in Sicily but failed. Mazzini died before his dream of a united republican Italy was fulfilled.

Mead, Margaret (1901–1978), an anthropologist, made firsthand studies of island societies in the South Pacific. She was also a commentator on the problems of contemporary American society. She was curator of technology at the American Museum of Natural History in New York City. Among her writings are *Coming of Age in Samoa, Growing Up in New Guinea,* and *Male and Female.*

Medici, Lorenzo (1449–1492), known as "the Magnificent," was a member of the Medici family that ruled Florence, Italy, during the Renaissance. Although an immoral and tyrannical ruler, he encouraged the building of libraries and other public structures, making Florence one of the world's most beautiful cities. He himself was a learned man and an accomplished writer and poet.

Meir, Golda (1898–1978), born in Russia and a long-time resident of Milwaukee, emigrated to Palestine, became active in the Zionist movement, and served as prime minister of Israel from 1969 to 1974. She was also a minister to the Soviet Union, minister of labor, and minister for foreign affairs.

Melville, Herman (1819–1891), an American writer, based several of his books on his experiences as a seaman in the South Pacific. His most famous novel, *Moby Dick,* recounts the destructive efforts of Captain Ahab to capture a whale. Melville's other works, most of which are about the struggle between good and evil, include *Redburn, Billy Budd,* and *The Confidence-Man.*

Mendel, Gregor Johann (1822–1884), an Austrian monk and botanist, established that certain characteristics of animals and plants are inherited. He also determined that certain characteristics are dominant and others recessive. His conclusions were based on extensive work in breeding garden peas. Mendel laid the foundations for the modern study of heredity and genetics.

Mendeleev, Dmitri (1834–1907), a Russian chemist, developed the periodic table of the elements, which gave a system to the properties of elements. On the basis of the table, he predicted the existence of elements that were then unknown but were later discovered. He also made contributions to meteorology and petroleum chemistry.

Metternich, Prince von (1773–1859), an Austrian statesman and minister of foreign affairs, guided the establishment of the Holy Alliance in 1815 following the Napoleonic Wars. He created a European balance of power that lasted until 1914. Antidemocratic in his politics, Metternich helped suppress nationalistic and democratic revolts in Europe in the 1840's.

Michelangelo (1475–1564) was an Italian painter, architect, sculptor, and poet of the Renaissance. He painted the frescoes on the ceiling of the Sistine Chapel in Rome and *The Last Judgment* on one wall. Michelangelo designed a chapel and tombs for the Medici family. Among his sculptures are the *Pietà* and a colossal figure of David.

Mies van der Rohe, Ludwig (1886–1969), a German-born architect, used glass, steel, and brick to create buildings with simple, even austere, lines. His work includes the Seagram Building in New York City; several buildings on the campus of the Illinois Institute of Technology in Chicago, where he taught after 1938; and apartment buildings in Chicago.

Mill, John Stuart (1806–1873), an English economist and philosopher, favored women's rights, higher pay for workers, and cooperative agriculture, among other progressive causes. Among Mill's works are *System of Logic, On Liberty,* and *Principles of Political Economy.* His book *Utilitarianism* explains his philosophy that pleasure, in its widest sense, is the basis for human action.

Milton, John (1608–1674), an English poet, wrote his greatest works, *Paradise Lost, Paradise Regained,* and *Samson Agonistes,* after he had become totally blind. A Puritan, he wrote on politics and on religion in such works as *The Tenure of Kings and Magistrates* and *Of Reformation in England.* Milton also wrote *Areopagitica,* a defense of freedom of the press.

Molière (1622–1673), was the stage name of Jean Baptiste Poquelin, France's leading writer of comedy. Molière's plays deal with the theme of the contrast between how people see themselves and how others see them. His best known works include *The School for Wives, Tartuffe, The Misanthrope,* and *The Imaginary Invalid.*

Monet, Claude (1840–1926), a French painter, was a leader of impressionism, a name that derived from his painting *Impression: Sunrise.* His technique was to place separate spots of color side by side in such a way that the eye would blend them from a distance. Among his other paintings are *The Haystacks* and *The Thames.*

Montesquieu (1689–1755), was a French philosopher and writer who satirized contemporary French society and wrote a history of Rome. His *The Spirit of the Laws* deals with different forms of government. Montesquieu believed that governmental checks and balances among the executive, judicial, and legislative branches are necessary. His ideas formed the basis for the separation of powers in the United States Constitution.

Montezuma II (1480?–1520), was the Aztec Emperor of Mexico when the Spaniards under Hernando Cortés arrived in Tenochtitlan (now Mexico City). At first, Montezuma thought Cortés was Quetzalcóatl, the White God of the Aztec, and he welcomed the Spaniards with gifts of golden ornaments. Later, he tried to prevent the Spaniards from entering the city, but it was too late. Cortés captured the city, and Montezuma was stoned to death by his own people.

More, Saint Thomas (1477?–1535), an English statesman, served King Henry VIII as lord chancellor. He opposed Henry's plan to divorce his first wife. After Henry VIII established the Church of England, More continued his opposition and was tried for treason and beheaded. He wrote *Utopia,* a futuristic work describing practices such as communal ownership, universal education, and religious toleration.

Morgan, John Pierpont (1837–1913), was one of the most powerful financiers in American history. His banking house in New York City financed many new industries across the country and marketed government bonds. He helped organize the United States Steel Corporation. Although he gave much money for education and philanthropy, Morgan was criticized for the considerable financial power that he wielded.

Morse, Samuel F. B. (1791–1872), best known for his invention of the telegraph, was also a painter and a sculptor. He spent many years developing a device that would transmit sound by means of electric wires. He carried out a historic demonstration of the telegraph in 1844 at the U.S. Capitol.

Moses (1200? B.C.), a great leader of the Israelites, was born in Egypt. To escape persecution, Moses led his people across the Red Sea to the Promised Land of Palestine. On the journey, he received the Ten Commandments from God on Mount Sinai. Although he saw Palestine from a distance, Moses did not live to enter the Promised Land.

Mozart, Wolfgang Amadeus (1756–1791), an Austrian composer, wrote operas, chamber music, concertos, symphonies, and church music. He was a child prodigy. Among his most popular works are the operas *Don Giovanni* and *The Magic Flute*. Mozart wrote 41 symphonies, including the *Jupiter* (Number 41).

Muhammad (570?–632), the Prophet, founded the religion of Islam, whose followers are called Muslims. A trader in Mecca in Arabia, at about age 40 he experienced visions that led him to become a prophet and teacher. He became a civic as well as a religious leader in Medina and attracted many converts. Many of his teachings were collected in the Koran. (See "Religion").

Mussolini, Benito (1883–1945), founded the Fascist Party and in the 1920's became the dictator of Italy. Under his rule, Italy conquered Ethiopia and attacked Albania and Greece. Italy fought in support of Germany in World War II but was defeated by Allied armies in 1943. Mussolini was captured and executed by partisans.

Napoleon I (1769–1829), emperor of France, seized control of the government in 1799 and began to conquer Europe. A brilliant military leader, he created a vast empire but met a disastrous defeat in Russia in 1813. Exiled, Napoleon returned to France in 1815 but was defeated by English and Prussian forces at Waterloo. He died in exile.

Nasser, Gamal Abdel (1918–1970), an Egyptian army officer, led a revolt against King Farouk in 1952 and later became president of Egypt. He took control of the Suez Canal in 1956 and adopted a more militant policy toward Israel and the West. Nasser did not succeed in uniting Arab nations under Egyptian leadership, but he did bring about economic reforms in Egypt.

Nebuchadnezzar II (died 562 B.C.), a Babylonian king, built Babylon into one of the most beautiful cities of the ancient world. He may have been responsible for building the Hanging Gardens. He destroyed Jerusalem and placed the Israelites in captivity. According to the Bible, Nebuchadnezzar suffered periodically from debilitating delusions.

Nehru, Jawaharlal (1889–1964), was a leader in the independence movement in India and became the country's first prime minister in 1947. He supported state-controlled economy and favored neutrality in the Cold War between the Communist powers and the United States. Nehru retained control of the Ruling Congress Party and was prime minister until his death.

Nelson, Horatio (1758–1805), Viscount Nelson, was Great Britain's greatest admiral and naval hero. He defeated the combined French and Spanish fleets at Trafalgar in the greatest naval victory in British history. His victory broke France's naval power, and established Britain's rule of the seas for the rest of the 1800's.

Nero (37–68), an emperor of Rome, led a dissipated private life that included acts such as the murder of his mother. The creature of his advisers, he ruled well during the first part of his reign when he had competent aides. Under later advisers, his reign was marked by misrule and persecution of Christians. Nero was deposed as emperor, and he committed suicide.

Newton, Sir Isaac (1642–1727), an English scientist and mathematician, made revolutionary contributions in mathematics, astronomy, and physics that became the foundations of modern physical science. He developed the law of gravity, discovered that sunlight is a mixture of colors, established laws of motion, invented calculus, and constructed a reflecting telescope. His writings include *Mathematical Principles of Natural Philosophy* and *Optiks*.

Nietzsche, Friedrich (1844–1900), a German philosopher and writer, was a critic of Christianity who searched for a morality outside religion. He valued the "superman," a person who uses power creatively. As a psychologist,

Nietzsche valued power more than morality or feelings. *The Antichrist* and *Thus Spake Zarathustra* are among his writings.

Nightingale, Florence (1820–1910), an English nurse, hospital reformer, and philanthropist, introduced sanitary practices into hospitals and thereby reduced the incidence of infectious diseases. Born into wealth, she became a nurse and directed nursing operations in the Crimean War. Known as "The lady with the lamp," she later founded the Nightingale Home for Nurses in London and was an adviser for many countries concerning military hospitals.

Nkrumah, Kwame (1909–1972), led the African nation of Ghana to independence from Great Britain in 1957 and became the nation's president in 1960. He promoted education, health and welfare, and industrialization, but he tended to rule dictatorially. When the country had economic difficulties, the army ousted him in 1966. Nkrumah lived in exile in Guinea.

Nobel, Alfred Bernhard (1833–1896), a Swedish chemist, became a wealthy man through his invention of dynamite. The use of his invention in warfare troubled him, and he set up the Nobel Fund, with an initial sum of more than $9 million, to award annual prizes for those who make contributions to international peace and other fields. The Nobel prize has become the world's most important award.

Nyerere, Julius Kambarage (1922–   ), was a leader in the African independence movement. After Tanganyika became free from British rule in 1961, he became prime minister and then president of the country. As head of the government, Nyerere developed socialistic programs for his country, though he promoted democracy. Tanganyika later joined Zanzibar to become Tanzania.

O'Connor, Sandra Day (1930–   ), became the first woman to serve as an associate justice of the U.S. Supreme Court following her nomination by President Ronald Reagan in 1981. She served as a county judge and as a judge on the Arizona Court of Appeals before stepping up to the Supreme Court. Earlier in her career, she had served as an assistant attorney general of Arizona and as a member of the Arizona Senate, where she was majority leader in 1973.

O'Higgins, Bernardo (1778–1842), was the leader of the movement to free Chile from Spain. With José de San Martín of Argentina, he led an army across the Andes Mountains to defeat the Spanish at Chacabuco and won final victory in 1818. O'Higgins became the ruler of Chile but was deposed in 1823.

O'Keeffe, Georgia (1887–   ), an American artist, created lyrical paintings of flowers and scenes of the Southwest that often included animal skulls. She painted in both abstract and realistic styles. O'Keeffe's paintings include *Lake George, Black Iris, Canada, Farmhouse Window and Door,* and *A Cross by the Sea.*

O'Neill, Eugene (1888–1953), is considered America's greatest playwright. He wrote 45 plays, most expressing a pessimistic view of life. They vary in length from one act to the 11-act *Mourning Becomes Electra.* O'Neill's other major works include *Desire Under the Elms, The Iceman Cometh,* and *Long Day's Journey into Night.* O'Neill won the 1936 Nobel prize for literature, as well as four Pulitzer prizes.

Oppenheimer, J. Robert (1904–1967), an American physicist, became known as the man who built the atomic bomb. From 1943 to 1945, he directed the Los Alamos laboratory near Santa Fe, N. Mex., where the design and building of the first atomic bomb took place.

Ovid (43 B.C.–A.D. 17 or 18), was a great Roman poet best known for his witty, sophisticated love poems. His *Art of Love* is a humorous, satirical manual in verse on falling in love. In *Metamorphoses (Transformations),* Ovid included more than 200 tales taken from the favorite legends and myths of the ancient world.

Paine, Thomas (1737–1809), born in England, became

the foremost pamphleteer of the American Colonies. His most famous pamphlet, *Common Sense*, succinctly stated the patriot cause and inspired popular support for it. Later works included *Rights of Man* and *The Age of Reason*.

Pascal, Blaise (1623–1662), was a French religious philosopher, mathematician, and scientist. Pascal's Law states the principle that liquid in a vessel carries pressures equally in all directions. Pascal invented the theory of probability with Pierre de Fermat. He also invented a calculating machine.

Pasteur, Louis (1822–1895), a French chemist and bacteriologist, developed pasteurization, a process that destroyed bacteria in wine and milk. He also investigated plant diseases, advanced the knowledge of immunity from disease, and developed a successful vaccine against rabies. The Pasteur Institute in Paris was founded in his honor.

Peary, Robert E. (1856–1920), an American naval officer and explorer, led numerous Arctic expeditions. In 1909, with Matthew Henson and four Eskimos, he reached the North Pole. Controversy over prior discovery arose, however, between him and Frederick A. Cook, who claimed to have reached the pole on an earlier expedition. A congressional investigation awarded the honor to Peary.

Penn, William (1644–1718), an English Quaker, founded the colony of Pennsylvania in 1681, primarily as a refuge for those suffering religious persecution. Although he owned Pennsylvania, he visited America only twice.

Pepin the Short (714?–768) was the king of the Franks who founded the Carolingian dynasty. He helped Pope Stephen II expel the Lombards from Ravenna in northern Italy and expanded his own kingdom to include Aquitaine in France. Pepin carried out educational and religious reforms and left his kingdom to his sons Carloman and Charlemagne.

Pericles (490?–429 B.C.), an Athenian statesman, encouraged art, literature, and architecture during his rule, known as the "Age of Pericles." He expanded democracy in the city and Athenian influence throughout the Mediterranean world. Pericles also prepared Athens for war with Sparta; he led Athenians in the Peloponnesian War against Sparta from 431 B.C. to 429 B.C., when he died of the plague.

Pershing, John Joseph (1860–1948), commanded the American Expeditionary Forces (A.E.F.) in Europe during World War I. The A.E.F. was the first U.S. Army ever sent to Europe. After the war, he received the highest rank ever given to an American Army officer, General of the Armies of the United States. (The same title was granted to George Washington in 1976.) Pershing served as chief of staff of the U.S. Army from 1921 to 1924, when he retired.

Peter I (1672–1725), called "the Great," was a czar of Russia who expanded Russian power in wars with Turkey, Persia, and Sweden. He improved his army and built a navy. Peter modernized Russia, introducing Western civilization and making the country an important European power. He founded the city of St. Petersburg (now Leningrad) and made it his capital.

Philip II (1527–1598), king of Spain, was a defender of the Roman Catholic faith who promoted the Inquisition and Counter Reformation. Trying to invade and conquer Protestant England, he launched the Great Armada, a Spanish naval force that the English defeated in 1588. The defeat of the Armada marked the beginning of a decline in Spanish power.

Philip II (382–336 B.C.), king of Macedonia, was a military genius who conquered the Greek city-states. He organized the Greek cities into the League of Corinth, which later helped them mount their attack against Persia. Philip was assassinated and was succeeded by his son Alexander the Great.

Picasso, Pablo (1881–1973), a Spanish-born artist, painted in nearly every modern art form, including cub-

ism. He did most of his work in France and produced a prodigious number of paintings and drawings. Among his paintings are *The Three Musicians*, *Guernica*, and *Les Demoiselles d'Avignon*. Picasso also produced many sculptures.

Pitt, William (1708–1778), an English statesman, was an influential member of Parliament, who as secretary of state helped organize the British victory over France in the Seven Years' War. At times out of favor with the king, he later entered the House of Lords as Earl of Chatham and frequently spoke in favor of American colonial rights.

Pitt, William, the Younger (1759–1806), an English statesman, entered Parliament at the age of 21 and became prime minister almost three years later, serving until 1801 and again from 1804 to 1806. He is considered one of the greatest prime ministers of Britain, surpassing even the excellent reputation of his father. Pitt's most important foreign achievements were in dealing with the effects of the French Revolution, the early years of Napoleonic rule, and French expansion.

Pizarro, Francisco (1478?–1541), conquered the Inca empire in Peru and opened the way for Spain's colonization of most of South America. King Charles I of Spain made Pizarro governor of Peru. In 1535, Pizarro founded the city of Lima and made it Peru's capital.

Plato (427?–347? B.C.), a Greek philosopher who was a pupil of Socrates, opened an academy in Athens and made it the intellectual center of Greece. In his dialogues, Plato taught that ideas are more real than the physical world, and in *The Republic* described an ideal state ruled by philosopher kings. Aristotle, who succeeded Plato as the intellectual leader of Greece, was his pupil.

Pliny the Elder (23–79), a Roman writer, admiral, and lawyer, produced many works on history, science, rhetoric, and military tactics. Only one work survives, his monumental *Natural History*, an encyclopedia of science. Pliny was killed by the eruption of Mount Vesuvius that destroyed the city of Pompeii.

Pliny the Younger (61?–113?), a Roman writer who was a nephew of Pliny the Elder, served for a time as the Roman governor of Bithynia and Pontica in the Near East. His description of the treatment of early Christians was one of the first historical accounts of the new religion. In his *Letters*, Pliny described the scholarly and gentlemanly life he led.

Plutarch (A.D. 46?–120?), was a Greek biographer and essayist best known for his work, *Parallel Lives of Illustrious Greeks and Romans*. It consists of biographies of Greek and Roman statesmen and generals and is considered an important source of historical information.

Pocahontas (1595?–1617) was the daughter of the chief of the Powhatan tribe in Virginia. As a young girl, she reportedly saved the life of Captain John Smith. Colonists took her hostage during a conflict with her father and his warriors. She met John Rolfe, whom she married and accompanied to England. About to return to Virginia, Pocahontas died of smallpox.

Poe, Edgar Allan (1809–1849), an American writer created poems and short stories of mystery and horror that focused on human madness. His tales of mystery include "The Murders in the Rue Morgue," "The Purloined Letter," and "The Masque of the Red Death." Among his well-known poems are "Ulalume," "The Raven," and "Annabel Lee."

Polo, Marco (1254?–1324?), a member of a Venetian merchant family, made a journey to China with his father and uncle. During the visit, Marco entered the diplomatic service of the Chinese ruler, Kublai Khan. Leaving China, the Polos returned to Venice in 1295 after a 24-year absence. Marco wrote *Description of the World*.

Pompey (106–48 B.C.), a Roman statesman and general, gained prominence in the Roman civil wars and was elected consul. With Caesar and Marcus Crassus he ruled Rome as a part of the First Triumvirate. After disagreements with Caesar, he was defeated in battle, and fled to Egypt, where he was killed by Ptolemy.

Ponce de León, Juan (1474–1521), a Spanish explorer, accompanied Christopher Columbus on his second voyage and later became governor of Puerto Rico. Searching for Bimini, reputed to be the site of the mythical Fountain of Youth, he explored part of Florida. Trying to found a colony in Florida, he was wounded in a battle with Indians and died.

Ptolemy (A.D. 100?–165?) was one of the greatest astronomers and geographers of ancient times. He worked in Alexandria, Egypt, producing a 13-volume work called *Mathematike Syntaxis*. Ptolemy believed the earth was motionless, and around it, the sun, moon, and planets traveled at various speeds. His ideas were accepted in Europe until the mid-1500's.

Ptolemy I (367?–283 B.C.), a general under Alexander the Great, became king of Egypt after Alexander's death. Making Alexandria his capital, he expanded his rule to include Cyrene, Crete, and Cyprus. He encouraged education and was responsible for establishing the great library and museum at Alexandria.

Pulaski, Casimir (1748–1779), was a Polish patriot who, after an unsuccessful revolt against Russian rule, came to America to join in the Revolutionary War. After service under George Washington, he was made a brigadier general and was in charge of the cavalry corps. Pulaski died from wounds suffered during the American siege of Savannah, Ga.

Pulitzer, Joseph (1847–1911), was a Hungarian immigrant who became a great American newspaper publisher and founder of the Pulitzer prizes. He worked as a laborer, reporter, and editor before buying the *St. Louis Dispatch* and *Evening Post* newspapers and combining them into one newspaper—the *St. Louis Post-Dispatch*. He then bought *The World*, a New York City newspaper, and transformed it into a vigorous publication with the largest circulation in the nation. *The World* became one of the first papers to use color comics and the sensational reporting that gave rise to "yellow journalism."

Pythagoras (500's B.C.), a Greek mathematician and philosopher, developed the Pythagorean Theorem in geometry. As a philosopher, he taught that numbers are central to all things and believed in the transmigration of souls. Pythagoras apparently was the first philosopher to believe that the earth is a sphere and that the sun, moon, and planets move.

Raleigh, Sir Walter (1552?–1618), an English courtier, navigator, historian, and poet, attempted unsuccessfully to found a colony in America. He was at times a favorite of the English court and at other times was in disfavor. Charged with treason and imprisoned by King James I, he wrote *History of the World*. Released to conduct an expedition for gold in South America, he disobeyed the restrictions that had been placed on him, for which he was beheaded.

Raphael (1483–1520), ranks as one of the greatest and most influential painters of the Italian Renaissance. He painted altarpieces, frescoes of historical and mythological scenes, and portraits, including many of the Virgin Mary. His leading works include *Marriage of the Virgin* and *Madonna of the Goldfinch*.

Rembrandt (1606–1669), a Dutch artist, used sharp contrasts of light and dark in his paintings. In his many portraits, he often painted himself and members of his family. Rembrandt produced many drawings and etchings. Among his works are *The Night Watch, Aristotle Contemplating the Bust of Homer,* and *The Prodigal Son*.

Renoir, Pierre Auguste (1841–1919), a French painter who was a leader of the impressionists, produced many landscapes, paintings of flowers, and works featuring children and young girls. He frequently used his children and his wife as models. Among his works are *The Luncheon of the Boating Party, The Bathers,* and *Mme. Charpentier and Her Children*.

Revere, Paul (1735–1818), was a colonial silversmith and patriot who participated in the Boston Tea Party. In 1775, he was one of those who rode from Boston with a warning of the British advance on Lexington, Mass. He fought in the Revolutionary War and also cast bronze cannons for the army.

Richard I (1157–1199), the English king known as the Lion-Hearted, joined a crusade that captured some territories from the Muslims. On his return he was taken prisoner in Austria and freed only after ransom was paid. Leaving his government in his advisors' hands, Richard embarked on a war against France, during which he was killed.

Richardson, Henry Hobson (1838–1886), an American architect, first attracted attention with his design for Boston's Trinity Church, which he based on the Romanesque style of the Middle Ages. He eventually developed an innovative style in designs for commercial buildings, public buildings, and houses.

Richelieu, Cardinal (1585–1642), was a French cleric and statesman who virtually ran the government of King Louis XIII. He rescinded political privileges of the Huguenots, curbed the nobility's power, conducted war against Spain, and furthered French interests during the Thirty Years' War. Richelieu encouraged the arts and the founding of the French Academy.

Rivera, Diego (1886–1957), a Mexican artist, painted murals in which labor and revolution were the major themes. He was a Communist, and many of his paintings embodied his view of the oppression of workers. He has been credited with influencing social changes in Mexico that have improved the lives of the lower classes. Rivera helped persuade the Mexican government to allow artists to decorate the interiors of public buildings.

Robespierre (1758–1794), was a leader in the French Revolution. As a radical Jacobin, he successfully urged the execution of King Louis XVI. He was partially responsible for the Reign of Terror, which executed thousands of people. When his fortunes turned, Robespierre himself was executed by guillotine.

Rockefeller, John D. (1839–1937), founded the Standard Oil Company and became wealthy from the oil business. He was strongly criticized for building monopolies and for such business practices as demanding rebates on freight rates from railroad companies. He established the Rockefeller Foundation for philanthropic endeavors.

Rodin, Auguste (1840–1917), was an influential French sculptor. He developed a realistic and perfectionist style in early works like the *Age of Bronze* that many people found startling. Rodin's other statues and busts include *The Gate of Hell, Saint John the Baptist, The Bather, Adam and Eve,* and *The Thinker*.

Roentgen, Wilhelm (1845–1923), a German physicist, through investigations of the mysterious fogging that appeared on photographic plates placed near glass tubes charged with electricity, discovered X rays. He found that X rays would pass through flesh but not bone, a discovery that revolutionized medicine. Roentgen won the first Nobel prize in physics, in 1901, for his discovery.

Rousseau, Jean Jacques (1712–1778), a French philosopher and writer, believed that human beings are naturally good but are corrupted by social and political institutions. He championed the "natural" man and natural rights. Rousseau emphasized feelings over reason and impulsiveness over restraint, particularly in education. His writings include *Emile* and *The Social Contract*.

Rubens, Peter Paul (1577–1640), a Flemish painter, was also a diplomat and a scholar. A master of several languages, he undertook diplomatic missions to Spain and England. He is remembered chiefly as a painter, however. His landscapes, portraits, and religious and historical paintings include *Elevation of the Cross, The Descent from the Cross,* and *The Battle of the Amazons*.

Russell, Bertrand (1872–1970), an English philosopher and mathematician, wrote *Principles of Mathematics* and,

133

with Alfred North Whitehead, *Principia Mathematica,* works that established the foundations for modern mathematics and logic. He frequently espoused such unpopular causes as pacifism, which sometimes got him dismissed from teaching positions and arrested. A writer on many subjects, Russell won the 1950 Nobel prize in literature.

Rutherford, Ernest (1871–1937), Baron Rutherford of Nelson, a British physicist, is known as the "father of nuclear science." He developed the nuclear theory of the atom in 1911, and also discovered alpha and beta rays and protons.

Salk, Jonas (1914–   ), an American scientist, developed a vaccine against poliomyelitis that was tested on nearly two million children. Found safe, it became the first effective means of reducing frequent epidemics of polio. Salk made other important contributions in the field of immunization.

Sandburg, Carl (1878–1967), was an American poet, biographer, and historian. Many of his works reflect his enthusiasm for the common people of America. His *Complete Poems* won the 1951 Pulitzer prize for poetry. From 1920 to 1939, he completed a six-volume history of Abraham Lincoln and the Civil War, a work that won the 1940 Pulitzer prize for history. Sandburg's other works include *Always the Young Strangers,* an autobiography; *The American Songbag,* a collection of ballads and folk songs; and three volumes of humorous stories for children.

San Martín, José de (1778–1850), an Argentine soldier and statesman, helped free South America from Spanish rule. He joined Bernardo O'Higgins to defeat Spanish forces in Chile and later fought for the independence of Peru. He became disenchanted with political quarreling in South America and withdrew from politics. San Martin's achievements, however, allowed other statesmen to complete the battle for independence.

Schiller, Johann Christoph Friedrich von (1759–1805), a German playwright and poet, is generally considered to be the greatest dramatist ever to write in the German language. Political freedom is a frequent theme in his plays, which include *Wallenstein, Don Carlos, The Robbers, Maria Stuart,* and *William Tell.*

Schweitzer, Albert (1875–1965), a German clergyman, philosopher, physician, and musician, served for many years as a medical missionary in Africa. He established a hospital in what is now Gabon, and treated thousands of patients. When he won the Nobel peace prize in 1952, Schweitzer used the money to establish a leper colony. An organist, he was an authority on Bach.

Scipio, Publius Cornelius (236?–184? B.C.), a Roman general known as Scipio the Elder, defeated the Carthaginians in Spain and invaded Africa from Sicily. He defeated the great Carthaginian general Hannibal in battle at Zama. His victory ended the Second Punic War between Rome and Carthage and earned Scipio the title "Africanus Major."

Scott, Sir Walter (1771–1832), was a Scottish romantic writer who created and popularized historical novels in a long series of works called the *Waverly* novels. They include *Ivanhoe, The Heart of Midlothian,* and *The Talisman.* Scott also produced narrative poetry, including such works as *Marmion* and *The Lady of the Lake.*

Shakespeare, William (1564–1616), generally considered the greatest dramatist and poet in any language, prospered as an actor and playwright at the Globe Theatre in Elizabethan London. His comedies include *The Comedy of Errors, A Midsummer Night's Dream,* and *Taming of the Shrew.* Among his tragedies are *Romeo and Juliet, Hamlet,* and *Macbeth.*

Shaw, George Bernard (1856–1950), an Irish-born dramatist, critic, and essayist, used his work to promote various social reforms. He wrote more than 50 plays, including *Candida, Man and Superman, Major Barbara, Saint Joan,* and *Pygmalion.* He won the Nobel prize for literature in 1925.

Shelley, Percy Bysshe (1792–1822), an English poet, wrote romantic lyric poems. A revolutionary, he lived much of his life outside England. Many of his works reflect his hatred of tyranny and his belief in human perfectability. Among his poems are "Ode to the West Wind," "To a Skylark," and "Adonais."

Shepard, Alan Bartlett, Jr. (1923–   ), became the first American in space during a flight from Cape Canaveral, Fla., in 1961. Shepard traveled 117 miles (188 kilometers) into space and landed 15 minutes later, 302 miles (486 kilometers) out in the Atlantic Ocean. Shepard later became the fifth astronaut to set foot on the moon.

Sherman, William Tecumseh (1820–1891), was a Union general in the Civil War. He captured and burned Atlanta in a destructive "march to the sea" through Georgia that ended at Savannah. After the war, he became commanding general of the Army. Sherman wrote an account of his military experiences in his *Memoirs.*

Siqueiros, David Alfaro (1898–1974), a Mexican artist, painted frescoes and murals upholding revolutionary ideals. A radical, he joined revolutionary forces when he was 15 years old and was later imprisoned in Mexico and expelled from the United States. His murals can be seen in buildings in Mexico City.

Sitting Bull (1834?–1890), a Sioux leader and medicine man, helped prepare Sioux warriors for battle against the whites led by General George A. Custer at Little Bighorn. Retreating to Canada after the battle, Sitting Bull returned in 1881 and was imprisoned. He was later killed by an Indian policeman, allegedly while resisting arrest.

Smith, Adam (1723–1790), a Scottish economist, wrote *The Wealth of Nations,* arguing that labor is the basic source of wealth. He urged that markets and trade be free from government control. Smith believed that unfettered economic self-interest produces the greatest good for the greatest number of people.

Smith, John (1580?–1631), an English soldier and adventurer, helped establish the first permanent English colony in America, at Jamestown, Virginia, in 1607. He later explored the Massachusetts Bay area and named the region "New England." His book *The Generall Historie of Virginia, New-England and the Summer Isles* helped promote American colonization.

Smith, Joseph (1805–1844), was the founder of the Church of Jesus Christ of Latter-day Saints, or the Mormon Church. His converts met persecution in several Midwestern states, sometimes because of their practice of polygamy. When a mob killed Smith and his brother Hyrum in Illinois, many Mormons migrated to the Great Salt Lake Valley in Utah.

Socrates (369?–399 B.C.), a Greek philosopher, taught mainly by asking questions, a technique called the "Socratic method." He tried to develop principles for good conduct but was accused of corrupting youth by destroying their faith in the gods. Put on trial, he was found guilty and carried out his sentence by drinking poison hemlock. Socrates left no writings but is a character in most of the dialogues of his student Plato.

Solomon (around 973–around 933 B.C.) succeeded his father David as king of Israel. Under Solomon, the kingdom reached its peak in prosperity and influence. His greatest accomplishment was the building of the Temple of Jehovah in Jerusalem. Known for his wisdom, Solomon was the reputed author of books of the Bible, including Proverbs and Ecclesiastes.

Solon (639?–559? B.C.) was a Greek poet and lawgiver. Elected a ruler of Athens, he carried out many economic and political reforms. Solon's greatest achievement was a constitution that provided for rule by a council of 400 and for a system of public courts, a milestone in Athenian democracy.

Sophocles (496?–406? B.C.), a Greek tragedian, wrote 100 plays, of which only 7 have survived. His central characters are people who choose courses of action that can lead only to suffering or death, a fate they face heroically.

134

Among Sophocles' works are *Electra, Antigone,* and *Oedipus Rex.*

Stalin, Joseph (1879–1953), dictator of the Soviet Union from 1929 until his death, eliminated his political enemies and ruled his country through secret police terrorism. He formed agricultural collectives and developed industry. Stalin led the Soviet Union during World War II and later expanded Soviet influence in Eastern Europe.

Steinbeck, John (1902–1968), was an American author known for his novels about poor, oppressed California farmers and laborers. Steinbeck expressed his liberal political views in several novels, including his best-known work, *The Grapes of Wrath,* which won a Pulitzer prize. Steinbeck also won the Nobel prize for literature in 1962. His other major works include *Tortilla Flat, Of Mice and Men,* and *East of Eden.*

Stevenson, Robert Louis (1850–1894), a Scottish author, wrote many popular novels, essays, and poems. He traveled widely and lived the last few years of his life in Samoa in the South Pacific Ocean. His works include *Treasure Island, Kidnapped, The Strange Case of Doctor Jekyll and Mr. Hyde,* and *A Child's Garden of Verses.*

Stowe, Harriet Beecher (1811–1896), an American writer and the daughter of a noted Congregational minister, wrote the antislavery novel *Uncle Tom's Cabin.* The novel was very popular, but aroused much antipathy in the South. It was credited with making the question of slavery a moral issue.

Stuart, Gilbert Charles (1755–1828), an American artist, is perhaps best known for his unfinished portrait of George Washington. Washington sat for a total of three portraits by Stuart. Stuart's work as a portrait painter gained him recognition and popularity in England as well as the United States.

Sullivan, Louis (1856–1924), an American architect, changed American design from historical imitation to the development of a distinctly American style. He adapted traditional principles to modern requirements in his designs for skyscrapers. His buildings included the Wainwright Building in St. Louis and the Stock Exchange Building in Chicago.

Sun Yat-sen (1866–1925), a Chinese revolutionary, helped bring about the downfall of the Ch'ing dynasty. When the revolution succeeded in 1911, the Chinese Republic was established. Sun failed to unify China, however, and carried on several years of struggle with rival political leaders. It was only after his death that unity was achieved.

Swift, Jonathan (1667–1745), an English writer and Anglican clergyman who was born and lived much of his life in Ireland, satirized many of the cruelties and excesses of his time. His most famous work, *Gulliver's Travels,* satirized political institutions. He wrote about poverty in Ireland in *A Modest Proposal* and about religious corruption in *A Tale of a Tub.*

Tacitus (about 55–about 120), a Roman politician, orator, and historian, wrote several works on the history of the Roman Empire. Biased in favor of the republican form of government, he criticized the emperors and the imperial system. Among his works are *Histories, Annals, Germania, Life of Agricola,* and *Dialogue on Orators.*

Tchaikovsky, Peter Ilich (1840–1893), a Russian composer, wrote melodic and emotional romantic music. He composed the opera *Eugène Onégin,* the ballets *Swan Lake* and *Nutcracker,* and the symphonic poem *Romeo and Juliet.* Tchaikovsky's symphonies include *Symphony No. 5* and *Symphony No. 6,* the "Pathétique."

Tennyson, Lord (1809–1892), Alfred, Baron of Aldworth and Farringford, was a leading English poet of the 1800's. He succeeded William Wordsworth as poet laureate in 1850. Among his greatest works are *In Memoriam,* which consists of 133 poems, and *Idylls of the King,* 12 narrative poems dealing with King Arthur and his knights. He is also known for his patriotic poem "The Charge of the Light Brigade."

Tereshkova, Valentina (1937–), a Soviet cosmonaut, became the first woman in space in 1963, completing 48 orbits around the earth. Untrained as a pilot, she made parachuting a hobby before joining the Soviet space program.

Thomson, Sir Joseph John (1856–1940), an English physicist, discovered the electron. Experimenting with cathode tubes, he established that the rays they emitted were not light waves but were composed of particles of matter. Thomson also discovered the first isotopes of elements and in 1906 won the Nobel prize in physics.

Thoreau, Henry David (1817–1862), was an American writer and philosopher. Along with his friend Ralph Waldo Emerson, Thoreau elaborated the transcendentalist philosophy of individualism and mysticism. His works include *Walden, A Week on the Concord and Merrimack Rivers,* and the essay "Civil Disobedience."

Titian (1487?–1576), a Venetian painter of the Italian Renaissance, became one of the most influential and successful painters in art history. His works include portraits and paintings of myths and religious scenes. Among his notable paintings are *The Rape of Europa* and *Man in a Red Cap.*

Tocqueville, Alexis de (1805–1859), a French writer and politician, wrote *Democracy in America,* after a visit to the United States in 1831 to study prisons. In the book, he skillfully analyzed the American character and American politics. He also wrote *The Old Regime and the French Revolution.* De Tocqueville held several positions in the French government.

Tolstoy, Leo (1828–1910), a Russian novelist, believed in social reform and nonviolence. Born an aristocrat, he later gave up worldly pleasures, adopted a fundamentalist form of Christianity, and lived a simple, pious life. Tolstoy's novels include *War and Peace, Anna Karenina,* and *Resurrection.*

Toulouse-Lautrec, Henri de (1864–1901), a French artist, painted dance hall scenes, circus performers, and cabaret scenes. An accident early in life left him deformed, and dissipated living brought about his early death. A designer of posters and an illustrator and lithographer, his works include *The Ringmaster* and *In the Circus Fernando.*

Trotsky, Leon (1897–1940), a Russian revolutionary, led the army against forces opposed to the revolution of 1917. After Lenin's death, he lost the struggle for leadership to Stalin. Banished from the country, Trotsky was murdered in Mexico. He wrote several books, including *My Life.*

Tubman, Harriet (1820?–1913), born a slave, escaped to the North in 1849 and began a campaign against slavery. She worked with the Underground Railroad and helped more than 300 blacks escape from slavery. After the Civil War began, she offered her services to the Union Army and worked as a nurse, cook, and spy.

Turgenev, Ivan Sergeevich (1818–1883), a Russian novelist, usually portrayed liberals as ineffectual, even though he was a liberal. His most famous novel is *Fathers and Sons,* in which he popularized the term *nihilist.* Turgenev also wrote the short story "First Love" and the novels *Rudin, A Nest of Gentlefolk,* and *On the Eve.*

Tutankhamon (reigned about 1347–1335 B.C.), an Egyptian pharaoh, ruled for only a few years. After changes by his predecessor, he restored the traditional religion and moved the capital back to Thebes. When his tomb in the Valley of the Kings near Luxor was discovered in the 1920's, it was largely untouched by grave robbers. Thousands of objects, many of them solid gold, were removed from the tomb and placed in the Cairo Museum in Egypt.

Twain, Mark (1835–1910), whose real name was Samuel Langhorne Clemens, was an American writer whose novels and stories appealed to children but also made perceptive comments on American society. His boyhood experiences serve as background for *The Adventures of Tom Sawyer*, and *The Adventures of Huckleberry Finn*. Twain's many other writings include *A Connecticut Yankee in King Arthur's Court* and *The Mysterious Stranger*.

Tweed, William Marcy (1823–1878), whose name became synonymous with graft, was the political boss of New York City for many years. He and his associates in the Tweed Ring cost the city millions of dollars through fraudulent supply and building contracts. Tweed was arrested in 1871, convicted, and jailed.

Updike, John (1932–   ), is an American author of novels, short stories, essays, and poetry. Much of his fiction explores the materialism of middle-class American life. His works include the novels *Rabbit Run, The Centaur, Couples, Rabbit Redux*, and *Rabbit Is Rich*, and the short-story collections *Pigeon Feathers* and *Museums and Women*. Updike won the 1982 Pulitzer Prize for fiction.

Van Gogh, Vincent (1853–1890), a Dutch painter, used thick brushstrokes to produce works of brilliant color. Many of his paintings seem to reflect the mental illnesses that he experienced for much of his life. Mental disturbances finally drove him to suicide. Among Van Gogh's works are *Self Portrait, The Starry Night*, and *Le Pont d' Arles*.

Verdi, Giuseppe (1813–1901), an Italian composer, wrote operas with dramatic plots and beautiful melodies. Among his best known operas are *Il Trovatore, Rigoletto, La Traviata*, and *Aida*. Verdi also wrote the *Requiem Mass*. His operas are considered to be among the finest written and are often performed today.

Verne, Jules (1828–1905), a French author, wrote science fiction that accurately forecast many technological developments some years before they actually appeared. Among his novels are *A Journey to the Center of the Earth, Twenty Thousand Leagues Under the Sea, Around the World in Eighty Days, The Mysterious Island*, and *From the Earth to the Moon*.

Vespucci, Amerigo (1454–1512), an Italian-born explorer, made three known voyages to America, beginning in 1499. He also claimed to have reached what is now the American mainland in 1497. A German mapmaker who believed that Vespucci was the first European to reach the New World suggested that the land be named *America*. The name was quickly adopted, though historians today doubt Vespucci's claim.

Victoria (1819–1901), in 63 years as queen of Great Britain and Empress of India, had the longest reign of any English monarch. During her rule, the British Empire was at the peak of its size and power, and the queen commanded domestic and foreign affairs during the latter half of the 1800's. With Victoria as the symbol, the era became known as the Victorian Age.

Virgil (70–19 B.C.), a Roman poet, modeled his greatest work, the *Aeneid*, partly on Homer's *Iliad* and *Odyssey*. Virgil's epic poem, a tribute to Rome, deals with the founding of the city, the growth of its power, and the civilizing effects of the Roman empire. Virgil's other works include the *Eclogues* and the *Georgics*.

Voltaire (1694–1778) was the pen name of the French writer François Marie Arouet. Perhaps the most influential thinker of his time, he advocated religious toleration in his poem *La Henriade* and satirized social wrongs in *Candide*. Voltaire also wrote histories, encyclopedia articles, and dramas.

Von Braun, Wernher (1912–1977), a rocket engineer, was in charge of Germany's efforts to build rockets during World War II. He developed the V-2 rocket used against England in the latter days of the war. After the war, he worked for the United States contributing to the development of the powerful rockets used in space flights.

Wagner, Richard (1813–1883), a German composer, wrote operas that he called music dramas. His operas are long and costly to stage but are often performed today. His works *The Rhine Gold, The Valkyrie, Siegfried*, and *The Twilight of the Gods* comprise a group called The

Ring of the Nibelung, based on heroic themes and myths from the ancient German past. Wagner's other operas include *Tristan and Isolde* and *Parsifal*.

Washington, Booker T. (1856–1915), the best-known black leader of his time, organized Tuskegee Institute, a school for blacks in Alabama, and served as its president. Washington accepted separation of the races and believed that education and skills would eventually elevate blacks economically. He wrote *Up from Slavery*.

Watson, James D. (1928–   ), an American biologist and chemist, worked on the development of a model of deoxyribonucleic acid (DNA), the substance that acts as a code in conveying genetic information from one generation to the next. He shared a Nobel prize in 1962. Watson's writings include *The Double Helix*.

Watt, James (1736–1819), a Scottish engineer and inventor, improved the steam engine. He invented the condensing steam engine and made numerous other improvements on existing engines. The patent on the Watt steam engine made him wealthy. The watt, a unit of electric power, is named for him. Watt also did work in metallurgy and chemistry.

Webster, Daniel (1782–1852), a lawyer and politician, served many years as a United States senator from Massachusetts, beginning in 1827. He was an eloquent spokesman for the Union during the states' rights controversy before the Civil War. Webster was also secretary of state under Presidents William Henry Harrison and John Tyler.

Webster, Noah (1758–1843), an American educator and journalist, won fame for compiling a dictionary of the English language. He published his first dictionary in 1806, then produced the two-volume work, *An American Dictionary of the English Language*, in 1828. This work contained 12,000 words and 40,000 definitions that had never before appeared in a dictionary.

Wellington, Arthur Wellesley, Duke of (1769–1852), a British general and statesman, won decisive victories in the Peninsular War against Napoleon. His later victory at Toulouse in 1814 forced Napoleon to abdicate his throne. When Napoleon returned from exile, Wellington defeated him with the aid of Prussian troops at Waterloo in 1815.

Wesley, John (1703–1791), an English Anglican minister, founded the Methodist Church. The church grew out of societies that Wesley organized and before which he preached. Methodism spread rapidly in England and in America. Between 1735 and 1738, Wesley served as a chaplain and missionary to Indians in Georgia.

Wheatley, Phillis (1753?–1784), considered the first black woman poet in America, was brought to America as a slave in 1761. Purchased by John Wheatley, a Boston tailor, she became his wife's personal servant. A child prodigy, she published her first poem in 1770. She moved to England for a year and was very popular there. She published many religious poems.

Whistler, James Abbott McNeill (1834–1903), an American artist, is best known for his work *Arrangement in Gray and Black: Portrait of the Artist's Mother*, commonly called *Whistler's Mother*. He also produced about 440 etchings, including many illustrations of Venice and the River Thames.

Whitman, Walt (1819–1892), an American poet, wrote poems praising America and democracy. He was a newspaperman and editor, was active in the antislavery movement, worked as a nurse during the Civil War, and later held minor government jobs. Whitman is considered to be one of the first poets to write in a distinctively American style. His volume *Leaves of Grass* is considered a classic.

Whitney, Eli (1765–1825), an American inventor, developed the cotton gin that separated cotton fibers from the seeds. The invention vastly increased the amount of cotton that could be grown and harvested. Later he used interchangeable parts to mass-produce guns.

Willard, Emma Hart (1787–1870), made important contributions to education for women in the United States.

She founded a girls' boarding school in Vermont and later a girls' seminary in New York that became famous as the Emma Willard School. Her school emphasized teacher training and educated hundreds of young women. She also wrote history textbooks and poetry.

William I (1027?–1087), an English king known as "the Conquerer," led an invasion and conquest of England from Normandy in 1066. To centralize his power, he forced all landholders, including the nobility, to swear allegiance directly to him. During his reign, he took an extensive census and survey of the English land, which was compiled in the Domesday Book.

Williams, Roger (1603?–1683), an English clergyman, founded the colony of Rhode Island. He was a forceful advocate of religious and political liberty. Williams won the friendship and trust of the Indians in the area and compiled a dictionary of their language.

Wolfe, Thomas (1900–1938), wrote long and lyrical autobiographical novels. Born and raised in North Carolina, Wolfe taught at New York University from 1924 to 1930 before turning to writing full time. Among his works are *Look Homeward, Angel; Of Time and the River; You Can't Go Home Again;* and *The Web and the Rock.*

Wordsworth, William (1770–1850), an English poet, was a romantic writer of poems about nature. In collaboration with Samuel Taylor Coleridge, he wrote *Lyrical Ballads,* poems that denounce artificiality and glorify the senses. Among his poems are "I Wandered Lonely as a Cloud," "She Was a Phantom of Delight," "Lines Composed a Few Miles above Tintern Abbey," "The Prelude," and "Ode: Intimations of Immortality."

Wren, Sir Christopher (1632–1723), an English architect, designed plans for the rebuilding of some 50 churches, including St. Paul's Cathedral, after the London fire of 1666. He also designed a master plan for the city of London, but it was not adopted. Wren's other works include the library of Trinity College at Oxford and additions to Hampton Court Palace.

Wright, Frank Lloyd (1867–1959), an American architect, designed hundreds of houses and other buildings. He developed a horizontal "prairie style" for houses and other buildings, and he established architectural schools in Wisconsin and in Arizona. Wright also designed the Im-

perial Hotel in Tokyo and the Guggenheim Museum in New York City.

Wright, Wilbur and Orville (1867–1912 and 1871–1948), after experimenting with kites and gliders, constructed and flew the first powered airplane on December 17, 1903. They contracted with the United States government for military planes and established factories in France and in Germany.

Xerxes I (519?–465 B.C.), a Persian king descended from Cyrus the Great and Darius I, invaded Greece with nearly 200,000 men in 480 B.C. The Persians won at Thermopylae but were later defeated at Salamis and Plataea. Xerxes' invasion was the last Persian attempt to conquer the Greeks. He spent the last years of his life in dissolute living and was murdered by a soldier.

Young, Brigham (1801–1877), was a convert to the Mormon faith who became a leader in the church. Three years after the Mormon leader, Joseph Smith, was killed in Illinois in 1844, Young led the Mormons west to Great Salt Lake Valley where they established settlements. He was the first governor of the Territory of Utah. Partly because he practiced polygamy, the United States government removed him as governor. He was put on trial but was not convicted.

Zapata, Emiliano (1880?–1919), a Mexican revolutionary, joined the revolt against President Porfirio Diaz in 1910. An Indian who became a leader of other revolutionary movements, he was committed to land redistribution and refused to recognize the new Mexican government. Zapata continued his opposition, frequently with armed resistance, until his assassination.

Zenger, John Peter (1697–1746), born in Germany, emigrated to New York and became a printer. When his newspaper criticized the British governor, Zenger was arrested for seditious libel. Represented by the lawyer Andrew Hamilton, who argued truth as a defense for libel, Zenger was acquitted. The case helped establish the principle of freedom of the press in America.

Zwingli, Huldreich (1484–1531), a Swiss clergyman, was among the first clericals to demand reforms in the Roman Catholic Church and to support the Protestant Reformation. Although they had some religious differences, Zwingli supported Martin Luther.

Plants

There are more than 350,000 kinds of plants. Plants live in almost every part of the world—on mountaintops, in the oceans, in forests and grasslands, even in many desert and polar regions. For information about kinds of plants that grow in various regions of the world, see the Biomes map and table in the "Earth" section. Information about the early development of plant life on earth appears in the "Outline of earth history" table in the "Earth" section.

Scientific classification of the plant kingdom

Scientists classify plants by separating them according to their differences and by grouping them according to their likenesses. The classification below groups plants primarily by their (1) structure and (2) method of reproduction.

Classification	Description

Subkingdom Thallophyta (plants without true roots, stems, and leaves)

Algae

Phylum Euglenophyta
These microscopic, one-celled organisms live chiefly in warm, fresh water. Some scientists classify them as both plants and animals. Like most plants, they get energy from the sun. Like some simple animals, they move about by means of a hairlike structure called a *flagellum.*

Phylum Chrysophyta
This group consists of yellow-green and golden-brown algae and diatoms. Most species have only one cell, but some consist of colonies of cells. These tiny plants live in fresh water, salt water, and damp places. Diatoms are an important source of food for fish.

Phylum Pyrrophyta
Most members of this phylum are called *dinoflagellates.* These tiny marine plants give off a red substance that poisons fish. When present in large amounts, this red substance causes the so-called *red tide* that kills great numbers of fish.

Phylum Chlorophyta
The many species of this group are commonly called *green algae.* Most are microscopic, but some, such as sea lettuce, can be seen with the unaided eye. Green algae grow in both salt and fresh water. They sometimes form a green scum on the surface of lakes and ponds.

Phylum Phaeophyta
These brown algae are the largest of the algae. Kelp, for example, grow as long as 200 feet (61 meters). Most brown algae live along the shores of cold oceans. One specie, *sargassum.* grows in the Sargasso Sea, an area of the North Atlantic Ocean.

Phylum Rhodophyta
The red algae of this phylum usually have a branched appearance. Few grow over 3 feet (91 centimeters) tall. Most live attached to rocks along warm ocean shores. A few species grow on the ocean floor, sometimes 600 feet (180 meters) below the surface.

Fungi

Phylum Myxomycophyta
The tiny, simple plants in this phylum are called *slime molds* or *slime fungi.* They consist of a jellylike mass called *plasmodium* that moves slowly. This mass may be orange, red, or white. Most species are *saprophytes,* living on dead plants and animals. A few are *parasites,* which exist on living tissue of other plants or animals.

Phylum Eumycophyta
These true fungi vary widely in size and shape. All are either saprophytes or parasites. They are grouped into four classes: (1) Phycomycetes (algalike fungi), (2) Ascomycetes (sac fungi), (3) Basidiomycetes (club fungi), and (4) Deuteromycetes (imperfect fungi).

Classification	Description

Subkingdom Embryophyta (plants that grow from an embryo)

Mosses and liverworts

Phylum Bryophyta Mosses and liverworts make up most plants in this phylum. They reproduce by means of spores and sex cells. An embryo is formed during the sexual stage of reproduction. Mosses and liverworts lack xylem and phloem tissue and thus do not have true roots, stems, or leaves.

Class Hepaticae The plants in this class are called *liverworts*. Most are shaped like small, round leaves and grow close to the ground. Some have a more elongated appearance.

Class Musci True mosses make up this class. Most species have erect branches with many leaflike growths. They seldom grow over 8 inches (20 centimeters) long.

Vascular plants

Phylum Tracheophyta Plants in this phylum are sometimes called *vascular plants* because they have xylem and phloem tissues that carry materials from one part of the plant to another. All members of this phylum produce embryos during sexual reproduction.

Subphylum Psilopsida Most species of this subphylum are extinct. Those that remain have slender, leafless stems that grow from underground rhizomes.

Subphylum Lycopsida Club mosses are small plants with tiny leaves arranged in a spiral shape. During the Carboniferous Period, large tree species of club moss existed.

Subphylum Sphenopsida Horsetails, the only surviving species, have small leaves that occur in whorls at the nodes. They grow 3 to 4 feet (91 to 120 centimeters) tall, but were tree-size in early times.

Subphylum Pteropsida This subphylum consists of three important classes of plants—(1) ferns, (2) cone-bearing plants, and (3) flowering plants. About two-thirds of all plant species belong to this subphylum. These plants supply people with most of their food and many raw materials.

Class Filicineae All plants in this class are ferns. They have large leaves called *fronds*. Most species do not grow more than a few feet or a meter tall. But some tropical tree ferns may reach heights of 40 feet (12 meters). Ferns reproduce by means of spores and sex cells.

Cone-bearing and related plants

Class Gymnospermae All species of gymnosperms have naked seeds. Most are trees that produce their seeds on female cones. Some of these trees are the largest and oldest of all living things. The class is divided into two subclasses—Cycadophytae and Coniferophytae.

Subclass Cycadophytae Cycads have fernlike leaves and large seed cones. The leaves of some species are atop a tall stem. On others, the leaves grow from an underground stem.

Subclass Coniferophytae Most trees and shrubs of this subclass are evergreens with needlelike or scale-like leaves. A broadleaf tree called the *ginkgo* also belongs to this group.

Flowering plants

Class Angiospermae All angiosperms have covered seeds. These plants have their sex cells in flowers. After fertilization, the ovary grows and encloses the seeds in a fruit. Flowering plants are divided into two subclasses—Dicotyledoneae and Monocotyledoneae.

Subclass Dicotyledoneae Dicots have seeds with two tiny leaves called *cotyledons*. Their leaves have branching veins. Their flower petals usually grow in multiples of four or five.

Subclass Monocotyledoneae The seeds of monocots have only one cotyledon. The veins in their leaves run parallel to each other. Their flowers usually grow in multiples of three.

Flowering Plants

More than half of the more than 350,000 kinds of plants are flowering plants. In addition to garden flowers and wildflowers, this group includes most fruits, grains, herbs, shrubs, trees, and vegetables. Flowering plants have four main parts: (1) roots, (2) stems, (3) leaves, and (4) flowers.

Roots

Most roots grow underground, where they anchor a plant and absorb the water and minerals a plant needs to grow. The roots of some plants, such as carrots, also store food for the rest of the plant to use. The two main types of root systems are *fibrous* and *taproot.* Fibrous systems consist of many slender roots of about the same size that spread out in all directions. A taproot system has one root that is larger than the others.

When a plant begins to grow, a *primary root* emerges from the seed. *Secondary roots* quickly branch out from the primary root. A *rootcap* protects the delicate tip of each root as it pushes through the soil. Tiny *root hairs,* which grow farther back on the root, greatly increase a plant's ability to absorb water and minerals from the soil.

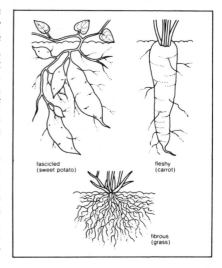

fascicled
(sweet potato)

fleshy
(carrot)

fibrous
(grass)

Stems

Stems support the leaves and flowers of a plant so they can receive sunlight. *Xylem* tissue in the stem carries water and minerals from the roots to the leaves. *Phloem* tissue carries food from the leaves to the other parts of the plant. *Woody* stems

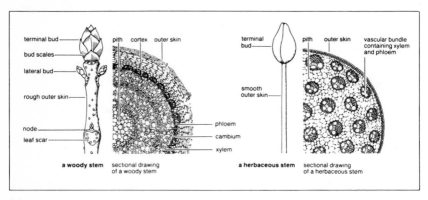

terminal bud
bud scales
lateral bud
rough outer skin
node
leaf scar

pith   cortex   outer skin

phloem
cambium
xylem

a woody stem   sectional drawing of a woody stem

terminal bud

smooth outer skin

pith   outer skin   vascular bundle containing xylem and phloem

a herbaceous stem   sectional drawing of a herbaceous stem

have a rough, brown skin and large amounts of xylem tissue. *Herbaceous* (nonwoody) stems are smooth and green and have small amounts of xylem tissue.

A *terminal bud* grows at the tip of each stem, making the plant grow taller. *Lateral buds* grow farther back along the stem, at places called *nodes.* Some of the lateral buds grow into branches, and others become leaves or flowers. *Bud scales* protect the growing ends of buds on some plants. On other plants, the buds are unprotected.

Leaves

Leaves produce most of the food a plant needs for growth and repair. The *blade* is the flat part of the leaf. The *petiole* attaches the blade to the stem and carries water and food to and from the blade. Tiny leaflike structures called *stipules* grow on some kinds of plants at the place where the petiole joins the stem. A network of *veins* helps hold the leaf up to the sun and carries water to the food-producing areas.

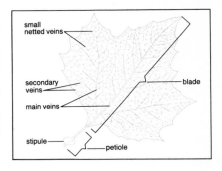

Leaves have many different forms. *Simple leaves* have one blade, and *compound leaves* have two or more blades. Other kinds of leaves include the needles of a pine tree and the spines of a cactus.

Flowers

Flowers contain the reproductive parts of a flowering plant. The male reproductive organ, called the *stamen,* consists of a *filament* and an *anther.* The anther produces pollen grains, which develop *sperm* (male sex cells). The female reproductive organ, called the *pistil,* consists of a *stigma,* a *style,* and an *ovary.* Female sex cells, called *eggs,* develop within the ovary. A flower that has both pistils and stamens is called a *perfect flower.* One that has either pistils or stamens is *imperfect.* Surrounding the reproductive organs are the petals. Together, all the petals make up the flower's *corolla.* The *calyx,* which consists of leaflike structures called *sepals,* holds the corolla. The base of the flower is the *receptacle.*

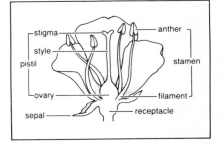

Plant Reproduction

Plants reproduce by either *asexual* or *sexual* reproduction. Asexual reproduction is common among simple plants. There are four methods of *asexual* reproduction. *Fission* occurs when a single-celled plant divides into two cells that then grow into separate plants. In *budding,* the parent plant produces a swelling called a bud, which grows and eventually splits from the parent. *Sporulation* takes place among plants that produce one-celled structures called spores, each of which grows into a new plant. *Vegetative propagation* occurs when a part of a plant—a root, stem, leaf, or flower—grows into a complete new plant.

Sexual reproduction involves the joining of male and female sex cells. Flowering plants, cone-bearing plants, and ferns and mosses all reproduce sexually. There are various methods of sexual reproduction. Flowering plants reproduce by a process called pollination.

Seeds

All seeds are either *naked* or *enclosed.* A pine seed is an example of a naked, or uncovered, seed. It forms on the upper surface of the scales of a pine cone. Flowering plants produce enclosed seeds, which form within an ovary. As seeds develop, the ovaries of some plants, such as apples and grapes, enlarge and form fleshy fruits. The ovaries form a dry fruit in such plants as beans and peas.

Seeds have three main parts: (1) the seed coat, which protects the inner parts; (2) the embryo, which contains all the parts of the new plant; and (3) the endosperm, which consists of food storage tissue to nourish the embryo until it can make its own food. *Cotyledons* are leaflike structures that absorb and digest food from the endosperm. Seeds of cone-bearing plants have from two to eight cotyledons. Seeds of flowering plants have one or two. Plants with one cotyledon are called *monocotyledons,* or *monocots.* Plants with two are called *dicotyledons,* or *dicots.* In some dicots, the cotyledons quickly absorb all the food from the endosperm and the cotyledons themselves become the food-storage structure.

Plant Growth

Four major processes occur in the growth of green plants: (1) germination, (2) water movement, (3) photosynthesis, and (4) respiration. Germination is the sprouting of a seed. In order to grow, a seed requires proper temperature, moisture, and oxygen.

Plants need a continuous supply of water. Water makes up much of a plant. In addition, water carries various important materials from one part of the plant to another. Most of a plant's water supply enters through the roots. Water, including various minerals dissolved in it, is absorbed by the roots in a process called *osmosis.* Water travels up the roots and stems to the leaves, where it can be used in the food-making process. Water also carries food from the leaves to the other parts of the plant. Plants give off water through a process called *transpiration.* Water escapes mainly through tiny pores called *stomata* on the surfaces of the leaves. Some scientists believe this water loss prevents the leaves from overheating in sunlight.

142

Photosynthesis is the process by which all green plants make food. It occurs chiefly in the leaves. A leaf needs three things in order to make food: (1) light, (2) carbon dioxide, and (3) water. The carbon dioxide and water are the raw materials, and the light provides the energy to convert them into food. Carbon dioxide enters a leaf from the air through the stomata. Water enters a leaf through the veins. Photosynthesis occurs within two kinds of cells in the leaf—palisade cells and spongy cells. Each of these cells has many *chloroplasts,* which contain the green pigment *chlorophyll.* When light strikes the chloroplasts, the chlorophyll absorbs energy. This energy splits water molecules into hydrogen and oxygen. The hydrogen joins with carbon from the carbon dioxide to produce a simple sugar. Oxygen is released through the stomata as a by-product of photosynthesis. The sugar produced during photosynthesis is carried to other parts of the plant, where it may be chemically changed to form fats and starches. It may also combine with various minerals to produce proteins, vitamins, and other essential substances; or it may be burned to provide energy needed for growth and other activities.

Respiration is the process that breaks down food and releases energy for the plant to use. When the sugar breaks down chemically, some of it combines with oxygen, releasing carbon dioxide, energy, and water. Respiration goes on day and night, throughout the life of a plant. Photosynthesis, on the other hand, takes place only during daylight.

A plant's growth and development depend to a large extent on heredity—the passing of characteristics from one generation to another. Heredity affects *all* living things, plants and animals. Each plant cell contains tiny structures called *chromosomes,* made up of hereditary units called *genes.* The chromosomes contain "instructions" that direct the plant's growth. As plant cells divide and multiply, the "instructions" are passed on to each new cell.

Leaves give off oxygen and water.

Carbon dioxide enters the leaves from the air.

Food is produced by the process called *photosynthesis.*

Sunlight strikes a green substance called *chlorophyll.*

Food is carried through the stems to all parts of the plant.

Stems carry water and minerals to the leaves.

Roots absorb water and minerals from the soil.

In the 1800's, an Austrian monk and botanist named Gregor Mendel developed the first basic laws of heredity as a result of his experiments with garden peas (see "People"). Mendel concluded that plant characteristics pass from one generation to another through the hereditary elements—what we now call genes—located in the sex cells. He reasoned that a plant receives a pair of genes—one from each parent—for each characteristic. As a result of his experiments, he determined that if a plant inherits two different genes for a particular characteristic, one gene will be *dominant* and the other will be *recessive*. The dominant gene determines the characteristic that appears in the plant. Mendel's *law of segregation* was based on his conclusion that pairs of genes *segregate* (separate) in a random manner when sex cells are formed, and a parent plant hands down only one gene of each pair to its offspring. Mendel also formulated the *law of independent assortment* as a result of his belief that a plant inherits each of its characteristics independently of all others. Scientists now know that independent assortment applies only to genes that are on different chromosomes. Genes that are linked, or on the same chromosome, tend to be inherited together.

Interesting facts about plants

The biggest plants of all are giant sequoia trees, found only in California. Sequoias are the largest living things on earth. Some sequoias stand more than 290 feet (88 meters) tall and measure more than 30 feet (9 meters) in diameter.

The smallest plants include *diatoms,* one-celled structures that can only be seen with a microscope. A single drop of water may contain as many as 500 diatoms.

The oldest plants on earth are bristlecone pine trees. One bristlecone pine in California is the oldest living thing. It began growing 4,000 to 5,000 years ago.

The smallest flower is the blossom of the duckweed plant. It can barely be seen with the naked eye.

The largest flower is the giant rafflesia, which grows in Indonesia. It measures up to 3 feet (91 centimeters) in diameter and can weigh 15 pounds (7 kilograms).

The largest leaves grow on raffia palm trees. They reach up to 50 feet (15 meters) long and 8 feet (2.4 meters) wide.

Seed sizes vary greatly. A tobacco plant produces more than 2,500 seeds in a pod less than ¾ of an inch (19 millimeters) long. On the other hand, the seed of a certain kind of coconut tree may weigh more than 20 pounds (9 kilograms).

The first plants appeared on earth about 3 billion years ago. No one knows exactly what they looked like, but they were probably simple plants similar to algae.

Plant medicines. Quinine, made from the bark of the cinchona tree, is used to treat malaria and other diseases. Digitalis, used in treating heart disease, comes from the dried leaves of the foxglove plant. Mold is the source of penicillin, a drug used to cure many illnesses. Cortisone, used to treat arthritis and many other diseases, comes from the roots of the Mexican yam plant.

Presidents

This section presents information about the U.S. Presidents and their administrations. The Presidents are listed in alphabetical order. A table of Presidents in chronological order, with places of birth, dates served, political party affiliations, and other information, appears in the "United States" section.

Adams, John (1735–1826), served one term as U.S. President after two terms as Vice-President under George Washington. Adams was a key figure in the American independence movement, serving in the First and Second Continental Congresses and helping to draft the Declaration of Independence. During the Revolutionary War, he was a diplomat in France and Holland. As President, Adams maintained U.S. neutrality during a war between France and Britain despite strong demands to join the fight against the French. Congress passed the Alien and Sedition Acts during Adams' presidency. Adams and his wife Abigail were the first occupants of the White House, moving in shortly before 1800.

Adams, John Quincy (1767–1848), the son of John Adams, was chosen President of the United States by the House of Representatives after a four-man race produced a stalemate in the Electoral College. Before becoming President, Adams served as a diplomat, member of the Massachusetts senate, U.S. senator, and secretary of state under James Monroe. Adams had a troubled presidency, winning little support for his policies. Two years after leaving office, he was elected to the House of Representatives, where he served until his death 18 years later.

Arthur, Chester A. (1829–1886), became President of the United States following the assassination of James A. Garfield. Arthur was a firm supporter of political patronage, but in response to public pressure, the nation's first civil service reform legislation—the Pendleton Civil Service Act—was passed during his presidency. Arthur signed the first law prohibiting Chinese immigration into the United States.

Buchanan, James (1791–1868), became President after a long political career as a legislator and diplomat. Buchanan was secretary of state under James K. Polk. Buchanan was President at a time when the slavery issue was reaching crisis proportions. He believed the federal government should not become involved in the issue, and his moderate, compromising stance eventually contributed to his unpopularity in both the North and the South. By the end of his presidency, seven Southern States had seceded from the Union.

Carter, James Earl, Jr. (1924–   ), was a naval officer and manager of his family's peanut farm before being elected governor of Georgia in 1970 and President of the United States in 1976. As President, Carter took a strong stand in favor of worldwide human rights. His mediation efforts helped produce a peace treaty between Egypt and Israel. The seizure of American hostages by Iranian revolutionaries in Teheran in 1979 created a foreign policy crisis during Carter's Administration. At home, his Administration was troubled by high unemployment and inflation.

Cleveland, Grover (1837–1908), was the only U.S. President to serve two nonconsecutive terms. He was a sheriff, mayor, and governor of New York before becoming President, gaining a nationwide reputation for honest government. Cleveland opposed increasing veterans' pensions and favored lower tariffs. He also favored the gold standard and opposed the free coinage of silver. These issues helped reduce his popularity. In 1888, he won the popular vote by 90,000 votes, but lost to Benjamin Harrison in the Electoral College. Four years later, however, Cleveland returned to the White House after defeating Harrison easily.

Coolidge, Calvin (1872–1933), known as "Silent Cal," succeeded to the U.S. presidency following the death of Warren G. Harding. Coolidge had had a long political career in Massachusetts before becoming Vice-President and then President. He believed that government involvement in the economy and in people's lives should be minimal. Under his Administration, taxes were reduced, tariffs were high, and farmers received little government aid. In foreign affairs, Coolidge opposed U.S. participation in the League of Nations and worked to improve relations with Mexico.

Eisenhower, Dwight David (1890–1969), known as "Ike," won acclaim as commander of the Allied forces in Europe during World War II before serving two terms as U.S. President. During his Administration, the Department of Health, Education, and Welfare (now the Department of Health and Human Services) was created, and the nation launched its first space satellite. Eisenhower sent federal troops to Little Rock, Ark., to enforce school integration there. In foreign affairs, the Korean War came to an end, and Eisenhower proposed an "Atoms for Peace" program.

Fillmore, Millard (1800–1874), succeeded to the U.S. presidency after the death of Zachary Taylor. Earlier, Fillmore had served in the New York assembly and the U.S. House of Representatives. As President, he supported and signed the Compromise of 1850, which admitted California as a free state and organized New Mexico and Utah as territories whose residents could decide the slavery issue for themselves. The Compromise also forbade the slave trade in the District of Columbia and strengthened fugitive slave legislation.

Ford, Gerald R. (1913–   ), was the only person to serve as both Vice-President and President of the United States without ever being elected to either office. Ford succeeded Richard M. Nixon as President, following Nixon's resignation because of the Watergate scandal. Ford had served in the U.S. House of Representatives for more than 20 years before Nixon appointed him Vice-President in 1973. As President, Ford pardoned Nixon for any federal crimes Nixon may have committed as President. During Ford's Administration, the United States celebrated its bicentennial, and the Vietnam War came to an end. Ford worked to improve relations with China and Russia; but at home, inflation and a recession caused problems.

Garfield, James A. (1831–1881), served as U.S. President for only a few months before being assassinated by Charles J. Guiteau, a disappointed government jobseeker. Garfield had taken office at a time when political corruption and the spoils system were widely condoned. His assassination helped spur public demands for civil service reform. Before being elected to the presidency, Garfield had served in the Ohio senate, in Congress, and in the U.S. Senate.

Grant, Ulysses S. (1822–1885), was a national hero as a result of his successful command of Union forces during the Civil War; but as President of the United States, he proved weak and ineffective. His Administration was marked by widespread political corruption and scandals involving some of his chief appointees. The Grant Administration did succeed in reducing the national debt, and reached agreement with Britain over payment of Civil War damages caused by Confederate ships built in Britain. An attempt to buy the Dominican Republic brought criticism to Grant. In addition, an economic depression that began in 1873 clouded his second term.

Harding, Warren Gamaliel (1865–1923), was elected President of the United States on a pledge to return the country to "normalcy" after World War I. He had held public office in Ohio and was a U.S. senator before winning election as President. Harding felt that Congress, rather than the President, should play a leading role in government policy. Under his Administration, Congress voted against membership in the League of Nations, raised tariffs to new highs, reduced taxes, and imposed immigration quotas for the first time. Corruption among some of Harding's top-level appointees led to the Teapot Dome scandal and other illegal activities. Harding died while on a cross-country speaking tour, shortly after hearing the first news of the Teapot Dome scandal.

Harrison, Benjamin (1833–1901), the grandson of William Henry Harrison, was an Indiana public official, Civil War commander, and U.S. senator before becoming President of the United States in 1889. Harrison's Administration increased veterans' benefits, set tariffs at the highest rate they had ever been, and adopted the Sherman Silver Purchase Act, which increased the amount of silver coins in circulation and led to a depletion of the nation's gold supply. The Sherman Antitrust Act was also passed during Harrison's Administration. In foreign affairs, Harrison negotiated trade treaties with Latin-American countries and hosted the first Pan-American Conference in Washington in 1899.

Harrison, William Henry (1773–1841), served as President of the United States for only 30 days—the shortest term of any President. Harrison caught a cold on his inauguration day in 1841 and died of pneumonia a month later. He was the first President to die in office. Harrison's military successes during the War of 1812 and against the Shawnee Indians in the Battle of Tippecanoe helped him win public office as an Ohio state senator, U.S. congressman, and senator. His 1840 presidential campaign was the most colorful ever staged up to that time, featuring "stump" speeches, parades, rallies, and campaign slogans and songs.

Hayes, Rutherford B. (1822–1893), won the first disputed presidential election in U.S. history. Hayes lost the 1876 election to Democrat Samuel J. Tilden by about 200,000 popular votes. But the returns were disputed, and both sides claimed victory. A congressional commission determined the outcome, making Hayes the winner by one electoral vote. Before becoming President, Hayes had been a U.S. congressman and three-term governor of Ohio. He earned a reputation for honesty, and as President he worked for a merit system for federal employees. Although his efforts failed, he paved the way for later civil service reform. Reconstruction came to an end during Hayes's Administration, with the last federal troops leaving the South in 1877.

Hoover, Herbert Clark (1874–1964), became President of the United States shortly before the nation plunged into the Great Depression. Hoover had earlier won a reputation as a brilliant engineer and an able administrator of World War I relief programs. He was also secretary of commerce under Warren G. Harding. But the stock market collapse of 1929 began a period of economic distress that brought widespread criticism and blame to the Hoover Administration. Hoover supported federal work projects and loans to businesses, but opposed direct federal aid to the unemployed. By 1932, 12 million workers were unemployed, and Hoover left office an unpopular man.

Jackson, Andrew (1767–1845), was a Tennessee supreme court justice, U.S. congressman, senator, and national military hero before becoming President in 1828. Jackson came from a poor frontier family and was known as a "man of the people." He believed in a strong presidency and wholeheartedly endorsed the "spoils" system of giving political jobs to party loyalists. He severed federal ties to the Bank of the United States and also opposed the idea that states could nullify federal laws. Dur-

ing his Administration, thousands of Indians were forced to migrate to lands west of the Mississippi. To bring land speculation under control, Jackson issued the *Specie Circular*, which required that payment for public lands be made in gold or silver. In foreign affairs, Jackson improved trade relations with the British and reached agreement with France on payment of damages for American ships attacked during the Napoleonic wars.

Jefferson, Thomas (1743–1826), was a political philosopher, writer, inventor, educational reformer, architect, scientist, statesman, and President of the United States. He was the author of the Declaration of Independence and the founder of the University of Virginia. Jefferson was a legislator in Virginia before becoming a delegate to the Second Continental Congress, where he drafted the declaration. During the Revolutionary War, he continued to serve in the legislature and was also elected governor of Virginia. After the war, he served in Congress, as U.S. minister to France, as George Washington's secretary of state, and as Vice-President under John Adams. One of the highlights of Jefferson's presidency was the Louisiana Purchase, which doubled the size of the United States. Foreign affairs troubled Jefferson's second term. British and French interference with American shipping led to curtailment of trade and economic distress. After leaving the presidency, Jefferson retired to his Virginia estate, Monticello. He died on July 4, 1826, exactly 50 years after the adoption of the Declaration of Independence.

Johnson, Andrew (1808–1875), succeeded to the U.S. presidency following the assassination of Abraham Lincoln in 1865. Johnson held a variety of public offices, including U.S. congressman, senator, and governor of Tennessee before becoming Lincoln's Vice-President. As President, he became involved in bitter controversies with Congress over the rebuilding of the nation in the wake of the Civil War. Johnson was impeached by Congress after he fired Secretary of War Edwin M. Stanton in defiance of the Tenure of Office Act. The Senate failed by one vote to convict Johnson.

Johnson, Lyndon Baines (1908–1973), became President of the United States following the assassination of John F. Kennedy in 1963. The following year, Johnson was elected in his own right by a huge majority. Johnson served in the U.S. Congress and was Senate majority leader before becoming Kennedy's Vice-President. As President, Johnson launched what he called the "Great Society," a program of civil rights laws, poverty programs, and other social legislation. The widening war in Vietnam led to Johnson's downfall. Troop commitments that had begun under Kennedy were expanded during Johnson's Administration, and the nation became increasingly divided over the unpopular war. Johnson did not run for re-election in 1968.

Kennedy, John Fitzgerald (1917–1963), was the youngest person ever elected to the U.S. presidency and the youngest to die in office. His assassination in 1963 by Lee Harvey Oswald was mourned around the world. Kennedy was a congressman and senator from Massachusetts before winning the presidency. As President, he proposed to lead the nation on a "New Frontier." He put forward legislation to deal with unemployment, civil rights, health care, and other matters; but Congress passed only some of his proposals. Kennedy's unsuccessful attempt to have American-trained Cuban exiles invade Cuba at the Bay of Pigs was sharply criticized. In 1962, the discovery of Soviet missile sites in Cuba caused a Cold War crisis. Kennedy forced the Russians to dismantle the sites. Kennedy's Administration, the United States launched its first man into space and negotiated a nuclear test ban treaty with the Russians. One of Kennedy's greatest achievements was the establishment of the Peace Corps in 1961.

Lincoln, Abraham (1809–1865), guided the nation through the Civil War as 16th President of the United States. Lincoln was a lawyer, Illinois legislator, and one-term member of Congress before gaining national recognition during a series of debates with Stephen A. Douglas in 1858. In the debates, Lincoln expressed his

Presidents

opposition to the extension of slavery. As the candidate of the new Republican Party in the 1860 presidential election, Lincoln did not win a majority of the popular votes, but he won election in the Electoral College. The Civil War began soon after his inauguration. His unswerving dedication to the preservation of the Union saved the United States from disintegration. Lincoln lost popularity as the war dragged on, but was elected to a second term. The Civil War ended shortly after his second inauguration. But less than a week later, Lincoln was assassinated by John Wilkes Booth, an actor and Confederate sympathizer.

Madison, James (1751–1836), served two terms as President of the United States, but is known primarily as the "Father of the Constitution." As a Virginia delegate to the Constitutional Convention in 1787, Madison won acceptance of his ideas for a two-house legislature and the separation of powers among the executive, legislative, and judicial branches of government. Madison served as a congressman from Virginia, and became a leading opponent of the Federalist Party, which favored business interests and a strong central government. He and Thomas Jefferson formed the Democratic-Republican Party, which favored states' rights. Madison served as secretary of state during Jefferson's Administration before winning election as President in 1808. His presidency was troubled by conflicts with Britain and France over interference with American shipping. The United States fought the War of 1812 during Madison's presidency. After the war, the country began a period of prosperity and expansion.

McKinley, William (1843–1901), served as U.S. President at a time of industrial and territorial expansion that marked the emergence of the nation as a world power. Earlier, McKinley had served in Congress, where he supported protective tariffs and the unlimited coinage of silver. He was also a two-term governor of Ohio. During McKinley's presidency, the United States fought the Spanish-American War, winning in four months. McKinley's first term was a time of prosperity for the nation, and he won re-election easily. But six months into his second term, he was assassinated by Leon F. Czolgosz while attending a reception at the Pan-American Exposition in Buffalo.

Monroe, James (1758–1831), became President of the United States in 1817, after a distinguished career as a Virginia legislator, U.S. senator, governor, diplomat, and Cabinet secretary. Monroe presided over the nation during a period called the "era of good feeling." The Democratic-Republican Party was the only one in existence at the time, and so Monroe's presidency was free of interparty battling. Monroe bought Florida from Spain in 1819 and a year later approved the Missouri Compromise, which temporarily settled a national debate on slavery. His most memorable achievement as President was the Monroe Doctrine, which warned European nations not to interfere in the affairs of free nations of the Western Hemisphere.

Nixon, Richard Milhous (1913–   ), was twice elected President of the United States, but in 1974 became the first person to resign from the office. Earlier in his political career, Nixon served as a congressman and senator from California, and was Vice-President under Dwight D. Eisenhower. During Nixon's presidency, the Vietnam War was a major foreign policy concern. Nixon withdrew U.S. troops from Vietnam, but ordered an invasion of Cambodia in 1970 that caused widespread protest. He took important steps toward improving relations with China and Russia. At home, inflation and recession were troublesome problems; but Nixon's downfall came as a result of the Watergate scandal, which involved burglaries, wiretapping, and other illegal activities during the re-election campaign. A number of Nixon's highest aides were found guilty of involvement in the scandal or in trying to cover it up. Nixon himself denied involvement, but threats of impeachment led to his resignation on Aug. 9, 1974.

Pierce, Franklin (1804–1869), became President in 1853, after serving earlier as a state legislator in New Hampshire, U.S. congressman, and senator. As President,

he approved the Gadsden Purchase, which gave the nation additional land from Mexico. The controversy over the extension of slavery became an overriding domestic issue during Pierce's Administration. He signed into law the Kansas-Nebraska bill, which turned Kansas into a battleground between pro- and anti-slavery settlers. Pierce found little support for renomination and left office after one term.

Polk, James K. (1795–1849), was elected President of the United States in 1844, having earlier served as a Tennessee legislator, U.S. congressman, and governor of Tennessee. Under his leadership, the United States reached a compromise with the British over the boundary of the Oregon Territory, and U.S. troops won the Mexican War. The victory led to the admission of Texas as a state and gave the United States the land that now forms most of the American West. In domestic affairs, Polk won a reduction in tariffs and passage of a bill to create an independent treasury for federal funds. Polk was the first President who did not seek re-election.

Reagan, Ronald (1911–   ), became President of the United States in 1981, after serving two terms as governor of California and spending nearly 30 years as an actor in motion pictures and television. Reagan stressed conservative themes as President. He won Congressional approval for a program of major tax cuts, large increases in defense spending, and cutbacks in spending on welfare and other social programs. High unemployment and huge budget deficits hampered Reagan's efforts to revitalize the economy, however. In foreign affairs, Reagan took a tough stance against Russia and other Communist nations and favored increased U.S. support for the government of El Salvador, which was fighting leftist guerilla insurgents.

Roosevelt, Franklin Delano (1882–1945), was elected to an unprecedented four terms as President of the United States, guiding the nation through the Great Depression of the 1930's and World War II in the 1940's. At the start of his political career, Roosevelt served in the New York senate and as assistant secretary of the Navy under Woodrow Wilson. In spite of being stricken by polio, he won two terms as governor of New York. As President, Roosevelt took decisive action to deal with the depression. His New Deal policies increased government involvement in the economy to an unprecedented level. Congress passed legislation for relief programs, public works projects, conservation projects, and other measures. In foreign affairs, Roosevelt favored using U.S. influence to counteract growing aggression by Japan and Germany in the 1930's. But neutrality laws prevented any action. By 1940, however, American sentiment supported increasing involvement. U.S. aid flowed to Britain, and Congress enacted a draft law. After the Japanese attacked Pearl Harbor, the United States entered World War II, and U.S. forces fought in Europe, Asia, Africa, and the Pacific. Roosevelt died of a cerebral hemorrhage before the war ended and several months after being elected to his fourth term.

Roosevelt, Theodore (1858–1919), became U.S. President in 1901, following the assassination of William McKinley. Roosevelt served in various government positions before becoming McKinley's Vice-President. His military record in the Spanish-American War, where he led a volunteer force known as the Rough Riders, helped him win the New York governorship. As President, Roosevelt moved successfully against business monopolies, supported wage increases for striking coal miners, and worked hard for national conservation measures. Legislation regulating the quality of foods and drugs was also passed during his Administration. Roosevelt took a strong stand in Latin-American affairs and secured the right to have the United States build the Panama Canal. William Howard Taft succeeded Roosevelt; but in 1912, Roosevelt ran again—as the unsuccessful candidate of the Progressive Republican "Bull Moose" ticket.

Taft, William Howard (1857–1930), served as President from 1909 to 1913 and later went on to achieve his highest goal—appointment as Chief Justice of the United States Supreme Court. Before becoming President, Taft

147

had served as a judge, civil governor of the Philippines, and secretary of war under Theodore Roosevelt. Taft did not enjoy the presidency, and he tried to steer a middle course between the liberal and conservative wings of the Republican Party. He supported antitrust action and set up a Tariff Board to study tariff rates. Powers of the Interstate Commerce Commission were enlarged and the postal savings and parcel post systems were established during his Administration. In foreign affairs, Taft favored the granting of loans to foreign countries by U.S. banks and businesses, thereby extending the nation's political and economic influence, especially in Latin America.

Taylor, Zachary (1784–1850), became President of the United States after 40 years of military service. He fought in Indian campaigns in Indiana, Wisconsin, and Florida before becoming a national military hero in the Mexican War. Taylor scored a brilliant victory in the Battle of Buena Vista in 1847, though his forces were outnumbered four-to-one. He was elected President a year later, at a time of controversy over the extension of slavery. Although Taylor was himself a slaveholder, he favored the admission of California as a free state. While Congress debated the issue, Taylor died, having served just 16 months as President.

Truman, Harry S. (1884–1972), succeeded to the U.S. presidency following the death of Franklin Roosevelt. Truman was a county judge in Kansas City and a U.S. senator before being selected as the Democrat's compromise candidate for the vice-presidency in 1944. A year later, he was President. Shortly after assuming the presidency, Truman forced Japanese surrender in World War II by ordering an atomic bomb to be dropped on Hiroshima and Nagasaki, Japan. Congress blocked many of Truman's plans for domestic programs, but he won greater support in foreign affairs. After World War II ended, Truman took steps to help war-torn nations revive. To counteract the growing influence of Communism, Truman announced the Truman Doctrine, which guaranteed American aid to any free nation resisting Communist propaganda or sabotage. The Marshall Plan and other foreign aid programs were enacted and the North Atlantic Treaty Organization was established. In a direct challenge to Communist aggression, Truman sent U.S. forces to South Korea at the start of the Korean War.

Tyler, John (1790–1862), was the first Vice-President to succeed to the presidency following the death of a Chief Executive. He succeeded William Henry Harrison, who had been President only one month. Earlier in his political career, Tyler served as a Virginia legislator, a U.S. congressman, governor of Virginia, and U.S. senator. Tyler was a southern Democrat who withdrew from his party because of opposition to President Andrew Jackson's handling of the nullification issue. The Whigs drafted him as their vice-presidential candidate in 1840. When Tyler became President, he clashed with the Whigs over a national bank and other issues. Tyler vetoed one bill after another, incurring the wrath of the Whigs. The Whigs tried to impeach Tyler, but failed.

Van Buren, Martin (1782–1862), became President of the United States in 1837, just before the nation slid into its first severe economic depression. Van Buren was a follower of Thomas Jefferson, and he believed the government should interfere as little as possible in American life. His refusal to provide government relief to ease the effects of depression brought him widespread criticism. Before becoming President, Van Buren had enjoyed a successful career in New York politics, serving as a state legislator, state attorney general, U.S. senator, and governor of New York. He also served as secretary of state and then Vice-President under Andrew Jackson.

Washington, George (1732–1799), the first President of the United States, is revered as the "Father of His Country." He commanded the Continental Army that won American independence from the British in the Revolutionary War and was president of the convention that wrote the U.S. Constitution. As a young man, Washington worked as a surveyor and began a military career with British and colonial forces during the French and Indian War. Although he suffered defeats and disappointments, by 1759 he was the best-known American-born soldier in the Colonies. He spent the years before the Revolutionary War managing his Virginia plantation, Mount Vernon, and serving in the Virginia legislature. He served in the First and Second Continental Congresses before being chosen to lead the Continental Army. The respect and admiration he won as a wartime leader made him the unanimous choice for the presidency. During Washington's Administration, the federal government assumed the Revolutionary War debts of the states, established the First Bank of the United States, and sent an army to put down a rebellion in western Pennsylvania. In foreign affairs, Washington steered a neutral course in conflicts between Britain and France. Washington was unanimously elected to a second term, but refused to be considered for a third term. He retired to Mount Vernon, where he died on Dec. 14, 1799.

Wilson, Woodrow (1856–1924), had a distinguished career as president of Princeton University and governor of New Jersey before becoming President of the United States in 1913. As U.S. President, Wilson achieved lower tariff rates, and the establishment of the Federal Reserve Board and the Federal Trade Commission. Foreign affairs became a major concern of the Wilson presidency. Conflicts with Mexico were eventually settled peacefully. During World War I, the United States at first was neutral. But after continued attacks on American ships by German submarines, Wilson led the nation in joining the war on the side of the Allies in 1917. After the war ended, Wilson took a leading role in negotiating a settlement. His efforts led to the establishment of the League of Nations. The U.S. Congress, however, refused to ratify the Treaty of Versailles, and so the United States did not participate in the league. Wilson suffered a stroke in 1919 and finished his second term as an invalid. His wife, Edith Bolling Galt Wilson, helped him carry out presidential duties.

Religion

Major religions of the world

Estimated number of members in each religion*

Christianity	951,059,000	**Islam**	537,713,000	**Shinto**	61,156,000
(includes 542,531,000 Roman Catholics, 323,725,000 Protestants, and 84,803,000 members of Eastern Orthodox churches		**Hinduism**	518,794,000	**Taoism**	29,284,000
		Buddhism	244,800,000	**Judaism**	14,533,000
		Confucianism	175,689,000		

*Membership figures for some of the major religions are very broad estimates. Some religions do not keep official records of the total number of their members. Various religions also have different standards for determining who is a member of the faith. In addition, many Asians belong to more than one religion. Source: Franklin H. Littell, Professor of Religion, Temple University, Philadelphia. Figures are for 1977.

The cross is the symbol of Christianity. Jesus Christ died on a cross in ancient Palestine.

Christianity is the religion based on the life and teachings of Jesus Christ, who lived in Palestine when it was part of the Roman Empire. Christianity has since spread throughout the world and is the dominant religion of the Western Hemisphere. Christians believe that God sent Jesus to the world as the Savior and that people can achieve salvation through Jesus.

Jesus traveled throughout Palestine with a group of followers called *disciples.* He chose 12 of them—the *apostles*—to spread His doctrine. Jesus preached justice toward others and humility toward God. He also preached mercy and brotherhood, and told of God's love for all creatures. The Jewish religious leaders of Jesus' time considered His claim to be the *Messiah* (promised deliverer of the Jews) to be blasphemy. The Roman authorities believed that Jesus' claim to be king of the Jews was treason. As a result, He was tried, condemned to death, and crucified. After His death, beginning on the first Easter morning, His followers reported seeing Him alive. This rising from the dead—the *Resurrection*—is a basic doctrine of the Christian faith. Christians believe Jesus remained on earth for 40 days after His Resurrection and then ascended into heaven. At Pentecost, 50 days after Easter, the disciples reported that the Holy Spirit had entered them, enabling them to perform unusual deeds, such as speaking in many languages. Some Christians believe the church began at this time.

The Bible is the most sacred book of Christianity. Christians accept both the Old Testament and the New Testament of the Bible. Some Christians also accept as part of the Bible a collection of writings called the *Apocrypha.* The Old Testament begins with the creation of the world and tells of the ancient Israelites. The New Testament records the life of Jesus and deals with the developments of the early

149

church and the meaning of faith in Jesus. The books of the Apocrypha cover a variety of subjects, including Jewish history and philosophy.

Splits among various Christian groups led to the development of three major divisions in Christianity: the Roman Catholic Church, the Protestant denominations, and the Eastern Orthodox churches. The largest Protestant denominations include Baptists, Congregationalists, Episcopalians, Lutherans, Methodists, and Presbyterians. The Eastern Orthodox churches are the major Christian churches in Greece, Russia, eastern Europe, and western Asia. Roman Catholics regard the Pope, who is the bishop of Rome, as their spiritual leader. A Catholic's faith is based on the Bible and on church teachings put forth by the popes, by church councils, and in statements called *creeds* and *dogmas*. Most Protestants believe the Bible should be the only authority for their religion. Eastern Orthodox beliefs are based on the Bible and on *holy tradition* (doctrines worked out mostly during the early centuries of Christianity). The three major divisions vary in other respects, including worship services. The central act of worship for Catholics is the *Eucharist,* also called the *Mass,* which is a celebration of the Lord's Supper that includes the distribution of Holy Communion—the body and blood of Christ in the form of bread and wine. Protestant services generally stress teaching the word of God through sermons. Eastern Orthodox churches perform various services, including the *Divine Liturgy,* also called the celebration of the Eucharist, which recalls Christ's entire life and includes the taking of Holy Communion.

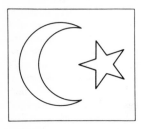

Islam's symbol, the crescent and star, appears on several national flags.

Islam is the religion based on the teachings of Muhammad, an Arab who began preaching in Mecca around A.D. 610. Followers of Islam are called *Muslims.* Islam is the major religion of northern Africa and the Middle East, as well as Bangladesh, Indonesia, Malaysia, and Pakistan.

Before Muhammad's time, the people in the region around Mecca worshiped *Allah* (God), as well as other deities. According the Islamic tradition, the angel Gabriel revealed the word of God to Muhammad, who then preached that there is only one God, and that he, Muhammad, was His messenger. Opposition to Muhammad led some Meccans to plot to kill him. In 622, he fled from Mecca to Medina, an event called the *Hegira.* In 630, Muhammad and his followers returned to Mecca and occupied the city. The Meccans eventually accepted Islam and acknowledged Muhammad as prophet. Mecca and Medina became the holy cities of Islam.

Muhammad's teachings are preserved in the *Koran,* the holy book of Islam. Muslims believe the Koran consists of the revelations to Muhammad of the words of God Himself. The Koran consists of verses grouped into 114 chapters called *suras.* The central teaching of the Koran is that there is only one God—Allah—the creator of the universe, who requires *Islam* (submission) to Himself. The Koran mentions various prophets who have been God's messengers to different peoples, including Abraham, Moses, Jesus, and others. It describes Muhammad as the last of the prophets. The Koran teaches ethics and morals, and such virtues as patience, kindness, and honesty. The Koran also speaks of a day of judgment, when people shall stand before God and be judged for their lives on earth. The good will go to heaven, and the bad to hell.

Muslim duties include prayer, almsgiving, fasting, and pilgrimage. Muslims pray five times daily. On Fridays, the Muslim Sabbath, they are expected to attend noon prayers at a *mosque,* a Muslim house of worship. Islam does not have an organized priesthood, but an *Imam* is a person who generally leads the people in prayer. Almsgiving consists of both required contributions and charity given voluntarily. Muslims observe *Ramadan,* the ninth month of the Islamic calendar, as a holy month of fasting, during which they may not eat or drink from dawn to sunset. All able Muslims are expected to make a pilgrimage, or *Hajj,* to Mecca at least once in their lives.

There are two major divisions within Islam: *Sunni* and *Shi'ah.* Sunnites, who make up the majority of Muslims, believe that Muslim leadership after Muhammad's death passed to *caliphs* elected from Muhammad's tribe. Shiites believe that leadership was restricted to descendants of Ali, Muhammad's son-in-law. Other minority groups include the *Wahhabis* and the *Ismaili Khoja* Muslims.

Hindus repeat the Sacred Word *Om* while meditating.

Hinduism, the chief religion of India, is the oldest living religion in the world. It dates from about 1500 B.C. and developed from the beliefs of many cultures. Hindus worship many gods. Early Hindus worshiped gods that represented powers in nature, such as the rain and the sun. Gradually, some Hindus came to believe that, though divinities appear in separate forms, they are part of one universal spirit called *Brahman.* The three most important divinities that make up Brahman are Brahma, creator of the universe; Vishnu, its preserver; and Shiva, its destroyer. Another important divinity, Shiva's wife, has several names. As Parvati or Uma, she is the beloved goddess of motherhood. As Durga or Kali, she is the feared goddess of destruction. For many Hindus, these contrasting forms represent the way in which time and matter constantly move from birth to death and from creation to destruction. Many Hindus find great religious truth in this symbolism and worship the goddess as their most important divinity. In addition to divinities, Hindus worship such animals as cows, monkeys, and snakes, as well as various local and regional saints.

Hindus worship as individuals, rather than as members of a congregation. Most Hindu homes have shrines devoted to a divinity of the family's choosing. Hindu temples generally have many shrines, each for a particular divinity. Each temple also has one principal shrine devoted to a single important divinity.

Hinduism teaches that the soul never dies. When the body dies, the soul is reborn in a continuous process of rebirth called *reincarnation.* The soul may be reborn in human or animal form. According to the law of *karma,* every action of a person influences the form in which his or her soul will be reborn in its next existence. Hindus believe that reincarnation continues until a person achieves spiritual perfection. The soul then enters a new level of existence, called *moksha,* from which it never returns.

Hinduism has many sacred writings. The four *Vedas* are the oldest. Each Veda has three parts: (1) the *Samhitas,* which contain prayers and hymns; (2) the *Brahmanas,* which deal with ritual and theology and include explanations of the Samhitas; and (3) the *Upanishads,* which are works of philosophy written as dialogues. Other major writings include the *Puranas,* long verse stories that contain many Hindu myths; the *Ramayana* and the *Mahabharata,* which are epics; and the *Manu Smriti (Code of Manu),* which is a basic source of Hindu religious and social law. Part of it sets forth the basis of the *caste system* that divides Hindus into hereditary social classes.

Six schools of Hindu philosophy have become prominent over the centuries. *Nyaya* deals with logic. *Vaisheska* concerns the nature of the world. *Sankhya* examines the origins and evolution of the universe. *Yoga* is a set of mental and physical exercises to free the soul from reliance on the body so it can unite with Brahman. *Purva-mimamsa* and *Vedanta* interpret the Vedas.

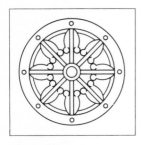

The Wheel is an important symbol of Buddhism.

Buddhism developed in India in the late 500's B.C., partly as a reaction against certain features of Hinduism. It evolved from the teachings of a prince named Siddhartha Gautama, who became known as *Buddha,* meaning *Enlightened One.* Buddha's teachings, called the *dharma,* include the idea that existence is a continuing cycle of death and rebirth. Each person's position and well-being in life is determined by his or her behavior in previous lives. Buddha taught that as long as people remain within the cycle of death and rebirth, they can never be completely free from pain and suffering. He said people could break out of the cycle by eliminating any attachment to worldly things, thereby gaining a kind of perfect peace and happiness he called *nirvana.*

Buddha taught that people who followed the *Middle Way* and the *Noble Eightfold Path* could achieve nirvana. The Middle Way is a way of life that avoids both the uncontrolled satisfaction of human desires and the extreme forms of self-denial and self-torture. The Noble Eightfold Path consists of (1) knowledge of the truth; (2) the intention to resist evil; (3) saying nothing to hurt others; (4) respecting life, morality, and property; (5) holding a job that does no injury to others; (6) striving to free one's mind of evil; (7) controlling one's feelings and thoughts; and (8) practicing proper forms of concentration.

The oldest of the many Buddhist schools that developed after Buddha's death compiled a scripture called the *Tripitika,* which means *Three Baskets.* The first part, the *Basket of Discipline,* deals with Buddhist monks. The second part, the *Basket of Discourses,* consists largely of sermons. The third part, the *Basket of the Higher Dharma,* contains later discussions of doctrine. Other Buddhist schools have added their own scriptures to Buddhism. The most influential schools of Buddhism today include the Theravada, which is the dominant religious tradition in Burma, Cambodia, Laos, Sri Lanka, and Thailand; the Mahayana, which has followers mainly in Japan, Korea, and other East Asian countries; the Mantrayana, which has centers primarily in the Himalayan regions, in Mongolia, and in Japan; and Zen, which is practiced chiefly in Japan.

Buddhist monks play an important role in preserving and spreading Buddhism. Members of the Buddhist laity are expected to honor Buddha and the images and objects associated with him; to follow basic moral rules; and to support the monks.

Confucianism is a Chinese religion based on the teachings of a philosopher named Confucius, who died about 479 B.C. Confucianism has no organization or clergy, and it does not teach the worship of a diety or the existence of a life after death. Some persons consider it simply a guide to morality and good government rather than a religion. Confucianism stresses respect for ancestors and government authority, and teaches that rulers must govern according to high moral standards. Confucius believed that virtuous behavior by rulers had a greater effect in governing than did laws and codes of punishment. Confucianism was the single most important force in Chinese life from the 100's B.C. to the A.D. 1900's. It influenced Chinese education, government, and attitudes toward correct behavior and the individual's duty to society. The Communist government that came to power in China in 1949 officially opposed Confucianism. However, Confucianism remains an important religious force among the Chinese people of Taiwan.

Confucius' philosophy was not widely known during his lifetime. His followers, including Mencius and Hsun-tzu, helped spread his ideas. His conversations and sayings were recorded in a book called the *Analects.* The Confucian philosophy was also preserved in works called the Five Classics and the Four Books. These volumes formed the basis of the Chinese educational system for centuries. Beginning in the 1000's, a movement known as *Neo-Confucianism* became widely popular. It also influenced Japanese moral codes and philosophy from the 1600's through the 1800's.

A wooden gate called a *torii* is Shinto's symbol. A torii stands at the entrance of Shinto shrines.

Shinto is the oldest surviving religion of Japan. The word *Shinto* means *the way of the gods.* Shintoists worship many gods, called *kami,* that are present in mountains, rivers, rocks, trees, and other parts of nature. Shintoists also consider kami to be the basic force in such processes as creativity, disease, growth, and healing. Shinto mythology states that Japan and the Japanese people were created by deities. Until the mid-1900's, the Japanese worshiped their emperor as a direct descendant of Amaterasu-Omikami, the sun goddess and most important Shinto deity.

Shinto does not have an elaborate philosophy, and

153

it does not stress life after death. It emphasizes rituals and moral standards. Many Shintoists worship at small shrines in their homes. Public shrines may consist of several buildings and gardens. Individual worshipers recite prayers and offer flowers and cakes to the kami.

On certain occasions, Shinto priests lead ceremonies called *matsuri*. One of these, the Great Purification Ceremony, consists of a confession of sins committed by individuals and the nation as a whole, followed by a request that the kami remove the impure conditions caused by these sins. Other ceremonies deal with such goals as long life, peace, good health, and abundant harvests.

The origins of Shinto are unknown. Beginning around the A.D. 500's, the philosophies of Buddhism and Confucianism influenced Shinto, helping to shape rituals and doctrines. Shinto myths are recorded in two works written in the 700's, the *Nihongi (Chronicles of Japan)* and the *Kojiki (The Record of Ancient Matters)*. The myths tell how the kami created the world and established customs and laws. In the mid-1800's, a movement called *State Shinto* stressed patriotism and the divine origins of the emperor. After Japan's defeat in World War II in 1945, the emperor denied his divinity, and State Shinto was abolished. Later Shinto movements, called *New Religions,* attracted followers in the 1800's and 1900's. They center around the teachings of a particular person or group, and some of them encourage group worship, charity work, and the organization of society on a cooperative basis.

Taoism's symbol stands for what Taoists consider the two basic forces—*yin* (female) and *yang* (male).

Taoism developed as an organized religion in China during the 100's B.C., though its roots go back farther in Chinese history to ancient folk traditions. Taoism teaches that everyone should try to achieve two goals, happiness and immortality. Aids to achieving these goals include prayer, magic, special diet, breath control, meditation, and recitation of scriptures. Taoists also believe in astrology, fortunetelling, witchcraft, and communication with the spirits of the dead. They worship more deities than the followers of almost any other religion. Deities include ancestors and spirits of famous people.

In its early years, Taoism was strongly influenced by Buddhism. By the A.D. 1000's, Taoists were divided into many sects. Members of some of these sects withdrew from society to live in monasteries. Other sects were based in temples, with hereditary priesthoods whose members lived among the common people. These priests gained a reputation as highly skilled magicians who could tell the future and protect believers from illness, accidents, and other misfortunes.

Chinese governments of the 1900's have opposed Taoism, and the religion is no longer officially practiced in China. Taoism is still practiced among Chinese people outside China, however, especially in Taiwan.

Judaism's symbol is the star of David, called the *Magen David,* or *Shield of David,* in Hebrew.

Judaism is the religion of the Jewish people. It is one of the oldest major religions and was the first to teach the belief in one God. Christianity and Islam both developed out of Judaism. Judaism began among the ancient Israelites in the Middle East. According to Jewish tradition, Abraham founded the religion around the 1700's B.C. Jews believe that God made a *covenant,* or special agreement, with Abraham, promising to bless Abraham and his descendants if they worshiped and remained faithful to Him. God later gave the Israelites the Ten Commandments and other laws through their leader Moses.

Judaism teaches that God wants people to do what is just and merciful. According to Jewish beliefs, a person serves God by studying the scriptures and practicing what they teach, especially concerning behavior toward others. Judaism teaches that all people are created in the image of God and should be treated with dignity and respect.

Judaism has two major collections of sacred writings, the Hebrew Bible (also called the Old Testament) and the *Talmud.* The *Torah,* the most important of all Jewish scriptures, consists of the first five books of the Hebrew Bible. The Torah contains the basic laws of Judaism and describes the history of the Jews until the death of Moses in the 1200's B.C. Jews traditionally believed that Moses actually wrote the Torah; but today, many scholars think that the teachings of Moses were passed down by word of mouth for many generations and were finally written down about 1000 B.C. In addition to the Torah, the Hebrew Bible contains books of history and moral teachings. The Talmud is a collection of legal and ethical writings, as well as Jewish history and folklore, produced between A.D. 200 and 500.

Jews worship both at home and at a public house of worship called a *synagogue.* The Jewish Sabbath begins at sundown on Friday and ends at sundown on Saturday. Home worship includes daily prayers, the lighting of candles on the Sabbath, and the blessing of wine and bread at the Sabbath meal. Jews also observe many holiday rituals at home (see "Holidays"). Synagogue worship consists primarily of readings from the Torah and the chanting of prayers from a prayerbook called the *siddur.* A *rabbi* serves as spiritual leader, teacher, and interpreter of Jewish law. Rabbis also deliver sermons during worship services and perform various other functions. A *cantor* chants the prayers during worship in the synagogue.

The three major branches of Judaism are *Orthodox, Reform,* and *Conservative.* These groups vary in their beliefs and practices. Orthodox Jews accept all the traditional Jewish beliefs and ways of life, including dietary rules and laws for keeping the Sabbath. They believe that God revealed the laws of the Torah and the Talmud directly to Moses on Mount Sinai. Reform Jews believe that moral and ethical teachings form the most important part of Judaism, and they regard the Bible as the principal source of their faith. They do not observe many of the traditional customs and ceremonies of Judaism. Conservative Jews accept both the Talmud and the Bible, but believe they should be interpreted in light of modern knowledge and culture. They do not stress the rituals of Judaism, but follow more traditional practices.

Scientific inventions and inventors

The following table lists in chronological order some of the world's great inventions and the inventors who created them. In some cases, the inventor listed was the first person to receive a patent for a successful device, though others may have contributed to its development. Since the mid-1900's, new technologies have continued to develop at an accelerated pace in such fields as computers, communications, medicine, space, and other areas. Corporations and government agencies have fostered the creation of countless new inventions through teams of researchers and engineers working together. In many cases, however, these modern technologies owe their success to the pioneering work done by individual inventors many years before. See also the "Awards" section with its table of winners of Nobel prizes in such fields as chemistry, physics, and medicine, and the "Transportation" section with its table of important dates in transportation.

Invention	Date	Inventor
Pump	200's B.C.	Ctesibius (Greek)
Archimedian screw (a device to raise water from a lower level to a higher level)	200's B.C.	*Archimedes (Greek)
Screw press (a device to squeeze juice from fruits)	100's B.C.	Hero (Greek)
Paper	c. A.D. 105	Ts'ai Lun (Chinese)
Movable type	1045	Pi Sheng (Chinese)
Printing from movable type	c. 1440	*Johannes Gutenberg (German)
Compound microscope	c. 1590	Zacharias Janssen (Dutch)
Thermometer	1593	*Galileo (Italian)
Sector (instrument used to draw and measure angles)	1597	*Galileo (Italian)
Telescope	1608	Hans Lippershey (Dutch)
Barometer	1643	Evangelista Torricelli (Italian)
Steam engine (first practical steam engine, used to pump water from mines)	1698	Thomas Savery (English)
Seed drill (device for planting seeds)	c.1700	Jethro Tull (English)
Mercury thermometer	1714	Gabriel D. Fahrenheit (German)
Flying shuttle (weaving machine)	1733	John Kay (English)
Improved steam engines	1760's–1780's	*James Watt (Scottish)
Spinning jenny (machine for spinning more than one thread at a time)	c.1764	James Hargreaves (English)
Hot-air balloon	1783	Jacques É. and Joseph M. Montgolfier (French)
Steam-powered loom	1786	Edmund Cartwright (English)
Cotton gin	1793	*Eli Whitney (American)
Food canning process	1795–1809	Nicolas Appert (French)
Lithography	1798	Alois Senefelder (German)
Steam-powered locomotive	1804	Richard Trevithick (English)
Stethoscope	1816	René Laënnec (French)
Electromagnet	1825	William Sturgeon (English)
Photography	1826	Joseph Nicéphore Niépce (French)
Electric generator	1832	Hippolyte Pixii (French)
Coal stove	1833	Jordan L. Mott (American)
Refrigerator (compression system)	1834	Jacob Perkins (American)
Reaper	1834	Cyrus McCormick (American)
Threshing machine	1834	John and Hiram Pitts (American)
Revolver	1835	Samuel Colt (American)
Telegraph	1836	*Samuel F. B. Morse (American)
Steel plow	1837	John Deere (American)

Invention	Date	Inventor
Steam hammer	1839	James Nasmyth (Scottish)
Vulcanization process for rubber	1839	Charles Goodyear (American)
Safety matches	1844	Gustave E. Pasch (Swedish)
Pneumatic tire	1845	Robert W. Thomson (Scottish)
Sewing machine	1846	*Elias Howe (American)
Safety pin	1849	Walter Hunt (American)
Photoengraving	1852	William Fox Talbot (English)
Hypodermic syringe	1853	Charles Pravaz (French)
Safety elevator	1854	Elisha G. Otis (American)
Gas burner	1855	Robert W. Bunsen (German)
Internal-combustion engine (fueled by illuminating gas)	1860	Jean Joseph Étienne Lenoir (French)
Pedal-powered bicycle	1866	Pierre Lallement (French)
Dynamite	1867	*Alfred Nobel (Swedish)
Typewriter	1868	Christopher Latham Sholes, Carlos Glidden, Samuel W. Soulé (American)
Air brake	1868	George Westinghouse (American)
Celluloid	1869	John W. Hyatt (American)
Barbed wire	1873	Joseph F. Glidden (American)
Telephone	1876	*Alexander Graham Bell (American)
Phonograph	1877	*Thomas Alva Edison (American)
Incandescent lamp	1879	*Thomas Alva Edison (American)
Synthetic fiber (later called rayon)	1884	Hilaire Chardonnet (French)
Linotype machine (used for typesetting)	1884	Ottmar Mergenthaler (German-born living in U.S.)
Gasoline engine	1885	Gottlieb Daimler, Karl Benz (German, working independently)
Kodak box camera	1888	George Eastman (American)
Kinetoscope (motion-picture device)	1889	*†Thomas A. Edison (American)
Automatic machine gun	1889	Hiram Maxim (American)
Diesel engine	1892	Rudolf Diesel (German)
Zipper	1893	Whitcomb L. Judson (American)
Wireless telegraph	1895	*Guglielmo Marconi (Italian)
Airplane	1903	*Orville and Wilbur Wright (American)
Diode (a vacuum tube that could detect radio signals)	1904	Sir John A. Fleming (English)
Triode (improved vacuum tube that amplified radio signals)	1907	Lee De Forest (American)
Helicopter (manned)	1907	Paul Cornu (French)
Cellophane	1908	Jacques E. Brandenberger (Swiss)
Bakelite (first synthetic resin)	1909	Leo H. Baekeland (American)
Electric self-starter for automobiles	1911	Charles F. Kettering (American)
Quick-freezing process of food preservation	1920's	Clarence Birdseye (American)
Iconoscope (television camera tube)	1923	Vladimir K. Zworykin (Russian-born American)
Kinescope (television picture tube)	1923	Vladimir K. Zworykin (Russian-born American)
Liquid-propellant rocket	1926	*Robert H. Goddard (American)
Analog computer	1930	Vannevar Bush (American)
Jet-aircraft engine	1930	Frank Whittle (English)
Frequency modulation (FM)	1933	Edwin H. Armstrong (American)
Nylon	1935	Wallace H. Carothers (American)
Radar	1935	Robert A. Watson-Watt (Scottish)
Electronic computer	1946	J. Presper Eckert, John W. Mauchly (American)
Transistor	1947	John Bardeen, Walter Brattain, William Shockley (American)
Polaroid land camera	1947	Edwin H. Land (American)
Polio vaccine	1953	*Jonas Salk (American)
Laser	1960	Theodore H. Maiman (American)

*See "People" section for biographical information.
†Some historians believe Edison's assistant, William Kennedy Laurie Dickson, may have invented the kinetoscope.

Signs and symbols

Signs and symbols commonly used in many different fields appear in this section. See "Astrology" for the signs of the zodiac, "Chemical elements" for the symbols used to represent the elements, and "Religion" for religious symbols. See also "Abbreviations" and "Alphabets and codes."

Business

Money

$ dollar
¢ cent(s)
₡ colón(es) (Costa Rica, El Salvador)
£ pounds sterling
/ , s. shilling, shillings
d old penny or pence: *The stamp cost 2½d.*
Cr.$ cruzeiro (Brazil)

D. Kr. krone (Denmark)
DM Deutsche Mark (Germany)
Drs. drachmae (Greece)
Esc. escudo (Portugal)
F franc (France)
N. Kr. krone (Norway)
P. peso (Mexico)
₱ peso (Philippines)

p new pence
Ptas. pesetas (Spain)
Rs. rupees (India)
RUB. ruble (U.S.S.R.)
S. Frs. francs (Switzerland)
S. Kr. krona (Sweden)
¥ yen (Japan)

Commerce

a/c account; account current
@ at
b/d, B/D bank draft
B/E, B E bill of exchange
B/L bill of lading
B/M bill of material
b/o (in bookkeeping) brought over
b/p, B/P bills payable
b/r, B/R bills receivable
b/s, B/S bill of sale
c/d, C/D (in bookkeeping) carried down
c/f, C/F (in bookkeeping) carried forward
c. & f. cost and freight

c.l., C/L carload, carload lots
C/N credit note
c/o care of; (in bookkeeping) carried over
c/s, C/S cases
D/N debit note
d/o, D/O delivery order
J/A joint account
l/a, L/A letter of authority
l/c, L/C letter of credit
n/a no account
n/f, N/F no funds
n/r, N/R not responsible
o/a on account of
o/c overcharge
O.D., O/D overdraft

o/d on demand
o/s, O/S out of stock
O.T., o/t, O/T overtime
P & L profit and loss; (in bookkeeping) a record to show net profit or loss
p/n, P/N promissory note
r/e, R/E rate of exchange
s. d., S/D sight draft
S/N shipping note
s/o, S/O shipping order
(before a figure) number: *# 10 envelopes*; (after a figure or figures) pounds
% per cent; order of
₱ per

Chemistry

+ plus; positive charge
− single bond; negative charge
◯ benzene ring
→ yields

⇌ reversible reaction
↓ precipitate
↑ gas expelled
%₀ salinity; parts per hundred
/ valence

— or ‿ joined
= give or form
≡ or ⇌ is equivalent

Mapping

▬ (red) superhighway, divided highway Other colors indicate toll or interstate
⫞ interchange
⫟ no interchange
▬ paved main highway (various colors)

— secondary road (various colors)
═ unpaved road
▦ broken line indicates under construction
⊞ bridge
⇥ tunnel

 railroad tracks
–·– international boundary
–··– state or provincial
······· county
— township
----- reservation

⊕ capital city
⊙ ○ cities, towns
🛢 U.S. Interstate Highways
🛢 🛢 🛢 U.S. Highways (Alternate, By-pass)
⑳ state and provincial highways
[284] secondary state, county, and provincial highways
κ county trunk highways
🛡 Trans-Canada Highway

⑪ Mexican and Central American Highways
🎿 U.S. and Canadian Nat'l Parks
⌂ U.S. National Cemeteries, Historic Sites
△ U.S. National Monuments
■ points of interest
⑰ interchange numbers and names
✈ ✈ ✈ airports (commercial, military, municipal)

⚓ state and provincial parks (with camping facilities)
⚓ state and provincial parks (no camping facilities)
⚓ state memorials, monuments, historic sites
⚓ recreational areas and campsites
⚓ colleges
⋏ ports of entry
⚲ springs and wells
□ ranger stations

Mathematics

+ plus; positive; denoting approximate accuracy: *pi is equal to 3.14159+*
− minus; negative; denoting approximate accuracy
× times; multiplied by
· multiplied by
÷ divided by
= equals, is equal to
≠ not equal to
≈ nearly equal to
± plus or minus; positive or negative
∓ minus or plus; negative or positive
< less than
> greater than
≦ equal to or less than
≧ equal to or greater than
≮ not less than
≯ not greater than
≡ identical with
≢ not identical with
∼ or ∝ proportional to
≐ approaches
→ approaches limits of
⟁ equivalent
: is to; divided by
! or ∟ factorial product

Σ sum
∝ varies as; is directly proportional to
√ radical sign, indicating square root of
^{1}, ^{2}, ^{3} (at the right of a symbol or numeral) indicating that it is raised to the first, second, third, etc., power
$\sqrt[\scriptstyle 3]{}$, $\sqrt[\scriptstyle 3]{}$, $\sqrt[\scriptstyle 3]{}$, $\sqrt[\scriptstyle 3]{}$, $\sqrt[\scriptstyle 3]{}$, the radical sign used with indices, indicating the second, third, fourth, fifth, sixth root of
0 infinitesimal; zero
∞ infinity
( ) parentheses ⎱ indicate that
[ ] brackets ⎰ the enclosed quantities
| | braces ⎱ should be
− vinculum (above letters) ⎰ treated as a single unit
f or F function
∫ integral
g the acceleration of gravity
∠; ⊿ angle; angles
△; ⊿ triangle; triangles
▱ parallelogram
▭ rectangle
□ square
O; ⑤ circle; circles
⊥ perpendicular to

∥ parallel to
π the Greek letter pi, representing the ratio of the circumference of any circle to its diameter; equal to 3.14159+
∂ or δ differential; variation
⌒ arc of circle
° degree, degrees
′ minute, minutes
″ second, seconds
≅ or ≡ congruent to
∴ therefore; hence
∵ since; because
⊥ equilateral
∨ equiangular
／ single bond of affinity (between letters)
∺ geometrical proportion
∹ difference between
{} or ∅ empty set
ε is a member of a set; j ε B
∤ is not a member of a set; j ∤ B
| such that
↔ is equivalent to; A ↔ Z
∪ universal set
⊂ is included in; A ⊂ N
∪ union; A ∪ B
∩ intersection; J ∩ K

Birthstones and flowers

Month	Birthstone	Flower
January	Garnet	Carnation or Snowdrop
February	Amethyst	Primrose
March	Aquamarine or Bloodstone	Violet
April	Diamond	Daisy or Sweet Pea
May	Emerald	Hawthorn or Lily of the Valley

Month	Birthstone	Flower
June	Moonstone, Alexandrite, or Pearl	Rose
July	Ruby	Water Lily
August	Peridot or Sardonyx	Gladiolus or Poppy
September	Sapphire	Morning Glory
October	Opal or Tourmaline	Calendula
November	Topaz	Chrysanthemum
December	Turquoise or Zircon	Holly, Narcissus, or Poinsettia

159

Traffic signs

Standard U.S. signs

Warning

Yield

Instructions
or directions

SPEED LIMIT 50

Railroad crossing

Complete stop
required

International signs

Uneven road

Right curve

Dangerous
curve

Intersection

Unguarded
level crossing

Slippery road

Road narrows

Pedestrian
crossing

Other danger

Stop at
intersection

Speed limit

All traffic
prohibited

No left turn

Stopping
prohibited

No entry

Automobiles
prohibited

Anniversary gifts

First	Paper, plastics
Second	Cotton
Third	Leather, any leatherlike article
Fourth	Linen, silk, rayon, nylon, other synthetic silks
Fifth	Wood and decorative accessories for the home
Sixth	Iron
Seventh	Wool, copper, brass
Eighth	Bronze, electrical appliances
Ninth	Pottery, china, glass or crystal
Tenth	Tin, aluminum
Eleventh	Steel
Twelfth	Linen, silk, nylon

Thirteenth	Lace
Fourteenth	Ivory, agate
Fifteenth	Crystal, glass
Twentieth	China or occasional furniture
Twenty-fifth	Silver
Thirtieth	Pearls or personal gifts
Thirty-fifth	Coral, jade
Fortieth	Rubies, garnets
Forty-fifth	Sapphires, tourmalines
Fiftieth	Gold
Fifty-fifth	Emeralds, turquoise
Sixtieth, Seventy-fifth	Diamonds, gold

Numerals

Arabic and Roman numerals from 1 to 10,000,000

1	I	16	XVI	130	CXXX	1,000	M
2	II	17	XVII	140	CXL	2,000	MM
3	III	18	XVIII	150	CL	3,000	MMM
4	IV	19	XIX	160	CLX	4,000	$M\overline{V}$
5	V	20	XX	170	CLXX	5,000	$\overline{V}$
6	VI	30	XXX	180	CLXXX	10,000	$\overline{X}$
7	VII	40	XL	190	CXC	15,000	$\overline{XV}$
8	VIII	50	L	200	CC	25,000	$\overline{XXV}$
9	IX	60	LX	300	CCC	50,000	$\overline{L}$
10	X	70	LXX	400	CD	100,000	$\overline{C}$
11	XI	80	LXXX	500	D	500,000	$\overline{D}$
12	XII	90	XC	600	DC	1,000,000	$\overline{M}$
13	XIII	100	C	700	DCC	5,000,000	$\overline{MMMMM}$
14	XIV	110	CX	800	DCCC	10,000,000	$\overline{MMMMMMMMMM}$
15	XV	120	CXX	900	CM		

Cats

The cats shown on these pages are some of the more common long-haired and short-haired breeds of cats. For more information about these cats, see the table in the "Animals" section.

Short-haired breeds

Rex

Russian blue

Burmese

Siamese

Abyssinian

Manx

161

Long-haired breeds

Birman

Maine coon

Persian

Balinese

Somali

Himalayan

Turkish angora

162

Dogs

The dogs shown on these pages are some of the most common breeds registered by the American Kennel Club (AKC). The AKC classifies breeds into seven groups: (1) toy dogs, (2) sporting dogs, (3) hounds, (4) working dogs, (5) herding dogs, (6) terriers, and (7) nonsporting dogs. For more information about these dogs, see the table in the "Animals" section.

Toy dogs

Yorkshire terrier

Maltese

Brussels griffon

Pomeranian

Affenpinscher

Chihuahua

Shih tzu

Silky terrier

163

Sporting dogs

Cocker spaniel

English springer spaniel

Vizsla

Golden retriever

German short-haired pointer

Irish setter

Labrador retriever

Brittany

Hounds

Basset hound

Norwegian elkhound

Afghan hound

Bloodhound

Basenji

Dachshund (wire-haired)

Borzoi

Beagle

Whippet

165

Working dogs

Alaskan malamute

Doberman pinscher

Great Dane

Siberian husky

Samoyed

Boxer

Great Pyrenees

Saint Bernard

Mastiff

Herding dogs

Collie

Bearded collie

Old English sheepdog

Belgian sheepdog

German shepherd dog

Australian cattle dog

Bouvier des Flandres

Terriers

Miniature schnauzer

Airedale terrier

Cairn terrier

West Highland white terrier

Bull terrier

Scottish terrier

Fox terrier

Kerry blue terrier

168

Nonsporting dogs

Poodle

Bulldog

Keeshond

Schipperke

Chow chow

Bichon frise

Boston terrier

French bulldog

Lhasa apso

Tibetan terrier

Dalmatian

169

Horses

The horses shown on these pages represent some of the various breeds and color types. See also the table in the "Animals" section.

American saddle horse

Tennessee walking horse

Morgan

Arabian

Quarter horse

Pinto

170

Thoroughbred

Standardbred

Albino

Appaloosa

Palomino

Lipizzaner

Belgian

Welsh pony

Percheron

Shetland pony

Suffolk

Shire

Przewalski's horse

Clydesdale

Hackney

World climate

The map on these pages shows the 12 major kinds of climate recognized by many *climatologists* — scientists who study climate. See the "Canada" and "United States" sections for more detailed information about the climates of those countries. A table of worldwide temperatures and average amounts of precipitation appears in the "Weather" section.

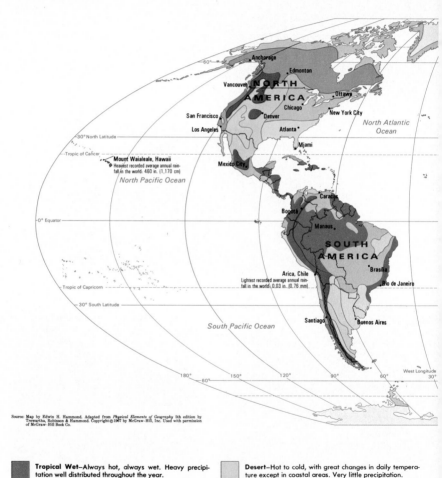

Source: Map by Edwin H. Hammond. Adapted from *Physical Elements of Geography* 5th edition by Trewartha, Robinson & Hammond. Copyright © 1967 by McGraw-Hill, Inc. Used with permission of McGraw-Hill Book Co.

Tropical Wet—Always hot, always wet. Heavy precipitation well distributed throughout the year.

Tropical Wet and Dry—Always hot, with alternate wet and dry seasons. Heavy precipitation in the wet season.

Highlands—These areas are affected by altitude and are generally cooler and wetter than the adjacent climates.

Desert—Hot to cold, with great changes in daily temperature except in coastal areas. Very little precipitation.

Steppe—Hot to cold, with great changes in daily temperature except in coastal areas. Little precipitation.

Subtropical Dry Summer—Hot, dry summers and mild, rainy winters. Moderate precipitation in winter.

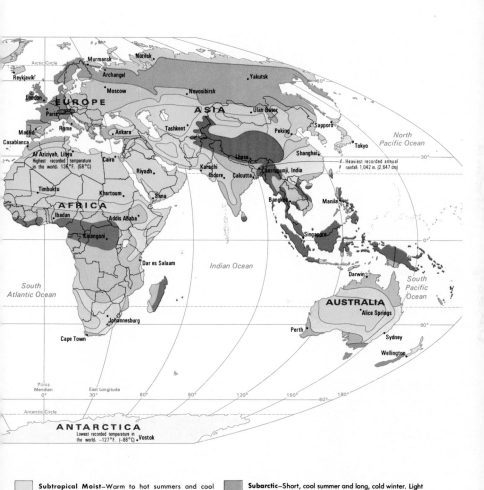

Subtropical Moist—Warm to hot summers and cool winters. Moderate precipitation in all seasons.

Oceanic Moist—Moderately warm summer and mild, cool winter. Moderate precipitation in all seasons.

Continental Moist—Warm to cool summer and cold winter. Moderate precipitation in all seasons.

Subarctic—Short, cool summer and long, cold winter. Light to moderate precipitation, mostly in summer.

Polar—Always cold, with a brief chilly summer. Little precipitation in all seasons.

Icecap—Always cold, average monthly temperature never above freezing. Precipitation always in the form of snow.

Decorations and Medals

See the tables in the "Decorations and Medals" section for information about decorations and medals awarded in the United States and other nations.

Decorations and medals of the United States

Medal of Honor (Army)

Medal of Honor (Air Force)

Medal of Honor (Navy)

Distinguished Service Cross (Army)

Air Force Cross

Navy Cross

(Army)

Distinguished Service Medal (Air Force)

(Navy)

Distinguished Flying Cross

Purple Heart

Silver Star

Victory Medal (World War I)

Victory Medal (World War II)

NASA Distinguished Service Medal

Legion of Merit
(Chief Commander)

Presidential Medal of Freedom

Young American
Medal for Bravery

Decorations and medals of other countries

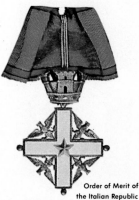

Iron Cross (Germany)

Legion of Honor (France)

Order of Merit of
the Italian Republic
(Italy)

Croix de Guerre
(France)

Victoria Cross
(Great Britain)

Distinguished
Service Order
(Great Britain)

Korean Service Medal
(United Nations)

Order of Lenin
(Russia)

177

Flags

For more information on flags, see the "Flags" section. International alphabet flags and semaphore flags appear in the "Alphabets and Codes" section.

Flags of the Americas

Antigua and Barbuda

Argentina

Bahamas

Barbados

Belize

Bolivia

Brazil

Canada

Chile

Colombia

Costa Rica

Cuba

Dominica

Dominican Republic

Ecuador

El Salvador

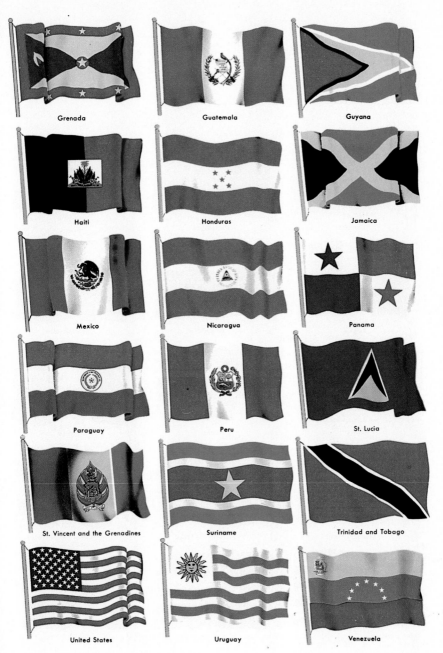

Grenada

Guatemala

Guyana

Haiti

Honduras

Jamaica

Mexico

Nicaragua

Panama

Paraguay

Peru

St. Lucia

St. Vincent and the Grenadines

Suriname

Trinidad and Tobago

United States

Uruguay

Venezuela

179

Flags of Europe

Albania

Andorra

Austria

Belgium

Bulgaria

Czechoslovakia

Denmark

Finland

France

Germany (East)

Germany (West)

Great Britain

Greece

Hungary

Iceland

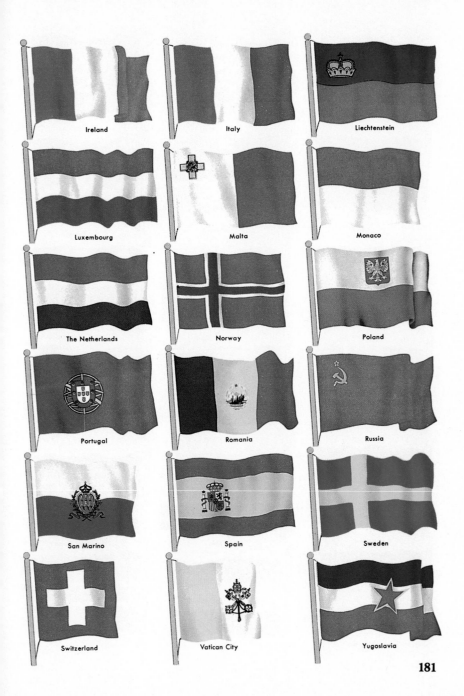

Ireland

Italy

Liechtenstein

Luxembourg

Malta

Monaco

The Netherlands

Norway

Poland

Portugal

Romania

Russia

San Marino

Spain

Sweden

Switzerland

Vatican City

Yugoslavia

Flags of Africa

Algeria

Angola

Benin

Botswana

Burundi

Cameroon

Cape Verde

Central African Republic

Chad

Comoros

Congo

Djibouti

Egypt

Equatorial Guinea

Ethiopia

Gabon

Gambia

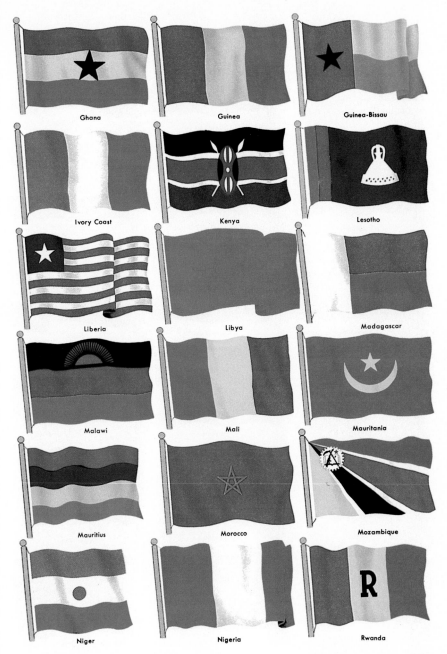

Ghana

Guinea

Guinea-Bissau

Ivory Coast

Kenya

Lesotho

Liberia

Libya

Madagascar

Malawi

Mali

Mauritania

Mauritius

Morocco

Mozambique

Niger

Nigeria

Rwanda

Flags of Africa
(continued)

St. Helena

São Tomé and Príncipe

Senegal

Seychelles

Sierra Leone

Somalia

South Africa

Sudan

Swaziland

Tanzania

Togo

Tunisia

Uganda

Upper Volta

Zaire

Zambia

Zimbabwe

Flags of Asia and the Pacific

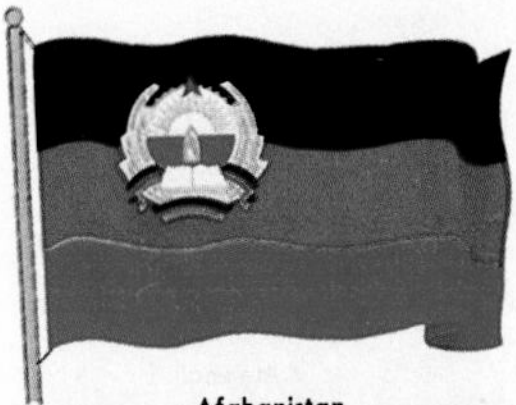

Afghanistan

Australia

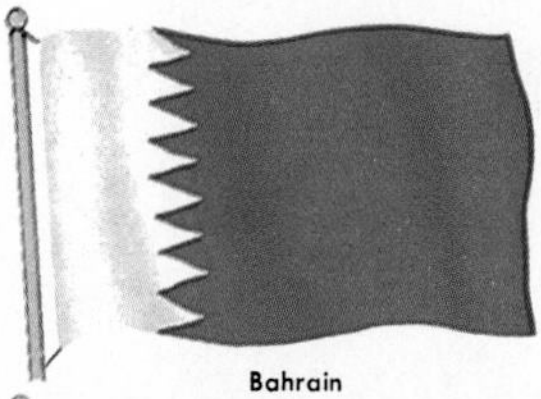

Bahrain

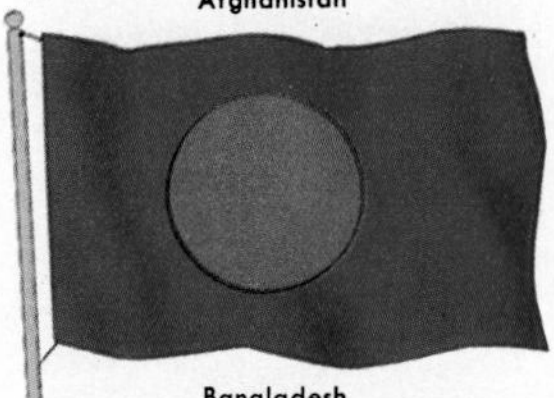

Bangladesh

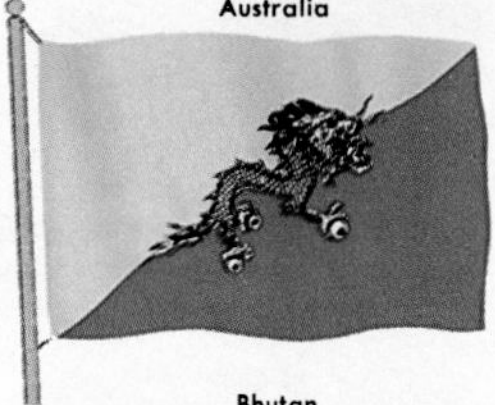

Bhutan

Brunei

Burma

Cambodia

China

Cyprus

Fiji

Hong Kong

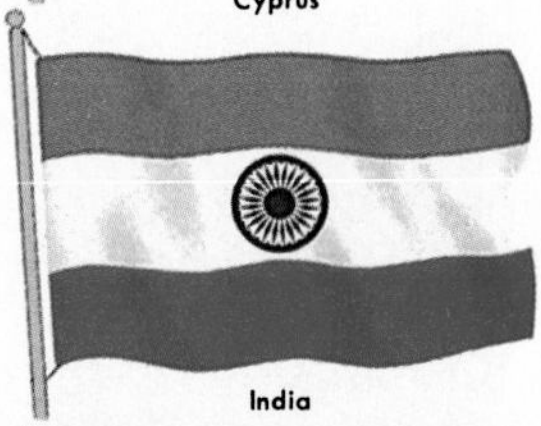

India

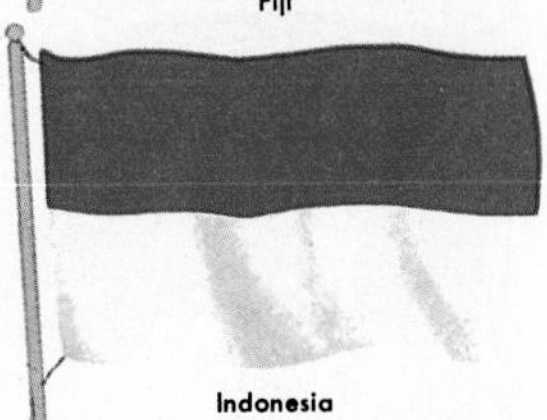

Indonesia

Iran

Iraq

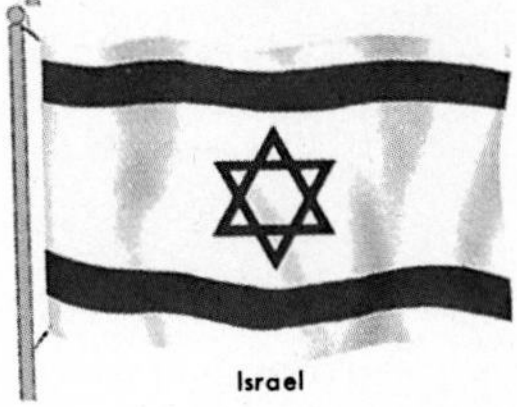

Israel

Japan

Jordan

Kiribati

Korea (North)

Korea (South)

Kuwait

Laos

Lebanon

Malaysia

Maldives

Mongolia

Nauru

Nepal

New Zealand

Oman

Pakistan

Papua New Guinea

Philippines

Qatar

Saudi Arabia

Singapore

Solomon Islands

Sri Lanka

Syria

Taiwan

Thailand

Tonga

Turkey

Tuvalu

United Arab Emirates

Vanuatu

Vietnam

Western Samoa

Yemen (Aden)

Yemen (Sana)

Flags of the states and territories

Alabama

Alaska

American Samoa

Arizona

Arkansas

California

Colorado

Connecticut

Delaware

District of Columbia

Florida

Georgia

Guam

Hawaii

Idaho

Illinois

Indiana

Iowa

Kansas

Kentucky

Louisiana

Maine

Maryland

Massachusetts

Michigan

Minnesota

Mississippi

Missouri

Montana

Nebraska

Nevada

New Hampshire

New Jersey

New Mexico

New York

North Carolina

North Dakota

Ohio

Oklahoma

Oregon

Pennsylvania

Puerto Rico

Rhode Island

South Carolina

South Dakota

Tennessee

Texas

Utah

Vermont

Virgin Islands

Virginia

Washington

West Virginia

Wisconsin

Wyoming

Some United States city flags

Baltimore

Boston

Chicago

Cleveland

Dallas

Detroit

Houston

Los Angeles

Milwaukee

New Orleans

New York

Philadelphia

Pittsburgh

Saint Louis

San Antonio

San Diego

San Francisco

190

Some flags in American history

Today's 50-Star United States Flag has the following dimensions: hoist (width) of flag, 1.0 unit; fly (length) of flag, 1.9; hoist of union, .5385 (7/13); fly of union, .76; width of each stripe, .0769 (1/13); and diameter of each star, .0616.

The Continental Colors served as America's first national flag from 1775 to 1777.

The Flag of 1777 had no official arrangement for the stars. The most popular design had alternating rows of 3, 2, 3, 2, and 3 stars. Another flag with 13 stars in a circle was rarely used.

The Flag of 1795 had 15 stripes, as well as 15 stars, to stand for the 15 states.

The Flag of 1818 went back to 13 stripes, and had 20 stars for the 20 states. One design had four rows of five stars each. The Great Star Flag, *right*, formed the 20 stars in a large star.

The Flag of 1861, used in the Civil War, had stars for 34 states, including the South.

The 48-Star Flag served as the national flag the longest of any flag, from 1912 to 1959.

Perry's Flag in 1813 bore the last words of James Lawrence, a hero of the War of 1812.

Texas Flags. The Alamo Flag of 1836, *left*, bore the date of Mexico's constitution, showing loyalty to the idea of constitutional government. The Texas Navy Flag, *right*, had a lone star.

The Bear Flag flew over an independent California republic for a few months in 1846.

 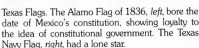 

Confederate Flags. The Stars and Bars, *left*, adopted in 1861, had stars for 7 seceding states. It looked too much like the U.S. flag, so troops carried a battle flag, *above*. It had stars for 11 states and for secession governments in Kentucky and Missouri, as did the flag of 1863, *above*. This looked too much like a flag of truce, so a red bar was added in 1865, *right*.

Flags of Canada

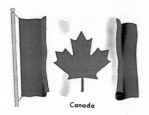

Canada

Royal Union

Queen

Governor General

Armed Forces

Flags of the provinces and territories of Canada

Alberta

British Columbia

Manitoba

New Brunswick

Newfoundland

Northwest Territories

Nova Scotia

Ontario

Prince Edward Island

Quebec

Saskatchewan

Yukon Territory

Space

This section presents information about space exploration and travel. For information about the planet earth and its moon, see the "Earth" Section. To find out about the solar system, stars, and other features of the universe, see the "Universe" section. Biographies of many famous space explorers and scientists appear in the "People" section.

Space begins about 100 miles (160 kilometers) above the surface of the earth, where the atmosphere is too thin to affect objects moving through it. *Cislunar space* exists between the earth and the moon—a distance of more than 220,000 miles (352,000 kilometers). *Translunar space* extends about 1,000,000 miles (1,600,000 kilometers) from earth, to the point where the combined gravities of the earth and the moon are no longer effective. Space between the planets is called *interplanetary space.* The sun's gravity controls this vast region. It extends as far as the sun's gravity is effective, a distance of perhaps 50 billion miles (80 billion kilometers) from earth. Space between the stars, called *interstellar space,* reaches even farther, to a distance greater than anyone can imagine. Beyond that, *intergalactic space,* space between the galaxies, extends with no known limits.

Space travel terms

Ablation is the melting away of a heat shield during reentry.

Aerospace includes the atmosphere and the regions of space beyond it.

Aphelion is the point farthest from the sun in the path of a solar satellite.

Apocynthion is the point farthest from the moon in the orbit of a lunar satellite.

Apogee is the point farthest from earth in the orbit of an earth satellite. .

Artificial Satellite is a spacecraft that circles the earth or other celestial body. The term is usually shortened to *satellite,* but it then also applies to natural moons.

Astro is a prefix meaning *star.* It also means *space* in such words as *astronautics* (the science of space flight).

Astronaut is a United States space pilot.

Attitude is the position of a spacecraft in relation to its direction of flight.

Biosatellite is an artificial satellite that carries animals or plants.

Booster is a launch vehicle's first stage.

Burnout is the point in the flight of a rocket when its propellant is used up. .

Capsule is a manned spacecraft or a small package of instruments carried by a larger spacecraft.

Cosmonaut is a Russian space pilot.

Decay is the slowing down of a satellite as it runs into air particles.

Drogue is a special parachute that slows and steadies a spacecraft as it returns to earth.

Eccentricity is the variation of a satellite's path from a perfect circle.

Escape Velocity is the speed a spacecraft must reach to coast away from the pull of gravity.

Exhaust Velocity is the speed at which the burning gases leave a rocket.

Gantry is a special crane or movable tower used to service launch vehicles.

Grain is a rubbery or plasticlike substance that consists of fuel and oxidizer in solid form.

Heat Shield is a covering on a spacecraft to protect the craft and astronaut from high temperatures of reentry.

Hypergol is a rocket fuel that ignites upon contact with an oxidizer.

LOX or **Liquid Oxygen** is a common oxidizer. It is made by cooling oxygen to $-183°$ C ($-297°$ F.).

Module is a single section of a spacecraft that can be disconnected and separated from other sections.

Orbit is the path of a satellite.

Oxidizer is a substance that mixes with the fuel in a rocket, furnishing oxygen that permits the fuel to burn.

Pericynthion is the point closest to the moon in the orbit of a lunar satellite.

Perigee is the point closest to earth in the orbit of an earth satellite.

Perihelion is the point closest to the sun in the path of a solar satellite.

Period is the time it takes for a satellite to make one revolution.

Propellant is a substance burned in a rocket to produce thrust. Propellants include fuels and oxidizers.

Reentry is that part of a flight when a returning spacecraft begins to descend through the atmosphere.

Rendezvous is a space maneuver in which two or more spacecraft meet.

Retrorocket is a rocket that fires in the direction a spacecraft is moving to slow it down or land it.

Spacecraft is a man-made object that travels through space.

Stage is one of two or more rockets combined to form a launch vehicle.

Thrust is the push given to a rocket by its engines.

Velocity is the speed and direction of a spacecraft.

Launch vehicles

Launch vehicle	Stages	Takeoff thrust		Payload
Vanguard*	3	28,000 lb.	125,000 N‡	50 lbs. (23 kg) in earth orbit
Jupiter C*	4	82,000 lb.	365,000 N	30 lbs. (14 kg) in earth orbit
Scout	4	107,200 lb.	476,850 N	410 lbs. (186 kg) in earth orbit; 85 lbs. (39 kg) to moon
Juno II*	4	150,000 lb.	667,000 N	100 lbs. (45 kg) in earth orbit
Mercury-Redstone*	1	82,000 lb.	365,000 N	3,000 lbs. (1,400 kg) suborbital
Delta	3	205,000 lb.	911,900 N	3,900 lbs. (1,770 kg) in earth orbit; 1,050 lbs. (476 kg) to moon
Mercury-Atlas*	1½†	367,000 lb.	1,632,000 N	3,000 lbs. (1,400 kg) in earth orbit
Atlas-Agena	2½†	400,000 lb.	1,800,000 N	7,700 lbs. (3,490 kg) in earth orbit; 1,430 lbs. (649 kg) to moon; 1,000 lbs. (450 kg) to Mars or Venus
Atlas-Centaur	2½†	400,000 lb.	1,800,000 N	10,300 lbs. (4,672 kg) in earth orbit; 2,500 lbs. (1,130 kg) to moon; 2,200 lbs. (998 kg) to Mars or Venus
Titan II*	2	430,000 lb.	1,910,000 N	8,600 lbs. (3,900 kg) in earth orbit
Titan IIIC	3 or 4	2,400,000 lb.	10,700,000 N	26,000 lbs. (11,800 kg) in earth orbit; 6,200 lbs. (2,810 kg) to moon
Titan-Centaur	4	2,400,000 lb.	10,700,000 N	35,000 lbs. (15,900 kg) in earth orbit; 11,500 lbs. (5,216 kg) interplanetary missions
Space Shuttle System	2	6,925,000 lb.	30,802,000 N	65,000 lbs. (29,500 kg) in earth orbit
Saturn V*	3	7,570,000 lb.	33,670,000 N	285,000 lbs. (129,300 kg) in earth orbit; 107,000 lbs. (48,530 kg) to moon; 70,000 lbs. (32,000 kg) to Mars or Venus

*No longer in use.
†Half stage is droppable booster engine.
‡N is the abbreviation for *newton,* the unit of force in the metric system. One newton is the force required to increase or decrease the velocity of a one-kilogram object by one meter per second every second.

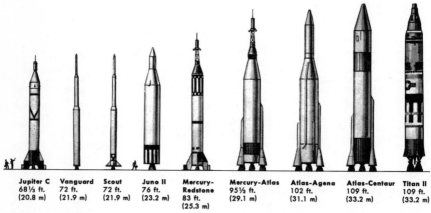

Jupiter C	Vanguard	Scout	Juno II	Mercury-Redstone	Mercury-Atlas	Atlas-Agena	Atlas-Centaur	Titan II
68⅓ ft.	72 ft.	72 ft.	76 ft.	83 ft.	95⅓ ft.	102 ft.	109 ft.	109 ft.
(20.8 m)	(21.9 m)	(21.9 m)	(23.2 m)	(25.3 m)	(29.1 m)	(31.1 m)	(33.2 m)	(33.2 m)

To get into space, a spacecraft must have the power to overcome gravity, the force that pulls everything to earth. Rockets provide this power by producing *thrust,* a pushing force. To do so, they burn huge amounts of *propellant* in a short time. Propellants consist of a fuel and an *oxidizer* (a substance that supplies oxygen). As the propellant burns, it creates hot gas. The heat causes extremely high pressure that pushes flaming gas out through the rocket nozzle and pushes the rocket forward.

Most spacecraft use liquid-propellant rockets. The fuel and oxidizer are liquids stored in separate tanks. The two elements meet in a combustion chamber. Most liquid propellants use an ignition system to begin combustion. But others ignite as soon as the fuel and oxidizer contact each other. Some spacecraft use solid-propellant rockets, which burn a rubbery or plasticlike substance called the *grain.* The grain is simply fuel and oxidizer in a solid form.

A launch vehicle can be a single rocket or a combination of rockets. Multistage rockets have two or more sections. Each section, or stage, has a propellant and a rocket engine. The first stage, called the *booster,* launches the rocket. After the first stage has used up all its propellant, it drops off the vehicle. The second stage ignites and carries the spacecraft into earth orbit or even farther into space. The rocket continues to use one stage after another. Most space rockets have two or three stages.

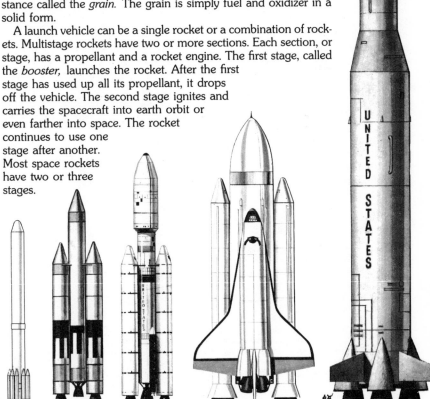

Delta	Titan IIIC	Titan-Centaur	Space Shuttle System	Saturn V
116 feet	135 ft.	160 ft.	184 ft.	363 ft.
(35.4 m)	(41.1 m)	(48.8 m)	(56.1 m)	(110.6 m)

Space travel

When a spacecraft is launched, it travels straight up for about a minute. Then it arches into the proper direction for its *orbit*—the path it will follow in space. Earth orbits may be circular or elliptical. A spacecraft in a circular orbit always maintains the same speed and stays the same distance from earth. In an elliptical orbit, a spacecraft's speed and distance from earth change continuously. The point of the orbit at which the spacecraft is closest to earth and its speed is greatest is called the *perigee*. The *apogee* is the point at which the spacecraft is farthest from earth and its speed is slowest. Spacecraft also vary in the directions of their orbits around the earth. A spacecraft may circle in an east-west direction, along the equator. A polar orbit carries a spacecraft in a north-south direction, over the poles. Most earth-orbiting spacecraft follow an inclined orbit, which forms an angle between the poles and the equator. In a synchronous orbit, a spacecraft circles the earth once every day.

The desired height of an earth orbit determines a spacecraft's required *velocity* (speed and direction). The higher the orbit, the lower the required velocity. But to reach the moon, a spacecraft needs much greater speed than it needs to orbit the earth. A spacecraft must travel about 24,300 miles (39,100 kilometers) per hour to reach the moon. At 25,000 miles (40,200 kilometers) per hour, a spacecraft reaches *escape velocity*. That is, it can escape the influence of the earth's gravity and travel into interplanetary space. There the spacecraft goes into orbit around the sun. To reach another planet, a spacecraft must go faster than escape velocity. The space age began on Oct. 4, 1957, when the Russians launched *Sputnik I,* the world's first artificial satellite. Since that time, many satellites have been launched. Weather satellites are used to forecast weather and study how weather develops. Communications satellites allow radio messages, telephone calls, and television programs to be sent between distant locations. Navigation satellites help pilots and sailors find their exact positions in all kinds of weather. Scientific satellites can provide data for research in astronomy, geophysics, and other fields.

Important satellites

Date launched	Name	Accomplishments

Communications satellites

1958	Dec. 18	*Project Score*	Broadcast first voice message from space.
1962	July 10	*Telstar I*	First satellite to relay television programs between United States and Europe.
1963	July 26	*Syncom II*	First synchronous satellite.
1965	Apr. 6	*Early Bird*	First commercial communications satellite.
1967	Jan. 11	*INTELSAT IIB*	First of a series of satellites in stationary orbit; used for television, data, or voice.
1971	Jan. 26	*INTELSAT IVA*	First high-capacity international communications satellite.
1974	May 30	*ATS-6*	Brought two-way voice and picture communication to isolated areas.
1977	Dec. 14	*CS*	First Japanese communications satellite.
1981	Feb. 21	*Comstar D*	Synchronous satellite; part of a worldwide communications system.

Weather satellites

1959	Feb. 17	*Vanguard II*	First satellite to send weather information back to earth.
1960	Apr. 1	*Tiros I*	Took the first detailed weather pictures.
1974	May 17	*SMS-1*	First full-time weather satellite in synchronous orbit.

Date launched	Name	Accomplishments
1975 Oct. 16	*GOES-1*	First weather satellite with enough speed to maintain same observational position over the earth.
1978 June 16	*GOES-3*	Equipped to provide both day and night pictures of the earth's weather patterns.
Oct. 24	*Nimbus-7*	Collected data for long-range weather forecasting and for evaluating the effects of fluorocarbons in the earth's atmosphere.
1980 Sept. 9	*GOES-D*	Designed to take readings of atmospheric moisture and temperature for the purpose of tracking storms.

Navigation satellites

1960 Apr. 13	*Transit IB*	First navigation satellite.
1961 June 29	*Transit IVA*	First satellite to use nuclear power.
Nov. 15	*Transit IVB*	Tested method of using earth's gravity to keep satellites in proper position.
1978 Feb. 21	*NAVSTAR*	First satellite of an 18-satellite system designed to provide navigational positions on a continuous basis.

Scientific satellites

1957 Oct. 4	*Sputnik I*	World's first artificial satellite; launched by Russia.
1958 Jan. 31	*Explorer I*	First U.S. satellite; discovered Van Allen radiation in space.
1962 Mar. 7	*OSO-I*	First orbiting solar observatory.
Apr. 26	*Ariel (U.K. No. 1)*	First international satellite; carried U.S. and British instruments.
Sept.28	*Alouette*	First Canadian satellite.
1963 Apr. 2	*Explorer XVII*	First satellite to study the atmosphere.
1967 Sept. 7	*Biosatellite II*	Carried living cells, plants, and animals into space and returned them to earth.
1968 Dec. 7	*OAO-II*	First orbiting astronomical observatory.
1972 July 23	*LandSat-1*	Photographed the earth with different wavelengths of light to provide information about earth's natural resources.
1973 June 10	*Explorer XLIX*	Conducted radio-astronomy research on the far side of the moon.
1976 May 4	*Lagoes*	First satellite designed for high-precision geographic measurements.
1977 Aug. 12	*HEAO-1*	Orbiting observatory used to locate objects in outer space that emit X rays.
Oct. 22	*ISEE's*	A pair of satellites launched by a single rocket to study the effects of the sun on the earth's atmosphere and climate.
1978 Nov. 13	*HEAO-2*	Transmitted data and photographs of quasars and other cosmic objects that emit X rays.
1979 Feb. 18	*SAGE*	Primarily designed to measure fluorocarbon content of the earth's stratosphere.
Sept.20	*HEAO-3*	Monitored and analyzed gamma rays and cosmic rays from deep space.
1980 Feb. 14	*S.M.M.*	Designed to study solar flares and the conditions on the sun that cause such eruptions.

Manned spacecraft

Four U.S. and two Russian spacecraft are shown on the following pages. Vostok and Mercury capsules each carried one space pilot. The Gemini capsule carried two astronauts who could change the orbit of the craft. Three astronauts can orbit the moon in the Apollo command module. Two of them can land on the moon in the lunar module. The Apollo service module carries a rocket engine used during the flight. The Russian Soyuz can carry three cosmonauts.

All manned spacecraft carry the following equipment: (1) life-support systems to supply the astronauts with oxygen, food, and water; (2) communications equipment for contact with scientists and engineers on the ground; (3) navigation equipment to determine the spacecraft's course and position; (4) control systems for maneuvering the spacecraft; and (5) reentry and landing equipment, such as retrorockets, heat shields, and parachutes.

Manned space flights

The Vostok, Voskhod, Soyuz, and Salyut spacecraft are Russian vehicles. All the others listed in this table were launched by the United States.

Date launched		Astronaut or cosmonaut	Spacecraft	Revolutions	Time of flight
1961	Apr. 12	Y. Gagarin	*Vostok 1*	1	1 hr. 48 min.
	May 5	A. Shepard, Jr.	*Freedom 7*	Suborbital	15 min.
	July 21	V. Grissom	*Liberty Bell 7*	Suborbital	16 min.
	Aug. 6	G. Titov	*Vostok 2*	16	1 day, 1 hr. 18 min.
1962	Feb. 20	J. Glenn, Jr.	*Friendship 7*	3	4 hr. 55 min.
	May 24	S. Carpenter	*Aurora 7*	3	4 hr. 56 min.
	Aug. 11	A. Nikolayev	*Vostok 3*	60	3 days, 22 hr. 22 min.
	Aug. 12	P. Popovich	*Vostok 4*	45	2 days, 22 hr. 57 min.
	Oct. 3	W. Schirra, Jr.	*Sigma 7*	6	9 hr. 13 min.
1963	May 15	G. Cooper, Jr.	*Faith 7*	22	1 day, 10 hr. 20 min.
	June 14	V. Bykovsky	*Vostok 5*	76	4 days, 23 hr. 6 min.
	June 16	V. Tereshkova	*Vostok 6*	45	2 days, 22 hr. 50 min.
1964	Oct. 12	V. Komarov, K. Feoktistov, B. Yegorov	*Voskhod 1*	15	1 day, 0 hr. 17 min.
1965	Mar. 18	P. Belyayev, A. Leonov	*Voskhod 2*	16	1 day, 2 hr. 2 min.
	Mar. 23	V. Grissom, J. Young	*Molly Brown*	3	4 hr. 53 min.
	June 3	J. McDivitt, E. White II	*Gemini 4*	62	4 days, 1 hr. 56 min.
	Aug. 21	G. Cooper, Jr., C. Conrad, Jr.	*Gemini 5*	120	7 days, 22 hr. 56 min.
	Dec. 4	F. Borman, J. Lovell, Jr.	*Gemini 7*	206	13 days, 18 hr. 35 min.
	Dec. 15	W. Schirra, Jr., T. Stafford	*Gemini 6*	16	1 day, 1 hr. 51 min.
1966	Mar. 16	N. Armstrong, D. Scott	*Gemini 8*	7	10 hr. 41 min.
	June 3	T. Stafford, E. Cernan	*Gemini 9*	44	3 days, 0 hr. 21 min.
	July 18	J. Young, M. Collins	*Gemini 10*	43	2 days, 22 hr. 47 min.

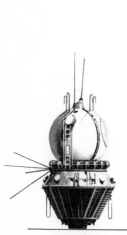

Russian Vostok
About 16 ft.
(4.9 m)

Mercury capsule
6⅞ ft.
(2.1 m)

Gemini capsule
19 ft.
(5.8 m)

Apollo command and service modules
35⅓ ft.
(10.8 m)

198

Date launched	Astronaut or cosmonaut	Spacecraft	Revolutions	Time of flight
1966 Sept. 12	C. Conrad, Jr., R. Gordon, Jr.	*Gemini 11*	44	2 days, 23 hr. 17 min.
Nov. 11	J. Lovell, Jr., E. Aldrin, Jr.	*Gemini 12*	59	3 days, 22 hr. 35 min.
1967 Apr. 23	V. Komarov	*Soyuz 1*	17	1 day, 2 hr. 37 min.
1968 Oct. 11	W. Schirra, Jr., D. Eisele, W. Cunningham	*Apollo 7*	163	10 days, 20 hr. 9 min.
Oct. 26	G. Beregovoi	*Soyuz 3*	60	3 days, 22 hr. 51 min.
Dec. 21	F. Borman, W. Anders, J. Lovell, Jr.	*Apollo 8*	Lunar flight	6 days, 3 hr. 1 min.
1969 Jan. 14	V. Shatalov	*Soyuz 4*	45	2 days, 23 hr. 23 min.
Jan. 15	B. Volynov, Y. Khrunov,* A. Yeliseyev*	*Soyuz 5*	46	3 days, 0 hr. 56 min.
Mar. 3	J. McDivitt, R. Schweickart, D. Scott	*Apollo 9*	151	10 days, 1 hr. 1 min.
May 18	T. Stafford, E. Cernan, J. Young	*Apollo 10*	Lunar flight	8 days, 0 hr. 3 min.
July 16	N. Armstrong, E. Aldrin, Jr., M. Collins	*Apollo 11*	Lunar landing	8 days, 3 hr. 19 min.
Oct. 11	V. Kubasov, G. Shonin	*Soyuz 6*	75	4 days, 22 hr. 42 min.
Oct. 12	A. Filipchenko, V. Gorbatko, V. Volkov	*Soyuz 7*	75	4 days, 22 hr. 41 min.
Oct. 13	V. Shatalov, A. Yeliseyev	*Soyuz 8*	75	4 days, 22 hr. 50 min.
Nov. 14	C. Conrad, Jr., A. Bean, R. Gordon, Jr.	*Apollo 12*	Lunar landing	10 days, 4 hr. 36 min.
1970 Apr. 11	J. Lovell, Jr., F. Haise, Jr., J. Swigert, Jr.	*Apollo 13*	Lunar flight	5 days, 22 hr. 55 min.
June 1	A. Nikolayev, V. Sevastyanov	*Soyuz 9*	268	17 days, 16 hr. 59 min.
1971 Jan. 31	A. Shepard, Jr., E. Mitchell, S. Roosa	*Apollo 14*	Lunar landing	9 days, 0 hr. 2 min.
Apr. 23	V. Shatalov, A. Yeliseyev, N. Rukavishnikov	*Soyuz 10*	30	1 day, 23 hr. 46 min.
June 6	G. Dobrovolsky, V. Volkov, V. Patsayev	*Soyuz 11* and *Salyut 1*	362	23 days, 18 hr. 22 min.
July 26	D. Scott, J. Irwin, A. Worden	*Apollo 15*	Lunar landing	12 days, 7 hr. 12 min.
1972 Apr. 16	J. Young, C. Duke, Jr., T. Mattingly	*Apollo 16*	Lunar landing	11 days, 1 hr. 51 min.
Dec. 7	E. Cernan, H. Schmitt, R. Evans	*Apollo 17*	Lunar landing	12 days, 13 hr. 52 min.
1973 May 25	C. Conrad, Jr., J. Kerwin, P. Weitz	*Skylab 1* and *2*	405	28 days, 0 hr. 50 min.
July 28	A. Bean, O. Garriott, J. Lousma	*Skylab 1* and *3*	859	59 days, 11 hr. 9 min.

*Transferred to *Soyuz 4* in orbit.

Apollo lunar module
22⅞ ft.
(7 m)

Russian Soyuz
23⅓ ft.
(7.1 m)

Manned space flights *(cont.)*

Date launched		Astronaut or cosmonaut	Spacecraft	Revolutions	Time of flight
1973	Sept. 27	V. Lazarev, O. Makarov	*Soyuz 12*	30	1 day, 23 hr. 16 min.
	Nov. 16	G. Carr, E. Gibson, W. Pogue	*Skylab 1* and *4*	1,214	84 days, 1 hr. 16 min.
	Dec. 18	P. Klimuk, V. Lebedev	*Soyuz 13*	119	7 days, 20 hr. 55 min.
1974	July 3	P. Popovich, Y. Artyukhin	*Soyuz 14* and *Salyut 3*	236	15 days, 17 hr. 30 min.
	Aug. 26	G. Sarafanov, L. Demin	*Soyuz 15*	30	2 days, 0 hr. 12 min.
	Dec. 2	A. Filipchenko, N. Rukavishnikov	*Soyuz 16*	90	5 days, 22 hr. 24 min.
1975	Jan. 10	A. Gubarev, G. Grechko	*Soyuz 17* and *Salyut 4*	436	29 days, 13 hr. 20 min.
	May 25	P. Klimuk, V. Sevastyanov	*Soyuz 18* and *Salyut 4*	930	62 days, 23 hr. 20 min.
	July 15	A. Leonov, V. Kubasov	*Soyuz 19*†	90	5 days, 22 hr. 31 min.
		V. Brand, D. Slayton, T. Stafford	*Apollo*†	148	9 days, 1 hr. 28 min.
1976	July 6	B. Volynov, V. Zholobov	*Soyuz 21* and *Salyut 5*	741	49 days, 6 hr. 24 min.
	Sept. 15	V. Bykovsky, V. Aksenov	*Soyuz 22*	119	7 days, 21 hr. 54 min.
	Oct. 14	V. Zudov, V. Rozhdestvensky	*Soyuz 23*	30	2 days, 0 hr. 6 min.
1977	Feb. 7	V. Gorbatko, Y. Glazkov	*Soyuz 24* and *Salyut 5*	267	17 days, 17 hr. 23 min.
	Oct. 9	V. Kovalenok, V. Ryumin	*Soyuz 25*	30	2 days, 0 hr. 46 min.
	Dec. 10	G. Grechko, Y. Romanenko‡	*Soyuz 26* and *Salyut 6*	553	37 days, 10 hr. 6 min.
1978	Jan. 10	V. Dzhanibekov, O. Makarov§	*Soyuz 27* and *Salyut 6*	959	64 days, 2 hr. 53 min.
	Mar. 2	A. Gubarev, V. Remek	*Soyuz 28* and *Salyut 6*	117	7 days, 22 hr. 17 min.
	June 15	V. Kovalenok, A. Ivanchenkov#	*Soyuz 29* and *Salyut 6*	1,177	79 days, 15 hr. 23 min.
	June 27	P. Klimuk, M. Hermaszewski	*Soyuz 30* and *Salyut 6*	117	7 days, 22 hr. 4 min.
	Aug. 26	V. Bykovsky, S. Jähn**	*Soyuz 31* and *Salyut 6*	930	67 days, 20 hr. 14 min.
1979	Feb. 25	V. Lyakhov, V. Ryumin††	*Soyuz 32* and *Salyut 6*	1,711	108 days, 4 hr. 24 min.
	Apr. 10	N. Rukavishnikov, G. Ivanov	*Soyuz 33*	31	1 day, 23 hr. 17 min.
1980	Apr. 9	L. Popov, V. Ryumin‡‡	*Soyuz 35* and *Salyut 6*	868	55 days, 1 hr. 29 min.
	May 26	V. Kubasov, B. Farkas§§	*Soyuz 36* and *Salyut 6*	1,040	65 days, 20 hr. 54 min.
	June 5	V. Malyshev, V. Akscnor	*Soyuz T-2*	62	3 days, 22 hr. 41 min.
	July 23	V. Gorbatko, P. Tuan##	*Soyuz 37* and *Salyut 6*	1,257	79 days, 15 hr. 17 min.
	Sept. 18	Y. Romanenko, A. Tamayo Mendez***	*Soyuz 38* and *Salyut 6*	124	7 days, 20 hr. 43 min.
	Nov. 27	L. Kizim, O. Makarov, G. Strekalov	*Soyuz T-3* and *Salyut 6*	204	12 days, 19 hr. 8 min.
1981	Mar. 12	V. Kovalenok, V. Savinykh	*Soyuz T-4* and *Salyut 6*	1,179	74 days, 18 hr. 38 min.
	Mar. 22	V. Dzhanibekov, J. Gurragcha	*Soyuz 39* and *Salyut 6*	124	7 days, 20 hr. 43 min.
	Apr. 12	J. Young, R. Crippen	*Columbia* space shuttle	36	2 days, 6 hr. 21 min.
	May 14	L. Popov, D. Prunariu	*Soyuz 40* and *Salyut 6*	124	7 days, 20 hr. 41 min.
	Nov. 12	J. Engle, R. Truly	*Columbia* space shuttle	36	2 days, 6 hr. 13 min.
1982	Mar. 22	J. Lousma, G. Fullerton	*Columbia* space shuttle	129	8 days, 1 hr. 5 min.
	June 24	V. Dzhanibekov, A. Ivanchenkov, J. Chretien	*Soyuz T-6* and *Salyut 7*	126	7 days, 21 hr. 51 min.
	June 27	T. Mattingly, H. Hartsfield	*Columbia* space shuttle	112	7 days, 1 hr. 9 min.
1983	Apr. 4	P. Weitz, K. Bobko, S. Musgrave, D. Peterson	*Challenger* space shuttle	121	5 days, 0 hr. 23 min.

†Joint U.S.-Soviet mission involving rendezvous and docking.
‡Remained in orbit for 96 days, 10 hr. before returning to the earth on *Soyuz 27*.
§Joined Grechko and Romanenko on board *Salyut 6* and remained in orbit for 5 days, 22 hr. 59 min. before returning to the earth on *Soyuz 26*.
#Remained in orbit for 139 days, 14 hr. 48 min. before returning to the earth on *Soyuz 31*.
**Joined Kovalenok and Ivanchenkov on board *Salyut 6* and remained in orbit for 7 days, 20 hr. 49 min. before returning to the earth on *Soyuz 29*.
††Remained in orbit for 184 days, 20 hr. 12 min. before returning to the earth on *Soyuz 37*.

‡‡Remained in orbit for 175 days, 36 min. before returning to the earth on *Soyuz 34*—a previously unmanned craft provided for re-entry.
§§Joined Popov and Ryumin on board *Salyut 6* and remained in orbit for 7 days, 20 hr. 46 min. before returning to the earth on *Soyuz 35*.
##Joined Popov and Ryumin on board *Salyut 6* and remained in orbit for 7 days, 20 hr. 42 min. before returning to the earth on *Soyuz 36*.
***Joined Popov and Ryumin on board *Salyut 6* and remained in orbit for about a week before returning to the earth.

From earth to moon

The Apollo missions of 1969 and the early 1970's included a total of six lunar landings. On July 20, 1969, astronauts Neil A. Armstrong and Edwin E. Aldrin, Jr., became the first persons to set foot on the moon. The third crew member, Michael Collins, piloted the command module in lunar orbit while Armstrong and Aldrin explored the moon. The following is a step-by-step description of how the Apollo astronauts reached the moon.

(1) A Saturn V rocket launches the spacecraft from the John F. Kennedy Space Center at Cape Canaveral, Fla. (2) After about 2½ minutes, with the spacecraft traveling about 6,200 miles (9,980 kilometers) per hour, the first stage separates from the vehicle and the second stage ignites. (3) About 116 miles (187 kilometers) above the earth, with the spacecraft traveling about 15,400 miles (24,780 kilometers) per hour, the second stage separates and the third stage ignites. (4) The spacecraft travels in a "parking orbit" 118 miles (190 kilometers) high. (5) The third stage reignites and sends the spacecraft toward the moon. (6) The spacecraft reaches a speed of 24,300 miles (39,110 kilometers) per hour. The command and service modules separate from the rest of the spacecraft. (7) The astronauts turn the command and service modules around. (8) The command and service modules dock with the lunar module (LM), which is atop the third stage. (9) The third stage separates from the spacecraft. (10) After determining the spacecraft's position, the crew puts the spacecraft back on course by firing small rockets. (11) A rocket engine in the service module retrofires to slow the spacecraft and put it into lunar orbit. (12) The spacecraft follows a lunar "parking orbit." (13) Two of the three astronauts enter the LM. (14) The LM separates from the command module, which is piloted by the one remaining astronaut. (15) The LM fires an engine to slow it down and allow it to descend to the moon. (16) When the LM is 5 feet (1.5 meters) from the moon's surface, the astronauts shut off its engines and the LM lands on the moon.

Space stations and the space shuttle

A space station is a large earth satellite designed so that many persons can live and work in it for a longer time than they could in an ordinary spacecraft. It provides living quarters and carries enough supplies to last for weeks or months at a time. A space station serves as a scientific laboratory, where experiments can be performed and data collected on the stars, the sun, solar wind, and other subjects.

Russia launched the first space station, *Salyut I,* in 1971. They placed several other Salyut stations in orbit during the 1970's and 1980's. The first U.S. space station, *Skylab 1,* was launched in 1973. It reentered the earth's atmosphere and disintegrated in 1979.

Both the Salyut and Skylab stations were put into orbit as unmanned spacecraft. Manned spacecraft later docked with the space stations, and crews then entered the stations.

The Russians have used both unmanned and manned spacecraft to carry fresh supplies to crews aboard the Salyut stations. Each delivery requires a new spacecraft. In 1981, the United States launched the first reusable space vehicle, the space shuttle *Columbia.* It is designed to take off like a rocket and land like an airplane. *Columbia* consists of an orbiter, an external tank for liquid fuels, and two solid rocket boosters. The orbiter can carry a crew of as many as seven astronauts and up to 65,000 pounds (29,500 kilograms) of cargo. A space shuttle will eventually be used to fly back and forth between earth and an orbiting space station.

Important space probes

Space probes are unmanned vehicles that explore space at various distances from earth. The probes listed in this table include lunar spacecraft, which collect information about the moon, and planetary probes, which gather data about the planets.

Date Launched		Name	Country	Accomplishments
1959	Sept. 12	*Luna 2*	Russia	First probe to strike the moon.
1962	Apr. 23	*Ranger IV*	U.S.A.	First U.S. probe to strike moon; failed to televise pictures to earth.
1964	Nov. 28	*Mariner IV*	U.S.A.	Photographed Mars on July 14, 1965; measured conditions in space.
1966	Jan. 31	*Luna 9*	Russia	Made first soft landing on the moon on Feb. 3; sent 27 pictures to the earth.
	Mar. 31	*Luna 10*	Russia	First spacecraft to orbit the moon; began orbiting on April 3.
1967	June 12	*Venera 4*	Russia	First spacecraft to transmit data on Venus' atmosphere.
	Sept. 8	*Surveyor 5*	U.S.A.	Landed on the moon; sent information on lunar soil back to earth for analysis.
1968	Sept. 14	*Zond 5*	Russia	First probe to orbit the moon and return to a soft landing on earth.
1970	Aug. 17	*Venera 7*	Russia	First spacecraft to transmit data from Venus' surface; landed Dec. 15, 1970.
	Sept. 12	*Luna 16*	Russia	First unmanned spacecraft to return lunar samples; landed on Sept. 20.
1971	May 28	*Mars 3*	Russia	Carried capsule that made first soft landing on Mars; landed Dec. 2, 1971.
	May 30	*Mariner IX*	U.S.A.	First probe to orbit Mars; began orbiting on Nov. 13, 1971.
1972	Mar. 2	*Pioneer X*	U.S.A.	Flew past Jupiter on Dec. 3, 1973, and sent back scientific data.
1973	Apr. 6	*Pioneer-Saturn*	U.S.A.	Passed close to Jupiter on Dec. 2, 1974, and flew past Saturn on Sept. 1, 1979; sent back scientific data and photos of both planets.
	Nov. 3	*Mariner X*	U.S.A.	First probe to fly by two planets; sent photos and data from Venus on Feb. 5, 1974, and Mercury on March 29 and Sept. 21, 1974, and March 16, 1975.
1975	June 8	*Venera 9*	Russia	First unmanned spacecraft to photograph surface of Venus; landed Oct. 21.
	Aug. 22	*Viking I*	U.S.A.	Sent photos and data from Mars; landed on July 20, 1976.
	Sept. 9	*Viking II*	U.S.A.	Landed on Mars Sept. 3, 1976; sent back photos and scientific data.
1977	Aug. 20	*Voyager 2*	U.S.A.	Flew past Jupiter in July 1979, and flew by Saturn in August 1981; sent back photos of the planets and their moons.
	Sept. 5	*Voyager 1*	U.S.A.	Passed Jupiter on March 5, 1979, and flew by Saturn on Nov. 12, 1980; made various discoveries about both planets and their moons.
1978	May 20	*Pioneer Venus 1*	U.S.A.	Transmitted radar images of Venus' surface; began orbiting on Dec. 4.
	Aug. 8	*Pioneer Venus 2*	U.S.A.	Entered Venus' atmosphere Dec. 9; measured its density and composition.
	Sept. 9	*Venera 11*	Russia	Made chemical analysis of Venus' lower atmosphere; landed Dec. 25.
	Sept. 14	*Venera 12*	Russia	Sent back data on atmosphere of Venus; landed Dec. 21.
1981	Oct. 30	*Venera 13*	Russia	Sent color photos of Venus and analyzed soil samples; landed March 1, 1982.
	Nov. 4	*Venera 14*	Russia	Landed on Venus four days after *Venera 13* and did similar experiments.

Sports winners

Automobile racing

Grand Prix world champions

Grand Prix races are a series of about 15 road races governed by the International Auto Sport Federation. The races take place in the United States, Canada, South America, Western Europe, and South Africa, and they range in length from 150 to 250 miles (241 to 402 kilometers). The winner and runners-up in each race receive points. The driver with the most points in a year wins the Grand Prix world championship. The first Grand Prix race was held in France in 1906. Unofficial world championship competition started in the 1920's. The first official world title was awarded in 1950.

Year	Driver	Country	Year	Driver	Country
1950	Giuseppe Farina	Italy	1967	Denis Hulme	New Zealand
1951	Juan M. Fangio	Argentina	1968	Graham Hill	Great Britain
1952	Alberto Ascari	Italy	1969	Jackie Stewart	Great Britain
1953	Alberto Ascari	Italy	1970	Jochen Rindt	Austria
1954	Juan M. Fangio	Argentina	1971	Jackie Stewart	Great Britain
1955	Juan M. Fangio	Argentina	1972	Emerson Fittipaldi	Brazil
1956	Juan M. Fangio	Argentina	1973	Jackie Stewart	Great Britain
1957	Juan M. Fangio	Argentina	1974	Emerson Fittipaldi	Brazil
1958	Mike Hawthorn	Great Britain	1975	Niki Lauda	Austria
1959	Jack Brabham	Australia	1976	James Hunt	Great Britain
1960	Jack Brabham	Australia	1977	Niki Lauda	Austria
1961	Phil Hill	United States	1978	Mario Andretti	United States
1962	Graham Hill	Great Britain	1979	Jody Scheckter	South Africa
1963	Jim Clark	Great Britain	1980	Alan Jones	Australia
1964	John Surtees	Great Britain	1981	Nelson Piquet	Brazil
1965	Jim Clark	Great Britain	1982	Keke Rosberg	Finland
1966	Jack Brabham	Australia			

Indianapolis *500* winners

The Indianapolis *500* is the most famous of a series of races—called the Championship Trail—sponsored by the United States Auto Club. The event is held each year during the Memorial Day weekend at the Indianapolis Motor Speedway. The winner is the first driver to complete 200 laps around the oval track—a total distance of 500 miles (805 kilometers).

Year	Driver	MPH	KPH	Year	Driver	MPH	KPH
1911	Ray Harroun	74.59	120.04	1923	Tommy Milton	90.95	146.37
1912	Joe Dawson	78.72	126.69	1924	L. L. Corum and Joe Boyer	98.23	158.09
1913	Jules Goux	75.93	122.20	1925	Peter De Paolo	101.13	162.75
1914	Rene Thomas	82.47	132.72	1926	Frank Lockhart	95.90	154.34
1915	Ralph De Palma	89.84	144.58	1927	George Souders	97.55	156.99
1916	Dario Resta	84.00	135.18	1928	Louis Meyer	99.48	160.10
1919	Howdy Wilcox	88.05	141.70	1929	Ray Keech	97.59	157.06
1920	Gaston Chevrolet	88.62	142.62	1930	Billy Arnold	100.45	161.66
1921	Tommy Milton	89.62	144.23	1931	Louis Schneider	96.63	155.51
1922	Jimmy Murphy	94.48	152.05	1932	Frederick Frame	104.14	167.60

203

Year	Driver	MPH	KPH
1933	Louis Meyer	104.16	167.63
1934	Bill Cummings	104.86	168.76
1935	Kelly Petillo	106.24	170.98
1936	Louis Meyer	109.07	175.53
1937	Wilbur Shaw	113.58	182.79
1938	Floyd Roberts	117.20	188.62
1939	Wilbur Shaw	115.04	185.14
1940	Wilbur Shaw	114.28	183.92
1941	Mauri Rose and Floyd Davis	115.12	185.27
1946	George Robson	114.82	184.78
1947	Mauri Rose	116.34	187.23
1948	Mauri Rose	119.81	192.82
1949	William Holland	121.33	195.26
1950	Johnny Parsons	124.00	199.56
1951	Lee Wallard	126.24	203.16
1952	Troy Ruttman	128.92	207.48
1953	Bill Vukovich	128.74	207.19
1954	Bill Vukovich	130.84	210.57
1955	Bob Sweikert	128.21	206.33
1956	Pat Flaherty	128.49	206.78
1957	Sam Hanks	135.60	218.23
1958	Jimmy Bryan	133.79	215.31
1959	Rodger Ward	135.86	218.65

Year	Driver	MPH	KPH
1960	Jim Rathmann	138.77	223.33
1961	A. J. Foyt	139.13	223.91
1962	Rodger Ward	140.29	225.77
1963	Parnelli Jones	143.14	230.36
1964	A. J. Foyt	147.35	237.14
1965	Jim Clark	150.69	242.51
1966	Graham Hill	144.32	232.26
1967	A. J. Foyt	151.21	243.35
1968	Bobby Unser	152.88	246.04
1969	Mario Andretti	156.87	252.46
1970	Al Unser	155.75	250.66
1971	Al Unser	157.74	253.86
1972	Mark Donohue	162.96	262.26
1973	Gordon Johncock	159.04	255.95
1974	Johnny Rutherford	158.59	255.22
1975	Bobby Unser	149.21	240.13
1976	Johnny Rutherford	148.73	239.36
1977	A. J. Foyt	161.33	259.64
1978	Al Unser	161.36	259.68
1979	Rick Mears	158.90	255.72
1980	Johnny Rutherford	142.86	229.87
1981	Bobby Unser	139.08	223.83
1982	Gordon Johncock	162.03	260.76
1983	Tom Sneva	162.12	259.39

Baseball

The World Series

The World Series brings together the champion baseball teams from the American League (AL) and the National League (NL). The first team to win four games in the series wins the world championship. The World Series has been played every year since 1903, except 1904.

Year	Winner	Loser	Games Won-Lost
1903	Boston (AL)	Pittsburgh (NL)	5-3
1905	New York (NL)	Philadelphia (AL)	4-1
1906	Chicago (AL)	Chicago (NL)	4-2
1907*	Chicago (NL)	Detroit (AL)	4-0
1908	Chicago (NL)	Detroit (AL)	4-1
1909	Pittsburgh (NL)	Detroit (AL)	4-3
1910	Philadelphia (AL)	Chicago (NL)	4-1
1911	Philadelphia (AL)	New York (NL)	4-2
1912*	Boston (AL)	New York (NL)	4-3
1913	Philadelphia (AL)	New York (NL)	4-1
1914	Boston (NL)	Philadelphia (AL)	4-0
1915	Boston (AL)	Philadelphia (NL)	4-1
1916	Boston (AL)	Brooklyn (NL)	4-1
1917	Chicago (AL)	New York (NL)	4-2
1918	Boston (AL)	Chicago (NL)	4-2
1919	Cincinnati (NL)	Chicago (AL)	5-3
1920	Cleveland (AL)	Brooklyn (NL)	5-2
1921	New York (NL)	New York (AL)	5-3

Year	Winner	Loser	Games Won-Lost
1922*	New York (NL)	New York (AL)	4-0
1923	New York (AL)	New York (NL)	4-2
1924	Washington (AL)	New York (NL)	4-3
1925	Pittsburgh (NL)	Washington (AL)	4-3
1926	St. Louis (NL)	New York (AL)	4-3
1927	New York (AL)	Pittsburgh (NL)	4-0
1928	New York (AL)	St. Louis (NL)	4-0
1929	Philadelphia (AL)	Chicago (NL)	4-1
1930	Philadelphia (AL)	St. Louis (NL)	4-2
1931	St. Louis (NL)	Philadelphia (AL)	4-3
1932	New York (AL)	Chicago (NL)	4-0
1933	New York (NL)	Washington (AL)	4-1
1934	St. Louis (NL)	Detroit (AL)	4-3
1935	Detroit (AL)	Chicago (NL)	4-2
1936	New York (AL)	New York (NL)	4-2
1937	New York (AL)	New York (NL)	4-1
1938	New York (AL)	Chicago (NL)	4-0
1939	New York (AL)	Cincinnati (NL)	4-0
1940	Cincinnati (NL)	Detroit (AL)	4-3

*Series included a tie game called off because of darkness.

Year	Winner	Loser	Games Won-Lost	Year	Winner	Loser	Games Won-Lost
1941	New York (AL)	Brooklyn (NL)	4-1	1962	New York (AL)	San Francisco (NL)	4-3
1942	St. Louis (NL)	New York (AL)	4-1	1963	Los Angeles (NL)	New York (AL)	4-0
1943	New York (AL)	St. Louis (NL)	4-1	1964	St. Louis (NL)	New York (AL)	4-3
1944	St. Louis (NL)	St. Louis (AL)	4-2	1965	Los Angeles (NL)	Minnesota (AL)	4-3
1945	Detroit (AL)	Chicago (NL)	4-3	1966	Baltimore (AL)	Los Angeles (NL)	4-0
1946	St. Louis (NL)	Boston (AL)	4-3	1967	St. Louis (NL)	Boston (AL)	4-3
1947	New York (AL)	Brooklyn (NL)	4-3	1968	Detroit (AL)	St. Louis (NL)	4-3
1948	Cleveland (AL)	Boston (NL)	4-2	1969	New York (NL)	Baltimore (AL)	4-1
1949	New York (AL)	Brooklyn (NL)	4-1	1970	Baltimore (AL)	Cincinnati (NL)	4-1
1950	New York (AL)	Philadelphia (NL)	4-0	1971	Pittsburgh (NL)	Baltimore (AL)	4-3
1951	New York (AL)	New York (NL)	4-2	1972	Oakland (AL)	Cincinnati (NL)	4-3
1952	New York (AL)	Brooklyn (NL)	4-3	1973	Oakland (AL)	New York (NL)	4-3
1953	New York (AL)	Brooklyn (NL)	4-2	1974	Oakland (AL)	Los Angeles (NL)	4-1
1954	New York (NL)	Cleveland (AL)	4-0	1975	Cincinnati (NL)	Boston (AL)	4-3
1955	Brooklyn (NL)	New York (AL)	4-3	1976	Cincinnati (NL)	New York (AL)	4-0
1956	New York (AL)	Brooklyn (NL)	4-3	1977	New York (AL)	Los Angeles (NL)	4-2
1957	Milwaukee (NL)	New York (AL)	4-3	1978	New York (AL)	Los Angeles (NL)	4-2
1958	New York (AL)	Milwaukee (NL)	4-3	1979	Pittsburgh (NL)	Baltimore (AL)	4-3
1959	Los Angeles (NL)	Chicago (AL)	4-2	1980	Philadelphia (NL)	Kansas City (AL)	4-2
1960	Pittsburgh (NL)	New York (AL)	4-3	1981	Los Angeles (NL)	New York (AL)	4-2
1961	New York (AL)	Cincinnati (NL)	4-1	1982	St. Louis (NL)	Milwaukee (AL)	4-3

Basketball

National Basketball Association champions

The National Basketball Association (NBA) holds a play-off tournament after its regular season to determine the champion team in professional basketball. Twelve teams compete in the play-offs, and the final pairing brings together the top teams from each conference.

Season	Eastern Division	Western Division	Play-Off Champions
1946–1947*	Washington Capitols	Chicago Stags	Philadelphia Warriors
1947–1948*	Philadelphia Warriors	St. Louis Bombers	Baltimore Bullets
1948–1949*	Washington Capitols	Rochester Royals	Minneapolis Lakers
1949–1950†			Minneapolis Lakers
1950–1951	Philadelphia Warriors	Minneapolis Lakers	Rochester Royals
1951–1952	Syracuse Nationals	Rochester Royals	Minneapolis Lakers
1952–1953	New York Knickerbockers	Minneapolis Lakers	Minneapolis Lakers
1953–1954	New York Knickerbockers	Minneapolis Lakers	Minneapolis Lakers
1954–1955	Syracuse Nationals	Fort Wayne Pistons	Syracuse Nationals
1955–1956	Philadelphia Warriors	Fort Wayne Pistons	Philadelphia Warriors
1956–1957	Boston Celtics	St. Louis Hawks	Boston Celtics
1957–1958	Boston Celtics	St. Louis Hawks	St. Louis Hawks
1958–1959	Boston Celtics	St. Louis Hawks	Boston Celtics
1959–1960	Boston Celtics	St. Louis Hawks	Boston Celtics
1960–1961	Boston Celtics	St. Louis Hawks	Boston Celtics
1961–1962	Boston Celtics	Los Angeles Lakers	Boston Celtics
1962–1963	Boston Celtics	Los Angeles Lakers	Boston Celtics

*Basketball Association of America champions.
†The NBA had three division champions: Eastern Division, Syracuse Nationals; Central Division, Minneapolis Lakers; Western Division, Indianapolis Olympians.

Season	Eastern Division	Western Division	Play-Off Champions
1963–1964	Boston Celtics	San Francisco Warriors	Boston Celtics
1964–1965	Boston Celtics	Los Angeles Lakers	Boston Celtics
1965–1966	Philadelphia 76ers	Los Angeles Lakers	Boston Celtics
1966–1967	Philadelphia 76ers	San Francisco Warriors	Philadelphia 76ers
1967–1968	Philadelphia 76ers	St. Louis Hawks	Boston Celtics
1968–1969	Baltimore Bullets	Los Angeles Lakers	Boston Celtics
1969–1970	New York Knickerbockers	Atlanta Hawks	New York Knickerbockers
	Eastern Conference	**Western Conference**	
1970–1971	Baltimore Bullets	Milwaukee Bucks	Milwaukee Bucks
1971–1972	New York Knickerbockers	Los Angeles Lakers	Los Angeles Lakers
1972–1973	New York Knickerbockers	Los Angeles Lakers	New York Knickerbockers
1973–1974	Boston Celtics	Milwaukee Bucks	Boston Celtics
1974–1975	Washington Bullets	Golden State Warriors	Golden State Warriors
1975–1976	Boston Celtics	Phoenix Suns	Boston Celtics
1976–1977	Philadelphia 76ers	Portland Trail Blazers	Portland Trail Blazers
1977–1978	Washington Bullets	Seattle SuperSonics	Washington Bullets
1978–1979	Washington Bullets	Seattle SuperSonics	Seattle SuperSonics
1979–1980	Philadelphia 76ers	Los Angeles Lakers	Los Angeles Lakers
1980–1981	Boston Celtics	Houston Rockets	Boston Celtics
1981–1982	Philadelphia 76ers	Los Angeles Lakers	Los Angeles Lakers
1982–1983	Philadelphia 76ers	Los Angeles Lakers	Philadelphia 76ers

National Collegiate Athletic Association (NCAA) basketball champions

1938–1939	Oregon	1954–1955	San Francisco	1970–1971	UCLA
1939–1940	Indiana	1955–1956	San Francisco	1971–1972	UCLA
1940–1941	Wisconsin	1956–1957	North Carolina	1972–1973	UCLA
1941–1942	Stanford	1957–1958	Kentucky	1973–1974	North Carolina State
1942–1943	Wyoming	1958–1959	California		
1943–1944	Utah	1959–1960	Ohio State	1974–1975	UCLA
1944–1945	Oklahoma A&M	1960–1961	Cincinnati	1975–1976	Indiana
1945–1946	Oklahoma A&M	1961–1962	Cincinnati	1976–1977	Marquette
1946–1947	Holy Cross	1962–1963	Loyola (Ill.)	1977–1978	Kentucky
1947–1948	Kentucky	1963–1964	UCLA	1978–1979	Michigan State
1948–1949	Kentucky	1964–1965	UCLA	1979–1980	Louisville
1949–1950	CCNY	1965–1966	Texas Western	1980–1981	Indiana
1950–1951	Kentucky	1966–1967	UCLA	1981–1982	North Carolina
1951–1952	Kansas	1967–1968	UCLA	1982–1983	North Carolina State
1952–1953	Indiana	1968–1969	UCLA		
1953–1954	La Salle	1969–1970	UCLA		

Boxing

Until the early 1960's, boxing champions were approved by the National Boxing Association, now called the World Boxing Association (WBA). In the early 1960's, the World Boxing Council (WBC) also began recognizing champions. In addition, some boxers claimed championships or were recognized as champions by other organizations. The table below lists champions recognized by both the WBA and WBC.

Years	Boxer
Heavyweights (WBA)	
1882–92	John L. Sullivan
1892–97	James J. Corbett
1897–99	Bob Fitzsimmons
1899–1905	James J. Jeffries
1905–06	Marvin Hart
1906–08	Tommy Burns
1908–15	Jack Johnson
1915–19	Jess Willard
1919–26	Jack Dempsey
1926–28	Gene Tunney
1928–30	None
1930–32	Max Schmeling
1932–33	Jack Sharkey
1933–34	Primo Carnera
1934–35	Max Baer
1935–37	James J. Braddock
1937–49	Joe Louis
1949–51	Ezzard Charles
1951–52	Joe Walcott
1952–56	Rocky Marciano
1956–59	Floyd Patterson
1959–60	Ingemar Johansson
1960–62	Floyd Patterson
1962–64	Sonny Liston
1964	Muhammad Ali
1965–67	Ernie Terrell
1967	Muhammad Ali
1968–70	Jimmy Ellis
1970–73	Joe Frazier
1973–74	George Foreman
1974–78	Muhammad Ali
1978	Leon Spinks
1978–79	Muhammad Ali
1979–80	John Tate
1980–	Mike Weaver
Heavyweights (WBC)	
1962–64	Sonny Liston
1964–71	Muhammad Ali
1971–73	Joe Frazier
1973–74	George Foreman
1974–78	Muhammad Ali
1978	Leon Spinks
1978	Ken Norton
1978–	Larry Holmes

Years	Boxer
Junior Heavyweights (WBA)	
1982–	Ossie Ocasio
Cruiserweights (WBC)	
1980	Marvin Camel
1980–82	Carlos DeLeón
1982–	S. T. Gordon
Light Heavyweights (WBA)	
1903	Jack Root
1903	George Gardner
1903–05	Bob Fitzsimmons
1905–12	Jack O'Brien
1912–16	Jack Dillon
1916–20	Battling Levinsky
1920–22	Georges Carpentier
1922	Gene Tunney
1922–23	Harry Greb
1923	Gene Tunney
1923–25	Mike McTigue
1925–26	Paul Berlenbach
1926–27	Jack Delaney
1927–29	Tommy Loughran
1930–32	Max Rosenbloom
1932–34	George Nichols
1934–35	Bob Olin
1935–39	John Henry Lewis
1939	Melio Bettina
1939–41	Billy Conn
1941	Anton Christoforidis
1941–48	Gus Lesnevich
1948–50	Freddie Mills
1950–52	Joey Maxim
1952–61	Archie Moore
1961–63	Harold Johnson
1963–65	Willie Pastrano
1965–66	José Torres
1966–68	Dick Tiger
1968–70	Bob Foster
1971–72	Vincente Rondon
1972–74	Bob Foster
1974–78	Victor Galindez
1978–79	Mike Rossman

Years	Boxer
1979	Victor Galindez
1979–80	Marvin Johnson
1980–81	Eddie Mustafa Muhammad
1981–	Michael Spinks
Light Heavyweights (WBC)	
1963–65	Willie Pastrano
1965–66	José Torres
1966–68	Dick Tiger
1968–74	Bob Foster
1974–77	John Conteh
1977–78	Miguel Cuello
1978	Mate Parlov
1978–79	Marvin Johnson
1979–81	Matthew Saad Muhammad
1981–	Dwight Braxton
Middleweights (WBA)	
1884–91	Jack "The Nonpareil" Dempsey
1891–97	Bob Fitzsimmons
1897–1907	Tommy Ryan
1908	Stanley Ketchel
1908	Billy Papke
1908–10	Stanley Ketchel
1910–13	Disputed
1913	Frank Klaus
1913–14	George Chip
1914–17	Al McCoy
1917–20	Mike O'Dowd
1920–23	Johnny Wilson
1923–26	Harry Greb
1926	Tiger Flowers
1926–31	Mickey Walker
1931–32	Gorilla Jones
1932–36	Marcel Thil
1936–38	Freddie Steele
1938	Al Hostak
1938–39	Solly Krieger
1939–40	Al Hostak
1940–47	Tony Zale
1947–48	Rocky Graziano
1948	Tony Zale

207

Boxing (cont.)

Years	Boxer
1948–49	Marcel Cerdan
1949–51	Jake LaMotta
1951	Ray Robinson
1951	Randy Turpin
1951–52	Ray Robinson
1953–55	Bobo Olson
1955–57	Ray Robinson
1957	Gene Fullmer
1957	Ray Robinson
1957–58	Carmen Basilio
1958–59	Ray Robinson
1959–62	Gene Fullmer
1962–63	Dick Tiger
1963–65	Joey Giardello
1965–66	Dick Tiger
1966–67	Emile Griffith
1967	Nino Benvenuti
1967–68	Emile Griffith
1968–70	Nino Benvenuti
1970–77	Carlos Monzón
1977–78	Rodrigo Valdes
1978–79	Hugo Carro
1979–80	Vito Antuofermo
1980	Alan Minter
1980–	Marvin Hagler

Middleweights (WBC)

Years	Boxer
1962–63	Dick Tiger
1963–65	Joey Giardello
1965–66	Dick Tiger
1966–67	Emile Griffith
1967	Nino Benvenuti
1967–68	Emile Griffith
1968–70	Nino Benvenuti
1970–74	Carlos Monzón
1974–76	Rodrigo Valdes
1976–77	Carlos Monzón
1977–78	Rodrigo Valdes
1978–79	Hugo Corro
1979–80	Vito Antuofermo
1980	Alan Minter
1980–	Marvin Hagler

Junior Middleweights (WBA)

Years	Boxer
1962–63	Denny Moyer
1963	Ralph Dupas
1963–65	Sandro Mazzinghi
1965–66	Nino Benvenuti
1966–67	Kim Ki-Soo
1967–70	Freddie Little
1970–71	Carmelo Bossi
1971–74	Koichi Wajima
1974–75	Oscar Albarado
1975	Koichi Wajima

Years	Boxer
1975–76	Yuh Jae-Do
1976	Koichi Wajima
1976–77	Miguel Castellini
1977–78	Eddie Gazo
1978–79	Masashi Kudo
1979–81	Ayub Kalule
1981	Ray Leonard
1981–82	Tadashi Mihara
1982–	Davey Moore

Super Welterweights (WBC)

Years	Boxer
1963–65	Sandro Mazzinghi
1965–66	Nino Benvenuti
1966–67	Kim Ki-Soo
1967–70	Freddie Little
1970–71	Carmelo Bossi
1971–74	Koichi Wajima
1974–75	Oscar Albarado
1975	Koichi Wajima
1975	Miguel De Oliveira
1975–76	Elisha Obed
1976–77	Eckhard Dagge
1977–79	Rocco Mattioli
1979–81	Maurice Hope
1981–	Wilfred Benitez

Welterweights (WBA)

Years	Boxer
1892–94	Mysterious Billy Smith
1894–96	Tommy Ryan
1896	Kid McCoy
1896–1900	Mysterious Billy Smith
1900	Rube Ferns
1900–01	Matty Matthews
1901	Rube Ferns
1901–04	Joe Walcott
1904	Dixie Kid
1904–06	Joe Walcott
1906–07	Honey Mellody
1907–10	Mike Sullivan
1910–15	Disputed
1915–19	Ted Lewis
1919–22	Jack Britton
1922–26	Mickey Walker
1926–27	Pete Latzo
1927–29	Joe Dundee
1929–30	Jackie Fields
1930	Jack Thompson
1930–31	Tommy Freeman
1931	Jack Thompson
1931–32	Lou Brouillard
1932–33	Jackie Fields
1933	Young Corbett
1933–34	Jimmy McLarnin
1934	Barney Ross

Years	Boxer
1934–35	Jimmy McLarnin
1935–38	Barney Ross
1938–40	Henry Armstrong
1940–41	Fritzie Zivic
1941–46	Freddie Cochrane
1946	Marty Servo
1946–51	Ray Robinson
1951	Johnny Bratton
1951–54	Kid Gavilan
1954–55	Johnny Saxton
1955	Tony DeMarco
1955–56	Carmen Basilio
1956	Johnny Saxton
1956–57	Carmen Basilio
1958	Virgil Akins
1958–60	Don Jordan
1960–61	Benny Paret
1961	Emile Griffith
1961–62	Benny Paret
1962–63	Emile Griffith
1963	Luis Rodríguez
1963–66	Emile Griffith
1966–69	Curtis Cokes
1969–70	José Nápoles
1970–71	Billy Backus
1971–75	José Nápoles
1975–76	Angel Espada
1976–80	José Cuevas
1980–81	Thomas Hearns
1981–	Ray Leonard

Welterweights (WBC)

Years	Boxer
1962–63	Emile Griffith
1963	Luis Rodríguez
1963–66	Emile Griffith
1966–69	Curtis Cokes
1969–70	José Nápoles
1970–71	Billy Backus
1971–75	José Nápoles
1975–76	John Stracey
1976–79	Carlos Palomino
1979	Wilfred Benitez
1979–80	Ray Leonard
1980	Roberto Durán
1980–	Ray Leonard

Junior Welterweights (WBA)

Years	Boxer
1946	Tippy Larkin
1946–59	division deactivated
1959–60	Carlos Ortiz
1960–62	Duilio Loi
1962	Eddie Perkins
1962–63	Duilio Loi
1963	Roberto Cruz

Years	Boxer
1963–65	Eddie Perkins
1965–66	Carlos Hernández
1966–67	Sandro Lopopolo
1967–68	Paul Fuji
1968–71	Nicolino Loche
1971–72	Alfonso Frazer
1972–76	Antonio Cervantes
1976	Wilfred Benitez
1977–80	Antonio Cervantes
1980–	Aaron Pryor

Super Lightweights (WBC)

Years	Boxer
1968–70	Pedro Adigue
1970–74	Bruno Arcari
1974–75	Perico Fernández
1975–76	Saensak Muangsurin
1976	Miguel Velázquez
1976–78	Saensak Muangsurin
1978–80	Kim Sang-Hyun
1980–82	Saoul Mamby
1982–	Leroy Haley

Lightweights (WBA)

Years	Boxer
1886–96	Jack McAuliffe
1896–99	Kid Lavigne
1899–1902	Frank Erne
1902–08	Joe Gans
1908–10	Battling Nelson
1910–12	Ad Wolgast
1912–14	Willie Ritchie
1914–17	Freddy Welsh
1917–25	Benny Leonard
1925	Jimmy Goodrich
1925–26	Rocky Kansas
1926–30	Sammy Mandell
1930	Al Singer
1930–33	Tony Canzoneri
1933–35	Barney Ross
1935–36	Tony Canzoneri
1936–38	Lou Ambers
1938–39	Henry Armstrong
1939–40	Lou Ambers
1940–41	Lew Jenkins
1941–44	Sammy Angott
1944–45	Juan Zurita
1945–51	Ike Williams
1951–52	Jimmy Carter
1952	Lauro Salas
1952–54	Jimmy Carter
1954	Paddy DeMarco
1954–55	Jimmy Carter
1955–56	Bud Smith
1956–62	Joe Brown
1962–65	Carlos Ortiz

Years	Boxer
1965	Ismael Laguna
1965–68	Carlos Ortiz
1968–69	Carlos Cruz
1969–70	Armando Ramos
1970	Ismael Laguna
1970–72	Ken Buchanan
1972–79	Roberto Durán
1979–80	Ernesto España
1980–81	Hilmer Kenty
1981	Sean O'Grady
1981–	Claude Noel

Lightweights (WBC)

Years	Boxer
1962–65	Carlos Ortiz
1965	Ismael Laguna
1965–68	Carlos Ortiz
1968–69	Carlos Cruz
1969–70	Armando Ramos
1970	Ismael Laguna
1970–71	Ken Buchanan
1971–72	Pedro Carrasco
1972	Armando Ramos
1972	Erubey Carmona
1972–74	Rodolfo González
1974–76	Gattu Ishimatsu
1976–78	Esteban De Jesús
1978–79	Roberto Durán
1979–81	Jim Watt
1981–	Alexis Arguello

Junior Lightweights (WBA)

Years	Boxer
1962–67	Flash Elorde
1967	Yoshiaki Numata
1967–71	Hiroshi Kobayashi
1971–72	Alfredo Marcano
1972–73	Ben Villaflor
1973	Kuniaki Shibata
1973–76	Ben Villaflor
1976–80	Sammy Serrano
1980–81	Yatsutsune Uehara
1981–	Sammy Serrano

Super Featherweights (WBC)

Years	Boxer
1962–67	Flash Elorde
1967	Yoshiaki Numata
1967–68	Hiroshi Kobayashi
1969–70	René Barrientos
1970–71	Yoshiaki Numata
1971–74	Ricardo Arredondo
1974–75	Kuniaki Shibata
1975–78	Alfredo Escalera
1978–80	Alexis Arguello

Years	Boxer
1980–81	Rafael Limón
1981	Cornelius Boza-Edwards
1981–82	Rolando Navarette
1982–	Rafael Limón

Featherweights (WBA)

Years	Boxer
1891–97	George Dixon
1897–98	Solly Smith
1898–1900	George Dixon
1900–01	Terry McGovern
1901–02	Young Corbett
1903–04	None
1905–12	Abe Attell
1912–23	Johnny Kilbane
1923	Eugene Criqui
1923–25	Johnny Dundee
1925–27	Kid Kaplan
1927–28	Benny Bass
1928	Tony Canzoneri
1928–29	André Routis
1929–32	Battling Battalino
1932–33	Tommy Paul
1933–36	Freddie Miller
1936–37	Petey Sarron
1937–38	Henry Armstrong
1938–41	Petey Scalzo
1941	Richard Lemos
1941–43	Jackie Wilson
1943	Jackie Callura
1943–44	Phil Terranova
1944–46	Sal Bartolo
1946–48	Willie Pep
1948–49	Sandy Saddler
1949–50	Willie Pep
1950–57	Sandy Saddler
1957–59	Hogan Bassey
1959–63	Davey Moore
1963–64	Sugar Ramos
1964–67	Vicente Saldívar
1968	Raul Rojas
1968–71	Shozo Saijyo
1971–72	Antonio Gómez
1972–74	Ernesto Marcel
1974	Ruben Olivares
1974–76	Alexis Arguello
1977	Rafael Ortega
1977–78	Cecilio Lastra
1978–	Eusebio Pedroza

Featherweights (WBC)

Years	Boxer
1963–64	Sugar Ramos
1964–67	Vicente Saldívar
1967–68	Howard Winstone
1968–69	José Legrá

Years	Boxer
1969–70	Johnny Famechon
1970	Vicente Saldívar
1970–72	Kuniaki Shibata
1972	Clemente Sánchez
1972–73	José Legrá
1973–74	Eder Jofre
1974–75	Bobby Chacón
1975	Ruben Olivares
1975–76	David Kotey
1976–80	Danny Lopez
1980–82	Salvador Sánchez

Junior Featherweights (WBA)

Years	Boxer
1977–78	Soon Hwang Hong
1978–80	Ricardo Cardona
1980	Leo Randolph
1980–82	Sergio Palma
1982–	Leo Cruz

Super Bantamweights (WBC)

Years	Boxer
1976	Rigoberto Riasco
1976	Royal Kobayashi
1976–77	Yum Dong Kyun
1977–	Wilfredo Gómez

Bantamweights (WBA)

Years	Boxer
1890–92	George Dixon
1893	None
1894–99	Jimmy Barry
1899–1900	Terry McGovern
1901–02	Harry Harris
1902–03	Harry Forbes
1903–04	Frankie Neil
1904	Joe Bowker
1905–07	Jimmy Walsh
1908–09	None
1910–14	Johnny Coulon
1914–17	Kid Williams
1917–20	Pete Herman
1920–21	Joe Lynch
1921	Pete Herman
1921–22	Johnny Buff
1922–24	Joe Lynch
1924	Abe Goldstein
1924–25	Eddie Martin
1925–27	Charley Rosenberg
1927–28	Bud Taylor
1929–35	Al Brown
1935–36	Baltazar Sangchili
1936	Tony Marino
1936–37	Sixto Escobar
1937–38	Harry Jeffra

Years	Boxer
1938–40	Sixto Escobar
1940	Georgie Pace
1940–42	Lou Salica
1942–47	Manuel Ortiz
1947	Harold Dade
1947–50	Manuel Ortiz
1950–52	Vic Toweel
1952–54	Jimmy Carruthers
1954–55	Robert Cohen
1955–57	Raul Macias
1957–59	Alphonse Halimi
1959–60	Joe Becerra
1961–65	Eder Jofre
1965–68	Masahiko Harada
1968–69	Lionel Rose
1969–70	Ruben Olivares
1970–71	Jesús Castillo
1971–72	Ruben Olivares
1972	Rafael Herrera
1972–73	Enrique Pínder
1973	Romeo Anaya
1973–74	Arnold Taylor
1974–75	Soon Hwan Hong
1975–77	Alfonso Zamora
1977–80	Jorge Lujan
1980	Julian Solis
1980–	Jeff Chandler

Bantamweights (WBC)

Years	Boxer
1963–65	Eder Jofre
1965–68	Masahiko Harada
1968–69	Lionel Rose
1969–70	Ruben Olivares
1970–71	Jesús Castillo
1971–72	Ruben Olivares
1972	Rafael Herrera
1972–73	Enrique Pínder
1973–74	Rafael Herrera
1974–76	Rodolfo Martínez
1976–79	Carlos Zárate
1979–	Lupe Pintor

Junior Bantamweights (WBA)

Years	Boxer
1981–82	Gustavo Ballas
1982	Rafael Pedroza
1982–	Jiro Watanabe

Super Flyweights (WBC)

Years	Boxer
1980–81	Rafael Oronó
1981–	Chul-Ho Kim

Flyweights (WBA)

Years	Boxer
1916–23	Jimmy Wilde
1923–25	Pancho Villa
1925–27	Fidel La Barba
1928–29	Frankie Genaro
1929	Spider Pladner
1929–31	Frankie Genaro
1931–32	Victor Perez
1932–35	Jackie Brown
1935–38	Benny Lynch
1938–41	Peter Kane
1941–42	None
1943–47	Jackie Paterson
1947–50	Rinty Monaghan
1950	Terry Allen
1950–52	Dado Marino
1952–54	Yoshio Shirai
1954–60	Pascual Perez
1960–62	Pone Kingpetch
1962–63	Masahiko Harada
1963	Pone Kingpetch
1963–64	Hiroyuki Ebihara
1964–65	Pone Kingpetch
1965–66	Salvatore Burruni
1966–68	Horacio Accavallo
1969	Hiroyuki Ebihara
1969–70	Bernabe Villacampo
1970	Berkrerk Chartvanchai
1970–73	Masao Ohba
1973–74	Chartchai Chionoi
1974–75	Susumu Hanagata
1975–76	Erbito Salavarría
1976	Alfonso López
1976–78	Guty Espadas
1978–79	Betulio González
1979–80	Luis Ibarra
1980	Kim Tae-Shik
1980–81	Peter Mathebula
1981	Santos Laciar
1981–	Luis Ibarra

Flyweights (WBC)

Years	Boxer
1963	Pone Kingpetch
1963–64	Hiroyuki Ebihara
1964–65	Pone Kingpetch
1965–66	Salvatore Burruni
1966	Walter MacGowan
1966–69	Chartchai Chionoi
1969–70	Efren Torres

Years	Boxer
1970	Chartchai Chionoi
1970–71	Erbito Salavarría
1971–72	Betulio González
1972–73	Venice Borkorsor
1973–74	Betulio González
1974–75	Shoji Oguma
1975–79	Miguel Canto
1979–80	Park Chan-Hee
1980–81	Shoji Oguma
1981–82	Antonio Avelar
1982	Prudencio Cardona
1982–	Freddie Castillo

Junior Flyweights (WBA)

Years	Boxer
1975–76	Jaime Rios
1976–81	Yoko Gushiken
1981	Pedro Flores
1981	Hwan-Jin Kim
1981–	Katsuo Tokashiki

Light Flyweights (WBC)

Years	Boxer
1975	Franco Udella
1975–78	Luis Estaba
1978	Freddy Castillo
1978	Netrnoi Vorasingh
1978–80	Kim Sung-Jun
1980	Shigeo Nakajima
1980–82	Hilario Zapata
1982	Amado Ursúa
1982	Tadashi Tomori
1982–	Hilario Zapata

Football

Professional football champions

National Football Conference (NFC)*

Year	Team	Year	Team
1933	Chicago Bears	1944	Green Bay Packers
1934	New York Giants	1945	Cleveland Rams
1935	Detroit Lions	1946	Chicago Bears
1936	Green Bay Packers	1947	Chicago Cardinals
1937	Washington Redskins	1948	Philadelphia Eagles
1938	New York Giants	1949	Philadelphia Eagles
1939	Green Bay Packers	1950	Cleveland Browns
1940	Chicago Bears	1951	Los Angeles Rams
1941	Chicago Bears		
1942	Washington Redskins	1952	Detroit Lions
		1953	Detroit Lions
1943	Chicago Bears		

Year	Team	Year	Team
1954	Cleveland Browns	1961	Green Bay Packers
1955	Cleveland Browns	1962	Green Bay Packers
1956	New York Giants	1963	Chicago Bears
1957	Detroit Lions	1964	Cleveland Browns
1958	Baltimore Colts	1965	Green Bay Packers
1959	Baltimore Colts		
1960	Philadelphia Eagles		

American Football Conference (AFC)†

Year	Team	Year	Team
1960	Houston Oilers	1963	San Diego Chargers
1961	Houston Oilers	1964	Buffalo Bills
1962	Dallas Texans	1965	Buffalo Bills

*National Football League (NFL) until 1970.
†American Football League (AFL) until 1970.

Super Bowl

The Super Bowl is played each January following the completion of the regular season and play-offs the preceding year. The 1966 NFL and AFL champions played in the first Super Bowl in January 1967. The NFL and AFL champions played through 1970, when the leagues merged. Beginning in 1971, the NFC and AFC champions played in the Super Bowl for the NFL title.

1967	Green Bay Packers (NFL) 35, Kansas City Chiefs (AFL) 10	1973	Miami Dolphins (AFC) 14, Washington Redskins (NFC) 7
1968	Green Bay Packers (NFL) 33, Oakland Raiders (AFL) 14	1974	Miami Dolphins (AFC) 24, Minnesota Vikings (NFC) 7
1969	New York Jets (AFL) 16, Baltimore Colts (NFL) 7	1975	Pittsburgh Steelers (AFC) 16, Minnesota Vikings (NFC) 6
1970	Kansas City Chiefs (AFL) 23, Minnesota Vikings (NFL) 7	1976	Pittsburgh Steelers (AFC) 21, Dallas Cowboys (NFC) 17
1971	Baltimore Colts (AFC) 16, Dallas Cowboys (NFC) 13	1977	Oakland Raiders (AFC) 32, Minnesota Vikings (NFC) 14
1972	Dallas Cowboys (NFC) 24, Miami Dolphins (AFC) 3	1978	Dallas Cowboys (NFC) 27, Denver Broncos (AFC) 10

1979	Pittsburgh Steelers (AFC) 35, Dallas Cowboys (NFC) 31
1980	Pittsburgh Steelers (AFC) 31, Los Angeles Rams (NFC) 19
1981	Oakland Raiders (AFC) 27, Philadelphia Eagles (NFC) 10
1982	San Francisco 49ers (NFC) 26, Cincinnati Bengals (AFC) 21
1983	Washington Redskins (NFC) 27, Miami Dolphins (AFC) 17

College bowl games

Each year after the regular season, the top-ranked college football teams in the United States participate in bowl games. The leading bowl games include the Rose Bowl in Pasadena, Calif.; the Orange Bowl in Miami, Fla.; the Sugar Bowl, in New Orleans, La.; and the Cotton Bowl, in Dallas, Tex. The bowl games are usually played on January 1.

Rose Bowl

1902	Michigan 49, Stanford 0
1903–15	No games
1916	Washington State 14, Brown 0
1917	Oregon 14, Pennsylvania 0
1918	Mare Island Marines 19, Camp Lewis Army 7
1919	Great Lakes Navy 17, Mare Island Marines 0
1920	Harvard 7, Oregon 6
1921	California 28, Ohio State 0
1922	Washington and Jefferson 0, California 0
1923	Southern California 14, Penn State 3
1924	Navy 14, Washington 14
1925	Notre Dame 27, Stanford 10
1926	Alabama 20, Washington 19
1927	Alabama 7, Stanford 7
1928	Stanford 7, Pittsburgh 6
1929	Georgia Tech 8, California 7
1930	Southern California 47, Pittsburgh 14
1931	Alabama 24, Washington State 0
1932	Southern California 21, Tulane 12
1933	Southern California 35, Pittsburgh 0
1934	Columbia 7, Stanford 0
1935	Alabama 29, Stanford 13
1936	Stanford 7, Southern Methodist 0
1937	Pittsburgh 21, Washington 0
1938	California 13, Alabama 0
1939	Southern California 7, Duke 3
1940	Southern California 14, Tennessee 0
1941	Stanford 21, Nebraska 13
1942*	Oregon State 20, Duke 16
1943	Georgia 9, UCLA 0
1944	Southern California 29, Washington 0
1945	Southern California 25, Tennessee 0
1946	Alabama 34, Southern California 14
1947	Illinois 45, UCLA 14
1948	Michigan 49, Southern California 0
1949	Northwestern 20, California 14
1950	Ohio State 17, California 14
1951	Michigan 14, California 6
1952	Illinois 40, Stanford 7
1953	Southern California 7, Wisconsin 0

1954	Michigan State 28, UCLA 20
1955	Ohio State 20, Southern California 7
1956	Michigan State 17, UCLA 14
1957	Iowa 35, Oregon State 19
1958	Ohio State 10, Oregon 7
1959	Iowa 38, California 12
1960	Washington 44, Wisconsin 8
1961	Washington 17, Minnesota 7
1962	Minnesota 21, UCLA 3
1963	Southern California 42, Wisconsin 37
1964	Illinois 17, Washington 7
1965	Michigan 34, Oregon State 7
1966	UCLA 14, Michigan State 12
1967	Purdue 14, Southern California 13
1968	Southern California 14, Indiana 3
1969	Ohio State 27, Southern California 16
1970	Southern California 10, Michigan 3
1971	Stanford 27, Ohio State 17
1972	Stanford 13, Michigan 12
1973	Southern California 42, Ohio State 17
1974	Ohio State 42, Southern California 21
1975	Southern California 18, Ohio State 17
1976	UCLA 23, Ohio State 10
1977	Southern California 14, Michigan 6
1978	Washington 27, Michigan 20
1979	Southern California 17, Michigan 10
1980	Southern California 17, Ohio State 16
1981	Michigan 23, Washington 6
1982	Washington 28, Iowa 0
1983	UCLA 24, Michigan 14

Orange Bowl

1933	Miami 7, Manhattan 0
1934	Duquesne 33, Miami 7
1935	Bucknell 26, Miami 0
1936	Catholic 20, Mississippi 19
1937	Duquesne 13, Mississippi State 12
1938	Auburn 6, Michigan State 0
1939	Tennessee 17, Oklahoma 0
1940	Georgia Tech 21, Missouri 7

*Played at Durham, North Carolina

1941	Mississippi State 14, Georgetown 7
1942	Georgia 40, Texas Christian 26
1943	Alabama 37, Boston College 21
1944	Louisiana State 19, Texas A & M 14
1945	Tulsa 26, Georgia Tech 12
1946	Miami 13, Holy Cross 6
1947	Rice 8, Tennessee 0
1948	Georgia Tech 20, Kansas 14
1949	Texas 41, Georgia 28
1950	Santa Clara 21, Kentucky 13
1951	Clemson 15, Miami 14
1952	Georgia Tech 17, Baylor 14
1953	Alabama 61, Syracuse 6
1954	Oklahoma 7, Maryland 0
1955	Duke 34, Nebraska 7
1956	Oklahoma 20, Maryland 6
1957	Colorado 27, Clemson 21
1958	Oklahoma 48, Duke 21
1959	Oklahoma 21, Syracuse 6
1960	Georgia 14, Missouri 0
1961	Missouri 21, Navy 14
1962	Louisiana State 25, Colorado 7
1963	Alabama 17, Oklahoma 0
1964	Nebraska 13, Auburn 7
1965	Texas 21, Alabama 17
1966	Alabama 39, Nebraska 28
1967	Florida 27, Georgia Tech 12
1968	Oklahoma 26, Tennessee 24
1969	Penn State 15, Kansas 14
1970	Penn State 10, Missouri 3
1971	Nebraska 17, Louisiana State 12
1972	Nebraska 38, Alabama 6
1973	Nebraska 40, Notre Dame 6
1974	Penn State 16, Louisiana State 9
1975	Notre Dame 13, Alabama 11
1976	Oklahoma 14, Michigan 6
1977	Ohio State 27, Colorado 10
1978	Arkansas 31, Oklahoma 6
1979	Oklahoma 31, Nebraska 24
1980	Oklahoma 24, Florida State 7
1981	Oklahoma 18, Florida State 17
1982	Clemson 22, Nebraska 15
1983	Nebraska 21, Louisiana State 20

Sugar Bowl

1935	Tulane 20, Temple 14
1936	Texas Christian 3, Louisiana State 2
1937	Santa Clara 21, Louisiana State 14
1938	Santa Clara 6, Louisiana State 0
1939	Texas Christian 15, Carnegie Tech 7
1940	Texas A & M 14, Tulane 13
1941	Boston College 19, Tennessee 13
1942	Fordham 2, Missouri 0
1943	Tennessee 14, Tulsa 7
1944	Georgia Tech 20, Tulsa 18
1945	Duke 29, Alabama 26
1946	Oklahoma A & M 33, St. Mary's (California) 13

1947	Georgia 20, North Carolina 10
1948	Texas 27, Alabama 7
1949	Oklahoma 14, North Carolina 6
1950	Oklahoma 35, Louisiana State 0
1951	Kentucky 13, Oklahoma 7
1952	Maryland 28, Tennessee 13
1953	Georgia Tech 24, Mississippi 7
1954	Georgia Tech 42, West Virginia 19
1955	Navy 21, Mississippi 0
1956	Georgia Tech 7, Pittsburgh 0
1957	Baylor 13, Tennessee 7
1958	Mississippi 39, Texas 7
1959	Louisiana State 7, Clemson 0
1960	Mississippi 21, Louisiana State 0
1961	Mississippi 14, Rice 6
1962	Alabama 10, Arkansas 3
1963	Mississippi 17, Arkansas 13
1964	Alabama 12, Mississippi 7
1965	Louisiana State 13, Syracuse 10
1966	Missouri 20, Florida 18
1967	Alabama 34, Nebraska 7
1968	Louisiana State 20, Wyoming 13
1969	Arkansas 16, Georgia 2
1970	Mississippi 27, Arkansas 22
1971	Tennessee 34, Air Force 13
1972	Oklahoma 40, Auburn 22
1972†	Oklahoma 14, Penn State 0
1973†	Notre Dame 24, Alabama 23
1974†	Nebraska 13, Florida 10
1975†	Alabama 13, Penn State 6
1977	Pittsburgh 27, Georgia 3
1978	Alabama 35, Ohio State 6
1979	Alabama 14, Penn State 7
1980	Alabama 24, Arkansas 9
1981	Georgia 17, Notre Dame 10
1982	Pittsburgh 24, Georgia 20
1983	Penn State 27, Georgia 23

Cotton Bowl

1937	Texas Christian 16, Marquette 6
1938	Rice 28, Colorado 14
1939	St. Mary's (California) 20, Texas Tech 13
1940	Clemson 6, Boston College 3
1941	Texas A & M 13, Fordham 12
1942	Alabama 29, Texas A & M 21
1943	Texas 14, Georgia Tech 7
1944	Randolph Field 7, Texas 7
1945	Oklahoma A & M 34, Texas Christian 0
1946	Texas 40, Missouri 27
1947	Louisiana State 0, Arkansas 0
1948	Southern Methodist 13, Penn State 13
1949	Southern Methodist 21, Oregon 13
1950	Rice 27, North Carolina 13
1951	Tennessee 20, Texas 14
1952	Kentucky 20, Texas Christian 7
1953	Texas 16, Tennessee 0
1954	Rice 28, Alabama 6

†Game played in December.

1955	Georgia Tech 14, Arkansas 6		1969	Texas 36, Tennessee 13
1956	Mississippi 14, Texas Christian 13		1970	Texas 21, Notre Dame 17
1957	Texas Christian 28, Syracuse 27		1971	Notre Dame 24, Texas 11
1958	Navy 20, Rice 7		1972	Penn State 30, Texas 6
1959	Air Force 0, Texas Christian 0		1973	Texas 17, Alabama 13
1960	Syracuse 23, Texas 14		1974	Nebraska 19, Texas 3
1961	Duke 7, Arkansas 6		1975	Penn State 41, Baylor 20
1962	Texas 12, Mississippi 7		1976	Arkansas 31, Georgia 10
1963	Louisiana State 13, Texas 0		1977	Houston 30, Maryland 21
1964	Texas 28, Navy 6		1978	Notre Dame 38, Texas 10
1965	Arkansas 10, Nebraska 7		1979	Notre Dame 35, Houston 34
1966	Louisiana State 14, Arkansas 7		1980	Houston 17, Nebraska 14
1966†	Georgia 24, Southern Methodist 9		1981	Alabama 30, Baylor 2
1968	Texas A & M 20, Alabama 16		1982	Texas 14, Alabama 12
			1983	Southern Methodist 7, Pittsburgh 3

†Game played in December

Golf

The following tables list the winners of some of the world's major golf tournaments. Both amateur and professional golfers participate in the British Open, the United States Open, the Masters Tournament, and the United States Women's Open. The championship tournaments sponsored by the Professional Golfers' Association of America (PGA) and the Ladies Professional Golf Association (LPGA) are for professionals only.

British Open

1914	Harry Vardon	1938	R. A. Whitcombe	1963	Bob Charles
1915–19	No tournaments	1939	Richard Burton	1964	Tony Lema
1920	George Duncan	1940–45	No tournaments	1965	Peter Thomson
1921	Jack Hutchison	1946	Sam Snead	1966	Jack Nicklaus
1922	Walter Hagen	1947	Fred Daly	1967	Roberto de Vicenzo
1923	Arthur G. Havers	1948	Henry Cotton	1968	Gary Player
1924	Walter Hagen	1949	Bobby Locke	1969	Tony Jacklin
1925	James M. Barnes	1950	Bobby Locke	1970	Jack Nicklaus
1926	Bobby Jones	1951	Max Faulkner	1971	Lee Trevino
1927	Bobby Jones	1952	Bobby Locke	1972	Lee Trevino
1928	Walter Hagen	1953	Ben Hogan	1973	Tom Weiskopf
1929	Walter Hagen	1954	Peter Thomson	1974	Gary Player
1930	Bobby Jones	1955	Peter Thomson	1975	Tom Watson
1931	Tommy Armour	1956	Peter Thomson	1976	Johnny Miller
1932	Gene Sarazen	1957	Bobby Locke	1977	Tom Watson
1933	Denny Shute	1958	Peter Thomson	1978	Jack Nicklaus
1934	Henry Cotton	1959	Gary Player	1979	Severiano Ballesteros
1935	Alf Perry	1960	Kel Nagle	1980	Tom Watson
1936	Alfred Padgham	1961	Arnold Palmer	1981	Bill Rogers
1937	Henry Cotton	1962	Arnold Palmer	1982	Tom Watson

U.S. Open

1914	Walter Hagen	1919	Walter Hagen	1923	Bobby Jones
1915	Jerome Travers	1920	Edward Ray	1924	Cyril Walker
1916	Charles Evans, Jr.	1921	James M. Barnes	1925	Willie Macfarlane
1917–18	No tournaments	1922	Gene Sarazen	1926	Bobby Jones

214

1927	Tommy Armour	1948	Ben Hogan	1966	Billy Casper, Jr.
1928	Johnny Farrell	1949	Cary Middlecoff	1967	Jack Nicklaus
1929	Bobby Jones	1950	Ben Hogan	1968	Lee Trevino
1930	Bobby Jones	1951	Ben Hogan	1969	Orville Moody
1931	Billy Burke	1952	Julius Boros	1970	Tony Jacklin
1932	Gene Sarazen	1953	Ben Hogan	1971	Lee Trevino
1933	John Goodman	1954	Ed Furgol	1972	Jack Nicklaus
1934	Olin Dutra	1955	Jack Fleck	1973	Johnny Miller
1935	Sam Parks, Jr.	1956	Cary Middlecoff	1974	Hale Irwin
1936	Tony Manero	1957	Dick Mayer	1975	Lou Graham
1937	Ralph Guldahl	1958	Tommy Bolt	1976	Jerry Pate
1938	Ralph Guldahl	1959	Billy Casper, Jr.	1977	Hubert Green
1939	Byron Nelson	1960	Arnold Palmer	1978	Andy North
1940	Lawson Little, Jr.	1961	Gene Littler	1979	Hale Irwin
1941	Craig Wood	1962	Jack Nicklaus	1980	Jack Nicklaus
1942–45	No tournaments	1963	Julius Boros	1981	David Graham
1946	Lloyd Mangrum	1964	Ken Venturi	1982	Tom Watson
1947	Lew Worsham	1965	Gary Player	1983	Larry Nelson

Masters Tournament

1934	Horton Smith	1952	Sam Snead	1968	Bob Goalby
1935	Gene Sarazen	1953	Ben Hogan	1969	George Archer
1936	Horton Smith	1954	Sam Snead	1970	Billy Casper, Jr.
1937	Byron Nelson	1955	Cary Middlecoff	1971	Charles Coody
1938	Henry Picard	1956	Jack Burke	1972	Jack Nicklaus
1939	Ralph Guldahl	1957	Doug Ford	1973	Tommy Aaron
1940	Jimmy Demaret	1958	Arnold Palmer	1974	Gary Player
1941	Craig Wood	1959	Art Wall, Jr.	1975	Jack Nicklaus
1942	Byron Nelson	1960	Arnold Palmer	1976	Ray Floyd
1943–45	No tournaments	1961	Gary Player	1977	Tom Watson
1946	Herman Keiser	1962	Arnold Palmer	1978	Gary Player
1947	Jimmy Demaret	1963	Jack Nicklaus	1979	Fuzzy Zoeller
1948	Claude Harmon	1964	Arnold Palmer	1980	Severiano Ballesteros
1949	Sam Snead	1965	Jack Nicklaus	1981	Tom Watson
1950	Jimmy Demaret	1966	Jack Nicklaus	1982	Craig Stadler
1951	Ben Hogan	1967	Gay Brewer	1983	Severiano Ballesteros

U.S. Women's Open

1946	Patty Berg	1959	Mickey Wright	1972	Susie Berning
1947	Betty Jameson	1960	Betsy Rawls	1973	Susie Berning
1948	Babe Didrikson Zaharias	1961	Mickey Wright	1974	Sandra Haynie
1949	Louise Suggs	1962	Murie Lindstrom	1975	Sandra Palmer
1950	Babe Didrikson Zaharias	1963	Mary Mills	1976	JoAnne Carner
1951	Betsy Rawls	1964	Mickey Wright	1977	Hollis Stacy
1952	Louise Suggs	1965	Carol Mann	1978	Hollis Stacy
1953	Betsy Rawls	1966	Sandra Spuzich	1979	Jerilyn Britz
1954	Babe Didrikson Zaharias	1967	Catherine Lacoste	1980	Amy Alcott
1955	Fay Crocker	1968	Susie Berning	1981	Pat Bradley
1956	Kathy Cornelius	1969	Donna Caponi	1982	Janet Alex
1957	Betsy Rawls	1970	Donna Caponi		
1958	Mickey Wright	1971	JoAnne Carner		

PGA Championship

1916	Jim Barnes	1939	Henry Picard	1961	Jerry Barber
1917–18	No tournaments	1940	Byron Nelson	1962	Gary Player
1919	Jim Barnes	1941	Vic Ghezzi	1963	Jack Nicklaus
1920	Jock Hutchison	1942	Sam Snead	1964	Bob Nichols
1921	Walter Hagen	1943	No tournament	1965	Dave Marr
1922	Gene Sarazen	1944	Bob Hamilton	1966	Al Geiberger
1923	Gene Sarazen	1945	Byron Nelson	1967	Don January
1924	Walter Hagen	1946	Ben Hogan	1968	Julius Boros
1925	Walter Hagen	1947	Jim Ferrier	1969	Ray Floyd
1926	Walter Hagen	1948	Ben Hogan	1970	Dave Stockton
1927	Walter Hagen	1949	Sam Snead	1971	Jack Nicklaus
1928	Leo Diegel	1950	Chandler Harper	1972	Gary Player
1929	Leo Diegel	1951	Sam Snead	1973	Jack Nicklaus
1930	Tommy Armour	1952	Jim Turnesa	1974	Lee Trevino
1931	Tom Creavy	1953	Walter Burkemo	1975	Jack Nicklaus
1932	Olin Dutra	1954	Chick Harbert	1976	Dave Stockton
1933	Gene Sarazen	1955	Doug Ford	1977	Lanny Wadkins
1934	Paul Runyan	1956	Jack Burke	1978	John Mahaffey
1935	Johnny Revolta	1957	Lionel Hebert	1979	David Graham
1936	Denny Shute	1958	Dow Finsterwald	1980	Jack Nicklaus
1937	Denny Shute	1959	Bob Rosburg	1981	Larry Nelson
1938	Paul Runyan	1960	Jay Hebert	1982	Ray Floyd

LPGA Championship

1955	Beverly Hanson	1965	Sandra Haynie	1975	Kathy Whitworth
1956	Marlene Hagge	1966	Gloria Ehret	1976	Betty Burfeindt
1957	Louise Suggs	1967	Kathy Whitworth	1977	Chako Higuchi
1958	Mickey Wright	1968	Sandra Post	1978	Nancy Lopez
1959	Betsy Rawls	1969	Betsy Rawls	1979	Donna Caponi Young
1960	Mickey Wright	1970	Shirley Englehorn	1980	Sally Little
1961	Mickey Wright	1971	Kathy Whitworth	1981	Donna Caponi
1962	Judy Kimball	1972	Kathy Ahern	1982	Jan Stephenson
1963	Mickey Wright	1973	Mary Mills		
1964	Mary Mills	1974	Sandra Haynie		

Hockey

The National Hockey League (NHL) is the only major professional hockey league in the United States and Canada. After postseason playoffs, the top two NHL teams compete for the Stanley Cup to determine the league champion.

Stanley Cup finals

Season	Winner	Loser	Games won-lost	Season	Winner	Loser	Games won-lost
1917–1918	Toronto Arenas	Vancouver Millionaires	3-2	1922–1923	Ottawa Senators	Edmonton Eskimos	2-0
1918–1919	No winner*			1923–1924	Montreal Canadiens	Calgary Tigers	2-0
1919–1920	Ottawa Senators	Seattle Metropolitans	3-2	1924–1925	Victoria Cougars†	Montreal Canadiens	3-1
1920–1921	Ottawa Senators	Vancouver Millionaires	3-2	1925–1926	Montreal Maroons	Victoria Cougars	3-1
1921–1922	Toronto St. Pats	Vancouver Millionaires	3-2	1926–1927	Ottawa Senators	Boston Bruins	2-0

Season	Winner	Loser	Games won-lost	Season	Winner	Loser	Games won-lost
1927–1928	New York Rangers	Montreal Maroons	3-2	1954–1955	Detroit Red Wings	Montreal Canadiens	4-3
1928–1929	Boston Bruins	New York Rangers	2-0	1955–1956	Montreal Canadiens	Detroit Red Wings	4-1
1929–1930	Montreal Canadiens	Boston Bruins	2-0	1956–1957	Montreal Canadiens	Boston Bruins	4-1
1930–1931	Montreal Canadiens	Chicago Black Hawks	3-2	1957–1958	Montreal Canadiens	Boston Bruins	4-2
1931–1932	Toronto Maple Leafs	New York Rangers	3-0	1958–1959	Montreal Canadiens	Toronto Maple Leafs	4-1
1932–1933	New York Rangers	Toronto Maple Leafs	3-1	1959–1960	Montreal Canadiens	Toronto Maple Leafs	4-0
1933–1934	Chicago Black Hawks	Detroit Red Wings	3-1	1960–1961	Chicago Black Hawks	Detroit Red Wings	4-2
1934–1935	Montreal Maroons	Toronto Maple Leafs	3-0	1961–1962	Toronto Maple Leafs	Chicago Black Hawks	4-2
1935–1936	Detroit Red Wings	Toronto Maple Leafs	3-1	1962–1963	Toronto Maple Leafs	Detroit Red Wings	4-1
1936–1937	Detroit Red Wings	New York Rangers	3-2	1963–1964	Toronto Maple Leafs	Detroit Red Wings	4-3
1937–1938	Chicago Black Hawks	Toronto Maple Leafs	3-1	1964–1965	Montreal Canadiens	Chicago Black Hawks	4-3
1938–1939	Boston Bruins	Toronto Maple Leafs	4-1	1965–1966	Montreal Canadiens	Detroit Red Wings	4-2
1939–1940	New York Rangers	Toronto Maple Leafs	4-2	1966–1967	Toronto Maple Leafs	Montreal Canadiens	4-2
1940–1941	Boston Bruins	Detroit Red Wings	4-0	1967–1968	Montreal Canadiens	St. Louis Blues	4-0
1941–1942	Toronto Maple Leafs	Detroit Red Wings	4-3	1968–1969	Montreal Canadiens	St. Louis Blues	4-0
1942–1943	Detroit Red Wings	Boston Bruins	4-0	1969–1970	Boston Bruins	St. Louis Blues	4-0
1943–1944	Montreal Canadiens	Chicago Black Hawks	4-0	1970–1971	Montreal Canadiens	Chicago Black Hawks	4-3
1944–1945	Toronto Maple Leafs	Detroit Red Wings	4-3	1971–1972	Boston Bruins	New York Rangers	4-2
1945–1946	Montreal Canadiens	Boston Bruins	4-1	1972–1973	Montreal Canadiens	Chicago Black Hawks	4-2
1946–1947	Toronto Maple Leafs	Montreal Canadiens	4-2	1973–1974	Philadelphia Flyers	Boston Bruins	4-2
1947–1948	Toronto Maple Leafs	Detroit Red Wings	4-0	1974–1975	Philadelphia Flyers	Buffalo Sabres	4-2
1948–1949	Toronto Maple Leafs	Detroit Red Wings	4-0	1975–1976	Montreal Canadiens	Philadelphia Flyers	4-0
1949–1950	Detroit Red Wings	New York Rangers	4-3	1976–1977	Montreal Canadiens	Boston Bruins	4-0
1950–1951	Toronto Maple Leafs	Montreal Canadiens	4-1	1977–1978	Montreal Canadiens	Boston Bruins	4-2
1951–1952	Detroit Red Wings	Montreal Canadiens	4-0	1978–1979	Montreal Canadiens	New York Rangers	4-1
1952–1953	Montreal Canadiens	Boston Bruins	4-1	1979–1980	New York Islanders	Philadelphia Flyers	4-2
1953–1954	Detroit Red Wings	Montreal Canadiens	4-3	1980–1981	New York Islanders	Minnesota North Stars	4-1
				1981–1982	New York Islanders	Vancouver Canucks	4-0
				1982–1983	New York Islanders	Edmonton Oilers	4-0

*Play-off between Montreal Canadiens and Seattle Metropolitans not finished because of influenza epidemic in Seattle.
†Member, Pacific Coast League.

Horse racing

The Kentucky Derby, the Preakness, and the Belmont Stakes are the most famous races for 3-year-old horses in the United States. Together, these events form the Triple Crown of U.S. horse racing.

Kentucky Derby winners

The Kentucky Derby is a 1¼-mile (2-kilometer) race held at Churchill Downs race track in Louisville, Ky.

Year	Winner	Jockey	Year	Winner	Jockey
1875	Aristides	Oliver Lewis	1921	Behave Yourself	Charles Thompson
1876	Vagrant	Robert Swim	1922	Morvich	Albert Johnson
1877	Baden Baden	Billy Walker	1923	Zev	Earl Sande
1878	Day Star	J. Carter	1924	Black Gold	John D. Mooney
1879	Lord Murphy	C. Shaver	1925	Flying Ebony	Earl Sande
1880	Fonso	George Lewis	1926	Bubbling Over	Albert Johnson
1881	Hindoo	Jimmy McLaughlin	1927	Whiskery	Linus McAtee
1882	Apollo	Babe Hurd	1928	Reigh Count	Chick Lang
1883	Leonatus	Billy Donahue	1929	Clyde Van Dusen	Linus McAtee
1884	Buchanan	Isaac Murphy	1930	Gallant Fox*	Earl Sande
1885	Joe Cotton	Erskine Henderson	1931	Twenty Grand	Charles Kurtsinger
1886	Ben Ali	P. Duffy	1932	Burgoo King	Eugene James
1887	Montrose	Isaac Lewis	1933	Brokers Tip	Don Meade
1888	Macbeth II	G. Covington	1934	Cavalcade	Mack Garner
1889	Spokane	Thomas Kiley	1935	Omaha*	Willie Saunders
1890	Riley	Isaac Murphy	1936	Bold Venture	Ira Hanford
1891	Kingman	Isaac Murphy	1937	War Admiral*	Charles Kurtsinger
1892	Azra	Alonzo Clayton	1938	Lawrin	Eddie Arcaro
1893	Lookout	E. Kunze	1939	Johnstown	James Stout
1894	Chant	Frank Goodale	1940	Gallahadion	Carroll Bierman
1895	Halma	James Perkins	1941	Whirlaway*	Eddie Arcaro
1896	Ben Brush	Willie Simms	1942	Shut Out	Wayne D. Wright
1897	Typhoon II	Buttons Garner	1943	Count Fleet*	Johnny Longden
1898	Plaudit	Willie Simms	1944	Pensive	Conn McCreary
1899	Manuel	Fred Taral	1945	Hoop Junior	Eddie Arcaro
1900	Lieutenant Gibson	Jimmy Boland	1946	Assault*	Warren Mehrtens
1901	His Eminence	Jimmy Winkfield	1947	Jet Pilot	Eric Guerin
1902	Alan-a-Dale	Jimmy Winkfield	1948	Citation*	Eddie Arcaro
1903	Judge Himes	Hal Booker	1949	Ponder	Steve Brooks
1904	Elwood	Frankie Prior	1950	Middleground	Bill Boland
1905	Agile	Jack Martin	1951	Count Turf	Conn McCreary
1906	Sir Huon	Roscoe Troxler	1952	Hill Gail	Eddie Arcaro
1907	Pink Star	Andy Minder	1953	Dark Star	Henry Moreno
1908	Stone Street	Arthur Pickens	1954	Determine	Ray York
1909	Wintergreen	Vince Powers	1955	Swaps	Bill Shoemaker
1910	Donau	Robert Herbert	1956	Needles	Dave Erb
1911	Meridian	George Archibald	1957	Iron Liege	Bill Hartack
1912	Worth	Carroll Shilling	1958	Tim Tam	Ismael Valenzuela
1913	Donerail	Roscoe Goose	1959	Tomy Lee	Bill Shoemaker
1914	Old Rosebud	John McCabe	1960	Venetian Way	Bill Hartack
1915	Regret	Joe Notter	1961	Carry Back	John Sellers
1916	George Smith	Johnny Loftus	1962	Decidedly	Bill Hartack
1917	Omar Khayyam	Charles Borel	1963	Chateaugay	Braulio Baeza
1918	Exterminator	Willie Knap	1964	Northern Dancer	Bill Hartack
1919	Sir Barton*	Johnny Loftus	1965	Lucky Debonair	Bill Shoemaker
1920	Paul Jones	Ted Rice	1966	Kauai King	Don Brumfield

*Winner of the Triple Crown (Kentucky Derby, Preakness Stakes, and Belmont Stakes).

Year	Winner	Jockey	Year	Winner	Jockey
1967	Proud Clarion	Bob Ussery	1975	Foolish Pleasure	Jacinto Vasquez
1968	Forward Pass†	Ismael Valenzuela	1976	Bold Forbes	Angel Cordero, Jr.
1969	Majestic Prince	Bill Hartack	1977	Seattle Slew*	Jean Cruguet
1970	Dust Commander	Mike Manganello	1978	Affirmed*	Steve Cauthen
1971	Canonero II	Gustavo Avila	1979	Spectacular Bid	Ron Franklin
1972	Riva Ridge	Ron Turcotte	1980	Genuine Risk	Jacinto Vasquez
1973	Secretariat*	Ron Turcotte	1981	Pleasant Colony	Jorge Velasquez
1974	Cannonade	Angel Cordero, Jr.	1982	Gato Del Sol	Eddie Delahoussaye
			1983	Sunny's Halo	Eddie Delahoussaye

*Winner of the Triple Crown (Kentucky Derby, Preakness Stakes, and Belmont Stakes).
†Dancer's Image finished first but was disqualified.

Preakness winners

The Preakness is a 1³⁄₁₆-mile (1.9-kilometer) race held at Pimlico Race Course in Baltimore, Md.

Year	Horse	Jockey	Year	Horse	Jockey
1873	Survivor	G. Barbee	1913	Buskin	Jimmy Butwell
1874	Culpepper	M. Donohue	1914	Holiday	Andy Schuttinger
1875	Tom Ochiltree	L. Hughes	1915	Rhine Maiden	D. Hoffman
1876	Shirley	G. Barbee	1916	Damrosch	Linus McAtee
1877	Cloverbrook	C. Hollaway	1917	Kalitan	E. Haynes
1878	Duke of Magenta	C. Hollaway	1918*	War Cloud	Johnny Loftus
1879	Harold	L. Hughes		Jack Hare Jr.	C. Peak
1880	Grenada	L. Hughes	1919	Sir Barton	Johnny Loftus
1881	Saunterer	W. Costello	1920	Man o' War	Clarence Kummer
1882	Vanguard	W. Costello	1921	Broomspun	Frank Coltiletti
1883	Jacobus	G. Barbee	1922	Pillory	L. Morris
1884	Knight of Ellerslie	S. H. Fisher	1923	Vigil	B. Marinelli
1885	Tecumseh	Jimmy McLaughlin	1924	Nellie Morse	J. Merimee
1886	The Bard	S. H. Fisher	1925	Coventry	Clarence Kummer
1887	Dunbine	W. Donoghue	1926	Display	John Maiben
1888	Refund	F. Littlefield	1927	Bostonian	A. Abel
1889	Buddhist	H. Anderson	1928	Victorian	Sonny Workman
1890–93	No race		1929	Dr. Freeland	Lou Schaefer
1894	Assignee	Fred Taral	1930	Gallant Fox	Earl Sande
1895	Belmar	Fred Taral	1931	Mate	George Ellis
1896	Margrave	Henry Griffin	1932	Burgoo King	Eugene James
1897	Paul Kauvar	Thorpe	1933	Head Play	Charles Kurtsinger
1898	Sly Fox	Willie Simms	1934	High Quest	R. Jones
1899	Half Time	R. R. Clawson	1935	Omaha	Willie Saunders
1900	Hindus	H. Spencer	1936	Bold Venture	George Woolf
1901	The Parader	Landry	1937	War Admiral	Charles Kurtsinger
1902	Old England	L. Jackson	1938	Dauber	Maurice Peters
1903	Flocarline	W. Gannon	1939	Challedon	George Seabo
1904	Bryn Mawr	Eugene Hildebrand	1940	Bimelech	F. A. Smith
1905	Cairngorm	W. Davis	1941	Whirlaway	Eddie Arcaro
1906	Whimsical	W. Miller	1942	Alsab	Basil James
1907	Don Enrique	G. Mountain	1943	Count Fleet	Johnny Longden
1908	Royal Tourist	Eddie Dugan	1944	Pensive	Conn McCreary
1909	Effendi	W. Doyle	1945	Polynesian	Wayne D. Wright
1910	Layminster	R. Estep	1946	Assault	Warren Mehrtens
1911	Watervale	Eddie Dugan	1947	Faultless	D. Dodson
1912	Colonel Halloway	Nash Turner	1948	Citation	Eddie Arcaro

*Race held in two divisions.

Year	Horse	Jockey	Year	Horse	Jockey
1949	Capot	Ted Atkinson	1966	Kauai King	Don Brumfield
1950	Hill Prince	Eddie Arcaro	1967	Damascus	Bill Shoemaker
1951	Bold	Eddie Arcaro	1968	Forward Pass	Ismael Valenzuela
1952	Blue Man	Conn McCreary	1969	Majestic Prince	Bill Hartack
1953	Native Dancer	Eric Guerin	1970	Personality	Eddie Belmonte
1954	Hasty Road	Johnny Adams	1971	Canonero II	Gustavo Avila
1955	Nashua	Eddie Arcaro	1972	Bee Bee Bee	Eldon Nelson
1956	Fabius	Bill Hartack	1973	Secretariat	Ron Turcotte
1957	Bold Ruler	Eddie Arcaro	1974	Little Current	Miguel Rivera
1958	Tim Tam	Ismael Valenzuela	1975	Master Derby	Darrel McHargue
1959	Royal Orbit	Willie Harmatz	1976	Elocutionist	John Lively
1960	Bally Ache	Bob Ussery	1977	Seattle Slew	Jean Cruguet
1961	Carry Back	John Sellers	1978	Affirmed	Steve Cauthen
1962	Greek Money	John Rotz	1979	Spectacular Bid	Ron Franklin
1963	Candy Spots	Bill Shoemaker	1980	Codex	Angel Cordero, Jr.
1964	Northern Dancer	Bill Hartack	1981	Pleasant Colony	Jorge Velasquez
1965	Tom Rolfe	Ron Turcotte	1982	Aloma's Ruler	Jack Kaenel
			1983	Deputed Testamony	Don Miller, Jr.

Belmont winners

The Belmont Stakes is a 1½-mile (2.4-kilometer) race held at Belmont Park in Elmont, N.Y.

Year	Horse	Jockey	Year	Horse	Jockey
1867	Ruthless	J. Gilpatrick	1897	Scottish Chieftain	J. Scherrer
1868	General Duke	Robert Swim	1898	Bowling Brook	P. Littlefield
1869	Fenian	C. Miller	1899	Jean Beraud	R. R. Clawson
1870	Kingfisher	W. Dick	1900	Ildrim	Nash Turner
1871	Harry Bassett	Walter Miller	1901	Commando	H. Spencer
1872	Joe Daniels	J. Rowe	1902	Masterman	J. Bullmann
1873	Springbok	J. Rowe	1903	Africander	J. Bullmann
1874	Saxon	G. Barbee	1904	Delhi	G. Odom
1875	Calvin	Robert Swim	1905	Tanya	Eugene Hildebrand
1876	Algerine	W. Donahue	1906	Burgomaster	L. Lyne
1877	Cloverbrook	C. Hollaway	1907	Peter Pan	G. Mountain
1878	Duke of Magenta	L. Hughes	1908	Colin	Joe Notter
1879	Spendthrift	S. Evans	1909	Joe Madden	Eddie Dugan
1880	Grenada	L. Hughes	1910	Sweep	Jimmy Butwell
1881	Saunterer	T. Costello	1911–12	No race	
1882	Forester	Jimmy McLaughlin	1913	Prince Eugene	Roscoe Troxler
1883	George Kinney	Jimmy McLaughlin	1914	Luke McLuke	M. Buxton
1884	Panique	Jimmy McLaughlin	1915	The Finn	G. Byrne
1885	Tyrant	P. Duffy	1916	Friar Rock	E. Haynes
1886	Inspector B	Jimmy McLaughlin	1917	Hourless	Jimmy Butwell
1887	Hanover	Jimmy McLaughlin	1918	Johren	Frank Robinson
1888	Sir Dixon	Jimmy McLaughlin	1919	Sir Barton	Johnny Loftus
1889	Eric	W. Hayward	1920	Man o' War	Clarence Kummer
1890	Burlington	S. Barnes	1921	Grey Lag	Earl Sande
1891	Foxford	Edward Garrison	1922	Pillory	C. H. Miller
1892	Patron	W. Hayward	1923	Zev	Earl Sande
1893	Comanche	Willie Simms	1924	Mad Play	Earl Sande
1894	Henry of Navarre	Willie Simms	1925	American Flag	Albert Johnson
1895	Belmar	Fred Taral	1926	Crusader	Albert Johnson
1896	Hastings	Henry Griffin	1927	Chance Shot	Earl Sande

Year	Horse	Jockey	Year	Horse	Jockey
1928	Vito	Clarence Kummer	1956	Needles	Dave Erb
1929	Blue Larkspur	Mack Garner	1957	Gallant Man	Bill Shoemaker
1930	Gallant Fox	Earl Sande	1958	Cavan	P. Anderson
1931	Twenty Grand	Charles Kurtsinger	1959	Sword Dancer	Bill Shoemaker
1932	Faireno	T. Malley	1960	Celtic Ash	Bill Hartack
1933	Hurryoff	Mack Garner	1961	Sherluck	Braulio Baeza
1934	Peace Chance	Wayne D. Wright	1962	Jaipur	Bill Shoemaker
1935	Omaha	Willie Saunders	1963	Chateaugay	Braulio Baeza
1936	Granville	James Stout	1964	Quadrangle	Manuel Ycaza
1937	War Admiral	Charles Kurtsinger	1965	Hail to All	John Sellers
1938	Pasteurized	James Stout	1966	Amberoid	Bill Boland
1939	Johnstown	James Stout	1967	Damascus	Bill Shoemaker
1940	Bimelech	F. A. Smith	1968	Stage Door Johnny	Heliodoro Gustines
1941	Whirlaway	Eddie Arcaro	1969	Arts and Letters	Braulio Baeza
1942	Shut Out	Eddie Arcaro	1970	High Echelon	John Rotz
1943	Count Fleet	Johnny Longden	1971	Pass Catcher	Walter Blum
1944	Bounding Home	G. L. Smith	1972	Riva Ridge	Ron Turcotte
1945	Pavot	Eddie Arcaro	1973	Secretariat	Ron Turcotte
1946	Assault	Warren Mehrtens	1974	Little Current	Miguel Rivera
1947	Phalanx	R. Donoso	1975	Avatar	Bill Shoemaker
1948	Citation	Eddie Arcaro	1976	Bold Forbes	Angel Cordero, Jr.
1949	Capot	Ted Atkinson	1977	Seattle Slew	Jean Cruguet
1950	Middleground	Willie Boland	1978	Affirmed	Steve Cauthen
1951	Counterpoint	Dave Gorman	1979	Coastal	Ruben Hernandez
1952	One Count	Eddie Arcaro	1980	Temperence Hill	Eddie Maple
1953	Native Dancer	Eric Guerin	1981	Summing	George Martens
1954	High Gun	Eric Guerin	1982	Conquistador Cielo	Laffit Pincay, Jr.
1955	Nashua	Eddie Arcaro	1983	Caveat	Laffit Pincay, Jr.

Soccer

Soccer teams from 24 nations compete in the World Cup championship every four years. Member nations of the Fédération Internationale de Football Association (FIFA) play in qualifying rounds to determine which teams will compete for the World Cup title.

World Cup finals

Date	Game	Location	Date	Game	Location
1930	Uruguay 4, Argentina 2	(in Montevideo, Uruguay)	1962	Brazil 3, Czechoslovakia 1	(in Santiago, Chile)
1934	Italy 2, Czechoslovakia 1	(in Rome)	1966	England 4, West Germany 2	(in London)
1938	Italy 4, Hungary 2	(in Paris)	1970	Brazil 4, Italy 1	(in Mexico City)
1950	Uruguay 2, Brazil 1	(in Rio de Janeiro, Brazil)	1974	West Germany 2, The Netherlands 1	(in Munich, W. Germany)
1954	West Germany 3, Hungary 2	(in Bern, Switzerland)	1978	Argentina 3, The Netherlands 1	(in Buenos Aires, Argentina)
1958	Brazil 5, Sweden 2	(in Stockholm, Sweden)	1982	Italy 3, West Germany 1	(in Madrid, Spain)

Tennis

All-England (Wimbledon) Championships

The All-England Championships are held annually in the London suburb of Wimbledon. Men's competition began in 1877, and women's competition in 1884. This table lists the Wimbledon singles champions since 1920.

Year	Winner	Country
Men's Singles		
1920	Bill Tilden	United States
1921	Bill Tilden	United States
1922	Gerald Patterson	Australia
1923	Bill Johnston	United States
1924	Jean Borotra	France
1925	René Lacoste	France
1926	Jean Borotra	France
1927	Henri Cochet	France
1928	René Lacoste	France
1929	Henri Cochet	France
1930	Bill Tilden	United States
1931	Sid Wood	United States
1932	Ellsworth Vines	United States
1933	Jack Crawford	Australia
1934	Fred Perry	Great Britain
1935	Fred Perry	Great Britain
1936	Fred Perry	Great Britain
1937	Don Budge	United States
1938	Don Budge	United States
1939	Bobby Riggs	United States
1940–45	No competition	
1946	Yvon Petra	France
1947	Jack Kramer	United States
1948	Bob Falkenburg	United States
1949	Ted Schroeder	United States
1950	Budge Patty	United States
1951	Dick Savitt	United States
1952	Frank Sedgman	Australia
1953	Vic Seixas	United States
1954	Jaroslav Drobny	Egypt
1955	Tony Trabert	United States
1956	Lew Hoad	Australia
1957	Lew Hoad	Australia
1958	Ashley Cooper	Australia
1959	Alex Olmedo	United States
1960	Neale Fraser	Australia
1961	Rod Laver	Australia
1962	Rod Laver	Australia
1963	Chuck McKinley	United States
1964	Roy Emerson	Australia
1965	Roy Emerson	Australia
1966	Manuel Santana	Spain
1967	John Newcombe	Australia
1968	Rod Laver	Australia
1969	Rod Laver	Australia
1970	John Newcombe	Australia
1971	John Newcombe	Australia

Year	Winner	Country
1972	Stan Smith	United States
1973	Jan Kodes	Czechoslovakia
1974	Jimmy Connors	United States
1975	Arthur Ashe	United States
1976	Bjorn Borg	Sweden
1977	Bjorn Borg	Sweden
1978	Bjorn Borg	Sweden
1979	Bjorn Borg	Sweden
1980	Bjorn Borg	Sweden
1981	John McEnroe	United States
1982	Jimmy Connors	United States
1983	John McEnroe	United States
Women's Singles		
1920	Suzanne Lenglen	France
1921	Suzanne Lenglen	France
1922	Suzanne Lenglen	France
1923	Suzanne Lenglen	France
1924	Kitty McKane	Great Britain
1925	Suzanne Lenglen	France
1926	Kitty McKane Godfree	Great Britain
1927	Helen Wills	United States
1928	Helen Wills	United States
1929	Helen Wills	United States
1930	Helen Wills Moody	United States
1931	Cilly Aussem	Germany
1932	Helen Wills Moody	United States
1933	Helen Wills Moody	United States
1934	Dorothy Round	Great Britain
1935	Helen Wills Moody	United States
1936	Helen Hull Jacobs	United States
1937	Dorothy Round	Great Britain
1938	Helen Wills Moody	United States
1939	Alice Marble	United States
1940–45	No competition	
1946	Pauline Betz	United States
1947	Margaret Osborne	United States
1948	Louise Brough	United States
1949	Louise Brough	United States
1950	Louise Brough	United States
1951	Doris Hart	United States
1952	Maureen Connolly	United States
1953	Maureen Connolly	United States
1954	Maureen Connolly	United States
1955	Louise Brough	United States
1956	Shirley Fry	United States
1957	Althea Gibson	United States
1958	Althea Gibson	United States
1959	Maria Bueno	Brazil

Year	Winner	Country	Year	Winner	Country
1960	Maria Bueno	Brazil	1972	Billie Jean King	United States
1961	Angela Mortimer	Great Britain	1973	Billie Jean King	United States
1962	Karen Hantze Susman	United States	1974	Chris Evert	United States
1963	Margaret Smith	Australia	1975	Billie Jean King	United States
1964	Maria Bueno	Brazil	1976	Chris Evert	United States
1965	Margaret Smith	Australia	1977	Virginia Wade	Great Britain
1966	Billie Jean King	United States	1978	Martina Navratilova	United States
1967	Billie Jean King	United States	1979	Martina Navratilova	United States
1968	Billie Jean King	United States	1980	Evonne Goolagong	Australia
1969	Ann Haydon Jones	Great Britain	1981	Chris Evert Lloyd	United States
1970	Margaret Smith Court	Australia	1982	Martina Navratilova	United States
1971	Evonne Goolagong	Australia	1983	Martina Navratilova	United States

United States Championships

The United States Championships are held annually in Flushing Meadows, N.Y. Men's competition began in 1881, and women's competition in 1887. This table lists the U.S. singles champions since 1920.

Year	Winner	Country	Year	Winner	Country
Men's Singles			1953	Tony Trabert	United States
			1954	Vic Seixas	United States
1920	Bill Tilden	United States	1955	Tony Trabert	United States
1921	Bill Tilden	United States	1956	Ken Rosewall	Australia
1922	Bill Tilden	United States	1957	Mal Anderson	Australia
1923	Bill Tilden	United States	1958	Ashley Cooper	Australia
1924	Bill Tilden	United States	1959	Neale Fraser	Australia
1925	Bill Tilden	United States	1960	Neale Fraser	Australia
1926	René Lacoste	France	1961	Roy Emerson	Australia
1927	René Lacoste	France	1962	Rod Laver	Australia
1928	Henri Cochet	France	1963	Rafael Osuna	Mexico
1929	Bill Tilden	United States	1964	Roy Emerson	Australia
1930	John Doeg	United States	1965	Manuel Santana	Spain
1931	Ellsworth Vines	United States	1966	Fred Stolle	Australia
1932	Ellsworth Vines	United States	1967	John Newcombe	Australia
1933	Fred Perry	Great Britain	1968	Arthur Ashe	United States
1934	Fred Perry	Great Britain	1969	Rod Laver	Australia
1935	Wilmer Allison	United States	1970	Ken Rosewall	Australia
1936	Fred Perry	Great Britain	1971	Stan Smith	United States
1937	Don Budge	United States	1972	Ilie Nastase	Romania
1938	Don Budge	United States	1973	John Newcombe	Australia
1939	Bobby Riggs	United States	1974	Jimmy Connors	United States
1940	Don McNeill	United States	1975	Manuel Orantes	Spain
1941	Bobby Riggs	United States	1976	Jimmy Connors	United States
1942	Ted Schroeder	United States	1977	Guillermo Vilas	Argentina
1943	Joe Hunt	United States	1978	Jimmy Connors	United States
1944	Frank Parker	United States	1979	John McEnroe	United States
1945	Frank Parker	United States	1980	John McEnroe	United States
1946	Jack Kramer	United States	1981	John McEnroe	United States
1947	Jack Kramer	United States	1982	Jimmy Connors	United States
1948	Pancho Gonzales	United States			
1949	Pancho Gonzales	United States	**Women's Singles**		
1950	Art Larsen	United States			
1951	Frank Sedgman	Australia	1920	Malla Bjurstedt Mallory	United States
1952	Frank Sedgman	Australia	1921	Molla Bjurstedt Mallory	United States

Year	Winner	Country	Year	Winner	Country
1922	Molla Bjurstedt Mallory	United States	1953	Maureen Connolly	United States
1923	Helen Wills	United States	1954	Doris Hart	United States
1924	Helen Wills	United States	1955	Doris Hart	United States
1925	Helen Wills	United States	1956	Shirley Fry	United States
1926	Molla Bjurstedt Mallory	United States	1957	Althea Gibson	United States
1927	Helen Wills	United States	1958	Althea Gibson	United States
1928	Helen Wills	United States	1959	Maria Bueno	Brazil
1929	Helen Wills	United States	1960	Darlene Hard	United States
1930	Betty Nuthall	Great Britain	1961	Darlene Hard	United States
1931	Helen Wills Moody	United States	1962	Margaret Smith	Australia
1932	Helen Hull Jacobs	United States	1963	Maria Bueno	Brazil
1933	Helen Hull Jacobs	United States	1964	Maria Bueno	Brazil
1934	Helen Hull Jacobs	United States	1965	Margaret Smith	Australia
1935	Helen Hull Jacobs	United States	1966	Maria Bueno	Brazil
1936	Alice Marble	United States	1967	Billie Jean King	United States
1937	Anita Lizana	Chile	1968	Virginia Wade	Great Britain
1938	Alice Marble	United States	1969	Margaret Smith Court	Australia
1939	Alice Marble	United States	1970	Margaret Smith Court	Australia
1940	Alice Marble	United States	1971	Billie Jean King	United States
1941	Sarah Palfrey Cooke	United States	1972	Billie Jean King	United States
1942	Pauline Betz	United States	1973	Margaret Smith Court	Australia
1943	Pauline Betz	United States	1974	Billie Jean King	United States
1944	Pauline Betz	United States	1975	Chris Evert	United States
1945	Sarah Palfrey Cooke	United States	1976	Chris Evert	United States
1946	Pauline Betz	United States	1977	Chris Evert	United States
1947	Louise Brough	United States	1978	Chris Evert	United States
1948	Margaret Osborne duPont	United States	1979	Tracy Austin	United States
1949	Margaret Osborne duPont	United States	1980	Chris Evert Lloyd	United States
1950	Margaret Osborne duPont	United States	1981	Tracy Austin	United States
1951	Maureen Connolly	United States	1982	Chris Evert Lloyd	United States
1952	Maureen Connolly	United States			

Davis Cup tournament

The Davis Cup is a silver trophy awarded annually to the nation that wins the world's men's tennis championship. Dwight F. Davis, a leading U.S. tennis player, established the competition in 1900.

Year	Winner	Runner-Up	Score	Year	Winner	Runner-Up	Score
1900	United States	Great Britain	3-0	1912	Great Britain	Australia and New Zealand	3-2
1901	No competition						
1902	United States	Great Britain	3-2	1913	United States	Great Britain	3-2
1903	Great Britain	United States	4-1	1914	Australia and New Zealand	United States	3-2
1904	Great Britain	Belgium	5-0	1915–18	No competition		
1905	Great Britain	United States	5-0	1919	Australia and New Zealand	Great Britain	4-1
1906	Great Britain	United States	5-0				
1907	Australia and New Zealand	Great Britain	3-2	1920	United States	Australia and New Zealand	5-0
1908	Australia and New Zealand	United States	3-2	1921	United States	Japan	5-0
1909	Australia and New Zealand	United States	5-0	1922	United States	Australia and New Zealand	4-1
1910	No competition			1923	United States	Australia and New Zealand	4-1
1911	Australia and New Zealand	United States	5-0	1924	United States	Australia and New Zealand	5-0

Year	Winner	Runner-Up	Score
1925	United States	France	5-0
1926	United States	France	4-1
1927	France	United States	3-2
1928	France	United States	4-1
1929	France	United States	3-2
1930	France	United States	4-1
1931	France	Great Britain	3-2
1932	France	United States	3-2
1933	Great Britain	France	3-2
1934	Great Britain	United States	4-1
1935	Great Britain	United States	5-0
1936	Great Britain	Australia	3-2
1937	United States	Great Britain	4-1
1938	United States	Australia	3-2
1939	Australia	United States	3-2
1940–45	No competition		
1946	United States	Australia	5-0
1947	United States	Australia	4-1
1948	United States	Australia	5-0
1949	United States	Australia	4-1
1950	Australia	United States	4-1
1951	Australia	United States	3-2
1952	Australia	United States	4-1
1953	Australia	United States	3-2
1954	United States	Australia	3-2

*Won by default.
†Fifth match suspended by mutual consent.

Year	Winner	Runner-Up	Score
1955	Australia	United States	5-0
1956	Australia	United States	5-0
1957	Australia	United States	3-2
1958	United States	Australia	3-2
1959	Australia	United States	3-2
1960	Australia	Italy	4-1
1961	Australia	Italy	5-0
1962	Australia	Mexico	5-0
1963	United States	Australia	3-2
1964	Australia	United States	3-2
1965	Australia	Spain	4-1
1966	Australia	India	4-1
1967	Australia	Spain	4-1
1968	United States	Australia	4-1
1969	United States	Romania	5-0
1970	United States	West Germany	5-0
1971	United States	Romania	3-2
1972	United States	Romania	3-2
1973	Australia	United States	5-0
1974	South Africa	India	*
1975	Sweden	Czechoslovakia	3-2
1976	Italy	Chile	4-1
1977	Australia	Italy	3-1†
1978	United States	Great Britain	4-1
1979	United States	Italy	5-0
1980	Czechoslovakia	Italy	4-1
1981	United States	Argentina	3-1†
1982	United States	France	4-1

Olympic Games

The Olympic Games rank as the world's largest and most popular international sports competition. Thousands of amateur athletes from all over the world compete in the Summer Games and Winter Games that make up the Olympics. Medals are awarded to the top three athletes in each event—gold for first place, silver for second, and bronze for third. The games take place every four years. The following tables show the results of the 1980 Olympic Games.

1980 Winter Olympic Games (Lake Placid, N.Y.)

Leading medal-winning nations

Nation	Gold	Silver	Bronze	Total
East Germany	9	7	7	23
Soviet Union	10	6	6	22
United States	6	4	2	12
Norway	1	3	6	10
Finland	1	5	3	9
Austria	3	2	2	7
Switzerland	1	1	3	5
West Germany	0	2	3	5
Sweden	3	0	1	4
Liechtenstein	2	2	0	4
The Netherlands	1	2	1	4

Winners, by event

Biathlon·†

Event	Winner	Nation
10 kilometers	Frank Ullrich	East Germany
20 kilometers	Anatoly Aljabiev	Soviet Union
Relay	Alikin, Tikhonov, Barnaschov, Aljabiev	Soviet Union

Bobsledding†

Event	Winner	Nation
Two-man	Schaerer, Benz	Switzerland
Four-man	Nehmer, Musiol, Germeshausen, Gerhardt	East Germany

Figure skating

Event	Winner	Nation
Men	Robin Cousins	Great Britain
Women	Anett Poetzsch	East Germany
Pairs	Irina Rodnina and Alexander Zaitsev	Soviet Union
Ice Dancing	Natalia Linichuk and Gennadi Karponosov	Soviet Union

·A combination of cross-country skiing and shooting.
†Competition limited to men only.

Ice hockey†

Event	Winner	Nation
———	United States	———

Skiing

Men

Event	Winner	Nation
Jump (70 meters)	Anton Innauer	Austria
Jump (90 meters)	Jouko Tormanen	Finland
Nordic combined	Ulrich Wehling	East Germany
Cross-country		
15 kilometers	Thomas Wassberg	Sweden
30 kilometers	Nikolai Zimyatov	Soviet Union
50 kilometers	Nikolai Zimyatov	Soviet Union
40-kilometer relay	Rochev, Bazhukov, Beliaev, Zimyatov	Soviet Union
Downhill	Leonhard Stock	Austria
Giant slalom	Ingemar Stenmark	Sweden
Slalom	Ingemar Stenmark	Sweden

Women

Event	Winner	Nation
Cross-country		
5 kilometers	Raisa Smetanina	Soviet Union
10 kilometers	Barbara Petzold	East Germany
20-kilometer relay	Rostock, Anding, Hesse, Petzold	East Germany
Downhill	Annemarie Proell-Moser	Austria
Giant slalom	Hanni Wenzel	Liechtenstein
Slalom	Hanni Wenzel	Liechtenstein

Speed skating

Men

Event	Winner	Nation
500 meters	Eric Heiden	United States
1,000 meters	Eric Heiden	United States
1,500 meters	Eric Heiden	United States
5,000 meters	Eric Heiden	United States
10,000 meters	Eric Heiden	United States

Event	Winner	Nation
Women		
500 meters	Karin Enke	East Germany
1,000 meters	Natalia Petruseva	Soviet Union
1,500 meters	Annie Borckink	The Netherlands
3,000 meters	Bjoerg Eva Jensen	Norway

Tobogganing (Luge)

Event	Winner	Nation
Single-seater (men)	Bernhard Glass	East Germany
Single-seater (women)	Vera Zozulia	Soviet Union
Two-seater (men)	Rinn, Hahn	East Germany

1980 Summer Olympic Games (Moscow)

Leading medal-winning nations

Nation	Gold	Silver	Bronze
Soviet Union	80	69	45
East Germany	47	36	43
Bulgaria	8	16	16
Hungary	7	10	15
Poland	3	14	15
Romania	6	6	13
Great Britain	5	7	9
Cuba	8	7	5
France	6	5	3
Czechoslovakia	2	3	8

Winners of team sports

Sport	Nation
Basketball (men)	Yugoslavia
Basketball (women)	Soviet Union
Field Hockey (men)	India
Field Hockey (women)	Zimbabwe
Handball (men)	East Germany
Handball (women)	Soviet Union
Soccer (men)	Czechoslovakia
Volleyball (men)	Soviet Union
Volleyball (women)	Soviet Union
Water Polo (men)	Soviet Union

Archery

Winner	Nation
Tomi Poikolainen (men)	Finland
Keto Losaberidze (women)	Soviet Union

Boxing·

Class	Winner	Nation
Light flyweight	Shamil Sabyrov	Soviet Union
Flyweight	Peter Lessov	Bulgaria
Bantamweight	Juan Hernandez	Cuba
Featherweight	Rudi Fink	East Germany
Lightweight	Angel Herrera	Cuba

·Competition limited to men only.

Class	Winner	Nation
Light welterweight	Patrizio Oliva	Italy
Welterweight	Andres Aldama	Cuba
Light middleweight	Armando Martinez	Cuba
Middleweight	Jose Gomez	Cuba
Light heavyweight	Slobodan Kacar	Yugoslavia
Heavyweight	Teofilo Stevenson	Cuba

Canoeing and kayaking

Event	Winner	Nation
Men		
500-meter kayak singles	Vladimir Parfenovich	Soviet Union
500-meter kayak tandems	Parfenovich, Chukhrai	Soviet Union
500-meter Canadian singles	Sergei Postrekhin	Soviet Union
500-meter Canadian tandems	Foltan, Vaskuti	Hungary
1,000-meter kayak singles	Rudiger Helm	East Germany
1,000-meter kayak tandems	Parfenovich, Chukhrai	Soviet Union
1,000-meter kayak fours	Helm, Olbricht, Marg, Duvigneau	East Germany
1,000-meter Canadian singles	Lubomir Lubenov	Bulgaria
1,000-meter Canadian tandems	Potzaichin, Simionov	Romania
Women		
500-meter kayak singles	Birgit Fischer	East Germany
500-meter kayak tandems	Genauss, Bischof	East Germany

Cycling

Event	Winner	Nation
Individual road race	Sergei Sukhoruchenkov	Soviet Union

227

Cycling *(cont.)*

Event	Winner	Nation
Sprint	Lutz Hesslich	East Germany
1,000-meter time trial	Lothar Thomas	East Germany
4,000-meter individual pursuit	Robert Dill-Bundi	Switzerland
4,000-meter team pursuit	Manakov, Movchan, Osokin, Petrakov	Soviet Union
100-kilometer team time trial	Kashirin, Logvin, Shelpakov, Yarkin	Soviet Union

Equestrian

Event	Winner	Nation
Three-day, team	Blinov, Salnikov, Volkov	Soviet Union
Three-day, individual	Frederico Euro Roman	Italy
Dressage, team	Kovshov, Ugryumov, Misevich	Soviet Union
Dressage, individual	Elisabeth Theurer	Austria
Prix des nation, individual	Jan Kowaiczyk	Poland
Prix des nation, team	Chukanov, Poganovsky, Asmaev	Soviet Union

Fencing

Individual Competition

Event	Winner	Nation
Foil (men)	Vladimir Smirnov	Soviet Union
Foil (women)	Pascale Trinquet	France
Epée (men)	John Harmenberg	Sweden
Sabre (men)	Viktor Krovopuskov	Soviet Union

Team Competition

Event	Winning Nation
Foil (men)	France
Foil (women)	France
Epée (men)	France
Sabre (men)	Soviet Union

Gymnastics

Event	Winner	Nation

Men

All-around	Alexandr Ditiatin	Soviet Union
Long horse vault	Nikolai Andrianov	Soviet Union
Pommel horse	Zoltan Magyar	Hungary
Horizontal bar	Stoyan Deltchev	Bulgaria

Event	Winner	Nation
Parallel bars	Alexandr Tkachyov	Soviet Union
Rings	Alexandr Ditiatin	Soviet Union
Floor exercise	Roland Bruckner	East Germany
Team		Soviet Union

Women

All-around	Yelena Davydova	Soviet Union
Balance beam	Nadia Comaneci	Romania
Uneven parallel bars	Maxi Gnauck	East Germany
Side horse vault	Natalie Shaposhnikova	Soviet Union
Floor exercise	Nelli Kim and Nadia Comaneci (tie)	Soviet Union and Romania
Team		Soviet Union

Judo·

Class	Winner	Nation
132 pounds or less	Thierry Rey	France
143 pounds or less	Nikolay Solodukhin	Soviet Union
157 pounds or less	Ezio Gamba	Italy
172 pounds or less	Shota Khabareli	Soviet Union
190 pounds or less	Juerg Roethlisberger	Switzerland
209 pounds or less	Robert Van De Walle	Belgium
209 pounds and over	Angelo Parisi	France
Open weight	Dietmar Lorenz	East Germany

Modern pentathlon· (fencing, horseback riding, pistol shooting, running, and swimming)

Individual Winner	Team Winner
Anatoly Starostin, Soviet Union	Soviet Union

Rowing

Event	Winner	Nation

Men

Single sculls	Pertti Karppinen	Finland
Double sculls	Dreipke, Kroppelien	East Germany
Four sculls	Dundr, Bunk, Heppner, Winter	East Germany
Pairs without coxswain	Landvoigt, Landvoigt	East Germany
Pairs with coxswain	Jahrling, Ulrich, Spohr	East Germany
Fours without coxswain	Thiele, Decker, Semmler, Brietzke	East Germany

*Competition limited to men only.

Event	Winner	Nation
Fours with coxswain	Wendisch, Diessner, Diessner, Dohn, Gregor	East Germany
Eights with coxswain	Krauss, Kope, Kons, Friedrich, Doberschutz, Karnatz, Duhring, Hoing, Ludwig	East Germany

Women

Single sculls	Sanda Toma	Romania
Double sculls	Khloptseva, Popova	Soviet Union
Four sculls with coxswain	Reinhardt, Ploch, Lau, Zobelt, Buhr	East Germany
Pairs without coxswain	Steindorf, Klier	East Germany
Fours with coxswain	Kapheim, Frohlich, Noack, Saalfeld, Wenzel	East Germany

Event	Winner	Nation
Eights with coxswain	Boesler, Neisser, Kopke, Schutz, Kuhn, Richter, Sandig, Metze, Wilke	East Germany

Shooting

Event	Winner	Nation
Skeet	Hans Rasmussen	Denmark
Trapshooting	Luciano Giovannetti	Italy
Free pistol	Alexandr Melentev	Soviet Union
Rapid-fire pistol	Corneliu Ion	Romania
Small bore rifle—prone	Karoly Varga	Hungary
Small bore rifle—three positions	Viktor Vlasov	Soviet Union
Running game target	Igor Sokolov	Soviet Union

Swimming and diving

Event	Winner	Nation	Time

Men

Event	Winner	Nation	Time
100-meter freestyle	Jorg Woithe	East Germany	50.40 s.
200-meter freestyle	Sergei Kopliakov	Soviet Union	1 m. 49.81 s†
400-meter freestyle	Vladimir Salnikov	Soviet Union	3 m. 51.31 s†
1,500-meter freestyle	Vladimir Salnikov	Soviet Union	14 m. 58.27 s.†
100-meter backstroke	Bengt Baron	Sweden	56.53 s.
200-meter backstroke	Sandor Wlador	Hungary	2 m. 01.93 s.
100-meter breaststroke	Duncan Goodhew	Great Britain	1 m. 03.34 s.
200-meter breaststroke	Robertas Zulpa	Soviet Union	2 m. 15.85 s.
100-meter butterfly	Par Arvidsson	Sweden	54.92 s.
200-meter butterfly	Sergei Fesenko	Soviet Union	1 m. 59.76 s.
400-meter medley	Alexandr Sidorenko	Soviet Union	4 m. 22.89 s.†
400-meter medley relay	Kerry, Evans, Tonelli, Brooks	Australia	3 m. 45.70 s.
800-meter freestyle relay	Kapliakov, Salnikov, Stukolkin, Krylov	Soviet Union	7 m. 23.50 s.
Platform diving	Falk Hoffmann	East Germany	
Springboard diving	Alexandr Portnov	Soviet Union	

Women

Event	Winner	Nation	Time
100-meter freestyle	Barbara Krause	East Germany	54.79 s.†
200-meter freestyle	Barbara Krause	East Germany	1 m. 58.33 s.†
400-meter freestyle	Ines Diers	East Germany	4 m. 08.76 s.†
800-meter freestyle	Michelle Ford	Australia	8 m. 28.90 s.†
100-meter backstroke	Rica Reinisch	East Germany	1 m. 00.86 s.†
200-meter backstroke	Rica Reinisch	East Germany	2 m. 11.77 s.†
100-meter breaststroke	Ute Geweniger	East Germany	1 m. 10.11 s.†
200-meter breaststroke	Lina Kachushite	Soviet Union	2 m. 29.54 s.†
100-meter butterfly	Caren Metschuck	East Germany	1 m. 00.42 s.
200-meter butterfly	Ines Geissler	East Germany	2 m. 10.44 s.†
400-meter medley	Petra Schneider	East Germany	4 m. 36.29 s.†
400-meter freestyle relay	Krause, Metschuck, Diers, Hulsenbeck	East Germany	3 m. 42.71 s.†
400-meter medley relay	Reinisch, Geweniger, Pollack, Metschuck	East Germany	4 m. 06.67 s.†
Platform diving	Martina Jaschke	East Germany	
Springboard diving	Irinia Kalinina	Soviet Union	

†Olympic record.

229

Track and field

Event	Winner	Nation	Time or Distance
Men			
100 meters	Allan Wells	Great Britain	10.25 s.
200 meters	Pietro Mennea	Italy	20.19 s.
400 meters	Viktor Markin	Soviet Union	44.60 s.
800 meters	Steve Ovett	Great Britain	1 m. 45.40 s.
1,500 meters	Sebastian Coe	Great Britain	3 m. 38.40 s.
5,000 meters	Miruts Yifter	Ethiopia	13 m. 21.00 s.
10,000 meters	Miruts Yifter	Ethiopia	27 m. 42.70 s.
110-meter hurdles	Thomas Munkelt	East Germany	13.39 s.
400-meter hurdles	Volker Beck	East Germany	48.70 s.
3,000-meter steeplechase	Bronislaw Malinowski	Poland	8 m. 09.70 s.
Marathon	Waldemar Cierpinski	East Germany	2 h. 11 m. .03 s.
400-meter relay	Muravyov, Sidorov, Aksinin, Prokofev	Soviet Union	38.26 s.
1,600-meter relay	Valiulis, Linge, Chernetsky, Markin	Soviet Union	3 m. 01.10 s.
20-kilometer walk	Maurizio Damilano	Italy	1 h. 23 m. 35.50 s.
50-kilometer walk	Hartwig Gauder	East Germany	3 h. 49 m. 24.00 s.
High jump	Gerd Wessig	East Germany	7 ft. 8¾ in. (2.36 m)†
Long jump	Lutz Dombrowski	East Germany	28 ft. ¼ in. (8.54 m)
Triple jump	Jaak Uudmae	Soviet Union	56 ft. 11 in. (17.35 m)
Pole vault	Wladyslaw Kozakiewicz	Poland	18 ft. 11½ in. (5.78 m)†
Discus	Viktor Rasshchupkin	Soviet Union	218 ft. 7 in. (66.62 m)
Javelin	Dainis Kula	Soviet Union	299 ft. 2 in. (91.20 m)
Shot-put	Vladimir Kiselyov	Soviet Union	70 ft. ½ in. (21.35 m)†
Hammer	Yuri Sedykh	Soviet Union	268 ft. 4 in. (81.79 m)†
Decathlon	Daley Thompson	Great Britain	8,495 pts.
Women			
100 meters	Ludmila Kondrateva	Soviet Union	11.06 s.
200 meters	Barbel Wockel	East Germany	22.03 s.†
400 meters	Marita Koch	East Germany	48.88 s.†
800 meters	Nadezhda Olizarenko	Soviet Union	1 m. 53.50 s.†
1,500 meters	Tatyana Kazankina	Soviet Union	3 m. 56.60 s.†
100-meter hurdles	Vera Komisova	Soviet Union	12.56 s.†
400-meter relay	Muller, Wockel, Auerswald, Gohr	East Germany	41.60 s.†
1,600-meter relay	Prorochenko, Goistchik, Zyuskova, Nazarova	Soviet Union	3 m. 20.20 s.
High jump	Sara Simeoni	Italy	6 ft. 5½ in. (1.97 m)†
Long jump	Tatiana Kolpakova	Soviet Union	23 ft. 2 in. (7.06 m)†
Discus	Evelin Jahl	East Germany	229 ft. 6 in. (69.95 m)†
Javelin	Maria Colon	Cuba	224 ft. 5 in. (68.40 m)†
Shot-put	Ilona Slupianek	East Germany	73 ft. 6¼ in. (22.41 m)†
Pentathlon	Nadezhda Tkachenko	Soviet Union	5,083 pts.†

†Olympic record.

Weight lifting*

Class	Winner	Nation	Weight
115 pounds or less	Kanybek Osmanoliev	Soviet Union	540 lbs. (245 kg)†
123 pounds or less	Daniel Nunez	Cuba	606 lbs. (275 kg)†
132 pounds or less	Viktor Mazin	Soviet Union	639 lbs. (290 kg)†
149 pounds or less	Yanko Roussev	Bulgaria	755 lbs. (343 kg)†
165 pounds or less	Assen Zlatev	Bulgaria	794 lbs. (360 kg)†
182 pounds or less	Yurik Vardanyan	Soviet Union	882 lbs. (400 kg)†
198 pounds or less	Peter Baczako	Hungary	832 lbs. (377 kg)
220 pounds or less	Ota Zaremba	Czechoslovakia	871 lbs. (395 kg)†
242 pounds or less	Leonid Taranenko	Soviet Union	931 lbs. (422 kg)†
Over 242 pounds	Sultan Rakhmanov	Soviet Union	970 lbs. (440 kg)†

*Competition limited to men only.
†Olympic record. Weight is total of two lifts.

Wrestling*

Class	Winner	Nation
Freestyle		
106 pounds or less	Claudio Pollio	Italy
115 pounds or less	Anatoly Beloglazov	Soviet Union
126 pounds or less	Sergei Beloglazov	Soviet Union
137 pounds or less	Magomedgasan Abushev	Soviet Union
149 pounds or less	Saipulla Absaidov	Soviet Union
163 pounds or less	Valentin Raitchev	Bulgaria
181 pounds or less	Ismail Abilov	Bulgaria
198 pounds or less	Sanasar Oganesyan	Soviet Union
220 pounds or less	Ilya Mate	Soviet Union
Over 220 pounds	Soslan Andlev	Soviet Union
Greco-Roman Style		
106 pounds or less	Zaksylik Ushkempirov	Soviet Union
114 pounds or less	Vakhtang Blagidze	Soviet Union
125 pounds or less	Shamil Serikov	Soviet Union
136 pounds or less	Stilianos Migiakis	Greece
150 pounds or less	Stefan Rusu	Romania
163 pounds or less	Ferenc Kocsis	Hungary
180 pounds or less	Gennady Korban	Soviet Union
198 pounds or less	Norbert Nottny	Hungary
220 pounds or less	Gheorghi Raikov	Bulgaria
Over 220 pounds	Alexandr Kolchinsky	Soviet Union

*Competition limited to men only.

Yachting

Class	Winner	Nation
Finn dinghy	Esko Rechardt	Finland
Tornado	Welter, Bjorkstrom	Brazil
470	Soares, Penido	Brazil
Soling	Jensen, Bandolowski, Hansen	Denmark
Flying Dutchman	Abascal, Noguer	Spain
Star	Mankin, Muzychenko	Soviet Union

Time zones

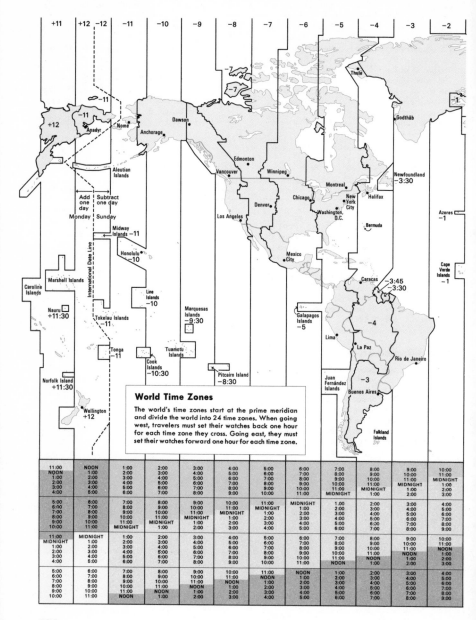

Add one day Monday | **Subtract one day** Sunday

World Time Zones

The world's time zones start at the prime meridian and divide the world into 24 time zones. When going west, travelers must set their watches back one hour for each time zone they cross. Going east, they must set their watches forward one hour for each time zone.

+11	+12 −12	−11	−10	−9	−8	−7	−6	−5	−4	−3	−2
11:00	NOON	1:00	2:00	3:00	4:00	5:00	6:00	7:00	8:00	9:00	10:00
NOON	1:00	2:00	3:00	4:00	5:00	6:00	7:00	8:00	9:00	10:00	11:00
1:00	2:00	3:00	4:00	5:00	6:00	7:00	8:00	9:00	10:00	11:00	MIDNIGHT
2:00	3:00	4:00	5:00	6:00	7:00	8:00	9:00	10:00	11:00	MIDNIGHT	1:00
3:00	4:00	5:00	6:00	7:00	8:00	9:00	10:00	11:00	MIDNIGHT	1:00	2:00
4:00	5:00	6:00	7:00	8:00	9:00	10:00	11:00	MIDNIGHT	1:00	2:00	3:00
5:00	6:00	7:00	8:00	9:00	10:00	11:00	MIDNIGHT	1:00	2:00	3:00	4:00
6:00	7:00	8:00	9:00	10:00	11:00	MIDNIGHT	1:00	2:00	3:00	4:00	5:00
7:00	8:00	9:00	10:00	11:00	MIDNIGHT	1:00	2:00	3:00	4:00	5:00	6:00
8:00	9:00	10:00	11:00	MIDNIGHT	1:00	2:00	3:00	4:00	5:00	6:00	7:00
9:00	10:00	11:00	MIDNIGHT	1:00	2:00	3:00	4:00	5:00	6:00	7:00	8:00
10:00	11:00	MIDNIGHT	1:00	2:00	3:00	4:00	5:00	6:00	7:00	8:00	9:00
11:00	MIDNIGHT	1:00	2:00	3:00	4:00	5:00	6:00	7:00	8:00	9:00	10:00
MIDNIGHT	1:00	2:00	3:00	4:00	5:00	6:00	7:00	8:00	9:00	10:00	11:00
1:00	2:00	3:00	4:00	5:00	6:00	7:00	8:00	9:00	10:00	11:00	NOON
2:00	3:00	4:00	5:00	6:00	7:00	8:00	9:00	10:00	11:00	NOON	1:00
3:00	4:00	5:00	6:00	7:00	8:00	9:00	10:00	11:00	NOON	1:00	2:00
4:00	5:00	6:00	7:00	8:00	9:00	10:00	11:00	NOON	1:00	2:00	3:00
5:00	6:00	7:00	8:00	9:00	10:00	11:00	NOON	1:00	2:00	3:00	4:00
6:00	7:00	8:00	9:00	10:00	11:00	NOON	1:00	2:00	3:00	4:00	5:00
7:00	8:00	9:00	10:00	11:00	NOON	1:00	2:00	3:00	4:00	5:00	6:00
8:00	9:00	10:00	11:00	NOON	1:00	2:00	3:00	4:00	5:00	6:00	7:00
9:00	10:00	11:00	NOON	1:00	2:00	3:00	4:00	5:00	6:00	7:00	8:00
10:00	11:00	NOON	1:00	2:00	3:00	4:00	5:00	6:00	7:00	8:00	9:00

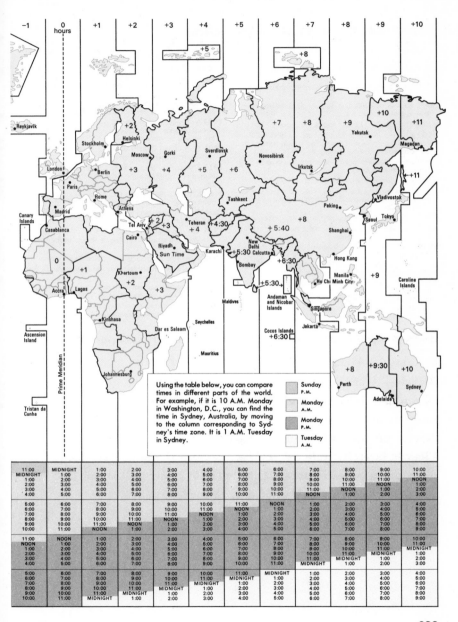

Using the table below, you can compare times in different parts of the world. For example, if it is 10 A.M. Monday in Washington, D.C., you can find the time in Sydney, Australia, by moving to the column corresponding to Sydney's time zone. It is 1 A.M. Tuesday in Sydney.

Sunday P.M.

Monday A.M.

Monday P.M.

Tuesday A.M.

11:00	MIDNIGHT	1:00	2:00	3:00	4:00	5:00	6:00	7:00	8:00	9:00	10:00
MIDNIGHT	1:00	2:00	3:00	4:00	5:00	6:00	7:00	8:00	9:00	10:00	11:00
1:00	2:00	3:00	4:00	5:00	6:00	7:00	8:00	9:00	10:00	11:00	NOON
2:00	3:00	4:00	5:00	6:00	7:00	8:00	9:00	10:00	11:00	NOON	1:00
3:00	4:00	5:00	6:00	7:00	8:00	9:00	10:00	11:00	NOON	1:00	2:00
4:00	5:00	6:00	7:00	8:00	9:00	10:00	11:00	NOON	1:00	2:00	3:00
5:00	6:00	7:00	8:00	9:00	10:00	11:00	NOON	1:00	2:00	3:00	4:00
6:00	7:00	8:00	9:00	10:00	11:00	NOON	1:00	2:00	3:00	4:00	5:00
7:00	8:00	9:00	10:00	11:00	NOON	1:00	2:00	3:00	4:00	5:00	6:00
8:00	9:00	10:00	11:00	NOON	1:00	2:00	3:00	4:00	5:00	6:00	7:00
9:00	10:00	11:00	NOON	1:00	2:00	3:00	4:00	5:00	6:00	7:00	8:00
10:00	11:00	NOON	1:00	2:00	3:00	4:00	5:00	6:00	7:00	8:00	9:00
11:00	NOON	1:00	2:00	3:00	4:00	5:00	6:00	7:00	8:00	9:00	10:00
NOON	1:00	2:00	3:00	4:00	5:00	6:00	7:00	8:00	9:00	10:00	11:00
1:00	2:00	3:00	4:00	5:00	6:00	7:00	8:00	9:00	10:00	11:00	MIDNIGHT
2:00	3:00	4:00	5:00	6:00	7:00	8:00	9:00	10:00	11:00	MIDNIGHT	1:00
3:00	4:00	5:00	6:00	7:00	8:00	9:00	10:00	11:00	MIDNIGHT	1:00	2:00
4:00	5:00	6:00	7:00	8:00	9:00	10:00	11:00	MIDNIGHT	1:00	2:00	3:00
5:00	6:00	7:00	8:00	9:00	10:00	11:00	MIDNIGHT	1:00	2:00	3:00	4:00
6:00	7:00	8:00	9:00	10:00	11:00	MIDNIGHT	1:00	2:00	3:00	4:00	5:00
7:00	8:00	9:00	10:00	11:00	MIDNIGHT	1:00	2:00	3:00	4:00	5:00	6:00
8:00	9:00	10:00	11:00	MIDNIGHT	1:00	2:00	3:00	4:00	5:00	6:00	7:00
9:00	10:00	11:00	MIDNIGHT	1:00	2:00	3:00	4:00	5:00	6:00	7:00	8:00
10:00	11:00	MIDNIGHT	1:00	2:00	3:00	4:00	5:00	6:00	7:00	8:00	9:00

Transportation

Important dates in transportation

c.5000 B.C. People begin to use donkeys and oxen as pack animals.

c.3500 B.C. The Mesopotamians build the first wheeled vehicles.

c.3200 B.C. The Egyptians invent sails and produce the first sailboats.

300's B.C.—A.D. 200's The Romans build the first extensive system of paved roads.

c.800 The rigid horse collar appears in Europe.

1100's Wagon makers in Europe build the first traveling carriages. Carriages with spring suspension systems become known as *coaches* during the 1400's.

1490's Improvements in ship construction help make long ocean voyages possible.

1660's The first city coach line opens in Paris.

c.1670 The first long-distance stagecoach line begins operating between London and Edinburgh, a distance of 392 miles (631 kilometers).

1700's British inventors develop the steam engine.

1807 The first commercially successful steamboat service begins in the United States.

1819 The American ship *Savannah* becomes the first steam-powered vessel to cross the Atlantic Ocean, though it uses its engines only about 85 hours during the 29-day voyage. The *Savannah* uses sails the rest of the trip.

1825 The first successful steam railroad begins operations in England.

1838 Great Britain's *Sirius* becomes the first ship to cross the Atlantic Ocean under steam power alone.

1869 The world's first transcontinental rail line is completed across the United States.

1880's German inventors build the first gasoline engines and use them to power bicycles. The first electric trains and streetcars appear in Europe and the United States.

1890's French engineers build the first gasoline-powered vehicles with automobile bodies. The first gasoline-powered buses and trucks are built in Germany.

1903 An airplane built by Orville and Wilbur Wright of the United States becomes the first one to lift a person into the air and fly successfully.

1905 Charles and Gabriel Voisin of France start the first airplane-manufacturing company.

1919 The world's first successful scheduled airlines begin to operate in Europe, using converted World War I bombers.

1920's Automobiles become the chief means of passenger transportation in the United States.

1926 The first successful scheduled airlines in the United States begin operations.

1934 The Burlington *Zephyr*, the first streamlined diesel-electric passenger train, begins service in the United States.

1950's The first commercial jet airliners begin service.

1959 The United States launches the *Savannah*, the first nuclear-powered merchant ship.

1964 Japanese passenger trains begin operating between Tokyo and Osaka at speeds up to 130 mph (209 kph).

1976 The first supersonic passenger airliner, the Concorde, begins service between Europe and the United States.

Average speeds of selected kinds of passenger transportation

Walking—3–4 mph (5–6 kph)

Bicycle—10 mph (16 kph)

Ocean liner *(Queen Elizabeth 2)*—33 mph (53 kph)

Intercity bus (Eastern U.S.)—52 mph (84 kph)

Hovercraft (Great Britain)—69 mph (111 kph)

Electric intercity train (*Metroliner***, Eastern U.S.)**—80 mph (130 kph)

Aerodynamic electric intercity train (*TGV***, France)**—165 mph (265 kph)

Jet airliner (Boeing 747)—560 mph (901 kph)

Air mileage for world and U.S. cities

To find the distance between two cities, trace along the horizontal line for one city to the intersection with the vertical column for the second city. All distances are given in miles.

One mile equals 1.6093 kilometers.

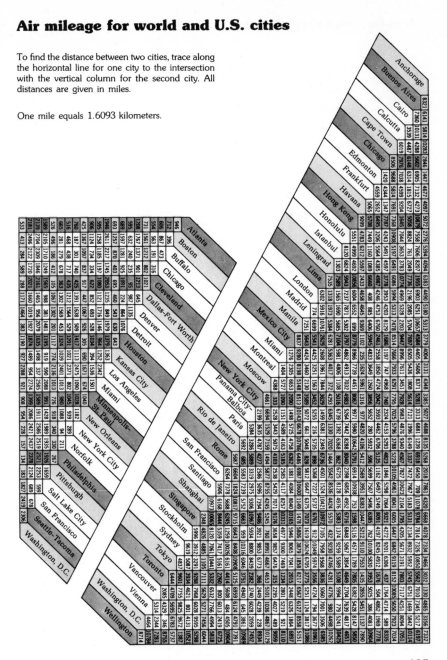

Interstate highway system

Highway distances for U.S. and Canadian cities

To figure the distance between two cities, trace down the vertical column for one city to the intersection with the horizontal row of the second city. All distances are given in miles. A mile equals 1.6093 kilometers.

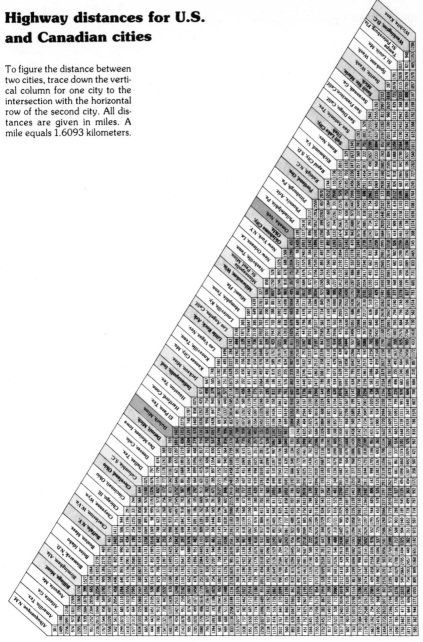

World's 25 busiest airports

Airport	Passenger departures and arrivals*	Aircraft take-offs and landings*
1. Chicago-O'Hare International	47,927,000	738,700
2. Hartsfield International (Atlanta)	41,665,000	550,400
3. Los Angeles International	34,857,000	455,100
4. Heathrow (London)	27,979,000	276,200
5. John F. Kennedy International (New York City)	26,971,000	284,200
6. San Francisco International	23,053,000	294,700
7. Dallas-Fort Worth Regional	22,782,000	409,500
8. Stapleton International (Denver)	20,542,000	359,300
9. Tokyo International	20,000,000	†
10. Miami International	19,628,000	305,600
11. La Guardia (New York City)	18,391,000	266,300
12. Osaka International	16,824,000	127,300
13. Frankfurt	16,566,000	208,100
14. Logan International (Boston)	15,196,000	271,900
15. Orly (Paris)	14,546,000	168,900
16. Honolulu International	14,530,000	218,800
17. Washington National (District of Columbia)	14,278,000	207,100
18. Toronto International	13,800,000	173,000
19. Detroit Metropolitan	11,178,000	209,300
20. Greater Pittsburgh International	11,139,000	278,800
21. Houston Intercontinental	10,901,000	236,000
22. McCarran International (Las Vegas)	10,574,000	185,500
23. Leonardo da Vinci International (Rome)	10,497,000	143,400
24. Philadelphia International	10,434,000	259,300
25. Mexico City International	10,206,000	118,700

*Includes only commercial airline traffic in 1979.
†Figure not available.
Source: International Civil Aviation Organization.

Leading merchant fleets of the world

Gross tons of ships registered in each country.*

Country	Tons	Ships
1. Liberia	74,906,000	2,281
2. Greece	42,005,000	3,710
3. Japan	40,836,000	10,422
4. Panama	27,657,000	4,461
5. Great Britain	25,419,000	2,975
6. Russia	23,493,000	7,867
7. Norway	21,675,000	2,409
8. United States	18,908,000	5,869
9. France	11,455,000	1,199
10. Italy	10,641,000	1,677

*Includes ships of 100 gross tons or more.
Source: *Lloyd's Register of Shipping, Statistical Tables, 1981.*

Leading ports of the world

Tons of dry cargo, petroleum, and petroleum products handled each year*

Port	Short tons	Metric tons
1. Ras Tanura, Saudi Arabia	416,332,000	377,690,000
2. Rotterdam	321,967,000	290,085,000
3. Khark, Iran	209,818,000	190,344,000
4. Chiba, Japan	161,073,000	146,123,000
5. Kobe, Japan	157,385,000	142,777,000
6. New Orleans	145,558,000	132,048,000
7. Yokohama	136,863,000	124,160,000
8. Marseille	119,810,000	108,690,000
9. Nagoya, Japan	118,787,000	107,762,000
10. New York City	107,889,000	97,875,000

Figures for ports in most Communist countries are not available.
*Includes imports and exports and coastwide shipments; excludes local harbor traffic and cargo transferred between ships. Figures are for 1975 for Ras Tanura, 1976 for Khark, 1977 for U.S. ports, and 1979 for all others.
Source: *Monthly Bulletin of Statistics,* May 1981, UN

Important canals of the world

Canal	Location	Length In mi.	Length In km	Width In ft.	Width In m	Depth In ft.	Depth In m
Albert	Belgium	80.8	130	335	102	16	5
Amsterdam-Rhine	Netherlands	45	72.4	246–394	75–120	14	4.2
Cape Cod	Massachusetts	17.5	28.2	450–700	137–213	32	9.8
Chesapeake and Delaware	Delaware, Maryland	14	23	450	137.1	35	10.7
Chicago Sanitary and Ship	Illinois	30	48	202	61.5	24	7.3
Corinth	Greece	3.9	6.3	81	24.6	26	8
Houston Ship Channel	Texas	50.6	81.4	300–400	91.4–121.9	36–40	11–12.2
Inner Harbor Navigation	New Orleans, La.	5.2	8.4	200	61	32	10
Kiel (Nord-Ostsee)	West Germany	61.3	98.7	336–531	102.5–162	36	11
Lake Washington Ship	Seattle, Wash.	8	13	300	91.4	30–34	9.1–10.4
Manchester Ship	England	36	58	121	37	28–30	8.5–9.1
Moscow	Russia	80	128	98	30	18	5.5
New York State Barge System	New York	524	843	45	13.7	12	3.7
North Sea	Netherlands	15	24.7	525	160	50	15.1
Panama	Panama	50.7	81.6	110–500	33.5–152.4	37–40	11.3–12.2
Sabine-Neches Waterway	Texas	52.8	85	200–800	61–243.8	30–40	9.1–12.2
Sacramento River Deepwater Ship	California	42.8	68.9	200	61	30	9.1
Saint Lawrence Seaway	Canada, New York	182	293	80–800	24.4–243.8	27	8.2
Soo (Sault Sainte Marie)	Canada	1.4	2.3	60–150	18.3–45.7	18–22	5.5–6.7
Soo (St. Marys Falls Canal and Locks)	Michigan	1.8	2.9	80–110	24.4–33.5	23.1–32	7–9.8
Suez	Egypt	117.9	189.8	741	226	64	19.5
Volga-Baltic	Russia	528	850	70	21.4	11	3.5
Volga-Don	Russia	62.8	101	59	18	11	3.5
Welland Ship	Canada	26	42	80–200	24.4–61	27	8.2
White Sea-Baltic	Russia	138	222	46	14	10	3.2

Leading countries in railroad transportation

Passenger service*

Country	In passenger-miles	In passenger-kilometers
Russia	200,205,700,000	322,200,000,000
Japan	193,778,300,000	311,856,000,000
India	108,908,900,000	175,272,000,000
France	32,189,500,000	51,804,000,000
China	28,378,000,000	45,670,000,000
Poland	27,536,700,000	44,316,000,000
Italy	24,166,400,000	38,892,000,000
West Germany	23,860,700,000	38,400,000,000
Great Britain	18,193,700,000	29,280,000,000
Romania	13,906,300,000	22,380,000,000

Freight service†

Country	In ton-miles	In ton-kilometers
Russia	2,284,976,500,000	3,336,000,000,000
United States	826,290,300,000	1,206,360,000,000
China	206,168,400,000	301,000,000,000
Canada	137,608,200,000	200,904,000,000
India	105,692,500,000	154,308,000,000
Poland	92,747,000,000	135,408,000,000
South Africa	54,913,400,000	80,172,000,000
Czechoslovakia	49,011,900,000	71,556,000,000
Romania	46,274,900,000	67,560,000,000
France	45,362,500,000	66,228,000,000

*A passenger-mile is one passenger carried one mile. A passenger-kilometer is one passenger carried one kilometer. Figures are for 1977, except for China and Romania. The figure for China is for 1959, and that for Romania is for 1975, the latest years for which data are available.
†A ton-mile is one short ton carried one mile. A ton-kilometer is one metric ton carried one kilometer. Figures are for 1977, except for China and Romania. The figure for China is for 1971, and the figure for Romania is for 1976, the latest years for which data are available.
Sources: *Monthly Bulletin of Statistics,* January 1979, UN; *The Statesman's Year-Book, 1978–79,* The Macmillan Press Ltd., London *Statistical Yearbook,* 1968 and 1977, UN.

Railroad passenger routes

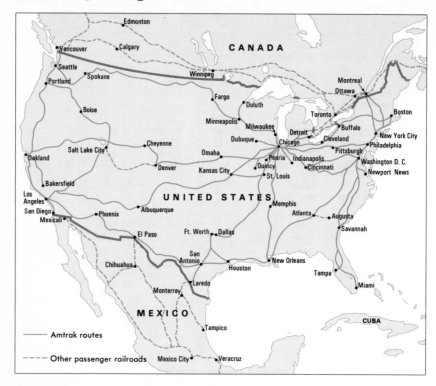

This map shows the major railroad passenger routes in North America. The National Railroad Passenger Corporation, (Amtrak), created in 1970, provides most of the passenger service in the United States. In Canada and Mexico, passenger service exists along with freight service on many minor routes not shown on the map. The cities shown are important rail passenger terminals.

United Nations

The United Nations was established on Oct. 24, 1945, with a charter membership of 50 nations. In the list below, the original members do not have dates after their names. Other nations are listed with their years of admission to the UN.

Members of the United Nations

Afghanistan (1946)
Albania (1955)
Algeria (1962)
Angola (1976)
Antigua and Barbuda (1981)
Argentina
Australia
Austria (1955)
Bahamas (1973)
Bahrain (1971)
Bangladesh (1974)
Barbados (1966)
Belgium
Belize (1981)
Benin (1960)
Bhutan (1971)
Bolivia
Botswana (1966)
Brazil
Bulgaria (1955)
Burma (1948)
Burundi (1962)
Byelorussian S.S.R.
Cambodia (1955)
Cameroon (1960)
Canada
Cape Verde (1975)
Central African Republic (1960)
Chad (1960)
Chile
China*
Colombia
Comoros (1975)
Congo (1960)
Costa Rica
Cuba
Cyprus (1960)
Czechoslovakia
Denmark
Djibouti (1977)

Dominica (1978)
Dominican Republic
Ecuador
Egypt
El Salvador
Equatorial Guinea (1968)
Ethiopia
Fiji (1970)
Finland (1955)
France
Gabon (1960)
Gambia (1965)
Germany (East) (1973)
Germany (West) (1973)
Ghana (1957)
Great Britain
Greece
Grenada (1974)
Guatemala
Guinea (1958)
Guinea-Bissau (1974)
Guyana (1966)
Haiti
Honduras
Hungary (1955)
Iceland (1946)
India
Indonesia (1950)
Iran
Iraq
Ireland (1955)
Israel (1949)
Italy (1955)
Ivory Coast (1960)
Jamaica (1962)
Japan (1956)
Jordan (1955)
Kenya (1963)
Kuwait (1963)
Laos (1955)
Lebanon

Lesotho (1966)
Liberia
Libya (1955)
Luxembourg
Madagascar (1960)
Malawi (1964)
Malaysia (1957)
Maldives (1965)
Mali (1960)
Malta (1964)
Mauritania (1961)
Mauritius (1968)
Mexico
Mongolia (1961)
Morocco (1956)
Mozambique (1975)
Nepal (1955)
Netherlands
New Zealand
Nicaragua
Niger (1960)
Nigeria (1960)
Norway
Oman (1971)
Pakistan (1947)
Panama
Papua New Guinea (1975)
Paraguay
Peru
Philippines
Poland
Portugal (1955)
Qatar (1971)
Romania (1955)
Russia (U.S.S.R.)
Rwanda (1962)
St. Lucia (1979)
St. Vincent and the Grenadines (1980)
São Tomé and Príncipe (1975)

Saudi Arabia
Senegal (1960)
Seychelles (1976)
Sierra Leone (1961)
Singapore (1965)
Solomon Islands (1978)
Somalia (1960)
South Africa
Spain (1955)
Sri Lanka (1955)
Sudan (1956)
Suriname (1975)
Swaziland (1968)
Sweden (1946)
Syria
Tanzania (1961)
Thailand (1946)
Togo (1960)
Trinidad and Tobago (1962)
Tunisia (1956)
Turkey
Uganda (1962)
Ukrainian S.S.R.
United Arab Emirates (1971)
United States
Upper Volta (1960)
Uruguay
Vanuatu (1981)
Venezuela
Vietnam (1977)
Western Samoa (1976)
Yemen (Aden) (1967)
Yemen (Sana) (1947)
Yugoslavia
Zaire (1960)
Zambia (1964)
Zimbabwe (1980)

*Nationalist China held a seat in the UN until October 1971, when the General Assembly voted to expel Nationalist China and admit Communist China.

Major organs of the United Nations

General Assembly—The only major organ in which all members are represented. Provides a forum for discussion; controls the UN budget; elects or takes part in electing members of the other major organs.

Security Council—15 members; decides what action the UN should take to settle international disputes; approves all applications for membership in the UN.

Secretariat—Secretary-general and various assistants; manages the day-to-day business of the UN and provides services for all other UN organs.

Economic and Social Council—27 member nations; works to encourage higher standards of living, better health, cultural, and educational cooperation among nations, and observance of human rights.

International Court of Justice—15 judges; deals with legal problems of the UN and helps settle disputes between countries.

Trusteeship Council—Oversees the governing of the trust territories and works to help the territories become self-governing or independent.

Selected other organs and committees of the United Nations

United Nations Children's Fund (UNICEF)—Provides aid for child development and care, job training, and family planning.

Office of the United Nations High Commissioner for Refugees—Protects the rights of refugees in foreign countries.

United Nations Environment Program (UNEP)—Encourages international cooperation to fight pollution and preserve the earth's natural resources.

United Nations Development Program (UNDP)—Helps nations make studies of their unused natural resources and helps people learn the skills needed to develop the resources.

United Nations Industrial Development Organization (UNIDO)—Encourages industrial development in developing countries.

United Nations Relief and Works Agency for Palestine Refugees in the Middle East (UNRWA)—Provides food, shelter, medical care, and other services to Palestinian refugees.

United Nations Conference on Trade and Development (UNCTAD)—Works to encourage international trade, especially between developed and developing nations.

United Nations University (UNU)—Promotes joint study and exchange of knowledge among cooperating institutions and scholars to deal with such issues as world hunger and the use of natural resources.

World Food Council—Coordinates delivery of food to developing nations and accumulates world food reserves for use in time of famine.

Specialized agencies of the United Nations

Food and Agriculture Organization of the United Nations (FAO)—Helps nations improve the production of farms, forests, and fishing waters.

Inter-Governmental Maritime Consultative Organization (IMCO)—Encourages cooperation in shipping practices and regulations.

International Civil Aviation Organization (ICAO)—Works for greater safety in air service and for standard international flying regulations.

International Development Association (IDA)—Works with the World Bank. It lends money on easier terms than does the World Bank or the International Finance Corporation.

International Finance Corporation (IFC)—Works with the World Bank. It encourages smaller, private developments. The World Bank mostly lends money for large governmental projects.

International Fund for Agricultural Development (IFAD)—Helps finance projects to increase food production in developing countries.

International Labor Organization (ILO)—Helps improve working and living conditions throughout the world.

International Monetary Fund (IMF)—Helps adjust differences between the money systems used by various countries, making it easier for nations to trade with one another.

International Telecommunication Union (ITU)—Helps nations cooperate to solve problems dealing with radio, telephone, telegraph, and satellite communications.

UNESCO (United Nations Educational, Scientific and Cultural Organization)—Encourages educational, scientific, and cultural progress to increase understanding among nations.

Universal Postal Union (UPU)—Works for international cooperation in the delivery of mail.

World Bank—Officially called the International Bank for Reconstruction and Development (IBRD). It lends money to help countries with such projects as dams, irrigation works, power plants, and railroads.

World Health Organization (WHO)—The world's principal agency for dealing with health problems.

World Intellectual Property Organization (WIPO)—Works for international cooperation to protect artistic and literary works, inventions, and trademarks against copying.

World Meteorological Organization (WMO)—Encourages nations to cooperate in weather forecasting.

The United Nations system

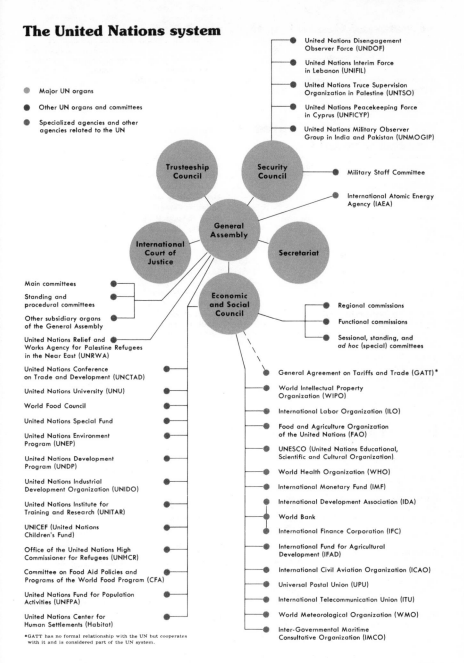

- Major UN organs
- Other UN organs and committees
- Specialized agencies and other agencies related to the UN

United Nations Disengagement Observer Force (UNDOF)

United Nations Interim Force in Lebanon (UNIFIL)

United Nations Truce Supervision Organization in Palestine (UNTSO)

United Nations Peacekeeping Force in Cyprus (UNFICYP)

United Nations Military Observer Group in India and Pakistan (UNMOGIP)

Trusteeship Council

Security Council

General Assembly

International Court of Justice

Secretariat

Economic and Social Council

Military Staff Committee

International Atomic Energy Agency (IAEA)

Regional commissions

Functional commissions

Sessional, standing, and ad hoc (special) committees

Main committees

Standing and procedural committees

Other subsidiary organs of the General Assembly

United Nations Relief and Works Agency for Palestine Refugees in the Near East (UNRWA)

United Nations Conference on Trade and Development (UNCTAD)

United Nations University (UNU)

World Food Council

United Nations Special Fund

United Nations Environment Program (UNEP)

United Nations Development Program (UNDP)

United Nations Industrial Development Organization (UNIDO)

United Nations Institute for Training and Research (UNITAR)

UNICEF (United Nations Children's Fund)

Office of the United Nations High Commissioner for Refugees (UNHCR)

Committee on Food Aid Policies and Programs of the World Food Program (CFA)

United Nations Fund for Population Activities (UNFPA)

United Nations Center for Human Settlements (Habitat)

General Agreement on Tariffs and Trade (GATT)*

World Intellectual Property Organization (WIPO)

International Labor Organization (ILO)

Food and Agriculture Organization of the United Nations (FAO)

UNESCO (United Nations Educational, Scientific and Cultural Organization)

World Health Organization (WHO)

International Monetary Fund (IMF)

International Development Association (IDA)

World Bank

International Finance Corporation (IFC)

International Fund for Agricultural Development (IFAD)

International Civil Aviation Organization (ICAO)

Universal Postal Union (UPU)

International Telecommunication Union (ITU)

World Meteorological Organization (WMO)

Inter-Governmental Maritime Consultative Organization (IMCO)

*GATT has no formal relationship with the UN but cooperates with it and is considered part of the UN system.

Secretaries-General of the United Nations

Name	Country	Dates served	Name	Country	Dates served
Trygve Lie	Norway	1946–1953	Kurt Waldheim	Austria	1972–1982
Dag Hammarskjöld	Sweden	1953–1961	Javier Pérez de Cuéllar	Peru	1982–
U Thant	Burma	1961–1972			

Presidents of the United Nations General Assembly

Name	Country	Dates	Name	Country	Dates
Paul-Henri Spaak	Belgium	1946	Carlos Sosa Rodríguez	Venezuela	1963
Oswaldo Aranha	Brazil	1947	Alex Quaison-Sackey	Ghana	1964–65
José Arce	Argentina	1948	Amintore Fanfani	Italy	1965
Herbert V. Evatt	Australia	1948–49	Abdul Rahman Pazhwak	Afghanistan	1966–67
Carlos P. Romulo	Philippines	1949	Corneliu Manescu	Romania	1967–68
Nasrollah Entezam	Iran	1950–51	Emilio Arenales	Guatemala	1968
Luis Padilla Nervo	Mexico	1951–52	Angie E. Brooks	Liberia	1969
Lester B. Pearson	Canada	1952–53	Edvard Hambro	Norway	1970–71
Mme. Vijaya Pandit	India	1953–54	Adam Malik	Indonesia	1971–72
Eelco N. van Kleffens	Netherlands	1954	Stanisław Trepczyński	Poland	1972–73
José Maza	Chile	1955	Leopoldo Benites	Ecuador	1973–74
Rudecindo Ortega	Chile	1956	Abdelaziz Bouteflika	Algeria	1974–75
Prince Wan Waithayakon	Thailand	1956–57	Gaston Thorn	Luxembourg	1975–76
Sir Leslie Munro	New Zealand	1957–58	Hamilton Shirley Amerasinghe	Sri Lanka	1976–77
Charles Malik	Lebanon	1958–59	Lazar Mojsov	Yugoslavia	1977–78
Victor Andrés Belaúnde	Peru	1959–60	Indalecio Lievano Aguirre	Colombia	1978–79
Frederick H. Boland	Ireland	1960–61	Salim A. Salim	Tanzania	1979–80
Mongi Slim	Tunisia	1961–62	Rüdiger von Wechmar	West Germany	1980–81
Sir Muhammad Zafrulla Khan	Pakistan	1962–63	Ismat T. Kittani	Iraq	1981–82

Present and former United Nations trust territories

This table lists the 11 original trust areas, their trustees, and the dates that some have achieved independence.

Name	Trustee	Status	Name	Trustee	Status
Cameroons	Great Britain	Independent as parts of Cameroon and Nigeria, 1961	Ruanda-Urundi	Belgium	Independent as Rwanda and Burundi, 1962
Cameroons	France	Independent as Cameroon, 1960	Somaliland	Italy	Independent as Somalia, 1960
Nauru	Australia	Independent, 1968	Tanganyika	Great Britain	Independent, 1961
New Guinea	Australia	Independent as part of Papua New Guinea, 1975	Togoland	France	Independent as Togo, 1960
			Togoland	Great Britain	Independent as part of Ghana, 1957
Pacific Islands (Carolines, Marianas except Guam, Marshalls)	United States	Strategic Area Trusteeship (under the Security Council)	Western Samoa	New Zealand	Independent, 1962

United States

Facts in brief

Capital: Washington, D.C.

Form of government: Republic.

Area: 3,618,465 sq. mi. (9,371,781 km²), including 74,389 sq. mi. (192,667 km²) of inland water but excluding 60,788 sq. mi. (157,440 km²) of Great Lakes and Lake Saint Clair and 13,942 sq. mi. (36,110 km²) of coastal water. *Greatest distances excluding Alaska and Hawaii*—east-west, 2,807 mi. (4,517 km); north-south, 1,598 mi. (2,572 km). *Greatest distances in Alaska*—north-south, about 1,200 mi. (1,930 km); east-west, about 2,200 mi. (3,540 km). *Greatest distance in Hawaii*—north-west-southeast, about 1,610 mi. (2,591 km). *Extreme points including Alaska and Hawaii*—northernmost, Point Barrow, Alaska; southernmost, Ka Lae, Hawaii; easternmost, West Quoddy Head, Me.; westernmost, Cape Wrangell, Attu Island, Alaska. *Coastline*—4,993 mi. (8,035 km), excluding Alaska and Hawaii; 12,383 mi. (19,929 km), including Alaska and Hawaii.

Elevation: *Highest*—Mount McKinley in Alaska, 20,320 ft. (6,194 m) above sea level. *Lowest*—In Death Valley in California, 282 ft. (86 m) below sea level.

Physical features: *Longest river*—Mississippi, 2,348 mi. (3,779 km). *Largest lake within the United States*—Michigan, 22,300 sq. mi. (57,757 km²). *Largest island*—island of Hawaii, 4,038 sq. mi. (10,458 km²).

Climate: Winters are mildest in the south and far west and coldest in Alaska. Elsewhere, average January temperatures generally increase from north to south, ranging from 0° to 15° F. (−18° to −9° C) in some northern and mountain areas and exceeding 60° F. (16° C) in Hawaii, southern Florida, and southern Texas. Average July temperatures range from 60° to 75° F. (16° to 24° C) in much of the north and west, and from 75° to 90° F. (24° to 32° C)

in most of the rest of the country. Summers are cooler in Alaska and some mountain areas and hotter in the southwestern deserts. Average annual precipitation generally increases from west to east. But the greatest amount falls in parts of the Pacific coast area, Alaska, and Hawaii. *Lowest average annual temperature*—9° F. (−3° C) in Barrow, Alaska. *Highest average annual temperature*—78.2° F (25.7° C) in Death Valley, Calif. *Lowest average annual precipitation*—less than 2 inches (5 centimeters) in Death Valley, Calif. *Highest average annual precipitation*—about 460 inches (1,170 centimeters) in Mount Waialeale, Hawaii. (See also "Weather.")

Population: *Estimated 1983 population*—233,450,000; density, 65 persons per sq. mi. (25 per km²). Distribution, 74 per cent urban, 26 per cent rural. *1980 Census*—226,504,825. *Estimated 1988 population*—248,561,000.

Chief products: *Agriculture*—beef cattle, milk, corn, soybeans, hogs, wheat, cotton. *Fishing industry*—shrimp, salmon, crabs. *Manufacturing*—nonelectric machinery; transportation equipment; chemicals; food products; electric machinery and equipment; fabricated metal products; primary metals; printed materials; paper products; rubber and plastics products; clothing. *Mining*—petroleum, natural gas, coal.

Flag: Adopted June 14, 1777. (For illustrations, see page 191. See also "Flags.")

Motto: *In God We Trust,* adopted July 30, 1956.

National anthem: "The Star-Spangled Banner," adopted March 3, 1931.

Bird: Bald eagle, adopted June 20, 1782.

Money: *Basic unit*—dollar.

Main outlying areas of the United States

Name	Acquired	Status	Name	Acquired	Status
American Samoa	1900	Unorganized unincorporated territory	**Palmyra Island**	1898	Unincorporated territory
Guam	1898	Organized unincorporated territory	**Puerto Rico**	1898	Commonwealth
Howland, Baker, and Jarvis Islands	1856	Unincorporated territory	**Trust Territory of the Pacific Islands**	1947	UN trust territory (U.S. administration)
Johnston Island and Sand Island	1858	Unincorporated territory	**Virgin Islands of the United States**	1917	Organized unincorporated territory
Kingman Reef	1922	Unincorporated territory	**Wake Island**	1898	Unincorporated territory
Midway Island	1867	Unincorporated territory			

Population of the United States

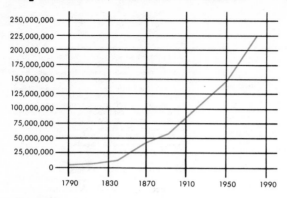

Census year	Population
1790	3,929,214
1800	5,308,483
1810	7,239,881
1820	9,638,453
1830	12,866,020
1840	17,069,453
1850	23,191,876
1860	31,443,321
1870	39,818,449
1880	50,155,783
1890	62,974,714
1900	75,994,575
1910	91,972,266
1920	105,710,620
1930	122,775,046
1940	131,669,275
1950	150,697,361
1960	179,323,175
1970	203,235,298
1980	226,504,825

Urban-rural population

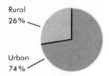

Rural 26%
Urban 74%

Racial groups

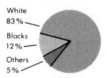

White 83%
Blacks 12%
Others 5%

Age groups by years

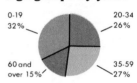

0-19 32%
20-34 26%
35-59 27%
60 and over 15%

The pie charts above show the urban-rural, racial, and age-group breakdowns of the U.S. population in 1980. Nearly 75 per cent of the people live in urban areas. Whites account for about 83 per cent of the population, and blacks for about 12 per cent. Persons under 20 make up the largest age group. This group accounts for about 32 per cent of the country's population.

50 largest cities in the United States

1. **New York City** 7,071,030
2. **Chicago** 3,005,072
3. **Los Angeles** 2,966,763
4. **Philadelphia** 1,688,210
5. **Houston** 1,594,086
6. **Detroit** 1,203,399
7. **Dallas** 904,078
8. **San Diego** 875,504
9. **Baltimore** 786,775
10. **San Antonio** 785,410
11. **Phoenix** 764,911
12. **Indianapolis** 700,807
13. **San Francisco** 678,974
14. **Memphis** 646,356
15. **Washington, D.C.** 637,651
16. **San Jose** 636,550
17. **Milwaukee** 636,212
18. **Cleveland** 573,822
19. **Columbus, O.** 564,871
20. **Boston** 562,994
21. **New Orleans** 557,482
22. **Jacksonville, Fla.** 540,898
23. **Seattle** 493,846
24. **Denver** 491,396
25. **Nashville** 455,651
26. **St. Louis** 453,085
27. **Kansas City, Mo.** 448,159
28. **El Paso** 425,259
29. **Atlanta** 425,022
30. **Pittsburgh** 423,938
31. **Oklahoma City** 403,213
32. **Cincinnati** 385,457
33. **Fort Worth** 385,141
34. **Minneapolis** 370,951
35. **Portland, Ore.** 366,383
36. **Honolulu** 365,048
37. **Long Beach** 361,334
38. **Tulsa** 360,919
39. **Buffalo** 357,870
40. **Toledo** 354,635
41. **Miami** 346,931
42. **Austin** 345,496
43. **Oakland** 339,288
44. **Albuquerque** 331,767
45. **Tucson** 330,537
46. **Newark** 329,248
47. **Charlotte** 314,447
48. **Omaha** 311,681
49. **Louisville** 298,451
50. **Birmingham** 284,413

Major waves of immigration in the United States

The United States has received more immigrants than any other nation in the world. Immigration reached its peak between 1890 and 1930, when nearly 22 million persons poured into the United States—more than the total that had arrived since colonial times. The table below lists some of the largest waves of immigration at various times in U.S. history.

Who	When	Number	Why
Irish	1840's and 1850's	About 1½ million	Famine resulting from potato crop failure
Germans	1840's to 1880's	About 4 million	Severe depression and unemployment; political unrest and failure of liberal revolutionary movement
Danes, Norwegians, and Swedes	1870's to 1900's	About 1½ million	Poverty; shortage of farmland
Poles	1880's to 1920's	About 1 million	Poverty; political repression; cholera epidemics
Jews from eastern Europe	1880's to 1920's	About 2½ million	Religious persecution
Austrians, Czechs, Hungarians, and Slovaks	1880's to 1920's	About 4 million	Poverty; overpopulation
Italians	1880's to 1920's	About 4½ million	Poverty; overpopulation
Mexicans	1910 to 1920's	About 700,000	Mexican Revolution of 1910; low wages and unemployment
	1950's to 1980's	About 1½ million	Poverty; unemployment
Cubans	1960's to 1980's	About 600,000	Take-over by Fidel Castro in 1959
Cambodians, Laotians, and Vietnamese	1970's and 1980's	About 165,000	Vietnam War (1959-1975); Communist take-overs

Regions of the United States

New England Connecticut, Maine, Massachusetts, New Hampshire, Rhode Island, Vermont

Middle Atlantic States New Jersey, New York, Pennsylvania

Southern States Alabama, Arkansas, Delaware, Florida, Georgia, Kentucky, Louisiana, Maryland, Mississippi, North Carolina, South Carolina, Tennessee, Virginia, West Virginia

Midwestern States Illinois, Indiana, Iowa, Kansas, Michigan, Minnesota, Missouri, Nebraska, North Dakota, Ohio, South Dakota, Wisconsin

Rocky Mountain States Colorado, Idaho, Montana, Nevada, Utah, Wyoming

Southwestern States *Arizona, *New Mexico, Oklahoma, Texas

Pacific Coast States California, Oregon, Washington

*Arizona and New Mexico are often grouped with the Rocky Mountain States.

The states of the United States, excluding Alaska and Hawaii, may be divided into seven major regions. The states within these regions have similarities in geography, climate, economy, traditions, and history. Regions are: (1) New England, (2) the Middle Atlantic States, (3) the Southern States, (4) the Midwestern States, (5) the Rocky Mountain States, (6) the Southwestern States, (7) the Pacific Coast States.

New England is a small region known for picturesque rural villages, many fishing harbors, and colorful autumn scenery. Manufacturing is the leading source of income, but the region also produces large amounts of dairy and poultry products. Historic sites, including many from colonial times, attract large numbers of tourists. Many New Englanders, especially in the rural north, are descendants of English Puritans who settled in the region during the 1600's. The more densely populated

(Continued on page 254)

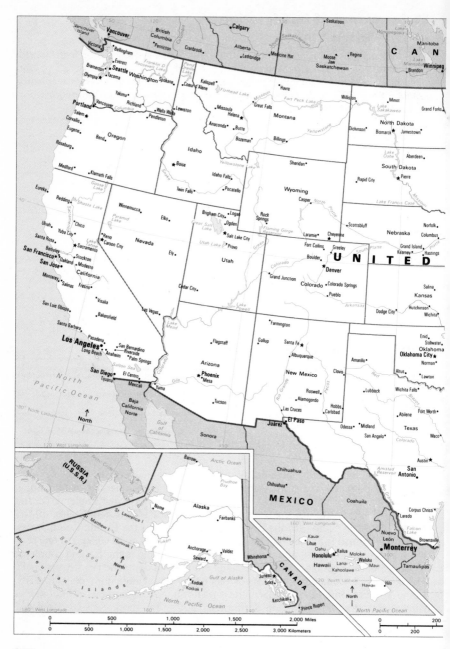

**United States
Political Map**

International boundary

State boundary

⊛ National capital

★ State capital

• Other city or town

Facts in brief about the states

State	Capital	Popular name	Area (sq. mi.)	(km²)	Rank in area	Population	Rank in pop.	Population density (sq. mi.)	(km²)
Alabama	Montgomery	Yellowhammer State	51,609	133,667	29	3,890,061	22	75	29
Alaska	Juneau	Last Frontier	589,757	1,527,464	1	400,481	50	0.7	0.3
Arizona	Phoenix	Grand Canyon State	113,909	295,023	6	2,717,866	29	24	9
Arkansas	Little Rock	Land of Opportunity	53,104	137,539	27	2,285,513	33	43	17
California	Sacramento	Golden State	158,693	411,013	3	23,668,562	1	149	58
Colorado	Denver	Centennial State	104,247	269,998	8	2,888,834	28	28	11
Connecticut	Hartford	Constitution State	5,009	12,973	48	3,107,576	25	620	239
Delaware	Dover	First State	2,057	5,328	49	595,225	47	289	112
Florida	Tallahassee	Sunshine State	58,560	151,670	22	9,739,992	7	166	64
Georgia	Atlanta	Empire State of the South	58,876	152,488	21	5,464,265	13	93	36
Hawaii	Honolulu	Aloha State	6,450	16,705	47	965,000	39	150	58
Idaho	Boise	Gem State	83,557	216,412	13	943,935	41	11	4
Illinois	Springfield	Land of Lincoln	56,400	146,075	24	11,418,461	5	202	78
Indiana	Indianapolis	Hoosier State	36,291	93,993	38	5,490,179	12	151	58
Iowa	Des Moines	Hawkeye State	56,290	145,790	25	2,913,387	27	52	20
Kansas	Topeka	Sunflower State	82,264	213,063	14	2,363,208	32	29	11
Kentucky	Frankfort	Bluegrass State	40,395	104,623	37	3,661,433	23	91	35
Louisiana	Baton Rouge	Pelican State	48,523	125,674	31	4,203,972	19	87	34
Maine	Augusta	Pine Tree State	33,215	86,026	39	1,124,660	38	34	13
Maryland	Annapolis	Old Line State	10,577	27,394	42	4,216,446	18	399	154
Massachusetts	Boston	Bay State	8,257	21,386	45	5,737,037	11	695	268
Michigan	Lansing	Wolverine State	58,216	150,779	23	9,258,344	8	159	61
Minnesota	St. Paul	Gopher State	84,068	217,735	12	4,077,148	21	48	19
Mississippi	Jackson	Magnolia State	47,716	123,584	32	2,520,638	31	53	20
Missouri	Jefferson City	Show Me State	69,686	180,486	19	4,917,444	15	71	27
Montana	Helena	Treasure State	147,138	381,086	4	786,690	44	5	2
Nebraska	Lincoln	Cornhusker State	77,227	200,017	15	1,570,006	35	20	8
Nevada	Carson City	Silver State	110,540	286,297	7	799,184	43	7	3
New Hampshire	Concord	Granite State	9,304	24,097	44	920,610	42	99	38
New Jersey	Trenton	Garden State	7,836	20,295	46	7,364,158	9	940	363

250

State bird	State flower	State tree	State song	Admitted to the Union	Order of admission	Members of Congress Senate	House
Yellowhammer	Camellia	Southern pine (Longleaf pine)	"Alabama"	1819	22	2	7
Willow ptarmigan	Forget-me-not	Sitka spruce	"Alaska's Flag"	1959	49	2	1
Cactus wren	Saguaro (Giant cactus)	Paloverde	"Arizona"	1912	48	2	5
Mockingbird	Apple blossom	Pine	"Arkansas"	1836	25	2	4
California valley quail	Golden poppy	California redwood	"I Love You, California"	1850	31	2	45
Lark bunting	Rocky Mountain columbine	Blue spruce	"Where the Columbines Grow"	1876	38	2	6
Robin	Mountain laurel	White oak	"Yankee Doodle"	1788	5	2	6
Blue hen chicken	Peach blossom	American holly	"Our Delaware"	1787	1	2	1
Mockingbird	Orange blossom	Cabbage (Sabal) palm	"Swanee River"	1845	27	2	19
Brown thrasher	Cherokee rose	Live oak	"Georgia on My Mind"	1788	4	2	10
Nene (Hawaiian goose)	Hibiscus	Kukui	"Hawaii Ponoi (Hawaii's Own)"	1959	50	2	2
Mountain bluebird	Syringa (Mock orange)	Western white pine	"Here We Have Idaho"	1890	43	2	2
Cardinal	Native violet	White Oak	"Illinois"	1818	21	2	22
Cardinal	Peony	Tulip tree, or yellow poplar	"On the Banks of the Wabash"	1816	19	2	10
Eastern goldfinch	Wild rose	Oak	"The Song of Iowa"	1846	29	2	6
Western meadow lark	Sunflower	Cottonwood	"Home on the Range"	1861	34	2	5
Kentucky cardinal	Goldenrod	Kentucky coffeetree	"My Old Kentucky Home"	1792	15	2	7
Brown pelican	Magnolia	Bald cypress	"Give Me Louisiana"; "You Are My Sunshine"	1812	18	2	8
Chickadee	White pine cone and tassel	White pine	"State of Maine Song"	1820	23	2	2
Baltimore oriole	Black-eyed Susan	White oak (Wye oak)	"Maryland, My Maryland"	1788	7	2	8
Chickadee	Arbutus	American elm	"All Hail to Massachusetts"	1788	6	2	11
Robin	Apple blossom	White pine	"Michigan, My Michigan"	1837	26	2	18
Common loon	Pink and white lady's-slipper	Norway, or red, pine	"Hail! Minnesota"	1858	32	2	8
Mockingbird	Magnolia	Magnolia	"Go Mis-sis-sip-pi"	1817	20	2	5
Bluebird	Hawthorn	Flowering dogwood	"Missouri Waltz"	1821	24	2	9
Western meadow lark	Bitterroot	Ponderosa pine	"Montana"	1889	41	2	2
Western meadow lark	Goldenrod	Cottonwood	"Beautiful Nebraska"	1867	37	2	3
Mountain bluebird	Sagebrush	Single-leaf piñon	"Home Means Nevada"	1864	36	2	2
Purple finch	Purple lilac	White birch	"Old New Hampshire"	1788	9	2	2
Eastern goldfinch	Purple violet	Red oak	None	1787	3	2	14

State	Capital	Popular name	Area (sq. mi.)	(km²)	Rank in area	Population	Rank in pop.	Population density (sq. mi.)	(km²)
New Mexico	Santa Fe	Land of Enchantment	121,666	315,113	5	1,299,968	37	11	4
New York	Albany	Empire State	49,576	128,401	30	17,557,288	2	354	137
North Carolina	Raleigh	Tar Heel State	52,586	136,197	28	5,874,429	10	112	43
North Dakota	Bismarck	Flickertail State	70,665	183,022	17	652,695	46	9	3
Ohio	Columbus	Buckeye State	41,222	106,764	35	10,797,419	6	262	101
Oklahoma	Oklahoma City	Sooner State	69,919	181,089	18	3,025,266	26	43	17
Oregon	Salem	Beaver State	96,981	251,180	10	2,632,663	30	27	10
Pennsylvania	Harrisburg	Keystone State	45,333	117,412	33	11,866,728	4	262	101
Rhode Island	Providence	Ocean State	1,214	3,144	50	947,154	40	780	301
South Carolina	Columbia	Palmetto State	31,055	80,432	40	3,119,208	24	100	39
South Dakota	Pierre	Sunshine State	77,047	199,551	16	690,178	45	9	3
Tennessee	Nashville	Volunteer State	42,244	109,411	34	4,590,750	17	109	42
Texas	Austin	Lone Star State	267,336	692,397	2	14,228,383	3	53	20
Utah	Salt Lake City	Beehive State	84,916	219,931	11	1,461,037	36	17	7
Vermont	Montpelier	Green Mountain State	9,609	24,887	43	511,456	48	53	20
Virginia	Richmond	Old Dominion	40,817	105,716	36	5,346,279	14	131	50
Washington	Olympia	Evergreen State	68,192	176,616	20	4,130,163	20	61	24
West Virginia	Charleston	Mountain State	24,181	62,628	41	1,949,644	34	81	31
Wisconsin	Madison	Badger State	56,154	145,438	26	4,705,335	16	84	32
Wyoming	Cheyenne	Equality State	97,914	253,596	9	470,816	49	5	2

State bird	State flower	State tree	State song	Admitted to the Union	Order of admission	Members of Congress Senate	House
Roadrunner	Yucca flower	Piñon, or nut pine	"O, Fair New Mexico"	1912	47	2	3
Bluebird	Rose	Sugar maple	"I Love New York"	1788	11	2	34
Cardinal	Flowering dogwood	Pine	"The Old North State"	1789	12	2	11
Western meadow lark	Wild prairie rose	American elm	"North Dakota Hymn"	1889	39	2	1
Cardinal	Scarlet carnation	Buckeye	"Beautiful Ohio"	1803	17	2	21
Scissor-tailed flycatcher	Mistletoe	Redbud	"Oklahoma!"	1907	46	2	6
Western meadow lark	Oregon grape	Douglas fir	"Oregon, My Oregon"	1859	33	2	5
Ruffed grouse	Mountain laurel	Hemlock	None	1787	2	2	23
Rhode Island Red	Violet	Red maple	"Rhode Island"	1790	13	2	2
Carolina wren	Carolina jessamine	Palmetto	"Carolina"	1788	8	2	6
Ring-necked pheasant	American pasqueflower	Black Hills spruce	"Hail, South Dakota"	1889	40	2	1
Mockingbird	Iris	Tulip poplar	"My Homeland, Tennessee"; "My Tennessee"; "Rocky Top"; "The Tennessee Waltz"; "When It's Iris Time in Tennessee"	1796	16	2	9
Mockingbird	Bluebonnet	Pecan	"Texas, Our Texas"	1845	28	2	27
Sea gull	Sego lily	Blue spruce	"Utah, We Love Thee"	1896	45	2	3
Hermit thrush	Red clover	Sugar maple	"Hail, Vermont!"	1791	14	2	1
Cardinal	Dogwood	Dogwood	"Carry Me Back to Old Virginia"	1788	10	2	10
Willow goldfinch	Coast rhododendron	Western hemlock	"Washington, My Home"	1889	42	2	8
Cardinal	Rhododendron	Sugar maple	"The West Virginia Hills"; "This is My West Virginia"; "West Virginia, My Home Sweet Home"	1863	35	2	4
Robin	Wood violet	Sugar maple	"On, Wisconsin!"	1848	30	2	9
Meadow lark	Indian paintbrush	Cottonwood	"Wyoming"	1890	44	2	1

Editor's note: Flags of the states appear on pages 188–189. See also "Abbreviations" section for postal and traditional abbreviations of state names.

(continued from page 247)

southern section has people of many backgrounds, including blacks, Irish, Italians, and French Canadians. Boston is New England's largest city.

The Middle Atlantic States form the most densely populated region of the United States. Major cities include New York City, the largest city in the United States; Philadelphia, Pittsburgh, Buffalo, and Newark. The region is a major center of international trade and manufacturing. Coal mining and related industries and farming are also important. The region's urban population has people of varied European backgrounds, as well as large groups of people of black African, Latin-American, and Asian descent. Many of the region's rural dwellers are of British descent.

The Southern States have long been known for the production of cotton, tobacco, sugar cane, and other warm-weather crops. Industrial development since the mid-1900's has made manufacturing a major economic activity as well. Tourists flock to the region's coastal beaches. The South does not have many large groups of people with varied ethnic backgrounds. Many Southerners are descended from early English, Irish, and Scottish immigrants. Blacks, descended from African slaves, form a large minority group. Baltimore is the region's largest city.

The Midwestern States have huge expanses of fertile soil, where corn, wheat, and other crops are grown. Farms in the region also produce dairy products and livestock. The Midwest has a number of large industrial cities, including Chicago, Detroit, Indianapolis, Milwaukee, and Cleveland. The Mississippi River system, the Great Lakes, and many railroads give the region an excellent transportation network. Large groups of rural Midwesterners are descendants of settlers from Germany, Great Britain, Norway, Sweden, and eastern and southern Europe. The region's urban population includes people from various European backgrounds and a large black minority group.

The Rocky Mountain States include many thinly populated wilderness areas of rugged mountains and deserts. A number of cities and towns in the region are growing rapidly, however. Denver ranks as the largest city in the Rocky Mountain region. Manufacturing is the area's chief source of income. Mining and farming are also important. Tourists come to enjoy the region's natural beauty and many ski resorts. Inhabitants of this region include persons of European descent, as well as blacks, Mexican Americans, and American Indians. Mormons form an important cultural group in this region.

The Southwestern States include vast areas of open space, much of it occupied by cattle ranches and huge fields of cotton and other crops. This region also has many of the nation's fastest growing cities, including Houston, Dallas, San Antonio, and Phoenix. Large deposits of petroleum, natural gas, and other minerals provide the region with much of its income. Refineries and petrochemical factories are major industrial employers. Many retirement communities are located in the Southwest. The region's population includes people of various European backgrounds, as well as black, Mexican-American, and American Indian minority groups.

The Pacific Coast States are known for their dense forests, rugged mountains, and dramatic coastline. Much of the nation's harvest of fruits, nuts, vegetables, and wine grapes comes from this region. The Pacific Coast States also have abundant timber, minerals, and fish. Major manufacturing centers include such cities as Los Angeles, San Diego, San Francisco, San Jose, and Seattle. Most of the people are of European ancestry. Blacks and Mexican Americans form the largest minority groups. The region also has a large number of American Indians and more persons of Asian ancestry than any other region.

Economy

The United States ranks first among the nations of the world in *gross national product (GNP)*—the total value of all the goods and services produced. The nation's GNP totaled about $2⅔ trillion in 1980. In general, Americans enjoy one of the highest standards of living in the world. (See "World.")

The U.S. economy is based largely on a *free enterprise system,* in which individuals and companies make many of their own economic decisions. Individuals and companies own the raw materials, equipment, factories, and other items needed for production, and they decide how best to use them to earn a profit. In practice, government regulations affect the operation of the free enterprise system in many ways. Examples of such regulations include anti-trust laws, job safety standards, minimum wage laws, and pollution control legislation.

Much of the strength of the U.S. economy is a result of the nation's abundant natural resources. In addition to a moderate climate, these resources include fertile soils, sufficient water, and valuable minerals, forests, and fish. Some of the best soils in the country occur in the Interior Plains and along the lower Mississippi River Valley and other smaller river valleys. Lakes, rivers, and underground deposits provide the nation's water supply. The country uses about 400 billion gallons (1,500 billion liters) of water daily, mainly to irrigate farmland and to operate manufacturing industries. Households consume only about 10 per cent of the total. The United States has large deposits of coal, iron ore, natural gas, and petroleum. Its many other important mineral resources include copper, gold, lead, nickel, phosphates, potash, silver, sulfur, and zinc. Forests cover nearly a third of the country, providing lumber, wood pulp, and other products. The annual fish catch in the United States totals about 3.9 million short tons (3.5 million metric tons).

Manufacturing is the most important economic activity in the United States. The value of U.S. manufactured goods is greater than that of any other country. The leading U.S. manufactured products are, in order of value, nonelectric machinery, transportation equipment, chemicals, food products, electric machinery and equipment, fabricated metal products, primary metals, printed materials, paper products, and rubber and plastic products. California ranks first among the states in the value of its manufactured goods, followed by New York, Ohio, Illinois, Michigan, and Pennsylvania.

The United States leads the world in farm production. The country has about 2,300,000 farms, with an average size of about 440 acres (178 hectares). On the average, a U.S. farmer produces enough to feed nearly 80 persons. This is enough to take care of the nation's food needs, with food left over for export. About a sixth of the total world food exports come from the United States. Beef cattle rank as the most valuable U.S. farm product. Other leading farm products, in order of value, include milk, corn, soybeans, hogs, wheat, and cotton.

The United States ranks as the world leader in the value of its mineral production. The chief mineral products are, in order of value, petroleum, natural gas, and coal.

Other important minerals include building stone, copper, gold, iron ore, lead, phosphate, potassium, salt, sand and gravel, silver, uranium, and zinc.

A sprawling transportation network serves all parts of the United States. The nation has about 4,000,000 miles (6,400,000 kilometers) of streets, roads, and highways, and about 348,000 miles (560,100 kilometers) of railroad track. Trucks carry nearly a fourth of the freight in the United States and railroads handle more than a third. Pipelines that carry petroleum products, crude oil, and natural gas account for nearly 25 per cent of the total freight handled in the United States. The country

U.S. gross national product

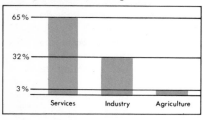

The U.S. gross national product (GNP) was $2,925,500,000,000 in 1981. The GNP is the total value of goods and services produced by a country in a year. Services include education, banking, transportation, trade, and many other economic activities. The GNP measures a nation's total economic performance and can also be used to compare the economic output and growth of countries.

*Based on gross domestic product (GDP). GDP is gross national product adjusted for net income sent or received from abroad.
†Included with Transportation.
Sources: U.S. Bureau of Economic Analysis; U.S. Bureau of Labor Statistics; U.S. Department of Agriculture.

Production and workers by economic activities

| | Per cent of GDP* produced | Employed workers | |
		Number of persons	Per cent of total
Economic activities			
Manufacturing	23	20,261,000	21
Wholesale & retail trade	16	20,738,000	22
Finance, insurance, & real estate	15	5,331,000	6
Community, social, & personal services	13	18,598,000	20
Government	11	16,054,000	17
Construction	5	4,307,000	4
Mining	4	1,104,000	1
Transportation	4	5,151,000	5
Agriculture	3	3,705,000	4
Communication	3	†	†
Utilities	3	†	†
Total	100	95,249,000	100

Family income in the United States

This graph shows how median family income in the United States has risen. The median is the middle value in the range of all incomes. On the average, U.S. families earned almost six times as much in 1980 as did families in 1950. During the same period, however, price increases, or *inflation,* took away some of the purchasing power of the higher incomes.

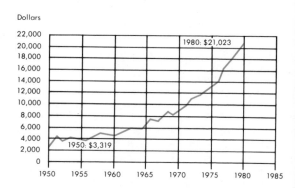

has about 1,250,000 miles (2,012,000 kilometers) of pipelines. About 15 per cent of all U.S. freight traffic travels on waterways. The Mississippi River system and the Great Lakes form the nation's major inland waterways. The busiest port in the United States is New York, followed by New Orleans, Houston, Baton Rouge, Baltimore, and Philadelphia. Airlines provide an important means of passenger travel in the United States, but they account for less than two-tenths of 1 per cent of the nation's freight traffic. More than 30 domestic and international airlines serve the country. (See "Transportation.")

The communications industry in the United States includes about 1,800 daily newspapers with a total circulation of more than 60 million copies. The country also has about 7,150 weekly and 540 semiweekly newspapers. About 9,000 radio stations and about 1,000 television stations operate in the United States.

The factories, farms, households, and vehicles of the United States consume a tremendous amount of energy annually. Petroleum alone supplies nearly half the nation's energy needs. Natural gas provides about 25 per cent, coal about 20 per cent, and water and nuclear power each about 4 per cent.

Personal consumption expenditures

Goods and services purchased by individuals and nonprofit institutions in the United States

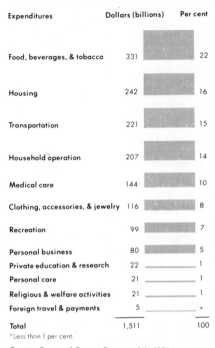

Expenditures	Dollars (billions)	Per cent
Food, beverages, & tobacco	331	22
Housing	242	16
Transportation	221	15
Household operation	207	14
Medical care	144	10
Clothing, accessories, & jewelry	116	8
Recreation	99	7
Personal business	80	5
Private education & research	22	1
Personal care	21	1
Religious & welfare activities	21	1
Foreign travel & payments	5	*
Total	1,511	100

*Less than 1 per cent.

Source: *Survey of Current Business*, July 1981, U.S. Department of Commerce.

Minerals—especially petroleum—rank as the leading import into the United States. Other major imports are machinery and transportation equipment, such as radios, stereo equipment, television sets, and automobiles and their parts; and manufactured goods, including iron and steel and other metals, newsprint, and textiles. The United States exports a variety of products. They include machinery and transportation equipment, such as computers, electronic power generators, aircraft, automobiles, trucks, and tractors; agricultural products, including corn, cotton, feed grains, livestock, soybeans, and wheat; chemicals, such as dyes, fertilizers, medicines, and plastic material and resins; and crude materials, including cotton and metal ores. Canada ranks as the leading trading partner of the United States. Other U.S. trading partners, in order of importance, include Japan, West Germany, and Great Britain.

The Presidency

Facts in brief about the President

Qualifications: The United States Constitution provides that a candidate for the presidency must be a "natural-born" U.S. citizen. The candidate must also be at least 35 years old, and must have lived in the United States for at least 14 years. No law or court decision has yet defined the exact meaning of *natural-born*. Authorities assume the term applies to citizens born in the United States and its territories. But they are not sure if it also includes children born to U.S. citizens in other countries.

How nominated: By a national political party convention.

How elected: By a majority vote of the Electoral College, held in December following the general election held on the first Tuesday after the first Monday in November of every fourth year.

Inauguration: Held at noon on January 20 after election. If January 20 is a Sunday, the ceremony may be held privately that day and again in public on January 21.

Term: The President is elected to a four-year term. A President may not be elected more than twice.

Income: $200,000 a year salary, a $50,000 annual allowance for expenses, and other allowances for travel, staff support, and maintenance of the White House. After leaving office, the President is eligible for a $69,630-a-year pension, clerical assistants, office space, and free mailing privileges. Widowed spouses of former Presidents get a $20,000-a-year pension.

Removal from office: Impeachment by a majority vote of the House of Representatives, and trial and conviction by a two-thirds vote of those present in the Senate.

Roads to the presidency

Presidential election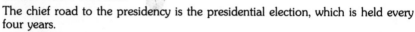

The chief road to the presidency is the presidential election, which is held every four years.

Political parties nominate their candidates for President and Vice-President at national conventions.

The nation's voters select a President and Vice-President by casting ballots for presidential electors.

The Electoral College, made up of electors chosen by all the states and the District of Columbia, elects the President and Vice-President.

Selection by Congress

If the Electoral College fails to give any candidate a majority, these steps can follow:

The House of Representatives chooses the President from among the top three candidates. Each state's House delegation has only one vote, and the winner must receive a majority of the votes that are cast.

If the House fails to choose a President, the Vice-President, chosen by the Electoral College or the Senate, becomes President.

If both Houses fail to choose a President or Vice-President, Congress shall by law deal with the situation. Congress would probably make the terms of the Presidential Succession Act applicable in this case. The speaker of the House would then become President.

Presidential succession

If the President dies, resigns, or is removed from office, the Vice-President becomes President. If the President becomes unable to perform the duties of office, the Vice-President serves as acting President during the President's disability.

The Vice-President, upon succeeding to the presidency, may then nominate a new Vice-President who takes office after being approved by Congress.

Next in line to the presidency after the Vice-President are the following government officials:

1. Speaker of the House
2. President *Pro Tempore* of the Senate
3. Secretary of State
4. Secretary of the Treasury
5. Secretary of Defense
6. Attorney General
7. Secretary of the Interior
8. Secretary of Agriculture
9. Secretary of Commerce
10. Secretary of Labor
11. Secretary of Health and Human Services
12. Secretary of Housing and Urban Development
13. Secretary of Transportation
14. Secretary of Energy
15. Secretary of Education

Presidential and Vice-Presidential candidates

Names of elected candidates are in italics. See the "Presidents" section for biographies of all the Presidents.

Year	President	Vice-President

Democratic

1828	*Andrew Jackson*	John Calhoun
1832	*Andrew Jackson*	*Martin Van Buren*
1836	*Martin Van Buren*	*Richard M. Johnson*
1840	Martin Van Buren	Richard M. Johnson
1844	*James K. Polk*	*George M. Dallas*
1848	Lewis Cass	William O. Butler
1852	*Franklin Pierce*	*William R. D. King*
1856	James Buchanan	John C. Breckinridge
1860	*Stephen A. Douglas	Herschel V. Johnson
1864	George B. McClellan	George H. Pendleton
1868	Horatio Seymour	Francis P. Blair, Jr.
1872	*Horace Greeley	B. Gratz Brown
1876	Samuel J. Tilden	Thomas A. Hendricks
1880	Winfield S. Hancock	William H. English
1884	*Grover Cleveland*	*Thomas A. Hendricks*
1888	Grover Cleveland	Allen G. Thurman
1892	*Grover Cleveland*	*Adlai E. Stevenson*
1896	*William Jennings Bryan	Arthur Sewall
1900	*William Jennings Bryan	Adlai E. Stevenson
1904	Alton B. Parker	Henry G. Davis
1908	*William Jennings Bryan	John W. Kern
1912	*Woodrow Wilson*	*Thomas R. Marshall*
1916	*Woodrow Wilson*	*Thomas R. Marshall*
1920	James M. Cox	Franklin D. Roosevelt
1924	John W. Davis	Charles W. Bryan
1928	Alfred E. Smith	Joseph T. Robinson
1932	*Franklin D. Roosevelt*	*John Nance Garner*
1936	*Franklin D. Roosevelt*	*John Nance Garner*
1940	*Franklin D. Roosevelt*	*Henry A. Wallace*
1944	*Franklin D. Roosevelt*	*Harry S. Truman*
1948	*Harry S. Truman*	*Alben W. Barkley*
1952	Adlai E. Stevenson	John J. Sparkman
1956	Adlai E. Stevenson	Estes Kefauver

1960	*John F. Kennedy*	*Lyndon B. Johnson*
1964	*Lyndon B. Johnson*	*Hubert H. Humphrey*
1968	Hubert H. Humphrey	Edmund S. Muskie
1972	George S. McGovern	Sargent Shriver
1976	*James E. Carter, Jr.*	*Walter F. Mondale*
1980	James E. Carter, Jr.	Walter F. Mondale

Republican

1856	*John C. Frémont	William L. Dayton
1860	*Abraham Lincoln*	*Hannibal Hamlin*
1864	*Abraham Lincoln*	*Andrew Johnson*
1868	*Ulysses S. Grant*	*Schuyler Colfax*
1872	*Ulysses S. Grant*	*Henry Wilson*
1876	*Rutherford B. Hayes*	*William A. Wheeler*
1880	*James A. Garfield*	*Chester A. Arthur*
1884	James G. Blaine	John A. Logan
1888	*Benjamin Harrison*	*Levi P. Morton*
1892	Benjamin Harrison	Whitelaw Reid
1896	*William McKinley*	*Garret A. Hobart*
1900	*William McKinley*	*Theodore Roosevelt*
1904	*Theodore Roosevelt*	*Charles W. Fairbanks*
1908	*William Howard Taft*	*James S. Sherman*
1912	William Howard Taft	James S. Sherman
1916	Charles Evans Hughes	Charles W. Fairbanks
1920	*Warren G. Harding*	*Calvin Coolidge*
1924	*Calvin Coolidge*	*Charles G. Dawes*
1928	*Herbert Hoover*	*Charles Curtis*
1932	Herbert Hoover	Charles Curtis
1936	Alfred M. Landon	Frank Knox
1940	Wendell L. Willkie	Charles L. McNary
1944	Thomas E. Dewey	John W. Bricker
1948	Thomas E. Dewey	Earl Warren
1952	*Dwight D. Eisenhower*	*Richard M. Nixon*
1956	*Dwight D. Eisenhower*	*Richard M. Nixon*
1960	Richard M. Nixon	Henry Cabot Lodge, Jr.
1964	Barry M. Goldwater	William E. Miller
1968	*Richard M. Nixon*	*Spiro T. Agnew*
1972	*Richard M. Nixon*	*†Spiro T. Agnew*
1976	Gerald R. Ford	Robert J. Dole
1980	*Ronald W. Reagan*	*George H. W. Bush*

*See the "People" section for biographical information.
†Resigned Oct. 10, 1973, and was later replaced by Gerald R. Ford. Ford was inaugurated as President on Aug. 9, 1974 to replace Nixon, who resigned that same day. Nelson A. Rockefeller was inaugurated as Ford's Vice-President on Dec. 19, 1974.

The Presidents of the United States

	Born	Birthplace	College or university
1. George Washington	Feb. 22, 1732	Wakefield, Va.	
2. John Adams	Oct. 30, 1735	Braintree, Mass.	Harvard
3. Thomas Jefferson	Apr. 13, 1743	Albemarle County, Va.	William and Mary
4. James Madison	Mar. 16, 1751	Port Conway, Va.	Princeton
5. James Monroe	Apr. 28, 1758	Westmoreland County, Va.	William and Mary
6. John Quincy Adams	July 11, 1767	Braintree, Mass.	Harvard
7. Andrew Jackson	Mar. 15, 1767	Waxhaw settlement, S.C. (?)	
8. Martin Van Buren	Dec. 5, 1782	Kinderhook, N.Y.	
9. William H. Harrison	Feb. 9, 1773	Berkeley, Va.	Hampden-Sydney
10. John Tyler	Mar. 29, 1790	Greenway, Va.	William and Mary
11. James K. Polk	Nov. 2, 1795	near Pineville, N.C.	U. of N. Carolina
12. Zachary Taylor	Nov. 24, 1784	Orange County, Va.	
13. Millard Fillmore	Jan. 7, 1800	Locke, N.Y.	
14. Franklin Pierce	Nov. 23, 1804	Hillsboro, N.H.	Bowdoin
15. James Buchanan	Apr. 23, 1791	near Mercersburg, Pa.	Dickinson
16. Abraham Lincoln	Feb. 12, 1809	near Hodgenville, Ky.	
17. Andrew Johnson	Dec. 29, 1808	Raleigh, N.C.	
18. Ulysses S. Grant	Apr. 27, 1822	Point Pleasant, Ohio	U.S. Mil. Academy
19. Rutherford B. Hayes	Oct. 4, 1822	Delaware, Ohio	Kenyon
20. James A. Garfield	Nov. 19, 1831	Orange, Ohio	Williams
21. Chester A. Arthur	Oct. 5, 1829	Fairfield, Vt.	Union
22. Grover Cleveland	Mar. 18, 1837	Caldwell, N.J.	
23. Benjamin Harrison	Aug. 20, 1833	North Bend, Ohio	Miami
24. Grover Cleveland	Mar. 18, 1837	Caldwell, N.J.	
25. William McKinley	Jan. 29, 1843	Niles, Ohio	Allegheny College
26. Theodore Roosevelt	Oct. 27, 1858	New York, N.Y.	Harvard
27. William H. Taft	Sept. 15, 1857	Cincinnati, Ohio	Yale
28. Woodrow Wilson	Dec. 29, 1856	Staunton, Va.	Princeton
29. Warren G. Harding	Nov. 2, 1865	near Blooming Grove, Ohio	
30. Calvin Coolidge	July 4, 1872	Plymouth Notch, Vt.	Amherst
31. Herbert C. Hoover	Aug. 10, 1874	West Branch, Iowa	Stanford
32. Franklin D. Roosevelt	Jan. 30, 1882	Hyde Park, N.Y.	Harvard
33. Harry S. Truman	May 8, 1884	Lamar, Mo.	
34. Dwight D. Eisenhower	Oct. 14, 1890	Denison, Tex.	U.S. Mil. Academy
35. John F. Kennedy	May 29, 1917	Brookline, Mass.	Harvard
36. Lyndon B. Johnson	Aug. 27, 1908	near Stonewall, Tex.	Southwest Texas State
37. Richard M. Nixon	Jan. 9, 1913	Yorba Linda, Calif.	Whittier
38. Gerald R. Ford‡	July 14, 1913	Omaha, Nebr.	Michigan
39. James E. Carter, Jr.	Oct. 1, 1924	Plains, Ga.	U.S. Naval Academy
40. Ronald W. Reagan	Feb. 6, 1911	Tampico, Ill.	Eureka

Editor's note: See the "Presidents" section for more information about each President.
*Church preference; never joined any church.
†The National Union Party consisted of Republicans and War Democrats. Johnson was a Democrat.
‡Inaugurated Aug. 9, 1974, to replace Nixon, who resigned that same day.

	Religion	Occupation or profession	Political party	Age at inauguration	Served	Died	Age at death
1.	Episcopalian	Planter	None	57	1789–1797	Dec. 14, 1799	67
2.	Unitarian	Lawyer	Federalist	61	1797–1801	July 4, 1826	90
3.	Unitarian*	Planter, lawyer	Democratic-Republican	57	1801–1809	July 4, 1826	83
4.	Episcopalian	Lawyer	Democratic-Republican	57	1809–1817	June 28, 1836	85
5.	Episcopalian	Lawyer	Democratic-Republican	58	1817–1825	July 4, 1831	73
6.	Unitarian	Lawyer	Democratic-Republican	57	1825–1829	Feb. 23, 1848	80
7.	Presbyterian	Lawyer	Democrat	61	1829–1837	June 8, 1845	78
8.	Dutch Reformed	Lawyer	Democrat	54	1837–1841	July 24, 1862	79
9.	Episcopalian	Soldier	Whig	68	1841	Apr. 4, 1841	68
10.	Episcopalian	Lawyer	Whig	51	1841–1845	Jan. 18, 1862	71
11.	Methodist	Lawyer	Democrat	49	1845–1849	June 15, 1849	53
12.	Episcopalian	Soldier	Whig	64	1849–1850	July 9, 1850	65
13.	Unitarian	Lawyer	Whig	50	1850–1853	Mar. 8, 1874	74
14.	Episcopalian	Lawyer	Democrat	48	1853–1857	Oct. 8, 1869	64
15.	Presbyterian	Lawyer	Democrat	65	1857–1861	June 1, 1868	77
16.	Presbyterian*	Lawyer	Republican	52	1861–1865	Apr. 15, 1865	56
17.	Methodist*	Tailor	Nat'l. Union†	56	1865–1869	July 31, 1875	66
18.	Methodist	Soldier	Republican	46	1869–1877	July 23, 1885	63
19.	Methodist*	Lawyer	Republican	54	1877–1881	Jan. 17, 1893	70
20.	Disciples of Christ	Lawyer	Republican	49	1881	Sept.19, 1881	49
21.	Episcopalian	Lawyer	Republican	51	1881–1885	Nov. 18, 1886	57
22.	Presbyterian	Lawyer	Democrat	47	1885–1889	June 24, 1908	71
23.	Presbyterian	Lawyer	Republican	55	1889–1893	Mar. 13, 1901	67
24.	Presbyterian	Lawyer	Democrat	55	1893–1897	June 24, 1908	71
25.	Methodist	Lawyer	Republican	54	1897–1901	Sept.14, 1901	58
26.	Dutch Reformed	Author	Republican	42	1901–1909	Jan. 6, 1919	60
27.	Unitarian	Lawyer	Republican	51	1909–1913	Mar. 8, 1930	72
28.	Presbyterian	Educator	Democrat	56	1913–1921	Feb. 3, 1924	67
29.	Baptist	Editor	Republican	55	1921–1923	Aug. 2, 1923	57
30.	Congregationalist	Lawyer	Republican	51	1923–1929	Jan. 5, 1933	60
31.	Friend (Quaker)	Engineer	Republican	54	1929–1933	Oct. 20, 1964	90
32.	Episcopalian	Lawyer	Democrat	51	1933–1945	Apr. 12, 1945	63
33.	Baptist	Businessman	Democrat	60	1945–1953	Dec. 26, 1972	88
34.	Presbyterian	Soldier	Republican	62	1953–1961	Mar. 28, 1969	78
35.	Roman Catholic	Author	Democrat	43	1961–1963	Nov. 22, 1963	46
36.	Disciples of Christ	Teacher	Democrat	55	1963–1969	Jan. 22, 1973	64
37.	Friend (Quaker)	Lawyer	Republican	56	1969–1974		
38.	Episcopalian	Lawyer	Republican	61	1974–1977		
39.	Baptist	Businessman	Democrat	52	1977–1981		
40.	Disciples of Christ	Actor	Republican	69	1981–		

Executive Office of the President

The Executive Office of the President consists of many assistants and advisors who provide services and help the President handle his many duties. The components of the Executive Office of the President are listed below.

White House Office. Includes presidential assistants and other staff members that aid the President in such duties as appointing government officials and developing domestic and foreign policies. The office also includes the President's military aide and physician, and personal and social secretaries to assist the First Family with official functions.

Foreign Intelligence Advisory Board. Evaluates the adequacy of information collected and analyzed by U.S. intelligence agencies. The board also analyzes the management and organization of these agencies and recommends ways to improve intelligence efforts of the United States.

Office of Management and Budget. Evaluates and coordinates federal programs and prepares the federal budget that the President presents to Congress each year. The office also seeks to develop executive talent and to improve government organization, information, and management systems. A director is in charge of the office.

Council of Economic Advisers. Studies the national economy, evaluates federal economic policies and programs, and recommends ways to promote economic growth and stability. The council helps the President prepare the annual economic report to Congress. A chairperson and two other members form the council.

Intelligence Oversight Board. Reviews and reports on the activities of the Central Intelligence Agency and other groups that gather political and military information. The board works to ensure that U.S. intelligence operations meet legal and ethical guidelines.

Office of Science and Technology Policy. Advises the President on matters involving science and technology. The office evaluates the scientific and technological programs of the federal government and helps develop new programs and policies.

Council on Environmental Quality. Studies the forces that affect the nation's environment, coordinates federal environmental programs, and develops new programs and policies. The council helps the President prepare the annual environmental report to Congress. A chairperson and two other members form the council.

National Security Council. Includes the President, Vice-President, secretaries of state and defense, and other officials. It coordinates federal programs that affect U.S. security. The Central Intelligence Agency informs the council about U.S. intelligence operations.

Office of the United States Trade Representative. Works to increase United States trade with other countries. The trade representative and two deputies make agreements with other countries for reducing tariffs. These officials also advise the President on many international trade matters.

Domestic Policy Staff. Assists the President in developing and coordinating federal domestic policies and in reviewing ongoing programs to ensure that they meet the nation's needs. An executive director heads the staff.

Office of Administration. Handles clerical, personnel, and other administrative matters for the Executive Office of the President. The Office of Administration also provides office supplies and other needs for the Executive Office Building.

Office of the Vice-President. Provides staff support to the Vice-President. The office includes the Vice-President's chief of staff, legal counsel, press secretary, and other assistants.

Administrations in office

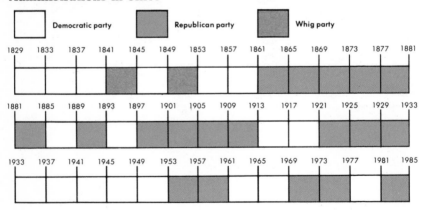

Executive Departments

The heads of the 13 executive departments described below make up what is commonly called the President's *Cabinet*. Twelve of the department heads are called *secretaries*. The *attorney general* heads the Department of Justice. The President appoints the department heads with the approval of the Senate. Over the years, the composition of the Cabinet has changed as new departments have been created and old ones dissolved or merged. Some Presidents discontinued Cabinet meetings altogether. Others expanded them to include the Vice-President and other officials.

Department of State. Plans and carries out, with the President's approval, the foreign policy of the United States and coordinates other executive departments' actions that affect foreign policy. The department negotiates treaties and agreements with other governments, handles official business with foreign embassies in Washington, D.C., speaks for the United States in the United Nations and other international organizations, and arranges for U.S. participation in international conferences.

Department of the Treasury. Collects federal taxes and customs duties and receives all money paid to the government. The department serves as custodian of the government's revenues, pays government expenses, and keeps accounts of government revenues and expenditures. It prepares all paper money, coins, and federal securities and supervises the operation of national banks. Upon authorization from Congress, the department borrows money for the federal government and manages the national debt. It also makes and carries out policies relating to the international economic, financial, and monetary field.

Department of Defense. Directs the operations of the nation's armed forces, including the army, navy, and air force. The secretary of defense, a civilian, is a member of the National Security Council and the North Atlantic Council.

Department of Justice. Enforces federal laws and provides legal advice for the President and the heads of the executive departments. The department argues all suits in the Supreme Court that concern the U.S. government. It supervises penal institutions and investigates and prosecutes violations of federal laws.

Department of the Interior. Supervises the nation's natural resources. The department manages federal lands and has trust responsibilities for land, primarily Indian reservations. It coordinates federal and state recreation programs and preserves and manages scenic and historic areas. The department conducts geological surveys of land and water resources and administers the Land and Water Conservation Fund to help acquire recreation areas and parklands for federal, state, and local governments. It operates and coordinates manpower and youth training programs. It administers hydroelectric power systems and the reclamation of arid lands through irrigation. The department is involved in the social and economic development of the territories of the United States and in the Trust Territory of the Pacific Islands. It administers programs providing services to Indians and Alaska Native people.

Department of Agriculture. Works to maintain adequate supplies of farm products and to insure reasonable prices for both farmers and consumers. The department works to safeguard the food supply through inspection of food processing plants and grades meat, poultry, and dairy products to indicate their quality. It establishes standards of quality for grain exports and administers a nationwide system of grain inspection. Much of the department's budget goes to provide food stamps.

Department of Commerce. Promotes the nation's economic development, international trade, and technological advancement. The department helps the President form national economic policy and provides economic data, studies, and advice to other federal agencies and to private enterprise. The department issues patents, registers trademarks, and establishes weights, measures, and standards for commodities. It includes the Bureau of the Census.

Department of Labor. Administers and enforces laws that seek to promote the welfare of U.S. workers. The department administers federal laws on child labor, minimum wages, overtime, and public contracts. It carries out federal laws on workers' compensation programs and handles appeals from federal workers regarding compensation. The department administers laws dealing with the election of labor union officers and with union financial reports. It collects, analyzes, and publishes information on employment and unemployment, industrial relations, occupational safety and health, price trends, and productivity and technology. It administers the public employment service and unemployment insurance programs.

Department of Health and Human Services. Deals with public health, social welfare, and income security. The department supports and conducts research into the causes and prevention of disease, administers community health services, and enforces laws designed to insure the purity, effectiveness, and truthful labeling of food, drugs, and cosmetics. It administers the Medicare and Medicaid programs, as well as the federal social security programs.

Department of Housing and Urban Development. Makes grants to state and local governments to help finance community development and housing programs. The department administers programs for home mortgages, home improvement loans, and rent subsidies.

Department of Transportation. Develops and promotes national transportation policies and programs. The department carries on research and development programs in cooperation with private industry and conducts studies to identify and solve transportation problems.

Department of Energy. Develops and coordinates national energy policies and programs. The department investigates, develops, and promotes new sources of energy and new ways to save existing supplies. It regulates the electric power, natural gas, and oil pipeline companies that conduct interstate operations. The department collects, analyzes, and publishes energy statistics. It develops and manages activities related to the international aspects of energy policy.

Department of Education. Develops and coordinates national educational policies and programs. The department administers programs to maintain and upgrade the nation's educational system and to supplement state and local educational efforts. It provides financial aid for elementary, high school, and college education. The department serves as the government's chief fact-finding agency in education, and sponsors research on teaching methods and educational programs.

263

The Congress

Facts in brief about members of Congress

Number: The Senate has 100 members, and the House of Representatives consists of 435 members.

Qualifications: A candidate for the Senate must be: (1) at least 30 years old, (2) a citizen of the United States for at least 9 years, and (3) a resident of the state from which he or she seeks election.

A candidate for the House of Representatives must be: (1) at least 25 years old, (2) a citizen of the United States for at least 7 years, and (3) a resident of the state from which he or she seeks election.

Nomination: Candidates for Congress are nominated by primary election or by party convention.

Election: A senator is elected by the voters from all parts of the state. A representative may (1) be elected by the voters of one congressional district of the state, or (2) be elected *at large* (by voters throughout the state).

Term: Senators are elected to six-year terms, and representatives are elected to two-year terms. A member of Congress can serve an unlimited number of terms.

Income: The speaker of the House receives a salary of $79,125 a year, and other members of Congress receive $60,662.50 a year. All members also receive free office space and allowances for office expenses, staff salaries, travel, and similar expenses.

Removal from office: Members of Congress may be expelled by a two-thirds vote of their house.

How a bill becomes a law in the United States

Federal laws are enacted in the United States through a process that involves both houses of Congress and the President. Thousands of bills are introduced during each Congress, which lasts two years, and hundreds become law. All bills not enacted by the end of the two-year period are killed.

Ideas for new laws come from many sources. The President, members of Congress, and other government officials may propose laws. Suggestions also come from individual citizens; special-interest groups, such as farmers, industry, and labor; newspaper editorials; and public protests. Congressional committees, in addition to lawyers who represent special-interest groups, actually write most bills and put them into proper legal form. Specialists called *legislative counsels* in the Senate and House of Representatives help prepare many bills for congressional action.

Each bill must be sponsored by a member of the House or Senate. Up to 25 representatives and any number of senators may co-sponsor a bill. A bill may originate in either house of Congress unless it deals with taxes or spending. The Constitution provides that all such bills must be introduced in the House. The tradition that money bills must begin in the lower house of the legislature came from England. There, the lower house—the House of Commons—is more likely to reflect the people's wishes because the people elect its members. They do not elect the upper house, the House of Lords. The rule has little meaning in the United States because voters elect both houses.

The following description follows the path of a bill introduced in the House of Representatives. The process is the same for a bill introduced in the Senate, except that the House action comes after the Senate action. A bill may die at almost any stage of the lawmaking process if no action is taken on it.

In the House of Representatives, a sponsor introduces a bill by giving it to the clerk of the House or placing it in a box called the *hopper.* The clerk reads the title of the bill into the *Congressional Record* in a procedure called the *first reading.* The Government Printing Office prints the bill and distributes copies. The speaker of the House then assigns the bill to a committee for study. The House has about 20 *standing* (permanent) committees, each with jurisdiction over bills in a certain area. The committee hears testimony from experts and other interested persons.

In some cases, a subcommittee conducts the study. The committee may release the bill with a recommendation to pass it, revise the bill and release it, or lay it aside so that the House cannot vote on it. Releasing the bill is called *reporting it out,* and laying the proposed law aside is called *tabling.* A bill that has been reported out goes on a *calendar,* a list of bills awaiting action. The Rules Committee may call for quick action on the bill, limit debate, and limit or prohibit amendments. Without the committee's help, a bill might never reach the floor of the House. Consideration by the full House begins with a second reading of the bill, the only complete reading in most cases. A third reading, by title only, comes after any amendments have been added and before the final vote. If the bill passes by a *simple majority* (one more than half the votes), it goes on to the Senate.

To introduce a bill in the Senate, a senator must be recognized by the presiding officer and announce the introduction of the bill. A bill that has passed either house of Congress is sometimes called an *act,* but the term usually means legislation that has passed both houses of Congress and become law. The Vice-President of the United States, who is the presiding officer of the Senate, assigns the proposed law to a committee for study. The Senate has about 15 standing committees. The committee or one of its subcommittees may hold hearings as part of its study. The committee may approve the bill as it stands, revise the bill, or table it. Bills normally reach the Senate floor in the order that they come from committee. But if a bill is urgent, the leaders of the majority party might push it ahead. When a bill is being considered by the Senate, senators can debate it indefinitely, unless they vote to limit discussion. When there is no further debate, the Senate votes. Most bills must have a simple majority to pass.

A *conference committee* made up of members of both houses works out any differences between the House and Senate versions of the bill. The revised bill is sent back to both houses for their final approval. The bill is then printed by the Government Printing Office in a process called *enrolling.* The clerk of the house of Congress that originated the bill certifies the final version. The speaker of the House signs the enrolled bill, and then the Vice-President signs it. Finally, Congress sends the proposed new legislation to the President for consideration.

The President has 10 days—not including Sundays—to consider a bill that has been passed by Congress. The President may approve the bill, veto it, or take no action. After approving a bill, the President signs it, dates it, and often writes the word *approved* on it. If the bill has been vetoed, it must be returned to Congress with an explanation of the President's objections. Congress then reconsiders the bill. If a two-thirds majority of both houses approves the vetoed bill, it becomes law despite the President's veto. The President might not veto the bill, but may fail to sign it to show disapproval of some parts. If the President holds the bill for 10 days—excluding Sundays—while Congress is in session, it becomes law without the signature of the chief executive. A bill that reaches the President fewer than 10 days—excluding Sundays—before Congress adjourns cannot become law without the President's signature. If the President fails to sign the proposed law, it dies. This procedure is called a *pocket veto.*

When a bill becomes a law, it is given a number that indicates which Congress passed it. For example, a law enacted by the 98th Congress might be designated Public Law 98-250.

Speakers of the House of Representatives

Speaker	Party	Years served
Frederick A. C. Muhlenberg	Federalist	1789–1791
Jonathan Trumbull	Federalist	1791–1793
Frederick A. C. Muhlenberg	Federalist	1793–1795
Jonathan Dayton	Federalist	1795–1799
Theodore Sedgwick	Federalist	1799–1801
Nathaniel Macon	Dem.-Rep.*	1801–1807
Joseph B. Varnum	Dem.-Rep.*	1807–1811
‡Henry Clay	Nat. Rep.†	1811–1814
Langdon Cheves	Dem.-Rep.*	1814–1815
‡Henry Clay	Nat. Rep.†	1815–1820
John W. Taylor	Dem.-Rep.*	1820–1821
Philip P. Barbour	Dem.-Rep*	1821–1823
‡Henry Clay	Nat. Rep.†	1823–1825
John W. Taylor	Dem.-Rep.*	1825–1827
Andrew Stevenson	Dem.-Rep.*	1827–1834
John Bell	Whig	1834–1835
§James K. Polk	Democratic	1835–1839
Robert M. T. Hunter	Democratic	1839–1841
John White	Whig	1841–1843
John W. Jones	Democratic	1843–1845
John W. Davis	Democratic	1845–1847
Robert C. Winthrop	Whig	1847–1849
Howell Cobb	Democratic	1849–1851
Linn Boyd	Democratic	1851–1855
Nathaniel P. Banks	American	1855–1857
James L. Orr	Democratic	1857–1859
William Pennington	Whig	1859–1861
Galusha A. Grow	Republican	1861–1863
Schuyler Colfax	Republican	1863–1869
Theodore M. Pomeroy	Republican	1869
James G. Blaine	Republican	1869–1875
Michael C. Kerr	Democratic	1875–1876
Samuel J. Randall	Democratic	1876–1881
J. Warren Keifer	Republican	1881–1883
John G. Carlisle	Democratic	1883–1889
Thomas B. Reed	Republican	1889–1891
Charles F. Crisp	Democratic	1891–1895
Thomas B. Reed	Republican	1895–1899
David B. Henderson	Republican	1899–1903
Joseph G. Cannon	Republican	1903–1911
James B. Clark	Democratic	1911–1919
Frederick H. Gillett	Republican	1919–1925
Nicholas Longworth	Republican	1925–1931
John N. Garner	Democratic	1931–1933
Henry T. Rainey	Democratic	1933–1935
Joseph W. Byrns	Democratic	1935–1936
William B. Bankhead	Democratic	1936–1940
Sam Rayburn	Democratic	1940–1947
Joseph W. Martin, Jr.	Republican	1947–1949
Sam Rayburn	Democratic	1949–1953
Joseph W. Martin, Jr.	Republican	1953–1955
Sam Rayburn	Democratic	1955–1961
John W. McCormack	Democratic	1962–1971
Carl B. Albert	Democratic	1971–1977
Thomas P. O'Neill	Democratic	1977–

*Democratic-Republican
†National Republican
‡See "People" section for biographical information.
§See "Presidents" section for biographical information.

The Supreme Court

The Supreme Court consists of a chief justice and eight associate justices. The President appoints the justices to life terms with the approval of the Senate.

U.S. Supreme Court justices

Name	Term	Appointed by
Chief justices		
*John Jay	1790–1795	Washington
John Rutledge	1795	†Washington
Oliver Ellsworth	1796–1800	Washington
*John Marshall	1801–1835	J. Adams
Roger B. Taney	1836–1864	Jackson
Salmon P. Chase	1864–1873	Lincoln
Morrison R. Waite	1874–1888	Grant
Melville W. Fuller	1888–1910	Cleveland
Edward D. White	1910–1921	Taft
‡William H. Taft	1921–1930	Harding
Charles E. Hughes	1930–1941	Hoover
Harlan F. Stone	1941–1946	F. D. Roosevelt
Frederick M. Vinson	1946–1953	Truman
Earl Warren	1953–1969	Eisenhower
Warren E. Burger	1969–	Nixon

Name	Term	Appointed by
Associate justices		
James Wilson	1789–1798	Washington
John Rutledge	1790–1791	Washington
William Cushing	1790–1810	Washington
John Blair	1790–1796	Washington
James Iredell	1790–1799	Washington
Thomas Johnson	1792–1793	Washington
William Paterson	1793–1806	Washington
Samuel Chase	1796–1811	Washington
Bushrod Washington	1799–1829	J. Adams
Alfred Moore	1800–1804	J. Adams
William Johnson	1804–1834	Jefferson
H. Brockholst Livingston	1807–1823	Jefferson
Thomas Todd	1807–1826	Jefferson
Gabriel Duvall	1811–1835	Madison
Joseph Story	1812–1845	Madison
Smith Thompson	1823–1843	Monroe
Robert Trimble	1826–1828	J. Q. Adams
John McLean	1830–1861	Jackson
Henry Baldwin	1830–1844	Jackson
James M. Wayne	1835–1867	Jackson
Philip P. Barbour	1836–1841	Jackson
John Catron	1837–1865	Van Buren
John McKinley	1838–1852	Van Buren
Peter V. Daniel	1842–1860	Van Buren
Samuel Nelson	1845–1872	Tyler
Levi Woodbury	1845–1851	Polk
Robert C. Grier	1846–1870	Polk
Benjamin R. Curtis	1851–1857	Fillmore
John A. Campbell	1853–1861	Pierce
Nathan Clifford	1858–1881	Buchanan
Noah H. Swayne	1862–1881	Lincoln
Samuel F. Miller	1862–1890	Lincoln
David Davis	1862–1877	Lincoln
Stephen J. Field	1863–1897	Lincoln
William Strong	1870–1880	Grant
Joseph P. Bradley	1870–1892	Grant
Ward Hunt	1873–1882	Grant
John M. Harlan	1877–1911	Hayes
William B. Woods	1881–1887	Hayes
Stanley Matthews	1881–1889	Garfield
Horace Gray	1882–1902	Arthur
Samuel Blatchford	1882–1893	Arthur
Lucius Q. C. Lamar	1888–1893	Cleveland
David J. Brewer	1890–1910	Harrison
Henry B. Brown	1891–1906	Harrison
George Shiras, Jr.	1892–1903	Harrison
Howell E. Jackson	1893–1895	Harrison
Edward D. White	1894–1910	Cleveland
Rufus W. Peckham	1896–1909	Cleveland
Joseph McKenna	1898–1925	McKinley
Oliver W. Holmes, Jr.	1902–1932	T. Roosevelt
William R. Day	1903–1922	T. Roosevelt
William H. Moody	1906–1910	T. Roosevelt
Horace H. Lurton	1910–1914	Taft
Charles E. Hughes	1910–1916	Taft
Willis Van Devanter	1911–1937	Taft
Joseph R. Lamar	1911–1916	Taft
Mahlon Pitney	1912–1922	Taft
James C. McReynolds	1914–1941	Wilson
Louis D. Brandeis	1916–1939	Wilson
John H. Clarke	1916–1922	Wilson
George Sutherland	1922–1938	Harding
Pierce Butler	1923–1939	Harding
Edward T. Sanford	1923–1930	Harding
Harlan F. Stone	1925–1941	Coolidge
Owen J. Roberts	1930–1945	Hoover
Benjamin N. Cardozo	1932–1938	Hoover
Hugo L. Black	1937–1971	F. D. Roosevelt
Stanley F. Reed	1938–1957	F. D. Roosevelt
Felix Frankfurter	1939–1962	F. D. Roosevelt
*William O. Douglas	1939–1975	F. D. Roosevelt
Frank Murphy	1940–1949	F. D. Roosevelt
James F. Byrnes	1941–1942	F. D. Roosevelt
Robert H. Jackson	1941–1954	F. D. Roosevelt
Wiley B. Rutledge	1943–1949	F. D. Roosevelt
Harold H. Burton	1945–1958	Truman
Tom C. Clark	1949–1967	Truman
Sherman Minton	1949–1956	Truman
John M. Harlan	1955–1971	Eisenhower
William J. Brennan, Jr.	1956–	Eisenhower
Charles E. Whittaker	1957–1962	Eisenhower
Potter Stewart	1958–1981	Eisenhower
Byron R. White	1962–	Kennedy
Arthur J. Goldberg	1962–1965	Kennedy
Abe Fortas	1965–1969	Johnson
*Thurgood Marshall	1967–	Johnson
Harry A. Blackmun	1970–	Nixon
Lewis F. Powell, Jr.	1972–	Nixon
William H. Rehnquist	1972–	Nixon
John P. Stevens	1975–	Ford
*Sandra Day O'Connor	1981–	Reagan

*See "People" section for biographical information.
†Appointment not confirmed by the United States Senate.
‡See "Presidents" section for biographical information.

Landmark decisions of the Supreme Court

Powers of the court, federal government, and states

1803   *Marbury v. Madison.* If a law passed by Congress conflicts with the Constitution, the Supreme Court must base its decision on the Constitution. This ruling established the court's power of *judicial review*—that is, its authority to declare laws unconstitutional.

1810   *Fletcher v. Peck.* Georgia could not revoke a land grant after the land had been sold to a third party. The Constitution protects contracts against interference by the states, and a sales agreement is a type of contract.

1819   *McCulloch v. Maryland.* The Constitution gives *implied powers* to the federal government in addition to the *express powers* that are specifically granted. Implied powers are those necessary to carry out express powers.

1819   *Dartmouth College v. Woodward.* New Hampshire could not alter a royal charter and make Dartmouth a state college. A charter is a contract, and the Constitution protects contracts against state interference.

Powers of the President

1952   *Youngstown Sheet and Tube Company v. Sawyer.* The President exceeded his lawful power when he seized the nation's steel mills to prevent a strike during the Korean War.

1974   *United States v. Nixon.* The President cannot withhold evidence needed in a criminal trial. This ruling established that the President's *executive privilege*—the right to keep records confidential—is not unlimited.

Regulation of business and industry

1824   *Gibbons v. Ogden.* The powers of the federal government are superior to those of the states in all matters of *interstate commerce* (trade between states).

1905   *Lochner v. New York.* A law limiting bakers to a 60-hour work week was unconstitutional because it violated "freedom of contract" between employer and employee. The court reversed this decision in 1937.

1935   *Schechter v. United States.* The National Industrial Recovery Act of 1933, which provided for the establishment of fair-competition codes for businesses, was unconstitutional.

1937   *National Labor Relations Board v. Jones and Laughlin Steel Corporation.* The federal government has the power to regulate the local activities of labor unions because these activities may affect interstate commerce.

Election districts

1962   *Baker v. Carr.* Citizens can challenge unfair election districting before a federal court.

1964   *Reynolds v. Sims.* The U.S. House of Representatives and both houses of a state legislature must follow the rule of "one person, one vote" and create election districts roughly equal in population.

Freedom of speech and of the press

1919   *Schenck v. United States.* The government cannot restrict freedom of speech unless the speech creates a "clear and present danger" of violence or some other evil that the government has a right to prevent.

1957   *Roth v. United States.* Freedom of the press, guaranteed by the First Amendment to the Constitution, does not protect publication of obscene material.

1964   *New York Times Co. v. Sullivan.* A newspaper cannot be punished for untrue statements about a public official unless it deliberately published a falsehood.

1971   *New York Times Co. v. United States.* The government could not prevent publication of the *Pentagon papers,* a secret study of the Vietnam War. The court held that the danger to national security did not justify such censorship.

1973   *Miller v. California.* Material can be considered obscene if it fulfills certain requirements established by the court.

School prayer

1962   *Engel v. Vitale.* Public schools cannot require the recitation of prayers.

Rights of persons accused of crime

1866   *Ex Parte Milligan.* Military courts cannot try civilians outside military areas if civilian courts are available.

1932   *Powell v. Alabama.* If a person on trial for his or her life cannot hire a lawyer, the state must provide one. The legal help must be furnished in time to prepare the case.

1961   *Mapp v. Ohio.* Evidence obtained by illegal means cannot be used in a criminal trial.

1963   *Gideon v. Wainwright.* The states must provide free legal counsel to any person accused of a felony who cannot afford a lawyer.

1964   *Escobedo v. Illinois.* A confession cannot be used as evidence if it is obtained after the accused person has been denied permission to see a lawyer.

1966   *Miranda v. Arizona.* An accused person must be informed of his or her constitutional rights, including the right to remain silent, before being questioned.

1972   *Argersinger v. Hamlin.* The states must provide free legal counsel to any person accused of a misdemeanor that involves a jail term if the person cannot afford a lawyer.

1972   *Furman v. Georgia.* The death penalty, as it was then administered, was cruel and unusual punishment in violation of the Eighth Amendment to the Constitution.

Rights of women and minority groups

1857   *Dred Scott v. Sandford.* Blacks could not be U.S. citizens, and Congress could not prohibit slavery in the U.S. territories. The first part of this ruling was overturned in 1868 by the 14th Amendment. The second part was struck down in 1865 by the 13th Amendment.

1896   *Plessy v. Ferguson.* "Separate but equal" public facilities for whites and blacks did not violate the Constitution. The court reversed this decision in 1954.

1944   *Korematsu v. United States.* The government could lawfully remove persons of Japanese ancestry from areas threatened by Japanese attack during World War II.

1948   *Shelley v. Kraemer.* State or federal courts cannot enforce *restrictive covenants,* which are agreements to prevent real-estate owners from selling their property to members of minority groups.

1954   *Brown v. Board of Education of Topeka* (Kans.). Separate but equal facilities for blacks in public schools do not meet the constitutional requirement for equal protection of the law.

1964   *Heart of Atlanta Motel, Inc. v. United States.* The Civil Rights Act of 1964 is constitutional. This act bans racial discrimination in all public accommodations that affect commerce, including hotels, motels, and restaurants.

1969   *Alexander v. Holmes County* (Miss.) *Board of Education.* Desegregation of all public school systems must take place "at once."

1973   *Doe v. Bolton* and *Roe v. Wade.* The states may not prohibit a woman's right, under certain conditions, to have an abortion during the first six months of pregnancy.

1978   *Regents of the University of California v. Allan Bakke,* also called the *Bakke* case. University and college admissions programs may not use specific quotas to achieve racial balance. But they may give special consideration to members of minority groups.

1979   *United Steelworkers of America v. Weber.* Employers can give preference to minorities and females in hiring and promotion for "traditionally segregated job categories."

Major speeches and documents in United States history

Articles of Confederation—Adopted in 1781 by the 13 original colonies to establish a government of states. Served as the basic law of the land until the present Constitution went into effect in 1789. Under the Articles, the confederation used the name United States of America and the Congress of the Confederation operated the government.

Atlantic Charter—Adopted in 1941 by U.S. President Franklin D. Roosevelt and British Prime Minister Winston Churchill to express the post-World War II aims of the United States and Britain. Those aims included a restoration of self-government in occupied nations, economic collaboration among nations, and worldwide disarmament.

Constitution of the United States—Signed Sept. 17, 1787; took effect June 21, 1788, after New Hampshire became the ninth state to ratify it. Sets forth the basic laws of the United States, establishes the form of national government, and lists the aims of the government and the methods of achieving them. The first 10 amendments form the Bill of Rights, which describes and guarantees the rights and liberties of the American people. The Bill of Rights took effect on Dec. 15, 1791.

Declaration of Independence—Adopted by representatives of the American Colonies on July 4, 1776, to proclaim their freedom from British rule.

Emancipation Proclamation—Issued by President Abraham Lincoln on Jan. 1, 1863. Declared freedom for slaves in all areas of the Confederacy that were still in rebellion against the Union. Provided for blacks to serve in the Union Army and Navy. Although the proclamation itself did not actually free any slaves, it led to the 13th Amendment to the Constitution, which took effect Dec. 18, 1865, ending slavery in all parts of the United States.

Four Freedoms—Expressed by President Franklin D. Roosevelt in a message to Congress on Jan. 6, 1941, as the basis for any settlement of World War II. Roosevelt defined the four freedoms as freedom of speech, freedom of worship, freedom from want, and freedom from fear.

Fourteen Points—Proposed by President Woodrow Wilson in a speech before Congress on Jan. 8, 1918, as the basis for ending World War I and keeping the peace. They included "open covenants openly arrived at," "adjustment of all colonial claims," and the formation of a "general association of nations."

Gettysburg Address—Delivered by President Abraham Lincoln on Nov. 19, 1863, at the site of the Battle of Gettysburg in Pennsylvania. In the speech, Lincoln reaffirmed the principles of freedom that guided the Founding Fathers, declaring that ". . . government of the people, by the people, for the people, shall not perish from the earth."

Mayflower Compact—First agreement for self-government ever put into force in America. Signed by 41 male Pilgrim adults aboard the ship *Mayflower* on Nov. 21 (then Nov. 11), 1620.

Monroe Doctrine—Set forth by President James Monroe in a message to Congress on Dec. 2, 1823. Warned European nations not to interfere in the affairs of the independent nations of the Western Hemisphere.

Northwest Ordinance—Passed by Congress on July 13, 1787. Provided for the government of the Northwest Territory, a region north of the Ohio River and west of Pennsylvania. Became a model for all territories that later entered the Union as states.

Signers of the Declaration of Independence

Fifty-six members of the Continental Congress signed the engrossed parchment copy of the Declaration. Most members signed on Aug. 2, 1776. The rest signed on later dates. The signers, in alphabetical order, follow.

*John Adams (Mass.)
†Samuel Adams (Mass.)
Josiah Bartlett (N.H.)
Carter Braxton (Va.)
Charles Carroll (Md.)
Samuel Chase (Md.)
Abraham Clark (N.J.)
George Clymer (Pa.)
William Ellery (R.I.)
William Floyd (N.Y.)
†Benjamin Franklin (Pa.)
Elbridge Gerry (Mass.)
Button Gwinnett (Ga.)
Lyman Hall (Ga.)
†John Hancock (Mass.)
Benjamin Harrison (Va.)
John Hart (N.J.)
Joseph Hewes (N.C.)
Thomas Heyward, Jr. (S.C.)

William Hooper (N.C.)
Stephen Hopkins (R.I.)
Francis Hopkinson (N.J.)
Samuel Huntington (Conn.)
*Thomas Jefferson (Va.)
Francis Lightfoot Lee (Va.)
Richard Henry Lee (Va.)
Francis Lewis (N.Y.)
Philip Livingston (N.Y.)
Thomas Lynch, Jr. (S.C.)
Thomas McKean (Del.)
Arthur Middleton (S.C.)
Lewis Morris (N.Y.)
Robert Morris (Pa.)
John Morton (Pa.)
Thomas Nelson, Jr. (Va.)
William Paca (Md.)
Robert T. Paine (Mass.)
John Penn (N.C.)

George Read (Del.)
Caesar Rodney (Del.)
George Ross (Pa.)
Benjamin Rush (Pa.)
Edward Rutledge (S.C.)
Roger Sherman (Conn.)
James Smith (Pa.)
Richard Stockton (N.J.)
Thomas Stone (Md.)
George Taylor (Pa.)
Matthew Thornton (N.H.)
George Walton (Ga.)
William Whipple (N.H.)
William Williams (Conn.)
James Wilson (Pa.)
John Witherspoon (N.J.)
Oliver Wolcott (Conn.)
George Wythe (Va.)

*See "Presidents" section for biographical information.
†See "People" section for biographical information.

Signers of the Constitution

On Sept. 17, 1787, 39 of the 55 delegates to the Constitutional Convention signed the Constitution. One delegate, John Dickinson, had left the convention but asked a delegate to sign for him. The signers, in alphabetical order, follow.

Abraham Baldwin (Ga.)	Thomas FitzSimons (Pa.)	Thomas Mifflin (Pa.)
Richard Bassett (Del.)	*Benjamin Franklin (Pa.)	Gouverneur Morris (Pa.)
Gunning Bedford, Jr. (Del.)	Nicholas Gilman (N.H.)	Robert Morris (Pa.)
John Blair (Va.)	Nathaniel Gorham (Mass.)	William Paterson (N.J.)
William Blount (N.C.)	*Alexander Hamilton (N.Y.)	Charles Cotesworth Pinckney (S.C.)
David Brearley (N.J.)	Jared Ingersoll (Pa.)	Charles Pinckney (S.C.)
Jacob Broom (Del.)	Daniel of St. Thomas Jenifer (Md.)	George Read (Del.)
Pierce Butler (S.C.)	William S. Johnson (Conn.)	John Rutledge (S.C.)
Daniel Carroll (Md.)	Rufus King (Mass.)	Roger Sherman (Conn.)
George Clymer (Pa.)	John Langdon (N.H.)	Richard D. Spaight (N.C.)
Jonathan Dayton (N.J.)	William Livingston (N.J.)	†George Washington (Va.)
John Dickinson (Del.)	†James Madison, Jr. (Va.)	Hugh Williamson (N.C.)
William Few (Ga.)	James McHenry (Md.)	James Wilson (Pa.)

*See "People" section for biographical information.
†See "Presidents" section for biographical information.

Important dates in United States history

1492	Christopher Columbus sails from Spain and lands in the Western Hemisphere.	**1672**	The completion of the Boston Post Road links Boston and New York City.
1513	Ponce de León of Spain searches for the Fountain of Youth; he finds instead a place he names Florida.	**1681**	Quaker William Penn founds the colony of Pennsylvania as a haven for persecuted English Quakers.
1540–1542	Francisco Coronado of Spain explores the American Southwest.	**1704**	*The Boston News-Letter,* the first successful colonial newspaper, begins publication.
1565	Spaniards found St. Augustine, Fla., the oldest city in what is now the United States.	**1733–1758**	Benjamin Franklin publishes his *Poor Richard's Almanac.*
1585–1586	Sir Walter Raleigh fails in his attempt to form a permanent English settlement in what is now the United States.	**1735**	New York newspaper publisher John Peter Zenger is acquitted of a libel charge that grew out of his criticism of the British government.
1607	About 100 colonists found Jamestown, the first permanent English settlement in North America.	**1752**	Benjamin Franklin flies a homemade kite during a storm to prove that lightning is a form of electricity.
1619	A Dutch vessel brings the first blacks in the English colonies to Jamestown.	**1756**	A stagecoach line links New York City and Philadelphia.
1619	Virginia establishes the House of Burgesses, the first representative legislature in America.	**c. 1757**	The first street lights in the colonies are installed in Philadelphia.
1620	The Pilgrims found Plymouth Colony, the second permanent British settlement in North America.	**c. 1760**	The first Conestoga wagons are built.
1624	The Dutch establish the settlement of New Netherland.	**1763**	Britain defeats France in the French and Indian War and gains control of eastern North America.
1636	Harvard, the first college in the colonies, is founded.	**1763**	Britain stations a standing army in North America and prohibits colonists from settling west of the Appalachian Mountains.
1638	Swedes establish the settlement of New Sweden.	**1765**	Colonists protest taxation without representation after the British Parliament passes the Stamp Act.
1646	The first successful American ironworks is built north of Boston.	**1769**	The first Catholic mission in California is established near what is now San Diego.
1647	Massachusetts establishes the first colonial public school system.	**1770**	British troops kill American civilians in the Boston Massacre.
1649	Maryland passes the first religious toleration act in North America.	**1773**	Colonists stage the Boston Tea Party to protest British laws, dumping British tea into Boston Harbor.
1664	England takes control of New Netherland and New Sweden.		

The thirteen colonies stretched along the eastern coast of North America. French territory lay to the north and west of the colonies, and Spanish territory lay to the south.

1774	The British Parliament passes the Intolerable Acts as punishment for colonial rebellion.
1774	The First Continental Congress meets in Philadelphia to consider action against the British.
1775	The Revolutionary War begins on April 19, as British soldiers attack the patriots at Lexington and Concord.
1776	Tom Paine publishes *Common Sense,* a pamphlet containing a stirring demand for independence.
1776	The Declaration of Independence is adopted on July 4.
1781	The Americans defeat the British at Yorktown, Va., in the last major battle of the Revolutionary War.
1781	The first U.S. central government is established by the Articles of Confederation.
1783	The Americans and the British sign the Treaty of Paris to officially end the Revolutionary War.
1787	The Constitution of the United States is written and signed.
1787–1788	Alexander Hamilton, James Madison, and John Jay write most of the essays later published as *The Federalist,* outlining the need for a strong central government.
1789	George Washington is elected first President of the United States.
1790's	The first U.S. political parties develop.
1790	Samuel Slater builds the country's first successful water-powered machines for spinning cotton.
1791	The Bill of Rights is adopted on December 15.

1793	Eli Whitney invents the cotton gin.
1800	Washington, D.C. replaces Philadelphia as the nation's capital.
1803	The Louisiana Purchase doubles the nation's size.
1804–1806	The Lewis and Clark Expedition explores the lands west of the Mississippi River.
1807	Robert Fulton demonstrates the first commercially successful steamboat.
1811	Work begins on the National Road, which, when completed, links the East and the Midwest.
1812–1814	The United States and Great Britain fight the War of 1812.
1814	Francis Scott Key writes "The Star-Spangled Banner."
1820	Congress approves the Missouri Compromise to end a slavery dispute.
1823	The Monroe Doctrine warns European nations not to interfere with free nations in the Western Hemisphere.
1825	The Erie Canal opens, providing a water route from the Atlantic Ocean to the Great Lakes.
1830	The *Tom Thumb,* the nation's first commercial steam locomotive, runs in Baltimore.
1834	Cyrus McCormick patents a reaping machine that makes it possible to harvest larger wheat crops.
1836	Massachusetts passes the first law limiting child labor in the United States.
1837	John Deere builds the first steel plow to effectively turn heavy prairie sod.
1837	Samuel F.B. Morse demonstrates the first successful telegraph in the United States.

1845	Many Americans come to believe that it is their "manifest destiny" to control all of North America.
1846	Britain cedes the southern part of the Oregon Country to the United States.
1846–1848	A dispute over territory leads to the Mexican War. Victory gives the United States vast new territory in the West.
1847	Mormon leader Brigham Young starts a Mormon settlement in the Great Salt Lake Valley in what is now Utah.
1848	The discovery of gold at Sutter's Mill in California triggers a gold rush.
1848	Delegates to the first Women's Rights Convention meet in Seneca Falls, N.Y.
1850	The Compromise of 1850 temporarily ends a national crisis over the slavery issue.
1851–1852	Harriet Beecher Stowe writes *Uncle Tom's Cabin,* a famous antislavery novel.
1854	Passage of the Kansas-Nebraska Act leads to nationwide turmoil over the slavery issue.
1859	The first commercially successful oil well is drilled near Titusville, Pa.
1860	Pony express riders begin carrying mail from St. Joseph, Mo., to the Far West.
1860	In December, South Carolina becomes the first state to secede from the Union.
1861	On February 4, South Carolina and five other states that have seceded meet in Montgomery, Ala., and declare the formation of the Confederate States of America. The Confederacy eventually consists of 11 states.

1861	On April 12, Southern troops fire on Fort Sumter in Charleston Harbor. The Civil War begins.
1862	The Homestead Act offers free land to settlers in the West.
1862	The Morrill, or Land-Grant, Act, provides land to each state; the land is to be sold to finance a college for agriculture and the mechanical arts in each state.
1863	The Emancipation Proclamation declares freedom for all slaves in Confederate-held territory.
1863	Union forces defeat Confederate troops at the Battle of Gettysburg, a turning point in the war.
1865	On April 9, General Robert E. Lee surrenders to General Ulysses S. Grant at Appomattox Court House in Virginia, ending the Civil War.
1865	On April 14, John Wilkes Booth assassinates President Abraham Lincoln.
1865–1877	The South is gradually returned to the Union during the Reconstruction era.
1866	A telegraph cable is laid across the Atlantic.
1867	The United States buys Alaska from Russia for $7.2 million.
1868	The House of Representatives impeaches President Andrew Johnson, but the Senate votes not to remove him from office.
1869	Susan B. Anthony and Elizabeth Cady Stanton found the National Woman Suffrage Association.
1869	In Promontory, Utah, the last spike is driven into the first transcontinental railway line.

The United States after the revolution extended from the Atlantic Ocean to the Mississippi River. British territory lay to the north, and Spanish territory lay to the west and south.

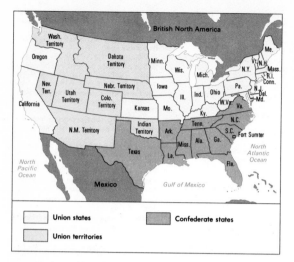

The Civil War (1861–1865) split the nation into two parts—the Confederacy and the Union. The Confederacy was made up of 11 Southern States that withdrew from the Union in 1860 and 1861.

1870–1916	More than 25 million immigrants enter the United States, more than doubling the country's population.
1876	Sioux and Cheyenne Indians defeat Lieutenant Colonel George Custer at the Little Bighorn River in Montana.
1876	Alexander Graham Bell invents telephone.
1877	Thomas Edison invents the phonograph.
1879	Edison invents the electric light.
1881	Clara Barton helps establish the American branch of the Red Cross.
1884	The people of France give the Statue of Liberty to the United States.
1884–1885	One of the world's first skyscrapers, the Home Insurance Building, is erected in Chicago.
1886	Samual Gompers founds the American Federation of Labor (AFL).
1894	Federal troops battle strikers at the Pullman plant in Chicago and elsewhere, with heavy loss of life and considerable property damage.
1896	Henry Ford builds his first automobile.
1897	The first U.S. subway is built in Boston.
1898	The United States annexes the Hawaiian Islands.
1898	The United States defeats Spain in the Spanish-American War and gains possession of Guam, Puerto Rico, and the Philippines.
1901	President McKinley is assassinated.
1903	Wilbur and Orville Wright make the first successful plane flight at Kitty Hawk, N.C.
1909	The National Association for the Advancement of Colored People (NAACP) is founded.
1909	Commander Robert E. Peary of the U.S. Navy is the first person to reach the North Pole.

1913	The 16th Amendment gives the federal government power to levy income tax.
1917–1918	The United States fights with the Allies in World War I.
1919	Police in Boston stage the first strike by public workers in the United States.
1920	The 18th Amendment goes into effect, prohibiting the manufacture and sale of alcoholic beverages.
1920	The 19th Amendment grants women the right to vote.
1920	The Senate votes against the Treaty of Versailles, which ended World War I, rejecting participation in the League of Nations.
1920	The Panama Canal opens with official proclamation.
1924	A Senate investigation uncovers the Teapot Dome scandal in the Administration of President Warren G. Harding.
1924	An Act of Congress declares Indians born in the United States are citizens.
1925	The Scopes Trial in Dayton, Tenn., upholds the right of a state to ban the teaching of evolution in public schools.
1926	Robert H. Goddard launches the first successful liquid-fuel rocket.
1927	*The Jazz Singer*, the first motion picture "talkie," appears.
1927	Charles A. Lindbergh makes the first nonstop solo flight across the Atlantic Ocean.
1929	On October 24, the stock market crashes, marking the start of the Great Depression.
1933	President Franklin D. Roosevelt begins the "New Deal" in an effort to end the depression.
1939–1940	The United States remains officially neutral as Germany invades Poland and World War II begins.
1941	On December 7, Japan attacks Pearl Harbor on the island of Oahu in Hawaii.

1941	On December 11, Germany and Italy declare war on the United States, which then declares war on them.
1942	The Manhattan Project is organized to supervise the development of an atomic bomb.
1945	Germany surrenders on May 7.
1945	The United States and 49 other nations adopt the United Nations (UN) Charter on June 26.
1945	U.S. aircraft drop atomic bombs on Hiroshima, Japan, on August 6, and on Nagasaki, Japan, on August 9.
1945	Japan signs documents of surrender on September 2.
1947	President Harry S. Truman announces the Truman Doctrine, pledging aid to nations threatened by Communism.
1949–1951	The number of television sets in American homes expands from 1 million to 10 million.
1950	Senator Joseph R. McCarthy accuses the U.S. Department of State of harboring Communists.
1950	On June 30, President Truman sends troops to South Korea, which had been invaded by North Korea.
1951	The UNIVAC is the first of a variety of electronic computers mass-produced during the 1950's.
1953	A truce ending the Korean War is signed on July 27.
1954	Senator Joseph R. McCarthy begins nationally televised hearings on possible Communist influences in the U.S. Army. The Senate later votes to condemn McCarthy for "contemptuous" conduct.
1955	Dr. Martin Luther King, Jr., begins organizing a movement to protest discrimination against blacks.
1955	The Congress of Industrial Organizations (CIO) merges with the American Federation of Labor (AFL).
1957	President Dwight D. Eisenhower sends federal troops to Little Rock, Ark., to permit black students to attend Central High School.
1957	The first full-scale U.S. nuclear power plant opens in Shippingport, Pa.
1959	Alaska and Hawaii are admitted as the 49th and 50th states.
1961	Astronaut Alan B. Shepard, Jr., becomes the first American in space.

1962	The United States learns that Russia has missile bases in Cuba; President John F. Kennedy orders a naval blockade of Cuba and forces removal of the missiles.
1962	Astronaut John Glenn becomes the first American to orbit the earth.
1963	More than 200,000 persons take part in a civil rights demonstration called the March on Washington.
1963	President John F. Kennedy is assassinated in Dallas, Tex., on November 22.
1964	Congress passes civil rights legislation guaranteeing blacks equal protection under the law.
1965	The first of a series of urban riots by blacks breaks out in the Watts section of Los Angeles.
1968	Dr. Martin Luther King, Jr. is killed in Memphis, Tenn., on April 4.
1969	Astronaut Neil Armstrong becomes the first person to set foot on the moon.
1973	A cease-fire agreement ends the Vietnam War.
1973–1974	Investigators reveal that high officials of the Nixon Administration were involved in covering up the Watergate break-in in 1972.
1974	Richard M. Nixon becomes the first American President to resign from office.
1976	The United States celebrates its bicentennial.
1978	The Senate approves a treaty that will give Panama control of the Panama Canal on Dec. 31, 1999.
1978	Egypt and Israel agree to a framework for peace as a result of talks mediated by President Jimmy Carter at Camp David, Md.
1979	The United States and China establish full diplomatic relations after a break of nearly 30 years.
1979	A failure in the cooling system of the Three Mile Island nuclear power plant near Harrisburg, Pa., causes the worst nuclear accident in U.S. history.
1979	Shortages of gasoline lead to sharp price increases and long lines of motorists waiting for service at gas stations.
1979–1981	Militant Iranians seize 53 Americans and hold them hostage for 14 months at the U.S. embassy in Teheran, Iran.
1981–1982	A recession leads to the highest rate of unemployment in the United States since the Great Depression.

Wars involving the United States

Wars	U.S. military deaths	U.S. war costs
Revolutionary War	25,324*	$101,100,000
War of 1812	2,260	$90,000,000
Mexican War	13,283	$71,400,000
Civil War		
Union Forces	364,511	$3,183,000,000
Confederate Forces	164,821	$2,000,000,000

Wars	U.S. military deaths	U.S. war costs
Spanish-American War	2,446	$283,200,000
World War I	116,516	$18,676,000,000
World War II	405,399	$263,259,000,000
Korean War	54,246	$67,386,000,000
Vietnam War	56,992	$140,857,000,000

*Estimate.

275

Universe

The universe consists of everything known to exist—all matter, light, and other forms of energy and radiation. It also includes everything that scientists, as a result of their theories, believe exists somewhere in time and space. The earth and the sun and the rest of the solar system form just a tiny part of the universe. Stars—huge, glowing balls of gas—are the basic units of the universe. The sun is a star. It is just one of more than 100 billion stars that are grouped together in an immense, circular *galaxy* (star system) called the Milky Way. The Milky Way, in turn, is just one of countless other galaxies that exist in the universe. Some galaxies appear to be alone in space. Others tend to be grouped together in *clusters.* The clusters, in turn, form *superclusters.* Superclusters are the largest known groupings in the universe. Astronomers do not know if the universe has a definite size. Most believe it is expanding constantly, and some believe it has no boundaries.

Various theories have tried to explain the creation of the universe. The one most scientists accept is called the *big bang* theory. According to this theory, the universe began 10 billion to 20 billion years ago with a huge explosion—the big bang. At first, the universe consisted chiefly of radiation, which formed a rapidly expanding sphere called the *primordial fireball.* Faint radio waves are all that remain today of the original radiation. Eventually, most of the fireball changed into matter—chiefly hydrogen—that continued to move away from the point of the explosion. The matter then broke apart in huge clumps that became galaxies. Smaller clumps within the galaxies formed the stars.

The solar system is the part of the universe that is most familiar to us. Scientists believe there are many other solar systems in the universe. Our solar system consists of the star we call the sun and the various objects that orbit around it. These orbiting objects are (1) the nine planets, including Earth, and their moons; (2) asteroids; (3) meteoroids; (4) comets; and (5) particles of dust and gas.

The four planets closest to the sun—Mercury, Venus, Earth, and Mars—are rocky and relatively small. The next four planets from the sun—Jupiter, Saturn, Uranus, and Neptune—are gaseous and relatively large. Scientists know little about Pluto, the outermost planet. Asteroids are irregularly shaped objects, similar to planets, but much smaller. They are also called *minor planets,* or *planetoids.* Most asteroids orbit in a belt between Mars and Jupiter. Meteoroids are small chunks of iron and rock. They result from collisions of asteroids, or they may be formed when comets disintegrate. Meteoroids that are falling through the earth's atmosphere are called *meteors.* Those that hit the earth's surface are called *meteorites.* Most meteors burn up before they reach the earth. Comets are balls of dust, ice, and frozen gases. When some of the brightest comets come near the sun, their long glowing tails of dust and gas create a spectacular sight in the night sky.

The tables and other text in this section give more details about the planets, the sun, the stars, and galaxies. For additional details about the planet Earth and its moon, see the "Earth" section. See the "Space" section for information about space travel and exploration of the solar system. For information about how some people use the positions of the stars and planets to predict future events, see the "Astrology" section.

Astronomy terms

Asterism is a small group of stars that are part of a larger constellation.

Astronomical unit (AU) is the average distance between the earth and the sun—about 93 million miles (150 million kilometers). This unit is used to measure distances within the solar system.

Astrophysics is the study of the chemical composition of astronomical bodies and of the physical processes that occur in space.

Big bang refers to the explosion that nearly all astronomers believe started the universe.

Binary star is a pair of stars revolving around each other.

Black hole is an object that is invisible because it has so much gravitational force that not even light can escape from it.

Celestial equator is an imaginary line through the sky directly over the earth's equator.

Celestial poles are points in the sky directly above the North Pole and the South Pole.

Constellation is a group of stars within a particular region of the sky. Ancient Greeks, Egyptians, and other peoples named the star groups after characters or animals associated with heroic stories. Astronomers divide the sky into 88 constellations for mapping purposes.

Cosmology is the study of the structure and history of the entire universe.

Declination tells how far north or south of the celestial equator a place is in the sky. Declination is measured in degrees.

Eclipsing binary is a binary that revolves in such an orbit that one star periodically blocks the other's light.

Ecliptic refers to the apparent yearly path of the sun through the sky with respect to the stars.

Giants and **supergiants** are stars that are larger and brighter than main sequence (common) stars.

Hertzsprung-Russell diagram is a graph that shows the relationship between the absolute magnitude and spectral class of stars.

Light-Year is the distance light travels in one year—about 5.88 trillion miles (9.46 trillion kilometers). Astronomers use this unit to measure distances outside the solar system.

Magnitude is a measurement of the brightness of an astronomical object. *Apparent magnitude* is an object's brightness as seen from the earth. *Absolute magnitude* is a measure of how bright an object would be if it were 32.6 light-years from the earth.

Main sequence, a band of points on the Hertzsprung-Russell diagram, represents the most common kinds of stars.

Nebula means a cloud of gas and dust among the stars.

Neutron star is a small, extremely dense star composed of tightly packed neutrons.

Nova is a star that explodes, becomes thousands of times brighter, and then becomes dim again.

Proper motion is the change in a star's position among other stars.

Pulsar is a neutron star that sends forth regular bursts of radio waves.

Pulsating variable is a star that changes in brightness as it expands and contracts.

Quasar is an object that looks much like a star but has a tremendous red shift. Quasars are the most distant objects yet detected in the universe. They are probably extreme types of galaxies that give off enormous amounts of energy from their central areas.

Red shift refers to a shift in the *spectrum* (color pattern) of radiation from an astronomical object toward the longer wavelengths. In the visible part of the spectrum, the longer wavelengths are red. The presence of red shift indicates that an object is moving away from the earth.

Right ascension tells how far east a place in the sky is from the point where the sun crosses the celestial equator on about March 21. Right ascension is measured in *hours*. One hour equals an angle of 15 degrees.

Spectral class identifies a star's color and surface temperature.

Supernova .is a star that explodes, becomes billions of times brighter for a few weeks, and then becomes dim again.

Variable star is a star whose brightness changes.

White dwarf is a small, white star with a large amount of material packed into an extremely small space.

The Sun

The sun is one of billions of stars in the universe. But it is more important to people than any other object in the sky. It gives off tremendous amounts of heat, light, and other forms of energy. Only about one two-billionth of the sun's energy reaches the earth. The rest is scattered in space. But all life on earth depends on the sun's warmth and light. Without the sun there would be no life on earth.

The sun at a glance

Distance from the earth: *Shortest*—about 91,400,000 miles (147,100,000 kilometers); *Greatest*—about 94,500,000 miles (152,100,000 kilometers); *Mean*—about 93 million miles (150 million kilometers). Sunlight takes about 8 minutes and 20 seconds to reach the earth, traveling at 186,282 miles (299,792 kilometers) per second.

Diameter: About 865,000 miles (1,392,000 kilometers), approximately 109 times that of the earth.

Volume: About 1,300,000 times that of the earth.

Mass: 99.8 per cent of the mass of the solar system; about 333,000 times that of the earth.

Temperature: *Surface*—about 10,000° F. (about 5500° C); *Center*—about 27,000,000° F. (about 15,000,000° C).

Age: About 4,600,000,000 years.

Rotation period: About 1 month.

Revolution period in the Milky Way: About 225 million years.

Chemical makeup: Hydrogen, about 75 per cent; helium, almost 25 per cent; at least 70 other elements make up the remaining 1 to 2 per cent.

Density: *Convection zone*—about $\frac{1}{10}$ that of water; *Radiative zone*—about equal to that of water; *Core*—about 100 times that of water.

Radiations: Heat, light, radio waves, ultraviolet rays, X rays. The sun converts about 4 million short tons (3.6 million metric tons) of its mass into energy every second.

Sun terms

Chromosphere is the middle region of the sun's atmosphere.

Convection zone is the outermost third of the sun's interior. It ends just below the sun's surface.

Core is the center of the sun, the region in which nuclear reactions produce the sun's energy.

Corona is the region of the sun's atmosphere above the chromosphere.

Disk is the part of the sun that can be seen from the earth.

Flares are bursts of light on the sun's surface. They release huge amounts of the sun's energy.

Granules are small patches of gas that make up the photosphere of the sun.

Photosphere is the visible surface of the sun, the innermost part of the sun's atmosphere.

Prominences are huge, bright arches of gas that rise from the edge of the disk and flow back into the sun.

Radiative zone is the middle third of the sun's interior.

Solar radiation is the sun's energy given off as light and heat and in other forms, including radio waves, ultraviolet rays, and X rays.

Solar wind is the expansion of gases from the sun's corona.

Spicules are streams of gas that shoot up briefly from the chromosphere.

Sunspots are dark patches on the sun's surface that appear and disappear in regular cycles. A complete sunspot cycle consists of two 11-year periods of sunspot activity.

Total solar eclipses, 1977–1992

Date	Path of total eclipse
Oct. 12, 1977	North Pacific Ocean, Venezuela
Feb. 26, 1979	Pacific Ocean, Montana, Greenland
Feb. 16, 1980	Atlantic Ocean, Africa, India, China
July 31, 1981	Black Sea, Mongolia, Pacific Ocean
June 11, 1983	Indian Ocean, Java, Fiji Islands
Nov. 22, 1984	New Guinea, New Caledonia, Pacific Ocean

Date	Path of total eclipse
Nov. 12, 1985	Pacific Ocean, Antarctica
Mar. 18, 1988	Indian Ocean, Borneo, Philippines
July 22, 1990	Finland, North Siberia, Pacific Ocean
July 11, 1991	Hawaii, Mexico, Panama, Brazil
June 30, 1992	Uruguay, Atlantic and Indian oceans

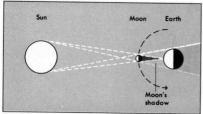

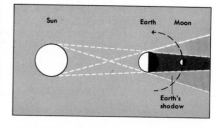

A solar eclipse occurs when the moon passes between the sun and the earth. The sun is blocked out by the moon and cannot be seen from areas on the earth that lie in the moon's shadow.

A lunar eclipse takes place when the earth is directly between the sun and the moon. The moon gradually becomes darker as it moves into the shadow of the earth.

Stars at a glance

Number: About 200 billion billion stars in the known universe.

Age: Up to 12 billion years. Most stars are between 1 million and 10 billion years old.

Composition: About 75 per cent hydrogen; 22 per cent helium; and traces of most other elements, including—in order of next highest percentages—oxygen, neon, carbon, and nitrogen.

Mass: From $\frac{1}{50}$ the mass of the sun to 50 times the mass of the sun.

Nearest star excluding the sun: Proxima Centauri, 4.3 light-years away.

Farthest stars: In galaxies billions of light-years away.

Brightest star excluding the sun: Sirius (according to apparent magnitude).

Largest stars: Have a diameter of about 1 billion miles (1.6 billion kilometers)—about 1,000 times that of the sun.

Smallest known stars: Neutron stars that have a diameter of 10 miles (16 kilometers).

Colors: From blue through white, yellow, and orange, to red, depending on the star's surface temperature.

Temperature: *Surface,* from about 50,000° F. (28,000° C) on blue stars to about 5000° F. (2800° C) on red stars; *interior,* more than 2,000,000° F. (1,100,000° C).

Radiations: Heat, light, radio waves, ultraviolet rays, X rays.

Energy source: Nuclear fusion process and other processes that change hydrogen into helium and energy.

The 20 brightest stars

Star	Distance (Light-Years)	Star	Distance (Light-Years)	Star	Distance (Light-Years)
1. Sirius	8.8	8. Procyon	11	15. Spica	300
2. Canopus	98	9. Betelgeuse	490	16. Antares	250
3. Alpha Centauri	4.3	10. Achernar	114	17. Pollux	35
4. Arcturus	36	11. Beta Centauri	290	18. Fomalhaut	23
5. Vega	26	12. Altair	16	19. Deneb	1,630
6. Capella	46	13. Alpha Crucis	390	20. Beta Crucis	490
7. Rigel	900	14. Aldebaran	68		

The Galaxies

A galaxy is a system of stars, dust, and gas held together by gravity. Scientists believe there are billions of galaxies scattered throughout the universe. Their diameters range from a few thousand to half a million *light-years*. A light-year, the distance that light travels in a year, equals about 5.88 trillion miles (9.46 trillion kilometers). Galaxies may contain anywhere from fewer than a billion to more than a trillion stars.

Scientists classify galaxies into two main types, according to shape. Most galaxies are *elliptical galaxies,* having an oval shape. A *spiral galaxy* looks like a pinwheel with bright arms curving outward from a bulging center. The remaining galaxies are irregular in shape. All galaxies rotate. Oval galaxies rotate more slowly than spirals.

The Milky Way is a spiral galaxy, about 100,000 light years in diameter, that contains our own solar system. Our solar system is a tiny speck located in one of the curving arms, about 30,000 light-years from the center of the Milky Way. The Milky Way is one of a group of galaxies called the *Local Group,* which consists of 3 spiral galaxies, 4 irregular galaxies, and about 25 elliptical galaxies. The Local Group, in turn, is part of a larger group called the *Virgo Cluster.*

Some scientists believe that invisible objects called *black holes* make up as much as a third of the material in the Milky Way. Black holes may form when a large star collapses inward from its own weight and becomes highly compressed. The greatly increased density of the collapsed star creates a tremendous gravitational force. This force is so great that even light cannot escape it, and the star becomes invisible. The gravitation around the "hole" in space may attract and hold nearby orbiting objects, including planets and comets.

Three galaxies outside the Milky Way can be seen from earth without a telescope. People in the Northern Hemisphere can see the Andromeda Nebula, a galaxy more

The stars and constellations of the Northern Hemisphere

This map shows the sky as it appears from the North Pole with Polaris, the North Star, directly overhead. Elsewhere in the Northern Hemisphere, Polaris appears lower in the sky, and only some constellations can be seen at any particular time of year. To use the map, face south and turn the map so that the current month appears at the bottom. The stars in about the bottom two-thirds of the map will be visible at some time of the night from most areas of the U.S. and Canada.

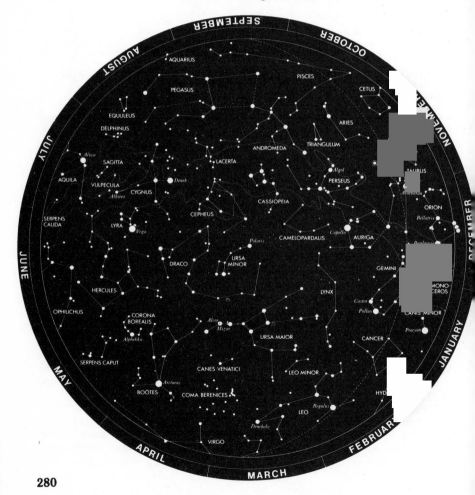

than 2 million light-years away. The Small and Large Magellanic Clouds are two galaxies that can be seen from the Southern Hemisphere. They are about 200,000 light-years away. Viewed without a telescope, these three galaxies look like small, hazy patches of light.

The stars and constellations of the Southern Hemisphere

This map shows the sky as it appears from the South Pole. There is no "South Star," but the constellation Octans is almost directly overhead. From other areas of the Southern Hemisphere, Octans appears lower in the sky and only some of the constellations are visible at any particular time of year. To use the map, an observer in the Southern Hemisphere would face north and turn the map so that the current month appears at the bottom.

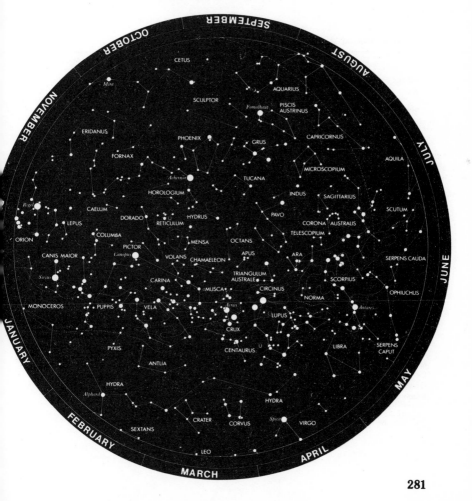

The Planets

The planets are large, dark, solid objects that orbit around the sun. Unlike the stars, the planets do not produce their own heat and light. Nearly all the heat and light on the planets comes from the sun. Some planets have one or more *satellites* (moons). Others have none.

All the planets move around the sun in the same direction, following *elliptical* (oval-shaped) orbits. The point of the orbit at which a planet is closest to the sun is called the *perihelion*. The orbit point farthest from the sun is the *aphelion*. A planet moves faster when it is close to the sun, and slower when it is far from the sun. In addition to revolving around the sun, each planet spins on its *rotational axis*, an imaginary line through its center.

The planets at a glance*

	Mercury ☿	Venus ♀	Earth ⊕	Mars ♂
Distance from the sun:				
Mean	36,000,000 mi. (57,900,000 km)	67,230,000 mi. (108,200,000 km)	92,960,000 mi. (149,600,000 km)	141,700,000 mi. (228,000,000 km)
Shortest	28,600,000 mi. (46,000,000 km)	66,800,000 mi. (107,500,000 km)	91,400,000 mi. (147,100,000 km)	128,500,000 mi. (206,800,000 km)
Greatest	43,000,000 mi. (69,200,000 km)	67,700,000 mi. (108,900,000 km)	94,500,000 mi. (152,100,000 km)	154,900,000 mi. (249,200,000 km)
Closest approach to Earth	57,000,000 mi. (91,700,000 km)	25,700,000 mi. (41,400,000 km)		48,700,000 mi. (78,390,000 km)
Length of year (Earth-days)	88	225	365	687
Average orbital speed	30 mi. per sec. (48 km per sec.)	22 mi. per sec. (35 km per sec.)	19 mi. per sec. (31 km per sec.)	15 mi. per sec. (24 km per sec.)
Diameter at equator	3,031 mi. (4,878 km)	7,520 mi. (12,100 km)	7,926 mi. (12,756 km)	4,200 mi. (6,790 km)
Rotation period	59 earth-days	243 earth-days	23 hrs. 56 min.	24 hrs. 37 min.
Tilt of axis (degrees)	about 0	175	23½	25
Temperature	−315° to 648° F. (−193° to 342° C)	850° F. (455° C)	−126.9° to 136° F. (− 88.29° to 58° C)	−191° to −24° F. (−124° to −31° C)
Atmosphere:				
Pressure	0.00000000003 lb. per sq. in. (0.000000000002 kg per cm²)	1.5 to 1,323 lbs. per sq. in. (0.1 to 93 kg per cm²)	14.7 lbs. per sq. in. (1.03 kg per cm²)	0.1 lbs. per sq. in. (0.007 kg per cm²)
Gases	Helium, hydrogen, oxygen	Carbon dioxide, nitrogen, helium, neon, argon, water vapor, sulfur, hydrogen, carbon, oxygen	Nitrogen, oxygen, carbon dioxide, water vapor	Carbon dioxide, nitrogen, argon, oxygen, carbon monoxide, neon, krypton, xenon, water vapor
Mass (Earth = 1)	0.06	0.82	1	0.11
Density (g/cm³)	5.44	5.27	5.52	3.95
Gravity (Earth = 1)	0.38	0.9	1	0.38
Number of satellites	0	0	1	2

*All figures are approximate.

The orbits of the planets

These diagrams show the orbits of the planets around the sun. Two diagrams are necessary because the orbits of the outer planets would extend off the page if they were drawn to the same scale as the orbits of the inner planets.

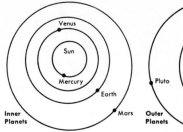

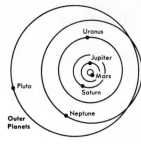

Jupiter ♃	Saturn ♄	Uranus ♅	Neptune ♆	Pluto ♇
483,700,000 mi. (778,400,000 km)	885,200,000 mi. (1,424,600,000 km)	1,781,000,000 mi. (2,866,900,000 km)	2,788,000,000 mi. (4,486,100,000 km)	3,660,000,000 mi. (5,890,000,000 km)
460,000,000 mi. (740,000,000 km)	838,000,000 mi. (1,349,000,000 km)	1,700,000,000 mi. (2,740,000,000 km)	2,754,000,000 mi. (4,432,500,000 km)	2,748,000,000 mi. (4,423,200,000 km)
507,000,000 mi. (816,000,000 km)	932,000,000 mi. (1,500,000,000 km)	1,860,000,000 mi. (2,999,000,000 km)	2,821,000,000 mi. (4,539,800,000 km)	4,571,200,000 mi. (7,356,000,000 km)
390,000,000 mi. (628,760,000 km)	762,700,000 mi. (1,277,400,000 km)	1,700,000,000 mi. (2,720,000,000 km)	2,700,000,000 mi. (4,350,000,000 km)	3,583,000,000 mi. (5,765,500,000 km)
4,333	10,759	30,685	60,188	90,700
8 mi. per sec. (13 km per sec.)	6 mi. per sec. (10 km per sec.)	4 mi. per sec. (6 km per sec.)	3 mi. per sec. (5 km per sec.)	3 mi. per sec. (5 km per sec.)
88,700 mi. (142,700 km)	74,600 mi. (120,000 km)	31,570 mi. (50,800 km)	30,200 mi. (48,600 km)	1,900 mi. (3,000 km)
9 hrs. 55 min.	10 hrs. 39 min.	16 to 28 hrs.	18 to 20 hrs.	6 earth-days
3	27	98	29	90
−236° F. (−149° C)	−285° F. (−176° C)	−357° F. (−216° C)	−360° F. (−218° C)	About −300° F. (−150° C)
2.35 to 1,470 lbs. per sq. in. (0.17 to 103 kg per cm²)	1.5 to 15 lbs. per sq. in. (0.1 to 1 kg per cm²) or higher	?	?	?
Hydrogen, helium, methane, ammonia, ethane, acetylene, phosphine, water vapor, carbon monoxide	Hydrogen, helium, methane, ammonia, ethane, phosphine (?)	Hydrogen, helium, methane	Hydrogen, helium, methane, ethane	Methane, ammonia (?), water(?)
318	95	14.6	17.2	0.0017 (?)
1.31	0.704	1.21	1.66	1.0 (?)
2.87	1.32	0.93	1.23	0.03 (?)
16	23	5	2	1

Weather

Weather around the world

The following table lists average minimum and maximum temperatures for cities around the world, as well as the number of days with rain or snow. Temperatures are given in Fahrenheit. To convert to Celsius, subtract 32 from the Fahrenheit reading and multiply by .55. See also the sections "Canada" and "United States" for general information about the climates of those countries.

City	January Max.	Min.	Precipitation days	July Max.	Min.	Precipitation days
United States and Canada						
Atlanta, Ga.	53° F.	36° F.	11	89° F.	70° F.	12
Boston, Mass.	40° F.	20° F.	12	84° F.	60° F.	9
Calgary, Alta.	26° F.	5° F.	7	76° F.	49° F.	10
Charlottetown, P.E.I.	26° F.	11° F.	15	74° F.	59° F.	10
Chicago, Ill.	33° F.	17° F.	11	75° F.	64° F.	10
Cleveland, O.	36° F.	21° F.	16	85° F.	63° F.	10
Dallas, Tex.	55° F.	36° F.	7	95° F.	76° F.	5
Denver, Colo.	42° F.	16° F.	6	87° F.	58° F.	9
Detroit, Mich.	32° F.	19° F.	13	84° F.	63° F.	9
Halifax, N.S.	32° F.	17° F.	15	74° F.	56° F.	12
Honolulu, Hawaii	77° F.	67° F.	10	82° F.	74° F.	8
Houston, Tex.	61° F.	50° F.	11	88° F.	76° F.	10
Indianapolis, Ind.	37° F.	21° F.	11	88° F.	64° F.	9
Jacksonville, Fla.	70° F.	48° F.	8	90° F.	74° F.	15
Kansas City, Mo.	39° F.	21° F.	9	91° F.	71° F.	5
Las Vegas, Nev.	55° F.	33° F.	3	105° F.	76° F.	3
Los Angeles, Calif.	65° F.	45° F.	6	83° F.	62° F.	1
Louisville, Ky.	44° F.	26° F.	12	89° F.	67° F.	11
Miami, Fla.	76° F.	58° F.	7	89° F.	75° F.	16
Milwaukee, Wis.	29° F.	15° F.	11	81° F.	61° F.	10
Minneapolis, Minn.	23° F.	6° F.	9	85° F.	63° F.	10
Montreal, Que.	23° F.	8° F.	13	79° F.	62° F.	13
Nashville, Tenn.	49° F.	31° F.	11	91° F.	69° F.	10
New Orleans, La.	64° F.	48° F.	10	90° F.	76° F.	15
New York, N.Y.	40° F.	26° F.	11	82° F.	67° F.	11
Omaha, Neb.	32° F.	14° F.	7	89° F.	68° F.	9
Ottawa, Ont.	21° F.	3° F.	14	80° F.	58° F.	11
Philadelphia, Pa.	41° F.	25° F.	11	87° F.	66° F.	9
Phoenix, Ariz.	65° F.	35° F.	3	105° F.	75° F.	4
Pittsburgh, Pa.	37° F.	21° F.	16	83° F.	62° F.	11
Portland, Ore.	44° F.	35° F.	19	79° F.	58° F.	4
Regina, Sask.	12° F.	−7° F.	11	81° F.	52° F.	10
St. Louis, Mo.	41° F.	26° F.	8	90° F.	72° F.	9
Salt Lake City, Utah	36° F.	17° F.	10	92° F.	61° F.	4
San Francisco, Calif.	56° F.	40° F.	11	69° F.	52° F.	0
Seattle, Wash.	43° F.	31° F.	19	75° F.	53° F.	5
Toronto, Ont.	31° F.	18° F.	16	81° F.	61° F.	10
Vancouver, B.C.	42° F.	33° F.	19	74° F.	55° F.	6
Washington, D.C.	44° F.	29° F.	10	87° F.	68° F.	10
Winnipeg, Man.	9° F.	−8° F.	12	80° F.	57° F.	10

City	January Max.	Min.	Precipitation days	July Max.	Min.	Precipitation days
Other places in North America						
Nassau, Bahamas	77° F.	65° F.	6	88° F.	75° F.	14
Hamilton, Bermuda	68° F.	58° F.	14	85° F.	73° F.	10
Mexico City, Mexico	66° F.	42° F.	4	74° F.	54° F.	27
San Juan, Puerto Rico	81° F.	67° F.	20	87° F.	74° F.	19
South America						
Buenos Aires, Argentina	85° F.	63° F.	7	57° F.	42° F.	8
Rio de Janeiro, Brazil	84° F.	73° F.	13	75° F.	63° F.	7
Bogotá, Colombia	67° F.	48° F.	6	64° F.	50° F.	18
Caracas, Venezuela	75° F.	56° F.	6	78° F.	61° F.	15
Europe						
Vienna, Austria	34° F.	26° F.	15	75° F.	59° F.	13
Prague, Czechoslovakia	34° F.	25° F.	13	74° F.	58° F.	13
Copenhagen, Denmark	36° F.	29° F.	17	72° F.	55° F.	14
London, England	44° F.	35° F.	17	73° F.	55° F.	13
Helsinki, Finland	27° F.	17° F.	20	71° F.	57° F.	14
Paris, France	42° F.	32° F.	17	76° F.	55° F.	12
Berlin, Germany	35° F.	26° F.	17	74° F.	55° F.	14
Athens, Greece	54° F.	42° F.	16	90° F.	72° F.	2
Budapest, Hungary	35° F.	26° F.	13	82° F.	61° F.	10
Dublin, Ireland	47° F.	35° F.	11	67° F.	51° F.	12
Rome, Italy	54° F.	39° F.	8	88° F.	64° F.	1
Amsterdam, The Netherlands	40° F.	34° F.	19	69° F.	59° F.	14
Oslo, Norway	30° F.	20° F.	15	73° F.	56° F.	15
Warsaw, Poland	30° F.	21° F.	15	75° F.	56° F.	16
Lisbon, Portugal	56° F.	46° F.	15	79° F.	63° F.	2
Moscow, Russia	21° F.	9° F.	18	76° F.	55° F.	15
Madrid, Spain	47° F.	33° F.	8	87° F.	62° F.	2
Stockholm, Sweden	31° F.	23° F.	16	70° F.	55° F.	13
Bern, Switzerland	35° F.	26° F.	11	74° F.	56° F.	13
Istanbul, Turkey	45° F.	36° F.	18	81° F.	65° F.	4
Africa						
Cairo, Egypt	65° F.	47° F.	1	96° F.	70° F.	0
Nairobi, Kenya	77° F.	54° F.	5	69° F.	51° F.	6
Casablanca, Morocco	63° F.	44° F.	8	79° F.	64° F.	0
Lagos, Nigeria	88° F.	74° F.	2	83° F.	74° F.	16
Asia						
Hong Kong	64° F.	56° F.	4	87° F.	78° F.	17
New Delhi, India	71° F.	43° F.	2	95° F.	80° F.	8
Teheran, Iran	45° F.	27° F.	4	99° F.	72° F.	1
Jerusalem, Israel	55° F.	41° F.	9	87° F.	63° F.	0
Manila, Philippines	86° F.	69° F.	6	88° F.	75° F.	24
Tokyo, Japan	47° F.	29° F.	5	83° F.	70° F.	10
Other areas						
Sydney, Australia	78° F.	65° F.	14	60° F.	46° F.	12
Wellington, New Zealand	69° F.	56° F.	10	53° F.	42° F.	18

Weather extremes around the world

Highest temperature recorded was 136.4° F. (58.0° C) at Al Aziziyah, Libya, on Sept. 13, 1922. The highest temperature recorded in North America was 134° F. (57° C) in Death Valley, Calif., on July 10, 1913.

Lowest temperature observed on the earth's surface was −126.9° F. (−88.28° C) at Vostok, Antarctica, on Aug. 24, 1960. The record low in the United States was −79.8° F. (−62.1° C) at Prospect Creek, Alaska, on Jan. 23, 1971.

Highest air pressure at sea level was recorded at Agata, Russia, on Dec. 31, 1968, when the barometric pressure reached 32.01 inches (81.31 centimeters or 108.4 kilopascals).

Lowest air pressure at sea level was estimated at 25.87 inches (65.71 centimeters or 87.61 kilopascals), during a typhoon in the Philippine Sea on Nov. 19, 1975.

Strongest winds measured on the earth's surface were recorded at Mount Washington, N.H., on April 12, 1934. For five minutes the wind blew at 188 mph (303 kph). One gust reached 231 mph (372 kph).

Driest place on earth is Arica, Chile. In one 59-year period, the average annual rainfall was ⁴⁄₁₀₀ inch (0.76 millimeter). No rain fell in Arica for a 14-year period.

Heaviest rainfall recorded in 24 hours was 73.62 inches (186.99 centimeters) on March 15–16, 1952, at Cilaos, on the island of Reunion in the Indian Ocean. The most rain in one year was at Cherrapunji, India. From August 1860 to July 1861, 1,041.78 inches (2,646.12 centimeters) fell. The wettest place is Mount Waialeale, on the island of Kauai in Hawaii, with an average annual rainfall of 460 inches (1,168 centimeters).

Heaviest snowfall recorded in North America in 24 hours—76 inches (193 centimeters)—fell at Silver Lake, Colo., on April 14–15, 1921. The most snow recorded in North America in one winter—1,122 inches (2,850 centimeters)—fell at Rainier Paradise Ranger Station in Washington in 1971–1972.

Largest hailstone in the United States fell on Coffeyville, Kans., on Sept. 3, 1970. It measured 17½ inches (44.5 centimeters) in circumference and weighed 1 pound 11 ounces (0.77 kilogram).

Wind Chill

Wind Chill is an estimate of how cold the wind makes a person feel in cold weather. The table at right shows wind speed in miles per hour and temperature in Fahrenheit. To convert miles to kilometers, multiply by 1.6. To convert Fahrenheit to Celsius, subtract 32 from the Fahrenheit reading and multiply by 55.

Equivalent wind chill temperatures

Wind (mph) calm	Thermometer reading (°F.)								
	40	30	20	10	0	−10	−20	−30	−40
5	37	27	16	6	5	−15	−26	−36	−47
10	26	16	3	−9	−22	−34	−46	−58	−71
20	19	4	−10	−24	−39	−53	−67	−81	−95
30	13	−2	−18	−33	−49	−64	−79	−93	−109
40	11	−5	−21	−37	−53	−69	−84	−100	−115

Weights and measures

Two major systems of measurement standards are used worldwide. One is the metric system, which is used in nearly all countries, including England. People in the United States and a few other countries, however, use the *customary,* or *English,* system.

The following tables will show you how to convert from customary to metric units and from metric to customary units.

Metric conversion table

When you know:	Multiply by:	To find:	When you know:	Multiply by:	To find:
Length and distance			**Volume and capacity**		
inches	25	millimeters	**ounces (fluid)**	30	milliliters
feet	30	centimeters	**pints**	0.47	liters
yards	0.9	meters	**quarts**	0.95	liters
miles	1.6	kilometers	**gallons**	3.8	liters
millimeters	0.04	inches	**milliliters**	0.034	ounces (fluid)
centimeters	0.4	inches	**liters**	2.1	pints
meters	1.1	yards	**liters**	1.06	quarts
kilometers	0.6	miles	**liters**	0.26	gallons
Surface or area			**Weight and mass**		
square inches	6.5	square centimeters	**ounces**	28	grams
square feet	0.09	square meters	**pounds**	0.45	kilograms
square yards	0.83	square meters	**tons**	0.9	metric tons
square miles	2.6	square kilometers	**grams**	0.035	ounces
acres	0.4	hectares	**kilograms**	2.2	pounds
square centimeters	0.16	square inches	**metric tons**	1.1	tons
square meters	1.2	square yards	**Temperature**		
square kilometers	0.4	square miles	**degrees Fahrenheit**	0.55 (after subtracting 32)	degrees Celsius
hectares	2.4	acres	**degrees Celsius**	1.8 (then add 32)	degrees Fahrenheit

Length and distance

Customary		Metric	Metric		Customary
1 inch (in.)		2.54 cm	**1 nanometer (nm)**		0.00000003937 in.
1 foot (ft.)	12 in.	30.48 cm	**1 micron (μ)**	1,000 nm	0.00003937 in.
1 yard (yd.)	3 ft.	0.9144 m	**1 millimeter (mm)**	1,000 μ	0.03937 in.
1 rod (rd.)	5½ yd.	5.0292 m	**1 centimeter (cm)**	10 mm	0.3937 in.
1 furlong (fur.)	40 rd., or ⅛ mi.	201.168 m	**1 decimeter (dm)**	10 cm	3.937 in.
1 statute mile (mi.)	5,280 ft.	1.6093 km	**1 meter (m)**	10 dm	39.37 in.
1 league (statute)	3 mi.	4.8280 km	**1 dekameter (dkm)**	10 m	393.7 in.
			1 hectometer (hm)	10 dkm	328.0833 ft.
			1 kilometer (km)	10 hm	0.62137 mi.

Surface or area

Customary				Metric
1 square inch (sq. in.)			=	6.4516 cm²
1 square foot (sq. ft.)	=144	sq. in.	=	0.0929 m²
1 square yard (sq. yd.)	= 9	sq. ft.	=	0.8361 m²
1 square rod (sq. rd.)	= 30¼	sq. yd.	=	25.293 m²
1 acre	=160	sq. rd.	=	0.4047 ha
1 square mile (sq. mi.)	=640	acres	=	258.9988 ha, or 2.590 km²

Metric				Customary
1 square millimeter (mm²)			=	0.002 sq. in.
1 square centimeter (cm²)	=100 mm²		=	0.155 sq. in.
1 square decimeter (dm²)	=100 cm²		=	15.5 sq. in.
1 square meter (m²)	=100 dm²		=1,550	sq. in.
1 square dekameter (dkm²)	=100 m²		=	119.6 sq. yd.
1 square hectometer (hm²)	=100 dkm²		=	2.4711 acres
1 square kilometer (km²)	=100 hm²		=	247.105 acres, or 0.3861 sq. mi.

Metric land measurement

Metric			Customary
1 centiare (ca)		= 1,550	sq. in.
1 are (a)	= 100 ca	= 119.6	sq. yd.

Metric			Customary
1 hectare (ha)	= 100 a	=	2.4711 acres
1 square kilometer (km²)	= 100 ha	=	247.105 acres, or 0.3861 sq. mi.

Weight and mass

Avoirdupois weight

		Metric
1 grain (gr.)		0.0648 g
1 dram (dr.)	27.34375 gr.	1.7718 g
1 ounce (oz.)	16 dr.	28.3495 g
1 pound (lb.)	16 oz.	453.5924 g, or 0.4536 kg
1 hundredweight (cwt.)	100 lb.	45.3592 kg
1 short ton (s.t.)	2,000 lb.	907.18 kg, or 0.9072 M.T.

Metric weight

		Avoirdupois
1 milligram (mg)		0.0154 gr.
1 centigram (cg)	10 mg	0.1543 gr.
1 decigram (dg)	10 cg	1.5432 gr.
1 gram (g)	10 dg	15.4323 gr.
1 dekagram (dkg)	10 g	0.3527 oz.
1 hectogram (hg)	10 dkg	3.5274 oz.
1 kilogram (kg)	10 hg	2.2046 lb.
1 quintal (q)	100 kg	220.46 lb.
1 metric ton (M.T.)	10 q, or 1,000 kg	2,204.62 lb.

Volume and capacity

Volume measurement

Customary		Metric
1 cubic inch (cu. in.)		16.387 cm³
1 cubic foot (cu. ft)	1,728 cu. in.	0.0283 m³
1 cubic yard (cu. yd.)	27 cu. ft.	0.7646 m³

Metric		Customary
1 cubic millimeter (mm³)		0.00006 cu. in.
1 cubic centimeter (cm³)	1,000 mm³	0.0610 cu. in.
1 cubic decimeter (dm³)	1,000 cm³	0.0353 cu. ft.
1 cubic meter (m³)	1,000 dm³	1.3079 cu. yd.
1 cubic dekameter (dkm³)	1,000 m³	1,307.9 cu. yd.
1 cubic hectometer (hm³)	1,000 dkm³	1,307,900 cu. yd.

Metric capacity measure

Metric		Customary
1 milliliter (ml)		0.0610 cu. in.
1 centiliter (cl)	10 ml	0.6102 cu. in.
1 deciliter (dl)	10 cl	6.1025 cu. in.
1 liter (l)	10 dl	61.025 cu. in., or 1.057 liquid qt., or 0.908 dry qt.
1 dekaliter (dkl)	10 l	610.25 cu. in.
1 hectoliter (hl)	10 dkl	6,102.50 cu. in.
1 kiloliter (kl)	10 hl	35.315 cu. ft., or 264.178 gal., or 28.38 bu.

Household capacity measurement

Customary			Metric
1 teaspoon		⅙ fl. oz.	4.9 ml
1 tablespoon	3 teaspoons	½ fl. oz.	14.8 ml
1 cup	16 tablespoons	8 fl. oz.	236.6 ml
1 pint	2 cups	16 fl. oz.	473.2 ml
1 quart	2 pints	32 fl. oz.	946.4 ml
1 gallon	4 quarts	128 fl. oz.	3.785 l

Customary liquid capacity measurement

Customary			Metric
1 gill (gi.)		7.219 cu. in.	0.1183 l
1 pint (pt.)	4 gi.	28.875 cu. in.	0.4732 l
1 quart (qt.)	2 pt.	57.75 cu. in.	0.9463 l
1 gallon (gal.)	4 qt.	231 cu. in.	3.7853 l
1 barrel (liquids) (bbl.)	31.5 gal.	4.21 cu. ft.	119.24 l
1 barrel (petroleum) (bbl.)	42 gal.	5.61 cu. ft.	158.98 l

Customary dry capacity measurement

Customary			Metric
1 pint (pt.)		33.600 cu. in.	550.60 cm³
1 quart (qt.)	2 pt.	67.20 cu. in.	1,101.21 cm³
1 peck (pk.)	8 qt.	537.61 cu. in.	8,809.85 cm³
1 bushel (bu.)	4 pk.	2,150.42 cu. in.	0.035239 m³
1 barrel (bbl.)		4.08 cu. ft.	0.115627 m³

Imperial	Customary		Metric
1 imperial dry quart	1.0320 U.S. qt.	69.354 cu. in.	1,136.5 cm³
1 imperial bushel	1.032 U.S. bu.	1.284 cu. ft.	0.03636 m³

289

Wonders of the world

The practice of listing Seven Wonders of the World began in ancient times, when Greeks and Romans compiled lists of things that travelers should see. Many different lists were compiled, but they all included structures made by human beings and considered notable because of their size or some other unusual quality. Since that time, writers, explorers, and world travelers have produced lists of natural wonders, in addition to the ancient wonders. The following lists consist of the most commonly mentioned wonders in each category.

Seven wonders of the ancient world

The Pyramids of Egypt, the only ancient wonder still standing, were built about 2600 to 2500 B.C. as tombs for Egyptian kings. The ruins of about 35 pyramids remain today. The three largest are at Giza (Al Jizah), outside Cairo. The *Great Pyramid,* the largest of all, was built for King Khufu (called Cheops by the Greeks). It contains more than 2 million stone blocks averaging 2½ short tons (2.3 metric tons) each. The pyramid was originally 481 feet (147 meters) tall, and its base covers about 13 acres (5 hectares).

The Hanging Gardens of Babylon, near what is now Baghdad, Iraq, were probably built by King Nebuchadnezzar II for one of his wives. Nebuchadnezzar ruled Babylon from 605 to 562 B.C. The gardens are described as being laid out on a brick terrace about 400 feet (120 meters) square and 75 feet (23 meters) above the ground. Slaves worked in shifts to irrigate the flowers and trees in the gardens.

The Temple of Artemis at Ephesus, built about 550 B.C., was one of the largest and most complicated temples built in ancient times. The temple, dedicated to the Greek goddess Artemis, stood in the Greek city of Ephesus on the west coast of what is now Turkey. It was made entirely of marble, except for a tile-covered wooden roof. The foundation of the temple measured 377 by 180 feet (115 by 55 meters). A double row of 106 columns, about 40 feet (12 meters) high, surrounded the inner area of the temple. It was designed by the architect Chersiphron and his son, Metagenes.

The Statue of Zeus at Olympia, Greece, was constructed about 435 B.C. by the sculptor Phidias. The work featured Zeus, king of the Greek gods, seated on his throne, holding a figure of Victory in his right hand and a scepter with an eagle in his left. The body of Zeus was made of ivory and his robe and ornaments of gold.

The Mausoleum at Halicarnassus, in what is now southwestern Turkey, was a huge marble building built as a tomb for Mausolus, an official of the Persian Empire. The word *mausoleum,* meaning large tomb, comes from this building. The tomb was about 135 feet (41 meters) high, with a rectangular basement beneath a colonnade formed by 36 columns. A stepped pyramid capped the colonnade, and a statue of Mausolus in a chariot probably stood on top of the pyramid. The Greek architects Satyros and Pythios designed the tomb.

The Colossus of Rhodes was a huge bronze statue that stood near the harbor of Rhodes on the Aegean Sea. The statue, which honored the sun god Helios, stood about 120 feet (37 meters) tall, or about as high as the Statue of Liberty. The sculptor Chares worked for 12 years to build the statue in the early 200's B.C. He used stone blocks and about 7½ short tons (6.8 metric tons) of iron bars to support the hollow figure. The statue was destroyed by an earthquake soon after completion.

The Lighthouse of Alexandria, on the island of Pharos in the harbor of Alexandria, Egypt, was the world's first important lighthouse. It was designed by the Greek architect Sostratos about 270 B.C. and stood about 440 feet (134 meters) high. A fire provided the light at the top of the structure. The lighthouse guided ships into Alexandria's harbor for more than 1,000 years before being toppled by an earthquake.

Seven natural wonders of the world

Mount Everest, the world's highest mountain peak, rises in the Himalaya range on the Nepal-Tibet border. (See the table of Famous Mountains on page 83).

Victoria Falls, sighted by explorer David Livingstone in 1855 and named for Queen Victoria of England, is located on the Zambia-Zimbabwe border. (See the table of Famous Waterfalls on page 82).

Grand Canyon of the Colorado River extends 277 miles (446 kilometers) in northwestern Arizona. Parts of the canyon are 1 mile (1.6 kilometers) deep and 18 miles (29 kilometers) wide.

Great Barrier Reef, the world's largest coral formation, extends in broken chains of reefs for about 1,250 miles (2,012 kilometers) along the northeastern coast of Australia.

Caves in France and Spain have many of the finest prehistoric paintings ever found. Most of the works are realistic portrayals of animals.

Parícutin, the first volcano to form in the Western Hemisphere since 1770, appeared in a cornfield 180 miles (290 kilometers) west of Mexico City on Feb. 20, 1943, after two weeks of earthquakes. (See the table of Famous Volcanoes on page 83).

The harbor at Rio de Janeiro in Brazil ranks as one of the world's most beautiful harbors.

World

Independent countries of the world

Name	Capital	Area In sq. mi.	In km²	Population*
Afghanistan	Kabul	250,000	647,497	14,238,000
Albania	Tiranë	11,100	28,748	2,944,000
Algeria	Algiers	919,595	2,381,741	20,377,000
Andorra	Andorra	175	453	39,000
Angola	Luanda	481,354	1,246,700	7,622,000
Antigua and Barbuda	St. John's	171	442	79,000
Argentina	Buenos Aires	1,072,163	2,776,889	28,964,000
Australia	Canberra	2,966,150	7,682,300	15,150,000
Austria	Vienna	32,374	83,849	7,530,000
Bahamas	Nassau	5,380	13,935	240,000
Bahrain	Manama	240	622	414,000
Bangladesh	Dacca	55,598	143,998	91,281,000
Barbados	Bridgetown	166	431	253,000
Belgium	Brussels	11,781	30,513	9,887,000
Belize	Belmopan	8,867	22,965	158,000
Benin	Porto-Novo	43,484	112,622	3,875,000
Bhutan	Thimphu	18,147	47,000	1,390,000
Bolivia	Sucre (official); La Paz (administrative)	424,164	1,098,581	6,048,000
Botswana	Gaborone	231,805	600,372	885,000
Brazil	Brasília	3,286,487	8,511,965	127,427,000
Bulgaria	Sofia	42,823	110,912	9,049,000
Burma	Rangoon	261,218	676,552	37,670,000
Burundi	Bujumbura	10,747	27,834	4,355,000
Cambodia	Phnom Penh	69,898	181,035	9,360,000
Cameroon	Yaoundé	183,569	475,442	9,103,000
Canada	Ottawa	3,831,033	9,922,330	24,541,000
Cape Verde	Praia	1,557	4,033	342,000
Central African Republic	Bangui	240,535	622,984	2,385,000
Chad	N'Djamena	495,755	1,284,000	4,843,000
Chile	Santiago	292,258	756,945	11,675,000
China	Peking	3,678,470	9,527,200	1,025,844,000
Colombia	Bogotá	439,737	1,138,914	29,810,000
Comoros	Moroni	838	2,171	358,000
Congo	Brazzaville	132,047	342,000	1,660,000
Costa Rica	San José	19,575	50,700	2,411,000
Cuba	Havana	44,218	114,524	10,252,000
Cyprus	Nicosia	3,572	9,251	635,000
Czechoslovakia	Prague	49,370	127,869	15,682,000
Denmark	Copenhagen	16,629	43,069	5,169,000
Djibouti	Djibouti	8,494	22,000	355,000
Dominica	Roseau	290	751	80,000
Dominican Republic	Santo Domingo	18,816	48,734	5,935,000
Ecuador	Quito	109,484	283,561	9,235,000
Egypt	Cairo	386,662	1,001,449	44,697,000
El Salvador	San Salvador	8,124	21,041	5,229,000
Equatorial Guinea	Malabo	10,830	28,051	389,000
Ethiopia	Addis Ababa	471,778	1,221,900	33,552,000
Fiji	Suva	7,056	18,274	664,000
Finland	Helsinki	130,129	337,032	4,821,000

*Populations are 1983 estimates based on the latest figures
from official government and United Nations sources.

291

Name	Capital	Area In sq. mi.	In km²	Population*
France	Paris	211,208	547,026	54,360,000
Gabon	Libreville	103,347	267,667	569,000
Gambia, The	Banjul	4,361	11,295	653,000
Germany (East)	East Berlin	41,768	108,178	16,637,000
Germany (West)	Bonn	96,005	248,651	61,412,000
Ghana	Accra	92,100	238,537	12,585,000
Great Britain	London	94,249	244,104	55,705,000
Greece	Athens	50,944	131,944	9,919,000
Grenada	St. George's	133	344	115,000
Guatemala	Guatemala City	42,042	108,889	7,935,000
Guinea	Conakry	94,926	245,857	5,415,000
Guinea-Bissau	Bissau	13,948	36,125	834,000
Guyana	Georgetown	83,000	214,969	919,000
Haiti	Port-au-Prince	10,714	27,750	5,284,000
Honduras	Tegucigalpa	43,277	112,088	4,104,000
Hungary	Budapest	35,919	93,030	10,818,000
Iceland	Reykjavík	39,769	103,000	236,000
India	New Delhi	1,269,346	3,287,590	726,154,000
Indonesia	Jakarta	788,425	2,042,012	156,864,000
Iran	Teheran (Tehran)	636,296	1,648,000	40,919,000
Iraq	Baghdad	167,925	434,924	14,506,000
Ireland	Dublin	27,136	70,283	3,575,000
Israel	Jerusalem	8,019	20,770	4,152,000
Italy	Rome	116,314	301,252	57,902,000
Ivory Coast	Abidjan	124,504	322,463	9,018,000
Jamaica	Kingston	4,244	10,991	2,292,000
Japan	Tokyo	145,834	377,708	120,246,000
Jordan	Amman	37,738	97,740	2,460,000
Kenya	Nairobi	224,961	582,646	18,185,000
Kiribati	Tarawa	278	719	56,000
Korea (North)	Pyongyang	46,540	120,538	19,291,000
Korea (South)	Seoul	38,025	98,484	39,275,000
Kuwait	Kuwait	7,780	20,150	1,610,000
Laos	Vientiane	91,429	236,800	3,995,000
Lebanon	Beirut	4,015	10,400	3,404,000
Lesotho	Maseru	11,720	30,355	1,442,000
Liberia	Monrovia	43,000	111,369	2,071,000
Libya	Tripoli	679,362	1,759,540	3,226,000
Liechtenstein	Vaduz	61	157	28,000
Luxembourg	Luxembourg	998	2,586	368,000
Madagascar	Antananarivo	226,658	587,041	9,387,000
Malawi	Lilongwe	45,747	118,484	6,427,000
Malaysia	Kuala Lumpur	127,317	329,749	14,554,000
Maldives	Male	115	298	159,000
Mali	Bamako	478,767	1,240,000	7,481,000
Malta	Valletta	122	316	377,000
Mauritania	Nouakchott	397,956	1,030,700	1,775,000
Mauritius	Port Louis	790	2,045	1,003,000
Mexico	Mexico City	758,136	1,963,564	74,507,000
Monaco	Monaco	0.58	1.49	27,000
Mongolia	Ulan Bator	604,250	1,565,000	1,795,000
Morocco	Rabat	172,414	446,550	22,119,000
Mozambique	Maputo	309,496	801,590	12,910,000
Nauru	(none)	8	21	8,000

Name	Capital	Area In sq. mi.	In km²	Population*
Nepal	Kathmandu	54,362	140,797	14,955,000
Netherlands	Amsterdam	15,892	41,160	14,427,000
New Zealand	Wellington	103,883	269,057	3,136,000
Nicaragua	Managua	50,193	130,000	2,980,000
Niger	Niamey	489,191	1,267,000	5,780,000
Nigeria	Lagos	356,669	923,768	84,721,000
Norway	Oslo	125,182	324,219	4,128,000
Oman	Muscat	82,030	212,457	976,000
Pakistan	Islamabad	310,404	803,943	89,230,000
Panama	Panama City	29,762	77,082	2,013,000
Papua New Guinea	Port Moresby	178,260	461,691	3,348,000
Paraguay	Asunción	157,048	406,752	3,361,000
Peru	Lima	496,225	1,285,216	19,317,000
Philippines	Manila	115,831	300,000	58,378,000
Poland	Warsaw	120,725	312,677	36,463,000
Portugal	Lisbon	35,553	92,082	10,264,000
Qatar	Doha	4,247	11,000	242,000
Romania	Bucharest	91,699	237,500	22,874,000
Russia	Moscow	8,649,500	22,402,000	272,775,000
Rwanda	Kigali	10,169	26,338	5,450,000
St. Lucia	Castries	238	616	121,000
St. Vincent and the Grenadines	Kingstown	150	388	126,000
San Marino	San Marino	24	61	22,000
Sao Tomé and Príncipe	Sao Tomé	372	964	88,000
Saudi Arabia	Riyadh	830,000	2,149,690	9,169,000
Senegal	Dakar	75,750	196,192	6,114,000
Seychelles	Victoria	171	443	69,000
Sierra Leone	Freetown	27,699	71,740	4,071,000
Singapore	Singapore	238	616	2,577,000
Solomon Islands	Honiara	10,983	28,446	241,000
Somalia	Mogadiscio	246,201	637,657	3,914,000
South Africa	Cape Town; Pretoria; Bloemfontein	471,445	1,221,037	31,444,000
Spain	Madrid	194,897	504,782	38,679,000
Sri Lanka	Colombo	25,332	65,610	15,640,000
Sudan	Khartoum	967,500	2,505,813	20,246,000
Suriname	Paramaribo	63,037	163,265	361,000
Swaziland	Mbabane; Lobamba	6,704	17,363	603,000
Sweden	Stockholm	173,732	449,964	8,370,000
Switzerland	Bern	15,941	41,288	6,348,000
Syria	Damascus	71,498	185,180	9,869,000
Taiwan	Taipei	13,885	35,961	18,783,000
Tanzania	Dar es Salaam	364,900	945,087	20,629,000
Thailand	Bangkok	198,457	514,000	50,027,000
Togo	Lomé	21,622	56,000	2,793,000
Tonga	Nukualofa	270	699	98,000
Trinidad and Tobago	Port-of-Spain	1,981	5,130	1,232,000
Tunisia	Tunis	63,170	163,610	7,083,000
Turkey	Ankara	301,382	780,576	48,410,000
Tuvalu	Funafuti	10	26	7,000
Uganda	Kampala	91,134	236,036	15,117,000
United Arab Emirates	Abu Dhabi	32,278	83,600	1,256,000
United States	Washington, D.C.	3,618,465	9,371,781	233,450,000
Upper Volta	Ouagadougou	105,869	274,200	7,439,000
Uruguay	Montevideo	68,037	176,215	2,952,000

*Populations are 1983 estimates based on the latest figures from official government and United Nations sources.

Name	Capital	Area In sq. mi.	In km²	Population*
Vanuatu	Port-Vila	5,700	14,763	125,000
Vatican City	(none)	0.17	0.44	1,000
Venezuela	Caracas	352,145	912,050	15,203,000
Vietnam	Hanoi	127,242	329,556	57,990,000
Western Samoa	Apia	1,097	2,842	160,000
Yemen (Aden)	Aden	128,560	332,968	2,083,000
Yemen (Sana)	Sana	75,290	195,000	6,270,000
Yugoslavia	Belgrade	98,766	255,804	23,129,000
Zaire	Kinshasa	905,568	2,345,409	30,824,000
Zambia	Lusaka	290,586	752,614	6,243,000
Zimbabwe	Harare (Salisbury)	150,804	390,580	7,926,000

*Populations are 1983 estimates based on the latest figures
from official government and United Nations sources.

Other political units of the world*

Name	Area In sq. mi.	In km²	Population†
American Samoa (United States)	76	197	34,000
Andaman and Nicobar Islands (India)	3,202	8,293	115,133
Anguilla (Great Britain)	35	91	6,500
Azores (Portugal)	905	2,344	273,400
Bermuda (Great Britain)	21	54	63,000
British Indian Ocean Territory (Great Britain)	23	60	2,000
Brunei (Great Britain)	2,226	5,765	277,000
Canary Islands (Spain)	2,808	7,273	1,487,000
Cayman Islands (Great Britain)	100	259	19,000
Channel Islands (Great Britain)	75	195	133,000
Cook Islands (New Zealand)	91	236	20,000
Easter Island (Chile)	63	163	2,600
Faeroe Islands (Denmark)	540	1,399	41,000
Falkland Islands (Great Britain)	4,700	12,173	2,000
French Guiana	35,135	91,000	67,000
French Polynesia	1,544	4,000	142,000
Gaza Strip (Egypt)‡	146	378	467,000
Gibraltar (Great Britain)	2.3	6	35,000
Greenland (Denmark)	840,004	2,175,600	52,000
Guadeloupe (France)	687	1,779	373,000
Guam (United States)	212	549	113,000
Hong Kong (Great Britain)	1,126	2,916	5,315,000
Macao (Portugal)	6	16	286,000
Madeira Islands (Portugal)	308	797	245,000
Man, Isle of (Great Britain)	227	588	73,000
Martinique (France)	425	1,102	381,000
Midway Island (United States)	2	5	2,220
Montserrat (Great Britain)	38	98	12,000
Namibia, or South West Africa (South Africa)	318,261	824,292	1,097,000
Netherlands Antilles	383	993	256,000
New Caledonia (France)	7,376	19,103	148,000
Niue Island (New Zealand)	100	259	4,000
Norfolk Islands (Australia)	14	36	2,000

*The political units listed are administered by the country shown in parentheses.
†Populations are 1983 and earlier estimates based on the latest figures from official government and United Nations sources.
‡Claimed by Israel.

Name	Area		Population†
	In sq. mi.	In km²	
Pacific Islands Trust Territory			
of the (United States)	717	1,857	119,440
Caroline Islands	463	1,199	75,394
Mariana Islands	184	477	14,335
Marshall Islands	70	181	29,511
Pitcairn Islands Group (Great Britain)	2	5	63
Puerto Rico (United States)	3,435	8,897	3,188,000
Reunion (France)	969	2,510	539,000
St. Christopher Nevis (Great Britain)	101	262	41,000
Saint Helena (Great Britain)	162	419	6,300
Saint Pierre and Miquelon (France)	93	242	5,000
South West Africa (South Africa), see Namibia			
Takelau (New Zealand)	4	10	2,000
Turks and Caicos Islands (Great Britain)	166	430	7,000
Virgin Islands (Great Britain)	59	153	14,000
Virgin Islands (United States)	133	344	104,000
Wake Island (United States)	3	8	1,647
Wallis and Futuna Islands (France)	106	275	9,000
Western Sahara§	102,703	66,000	165,000

†Populations are 1983 and earlier estimates based on the latest figures from official government and United Nations sources.
§Claimed by Morocco.

25 largest countries of the world in area

Rank	Country	Area	
		In sq. mi.	In km²
1.	**Russia**	8,649,500	22,402,000
2.	**Canada**	3,831,033	9,922,330
3.	**China**	3,678,470	9,527,200
4.	**United States**	3,618,465	9,371,781
5.	**Brazil**	3,286,487	8,511,965
6.	**Australia**	2,966,150	7,682,300
7.	**India**	1,269,346	3,287,590
8.	**Argentina**	1,072,163	2,776,889
9.	**Sudan**	967,500	2,505,813
10.	**Algeria**	919,595	2,381,741
11.	**Zaire**	905,568	2,345,409
12.	**Saudi Arabia**	830,000	2,149,690
13.	**Indonesia**	788,425	2,042,012
14.	**Mexico**	761,607	1,972,552
15.	**Libya**	679,362	1,759,540
16.	**Iran**	636,296	1,648,000
17.	**Mongolia**	604,250	1,565,000
18.	**Peru**	496,225	1,285,216
19.	**Chad**	495,755	1,284,000
20.	**Niger**	489,191	1,267,000
21.	**Angola**	481,354	1,246,700
22.	**Mali**	478,767	1,240,000
23.	**Ethiopia**	471,778	1,221,900
24.	**South Africa**	471,445	1,221,037
25.	**Colombia**	439,737	1,138,914

25 largest countries of the world in population

Rank	Country	Population
1.	**China**	1,025,844,000
2.	**India**	726,154,000
3.	**Russia**	272,775,000
4.	**United States**	233,450,000
5.	**Indonesia**	156,864,000
6.	**Brazil**	127,427,000
7.	**Japan**	120,246,000
8.	**Bangladesh**	91,281,000
9.	**Pakistan**	89,230,000
10.	**Nigeria**	84,721,000
11.	**Mexico**	74,507,000
12.	**West Germany**	61,412,000
13.	**Philippines**	58,378,000
14.	**Vietnam**	57,990,000
15.	**Italy**	57,902,000
16.	**Great Britain**	55,705,000
17.	**France**	54,360,000
18.	**Thailand**	50,027,000
19.	**Turkey**	48,410,000
20.	**Egypt**	44,697,000
21.	**Iran**	40,919,000
22.	**South Korea**	39,275,000
23.	**Spain**	38,679,000
24.	**Burma**	37,670,000
25.	**Poland**	36,463,000

50 Largest cities in the world in population

1. Shanghai 10,820,000
2. Mexico City 9,373,353
3. Tokyo 8,349,209
4. Moscow 7,831,000
5. Peking 7,570,000
6. New York City 7,071,030
7. São Paulo 7,033,529
8. Seoul 6,889,502
9. London 6,696,008
10. Cairo 6,133,000
11. Bombay 5,970,575
12. Jakarta 5,490,000
13. Hong Kong 5,315,000
14. Bangkok 5,153,902
15. Rio de Janeiro 5,093,232
16. Teheran 4,716,000
17. Tientsin 4,280,000
18. Leningrad 4,073,000
19. Santiago 3,899,495
20. Karachi 3,515,402
21. Ho Chi Minh City 3,460,500
22. Delhi 3,287,883
23. Madrid 3,201,234
24. Calcutta 3,148,746
25. Berlin (East and West) 3,038,689
26. Chicago 3,005,072
27. Baghdad 2,969,000
28. Los Angeles 2,966,763
29. Lima 2,941,473
30. Buenos Aires 2,908,001
31. Sydney 2,874,415
32. Rome 2,868,248
33. Bogotá 2,850,000
34. Yokohama 2,773,822
35. Osaka 2,648,158
36. Melbourne 2,578,527
37. Istanbul 2,547,364
38. Pyongyang 2,500,000
39. Madras 2,469,449
40. Pusan 2,453,173
41. Shen-yang 2,411,000
42. Alexandria 2,320,000
43. Singapore 2,308,200
44. Paris 2,299,830
45. Taipei 2,200,427
46. Lahore 2,169,742
47. Wu-han 2,146,000
48. Kiev 2,144,000
49. Ch'ung-ch'ing 2,121,000
50. Budapest 2,093,187

50 Largest metropolitan areas in the world in population

1. Mexico City 14,445,000
2. São Paulo 12,588,439
3. Tokyo 11,615,069
4. Shanghai 10,820,000
5. Buenos Aires 9,927,404
6. New York City 9,119,737
7. Rio de Janeiro 9,018,637
8. Paris 8,549,898
9. Moscow 8,011,000
10. Peking 7,570,000
11. Los Angeles-Long Beach 7,477,657
12. Chicago 7,102,328
13. Calcutta 7,031,382
14. Seoul 6,889,502
15. London 6,696,008
16. Cairo 6,133,000
17. Bombay 5,970,575
18. Jakarta 5,490,000
19. Hong Kong 5,315,000
20. Bangkok 5,153,902
21. Manila 4,970,006
22. Philadelphia 4,716,818
23. Teheran 4,716,000
24. Leningrad 4,588,000
25. Detroit 4,352,762
26. Tientsin 4,280,000
27. Santiago 3,899,495
28. Delhi 3,647,023
29. Karachi 3,515,402
30. Ho Chi Minh City 3,460,500
31. Istanbul 3,432,234
32. Lima 3,254,789
33. San Francisco-Oakland 3,252,721
34. Madrid 3,201,234
35. Madras 3,169,930
36. Bogotá 3,143,200
37. Washington, D.C. 3,060,240
38. Berlin (East and West) 3,038,689
39. Dallas-Fort Worth 2,974,878
40. Baghdad 2,969,000
41. Houston 2,905,350
42. Sydney 2,874,415
43. Rome 2,868,248
44. Guadalajara 2,856,000
45. Toronto 2,803,101
46. Montreal 2,802,485
47. Yokohama 2,773,822
48. Boston 2,763,357
49. Caracas 2,755,000
50. Osaka 2,648,158

Major languages

There are an estimated 3,000 spoken languages in the world. This table lists examples of the ones that are most widely spoken.

Language family	Number of speakers	Main languages
Indo-European	1,900,000,000	*Germanic or Teutonic branch:* English, German, Dutch-Flemish, Danish, Icelandic, Norwegian, Swedish
		Romance or Latin-Romance branch: French, Italian, Portuguese, Romanian, Spanish
		Balto-Slavic branch: Russian, Ukrainian, Polish, Czech, Slovak, Serbo-Croatian, Slovenian, Bulgarian, Latvian, Lithuanian
		Indo-Iranian branch: Hindustani, Bengali, Persian, Pashto
		Greek
		Celtic branch: Irish (Gaelic), Scots Gaelic, Welsh, Breton
		Albanian
		Armenian
Sino-Tibetan	970,000,000	Chinese, Thai, Tibetan, Cantonese, Burmese, Lao
Black African	290,000,000	*Nilo-Saharan branch:* Dinka, Kanuri, Masai, Nuer
		Niger-Kordofanian branch: Swahili, Fula, Yoruba, Ibo, Akan, Kongo, Ganda, Kikuyu, Rundi, Sotho, Zulu
		Khoisan branch: Hottentot, Bushman
Malayo-Polynesian	215,000,000	Indonesian, Malay, Pilipino, Javanese, Tagalog, Malagasy, Hawaiian
Dravidian	175,000,000	Tamil, Telugu
Afro-Asian	170,000,000	Arabic, Hebrew, Berber, Amharic, Somali, Galla, Hausa
Japanese and Korean	165,000,000	Japanese, Korean, Ainu
Uralic and Altaic	115,000,000	Finnish, Hungarian (Magyar), Turkish, Mongol, Manchu, Uzbek
Mon-Khmer	70,000,000	Cambodian, Vietnamese

Major languages (by percentage)

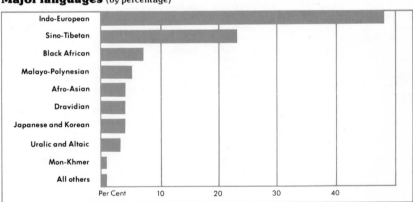

World economy

The nations of the world vary greatly in their wealth and level of economic development. One tool that economists use to measure a nation's economic performance is *gross national product (GNP)*. Gross national product is the value of all goods and services produced by a country during a given period. GNP figures do not tell everything about a nation's economy. For example, they do not tell about the well-being of individuals or families. The GNP *per capita* (for each person) is determined by dividing the GNP figure by the number of people in the country. The GNP per capita is an average measurement, and does not tell who, specifically, uses various goods and services. For example, it does not show how much of the GNP goes to the poorest 20 per cent of the population or the richest 20 per cent. Nor does it tell anything about the quality of the goods and services being produced.

Economists classify the United States, Canada, Japan, and most European countries among the so-called *developed,* or *industrial* nations of the world. Most other nations, including a majority of the countries of Africa, Asia, and Latin America, are called *developing nations.* In 1980, the United States had a per capita GNP of $11,536. The developed countries of Western Europe had a combined average annual per capita GNP of about $9,650. In contrast, the developing nations of the world had an average per capita GNP of $846.

Leading countries in total gross national product

Total value of goods and services produced in 1980

United States	$2,626,100,000,000
Russia	$1,280,146,000,000
Japan	$955,308,000,000
West Germany	$642,801,000,000
China	$591,653,000,000
France	$504,914,000,000
Italy	$303,455,000,000
Great Britain	$297,562,000,000
Brazil	$251,399,000,000
Canada	$236,889,000,000

Sources: U.S. Department of Commerce; *The Planetary Product in 1980,* Herbert Block.

Leading countries in gross national product per person

Value of goods and services produced per person in 1980

Qatar	$25,000
Kuwait	$13,000
Saudi Arabia	$12,000
United States	$11,536
Sweden	$11,000
West Germany	$10,500
United Arab Emirates	$10,400
Switzerland	$10,300
Norway	$10,200
Canada	$9,875

Sources: U.S. Department of Commerce; *The Planetary Product in 1980,* Herbert Block.

World history

The study of world history generally begins around 3000 B.C., when writing was developed and people had a way to record their experiences. The period of time before writing is called Prehistory. The information that follows gives a general description of the major periods of world history. For information about prehistoric times, see the "Human Being" section. For information about specific events, see the tables "Important Dates in World History" and "Famous Wars, Battles, and Treaties." See the "People" section for biographical information about many important figures in world history.

Ancient history (3000 B.C.-A.D. 476)

The world's first important civilizations developed in four river valleys known as "cradles of civilization." These were (1) the land between the Tigris and Euphrates rivers in the Middle East, (2) the Nile River Valley in Egypt, (3) the Indus River Valley in what is now Pakistan, and (4) the Huang Ho (Yellow River) Valley in China.

The Tigris-Euphrates Valley gave rise to a number of ancient civilizations, including those of the Sumerians, Babylonians, Hebrews, Phoenicians, Assyrians, Chaldeans, and Persians. The Sumerians had an advanced civilization of independent city-states as early as 3000 B.C. They invented a form of writing called *cuneiform* and devised a system of laws to govern weights, measures, and trade. The Babylonian ruler Hammurabi organized a code of laws that established what was probably the world's first social order based on the rights of the individual. The Hebrews made a major contribution to world religion with their idea of worshipping one God. The Phoenicians developed an alphabet that was the basis of the Greek alphabet and later Western alphabets. The Assyrians decorated their buildings with wall paintings, colored bricks, and carved stone slabs. They eventually formed the first empire in the Middle East. The Chaldeans built the magnificent Hanging Gardens of Babylon (see "Wonders of the World"). They also made important discoveries in astronomy and probably invented astrology as well (see "Astrology"). The Persians developed a just, efficient system of government to rule over a vast empire for more than 200 years.

The Nile Valley supported the civilization of ancient Egypt for more than 2,000 years. The Egyptians developed the world's first national government, and their religion was one of the first to emphasize a life after death. The Egyptians devised engineering techniques that enabled them to build huge pyramids as tombs for their *pharaohs* (rulers). Egyptian artists and craftsmen created exquisite works to decorate tombs, palaces, and temples. The Egyptians developed a kind of writing called *hieroglyphics* that used picture symbols. They were among the first peoples to use a kind of paper instead of clay tablets for writing. In addition, the Egyptians made important contributions to the fields of astronomy, medicine, surveying, architecture, and geometry.

In the Indus Valley, an advanced Bronze Age culture developed around the cities of Harappa and Mohenjo-daro. These cities had buildings made of brick, efficient sewerage systems, and streets laid out in rectangular patterns. Artists and craftsmen of the Indus civilization made metal utensils, and created decorated furniture, jewelry, and sculptures. The Indus people devised their own form of writing.

They probably traded with people of the Middle East, central Asia, southern India, and Persia.

In the Huang Ho Valley, the earliest records date from the Shang dynasty (1766–1122 B.C.), though civilizations probably developed at an earlier date. Under the Shang, the Chinese had a well organized government and a form of written language. They developed many artistic skills, including bronze casting. Art and learning flourished during the Chou dynasty, which arose in the Yangtze Valley and succeeded the Shang. During this period, such great scholars as Confucius and Lao Tzu developed their philosophies.

Civilization and its accomplishments eventually spread from the four cradle lands to other parts of the world. In Europe, the Greeks and Romans developed ideas and skills that formed the basis of later Western civilization. In Asia, the Indians and Chinese developed lasting forms of art, government, and philosophy.

The ancient Greeks were the first people to develop a democratic way of life, based on the idea that every citizen should take an active part in government. Their contributions to the arts and sciences included the monumental works of such persons as the poet Homer; the dramatists Aeschuylus, Sophocles, and Euripedes; the historian Herodotus; the physician Hippocrates; and the philosophers Socrates, Plato, and Aristotle. Greek culture reached great heights during the Hellenic Age, from 750 to 338 B.C. The Golden Age of Greece, from 461 to 431 B.C., was a particularly productive period for architecture, literature, and art. During the Hellenistic Age, from about 323 to 146 B.C., Greek culture spread and combined with other cultures. Alexandria, Egypt, became a center of scientific learning.

The Roman Empire, which reached its greatest extent in A.D. 117, adopted many aspects of Greek culture. The ancient Romans built well-planned cities, with many public buildings and monuments. They constructed huge aqueducts and bridges, and vast networks of roads. Famous Roman writers included Cicero, Julius Caesar, Livy, Ovid, Tacitus, and Virgil. Latin, the Roman language, became the foundation of modern Romance languages, such as Italian and French. Roman political and legal traditions influenced the governing systems of many modern-day nations. Christianity eventually became the official religion of the empire, spreading to many parts of the world and becoming a major force in Western civilization.

The ancient Indians achieved many important advances during the years of the Mauryan and Gupta empires. Hinduism and Buddhism developed during the Mauryan period, from about 321 to 185 B.C. During the Gupta dynasty, from A.D. 320 to about 500, Indian mathematicians invented the number system that was later adopted by the Arabs and became known as the "Arabic" system. The Indians invented the decimal system, with a symbol for zero. In addition, many fine paintings and sculptures and masterpieces of Sanskrit literature appeared during this period.

The ancient Chinese constructed the Great Wall of China during the Ch'in dynasty (221–206 B.C.), and China became a unified nation. During the 400 years of the Han dynasty that followed, Confucianism developed further, and Chinese scholars compiled one of the world's first dictionaries. Chinese inventions of this period included paper and the breast-strap harness, which allowed animals to pull heavy loads without choking.

300

The Middle Ages (A.D. 476-mid-1400's)

In Western Europe, the first part of the Middle Ages is generally referred to as the Dark Ages, a time when barbarian tribes roamed the land of the West Roman Empire they had conquered. The Roman Catholic Church became the chief civilizing force, exerting political and social influence, as well as religious influence. The church monasteries preserved much of the knowledge that had been accumulated during the Greek and Roman eras. Under a political system called *feudalism,* most of the land was owned by the church or powerful nobles. Most of the people worked as farmers, living under the protection of the landowners.

Palestine, the birthplace of Christianity, came under Muslim control during the Middle Ages. The Christian Europeans launched a series of military expeditions called the Crusades to win back the Holy Land. The Crusades brought Europe into contact with the advanced Muslim civilization, and they spurred an interest in trade with distant lands. Manufacturing and craftsmanship revived, and towns developed. Small feudal units merged into larger political units, which eventually became nations, such as England and France.

Widespread commerce brought wealth to the cities of Western Europe. An interest in learning led to the creation of many universities, where European scholars made important advances in the sciences, based largely on the earlier achievements of the Muslims. Medieval literature produced poems, songs, and ballads in popular languages, such as French and Italian. Dante's *Divine Comedy* and Chaucer's *Canterbury Tales* rank as masterpieces of medieval literature. In architecture, towering Gothic cathedrals came to symbolize the power of Christianity as a moving force in Western Europe during the Middle Ages.

The Byzantine Empire, which grew out of the East Roman Empire, had its capital in Constantinople (now Istanbul). The empire, which reached its greatest size in the A.D. 500's, became the chief civilizing force among the peoples of southeastern Europe. As in Western Europe, Christianity was a major element of the Byzantine Empire. In time, the Byzantine Church split from the Roman Catholic Church and later became known as the Eastern Orthodox Church. The Byzantine Empire followed Roman traditions of justice and a strong central government. In the arts, Greek art forms were combined with Oriental influences. Byzantine traders kept the empire in contact with central Asia and Russia.

The Muslim Empire of the Middle East became one of the most advanced cultures of the Middle Ages. Its Arab founders established a new religion, Islam, and converted millions of people. At its height, from about 750 to the 1200's, the Muslim Empire extended from the Atlantic Ocean to the borders of India. Within this vast expanse, the cultures of the Middle East, Egypt, India, and China came together. In addition, the Muslims preserved the works of Aristotle and other Greek scholars. Muslim scholars made major contributions to the fields of algebra, medicine, astronomy, mathematics, geography, and literature. The intricate designs of Islamic art decorated *mosques* (Muslim houses of worship) and were used in paintings, rugs, cloth, and other items.

In China during the Middle Ages, the period of the T'ang dynasty (618–907) became known as the golden age of Chinese civilization. During this period, the Chinese invented printing, and Chinese literature and other arts flourished. During the Sung dynasty (960–1279), the Chinese invented gunpowder, the magnetic compass, and movable type. Under both dynasties, scholars produced dictionaries, encyclopedias, and histories. In 1279, the great Mongol ruler Kublai Khan conquered China and eventually established the largest land empire in history. He encouraged contact with other civilized peoples and sponsored many of the travels of Marco Polo. The empire crumbled soon after his death, however, and the Chinese regained control of their country.

In Japan, Buddhist monks from China and Korea helped develop civilized ways of life during the Middle Ages. The Japanese adopted Chinese writing and other cultural elements. Like the Chinese, the Japanese were ruled by an emperor; but in Japan, the emperor was considered godlike. The Japanese developed great respect for soldiers and strict military codes of behavior. During Japan's Golden Age, from the late 700's to about 1150, Kyoto, the national capital, became one of the largest cities of the world. At this time, noblemen called *shoguns* assumed great political power, though they ruled in the name of the emperor.

In Africa, a number of powerful kingdoms and city-states developed. These included the kingdoms of Hafsid, Marinid, and Ziyanid in the northwest; Ashanti, Benin, Ghana, Mali, Mossi, Oyo, and the Hausa city-states in the west; Kilwa, Mogadiscio, Mombasa, and Sofala along the east coast; Kongo in the central region; and Zimbabwe in the south.

In North and South America during the Middle Ages, most of the people—called Indians—followed primitive ways of life. But some groups developed highly civilized societies. The Maya of Central America, for example, developed a culture that included a calendar, a system of writing, and a system of mathematics. They built huge temples similar to the pyramids of Egypt. The Aztec and Toltec peoples developed civilizations in what is now Mexico. The Inca controlled a huge empire in what is now Peru.

Modern times (1453-the present)

During the early period of Modern Times—up through the 1800's—major cultural advances occurred in Western Europe, and Western civilization came to dominate much of the rest of the world. The cultural advances began during a 300-year period called the *Renaissance,* which had actually begun in Italy during the 1300's. The idea of individual freedom was a Renaissance ideal that influenced developments in the arts and sciences. Many world masterpieces of architecture, literature, painting, and sculpture were created. Famous Renaissance artists and writers included Cervantes, Hans Holbein, Leonardo da Vinci, Michelangelo, Raphael, and William Shakespeare. In science, the discoveries of Nicolaus Copernicus and Galileo revolutionized physics and astronomy. The *humanist* philosophy, developed by Saint Thomas More, Desiderius Erasmus, and others, emphasized the importance of humanity and enjoyment of life. In religion, a movement called the *Reformation* led to the establishment of Protestant churches in England, Germany, and other countries.

The Renaissance spurred the great age of European discovery and exploration, as Christopher Columbus, Vasco da Gama, Ferdinand Magellan, and others set out to find the best trade routes to distant lands. Commerce flourished, and joint-stock companies—similar to present-day corporations—were formed. Fabrics, porcelains, foods, and other items brought from distant lands enabled Europeans to enjoy a higher standard of living than ever before. Overseas colonies were established, and a slave trade developed with Africa.

During the 1600's and 1700's, an intellectual revolution called the *Age of Reason* swept over Europe. The Age of Reason led to the development of the scientific method, which emphasized experimentation and the use of reason to study basic natural laws. Major discoveries in science were made by Isaac Newton, Benjamin Franklin, Robert Boyle, Joseph Priestley, René Descartes, William Harvey, and others. Scholars also used the principles of the scientific method to study problems in such fields as economics, government, education, and religion. The writings of Voltaire, Montesquieu, Jean Jacques Rousseau, and others attacked injustices of the times and expressed faith in people's ability to solve problems using reason as their primary tool. The Age of Reason also brought great achievements in the arts, through the works of such masters as Henry Fielding, Alexander Pope, Rembrandt, Johann Sebastian Bach, Joseph Haydn, and Wolfgang Amadeus Mozart.

Two powerful political forces—democracy and nationalism—shaped political events during the 1600's and 1700's. Revolutions in England, America, and France ended absolute rule by kings. The writings of John Locke helped spread the idea that people had a right to revolt against a bad government. In England, a series of struggles ended in 1689, when Parliament adopted a Bill of Rights. The American Revolution led to the establishment of the United States of America, and the French Revolution ended the monarchy in France. During the 1800's, the French leader Napoleon Bonaparte conquered many European nations and overthrew their monarchs. After his eventual defeat, European political leaders restored monarchies in various countries. But democratic movements regained strength and eventually led to the establishment of constitutions and some forms of democracy in many European nations. New nations such as Italy and Germany were created by the union of smaller states. In Latin America, colonial wars of independence led to the creation of Argentina, Brazil, Chile, Mexico, and other countries.

Another kind of revolution—the Industrial Revolution—brought about dramatic social and economic changes in the 1700's and 1800's. Factories were built, and more and more people left the countryside to work in cities. Middle class business people gained considerable control and influence over national economies. Many of them believed businesses should be controlled by the laws of supply and demand, without government interference. This idea formed the basis of the economic system known as *capitalism*. Poor working conditions led to widespread attacks on capitalism. *Socialism,* which called for government control of all industrial production, developed in opposition to capitalism. The German philosopher Karl Marx developed the theories of *communism* from earlier socialist ideas. Marx called for workers' revolutions against the middle class and the organization of state-owned economic systems.

During the 1800's, the industrial nations of Europe established many colonies in Africa and Asia. The colonies provided the European nations with essential raw materials for their factories and served as big markets for manufactured goods. By the late 1800's, huge European empires had been created in Africa and Asia. This colonial expansion became known as *imperialism.* The combined forces of industrialization and imperialism created an era of unprecedented wealth and political power in Europe.

The 1900's brought rapid, widespread change. The most destructive conflicts in world history—World War I and World War II—involved entire populations in the war efforts. Europe's colonial empires crumbled after World War II, and many nations in Africa, Asia, and the Middle East gained independence. A great struggle known as the Cold War developed between Communist nations and democratic nations. Each side promoted its own political and economic ideas and tried to win the support of certain neutral, or *nonaligned,* nations.

The development of nuclear weapons in the mid-1900's threatened to destroy civilization itself. At the same time, nations began to work together in such organizations as the United Nations (see "United Nations"). Tremendous advances in the technologies of transportation and communication brought the nations of the world closer together in some ways. But a large gap continued to separate the industrialized nations of the world and the developing nations. The invention of automobiles, airplanes, radios, televisions, synthetic materials, household appliances, computers, and countless other innovations changed the lifestyles of millions of people. Tremendous strides were made in the field of medicine, and space travel opened up a vast new frontier for exploration. But in some parts of the world, especially in Asia, Africa, and Latin America, millions of people still struggled to overcome poverty, hunger, and illiteracy.

Important dates in world history

This table lists major events in world history. A separate table of "Major wars, battles, and treaties" appears on page 307. See the "People" section for biographical information about many important world figures. See also the tables in the sections "Disasters," "Explorations," "Space," "Canada," "United States," and "Scientific inventions and inventors."

Ancient history

c. 3100 B.C. King Menes unites Lower and Upper Egypt and forms one of the world's first national governments.

c. 3000 B.C. Cuneiform writings of the Sumerians begin the recorded history of the Middle East.

2700 –2200 B.C. In a period often called the *Age of the Pyramids,* Egyptian art and architecture develop to their highest point.

c. 2500 B.C. The Indus Valley civilization begins in the cities of Harappa and Mohenjo-daro in what is now Pakistan.

c. 2300 B.C. Sargon of Akkad conquers the Sumerians and unites their city-states under his rule.

c. 2000 B.C. The kingdom of Kush arises south of Egypt, eventually becoming a major center of art, learning, and trade that lasts until A.D. 450.

1700's B.C. The Shang dynasty begins its rule of China.

c. 1750 B.C. Hammurabi conquers Sumer and establishes the Babylonian empire.

c. 1650 B.C. The Hittites form an empire in what is now Turkey and eventually become a leading power in the Middle East.

c. 1600 –1400 B.C. The Minoan civilization flourishes on the Mediterranean island of Crete.

c. 1500 B.C. The Aryans of central Asia invade India.

1490 –1436 B.C. The Egyptian Empire reaches its height during the reign of King Thutmose III.

1122 B.C. The Chou people of western China overthrow the Shang and set up a new dynasty that rules until 256 B.C.

c. 1100 B.C. Based mainly in the city of Tyre, the Phoenicians begin to expand their political and economic influence by establishing colonies around the Mediterranean Sea.

1100's B.C. The Dorians invade Greece during a period known as the *Dark Ages* of ancient Greece.

1090 –945 B.C. Egyptian priests and nobles struggle for royal power, leaving Egypt broken into small states.

c. 1020 B.C. The Twelve Tribes of Israel form a united kingdom under Saul.

c. 1000 B.C. King David makes Jerusalem the capital of the united Israelite tribes.

1000's B.C. Latin tribes settle south of the Tiber River, and Etruscans settle in the west central region of the Italian peninsula.

800's B.C. Assyria begins to build an empire that eventually includes Egypt and territory from the Mediterranean Sea to the Persian Gulf.

750 –338 B.C. Athens, Corinth, Sparta, and Thebes develop as the chief city-states of Greece during the Hellenic Age.

509 B.C. The Latins rebel against their Etruscan rulers and establish the Roman Republic.

500 B.C. The Achaemenid Empire of ancient Persia reaches its peak during the reign of Darius I.

390 B.C. The Gauls raid Italy and destroy Rome.

338 B.C. Philip II of Macedonia defeats the Greeks and makes Greece part of the Macedonian Empire.

331 B.C. Alexander the Great defeats the Persians at Arbela (Irbil) and opens his path of conquest to India.

323 B.C. Alexander the Great dies, leaving behind an empire that extends from Greece to India, with Babylon as its capital.

321–185 B.C. The Maurya Empire of northern India spreads over almost all of India and part of central Asia.

221–206 B.C. The Ch'in dynasty establishes China's first strong central government and completes the Great Wall that protects China from invaders.

202 B.C. The Han dynasty begins its 400-year rule of China.

146 B.C. The Romans destroy Corinth and conquer Greece.

55 –54 B.C. Julius Caesar leads the Roman invasion of Britain.

44 B.C. Brutus and other conspirators assassinate Caesar.

27 B.C. Augustus becomes the first Roman emperor.

A.D. 70 Roman forces under Titus capture and destroy Jerusalem.

50 –mid 200's The Kushan empire rules Afghanistan and northwestern India.

105 The Chinese invent paper.

293 Diocletian divides the Roman Empire into four prefectures and sets up two capitals—Nicomedia in Asia Minor, and Milan in Europe.

c. 300 The Maya develop an advanced civilization in Central America.

313 Constantine grants the Christians of the Roman Empire freedom of religion in the Edict of Milan.

317 The Huns conquer northern China, starting a series of nomadic invasions of Asia.

320 India begins its golden age under the Gupta dynasty.

330 Constantine moves the capital of the Roman Empire to Byzantium, which he renames Constantinople (now Istanbul).

395 The Roman Empire splits into the East Roman Empire and the West Roman Empire.

410 The Visigoths capture and sack Rome.

455 Vandal tribes attack Rome.

476 The German chieftain Odoacer deposes Romulus Augustulus, the last emperor of the West Roman Empire.

Middle Ages

486 Clovis becomes king of the Franks and founds the Merovingian dynasty, rulers of the first French state.

527–565 Justinian I rules the Byzantine Empire and develops the famous Justinian Code of law.

581–618 The Sui dynasty reunifies China after almost 400 years of division.

618 –907 The T'ang dynasty rules China during a period of prosperity and great cultural accomplishment.

661 The Omayyad Caliphate establishes the capital of the Muslim Empire at Damascus.

700's The kingdom of Kanem is founded south of the Sahara and lasts more than 1,000 years.

711 The Muslims invade Spain and begin an occupation that lasts about 700 years.

732 Charles Martel leads the Franks in defeating the invading Muslims at Tours. The victory prevents the Muslims from conquering Europe.

750 The Abbasid Caliphate replaces the Omayyads as ruler of the Muslim Empire and later establishes a new capital at Baghdad.

768 Charlemagne becomes ruler of the Franks.

c. 770 The Chinese invent wood-block printing.

800 Pope Leo III crowns Charlemagne Emperor of the Romans.

843 The Treaty of Verdun divides Charlemagne's empire into three parts and begins the national development of France, Germany, and Italy.

862 Rurik, chief of the Varangians (vikings), establishes his rule at Novgorod and founds the Russian Empire.

878 Alfred the Great of England defeats the Dutch in the Battle of Edington.

960 –1279 The Sung dynasty rules China and makes Neo-Confucianism the official state philosophy.

962 The Holy Roman Empire is established under Otto I.

969 The Fatimids conquer Egypt and make Cairo the center of the Muslim Empire.

987 Hugh Capet becomes king of France and founds the Capetian dynasty that rules until 1328.

c. 1000 Leif Ericson sails west from Greenland to the North American mainland. He leads what is probably the first European expedition to the mainland of America.

1016 Canute becomes king of England and brings the entire country under Danish rule.

1037 The Seljuk Turks conquer most of the Iranian kingdoms.

1066 Norman forces under William the Conqueror defeat the Anglo-Saxons in the Battle of Hastings, and end Anglo-Saxon rule of England.

1099 Christian forces capture Jerusalem, ending the First Crusade.

1187 Muslim troops under Saladin recapture Jerusalem.

1192 Yoritomo becomes the first shogun to rule Japan.

1215 Barons of England force King John to grant the Magna Carta.

1279 Kublai Khan leads the Mongols in completing the conquest of China.

1337 The Mali empire in West Africa reaches the height of its power.

1368 The Ming dynasty establishes its 300-year rule of China.

1438 The Hapsburg family of Austria begins almost continuous rule of the Holy Roman Empire.

1438 The Inca empire begins a period of expansion that makes it one of the largest and richest empires in the Americas.

c. 1440 Johannes Gutenberg, a German printer, invents movable type.

1440 Montezuma I becomes ruler of the Aztec empire in Mexico and begins a period of territorial expansion.

1453 The Ottoman Turks capture Constantinople and overthrow the Byzantine Empire.

Modern times (early period: 1453-1900)

1492 Christopher Columbus reaches America and claims it for Spain.

1492 The Spaniards capture Granada and end the rule of Spain by the Muslim Moors.

1493 Askia Muhammad becomes king of the Songhai Empire in West Africa and it reaches its peak of wealth and power under his rule.

1517 The Reformation begins in Germany.

1519 –1522 Ferdinand Magellan commands the first voyage around the world.

1521 Spanish forces led by Hernando Cortés destroy the Aztec empire.

1526 Babar, a Muslim ruler, conquers India and establishes the Mogul Empire.

1532 Francisco Pizarro invades Peru, beginning the Spanish conquest of the Inca empire.

1558 Elizabeth I becomes queen of England, ruling during what becomes known as the golden age of English history.

1588 The Royal Navy of England defeats the Spanish Armada and establishes England as a great naval power.

1589 Henry IV becomes the first Bourbon king of France, inaugurating the period of France's greatest influence over European politics and culture.

1613 Michael Romanov becomes czar of Russia and starts the 300-year rule of Russia by the Romanovs.

1639 Japan closes its doors to influences from Europe.

1644 Manchus conquer China and establish their rule, which lasts until 1912.

1688 The Glorious Revolution deposes James II of England.

1763 The Treaty of Paris ends the Seven Years' War in Europe and the French and Indian War in America.

1776 The 13 American colonies of England sign the Declaration of Independence.

1789 The French Revolution begins.

1799 Napoleon Bonaparte seizes control of the French government.

1814 –1815 The Congress of Vienna meets after the defeat of Napoleon to restore monarchies to power and to change the boundaries of European countries.

1824 Armies of Simón Bolívar and Antonio José de Sucre defeat the Spaniards at Ayacucho, ending the Latin-American wars of independence.

1842 The Treaty of Nanking ends the "Opium War" and grants important trading rights in China to Britain.

1847 Liberia is established as the first independent black republic in Africa.

1853 –1854 Commodore Matthew Perry visits Japan and opens two ports to U.S. trade, ending Japan's isolation.

1858 Great Britain takes over rule of India from the East India Company after the Sepoy Rebellion.

1865 Union forces defeat the Confederates in the American Civil War after four years of fighting.

1867 Japanese Emperor Mutsuhito regains his traditional power from the shogun.

1867 The British North America Act establishes the Dominion of Canada.

1869 The Suez Canal opens.

1871 Germany becomes united under the Prussian king, who rules the new empire as Kaiser Wilhelm I.

1882 Great Britain invades and occupies Egypt.

1885 Leopold II of Belgium establishes the Congo Free State and controls it as his personal possession.

1895 Japan takes control of Taiwan after the Chinese-Japanese War.

1898 The United States takes control of Guam, Puerto Rico, and the Philippines following the Spanish-American War.

The 1900's

1900 Secret societies attack and kill Westerners and Chinese Christians during the Boxer Rebellion.

1901 The Australian states unite to form a commonwealth.

1905 Japan defeats Russia and takes control of Russian interests in Korea and Manchuria.

1912 The Republic of China is established.

1914 The assassination of Archduke Francis Ferdinand of Austria-Hungary starts World War I.

1917 Revolutionaries overthrow Czar Nicholas II and the Bolsheviks seize power in Russia.

1920 The Panama Canal opens.

1920 The League of Nations is established.

1922 The Fascist party seizes control of Italy and Benito Mussolini becomes dictator.

1922 The Union of Soviet Socialist Republics is established.

1923 Mustafa Kemal (Atatürk) establishes the Republic of Turkey and modernizes Turkish institutions.

1928 The Nationalists, led by Chiang Kai-shek, unite China under one government.

1931 Japan invades and occupies Manchuria.

1933 Adolf Hitler becomes dictator of Germany.

1935 –1936 Italian troops invade and annex Ethiopia.

1939 Francisco Franco becomes dictator of Spain after 32 months of civil war.

1939 Germany invades Poland, starting World War II.

1941 The Japanese attack Pearl Harbor, and the United States enters World War II.

1945 The United Nations is established.

1945 The first atomic bombs used in warfare are dropped by U.S. planes on Hiroshima and Nagasaki.

1945 World War II ends in Europe on May 7 and in the Pacific on September 2.

1946 The United States grants independence to the Philippines.

1946 –1954 France fights Communist-led rebels in Indochina.

1947 Britain grants independence to India and Pakistan.

1948 The Arabs and Israelis fight the first of four wars.

1948 The United States starts the European Recovery Program (Marshall Plan) to aid Europe's economic recovery.

1949 The Chinese Communists conquer China.

1950 North Korean Communist troops invade South Korea, starting the Korean War.

1957 Russia opens the space age by launching Sputnik I, the first artificial satellite to circle the earth.

1957 Communist guerrilla forces of North Vietnam begin a terror campaign against U.S.-backed South Vietnam.

1962 Russia agrees to U.S. demands that missiles be removed from Cuba, ending a serious Cold War crisis.

1963 Russia, the United States, and Great Britain sign an agreement banning the testing of nuclear weapons above ground. Other nations sign later.

1965 The Vietnam War expands. Both the United States

and the Communists send in thousands of troops, and the United States begins bombing North Vietnam.

1965 The Second Vatican Council ends. Roman Catholic Church leaders modernize the church.

1967 Israel defeats Egypt, Jordan, Syria, and other Arab states in an Arab-Israeli war.

1969 Two American astronauts become the first people to walk on the moon.

1975 The Vietnam War ends when the non-Communist South Vietnam government surrenders to the Viet Cong.

1978 The leaders of Egypt and Israel meet with U.S. Presi-

dent Jimmy Carter and work out the Camp David Accords, which lead to the signing of a peace treaty between Egypt and Israel in 1979.

1979 Revolutionaries under the leadership of the Ayatollah Ruhollah Khomeini overthrow the shah of Iran and establish a fundamentalist Islamic republic.

1979 –1980 Russian forces invade Afghanistan and help the leftist government there fight rebel guerrillas.

1982 Britain defeats Argentina in air, sea, and land battles to retain control of the Falkland Islands in the South Atlantic Ocean.

Major wars, battles, and treaties

Wars

431 –404 B.C.—Peloponnesian War. Sparta and its allies fought against Athens. Ended in victory for Sparta, which became the most powerful Greek state.

264 –146 B.C.—Punic Wars. Three wars (264 –241 B.C., 218 –201 B.C., 149 –146 B.C.) fought between Rome and Carthage. Rome won all three and became the leading power of the Western world.

A.D. 1096 –1291—Crusades. Series of religious wars in which Christian Europeans tried to recapture the Holy Land from the Muslims. Ended with Muslims retaining control of the Holy Land.

1337-1453—Hundred Years' War. The British and French fought for control of France. France won, and England lost almost all its territory on the European continent.

1455-1485—Wars of the Roses. Struggle between the House of York and the House of Lancaster for the English throne. Ended when Henry VII, a Lancaster, married the daughter of Edward IV, a York, uniting the two houses and founding the Tudor dynasty.

1618 –1648—Thirty Years' War. A series of wars that began as a civil war between Catholics and Protestants in the German states and then became a general struggle for territory and political power among most of the nations of Europe. Caused widespread destruction in Germany and the loss of important German territory to France and Sweden.

1689 –1763—French and Indian Wars. A series of four wars between Britain and France over territorial claims in North America. King William's War took place from 1689 to 1697, Queen Anne's War from 1702 to 1713, King George's War from 1744 to 1748, and the French and Indian War from 1754 to 1763. The wars resulted in Britain's final victory over France, which gave up most of its possessions in North America.

1756 –1763—Seven Years' War. (Fought as the French and Indian War in North America.) Prussia, allied with England, fought against Austria, allied with France, for control of Germany. Prussia won and became the leader of the German states.

1775 –1783—American Revolution. American colonists fought for independence from Britain. American victory resulted in the formation of the United States of America and the acquisition of British territory extending to the Mississippi River.

1789 –1799—French Revolution. Led to the temporary overthrow of the French monarchy, the establishment of a series of other governments, and then the dictatorship of Napoleon.

1812 –1814—War of 1812. British seizure of U.S. mer-

chant ships and impressment of U.S. sailors during a war with France led to war with the United States. Ended with neither side gaining anything.

1846 –1848—Mexican War. Mexico and the United States fought over boundaries and control of Texas. The United States defeated Mexico and gained vast new territory in the southwest. Mexico gave up all claims to Texas.

1848 —Revolution of 1848. A series of popular uprisings against undemocratic rulers eventually spread through all the countries of Europe. Led to various democratic reforms.

1853 –1856—Crimean War. One of a series of wars between Russia and Turkey, which was allied with Britain, France, and Sardinia. Ended in Russian defeat and loss of dominance in the Balkans and Black Sea area.

1861 –1865—American Civil War. Union forces of the North fought against Confederate troops from the South over slavery and other issues. Ended in Union victory and the preservation of the United States of America.

1870 —Franco-Prussian War. A political dispute between France and Prussia eventually led to war between France and all the German states. Ended in French defeat and the establishment of a new German Empire.

1880 –1881—First Anglo-Boer War. *Boers* (Dutch farmers) of the Transvaal in South Africa successfully revolted against the British.

1894 –1895—Chinese-Japanese War. China and Japan fought over control of Korea. Japan defeated China and gained Taiwan and other territory. Korea became independent.

1898 —Spanish-American War. Spain and the United States fought over the issue of liberation for Cuba. U.S. victory marked its emergence as a world power and led to the independence of Cuba, and the acquisition by the U.S. of Guam, Puerto Rico, and the Philippines from Spain.

1899 –1902 —Second Anglo-Boer War. The Boer republics of Transvaal and the Orange Free State fought against Britain and were defeated. The republics then became British colonies.

1904 –1905—Russo-Japanese War. Japan defeated Russia, gained territory, and won recognition as a major world power.

1905 —Russian Revolution. Revolts by workers, peasants, and military groups led Czar Nicholas II to agree to the formation of an elected *Duma* (parliament).

1914 –1918—World War I. Britain, France, Russia, Japan, the United States, and 19 other Allied countries fought against the Central powers—Austria-Hungary, Germany, the Ottoman Empire, and Bulgaria. The war cost more than $337 billion. Servicemen killed totaled more than 5,000,000 on the Allied side and more than 3,300,000 on the side of the Central Powers. The war had widespread effects, including the establishment of new governments in Austria, Czechoslovakia, Estonia, Finland, Germany, Hungary, Latvia, Lithuania, Poland, Russia, Yugoslavia, and several countries of western Asia.

1917—February Revolution. Russian revolt that forced Czar Nicholas II to give up the throne.

1917—October Revolution. Russian revolt that led to the establishment of a Bolshevik government headed by V. I. Lenin.

1939–1945 —World War II. The Allies—Britain, Canada, China, France, Russia, the United States, and 43 other nations—defeated the Axis—Germany, Italy, Japan, and 6 other nations. The most costly and destructive war in history, World War II killed more than 10 million Allied servicemen and nearly 6 million Axis servicemen. In addition, countless civilians were killed, including an estimated 6 million Jews who died in German concentration camps. The war was fought in Europe, Africa, Asia, and the Pacific. Provisions in the peace treaties signed after the war

included the surrender of Axis territory; limitations on the size of the military forces allowed in Axis countries; Allied occupation of Germany, Italy, and Japan; and payment of reparations to the Allies.

1948 —Arab-Israeli War. First of a series of wars between the Israelis and Arabs in the Middle East. Israeli victory led to acquisition of Palestinian territory that the UN had planned for a new Arab state. Other full-scale Arab-Israeli wars erupted in 1956, 1967, and 1973.

1950–1953 —Korean War. United Nations forces fought against Communist Chinese and North Korean troops after North Korea invaded South Korea. Ended in a truce signed by the UN and North Korea.

1957–1975 —Vietnam War. Communist Vietnamese forces, called the *Viet Cong,* and North Vietnamese troops supported by China and Russia fought against South Vietnamese Army troops, U.S. troops, and forces from South Korea, Australia, New Zealand, and Thailand. Ended with Communist victory and control over all of Vietnam.

Editor's note: See also the "United States" section for the table of "Wars involving the United States."

Battles

490 B.C.—Marathon. Miltiades of Athens routed the Persians under Datis and Artaphernes and saved Greece from invasion.

414–413 B.C.—Syracuse. The Athenians under Nicias laid siege to the city of Syracuse, an ally of Sparta in the Peloponnesian War. They were repulsed by troops led by Hermocrates and Gylippus. The loss led to the fall of Athens as a great power.

331 B.C.—Arbela. Alexander the Great of Macedonia defeated Darius III of Persia near Gaugamela, northwest of Arbela. Alexander then ruled the Persian Empire.

207 B.C.—Metaurus. Roman armies of Marcus Livius Salinator and Claudius Nero destroyed the troops of Carthage under Hasdrubal in Italy. The battle marked a turning point in the Punic Wars between Carthage and Rome.

A.D. 9 —Teutoburg Forest. Arminius directed an army of Germans in destroying a Roman force under Publius Varus and halted Roman plans to conquer Germany.

451—Châlons. In northeast France, Roman legions of Aëtius and Visigoth cavalry under Theodoric I saved Europe from an invasion by Attila and his Hun armies.

732 —Poitiers. Charles Martel and the Franks turned back Abd-al-Rahman's warriors in west-central France, preventing the Moors from overrunning Europe. This conflict is also called the Battle of Tours.

1066—Hastings. The Normans under William, Duke of Normandy, invaded England and overthrew the Saxons led by King Harold II.

1429—Orléans. Joan of Arc with a French army forced the English, under the Earl of Suffolk, to give up the siege of Orléans in France.

1588—Spanish Armada. In a battle in the English Channel, Lord Howard's 197 warships smashed Spain's 130-ship "Invincible Armada" under the Duke of Medina Sidonia. The loss was a severe blow to the political prestige of Spain, the world's leading power at the time.

1704—Blenheim. An allied force under the Duke of Marlborough and Prince Eugene defeated the Bavarians and French led by Comte de Tallard.

1709 —Poltava. The soldiers of Peter the Great of Russia crushed an army under Charles XII of Sweden at Poltava in the Ukraine. The victory made Russia the dominant power in Eastern Europe.

1777—Saratoga. John Burgoyne's British army surrendered to Horatio Gates's American troops. The French then decided to help the colonists win independence.

1781—Yorktown. American and French armies under George Washington forced Charles Cornwallis to surrender his British troops. The surrender led to the end of the Revolutionary War in America.

1792—Valmy. A Prussian army under the Duke of Brunswick withdrew from a French army led by Charles Dumouriez. This action prevented the Prussians from advancing on Paris to put down the French Revolution.

1805 —Trafalgar. Napoleon's dreams of invading England were shattered when Lord Nelson's 27-ship British fleet defeated a force of 33 French and Spanish warships under Pierre de Villeneuve off the coast of southern Spain. The battle ended a 100-year struggle for domination of the seas.

1815 —Waterloo. An allied force under the Duke of Wellington and a Prussian force under Gebhard von Blücher crushed Napoleon I and ended his return to power.

1863 —Gettysburg and Vicksburg. George G. Meade's Union forces defeated Confederate troops led by Robert E. Lee in the Battle of Gettysburg. The next day, John C. Pemberton's Confederate army surrendered to the Union forces of Ulysses S. Grant at Vicksburg. These defeats led to the encirclement of the Confederate States.

1914 —Tannenberg and the Marne. A German army under Paul von Hindenburg defeated two invading Russian armies led by Pavel K. Rennenkampf and Alexander Samsonov at the Battle of Tannenberg. A week later, in the Battle of the Marne, the armies of Joseph Joffre of France and John French of Great Britain forced two armies of invading German troops led by Alexander von Kluck and Karl von Bülow to retreat from the approaches to Paris.

1939 —Polish Air Campaign. The 1,600-aircraft German *Luftwaffe* (air force) overwhelmed Polish forces in the Nazi *blitzkrieg* (lightning war). The battle seemed to confirm the Germans' mistaken belief that an air force serves mainly as an extension of artillery. As a result of this concept, the Luftwaffe met defeat when it encountered the Royal Air Force.

1940—Battle of Britain. The Luftwaffe, numbering more than 2,000 aircraft, tried to bomb the British into submission, but the much smaller R.A.F. repelled almost daily assaults. The battle saved Great Britain from invasion. It also proved that air forces could fight decisive actions by themselves, not just in support of infantry and artillery.

1941—Pearl Harbor. A 360-plane attack plunged the United States into World War II. The Japanese proved that airplanes could destroy armored naval vessels.

1942 —Midway. U.S. carrier forces fought a much larger Japanese force. Four Japanese carriers and one U.S. car-

rier were sunk. The decisive U.S. victory marked the end of Japanese expansion in World War II.

1944 —Normandy. Dwight D. Eisenhower's Allied force invaded Normandy, defended by Axis soldiers under Gerd von Rundstedt.

Treaties

840 —Treaty of Verdun. Divided Charlemagne's empire into three parts, marking the end of the political unity of the Christian countries of Western Europe.

1494 —Treaty of Tordesillas. Established a Line of Demarcation to settle conflicting land claims by Spain and Portugal in the Western Hemisphere. Portugal received most of what is now Brazil, and Spain received land west of the line.

1713 —Peace of Utrecht. Ended the War of the Spanish Succession in Europe and Queen Anne's War (one of the French and Indian Wars) in North America. The French Duke of Anjou was recognized as King of Spain, but France agreed that Spain and France would never be united under one ruler. Spain gave up various territories in Europe to Britain and Austria. In North America, France gave up part of its Canadian territory to Britain.

1750 —Treaty of Madrid. Spain recognized Portugal's claim to nearly all of what is now Brazil.

1763 —Treaty of Paris. Ended the Seven Years' War in Europe and the French and Indian War in America. France surrendered Canada to Britain. Britain also received all French territories east of the Mississippi River except New Orleans, as well as France's trading centers in India.

1783 —Treaty of Paris. Ended the Revolutionary War in America. Established peace between Britain and the United States and formally recognized the United States. Gave the United States British territory west as far as the Mississippi River and set the northern boundary of the United States.

1795 —Pinckney Treaty (Treaty of San Lorenzo el Real). Settled a dispute between the United States and Spain over the Florida border and gave both countries free use of the Mississippi River.

1814 —Treaty of Ghent. Ended the War of 1812 between the United States and Britain. Restored the situation that had existed before the war.

1814 —Treaty of Paris. Marked the end of Napoleon's domination over Europe. France was returned to its 1792 boundaries.

1815 —Treaty of Paris. Following Napoleon's final defeat at Waterloo, France was returned to its boundaries of 1790 and made to pay war damages.

1848 —Treaty of Guadalupe Hidalgo. Ended the Mexican War between the United States and Mexico. The United States gained vast amounts of territory in the West, and the Rio Grande became the boundary between Texas and Mexico. The United States agreed to pay Mexico $15 million.

1856 —Treaty of Paris. Ended the Crimean War between

Russia and the Ottoman Empire, which had been aided by France, Austria, Britain, and Sardinia. Forced Russia to return much of the territory it had taken from the Turks. Guaranteed the independence of the Ottoman Empire. Opened the Danube River to free navigation for all nations and the Black Sea to merchant vessels of all nations.

1898 —Treaty of Paris. Ended the Spanish-American War between Spain and the United States. Cuba gained independence, Spain surrendered Puerto Rico, Guam, and the Philippine Islands to the United States. The United States paid Spain $20 million for the Philippines.

1919 –1920 —Peace of Paris. Consists of five treaties signed after World War I. The 1919 Treaty of Versailles, signed by the Allies and Germany, officially ended the war and established the League of Nations. The Allies signed the Treaty of Saint Germain with Austria in 1919, the Treaty of Neuilly with Bulgaria in 1919, the Treaty of Sèvres with Turkey in 1920, and the Treaty of Trianon with Hungary in 1920. All the treaties included provisions for the Central Powers to give up territory, limit their armaments, and pay reparations.

1947—Inter-American Treaty of Reciprocal Assistance (Rio Treaty). Pledged the peaceful settlement of differences among the United States and 19 Latin-American republics, and declared that an armed attack against one would be considered an attack against all.

1949 —North Atlantic Treaty. Provided for the collective defense of Western nations by the establishment of the North Atlantic Treaty Organization (NATO). The twelve nations that signed the treaty in 1949 were Belgium, Canada, Denmark, France, Great Britain, Iceland, Italy, Luxembourg, The Netherlands, Norway, Portugal, and the United States. Greece and Turkey signed in 1951, West Germany in 1954, and Spain in 1982.

1951—Treaty of Paris. Established the European Coal and Steel Community (ECSC) among Belgium, France, Italy, Luxembourg, The Netherlands, and West Germany.

1955 —Warsaw Pact. Brought the Communist nations of Europe under a unified military command. Russia, Albania, Bulgaria, Czechoslovakia, East Germany, Hungary, Poland, and Romania signed the treaty. Albania withdrew in 1968.

1957—Rome Treaties. Established the European Atomic Energy Community and the European Economic Community among the six ECSC nations. The 1951 Treaty of Paris and the Rome Treaties form the basis of the European Community (European Common Market). Denmark, Ireland, and Great Britain joined the Community in 1973, and Greece joined in 1981.

Index

A

Abbreviations, 8–12
  See also Chemical
  elements; Signs and
  symbols; Sports; United
  Nations; Weights and
  measures
Aborigine, 100
Abraham, 116, 155
Academy Awards, 30–33
Academy of Motion Picture
  Arts and Sciences, 30
Act of Union. See Union,
  Act of
Actor, 31–32, 60–61
Actress, 31–32, 60–61
Adams, John, 145
Adams, John Quincy, 145
Adams, Samuel, 116
Addams, Jane, 116
Administrations, 262, graph
Aeschylus, 116
Aesop, 116
Afghan hound, 24; picture, 165
Africa, 302
  flags, 182–184, pictures
African, 100
Age of Reason, 303
Agriculture, Department
  of, 263
Air, 85
Airedale terrier, 25;
  picture, 168
Air mileage, 235
Airports, 238
Alberta, 65
Albertus Magnus, Saint, 116
Albino, 171, picture
Alcott, Louisa May, 116
Aldrin, Edwin E., Jr., 201
Alexander the Great, 116
Alexandria, Lighthouse of, 290
Alfred the Great, 116
Algae, 138
Allah, 150
All–England Championship,
  222–223
Alphabets and codes, 13–16
Alveoli, 104
America, 302
  flags of, 178–179, pictures
American Book Awards,
  39–40
American Football Conference,
  211
American Indian. See Indian,
  American
American League, 204–205
American Mongoloid, 100
Ampère, André Marie, 116
Amphibian, 20, 23
Amtrak, 240, with map
Amundsen, Roald, 116
Anabolism, 22
Ancient history, 299–300,
  304–305
Andersen, Hans Christian, 116
Animals, 17–27
  classification, scientific,
    18–20
  interesting facts, 17–18
  life spans, 23
  names of, 27
  speeds of, 26
  terms, 20
Anniversary, wedding, 160
Anther, 141, with picture
Anthony, Susan B., 116
Antony, Mark, 116
Apocrypha, 149–150
Apollo program, 197–199 with
  pictures; 201
Apostles, 149
Appaloosa, 25; picture, 171
Aquinas, Saint Thomas, 116
Arabian horse, 25; picture, 170
Arabic numerals, 160
Archery, 227
Archimedes, 116
Area codes, 28
Aristophanes, 116
Aristotle, 116
Armstrong, Neil A., 116, 201
Arnold, Benedict, 116–117
Artemis, Temple of, 290
Artery, 105–106, with picture
Arthur, Chester A., 145
Articles of Confederation, 269
Asexual reproduction, 21, 142
Asia
  flags, 185–187, pictures
  weather, 285
Asians, 100
Asteroid, 276
Astor, John Jacob, 117
Astrology, 29
Astronaut, 193, 201
Astronomy, 276–283, with
  pictures
  terms, 277
  See also Earth
Atahualpa, 117
Atatürk, Kemal, 117
Atlantic Charter, 269
Atlantic Provinces, 67
Atmosphere, 85
Attila, 117
Attucks, Crispus, 117
Audubon, John James, 117
Augustine, Saint, 117
Augustus Caesar, 117
Aurangzeb, 117
Austen, Jane, 117
Australoid, 100
Australopithecine, 98, pictures
Autobiography, 37, 39, 56–57
Auto Club, United States, 203
Automobile racing, 203–204
Autonomic nervous system,
  107–108, with picture
Awards, 30–61
  See also Decorations and
  medals, Sports winners
Axis (astronomy), 80, with
  picture; 282

B

Babylon, Hanging Gardens of.
  See Hanging Gardens of
  Babylon
Bach, Johann Sebastian, 117
Bacon, Francis, 117
Bacon, Roger, 117
Balboa, Vasco Núñez de, 117
Balzac, Honoré de, 117
Banneker, Benjamin, 117
Bantamweight, 210
Barnum, Phineas T., 117
Barton, Clara, 117
Baseball, 204–205
Basketball, 205–206
Basset hound, 24; picture, 165
Battles, 308–309
Beagle, 24; picture, 165
Beaufort scale, 286
Becket, Saint Thomas à, 117
Bede, 117
Beebe, William, 117
Beethoven, Ludwig van, 117
Bell, Alexander Graham, 117

Bellow, Saul, 118
Belmont Stakes, 220–221
Ben–Gurion, David, 118
Bentham, Jeremy, 118
Bessemer, Sir Henry, 118
Bethune, Mary McLeod, 118
Biathlon, 226
Bible, 149, 155
Big bang theory, 276–277
Bile, 103–104
Bill (document), 264–266
Bill of Rights, Canadian, 72
Binary fission, 21
Biography, 37, 39, 56–57
Biome, 88–89, with map
Biosphere, 81
Birds, 23
    state, 251, 253
Birthstone, 159
Bismarck, Otto von, 118
Black hole, 277, 279–280
Blackstone, Sir William, 118
Blackwell, Elizabeth, 118
Blade (botany), 141, with
    picture
Blake, William, 118
Blood, 105–106
Bloodhound, 24; picture, 165
Bobsledding, 226
Boccaccio, Giovanni, 118
Body, human. See Human
    body
Bohr, Niels, 118
Boleyn, Anne, 118
Bolívar, Simón, 118
Bone, 103; picture, 101
Book Awards, American,
    39–40
Book Awards, National, 36–38
Boone, Daniel, 118
Booth, John Wilkes, 118
Boston terrier, 25; picture, 169
Boxer (dog), 24; picture, 166
Boxing, 207–211, 227
Bradford, William, 118
Brahe, Tycho, 118
Brahman, 151
Brahms, Johannes, 118
Braille, 15
Braille, Louis, 118
Brain, 107–108, with picture
British Columbia, 65, 67
British North America Act, 72
British Open, 214
Brontë Sisters, 118
Brooks, Gwendolyn, 118
Brown, John, 118
Bryan, William Jennings,
    118–119

Buchanan, James, 145
Bud, 140–141, with pictures
Buddha, 119, 152
Buddhism, 149, 152–153, with
    picture
Budding, 21, 142
Bulldog, 25; pictures, 169
Burr, Aaron, 119
Business
    regulation, 268
    symbols, 158
Byrd, Richard, 119
Byron, Lord, 119
Byzantine Empire, 301

C

Cabinet (government)
    Canada, 70
    United States, 263
Cabot, John, 119
Caesar, Julius, 119
Cairn terrier, 25; picture, 168
Caldecott medal, 33–34
Calendars, 62–64
Calhoun, John C., 119
Calvin, John, 119
Calyx, 141
Canada, 65–72
    abbreviations, 12
    cities, 66–67
    facts in brief, 65
    flags, 95; pictures,
        178, 192
    highway distances, 237
    history of, 71–72
    holidays, 96
    map, 68–69
    prime ministers of, 70–71
    provinces, 65–67
    territories, 66–67
    weather, 284
Canal, 239
Canoeing, 227
Cantor, 155
Capillary, 105–106
Capitals of the states, 250, 252
Carbon dioxide, 104, 106
Cardiac muscle, 103
Carnegie, Andrew, 119
Carroll, Lewis, 119
Carter, James Earl, Jr., 145
Cartier, Jacques, 119
Caruso, Enrico, 119
Carver, George Washington,
    119
Cassatt, Mary, 119
Castro, Fidel, 119
Catabolism, 22

Catherine of Aragon, 119
Catherine II, 119
Cato, Marcus Porcius, the
    Elder, 119
Cats
    breeds of, 23
    pictures, 161–162
Caucasoid race, 100
Cavour, Camillo Benso, 119
Cell, 102
Celsius, 287
Cenozoic Era, 86–87
Census, 246
Central nervous system, 107,
    with picture
Cervantes, Miguel de, 119
Cézanne, Paul, 119
Championship Trail, 203
Champlain, Samuel de, 119
Chaparral, 89
Charlemagne, 119–120
Chaucer, Geoffrey, 120
Chavez, Cesar, 120
Cheever, John, 120
Chekhov, Anton, 120
Chemical elements. See
    Elements, chemical
Chemistry, 42–43, 158
Chiang Kai-shek, 120
Chief justice, 266
Chihuahua, 24; picture, 163
Children's literature, 38–39
China, 300–302
    calendar, 64
Chlorophyll, 143
Chopin, Frédéric, 120
Chow chow, 25; picture, 169
Christ, Jesus. See Jesus Christ
Christianity, 149–150, with
    picture
    See also Holidays
Chromosome, 143
Church calendar, 62
Churchill, Winston, 120
Chyme, 103
Cicero, 120
Cincinnatus, Lucius Quinctius,
    120
Circulatory system, 105–106,
    with picture
Cislunar space, 193
Cities
    air mileage, 235
    Canada, 66–67
    flags, 190, pictures
    highway distances, 237
    United States, 246
    weather, 284–285
    world, 296

Civil War, 273–275, *with map*
Clark, George Rogers, 120
Classification, scientific
  animals, 18–20
  plants, 138–139
Clay, Henry, 120
Cleopatra, 120
Cleveland, Grover, 145
Climate, 174–175, *with map*
  See also Weather
Clinton, De Witt, 120
Cluster (astronomy), 276
Clydesdale, 25; *picture,* 173
Coach horse, 25
Cochise, 120
Cocker spaniel, 24; *picture,*
  164
Codes, 15–16
Collie, 24; *pictures,* 167
Colonies, 272, map
Colossus of Rhodes, 290
Columbia space shuttle,
  200, 202
Columbus, Christopher, 120
Comet, 276
Commerce, Department of, •
  263
Communications satellite, 196
Communion, 150
Cone–bearing plant, 139
Confederacy, 274, map
Confederate flags, 191, *pictures*
Confucianism, 149, 153
Confucius, 120, 153
Congress, 258, 264–266
Connective tissue, 102
Conrad, Joseph, 120
Constantine, 120
Constellation, 277, 280–281,
  with pictures
Constitution Act, 72
Constitutional Act, 72
Constitution of the United
  States, 269, 271
Continents, 82
Cook, James, 120
Coolidge, Calvin, 145
Cooper, James Fenimore, 120
Copernicus, Nicolaus, 120
Core (geology), 81
Corolla, 141
Coronado, Francisco Vásquez
  de, 120
Cortés, Hernando, 120
Cotton Bowl, 213–214
Cotyledon, 142
Countries, 291–295
Cousteau, Jacques-Yves, 121
Crane, Stephen, 121

Crescent and star, 150, *picture*
Crockett, David, 121
Cro–Magnon man, 99, *picture*
Cromwell, Oliver, 121
Cruiserweight, 207
Crust (geology), 81
Curie, Marie, 121
Curie, Pierre, 121
Custer, George Armstrong, 121
Cycling, 227–228
Cyrillic alphabet, 13
Cyrus the Great, 121

D

Dachshund, 24; *picture,* 165
Da Gama, Vasco, 121
Dalmation, 25; *picture,* 169
Dalton, John, 121
Dante Alighieri, 121
Darius I, 121
Darwin, Charles, 121
David, 121
Da Vinci, Leonardo, 121
Davis cup, 224–225
Davis, Jefferson, 121
Davy, Sir Humphry, 121
Debs, Eugene V., 121
Declaration of Independence,
  269–270
Decorations and medals,
  76–77; *pictures,* 176–177
Defense, Department of, 263
Degas, Edgar, 121
De Gaulle, Charles, 121
Demosthenes, 121
Department of. . .
  Departments appear under
  their key words, as in
  State, Department of
Dermis, 103
Descartes, René, 121
Desert, 89
De Soto, Hernando, 121
Dewey decimal classification,
  109
Dewey, John, 121–122
Dias, Bartolomeu, 122
Dickens, Charles, 122
Dickinson, Emily, 122
Dicotyledon, 142
Didérot, Denis, 122
Differentiation, 22
Digestive system, 103–104,
  with picture

Diocletian, 122
Director, 30–31
Disasters, 78–79
Disraeli, Benjamin, 122
Distances
  air, 235
  highway, 237
Diving, 229
Doberman pinscher, 24;
  picture, 166
Dogs
  breeds of, 24–25
  pictures, 163–169
Doldrums, 88
Dostoevsky, Fyodor, 122
Douglas, Stephen A., 122
Douglas, William Orville, 122
Douglass, Frederick, 122
Draft horses, 25; *pictures,*
  172–173
Drake, Sir Francis, 122
Du Bois, W. E. B., 122
Dunbar, Paul Laurence, 122
Duns Scotus, 122
Dürer, Albrecht, 122

E

Earhart, Amelia, 122
Earth (planet), 80–89, 276,
  282
  See also World
Earthquake, 78–79
Eastern Orthodox churches,
  150
Eclipse, 278, *with pictures*
Economic Advisers, Council of,
  262
Economics, 48
Economy
  United States, 255–257
  world, 298
Edison, Thomas Alva, 122
Education, Department of, 263
Edward the Confessor, 122
Egg, 21, 106–107, 141
Egypt, 290
Egyptian mythology, 113, *with*
  pictures
Einstein, Albert, 122
Eisenhower, Dwight David, 145
Eleanor of Aquitaine, 122
Elements, chemical, 73–75
Eliot, T. S., 122–123
Elizabeth I, 123
Elizabeth II, 123
Emancipation Proclamation,
  269

Emerson, Ralph Waldo, 123
Endocrine gland, 108
Energy, Department of, 263
Engels, Friedrich, 123
Enzyme, 101, 103
Epidermis, 102
Epithelial tissue, 102
Epoch, 86–87
Equestrian, 228
Equinox, 88
Erasmus, Desiderius, 123
Ericson, Leif, 123
Escape velocity, 193, 196
Eucharist. See Mass (religion)
Euclid, 123
Euripides, 123
Europe, 301
    flags, 180–181, pictures
    weather, 285
Europeans, 100
Everest, Mount. See Mount
    Everest
Exchange rate, 110
Executive department, 263
Executive Office, 262
Exocrine gland, 108
Exosphere, 85
Explorations, 90–93
Exports and imports, 257

F

Fahrenheit, 287
Fallopian tube, 106
Faraday, Michael, 123
Farragut, David G., 123
Fates, 112
Faulkner, William, 123
Featherweight, 209–210
Fencing, 228
Fermi, Enrico, 123
Fertilization, 21, 106
Fibrous root, 140, with picture
Figure skating, 226
Filament, 141, with picture
Fillmore, Millard, 145
Finger alphabet, 14
Fish, 23
Fission, 142
Flag code, international, 16
Flags, 94–95; pictures,
    178–192
Fleming, Sir Alexander, 123
Flower, 141, with picture
    state, 251, 253
    symbols, 159
Flowering plant, 139–141, with
    pictures

Flyweight, 210–211
Football, 211–214
Ford, Gerald R., 145
Ford, Henry, 123
Foreign Intelligence Advisory
    Board, 262
Forest, 89
Four Freedoms, 269–270
Fourteen Points, 270
Fragmentation, 21
Francis of Assisi, Saint, 123
Franklin, Benjamin, 123
Frederick I, 123
Free enterprise system, 255
Freedom of speech, 268
Freedom of the press, 268
Frémont, John C., 123
Freud, Sigmund, 123
Frobisher, Sir Martin, 123
Frost, Robert Lee, 123
Fulton, Robert, 123–124
Fungi, 138

G

Gagarin, Yuri Alekseyevich,
    124
Galaxy, 276, 279–281
Galen, 124
Galileo, 124
Gandhi, Mohandas K., 124
Garfield, James A., 145
Garibaldi, Giuseppe, 124
Gauguin, Paul, 124
Gauss, Karl Friedrich, 124
Gautama. See Buddha
Gemini capsule, 197–198, with
    picture; 199
General Assembly, 242, 244
Gene, 143
Genghis Khan, 124
Geology, 86–87
German shepherd dog, 24;
    picture, 167
Germination, 142
Geronimo, 124
Gestation, 27
Gettysburg Address, 270
Giacometti, Alberto, 124
Giotto, 124
Gladstone, William Ewart, 124
Glenn, John, 124
GNP. See gross national
    product

God. See Mythology; Religion
Goddard, Robert Hutchings,
    124
Goethe, Johann Wolfgang von,
    124
Golden retriever, 24; picture,
    164
Golf, 214–216
Gompers, Samuel, 124
Gorgas, William Crawford, 124
Government
    Canada, 70
    United States, 258–269
Government Printing Office,
    264–265
Goya, Francisco, 124
Grand Canyon, 290
Grand Prix, 203
Grant, Ulysses S., 145–146
Grassland, 89
Great Barrier Reef, 290
Great Dane, 24; picture, 166
Greco, El, 124
Greece, ancient, 300
Greek alphabet, 13
Greek mythology, 112
Greeley, Horace, 124
Gregorian calendar, 62
Grimm, Jakob Ludwig, 124
Grimm, Wilhelm Karl, 124
Gropius, Walter, 124–125
Gross national product
    United States, 255–256
    world, 298
Growth, 22
Gutenberg, Johannes, 125
Gymnastics, 228

H

Hadrian, 125
Hale, Nathan, 125
Halicarnassus, Mausoleum at,
    290
Hall of Fame for Great
    Americans, 35
Hamilton, Alexander, 125
Hammurabi, 125
Hancock, John, 125
Handel, George Frideric, 125
Hanging Gardens of Babylon,
    290
Hannibal, 125
Harding, Warren Gamaliel, 146
Hardy, Thomas, 125
Harness horses, 25; pictures,
    171, 173

Harrison, Benjamin, 146
Harrison, William Henry, 146
Harvey, William, 125
Hawthorne, Nathaniel, 125
Haydn, Joseph, 125
Hayes, Rutherford B., 146
Health and Human Services,
    Department of, 263
Hearst, William Randolph, 125
Heart, 105–106, *with picture*
Heavyweight, 207
Hebrew alphabet, 14
Hebrew calendar, 62, 64
Hegel, Georg Wilhelm
    Friedrich, 125
Hegira, 150
Hemingway, Ernest, 125
Hemisphere, 88, 280–281,
    with pictures
Henry, Patrick, 125
Henry II, 125
Henry VIII, 125
Henson, Matthew, 125
Heraclitus, 125
Herbaceous stem, 140–141,
    with picture
Herding dogs, 24; *pictures*, 167
Heredity
    in animals, 22
    in plants, 143–144
Hermaphrodite, 21
Herodotus, 125
Hertz, Heinrich, 125
Heyerdahl, Thor, 126
Hidalgo, Miguel, 126
Highways, 236–237, *with map*
Hillary, Sir Edmund, 126
Hinduism, 149, 151–152, *with
    picture*
Hippocrates, 126
History
    awards, 37, 40, 57–58
    Canada, 71–72
    earth, 86–87
    flags, 191, *pictures*
    United States, 269–275
        important dates, 271–
        275
    world, 299–309
        important dates, 304–
        307
    See also Human being,
    People

Hitler, Adolf, 126
Hobbes, Thomas, 126
Ho Chi Minh, 126
Hockey, 216–217, 226
Holidays, 96
Holmes, Oliver Wendell, 126
Holmes, Oliver Wendell, Jr.,
    126
Holy Communion. *See*
    Communion
Homer, 126
Homer, Winslow, 126
Homo sapiens, 97, 100;
    picture, 99
Homo sapiens sapiens, 97;
    picture, 99
Hooke, Robert, 126
Hoover, Herbert Clark, 146
Hormone, 108
Horse latitudes, 88
Horse racing, 218–221
Horses
    breeds of, 25
    pictures, 170–173
Hounds, 24; *pictures,* 165
House of Representatives, 258,
    264–266
Housing and Urban
    Development, Department
    of, 263
Houston, Samuel, 126
Howe, Elias, 126
Huang Ho Valley, 300
Hudson, Henry, 126
Hughes, Langston, 126
Hugo, Victor Marie, 126
Human being, 97–100, *with
    pictures*
    See also Human body
Human body, 101–108, *with
    pictures*
Husky, 24; *picture,* 166
Huygens, Christian, 126
Hydrosphere, 81

I

Ibn Khaldun, 126
Ibsen, Henrik, 126
Ice hockey. *See* Hockey
Igneous rock, 81
Ikhnaton, 126
Immigration, 247
Import. *See* Exports and
    imports

Independence, Declaration of.
    See Declaration of
    Independence
Independent assortment, law
    of, 144
India, 100, 300
Indian, American, 100
Indianapolis 500, 203–204
Industrial Revolution, 303
Indus Valley civilization, 299–
    300
Innocent III, 126
Intelligence, 17
Intergalactic space, 193
Interior, Department of the,
    263
International Court of Justice,
    242
International flag code, 16
International Monetary Fund,
    242
International Morse Code, 15
Interplanetary space, 193
Interstate highways, 236, *map*
Interstellar space, 193
Interstitial fluid, 106
Inventions, 156–157
Invertebrate, 18
Involuntary muscle, 103
Ionosphere, 85
Irish setter, 24; *picture,* 164
Irving, Washington, 126–127
Isabella I, 127
Islam, 149, 150–151, *with
    picture*
    See also Holidays
Islamic calendar, 64
Islands, 82
Ivan IV, 127

J

Jackson, Andrew, 146
Jackson, Stonewall. *See*
    Jackson, Thomas J.
Jackson, Thomas J., 127
James, Henry, 127
Japan, 302
Jay, John, 127
Jefferson, Thomas, 146
Jenner, Edward, 127
Jesus Christ, 127, 149
Joan of Arc, Saint, 127
Johnson, Andrew, 146
Johnson, Lyndon Baines, 146
Joint (anatomy), 103

Jones, John Paul, 127
Jonson, Ben, 127
Journalism, 48–54
Joyce, James, 127
Juárez, Benito, 127
Judaism, 149, 155, *with picture*
  See also Holidays
Judo, 228
Julian calendar, 62
Jung, Carl, 127
Jupiter (planet), 276, 283
Justice (office), 266–267
Justice, Department of, 263
Justinian I, 127

K

Kant, Immanuel, 127
Karma, 152
Kayaking, 227
Keats, John, 127
Keller, Helen, 127
Kelvin, William Thomson,
  Lord, 127
Kennedy, John Fitzgerald, 146
Kentucky Derby, 218–219
Kenyatta, Jomo, 127
Kepler, Johannes, 127
Key, Francis Scott, 127–128
Keynes, John Maynard, 128
Kilogram, 288
Kilometer, 287–288
King, Martin Luther, Jr., 128
Kipling, Rudyard, 128
Klee, Paul, 128
Knox, John, 128
Koch, Robert, 128
Koran, 150
Kosciusko, Thaddeus, 128
Kublai Khan, 128, 302

L

Labor, Department of, 263
Labrador retriever, 24; *picture,*
  164
Lafayette, Marquis de, 128
Lakes, 82
Languages, 297, *with graph*
La Salle, Robert Cavelier, Sieur
  de, 128
Lateral bud, 140–141, *with
  picture*
Launch vehicles, 194–195,
  with pictures

Lavoisier, Antoine Laurent,
  128
Law, 264–266
Law of. . .
  Laws appear under their key
  words, as in Segregation,
  Law of
Leaf, 141, *with picture*
Le Corbusier, 128
Lee, Robert E., 128
Lewis, Meriwether, 128
Lhasa apso, 25; *picture,* 169
Library of Congress
  classification, 110
Life span, 23
Ligament, 103
Lighthouse of Alexandria, 290
Lightweight, 209
Light-year, 277, 279
Liliuokalani, 128
Lincoln, Abraham, 146–147
Lindbergh, Charles A., 128
Linnaeus, Carolus, 128
Lipizzaner, 171, *picture*
Lister, Sir Joseph, 128
Literature, 36–40, 45–46,
  54–58
Liverwort, 139
Livingstone, David, 128
Livy, 128
Local Group (astronomy), 279
Locke, John, 128–129
London, Jack, 129
Longfellow, Henry Wadsworth,
  129
Long-haired cats, 23; *pictures,*
  162
Louis XIV, 129
Louis XVI, 129
LPGA, 214, 216
Luge, 227
Lunar eclipse, 278, *picture*
Lunar module, 197, 199, *with
  picture;* 201
Lungs, 104, 106
Luther, Martin, 129
Lymphatic system, 106

M

MacArthur, Douglas, 129
Machiavelli, Niccoló, 129
Macromolecule, 101
Madison, James, 147
Magellan, Ferdinand, 129
Magellanic Clouds, 280
Mahayana, 153

Maltese, 24; *picture,* 163
Malthus, Thomas Robert, 129
Mammal, 20, 23
Management and Budget,
  Office of, 262
Manet, Édouard, 129
Manitoba, 65
Mann, Horace, 129
Mann, Thomas, 129
Manned space flights (table),
  198–200
Mantle (geology), 81
Mantrayana, 153
Manx, 23; *picture,* 161
Mao Tse-tung, 129
Map symbols, 158–159
Marconi, Guglielmo, 129
Marcus Aurelius, 129
Maria Theresa, 129
Marie Antoinette, 129
Marlowe, Christopher, 129
Marquette, Jacques, 129
Mars (planet), 276, 282
Marshall, John, 129
Marshall, Thurgood, 129
Marsupial, 20
Marx, Karl, 129
Mary, Queen of Scots, 130
Mass (religion), 150
Masters Tournament, 215
Mathematics symbols, 159
Mather, Cotton, 130
Mausoleum at Halicarnassus,
  290
Mayflower Compact, 270
Mazzini, Giuseppe, 130
McKinley, William, 147
Mead, Margaret, 130
Measurement, 287–289
Mecca, 150
Medals. See Decorations and
  medals
Medici, Lorenzo, 130
Medicine, 43–45
Medina, 150
Meir, Golda, 130
Melanesian-Papuan, 100
Melville, Herman, 130
Mendel, Gregor Johann, 130,
  143–144
Mendeleev, Dmitri, 130
Mercury (planet), 276, 282
Mercury capsule, 197–198,
  with picture
Mesosphere, 85
Mesozoic Era, 86–87
Messiah, 149
Metabolism, 22
Metamorphic rock, 81

315

Metamorphosis, 22
Meteor, 276
Meteorite, 276
Meteoroid, 276
Metric system, 287–289
Metropolitan area, 296
Metternich, Prince von, 130
Michelangelo, 130
Micronesian, 100
Middle Ages, 301–302, 305
Middle Atlantic States, 247, 254
Middle Way, 152
Middleweight, 207–208
Midwestern States, 247, 254
Mies van der Rohe, Ludwig, 130
Migration, 20
Milky Way, 276, 279
Mill, John Stuart, 130
Milton, John, 130
Minerals, 84, 255–256
Minor planet. See Asteroid
Minority groups, rights of, 269
Modern history, 302–304, 306–307
Mohorovičic discontinuity, 81
Molière, 130
Molting, 20
Monet, Claude, 130
Money, 110–111
    See also Signs and symbols
Mongoloids, 100
Monocotyledon, 142
Monroe, James, 147
Monroe Doctrine, 270
Montesquieu, 130
Montezuma II, 130
Moon, 81
More, Saint Thomas, 130
Morgan, John Pierpont, 130
Morgan horse, 25; picture, 170
Morse code, 15
Morse, Samuel F. B., 130
Moses, 130–131, 155
Mosque, 151, 301
Moss, 139
Motion (parliamentary procedure), 114–115
Motion picture, 30
Motion Picture Arts and Sciences, Academy of, 30
Mountains, 83
Mount Everest, 83, 290
Movable feast, 62
Mozart, Wolfgang Amadeus, 131

Muhammad, 131, 150
Muscle, 102–103, with picture
Muses, 112
Music, 58–59
Musical, 60
Muslims, 150, 301
Mussolini, Benito, 131
Mythology, 112–113, with pictures

N

Names, animal, 27
Napoleon I, 131
Nasser, Gamal Abdel, 131
National Basketball Association, 205
National Book Awards, 36–38
National Collegiate Athletic Association, 206
National Football Conference, 211
National Hockey League, 216
National League, 204–205
National Railroad Passenger Corporation. See Amtrak
National Security Council, 262
Natural resources, 84, 255
Navigation satellite, 196–197
NBA. See National Basketball Association
NCAA. See National Collegiate Athletic Association
Neanderthal man, 99, picture
Nebuchadnezzar II, 131
Nebula, 277, 280
Negroids, 100
Nehru, Jawaharlal, 131
Nelson, Horatio, 131
Nephron, 106
Neptune (planet), 276, 283
Nero, 131
Nervous system, 107–108, with picture
Nervous tissue, 102
Neuron, 107
Newbery, John, 34
Newbery medal, 34–35
New Brunswick, 65
New England, 247, 254
Newfoundland, 65
New Testament, 149
Newton, Sir Isaac, 131
Nietzsche, Friedrich, 131
Nightingale, Florence, 131
Nile Valley, 299

Nirvana, 152
Nixon, Richard Milhous, 147
Nkrumah, Kwame, 131
Nobel, Alfred Bernhard, 131
Nobel prizes, 40–48
Noble Eightfold Path, 152
Node, 140–141, with picture
Nonsporting dogs, 25; pictures, 169
Norse mythology, 113
North Star. See Polaris
Northern Hemisphere, 88; 280, with picture
Northwest Ordinance, 270
Northwest Territories, 66–67
Notochord, 18, 20
Nova, 277
Nova Scotia, 65
Numerals, 160
Nyerere, Julius Kambarage, 131

O

Ocean, 84
O'Connor, Sandra Day, 131
Octans (star), 281, with picture
Office of. . .
    Government offices appear under their key words, as in Management and Budget, Office of
O'Higgins, Bernardo, 131
O'Keeffe, Georgia, 131
Old Testament, 149, 155
Olympic Games, 226–231
Om, 151, picture
O'Neill, Eugene, 131
Ontario, 65, 67
Oppenheimer, J. Robert, 131
Orange Bowl, 212–213
Orbit, 193, 196, 282–283, with diagrams
Organ (anatomy), 102
Oscar (award), 30–33
Ovary, 106, 141
Ovid, 131
Oviparity, 21
Oxygen, 104, 106

P

Pacific Coast States, 247, 254–255
Pacific, flags of the, 185–187, *pictures*
Paine, Thomas, 131–132
Paleozoic Era, 86–87
Palomino, 25; *picture,* 171
Parasite, 20
Parícutin, 83, 290
Parliamentary procedure, 114–115
Parthenogenesis, 21
Pascal, Blaise, 132
Pasteur, Louis, 132
Peace, 46–48
Peary, Robert E., 132
Peking man, 98, *picture*
Penis, 106
Penn, William, 132
Pentathlon, 228
People, 116–137
    See also Awards, Canada, Elements, Chemical, Explorations, Presidents, Space, Scientific inventions and inventors, Sports winners, United States, World
Pepin the Short, 132
Pericles, 132
Perihelion, 193, 282
Peripheral nervous system, 107–108, *with picture*
Perpetual calendar, 62–63
Pershing, John Joseph, 132
Persian cat, 23; *picture,* 162
Peter I, 132
Petiole, 141, *with picture*
PGA, 214, 216
Philip II, 132
Phloem, 140, *with pictures*
Photosynthesis, 143
Phylum, 18, 138–139
Physics, 40–42
Picasso, Pablo, 132
Pierce, Franklin, 147
Pinto, 170, *picture*
Pistil, 141, *with picture*
Pitt, William, 132
Pitt, William, the Younger, 132
Pituitary gland, 108
Pizarro, Francisco, 132
Planet, 80, 276, 282–283
Planetoid. See Asteroid
Plants, 138–144
    earth, 86
      biome, 88–89
    interesting facts about, 144

Plasma, 106
Platelet, 106
Plate tectonics, 81
Plato, 132
Play (drama), 59–60
Pliny the Elder, 132
Pliny the Younger, 132
Plutarch, 132
Pluto (planet), 276, 283
Pocahontas, 132
Pocket veto, 265
Poe, Edgar Allan, 132
Poetry, 36, 40, 55
Pointer, 24; *picture,* 164
Polar exploration, 92–93
Polaris (star), 280, *with picture*
Political party, 258, 261–262
Political unit, 294–295
Polk, James K., 147
Polo, Marco, 132
Polynesian, 100
Pomeranian, 24; *picture,* 163
Pompey, 132–133
Ponce de León, Juan, 133
Ponies, 25; *pictures,* 172
Poodle, 25; *picture,* 169
Pope, 150
Population
    Canada, 65–67
    United States, 245–246, 250, 252
    world, 291–296
Port (shipping), 238, 257
Postal abbreviations, 12
Prairie Provinces, 67
Preakness, 219–220
Prehistoric people, 97–99, *with pictures and maps*
Presidency, 258–263, 268
Presidential succession, 258–259
Presidents, 145–148
    See also United States (table), 260–261
Press, freedom of the. See Freedom of the press
Prime ministers of Canada, 70–71
Primordial fireball, 276
Prince Edward Island, 66
Protective coloration, 20
Protective resemblance, 20
Protestant, 150
Province, Canadian, 65–67
    abbreviations, 12
    flags, 192, *pictures*
Ptolemy, 133
Ptolemy I, 133
Pulaski, Casimir, 133

Pulitzer, Joseph, 133
Pulitzer prizes, 48–59
Pulsar, 277
Pyramids, 290
Pythagoras, 133

Q

Quarter horse, 25; *picture,* 170
Quasar, 277
Quebec (province), 66–67
Quebec Act, 72

R

Rabbi, 155
Races, human, 100
Racial groups, U.S., 246
Railroad, 239–240, *with map*
Rain forest, 89
Raleigh, Sir Walter, 133
Ramadan, 151
Raphael, 133
Reagan, Ronald, 147
Reason, Age of. See Age of Reason
Receptacle (botany), 141, *with picture*
Red blood cell, 106
Red shift, 277
Regeneration, 21
Regions
    Canada, 67
    United States, 247, 254–255
Reincarnation, 152
Religion, 149–155, *with pictures*
Rembrandt, 133
Renaissance, 302–303
Renoir, Pierre Auguste, 133
Report on the Affairs of British North America, 72
Representatives, House of, 258, 264–266
Reproduction
    in animals, 21
    in human beings, 106–107
    in plants, 142
Reptile, 20, 23
Respiration, 21, 143
Respiratory system, 104
Resurrection, 149
Retriever, 24; *pictures,* 164

Revere, Paul, 133
Revolutionary War, 272–273, 275
Rhodes, Colossus of, 290
Richard I, 133
Richardson, Henry Hobson, 133
Richelieu, Cardinal, 133
Rio de Janeiro, 290
Rivera, Diego, 133
Rivers, 82
Roadster horses, 25; *pictures,* 171, 173
Robespierre, 133
Rockefeller, John D., 133
Rocky Mountain States, 247, 254
Rodin, Auguste, 133
Roentgen, Wilhelm, 133
Roman Catholic Church, 150
Roman Empire, 300
Roman mythology, 112
Roman numerals, 160
Roosevelt, Franklin Delano, 147
Roosevelt, Theodore, 147
Root, 140, *with pictures*
Rose Bowl, 212
Rotational axis, 282
Rousseau, Jean Jacques, 133
Routes, railroad, 240, *with map*
Rowing, 228–229
Rubens, Peter Paul, 133
Russell, Bertrand, 133–134
Russian alphabet, 13
Rutherford, Ernest, 134

S

Sabbath, 155
Saddle horses, 25; *pictures,* 170–171
Saint Bernard, 24; *picture,* 166
Saliva, 103
Salk, Jonas, 134
Salyut, 199–201
Sandburg, Carl, 134
San Martín, José de, 134
Saskatchewan, 66
Satellite (astronomy), 282
Satellite, artificial, 196–197
Saturn (planet), 276, 283
Saturn V, 194–195, *with picture*
Savanna, 89
Savannah (nuclear ship), 234
Savannah (steamship), 234

Schiller, Johann Christoph Friedrich von, 134
Schnauzer, 25; *picture,* 168
Schweitzer, Albert, 134
Scientific classification. *See* Classification, Scientific.
Scientific inventions and inventors, 156–157
  See also Awards, Transportation (table of important dates)
Scientific satellite, 196–197
Scipio, Publius Cornelius, 134
Scott, Sir Walter, 134
Scrotum, 106
Sea. *See* Ocean
Seasons, 88
Secretariat (government), 242
Secretary-general (UN), 244
Security Council, UN, 242
Sedimentary rock, 81
Seeds, 142
Segregation, law of, 144
Semaphore, 16
Senses, 17
Sepal, 141
Setter, 24; *picture,* 164
Seven Wonders of the World, 290
Sexual reproduction, 21, 106–107, 142
Shakespeare, William, 134
Shaw, George Bernard, 134
Sheepdog, 24; *pictures,* 167
Shelley, Percy Bysshe, 134
Shepard, Alan Bartlett, Jr., 134
Sherman, William Tecumseh, 134
Shetland pony, 25; *picture,* 172
Shih tzu, 24; *picture,* 163
Shiites, 151
Shinto, 149, 153–154, *with picture*
Shire horse, 25; *picture,* 173
Shooting, 229
Short-haired cats, 23; *pictures,* 161
Sial, 81
Siamese cat, 23; *picture,* 161
Siberian husky, 24; *picture,* 166
Siddhartha Gautama. *See* Buddha
Signs and symbols, 158–160, *with pictures*
  See also Astrology, Chemical elements, Religion, Abbreviations, Alphabets and codes

Sima, 81
Simple majority vote, 265
Siqueiros, David Alfaro, 134
Sirius (ship), 234
Sitting Bull, 134
Skating, 226
Skeleton, 103; *picture,* 101
Skiing, 226–227
Skin, 102–103
Skylab, 199–201
Smith, Adam, 134
Smith, John, 134
Smith, Joseph, 134
Smooth muscle, 103
Soccer, 221
Socrates, 134
Solar eclipse, 278, table, *picture*
Solar system, 276
Solomon, 134
Solon, 134
Solstice, 88
Songs, state, 251, 253
Sophocles, 134–135
Southern Hemisphere, 281, *with picture*
Southern States, 247, 254
Southwestern States, 247, 254
Soyuz, 197, 199, *with picture*
Space, 93, 193–202, *with pictures*
  terms, 193
  See also Earth, Universe, People
Space probe, 202
Space shuttle, 194–195, *with picture;* 201–202
Space station, 201–202
Spaniel, 24; *pictures,* 164
Speaker of the House, 264–266
Speech, freedom of. *See* Freedom of Speech
Speed, comparative, 26
Speed skating, 226
Sperm, 21, 106
Spinal reflex, 107
Spiracles, 21
Sporting dogs, 24; *pictures,* 164
Sports winners, 203–231
Sporulation, 21, 142
Sputnik I, 196–197
Stalin, Joseph, 135
Stamen, 141, *with picture*
Stanley Cup, 216–217
Star (astronomy), 276–277, 279–281, *with pictures*
Star of David, 155, *picture*

State
  abbreviations, 12
  birds, 251, 253
  capitals, 250, 252
  flags, 188–189, *pictures*
  flowers, 251, 253
  songs, 251, 253
State, Department of, 263
Statute of Westminster, 72
Steinbeck, John, 135
Stem, 140–141, *with pictures*
Stevenson, Robert Louis, 135
Stigma, 141, *with picture*
Stipule, 141, *with picture*
Stomata, 142–143
Stone Age, 98–99
Stowe, Harriet Beecher, 135
Stratosphere, 85
Stuart, Gilbert Charles, 135
Style (botany), 141, *with picture*
Subcutaneous tissue, 103
Succession, presidential. *See* Presidential succession
Sugar Bowl, 213
Sullivan, Louis, 135
Summer Olympics, 227–231
Summer solstice, 88
Sun, 277–278
Sunnites, 151
Sunspot, 278
Sun Yat-sen, 135
Super Bowl, 211–212
Supercluster, 276
Supernova, 277
Supreme Court, 266–269
Swift, Jonathan, 135
Swimming, 229
Symbols. *See* Signs and symbols
Synagogue, 155

T

Tacitus, 135
Taft, William Howard, 147–148
Talmud, 155
Taoism, 149, 154, *with picture*
Taproot, 140, *with picture*
Taylor, Zachary, 148
Tchaikovsky, Peter Ilich, 135
Temperature, 284–287
Tendon, 103
Tennis, 222–225
Tennyson, Lord, 135
Tereshkova, Valentina, 135

Terminal bud, 140–141, *with pictures*
Terriers, 25; *pictures,* 168
Territory, Canadian, 66–67
  abbreviations, 12
  flags, 192, *pictures*
Testicle, 106
Teutonic mythology, 113
Thermosphere, 85
Thirteen colonies, 272, *map*
Thomson, Sir Joseph John, 135
Thoreau, Henry David, 135
Thoroughbred, 25; *picture,* 171
Tigris-Euphrates Valley, 299
Time zones, 28, 232–233, *with maps*
Tissue, 102
Tissue respiration, 22
Titian, 135
Tobogganing, 227
Tocqueville, Alexis de, 135
Tolstoy, Leo, 135
Tony awards, 59–61
Torah, 155
Torii (symbol), 153, *picture*
Toulouse-Lautrec, Henri de, 135
Toy dogs, 24; *pictures,* 163
Track and field, 230
Traffic signs, 160, *with pictures*
Train, 234
  See also Railroad
Translunar space, 193
Transportation, 234–240, *with maps*
  average speeds of, 234
  important dates, 234
  United States, 256–257
Transportation, Department of, 263
Treasury, Department of the, 263
Treaties, 309
Triple Crown, 218
Tropical rain forest, 89
Troposphere, 85
Trotsky, Leon, 135
Truman, Harry S., 148
Trust territory, 244
Tubman, Harriet, 135
Tundra, 88
Turgenev, Ivan Sergeevich, 135
Tutankhamon, 135
Twain, Mark, 135–136
Tweed, William Marcy, 136
Tyler, John, 148

U

Undersea exploration, 93
UNESCO, 242
UNICEF, 242
Union, 274, *map*
Union, Act of, 72
United Nations, 241–244, *with diagram*
United Nations Children's Fund. *See* UNICEF
United Nations Educational, Scientific and Cultural Organization. *See* UNESCO
United Nations University, 242
United States, 245–275
  abbreviations, 12
  air mileage, 235
  area codes, 28
  census, 246
  cities, 246
  decorations and medals, 76; *pictures,* 176–177
  facts in brief, 245, 250–253
  flag, 95; *pictures,* 179, 188–189, 191
  highways, 236–237, *with map*
  holidays, 96
  maps, 248–249, 272–274
  population, 245–246, 250, 252
  regions, 247, 254–255
  wars, 275
  weather, 284
Universe, 276–283, *with pictures*
  See also Earth, Space
Updike, John, 136
Uranus, 276, 283
Urinary system, 106
U.S. Open, 214–215
U.S. Women's Open, 215

V

Vagina, 106–107
Van Buren, Martin, 148
Van Gogh, Vincent, 136
Vascular plant, 139
Vedas, 152
Vegetative propagation, 142
Vein, 105–106, 141, *with picture*
Velocity, 193, 196
Venus (planet), 276, 282

Verdi, Giuseppe, 136
Vernal equinox, 88
Verne, Jules, 136
Vertebrate, 18
Vespucci, Amerigo, 136
Veto, 265
Vice-President, 258–259, 262
Victoria, 136
Victoria Falls, 82, 290
Virgil, 136
Virgo Cluster (astronomy), 279
Viviparity, 21
Volcano, 78–79, 83
Voltaire, 136
Voluntary muscle, 103
Von Braun, Wernher, 136
Vostok, 197–198, *with picture*

W

Wagner, Richard, 136
Wars
  United States, 275
  world, 307–308
Washington, Booker T., 136
Washington, George, 148
Waterfalls, 82
Watson, James D., 136
Watt, James, 136
Weather, 284–286
Weather satellite, 196–197
Webster, Daniel, 136
Webster, Noah, 136
Wedding anniversary, 160
Weight lifting, 231
Weights and measures,
  287–289
Wellington, Arthur Wellesley,
  Duke of, 136
Welterweight, 208–209
Wesley, John, 136
Western Europe, 301
Westminster, Statute of, 72

Wheatley, Phillis, 136
Wheel (symbol), 152, *picture*
Whistler, James Abbott
  McNeill, 136
White blood cell, 106
White dwarf, 277
White House Office, 262
Whitman, Walt, 136
Whitney, Eli, 136
Willard, Emma Hart, 136–137
William I, 137
Williams, Roger, 137
Wilson, Woodrow, 148
Wimbledon, 222–223
Wind, 88, 286
Winter Olympics, 226–227
Winter solstice, 88
Wolfe, Thomas, 137
Women's rights, 269
Wonders of the world, 290
Woody stem, 140–141, *with
  picture*
Wordsworth, William, 137
Working dogs, 24; *pictures,*
  166
World, 290–309
  air mileage, 235
  airports, 238
  canals, 239
  climate, 174–175, *with
    map*
  economy, 298
  history, 299–309
  largest cities, 296
  largest countries, 295
  merchant fleets, 238
  population, 291–296
  ports, 238
  time zones, 232–233, *with
    map*
  wars, 307–308
  weather, 284–286
  wonders of, 290
World Bank, 242
World Cup, 221

World Health Organization,
  242
World Series, 204–205
Wren, Sir Christopher, 137
Wrestling, 231
Wright, Frank Lloyd, 137
Wright, Wilbur and Orville, 137

X

Xerxes I, 137
Xylem, 140, *with pictures*

Y

Yachting, 231
Yang, 154, *picture*
Yin, 154, *picture*
Yoga, 152
Yorkshire terrier, 24; *picture,*
  163
Young, Brigham, 137
Yukon Territory, 66–67

Z

Zapata, Emiliano, 137
Zen, 153
Zenger, John Peter, 137
Zephyr (train), 234
Zeus, statue of, 290
Zodiac, 29
Zwingli, Huldreich, 137